LAW AND THE FINANCIAL SYSTEM

SECURITIZATION AND ASSET BACKED SECURITIES: LAW, PROCESS, CASE STUDIES, AND SIMULATIONS

LAW AND THE FINANCIAL SYSTEM

SECURITIZATION AND ASSET BACKED SECURITIES: LAW, PROCESS, CASE STUDIES, AND SIMULATIONS

Tamar Frankel
Michaels Faculty Research Scholar, Professor of Law,
Boston University School of Law

&

Mark Fagan
Senior Fellow, Mossavar-Rahmani Center for Business & Government
Harvard Kennedy School, Harvard University

Vandeplas Publishing

United States of America

Law and the Financial System
Securitization and Asset Backed Securities: Law, Process, Case Studies, and Simulations

Frankel, Tamar and Fagan, Mark

Published by:

Vandeplas Publishing - December 2009

801 International Parkway, 5th Floor
Lake Mary, FL. 32746
USA

www.vandeplaspublishing.com

ISBN: 978-1-60042-095-5

Dedication

To Ray and to my children Anat and Michael
- Tamar

To Janet, Miriam, and Abigail for your love and support
- Mark

Acknowledgments

This book was hard to write because the topic is complex, involving lending and securities distribution and touching on numerous areas of the law, such as bank regulation, the Investment Company Act of 1940, and Article 9 of the U.C.C, regulation of rating agencies and appraisers. Since much of the materials were drawn from a treatise addressed to practicing lawyers it was unclear how much elaboration or summaries should be offered to the students.

Therefore, the text was given to a number of students that did not have exposure to securitization. They were asked to comment on the text and pose questions on concepts and words they did not understand or were not sure about. Their contribution was invaluable to guide us in shaping this book. Thus, we are thankful to Colin Darke, Stephanie Kao, and Iris Zhang for their comments on the manuscript. Our thanks to William Hecker, Esq. for his editing the manuscript and to Carol McGeehan for her invaluable comments. Needless to say, we bear the entire burden for the mistakes and lack of clarification in the book.

Tamar Frankel
Mark Fagan

LAW AND THE FINANCIAL SYSTEM

SECURITIZATION AND ASSET BACKED SECURITIES: LAW, PROCESS, CASE STUDIES, AND SIMULATIONS

Tamar Frankel and Mark Fagan

TABLE OF CONTENTS

TABLE OF CONTENTS

LAW AND THE FINANICAL SYSTEM
SECURITIZATION AND ASSET BACKED SECURITIES: LAW, PROCESS, CASE STUDIES AND SIMULATIONS

Tamar Frankel and Mark Fagan

Introduction

Securitization has risen to prominence during financial crises both as remedy to problems and as a cause of problems. During the 1970s and 1980s securitization was used to help failing Savings and Loan Associations by creating liquidity for them. In the years 2007-2008 it was considered to be one of the main triggers of a severe financial and economic crisis. In between these events, the process of securitization has been used to benefit lenders, borrowers, investors, market intermediaries, and the financial system.

The purpose of this Book is to examine securitization/asset backed securities from legal, financial-economic and public policy points of view. Each discipline plays a role in understanding, evaluating and giving advice about this process. Securitization poses interesting issues because it offers self-conflicting, yet beneficial, results. It starts with contract and ends in property. It starts with financing by lenders and ends in financing by investors. It starts in banks and similar institutions and ends in the markets. These transformations provide its advantages and its disadvantages. In this Book we examine each of these features and the possible ways to maintain securitization's benefits while limiting, if not eliminating, its disadvantages and risks.

A significant part of this Book's materials is derived from a treatise by Tamar Frankel, Securitization (2d ed. 2005). The case studies and simulation exercises were written by Mark Fagan. This Book is the product of their collaboration. When the materials in this Book are derived from the Treatise, the reader will find one cite for each subject, noting the section in the Treatise that contains many authorities for the statements in this Book. When the materials in this Book are not derived from the Treatise, there are cites that substantiate the statements in those materials in this text.

PART I: INTRODUCTION TO SECURITIZATION

Chapter 1: The Nature of the Financial System

Securitization is part of the financial system. Therefore, the study of securitization requires an understanding of the financial system, its purpose, structure, functions, problems, and regulation. Securitization is a process that starts with the making of loans, continues with their transfer to an entity (e.g., a corporation, a trust), and ends with the entity's issuance of securities, which are traded in the securities markets. The study of this process requires a focus on the actors as well as the financial products that the process produces. This chapter details the operation of the financial system as well as the nature of speculation, volatility and liquidity that accompany the financial system.

A. The Financial System: Markets and Institutions[1]

The following example demonstrates the need for a financial system. John Taste has been fascinated with cooking most of his life. He completed college and graduated with honors from a world-famous cooking school. He wanted to open his own restaurant and needed $50,000 to start the business. Having tasted his cooking, family members and friends gladly invested in his restaurant. John created a corporation. A number of family members and friends were offered and bought shares in the corporation. Others wished to invest in his notes to be paid at the end of two years. By that time he hoped to have earned and saved enough to repay the debt.

John was tremendously successful. His dishes were praised, his restaurant became famous, and the reservations extended months ahead. He decided to open another restaurant, and this time he needed $500,000. His savings amounted to $100,000. His family and friends did not have enough cash. There were many investors and lenders who might offer John the financing but he did not know them, and they did not know him.

This is when the financial system came to the assistance of John and potential investors. John was able to borrow from a bank and withdraw some of his savings under his life insurance policy. Moreover, a broker who befriended him suggested that he might create a closed-end corporation which is a non-public corporation that has a few shareholders, and offer to issue shares to some of the broker's clients if he needed additional capital. He may also borrow against his savings under his life policy, if the amount is significant, or perhaps ask a retired wealthy family member to do that. The banks, the insurance companies and the broker's customers, as well as others, we shall see, are a part of the financial system.

---

[1] 1 TAMAR FRANKEL, SECURITIZATION § 1.1 (Ann Taylor Schwing ed., 2d ed. 2005).

Thus, the main purpose of a financial system is to facilitate the transfer of money from savers--those who postpone consumption or production—to borrowers—those who require money for productive purposes, or for consumption (which creates production to meet the consumers' demand). In exchange for transferring their money to borrowers, savers receive the borrowers' obligations. These obligations promise to repay the savers in the future various sums under various conditions.

a. Forms and Names of Obligations and Obligors

Obligations can take the form of beneficial ownership (e.g., partnership interests, shares) in the enterprises that the borrowers create or expand. Alternatively obligations can take the form of debt (e.g., bonds, notes) to be paid on a specific date, subject to various conditions. We call the different obligations by different names, such as stocks, shares, notes, bonds, depending on the type of the obligations and the way they are distributed. We call the savers "investors" or "lenders." We call the borrowers "issuers" or "borrowers." The investors or lenders we describe here are passive, going about their own business. They expect payment not only of the amount they gave issuers or borrowers but an additional compensation for the risk that they might not receive their money back. The higher the risk—the higher the compensation will be. The lower the risk—the lower the compensation will be.

b. The Meaning and Nature of Intermediation

The intermediaries in the financial system are what their name implies: The middle man. They connect investors with issuers and lenders with borrowers, who do not know each other and are not aware of each others' needs. Throughout this Book we use the terms "intermediaries" and to "intermediate" to denote the function of intermediaries. Intermediaries are efficient because they have more information and skills to bring parties together and help them transact to benefit both.

The financial system offers two main avenues of intermediation by which savers and borrowers reach each other. One avenue of intermediation is the Markets in the borrowers' obligations, such as the New York Stock Exchange and Market intermediaries such as brokers, dealers and underwriters. The other channel of intermediation offered by the financial system is Institutions, such as banks, insurance companies, pension funds, hedge funds, and mutual funds.

c. Markets

To be formed and function efficiently, Markets in the savers' obligations, which we call securities, must meet a number of conditions. First, there are conditions with respect to the traded borrowers' obligations. The obligations should be in a standard form, and their terms must be very similar, if not identical, rather than custom-made. This condition reduces the information costs to investors. After all, no efficient Market can be created in a single $3,000.25 loan for 67 days. It would be very costly to find a buyer that desires precisely these terms.[2] In addition, obligations must be in denominations that many buyers can afford so as to facilitate trading. If the price of each unit to be traded is $300,000, the Market will be "thin" because fewer individuals will buy and trade in such large units. But if the price of each unit is $50, there is a greater chance for a larger number of buyers and traders. Finally, there must be usually a sufficient number of obligations offered to the public.

Second, the cost of obtaining information about the issuers and their obligations must be relatively low. If the cost of uncovering information about them and the terms of their obligations are high, it would be harder for traders to determine the value of the obligations and establish their price.

In sum, securities have these attributes: There are usually a sufficient number of such obligations offered to the public. The terms of the obligations are identical. Their amounts are usually not so high as to exclude a large number of buyers. And the obligors that issue the securities offer information about themselves and the obligations, whether voluntarily or by legal requirement. In contrast, the obligations we call debts or loans lack the attributes that facilitate Markets. Each debtor is unique, and the terms and amounts of a debt may differ from any other debt.[3]

Third, Markets require market intermediaries such as brokers, dealers, underwriters, advisers and analysts, who collect information about possible savers and borrowers and about their obligations and execute transactions among the parties. The fees of brokers-dealers and underwriters reflect their main function. The fees are usually paid only when the transactions close; otherwise, they receive nothing. In contrast, advisers-managers are paid a percentage of the assets they manage. Their fees provide the advisers-managers incentives to increase the amount under management. If the amount rises by their performance, they are rewarded by a percentage of that amount.

The initial offering of issuers' obligations is called a "primary Market." Thus, underwriters offer potential investors the obligations of the issuers, and the offering is successful if investors purchase all or most of the issued obligations at the offering price (or higher).

---

[2] There are indeed markets in unique items, such as old artists' paintings. The paintings are one of a kind. Their price, however, is not efficiently determined and may depend more on taste and emotions than on market value. Even these markets require a sufficient number of items. A gallery will not survive unless it offers a sufficient number of works of art, and sometimes would be successful if it offers many paintings of the same artist.

[3] Debts and loans are somewhat synonymous, but not quite. Both are obligations of one party to pay another. However, the source of the obligation of a loan is money received from another party, and the promise to pay it back. The source of a debt can be a requirement to compensate for harm inflicted or for a breach of fiduciary duty, among other things. The common understanding of the two terms signifies this difference. The word loan focuses on money received (and to be repaid); a debt focuses on the repayment.

However, a primary Market presents a problem for investors, who need or wish to have their money back before the payment under these obligations is due. This is especially important to investors in an enterprise, which in fact promises them only relatively small dividends and a return of the rest of their main investment only upon the liquidation or sale of the enterprise or repurchase of its shares by the enterprise.

What if the investors' money was used to build factories and other enterprises that cannot be and should not be liquidated so long as the enterprise maintains an operating business? To offer investors liquidity – the ability to get their money back when they need it or want it -- a second, "secondary Market" is usually available. In a secondary Market *investors trade with each other* in the borrowers' or issuers' obligations. The more investors are interested in trading particular obligations, the more "liquid" the obligations will be.

Thus, Markets offer issuers (borrowers) and investors (savers) one mechanism for transferring money from investors in exchange for the borrowers' obligations, and a second mechanism for liquidating ("liquefying" and converting into cash) these obligations by the investors transferring and trading in these obligations among themselves.

d. Institutions

When the conditions necessary for creating Markets are absent, for example, when savers prefer terms on which borrowers cannot or will not borrow, or when the terms, forms, and amounts of debts do not meet the conditions necessary to create securities markets, Institutions bridge the gap between the parties. Institutions borrow from savers on terms acceptable to savers, and lend the proceeds to borrowers on terms acceptable to borrowers. Institutions include banks, thrifts, mortgage bankers, and consumer banks, and insurance companies, pension funds, and investment companies (collectively "Institutions"). To be sure, Institutions offer other services to both depositors (lenders) and to borrowers. But the main function of Institutions is intermediation.

e. Banks

Banks are Institutional intermediaries. Banks borrow from savers (depositors, investors). They then turn around and lend the deposited money or investors' money to borrowers. The banks cover their cost of operation by paying less on the amounts they borrow (the deposits) and charging more on the amounts they lend. To do that, banks must issue obligations that pose lower risks to savers, such as bank deposits covered by the Federal Deposit Insurance Corporation. The investors in these deposits are paid very little, if anything, but receive services and low risk, safe keeping, liquid, bank obligations. Banks make loans to borrowers that pose higher risks, and therefore pay higher returns. Thus, the banks live off the "spread," that is, the difference between the interest they pay on their deposits and the interest they charge to borrowers.

The banks' financial structure, however, is vulnerable. Banks can fail when the market price of their assets falls below the amounts they owe (e.g., deposits, bonds). Institutions, such as banks and savings a loan associations, issue obligations that promise their depositors fixed amounts at fixed dates or on depositors' demand, regardless of whether the banks collect the money they lent to borrowers. If, for any reason, the borrowers to whom the banks have lent default, the banks might not be able to repay the depositors the amounts of their deposits. Therefore, the banks' basic structure poses risk to depositors.

Another type of Institution -- mutual funds -- offers a somewhat different intermediation model as compared to banks. Theoretically, mutual funds cannot fail. That is because mutual funds promise investors a pro rata share of whatever assets the funds hold. Not more and not less. The investors bear the entire risk of the funds' investments. And the mutual fund, as an Institution, always balances its assets and liabilities.

Markets and Institutions are distinguished throughout this Book, even though the difference between them is not necessarily relevant in other contexts. Because Markets and Institutions offer different intermediation models, different regulatory regimes apply to each model. In this Book, the distinction is important to understanding securitization because securitization is the technique by which loans, intermediated and held by Institutions, are transformed into securities, intermediated in the Markets. To understand securitization we must understand the two kinds of intermediation and the different regulatory regimes under which they function.

To simplify the analysis, Markets will be treated in this Book as one prototype, and so will Institutions, even though the financial system as a whole consists of different Markets and different Institutions. Markets and Institutions vary in ways that affect their benefits, drawbacks, and strengths; they differ by volume, nature, and size of transactions, the savers and borrowers they serve, and the regulations that governs them. Institutions also vary. Even so, the basic differences between them remain: Markets and Institutions emerge in different circumstances and each represents a particular mix of benefits, costs, and risks.

B. Risks in the Financial System[4]

The financial system is the lifeblood of the economy. Its very importance to the economy poses risks if it fails. Therefore, one of the greatest risks is that the system

[4] 1 TAMAR FRANKEL, SECURITIZATION § 1.2 (Ann Taylor Schwing ed., 2d ed. 2005).

might not function well. As the situation in 2007 and 2008 has demonstrated, the malfunction of the financial system can bring about the failure of the economy.

a. Risks Posed by Intermediaries

Most financial intermediaries hold the investors' money. Some of these intermediaries advise investors and others may merely point to the persons who might be interested in the exchange of money for obligations. But most of the intermediaries, be they banks or brokers or dealers, must hold or have control over the investors' money. In many cases they determine the degree of speculation and general investment of the investors whose money and assets they trade. This power is accompanied by temptation. After all, few intermediaries are exposed continuously to supervision. Some of intermediaries are experts, far more knowledgeable than the investors or the borrowers between whom they intermediate. The risks of misappropriating some of the entrusted money or misusing the entrusted power are inherent in the financial system.

b. Risks Posed by Behavior of Lenders and Borrowers

The transfer of money and assets from lenders to borrowers is founded on an agreement among the two, and the terms of the agreement. When the parties' bargaining power is imbalanced, either because of the dire need of the borrowers or sometimes that of the lenders, the terms of the agreement may be inherently unfair; there comes a point when the parties will not interact. It is at this point that the law usually intervenes. Congress sometimes provides incentives for the parties to interact or requires one party to provide certain terms to the other. Thus, for example, banks are required to make certain loans in certain depressed areas of the cities. Some loan terms are regulated as well.[5]

c. "Runs" on Institutions, such as Banks, and on the Markets

Markets and Institutions require a measure of reasonable equilibrium. If there is demand for securities in the Markets and no commensurate supply, the securities' prices will rise beyond their inherent value and the Markets may become inefficient. In such cases prices may rise far beyond the value of the obligations to represent a bubble (full of hot air). If there are too many withdrawals from a bank so that a bank must liquidate an increasing amount of assets, or if a bank cannot liquidate its long-term assets, the bank may fail. Such failures may pose systemic risks, that is, when not only one issuer or one type of Market or one Institution fails, but when the failure leads to pressure which undermines solid, essentially "healthy" Markets and Institutions.

---

[5] Community Reinvestment Act of 1977, 12 U.S.C. §§ 2901-2908 (2006).

d. Speculation, Volatility and Liquidity[6]

These terms are often used in connection with the financial system. Therefore, we offer a short definition of each term.

Speculation: The process of selecting high-risk investments in order to profit from an anticipated rising price movement. It means taking significant risks, especially by attempting to predict the future; gambling, in the hope of making quick, large gains. Speculators purchase risky investments that offer possible large profits, but also pose a higher-than-average possible loss. It is a profitable strategy over the long term if undertaken by professionals who hedge their portfolios to control the level of risk. Sophisticated investors will use a hedging strategy in combination with speculative investment in order to limit potential losses. They buy the other party's obligation, such as insurance, to cover at least part of the potential losses. Speculation should not be considered purely a form of gambling, as speculators do make informed decision before acquiring risky investments. Yet, speculation cannot be categorized as a traditional investment because the risk involved is higher than average investment risks.

Volatility: A measure of the dispersion of returns for a given security or market index. Volatility can be measured by using the standard deviation or by using the variance between returns from that same security or from a market index. In general, the higher the volatility is, the riskier the security is. In other words, volatility relates to the degree of uncertainty or risk about the magnitude of changes in a security's value. A higher volatility means that a security's value can potentially be spread out over a larger range of values. This means that the price of the security can change dramatically over a short time period in either direction (higher or lower). In contrast, a lower volatility means that a security's value does not fluctuate dramatically, and that its value changes at a steady pace over a period of time. One measure of the relative volatility of a particular stock to the market is its "beta." A beta approximates the overall volatility of a security's returns against the returns of a relevant benchmark (usually the Standard & Poor's [S&P]). For example, a stock with a beta value of 1.1 has historically moved 110% for every 100% move in the benchmark, based on price level. Conversely, a stock with a beta of .9 has historically moved 90% for every 100% move in the underlying index.

[6] 1 TAMAR FRANKEL, SECURITIZATION § 1.3 (Ann Taylor Schwing ed., 2d ed. 2005).

Liquidity: The opportunity of the holder of a financial asset to convert the asset into money--to sell the asset in an active Market or pursuant to a right to sell the asset for cash. The secondary Markets in securities, the bank accounts, and certain types of investment companies (open-end investment companies and unit investment trusts) provide investors with liquidity but do so in different ways. Markets provide buyers for security holders who wish to liquidate their investments; banks undertake to pay back deposits on demand or on short notice; open-end investment companies and unit investment trusts redeem the shares they issue at the value of a pro rata share of their portfolios on short notice.

Financial assets that offer liquidity benefit the economy by reducing the cost of capital. Investors will accept lower returns for the ability to liquidate their investments because liquidity lowers their risks and enables them to cut their losses. An investment in exchange-traded securities is liquid because investors can sell the securities any time the exchange is open. An investment in a limited partnership that owns raw land may not be as liquid if no one is interested in that parcel of land when the investor wants to sell his interest. If an investor cannot afford to keep an investment until a buyer is found, the investor can lower this risk by buying investments that enjoy an established market but these investments will bear lower returns. Borrowers will not benefit if intermediation costs exceed the liquidity premium that investors forgo or if competition is not sufficiently strong to induce intermediaries to share these premiums with borrowers, in full or in part.

Liquidity has drawbacks, however. It encourages speculation; it can cause volatility in Market prices and bank deposits. Extreme volatility, "bubbles" (rising prices, unsupported by current production and excess deposits unmatched by withdrawals), and "runs" (a free-fall of prices that does not reflect present economic conditions and excess of withdrawals over deposits) occur in both Markets and less frequently in banks. Both are triggered by excessive supply over demand for financial assets, or the reverse. But how much excess is excessive is subject to debate and depends on the circumstances.

Each type of intermediation produces its own brand of volatility. Runs in the Markets produce falling securities prices and consequent losses to investors; runs on banks produce bank failures and consequent losses to uninsured investors and to government deposit insurance systems. Therefore, market volatility exposes investors to market risks (that prices will fall) while bank volatility exposes investors to issuer risk (that the issuing bank will fail). These differences seem irrelevant, since ultimately investors bear both market risks and issuer risks. However, the levels and kinds of risks for investors, as well as the regulatory response to these risks, may differ.

C. Case Study: Assuring Confidence in the Financial System

The successful operation and even the existence of, the financial system are based on the confidence of all participants in the system. Those who place money in demand deposit accounts at banks (or other Institutions) must be confident that when they demand the money, it will be available and repaid. Those who purchase equity shares issued by a publicly traded corporation must be confident that the information on which they based their investment decision was accurate and that the rules for trading are transparent and stable. When confidence is lost, the results can be devastating, as was the case in the 1929 Stock Market Crash and subsequent Great Depression.

The Roaring Twenties was a period of great industrial expansion in the U.S. New technologies such as automobile, telephone, and radio created a cycle of growth and consumer confidence in the manufacturing sector. From 1921 to 1929 the U.S. gross domestic product (GDP) grew 45%.[7] The rapid growth of industrial production during this period was also reflected in the appreciating stock prices of publicly traded corporations. An index of the leading corporations of the day (the Dow Jones Industrial Average) increased from in 64 in August 1921 to 381 in September 1929.[8] The seemingly endless stock price appreciation led to speculation. "Buy a stock this week and next week it will be worth more" was the mantra on Wall Street and Main Street. A broad range of the population, not just the wealthy, invested in the stock market. Confidence in future appreciation of stock prices lead many investors to purchase stock on margin. That is, they bought stock with borrowed money. Margin-based investment, leveraging the investor's cash by only paying for a portion of the stock price and pledging the stock itself as collateral for the rest of the price which was borrowed, fueled the speculative bubble in the stock market.

While the industrial production was growing, the economic performance in the agricultural sector was not keeping pace. Between 1900 and 1930 the portion of the U.S. population was engaged in farming declined from 41% to 21.5%.[9] Agricultural output accounted for only 7.7%% of the country's GDP in 1929.[10] Prices for farm products fell dramatically in the early 1920s and remained depressed throughout the decade. Banks that served the agricultural regions of the country faced the dual

---

[7] Louis D. Johnston & Samuel H. Williamson, *What Was the U.S. GDP Then?*, MEASURINGWORTH (2008), http://www.measuringworth.org/usgdp/ (last visited July 17, 2009) (GDP in 2000 dollars increased from $595.1 billion to $865.2 billion); *see* OLIVIER BLANCHARD, MACROECONOMICS 204 Figure 10-1 (3d ed. 2003).

[8] *The Crash of 1929,* http://marketplace.publicradio.org/features/crash_1929/timeline.html (last visited July 8, 2009).

[9] CAROLYN DIMITRI ET AL., THE 20TH CENTURY TRANSFORMATION OF U.S. AGRICULTURE AND FARM POLICY 2 (2005) (U.S. Dep't of Agriculture), http://www.ers.usda.gov/publications/eib3/eib3.pdf (last visited July 8, 2009)..

[10] *Id.*

pressure of farmers defaulting on their mortgages and substantial withdrawals of savings. More than 500 banks went out of business from mid-1928 to mid-1929.[11] In addition to the liquidity crisis in the farm belt, the need for jobs to replace farm income caused a substantial migration of farm workers to the manufacturing sector. The expanding supply of labor kept manufacturing wages low. The combination of minimal farm income and low manufacturing wages led first to an expanded use of credit to fund purchases and then to a slow down in consumption.

In October 1929, the decade of confidence gave way, as signs of economic contraction became evident. On October 28, known as Black Monday, the Dow (market price of leading stocks) lost 12.8% of its value. At the end of the trading session, the Dow stood at only 260 compared to 380 only a month before.[12] The "run" on stocks was swift and deep. It also created a broader financial crisis. The first effect was an investor liquidity crunch. As investors were required to pay cash for margin calls, the need for ready cash increased. Investors had the alternative of selling the stocks to raise cash or using their bank savings. Banks came under pressure to provide more cash than they had in their vaults; banks at that time typically held less than 10% of deposits in cash.[13] Depositors, who feared losing their investments, demanded the money in their bank deposits. The "herd effect" took over, and lines formed at hundreds of banks around the country as depositors and investors clamored for their savings. The fallout for the banking sector was devastating. 9000 banks failed between 1930 and 1933.[14]

The Great Depression resulted in a vicious cycle. Firms reduced employment fearing lower sales. In turn, consumers reduced purchases fearing layoffs. And the downward spiral continued. The country had experienced numerous recessions since its founding. But unlike past slowdowns, which generally lasted less than three years, the Great Depression lasted from the end of 1929 through the entire 1930s. Unemployment exceeded a staggering 25% in 1933.[15] The human toll of the Depression cannot be overstated. People lost their homes: "Here were all these people living in old rusted-out car bodies. . . . One family . . . [was] living in a piano box. This wasn't just a little section; this was maybe 10 miles wide and 10 miles

---

[11] *Great Depression, in* WORLD BOOK ENCYCLOPEDIA 339 (1995)..

[12] *Timeline: A Selected Wall Street Chronology*, http://www.pbs.org/wgbh/amex/crash/timeline/timeline2.html (last visited Sept. 9, 2009) (noting September 3 peak of 381.17); *Market Data Center*, WSJ.COM, http://online.wsj.com/mdc/public/page/2_3047-djia_alltime.html (last visited Sept. 9, 2009) (noting October 28 close at 260.64)..

[13] Robert L. Stauffer, *Back to Basics: Reserve Requirements and Money Stock Changes, 1929-1936,* AM. ECON., Spring 2000, at 62, 62.

[14] *Great Depression, in* WORLD BOOK ENCYCLOPEDIA 340 (1995)..

[15] J. Bradford DeLong, *Slouching Toward Utopia?: The Economic History of the Twentieth Century – XIV. The Great Crash and the Great Slump* (1997), http://econ161.berkeley.edu/TCEH/Slouch_Crash14.html (last visited Sept. 9, 2009).

long. People living in whatever they could [join] together."[16] Finding any work was almost impossible. "In 1932, City of New York Police estimated that 7,000 persons over the age of 17 shined shoes for a living."[17] Food was scarce and even heating fuel had to be "hunted." "[S]everal hundred men risk[ing] their lives and several hundred women scrabbl[ing] in the mud for hours . . . searching eagerly for tiny chips of coal."[18]

The initial response to the financial crisis by the Hoover administration was to let the free market work through the "normal" business cycle. Leading economists of the time, including Secretary of the Treasury Mellon, Friedrich Hayek and Joseph Schumpeter argued that "liquidation" or purging of the economic ills was the right solution. "It [liquidation] will purge the rottenness out of the system. High costs of living and high living will come down. People will work harder, live a more moral life. Values will be adjusted, and enterprising people will pick up the wrecks from less competent people."[19] By 1932 there was mounting evidence that this recession was different. The liquidation concept failed to restart the economy. The newly-elected Franklin Roosevelt took a different tack. He and his advisors concluded that the government needed to step in and serve as the catalyst for new investments. The logic was that putting people to work would enable them to purchase goods and services again and that this in turn would encourage the private sector to increase output. The New Deal, a set of programs to reinvigorate the economy, was implemented throughout the 1930s. Examples of New Deal programs included the Public Works Administration which contracted with private sector companies to build public works. Another example was the Civil Works Administration which employed millions of workers on a temporary basis.

The process of rebuilding trust and confidence in the financial system was launched concurrently with the economic incentives. One of the first actions was to insure bank deposits and prevent future bank runs. President Roosevelt explained the problem to the public and vowed to prevent future runs. "I want to talk for a few minutes with the people of the United States about banking -- with the comparatively few who understand the mechanics of banking but more particularly with the overwhelming majority who use banks for the making of deposits and the drawing of checks. . . . First of all let me state the simple fact that when you deposit money in a bank the bank does not put the money into a safe deposit vault. . . . [T]he bank puts your money to work to keep the wheels of industry and of agriculture turning around. A comparatively small part of the money you put into the bank is kept in currency. . . . Because of undermined confidence on the part of the public, there was a general

---

[16] *Great Depression, in* WORLD BOOK ENCYCLOPEDIA 341 (1995)..

[17] *Id, at* 340.

[18] J. Bradford DeLong, *Slouching Toward Utopia?: The Economic History of the Twentieth Century – XIV. The Great Crash and the Great Slump* (Feb. 1997), , http://econ161.berkeley.edu/TCEH/Slouch_Crash14.html (last visited Sept. 9, 2009).

[19] *Id.*

rush by a large portion of our population to turn bank deposits into currency or gold. -- A rush so great that the soundest banks could not get enough currency to meet the demand. . . . By the afternoon of March 3 scarcely a bank in the country was open to do business. . . . Your Government does not intend that the history of the past few years shall be repeated. WE do not want and will not have another epidemic of bank failures."[20]

The solution was the establishment of the Federal Deposit Insurance Corporation (FDIC). "The Federal Deposit Insurance Corporation (FDIC) preserves and promotes public confidence in the U.S. financial system by insuring deposits in banks and thrift institutions for at least $250,000 [in 2009]; by identifying, monitoring and addressing risks to the deposit insurance funds; and by limiting the effect on the economy and the financial system when a bank or thrift institution fails."[21] The rationale for the FDIC was that if consumers knew their money was safe, runs on banks would cease. The funds to pay depositors in the event of a bank's failure were generated by premiums paid by member banks. Since its inception no depositor has lost money resulting from a bank failure.

Regulations of the securities markets were also imposed in the aftermath of the stock market crash. The Securities Act of 1933, also known as the "Truth in Securities Act," required issuers to disclose material information about their securities and explicitly prohibited and imposed criminal sanctions on fraud in the offer and sale of securities. The legislation was based on the rationale that comprehensive and accurate information would enable investors to make educated investment decisions. A year later the Securities Exchange Act of 1934 was enacted to improve the trust and confidence in the secondary markets where investors traded in securities through market intermediaries. Legislation established the Securities and Exchange Commission (SEC) to oversee the securities markets and specified the information to be disclosed by large issuers on an ongoing basis (such as the annual 10K and quarterly 10Q). The Act also brought broker-dealers under a self-regulatory organization subject to federal oversight.

The combined actions taken to restore faith in the operations of both institutions and markets were successful. Between 1940 and 1980 the number of bank failures was very small. During this same period the stock market prices fluctuated but did not crash. The savings and loan crisis of the 1980s and the "Black Monday" (October 19, 1987) market selloff put the "anti-run" measures that were adopted in the 1930s to the test. While there were instances of panic at that time and the resulting recession in 1991-1992 was painful, overall, the financial system weathered the storm. Within two years the stock market indexes were back to the pre-Black Monday levels.

[20] Transcript of Speech by President Franklin D. Roosevelt Regarding the Banking Crisis (Mar. 12, 1933), http://www.fdic.gov/about/history/3-12-33transcript.html (last visited Sept. 9, 2009)..

[21] FDIC, *Who Is the FDIC?* (June 9, 2009), http://www.fdic.gov/about/learn/symbol/index.html, (last visited Sept. 9, 2009).

Two decades passed without a significant threat to the financial system. By early 2007, signs of a brewing crisis were seen. As housing prices began to level off, fears grew that "subprime" mortgages (paying low interest for 2-3 years) to borrowers that could not afford them when the interest rates were automatically raised would lead to defaults. The subprime sector of the mortgage portfolio had grown rapidly since 2000. Six hundred and fifty billion dollars of the mortgage value initiated in 2006 was to subprime borrowers. The growth in subprime mortgages was also driven by pooling the mortgages and selling participations in the pools to investors. These participations were based on the logic of the law of large numbers – the risk of an individual default would be mitigated by investing in a large pool of mortgages. The fact that potential for default could be highly correlated was given little consideration. The slow-down in real estate appreciation, the wave of mortgages that adjusted upward, and the poor quality of most subprime loans created the unanticipated correlation of defaults. By 2008, thirteen percent of all subprime mortgage loans were delinquent and more than one million housing units were facing the prospect of foreclosure.

The investors in subprime mortgage-backed securities included commercial banks, investment banks, and hedge funds. Despite their level of sophistication, these financial institutions incurred significant losses in their subprime mortgage holdings. News of the losses triggered a crisis in confidence in both the banks and companies that held large positions in subprime loans, and more generally in the financial system itself. One of the first impacts of the subprime mortgages crisis was a tightening of credit and consequent loss of liquidity throughout financial system.

Uncertainty about potential losses inhibited banks from lending money to other financial institutions; for fear that the borrowers would not be able to prepay their obligations. Ironically, an early casualty of the U.S. subprime crisis was a British bank that held no subprime loans. Northern Rock was one of England's top five mortgage lenders. This bank's business model was to raise most of its capital for lending from secondary credit markets rather than from individual depositors. Thus Northern Rock raised money in the wholesale market and sold loans in the retail market. The bank profited from the spread between the wholesale and retail interest rates. For many years this model worked well and the bank grew rapidly because it was able to tap an ample supply of money on reasonable terms. However, when the liquidity crisis came in 2007, the bank was unable to draw capital. Depositors learned of the bank's limited access to funds, feared that their money was not safe, and began a run on the bank -- the first run on an English bank since 1866.[22] The bank had ample assets to meet its obligations to depositors but the assets were tied up in mortgage loans and could not cover immediate demands. In one day alone

[22] *The Bank that Failed,* ECONOMIST, Sept. 22, 2007, LEXIS, News Library, Curnws File.

customers withdrew 1 billion pounds from the bank. The run was stopped only when the government's Bank of England agreed to guarantee deposits.

Revelations of the subprime investment losses by Institutions and Market participants accelerated during the fourth quarter of 2007 and the first quarter of 2008. The concurrent erosion of confidence in the financial system triggered a "run" mentality. The flight from Bear Stearns stock is illustrative. Bear Stearns was a Blue Chip investment bank founded in 1923.[23] As recently as 2007, the bank was rated one of the "most admired" securities firms by *Fortune* magazine.[24] Its January 2007 share price was $172.[25] News of Bear Stearns' subprime losses became public in 2007 but the bank was able to survive the first round of losses. By March 2008, there were concerns that Bear Stearns might not survive. Shareholders ran, actually sprinted, from Bear Stearn's during the month of March 2008. The bank's stock price ended February above $80 per share. By mid-March the price had plummeted to a low of $2.

Fear of the Bear Stearns' collapse and a resulting chain reaction run on other subprime holders led the U.S. Treasury Department to broker a deal for JPMorgan to acquire Bear Stearn's at a fire-sale price. Moreover, the government offered loan guarantees in order to assure that the transaction would close.

By early 2008, the subprime crisis began taking its toll on commercial banks. IndyMac Bancorp became the second largest bank failure in U.S. history in July 2008. Independent National Mortgage Corporation operated as both a thrift and mortgage bank. Through organic growth and acquisitions IndyMac became the largest savings and loan association in the Los Angeles area and one of the top 10 mortgage originators in the U.S. The bank maintained a large portfolio of mortgage-backed securities. As the bank reported the declining value of those assets in 2007 and early 2008, it faced a liquidity crunch. Other potential lenders declined to provide the bank with the necessary operating cash, concerned that the bank will fail.

The run on IndyMac was triggered in part by a letter from Senator Charles Schumer to federal regulators, questioning the bank's viability. "I am concerned that IndyMac's financial deterioration poses significant risks to both taxpayers and borrowers, and that the regulatory community may not be prepared to take measures

---

[23] *A History of Bear Stearns,* N.Y. TIMES, Mar. 17, 2008, http://www.nytimes.com/imagepages/2008/03/17/business/20080317_BEAR_STEARNS_GRAPHIC.html (last visited Sept. 9, 2009).

[24] *The List of Industry Stars,* FORTUNE, Mar. 19, 2007, at 5, LEXIS, News Library, Arcnws File.

[25] William D. Cohan, *The Rise and Fall of Jimmy Cayne,* FORTUNE, Aug. 18, 2008, at 90, LEXIS, News Library, Curnws File.

that would help prevent the collapse of IndyMac or minimize the damage should such a failure occur.'"'"[26] When the letter became public, the race was on to withdraw funds from the bank notwithstanding the fact that most of the deposits were insured by the FDIC. One and a third billion dollars were withdrawn from the bank in only eleven days.[27] Even those that did not withdraw their money questioned their own decision. "[A]n IndyMac customer . . . said she almost withdrew her money after hearing about Mr. Schumer's letter two weeks ago. Once she felt assured that the F.D.I.C. would insure her money, she decided against it . . . because she felt a public duty not to contribute to 'mass panic.' 'Now I wish I had withdrawn it . . . .'"[28] On July 11, 2008, IndyMac "was closed by the Office of Thrift Supervision (OTS) and the Federal Deposit Insurance Corporation (FDIC) was named conservator."[29]

Bear Stearns and IndyMac are only examples of the runs that have occurred in conjunction with the subprime mortgage loans. Between January and August 2008, nine banks were added to the FDIC Failed Bank List. There were three in 2007 and none in 2006 and 2005.[30] Investor flight from Blue Chip financial sector corporations erased billion of dollars in market capitalization. In the period from 9/20/07 to 11/5/07 alone, the sector lost $120 billion in market capitalization.[31]

Discussion Topics

1. How do "runs" occur in Markets as compared to Institutions?
2. Who benefits and who loses from "runs" on the Markets and "runs" on Institutions?
3. Which "runs" are more easily stopped or controlled? Those on Markets or those on Institutions?

---

[26] Cheyenne Hopkins & Joe Adler, *Schumer Voices IndyMac Fears,* AM. BANKER, June 27, 2008, at 5, LEXIS, News Library, Curnws File.

[27] Louise Story, *Regulators Seize IndyMac After a Run on the Bank,* N.Y. TIMES, July 12, 2008, at 5, LEXIS, News Library, Nyt File..

[28] *Id.*

[29] FDIC, *Failed Bank Information* (last updated Aug. 6, 2009), http://www.fdic.gov/bank/individual/failed/IndyMac.html (last visited Sept. 9, 2009).C.

[30] FDIC, *Failed Bank List* (last updated Sept. 9, 2009), http://www.fdic.gov/bank/individual/failed/banklist.html (last visited Sept. 9, 2009).

[31] David Gaffen, *Erasing $120 Billion in Market Cap,* WSJ.COM, Nov. 5, 2007, http://blogs.wsj.com/marketbeat/2007/11/05/erasing-120-billion-in-market-cap/ (last visited Sept. 9, 2009).

Chapter 2: An Overview of Securitization

The nature of the financial system provides the context for understanding the process of securitization. This chapter provides an overview of that process. A prototype example is used to illustrate both the process and the participants. The differentiation between securitization and structured finance is also explained. The benefits and drawbacks of securitization are highlighted here and dealt with in greater detail in subsequent chapters. A case study covering the securitization of residential mortgages explains the mechanics of the securitization process in the sector where the technique has been most extensively used.

A. Securitization as a Process of Intermediation[32]

Securitization is an intermediation process that converts non-liquid assets (e.g. loans) into liquid, tradable financial assets (e.g. securities and bonds). There are a number of variations of the securitization process and the assets to which it applies, but its main form in the United States involves a large number of relatively small loans and to a smaller extent—receivables (short-term debts due usually for services and purchase). The steps to securitizing these loans or debts and the main actors involved are detailed below and illustrated in Figure 1.

First, lenders, usually Institutions, make loans to borrowers. Sometimes mortgage brokers contact borrowers and connect them with the lenders.
Second, often the loans are purchased by intermediaries that design and create the securitization. They are called "sponsors" or "Originators."
Third, the loans are pooled and transferred to an entity called Special Purpose Vehicle ("SPV") or Special Purpose Entity ("SPE"). This entity is organized by the lenders or by the Originators.[33]
Fourth, often the risk of the asset pool is supported by a collateral or other "credit enhancement mechanisms," such as guarantees.
Fifth, the SPV issues its securities which are then sold by Market intermediaries. These securities are often segmented into classes or "tranches" based on seniority of payment.
Sixth, a secondary market in the securities is developed by Market intermediaries, such as securities brokers.

Appraisers, rating agencies, securities brokers and servicers also participate in the securitization process. Their roles are detailed in subsequent chapters.

[32] 1 TAMAR FRANKEL, SECURITIZATION § 2.1 (Ann Taylor Schwing ed., 2d ed. 2005).

[33] The transfer must be a true sale to protect the ultimate investors in the securities that are issued by the SPV. See Chapter 9.

Figure 1: The Securitization Process

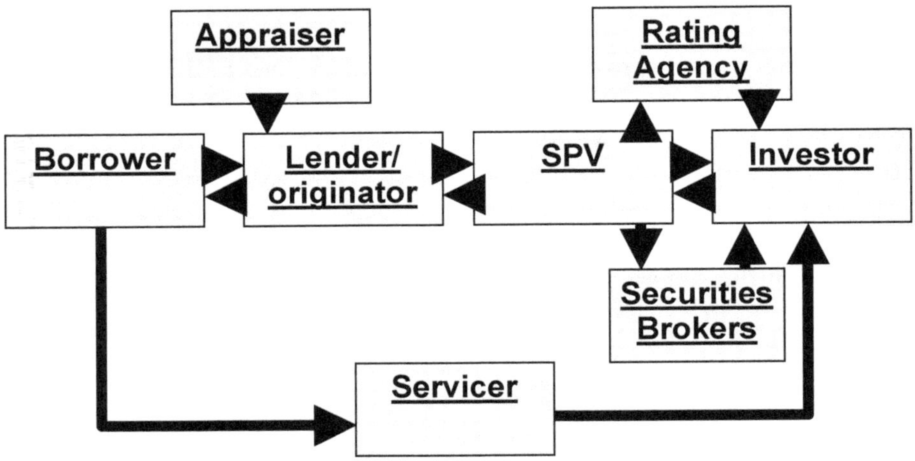

By this pooling technique and the guarantees of the securities issued by the pools (the SPVs), the United States Government propelled the securitization of mortgage loans into a huge secondary Market in mortgage-backed securities. The securities offered safe investments for pension funds, other institutional investors and individuals. This process served as a model for securitizing other types of loans and debt by the Government and the private sector.[34]

a. A Prototype of Securitization

The following is a description of a prototype securitization. Acorp is an auto manufacturer that offers financing to auto buyers through its dealers. Acorp has a finance subsidiary – Asub -- that raises funds in the Markets by issuing its own obligations, and transfers them through Acorp to the dealers in exchange for auto buyers' loan agreements and notes. Asub services the loans for a fee. It receives the buyers' payments and exercises lenders' rights in connection with the loans.

Acorp organizes a special purpose corporation, Spcorp. The equity of Spcorp is issued to the designated underwriter of Spcorp's securities. Spcorp issues three classes of debt securities. Class A bears 6 percent and matures in one year. Class B bears 6.5 percent and matures in two years. Class C bears 7 percent and matures in three years. While all classes are paid quarterly, Class A is paid principal and

[34] The government has supported mortgage backed securities. For example, Fannie Mae, which is a semi-government corporation established under a statute, guarantees securities that represent mortgage loans by persons whom this semi-government corporation qualifies. The corporation can issue guarantees which are backed by a guarantee of the United States. Guarantees reduce the interest rate, which the investors would demand, because the guarantees reduce the risk that the borrowers would default, and that their homes would not cover the loans. The lower interest benefits the borrowers as well.

interest; Classes B and C are paid interest quarterly but are paid the principal only during the last six months before maturity.

Acorp guarantees that it will pay Spcorp's losses from defaults on its portfolio loans up to 5 percent of the face amount of the portfolio. Bank1 issues a letter of credit to Spcorp promising to pay up to 6 percent of any additional defaults in Spcorp's portfolio. Spcorp's securities are rated AA by two rating agencies.

Bank2 enters into a guaranteed investment contract ("GIC") with SpCorp. Bank2 agrees to accept all payments on Spcorp's loan portfolio before they are due and pay on these amounts a specified interest rate. Bank2 also agrees to advance funds to Spcorp if borrowers pay late (but do not default), thus assuring prompt payment on Spcorp's securities.

Spcorp's securities are distributed by a syndicate in a public offering. Bank3 is appointed trustee-custodian for the security holders. After distribution of the securities, the borrowers make payments to Subcorp, which retains a servicing fee. Subcorp is required to transfer the rest of the funds to Bank3 within four weeks of receipt, getting the benefit of a four-week interest-free use of the funds (cash float). The funds are then transferred to a collection account at Bank3 that serves as trustee-custodian. Prepayments by the borrowers are transferred to Bank2, and interest is received by Bank3 from that bank. Bank3 then pays off the amounts due to each class of the securities.

b. Structured Financing

Another form of pooling and distributing financial assets to the Market is structured financing. Even though the terms "securitization" and "structured financing" are used interchangeably, we use them to denote a somewhat different type of conversion from illiquid to liquid financial assets. The difference between securitization and structured financing appears in the nature and number of the borrowers. "Securitization" usually is effected by the transfer to the SPV of numerous small obligations issued by numerous small obligors such as mortgagors or credit card borrowers. "Structured financing," on the other hand, usually is effected by the transfer to an entity, such as an SPV, of obligations issued by one large obligor backed by (collateralized) various properties, with or without recourse to the obligor. Even though such an obligor could either borrow from a bank or issue its own obligations to the Market, structured financing may offer the obligor a benefit of reducing the investors' risks from the other business of the corporation and limiting the risk to the obligations contained in the SPV.

For example, suppose a large construction company needs to finance its future building operations. Construction business is fairly risky and subject to market volatility. If the company issues bonds to the market, investors would demand interest commensurate with the risk of the company's business. Now suppose the company has real estate or rental properties, which have had historically a very high rate of occupancy. The company borrowed and mortgaged the property, and then transferred the mortgage loan to an SPV. The obligations under the loans would also carry the rents from the property as collateral. In such a case the investors might require a lower interest rate because the risk of the company's business has been removed and the risk from lower occupancy of the real estate is far lower, in light of the past performance of the rental property.

Another example is a small company that owns receivables of companies with a far higher credit rating. If the company borrows, its lower credit may require it to pay a higher interest rate than if it transferred the receivables to an SPV and offered investors securities in the SPV, backed by its clients' obligations. Since those obligations involve a higher credit, the company will pay a lower interest rate. In both cases we call the financing "structured financing."

> **Discussion Topic**
> What are the costs and benefits to the obligors, lenders, underwriters, Originators, and investors under the different methods of raising funds: (i) borrowing from banks, (ii) issuing their own obligations directly to investors, or (iii) issuing their obligations to an entity that in turn issues its own obligations to investors?

B. Benefits and Drawbacks of Markets, Institutions and Securitization[35]

a. Description of Pros and Cons

There are a number of criteria for determining the benefits of an intermediation system. One criterion is positive: the larger the number of savers and borrowers that an intermediation system can serve, the greater are its benefits. The second criterion is related to costs and risks: the lower the relative costs and risks of an intermediation system, the more beneficial the system is. Thus, a system is preferable if it involves relatively low information costs, or reduces risks by diversification, or shifts costs and risks to a party for whom the costs and risks are relatively lower, or routes long-term investments to Institutional investors with long-term rather than short-term liabilities so that their assets and liabilities can be better matched.

The concept of costs covers a broad spectrum and ranges from quantifiable dollars and cents to social and even individual emotional costs that cannot be quantified. The concept of risk also covers a broad spectrum, including the most prevalent risks: credit risk (that borrowers will default), Market risk (that the interest rate will change), and intermediary risk (that the intermediary will fail).

---

[35] 1 TAMAR FRANKEL, SECURITIZATION § 1.3 (Ann Taylor Schwing ed., 2d ed. 2005).

This section analyzes the traditional intermediation systems and securitization without offering a final calculus of the overall result. However, a comparison with the traditional systems suggests that under certain circumstances securitization may be preferable, notwithstanding its drawbacks. For example, a major benefit from securitization is that it enables Institutions and large organizations that hold long-term loans to covert these loans to securities, in which investors can trade in the Markets. Therefore, investors in the Markets will own the loans that otherwise banks would have held. This feature provides liquidity to Institutions. They can make loans, securitize them and sell the securities backed by the loans. Or they can sell the loans to originators who will securitize the loans. This feature strengthens the structure of Institutions. They can more easily match their liabilities and assets.

The drawback of securitization is that it feeds larger Markets, which are more volatile than Institutions. Making loans for sale enables banks to make many more loans than banks that make loans to keep. If Market volatility is extreme, bubbles and crashes may become the order of the day and render the economy unstable. To evaluate these benefits and drawbacks, liquidity and illiquidity are compared under various scenarios. Another drawback of securitization is the risks to investors from additional new intermediaries who participate in the securitization process. This process includes not only Institutions that make loans or organizations that hold receivables but also securities underwriters and securities brokers, and sometimes the brokers of the lenders. Additional intermediaries increase to investors what economists call "agency costs" and what lawyers call the risk of breach of fiduciary duties. Similar risks to investors stem from the new capacities in which traditional intermediaries serve. No longer are the banks or mortgage bankers the lenders. They have become sellers of the loans they make, and in that capacity their incentives have changed, and these incentives affect the investors.

Traditional intermediaries may lack experience performing in these capacities and may not be regulated adequately in these functions. To be sure, regulation can reduce such drawbacks and enhance the development of securitization and its benefits. And yet, as we shall discuss later, regulation did not stop the growth of securitization in sub-prime mortgage loans that ended in serious incapacity of the markets and drying up of liquidity. In fact, regulation did not prevent the scandalous behavior of Enron Corporation and did not reach the advisors of that corporation that caused so much harm to so many of its employees and investors. It may well be that other mechanisms should be put in place to prevent these events from reoccurring.

Discussion Topic

Good things, such as food, can turn into bad things, such as obesity and even death. Their "goodness" or "badness" depend on a balance under certain conditions. If that is so, what would be the question that should be asked with respect to speculation, volatility and liquidity?

b. Securitization in the Context of Markets and Institutions[36]

As an intermediation system, securitization combines traditional Markets and Institutions, but the system it produces differs from the system in which intermediaries have a discretely-assigned function, as they have operated in the past.

First, securitization "unbundles" and recombines Institutional functions. Traditionally, Institutions act as initial lenders and continue to hold the loans they make. Yet, many Institutions are better suited to perform only lending, and usually only to particular types of borrowers.

Securitization separates initial lenders from holders of the loans they made and enables the Market to allocate these functions to different actors. Rather than reserve loan origination for Institutions, securitization enables anyone to make loans if it is profitable to do so, and do it in a competitive environment. For example, lenders may raise funds for lending by attracting investors to a lending business (rather than attracting depositors). In addition, loans made for sale rather than for holding enable lenders to re-loan the money from the sale, thus profiting from the lending transactions perhaps more than from holding the loans.

This separation of functions can benefit borrowers by enlarging the pool of lenders. It may affect banks adversely by reducing their monopoly as lenders, but the virtue of monopoly is a weak argument against securitization.

Separating the making of loans and the holding of loans also helps lower the risks for Institutions and arguably to the financial system as well. The separation allows long-term illiquid loans to be routed to individual and Institutional investors with matching long-term liabilities. As mentioned, one of the dangers for Institutional intermediaries such as banks is that their liabilities and their assets do not match. They might have assets consisting of long-term loans (e.g., 30 year mortgages) and liabilities that are short-term (e.g., demand deposits). If, for any reason the demand deposit holders demand their money at a greater number than usual, the Institutions might not have sufficient cash to honor their obligations, even though the "good and solid" mortgage loans are being paid as required.

Moreover, Institutions that lend and hold loans cannot diversify their loan portfolios effectively. Demand for loans usually follows business cycles. In addition, Institutions have few groups of customers that they seek to keep and lend, as their loan officers become expert in their customers' businesses. Securitization allows Institutions, particularly banks, to continue their lending business and to diversify

---

[36] 1 TAMAR FRANKEL, SECURITIZATION § 3.2 (Ann Taylor Schwing ed., 2d ed. 2005).

their loan portfolios effectively by selling loans of similar vintage and industry and buying securities backed by other types of loans and borrowers.

Second, securitization separates two other functions that have been traditionally combined: originating loans and servicing loans. A lender that makes loans might wish to outsource the function of collecting on the loans. Another specialized institution may operate as the servicer, not only to the particular banker but to other bankers as well. The servicer has the list of borrowers and is charged with collecting the payments of the borrowers and paying the lenders-investors after deducting the servicing fees.[37]

Thus, this separation of functions helps reduce the cost of servicing when servicing requires substantial investment (e.g., computer facilities) beyond the capabilities of small Originators. Loan Originators that choose not to service can sell the servicing function for loans that they originate, especially if the buying servicer offers a better service at lower cost, and the servicing includes the collection of loans in default and foreclosure of collateral, both of which require expertise. Alternatively, loan Originators may sell the loans and retain the servicing functions for the income stream, and continued contact with the borrowers. Thus, under securitization, the Market allocates the servicing function to more efficient servicers.

Third, like other Institutions, securitization by pooling intermediates between investors and borrowers with different desires. It offers investments on different terms than those of the securitized loans (in amounts, maturities, and risks). Furthermore, it can satisfy investors with different desires by issuing more than one class of securities without changing the terms of the loans for borrowers.

These techniques help reduce the risks to Institutions. Initial lenders do not have to hold loans that do not match their liabilities. Securitization by pooling creates a new kind of Institution – the SPV -- that is more stable because it is able to match its assets and liabilities more closely. They issue securities that shift the risks created by the parties to different classes of investors. These investors, however, may have liabilities that match the terms of the SPV securities. Furthermore, if the SPVs miscalculate projected cash flows from the loans they hold, they will benefit one class of securities at the expense of another rather than the SPV as a whole.

[37] Investors in asset-backed securities do not wish to receive a trickle of payments from the pool of borrowers, as each of them might pay on another due date. Rather, investors may wish to receive larger lump sums at predictable dates. The servicer therefore serves this important function of collecting the money due from the borrowers, and distributing the larger sums to the ultimate investors. Often the servicer is the bank or institution that made the original loans which were securitized. It has the names and contact information of the borrowers and sometimes knows who they are. The bank often pays the investors the amounts due even if not all borrowers paid on time, and then charges a fee for the prepayment. Finally, the bank has the facility of holding the multitude of mortgage documents, because this is part of its business.

Fourth, securitization creates a secondary Market for investors to meet their liquidity needs, thus substituting for Institutions Market liquidity to pay investors on demand or on short notice, as banks must do. This substitution helps the sellers of loans to match the maturities of their liabilities with the maturities of their assets more closely and to reduce their liquidity risks, which is something banks and thrifts have always found difficult to do.

Fifth, by providing investors with market liquidity, securitization also reduces liquidity risks for banks that hold SPV securities because the securities can be quickly sold to pay the Institutions' short-term liabilities, for example, deposits and savings accounts. In sum, securitization reduces the cost of making loans, lowers the risks of holding them, and reduces liquidity and credit risks for Institutions by enabling them to design more flexible and rational financial structures.

C. Case study: MBS - Using Capital for One Mortgage and Then Another and Another

"One of the greatest innovations in US credit history in the past 30 years was the creation of the mortgage-backed securities (MBS) market. The securitization of mortgages brought new capital and led to more liquid assets and more efficient market pricing of mortgages. It also led to specialized intermediation of the mortgage markets. Together, these improvements lowered mortgage rates for borrowers, broadened homeownership and eliminated regional disparities in the deployment of capital for home mortgage lending."[38]

The creation of the Government National Mortgage Association, nicknamed Ginnie Mae, was a key actor in this new financial development. Congress established Ginnie Mae under the National Housing Act in 1968 as a government owned corporation within the Department of Housing and Urban Development. Title III of the Act, National Mortgage Associations, has as its purpose "to establish secondary market facilities for residential mortgages, to provide that the operations thereof shall be financed by private capital to the maximum extent feasible, and to authorize such facilities to- (1) provide stability in the secondary market for residential mortgages; (2) respond appropriately to the private capital market; (3) provide ongoing assistance to. . . mortgages on housing for low- and moderate income families . . . ; (4) promote access to mortgage credit throughout the Nation (including central cites, rural areas, and underserved areas) . . . ."[39]

[38] Ivo Kolev, *Primer: Mortgage-Backed Securities,* July 29, 2004 (Financial Policy Forum: Derivatives Study Center), http://www.financialpolicy.org/fpfprimermbs.htm (last visited Sept. 9, 2009), http://www.financialpolicy.org/fpfprimermbs.htm (last visited Sept. 9, 2009)..

[39] 12 U.S.C. § 1716 (2006).

Ginnie Mae was empowered to buy and sell mortgages that were insured under the National Housing Act, Servicemen's Readjustment Act or Public Health Services Act. In addition, the company could pool mortgages into securities and sell them to third party investors. The resulting MBS were particularly attractive because they were guaranteed by Ginnie Mae and backed by the "full faith and credit of the United States."[40] The funds to pay any defaults were generated through a guaranty fee applied to all transactions.

Why did the government need to create Ginnie Mae when there were banks around the country already offering mortgage loans to potential homeowners? At that time, banks, depository institutions as well as savings and loans (S&Ls), held their mortgage loans from initiation to maturity. Mortgages were difficult to sell to outside investors because they were not standardized and it was difficult to mitigate repayment risks. The lending institutions raised capital primarily from deposits and secondarily from equity and debt offerings. Since regulations capped the amount of bank debt and banks were only permitted to draw customers from defined geographic areas, funds for mortgage loans were limited. Moreover, economic conditions in the late 1960s reduced the banking industry's ability to attract deposits. Government spending for President Johnson's Great Society Program and the costs of the Vietnam War led to inflationary pressures on prices. The Consumer Price Index (CPI) increased from 29.8 in January 1961 to 37.8 in January 1970.[41] Fears of future inflation were realized as the CPI soared to nearly 100 in 1982.[42] Interest rates also rose, from 4.5% in 1961 to 7.9% in 1970 and to 14.8% in 1982.[43] Despite the rise in both inflation and interest rates, banks' regulations limited their ability to offer higher interest rates on deposits, further reducing the ability of these institutions to attract capital that could be used for mortgages. The solution to increase mortgage capital availability was to tap the funds of investment institutions by packaging mortgage loans into securities and creating a secondary market for the securities.

---

[40] 12 U.S.C. § 1721(g)(1) (2006).

[41] *Historical CPI,* http://inflationdata.com/inflation/Consumer_Price_Index/HistoricalCPI.aspx?rsCPI_currentPage=4 (last visited Sept. 9, 2009) (1950-61 data); *Historical CPI,* http://inflationdata.com/inflation/Consumer_Price_Index/HistoricalCPI.aspx?rsCPI_currentPage=3 (last visited Sept. 9, 2009) (1962-73 data).

[42] *Historical CPI,* http://inflationdata.com/inflation/Consumer_Price_Index/HistoricalCPI.aspx?rsCPI_currentPage=2 (last visited Sept. 9, 2009) (1974-85 data).

[43] *See, e.g., Prime Rate History,* http://www.wsjprimerate.us/wall_street_journal_prime_rate_history.htm (last visited Sept. 9, 2009).

GNMA was created to jump-start the process for securities backed by government guaranteed mortgage loans.[44]

GNMA issued the first MBS in 1970. Exhibit 1 shows the process for creating Ginnie Mae mortgage-backed securities. The process begins with lenders providing loans to borrowers that are guaranteed or insured by the Federal Housing Administration, the Veterans Administration or under the Public Health Services Act. Issuers, often the lenders themselves, pool loans and create the MBS. Broker-dealers in turn sell the securities directly to investors. Borrowers make their monthly interest and principal payments to a service agency which passes the funds, less administrative fees, directly to the investors. Ginnie Mae's role is to provide investors with a guarantee of timely payments. The initial MBS were designed as "pass-through" securities. All these securities had similar yields and maturities that generated interest and principal repayment funds that were passed through to the investors on a pro rata basis. The MBS issued by Ginnie Mae during the 1970s (know as GNMA I) consisted of securities backed by mortgage pools combined by a single lender, and holding primarily mortgage loans on individual family houses. These mortgages were insured or guaranteed by federal agencies.

Ginnie Mae's MBS program has been very successful. From an initial launch in 1970, Ginnie Mae recorded a cumulative amount of $2.66 trillion of mortgage-backed securities in 2007. Exhibit 2 shows this exponential increase. Part of the success is attributable to the growing global search for attractive investment opportunities. Ginnie Mae's full faith and credit backing by the Untied States is a strong selling point. The company has also introduced a broad array of MBS investment options.

In support of the social welfare component of Ginnie Mae's mission, the company securitizes mortgages on multifamily dwellings to increase affordability of rental units. Access to reasonably priced rental housing provides the renters with a stable living environment until they can enter the home ownership market. Ginnie Mae has also introduced the Targeted Lending Initiative to insure mortgage capital flows into underserved areas. The program offers reduced guarantee fees for loans initiated in the target areas.

Ginnie Mae is not alone in offering MBS. Both Fannie Mae and Freddie Mac also securitize mortgages. The key differentiators between Ginnie Mae and Fannie/Freddie are that (1) only Ginnie Mae's MBS are backed by the full faith and credit of the U.S. government and (2) all Ginnie Mae mortgages are insured by

---

[44] The Federal Home Loan Mortgage Association (Freddie Mac) and the Federal National Mortgage Association (Fannie Mae) were also used to provide a secondary market for conventional mortgage loans (those not guaranteed by the government) for the S&L and banking industries respectively.

federal programs. Both Fannie and Freddie are Government Sponsored Enterprises (GSEs.) As such both were created by federal legislation and have since been privatized into publicly traded shareholder corporations although the government retains some control in the choice of board members and top management as well as regulatory oversight. Both offer guarantees against credit loss but neither receives funding from the government. They do have, however, some special benefits such as certain tax exemptions and the ability to borrow funds from the Treasury. The close ties between Fannie and Freddie to U.S. public policies on home ownership have led investors to believe these entities would receive special treatment if they experienced financial difficulty which in fact happened in the wake of the 2008 financial crisis.

Fannie Mae focuses its securitization efforts on conventional mortgages which are not guaranteed by federal agencies. "Fannie Mae-issued mortgage-backed security[ies] represent[] an undivided beneficial ownership interest in a group or pool of one or more mortgages."[45] The MBS pools, created from loans that conform to Fannie Mae's requirements, are "guarantee[d] as to timely payment of principal and interest."[46] The growth in Fannie Mae MBS mirrored that of Ginnie Mae as shown in Exhibit 3.

Freddie Mac mortgage-backed securities are similar to those offered by Fannie Mae. The primary security issued by Freddie Mac initially was a Participation Certificate (PC.) These certificates are backed by pools of conventional mortgages. The PCs are created through a Cash Program where Freddie Mac buys mortgages from loan Originators, pools, and then sells the securities issued by the pool to investors. In response to liquidity problems in the thrift industry, Freddie Mac introduced the Guarantor/Swap Program where Freddie Mac allows originators to exchange (swap) pooled mortgages for PCs in those same pools. For example, if a thrift has $50 million of mortgages it can exchange these mortgages for a Freddie Mac PCs which are backed by a mortgage pool in the same $50 million in mortgage loans.[47] The swap program enabled thrifts to exchange mortgages that were trading below par (carrying interest rates below prevailing rates) for PCs without having to recognize the loss of value for financial reporting purposes. Another Freddie Mac innovation was the creation of Collateralized Mortgage Obligations (CMOs.) This product allows pools of mortgages to be subdivided into various bond classes with different levels of risk mitigation. The ability of investors to customize the payment stream

---

[45] Fannie Mae, *Basics of Fannie Mae MBS,* FANNIEMAE.COM,. http://www.fanniemae.com/mbs/mbsbasics/index.jhtml?p=Mortgage-Backed+Securities&s=Basics+of+Fannie+Mae+MBS (last modified June 16, 2009) (last visited Sept. 9, 2009).

[46] *Id.*

[47] FRANK J. FABOZZI & FRANCO MODIGLIANI, MORTGAGE AND MORTGAGE-BACKED SECURITIES MARKETS 23 (1992).

and risk management brought more liquidity into the secondary MBS market. Freddie Mac has evolved to offer a full range of MBS offerings covering single-family and multifamily housing as well as adjustable rate mortgages. The company's MBS business has grown rapidly since the early 1970s. Freddie Mac has financed the homes of 50 million families as of 2007, half of which support low- and moderate-income families.[48] The company estimates that the interest expense savings that it generates for a $150,000 mortgage is $18,000.

The foregoing discussion of MBS deals only with government owned or affiliated entities that issue MBS. There are also MBS instruments issued by private parties known as "private label" offerings. The MBS offered by Ginnie Mae, Freddie, and Fannie are for loans that conform to underwriting standards including loan to market value ratio and total loan size. The private sector has stepped into the securitization market for nonconforming loans, especially, "jumbo" mortgages, those that exceed the conforming loan dollar value. Bank of America was the first to offer private label MBS pass-through securities in the late 1970s. The growth of the private label offerings was limited because of nonstandardized products, SEC registration regulations (the final pool was not known at the time of registration), and unfavorable tax rules. Three government led actions overcame these constraints. First, The Secondary Mortgage Market Enhancement Act of 1984 permitted federally chartered banks and thrifts to invest in private label MBS if the security was rated AA or better. This Act opened a large pool of potential investment funds to the private labels. The second action was that the SEC altered its registration requirements for private label MBS "by permitting the registration of securities backed by blind pools, as long as the issue commits to obtain a specified quality rating and provides sufficient information about the potential pool in the prospectus."[49] Tax treatment was addressed in the Tax Reform Act of 1986 which set the framework for not taxing the issuer's distribution entity (known as a special purpose vehicle) on pass-through and REMIC structures.

Taken together, MBS have transferred trillions of dollars from the pockets of investors around the globe into the hands of new homeowners. What accounts of the rapid growth of MBS? The answer is the MBS offer "something for everyone." For borrowers MBS increase availability of mortgage funds, which in turn yield lower interest rates. Issuers are able to move long-term, illiquid assets off their books and obtain fresh cash for new loans. Fidelity Investment Company describes the benefits of MBS for investors to include (1) attractive yields, usually exceeding investment grade corporate bonds (see Exhibit 4); (2) credit quality, explicit or implicit federal guarantees against credit loss; and (3) liquidity, a robust secondary market for MBS

---

[48] FREDDIE MAC, 2006 ANNUAL REPORT, http://www.freddiemac.com/investors/ar/pdf/2006ar_cover.pdf (last visited Sept. 9, 2009).

[49] FRANK J. FABOZZI & FRANCO MODIGLIANI, MORTGAGE AND MORTGAGE-BACKED SECURITIES MARKETS 33 (1992).

securities. Finally, MBS have allowed policy makers to make the dream of homeownership a reality for millions of Americans.

Exhibit 1
Ginnie Mae Mortgage-Backed Securities Process

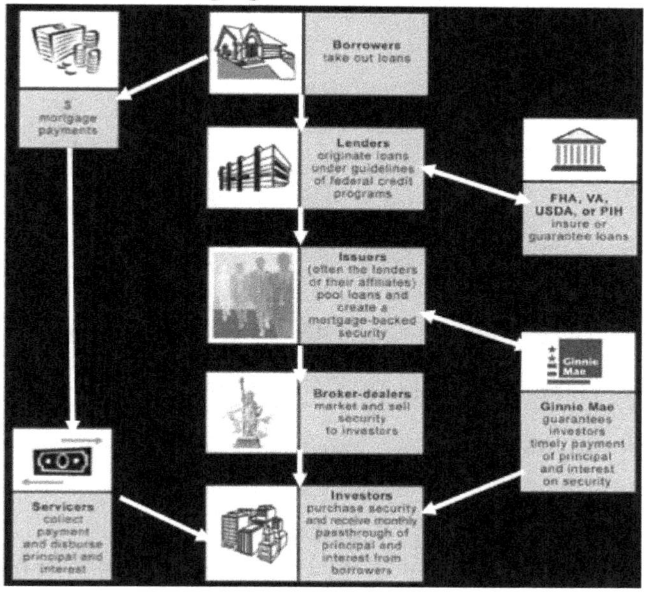

Source: Ginnie Mae, Annual Report 2007, at 2, http://www.ginniemae.gov/about/ann_rep/annual_report07.pdf (last visited Sept. 9, 2009)..

Exhibit 2
Cumulative Amount of Ginnie Mae Mortgage -Backed Securities

(Billions of Dollars)

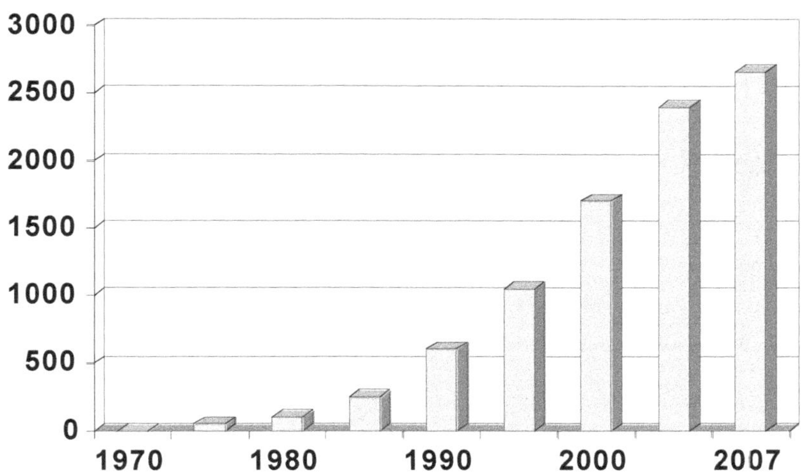

Source:Ginnie Mae, Annual Report 2007, at 6, http://www.ginniemae.gov/about/ann_rep/annual_report07.pdf (last visited Sept. 9, 2009).

Exhibit 3
Pass-through Originations by Agency
(Dollars in Billions)

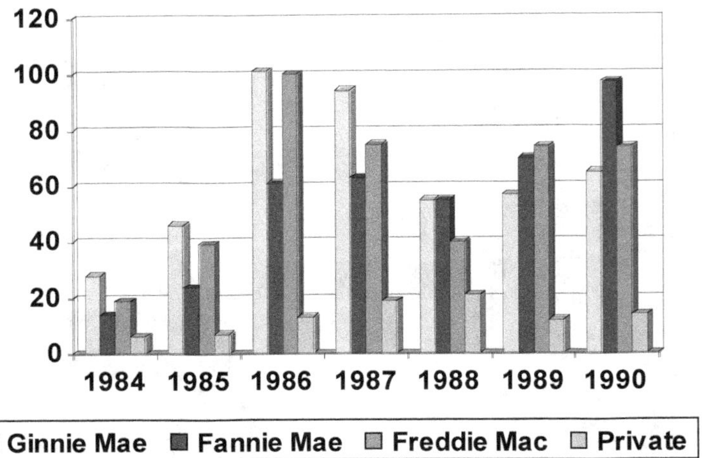

Source: Author estimation of data in Franco Modigliani & Frank J. Fabozzi, Mortgage and Mortgage-Backed Securities Markets 22 (1992).

Exhibit 4
Comparison of Yields on Bond-Like Investments
(October 12, 1984)

Investment Vehicle	Yield	GNMA Spread
U.S. Treasury 90 Day Bills	10.33	-2.66
U.S. Treasury Bonds	12.16	-0.83
Fannie Mae	12.49	-0.50
Adjustable Rate Mortgages	12.39	-0.60
Ginnie Mae	12.99	---

Source: Anthony Downs, The Revolution in Real Estate Finance 261 (1985).

Discussion Questions

Legal

- What areas of the law touch on MBS? Which are most relevant?
- What is the difference in legal status between Ginnie Mae and Fannie Mae?
- What are the legal implications of a Government Sponsored Enterprise?

Business

- Who are the actors involved in the creation and distribution of MBS?
- Who benefits from recycling mortgage capital? How?
- Does the growth of hedge fund and sovereign wealth fund capital affect the MBS business? If so, how?
- What would be the implications of eliminating MBS?
- What risks and advantages do MBS pose for bank lenders, mortgage lenders, mortgage brokers and securities brokers on the one hand, and borrowers and investors on the other hand? What strategies mitigate the risks for each of them? Are these strategies compatible with the interests of the actors?
- What are the risks and benefits of securitization to the financial system as a whole?

Public Policy

- Should the government be in the business of guaranteeing home loans? Why? Why not?
- What are the implications of MBS on macroeconomic policy?
- What are the implications of MBS on home ownership?

Chapter 3: The Evolution of Securitization

Securitization dates back to 1970. Since that time securitization has grown steadily in terms of dollar amounts and range of obligations that have been securitized. The motivations for the growth are provided below as are the concerns raised about securitization's role in the financial crisis beginning in 2008. A case study illustrates the expansion of the securitization concepts from mortgages to other assets. The chapter closes with a simulation exercise to identify new asset classes for securitization.

A. The Growth of Securitization[50]

Securitization began modestly in the 1970s with the conversion of government-backed residential mortgages into securities. Since that time literally trillions of dollars of residential mortgages have been securitized. For example in 2008, more than a trillion in mortgage-backed securities (MBS) were outstanding. Three federal agencies account for the majority of securitized mortgages. The first two are the Federal National Mortgage Association ("FNMA" or "Fannie Mae") and the Federal Home Loan Mortgage Corporation ("FHLMC" or "Freddie Mac"). These agencies have historically bought and sold mortgages. The FNMA and FHLMC began as government corporations and were gradually "privatized." In 1968, the third agency, the Government National Mortgage Association ("GNMA" or "Ginnie Mae"), was chartered to purchase and pool home mortgages and sell shares in these SPVs to public investors. To "encourage" securitization and reduce the investors' high cost of information about the borrowers and about the credit experience of the mortgage SPVs, the Government guaranteed the SPV securities of GNMA as to credit risk and timely payments. Thereafter FNMA and FHLMC began to support SPV securities by their own guarantees. FNMA focused on the secondary Market for SPV securities to provide liquidity for investors. All three entities encountered difficulties in recent years, discussed as appropriate throughout this Book.

The securitization of private residential mortgage loans also developed. Mortgages offered or guaranteed by FNMA, FHLMC and GNMA required conformance with a variety of terms. For example, the dollar value of the mortgage was limited. For borrowers who required larger loans, know as jumbo mortgages, private lenders stepped in. The logic of securitization applied to the nonconforming loans offered by private lenders. Thus "private label" mortgage-backed securities were offered to investors.

Commercial mortgage debt Markets were slower to join the increase in securitization, largely because the Government did not create a secondary Market for

---

[50] 1 TAMAR FRANKEL, SECURITIZATION § 1.3 (Ann Taylor Schwing ed., 2d ed. 2005).

commercial mortgages, as it had for residential mortgages. Further, the larger size and smaller number of commercial mortgages made for smaller loan pools and, thus, decreased diversification. Nevertheless, the commercial mortgage-backed securities Market grew in the late 1980s and 1990s. Commercial mortgage securitization grew more slowly than residential securitization because the commercial real estate lending Market historically had not had uniform underwriting standards. This obstacle became less significant as credit rating agencies began rating commercial mortgages. Securitization has also had a tremendous impact on the equity structure of real estate. Real estate investment trusts (REITs) accounted for over one-third of all institutional real estate in the United States in the late 1990s.

In the United States the rationale for securitizing mortgages was extended to other asset categories. After mortgages came auto and light truck loans, credit card loans and other receivables (including health care and pharmaceutical receivables, license and franchise fee receivables, airline ticket, hotel and other travel receivables, and tax receivables) and trade credits, equipment and automobile leases, taxicab medallions, computer leases, municipal leases, bad debts resulting from defaults by credit card debtors and junk bond issuers, student loans, cosmetic surgery receivables, vertical settlements, servicing rights, tax liens, loans made and held by the federal Government, royalties generated by performing celebrities, natural resource assets, mutual fund shares, athletic venue revenues, state indebtedness to finance easement acquisition, software financing obligations and insurance premium loans. There also exists a limited Market in securitized Third World loans and attempts are being made to extend and deepen this Market. Techniques also have developed to securitize negotiated litigation settlements and state lottery winnings. In sum, the movement to securitize loans has been sweeping the United States financial scene and has marched on to world markets.

The securitization of auto and truck loans provides a compelling case of how securitization adds value. The auto manufacturers have long financed vehicle purchases to make car ownership more affordable. The cash to cover these loans can be raised though equity, debt, or securitization. Equity is generally an expensive source of capital and rarely used to finance vehicle loans. Debt is more cost-effective but the manufacturers' ability to obtain funds depends on the strength of their financials. When times are good, the debt market is an attractive source of funds. However, the auto industry is very cyclical. During the periods of weak performance, debt financing is very costly. At these times the industry has turned to securitization for capital to fund consumer loans at a reasonable cost. Car loan securitization was developed by Salomon Brothers in January 1985, starting with private placement of $10 million followed in March 1985 by a first public offering of $60 million; "pass-through" certificates were backed by a pool of auto loans, each with credit insurance; the SPV was also insured by a private insurer. The importance of securitizing auto loans as a driver of economic growth was reinforced in early

2009 when the Federal Reserve Bank offered to loan funds to investors in such securities and backstop against default as part of the economic stimulus package.

Another example of the extension of the securitization concept is creating securities out of stranded asset recovery fees. In the 1990s many states restructured the regulation of their electric utilities to increase competition. In several cases the utilities were required to sell their electricity generating plants, transmission grids, and local distribution lines. Where prices were less than book value the states allowed the utilities to recapture the value of the "stranded assets" through a user fee to be paid over several years. In 1996, the California Legislature passed Assembly Bill 1890 providing for a special class of bonds to finance and buyout utilities' stranded costs.

B. Motivations for Securitization[51]

Economic factors, such as tight credit, prompted the Government to securitize mortgages. Nonbank intermediaries securitized consumer credit (offered by manufacturers or retailers) to gain liquidity and increase their financing activities.

Securitization also enables a holder of loans to raise funds at a lower cost than had it borrowed on its own credit such as the example of the construction firm that could securitize loans on its real estate at a lower interest rate because its own business was more risky than the business of renting its real estate described in Chapter 2. Thus, some loans may have a higher credit rating than the credit of their holder, and investors will accept lower returns for securities backed by such loans.

Also, eliminating the holder's bankruptcy risk, and adding intrinsic or third-party credit enhancement, permits a higher credit rating for the asset pool than for the original holder and transferor of the obligations, which in turn reduces the rate of return demanded by investors. Because the asset pool or special purpose entity or SPV, not the transferor, owns the receivables, the SPV investors can often make their investment decision without concern for the transferor's financial condition.

Opportunities for profit mobilized the securities industry to develop securitization techniques. Legal requirements, such as capital requirements, induced banks to sell their assets, reduce their short-term liabilities, and thereby increase their equity and long-term debt. For holders of loans, securitization lowered the cost of funding, and, for banks, it also reduced the cost of legally required capital. Accounting and tax regulation also provided incentives to securitize. An accounting rule that requires companies to include in their consolidated financial statements the assets and

[51] 1 TAMAR FRANKEL, SECURITIZATION §§ 3.3-.4 (Ann Taylor Schwing ed., 2d ed. 2005); *id.* § 2.2.3; *id.* § 2.9D.

liabilities of highly leveraged financial subsidiaries under their control may drive the companies to securitize loans owned by these subsidiaries and thereby reduce the effect of consolidation. The parent company would create a special purpose entity and cause the subsidiary to sell its loans to the SPV. The SPV would then sell its securities to investors.

For mortgage-backed securities, the Government has fostered a large distribution network. The law was amended to permit banks, in addition to investment bankers, to underwrite and deal in the secondary Markets for some of these instruments. The Market in mortgage-backed securities is the largest of the loan-backed securities. Mortgage-backed securities increasingly appear abroad, exporting both the American securities and the techniques of structuring them.

Before new species of loan-backed securities are publicly distributed and traded, they are tested in private placements. That is the distribution of the securities to a relatively small number of investors who are sophisticated and have a significant amount of investment assets. Market intermediaries are the main underwriters and traders in these securities because, except for government-sponsored mortgage-backed securities, banks were prohibited from underwriting and trading in loan-backed securities until the repeal of the Glass-Steagall Act in 1999. Since 1978, banks have battled the securities industry on banks' powers to deal and underwrite commercial paper and other ineligible securities. In the initial battles, the banks won only a partial victory, but, in November 1999, the Glass-Steagall Act was repealed by the Gramm-Leach-Bliley Act. Even before its repeal, the Act had been watered down by federal and state bank regulators and the courts. Banks have sought to escape the legal constraints that bind them by searching for nooks and crannies that are part of the mainstream of securitization, including engaging in business abroad, developing international networks for trading in foreign currencies government securities, short-term paper, and various permissible securities. They seem to have profited from these activities. Thus, during the past years, market intermediaries have engaged in the more lucrative portion of the securitization business. On occasion they have lent banks the use of their names to legalize bank transactions (for a fee and access to bank customers).

Securitization has fostered the development of Markets in loans. As private sector Institutions gain expertise in securitizing loans guaranteed by the Government, they seek to enlarge their loan inventories and buy loans to securitize. The demand has led to publications about loan pricing and networks to exchange information about available loans. Information about the financial situation of corporations, including middle-size corporations in various locations in the United States, is now readily available on the Internet and otherwise.

Securitization, well structured, can circumvent traditional Institutional intermediation. Loans can be made not only by banks but by other lenders, such as mortgage lenders or underwriters. Markets might charge lower interest than banks might. Thus, securitization can be analogized to the cell phones that circumvent the telephone system, which many developing countries have adopted rather than build the telephone exchanges infrastructures. Similarly, emerging markets lacking a solid banking structure could more easily resort to securitization.

C. Recent Concerns

Throughout the 1990s and up until 2007, securitization of mortgages and other assets showed strong steady growth. The resulting securities were highly rated and provided attractive returns at a time when interest rates on other forms of debt-based securities were very low. However, many of these mortgage loans were sold to persons who could not afford to pay them, and had hoped to cover their payments with rising values of the homes they held or bought. The terms of many of these loans required payments of far higher interest rates starting after certain periods. When an increasing number of borrowers defaulted, an increasing number of homes appeared for sale, and their prices declined. Thus began a vicious circle of lower home prices and higher number of foreclosures and bankruptcies. It became evident that the problem was systemic and that one of the main issues was the inability of the markets to price the securities backed by these loans correctly. In 2008, the problems with defaults in the mortgage sector began to spread to the other loans including auto loans and credit card debt bringing into question the effectiveness of securitization. We will deal with these issues throughout this book.

Another concern is that securitization can lead to fraud. The technique can lend itself to a Ponzi scheme where new investors' money is used to pay off higher and unearned returns to previous investors until no new investors are available. Barring a strong controlling hand over the whole operation or having the operation in the hands of those with intent to abuse, the complexity of the structure makes it difficult to uncover abuses. Enron Corporation demonstrates a classic abuse of securitization and structured finance.

D. Case Study: From MBS to ABS: The Securitization Concept Takes Hold

The term "securitization" first appeared in print in a 1977 article in the *Wall Street Journal* seven years after Ginnie Mae offered the first mortgage-backed securities (MBS). The "word" (it actually was not a word when it was first used) was coined by Lewis Ranieri to describe "the first conventional mortgage [in contrast to MBS issued by government affiliates secured by conforming mortgages] pass-through security."[52] It became the generic term used to describe the process of converting future cash flows into tradable securities.

---

[52] Lewis S. Ranieri, *The Origins of Securitization, Sources of Its Growth, and Its Future Potential, in* A PRIMER ON SECURITIZATION 31, 31 (Leon T. Kendall & Michael J. Fishman eds., 1996).

Securitization represented a major innovation in the financial services industry. Like most innovations, its development followed an "S-Shaped" curve - slow at the beginning when only the early adopters were onboard, gaining strength and speed as the concept became mainstream and then growing but at a slower rate as the idea matured. As shown in Exhibit 1, the early adoption phase took place in the 1970s as MBS proved the concept could work. Almost 10 years passed before the MBS market growth began to accelerate. During this time investors gained confidence that MBS could provide significant benefits and only minimal risks. By the mid-1980s, mainstream investors in addition to the innovators were ready to embrace the MBS market enabling that sector to grow rapidly.

As the market for MBS began to grow more rapidly in the 1980s, the idea of expanding the securitization concept to other assets was just beginning. The first adopter of asset-backed securities (ABS) was the Sperry Corporation which sought to securitize long-term lease payment streams on the computers it sold. Sperry was a leader in the manufacture, sales and support of mainframe computers in the mid-1980s. Computers at that time carried a multi-million price tag; therefore, many of Sperry's customers wanted to finance their purchases. The company offered to finance its sales, creating long-term leases to recapture the sale price of the computer and the associated financing costs. In 1984, the company determined that keeping the leases on their balance sheet was not advantageous from a capital structure perspective. They also were concerned about interest rate risk. Management's solution was to pursue a public offering of securities that produced cash flow from their customers' lease payments and were backed by the computer assets themselves. After a year of preparation, First Boston brought an offering of $192 million in 11% lease-backed notes to the market in March 1985. The notes, rated AAA by Standard and Poor's, had a maturity of six years and an average life of 2 years.

Sperry created a special purpose vehicle, the Sperry Lease Finance Corporation (SLFC), which purchased the lease payment stream from Sperry in exchange for the proceeds from the public offering. Thus, the lease payments and financing were moved from Sperry's books to those of SLFC. A true sale of the assets was made to SLFC to provide the investors with protection in the event of Sperry's bankruptcy. SLFC carried the leases as debt so that the "interest payments to the note holders by SLFC would be tax deductible, and thereby substantially offset the taxable income flowing to SLFC from the lease receivables."[53]

The Sperry asset-backed securities posed several risks for potential investors. While 40% of the lease holders were AAA rated corporations and almost two-thirds were rated A or above, 34% were unrated. Even though many of the contracts were not cancellable, customer bankruptcies could jeopardize timely and even eventual payment. Moreover, a sizable portion of the leases were with federal and state

[53] JAMES A. ROSENTHAL & JUAN M. OCAMPO, SECURITIZATION OF CREDIT 163 (1988)..

governments; these contracts were cancellable. Investors also faced risks associated with the performance of the computers themselves for if they malfunctioned, the lease payment stream could be interrupted. Sperry addressed these risks by offering "credit enhancement," added guarantees that reduced the investors' risk. Sperry, with the backing of UBS, offered to make investors whole for up to 20% of losses. This figure compares with an historical 3.5% loss in receivables.

The initial offering of Sperry's ABS was successful. "Investors received AAA rated debt securities at an attractive 49bp [basis point] spread to Treasuries."[54] Investor demand for such securities allowed Sperry to issue similar ABS in September of 1985 and again in December of 1986. The transaction also provided significant benefits to Sperry Corporation. The company was able to access capital at a lower rate than if it tried to raise the funds through traditional debt financing. A McKinsey & Company analysis of the transactions estimated that Sperry was able to secure funds at 14.26% through the ABS route in comparison to 17.33% using traditional debt funding.[55] (Exhibit 2) The ABS cost of the notes was marginally less than Sperry traditional debt (the difference between the ABS' AAA rating and Sperry's BBB+/A rating); however, this was offset by the costs of credit enhancement. The real gain for Sperry was that the company no longer needed to finance its balance sheet with as much equity since its debt was reduced with the transfer of the leases to SLFC. Equity is significantly more expensive than debt. The McKinsey analysis calculates that the equity financing costs amounted to 3.79%, a significant proportion of the overall 17.33% financing costs Sperry faced prior to issuing its ABS.[56]

ABS secured by computer equipment leases set a precedent for a wide range of other asset-backed securities including automobiles, credit card receivables, healthcare receivables and even lottery winnings. One of the largest ABS segments is securities backed by auto and light truck receivables. The first auto ABS was issued within a year of the Sperry lease ABS offering. Between 1985 and 1987, auto ABS accounted for almost 80% of securities backed by receivables.[57] In one issue alone, General Motors securitized $4.2 billion of car and light truck receivables. The auto industry was well suited to the use of ABS for financing. Cars were an expensive long-lived asset, most customers desired to finance the purchase, and the manufacturers desired to keep the financing off their balance sheets to free debt capacity to support production. The manufacturers' focus on financial structure can be seen in the ups and downs of ABS volume. (Exhibit 3) When the industry has weak financial performance such as during the 1990 recession, manufacturers turn to securitization

[54] *Id.* at 171.

[55] *Id.* at 168.

[56] *Id.*

[57] Dennis M. Cantwell, *How Public Corporations Use Securitization in Meeting Financial Needs, in* A PRIMER ON SECURITIZATION 55, 79 (Leon T. Kendall & Michael J. Fishman eds., 1996).

as a way to reduce financing costs. When profits are strong, ABS plays a less important, but still significant, role. Commercial banks and other finance companies, which also provide consumer auto loans, have also used ABS to convert auto receivables into cash. Exhibit 4 shows that the role of these lenders increased greatly during auto ABS' formative years. The structure of the auto ABS is similar to that used by Sperry. Finance companies, subsidiaries of the manufactures or other lenders buy the auto loan receivables from car dealerships. The receivables are then transferred to a bankruptcy-remote SPV. The SPV then creates securities, enhances their credit and sells them to investors. McKinsey's analysis of early General Motors ABS offerings find that the cost of the securities notes was 7.69% compared to 8.39% using traditional financing.[58] The rapid growth of auto receivables securitization is illustrated by comparing Chrysler's funding sources. (Exhibit 5) Between 1988 and 1993 securitization grew from 15% to 51% of funding.[59]

From modest beginnings in 1985, in only a decade ABS grew to 1,595 issues with a value of more than $850 billion in 2004.[60]

Exhibit 1
Adoption of Securitization

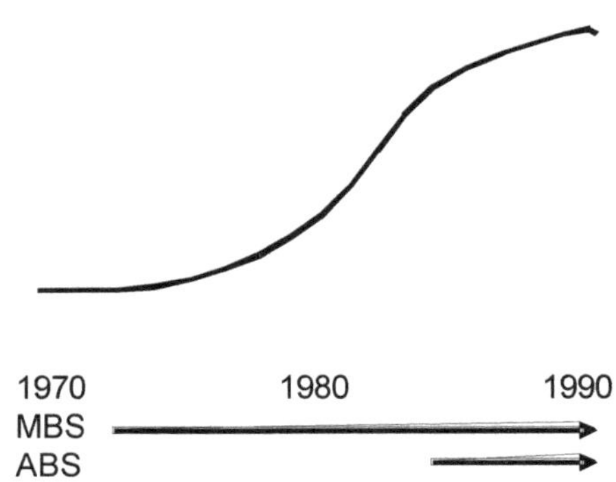

---

[58] *Id.* at 90.

[59] *Id.* at 58-59.

[60] *Thomson Financial League Tables, accessed through* WIKIPEDIA, http://en.wikipedia.org/wiki/Thomson_Financial_league_tables (last visited Sept. 9, 2009).

Exhibit 2
Comparison of Funding Cost of Sperry Leases

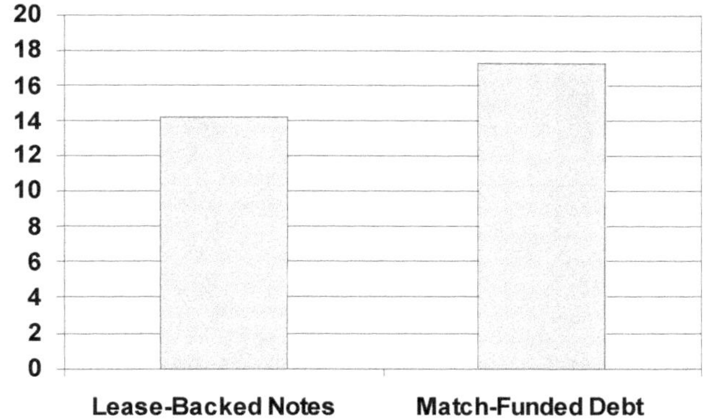

Source: Author estimation of data presented in James A. Rosenthal & Juan M. Ocampo, Securitization of Credit 168 (1988).

Exhibit 3
ABS Auto Issuance

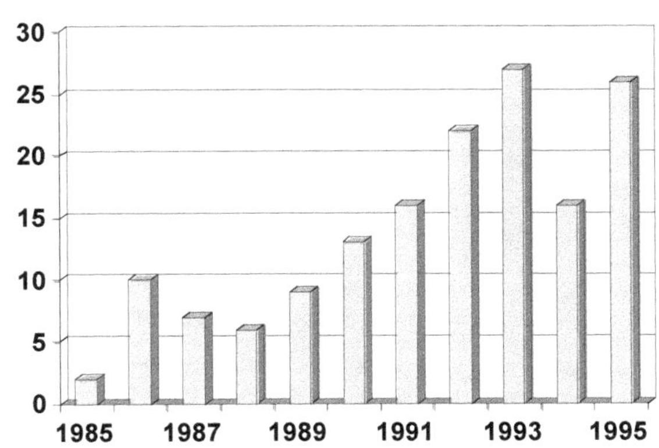

Source: Author estimation of data presented in Dennis M. Cantwell, *How Public Corporations Use Securitization in Meeting Financial Needs*, *in* A Primer on Securitization 55, 89 (Leon T. Kendall & Michael J. Fishman eds., 1996).

Exhibit 4
ABS Auto Issuance

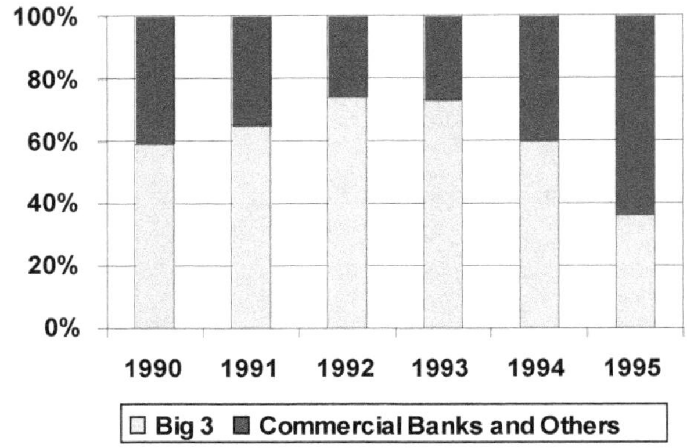

Source: Author estimation of data presented in Dennis M. Cantwell, *How Public Corporations Use Securitization in Meeting Financial Needs, in* A Primer on Securitization 55, 89 (Leon T. Kendall & Michael J. Fishman eds., 1996).

Exhibit 5
Chrysler Funding Sources

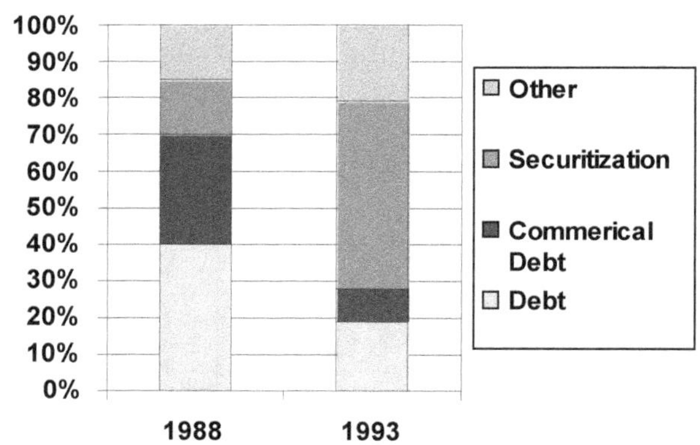

Source: Author estimation of data presented in Dennis M. Cantwell, *How Public Corporations Use Securitization in Meeting Financial Needs, in* A Primer on Securitization 55, 58-59 (Leon T. Kendall & Michael J. Fishman eds., 1996).

Discussion Questions

Legal

- What were the legal foundations for securitization of non-mortgage assets?
- What new legal issues were raised by the securitization of non-mortgage assets versus mortgages?

Business

- What was the attraction of securitization assets for corporations?
- What risks did corporations face as a result of securitization and how did they mitigate the risks?

Public Policy

- What are the implications of broadening the investor base in corporate assets?

E. Simulation Exercise: Creating New Securitization Products

Bill graduated with a joint JD/MBA in the spring of 2008. He had spent his last two summers working at the New York based global investment bank IBI.[61] His first summer was spent supporting the mergers and acquisitions (M&A) department and the second was in the Initial Public Offering (IPO) group. The work was stimulating, the environment was collegial, and the compensation was terrific so he accepted a full time position upon graduation. While he had the opportunity to work in IBI's M&A or IPO department he requested a position in the Securitization Group. During his final semester of school he took an interdisciplinary course on securitization and was excited by the combination of law, business, and even public policy issues that the topic entailed.

As his first day of work drew closer, he become even more excited about working in the securitization arena as the topic moved center stage in the growing financial crisis of 2008. A year earlier few of his fellow students had heard of securitization; now it was headline news. A range of politicos and pundits blamed securitization for the worst financial crisis since the Great Depression as non-performing sub-prime mortgage-backed securities led to a freeze in liquidity, a substantial decline in the stock market, the failure of financial icons including Bear Stearns and Lehman Brothers, the government bailout of the insurance giant AIG and the nationalization of Fannie Mae and Freddie Mac.

Bill's first day at work was a whirlwind. The day began with a brainstorming session - explain to the public the benefits of securitization and that the excesses responsible for the financial crisis did not mean that securitization should be regulated into extinction. Bill offered several examples of the benefits of securitization ranging from the Sperry computer leases to millions of prime-borrower home mortgages that saved consumers millions of dollars. Immediately following the meeting he was presented with a stack of presentations that explained the full range of securitization products offered by IBI and was told with a smile: "Become an expert by 3:00!" The materials covered the usual suspects - mortgage-backed securities (MBS), asset-backed securities (ABS) covering auto receivables, and products for securitizing credit card debt. He was surprised to read about IBI's securitization of lottery winnings and large legal settlements. He thought: "What will they think of next?"

[61] The events described in this case are not based on actual companies or individuals.

At 3:01 his boss walked into his office. She explained that the collapse of the subprime MBS market and broader financial crisis were significantly reducing the Securitization Group's revenue opportunities. After detailing the group's financial outlook and gap to budget, she said: "Now that you are an expert in our product offerings, we need you to fill our revenue shortfall. Your assignment is to 'invent' new securitization products for IBI to sell. I will look forward to hearing your ideas in the morning." As she left Bill's office she turned around to Bill and said: "The cafeteria is open all night!"

Assignment: Create a list of potential financial assets that can be securitized profitably. Then define a set of criteria for evaluating the market potential for the securities backed by these assets. Proceed to assess your list and ideas against the criteria; rank them by attractiveness to IBI. Finally, write an "elevator speech" describing your top two recommended asset-backed securities. (Note: An elevator speech is a short but compelling explanation that can be delivered in the time it takes to ride an elevator.)

PART II: THE PROCESS AND LAW OF SECURITIZATION

Chapter 4: The Special Purpose Vehicle (SPV)

The Special Purpose Vehicle (SPV) is the "processor" of securitization. Securitization is used to convert loans and debts into tradable securities. The SPV takes-in (buys) obligations, loans and debt, and puts out (issues and sells) securities. This Chapter begins with an introduction to SPVs and an explanation of SPVs' institutional features and financial structure. Next discussion focuses on the legal structure of SPVs, their regulation[62] and operation. The Chapter concludes with a case study that explores the uses and misuses of SPVs' structures.

A. Definition and Legal Form

a. Definition

The SPV is a legal entity. It can be organized in many legal forms. The main role of the SPV is converting the SPV's illiquid financial assets into liquid tradable securities. The SPV's assets are not actively managed, unless the assets convert into cash before they are due to the investors in the securities that the SPVs issue. In that case, a limited opportunity for reinvestment is permitted.

b. Alternative Legal Forms

SPVs can be organized in any legal form, such as trusts, corporations, limited partnerships, and Limited Liability Corporations (LLCs). In choosing the legal forms of SPVs, lawyers consider the protection of investors from the bankruptcy of the entities that made the loans and those who transferred the loans to the SPVs. If those entities become insolvent, their creditors may claim the SPVs assets. In such a case the investors, who paid for these assets, become unsecured creditors in the transferors' bankruptcy proceedings. That is why our study of the SPVs financial assets will follow the examination of the tax and bankruptcy issues involving SPVs.

The legal organization of SPVs is affected by the need to protect the investors in the securities that the SPVs issue against the claims of the creditors of the sponsor-Originator who transferred the financial assets to the SPV. This protection requires a

---

[62] Because SPVs may involve advisory services with respect to the securities they issue, they had to receive an exemption from the regulation of investment advisers under the Advisers Act of 1940. And because the SPVs' structure could be viewed as the structure of investment companies, they gained exemptions from the Investment Company Act of 1940, under certain conditions. These exemptions will be discussed at the end of this Chapter. Their importance lies in the fact that barring the exemptions SPVs cannot efficiently function as they do. We will examine these exemptions in light of the financial crisis to evaluate their scope and effectiveness. See Chapter 11.

total separation between the transferor-servicer-Originator and the SPV. On the other hand, there are situations in which the sponsor-Originator must continue to be involved and hold some of the SPV's securities. For example, if the sponsor-Originator transfers to the SPV a large amount of financial assets and the SPV issues bonds for a smaller amount, the excess amount of financial assets that the SPV holds serves as collateral. It supports the securities that the SPV issued and assures the investors of full payment under the securities. Consequently, the SPV's securities will offer a lower interest rate, which the investors are likely to accept in light of the lower risk that they will not be paid. The sponsor-Originator, however, must continue to hold the equity securities issued by the SPV in order to be able to collect any excess of the assets in the SPV that was not used to cover its obligations under the securities that it issued.

The legal design of the SPV is affected by the nature of its assets. For example, in the case of securitizing mortgages, the SPV would be organized as a trust or a corporation, and no additional structure is usually necessary. However, in the case of securitizing receivables and other revolving loans, the structure used is often master trusts as these are financial assets held by the SPVs that are paid earlier than the obligations which SPVs issue. For example, credit cards are expected to be paid every 30 days at the most, and sometimes earlier. The securities issued by the SPV backed by these securities might have a maturity of 6 months or one year. In that case the company that creates the credit card receivables establishes a trust and when the SPV's assets are paid and have cash, they acquire more credit card receivables.

Rather than issue their own obligations, Institutions or manufacturers may raise funds by creating SPVs that issue securities, including money market instruments.[63] These securities can be backed by financial assets in the SPV and the guarantees of the sponsor or Originator. If the sponsor holds the equity in the SPV, the SPV is called an "orphan finance subsidiary." Proceeds from the sale of the SPV's securities are transferred to the sponsor. A trustee takes possession of the securities held by the SPV on behalf of the purchasers and upon default has the rights of a secured creditor in the collateral. Thus, the trustee's holding of the equity securities issued by the SPV protects the investors, in the event that there is need to cover the investors' claims from the assets of the SPVs. However, to the extent that there remain assets in the SPVs after all investors have been paid, the trustee will return the equity securities representing the assets to the sponsor-Originator. The trust can be a mechanism for ensuring the performance of specific conditions under unknown future events (e.g., how much of the collateral remains in the SPV after the investors have been paid in full).

[63] 1 TAMAR FRANKEL, SECURITIZATION § 11.30 (Ann Taylor Schwing ed., 2d ed. 2005).

c. Taxation Considerations

The choice of legal form is often affected by tax considerations. These tax considerations, in turn, are affected by the assumptions and rules underlying the legal forms, such as the division of power and benefits between the investors and the managers of the SPVs. Most SPVs are passive, like their investors. Therefore, as the legal forms comport to the power structure, the forms permits the advantageous tax design of SPV. As we shall see, the designs allow the SPVs to "pass through" the returns from their assets to the investors without being taxed. (See Chapter 11)

B. SPV Structure[64,65]

a. The Institutional Features of SPVs

SPVs are Institutions. They raise funds by issuing their own obligations in the form of securities (e.g., commercial paper, bonds, equity securities, preferred stock) and invest the proceeds in the obligations of others (e.g., borrowers, debtors). Securitized financial assets include loans and debts, such as mortgages receivables owed by government (e.g., Medicare), financial institutions (e.g., insurance companies), commercial enterprises and individuals (e.g., customers' and credit card receivables). By investing in illiquid loans and debts and issuing liquid securities, SPVs act as conduits for securitizing these assets. Because of the nature of the assets, SPVs portfolios are rarely actively managed.

In terms of their assets and liabilities, SPVs represent a new type of Institutional intermediary; part investment company, part bank. Like investment companies, SPVs raise funds by issuing securities, in contrast to banks that raise funds mainly by offering unique obligations (bank deposits). Like banks, SPVs invest their funds in loans and debts, in contrast to investment companies that invest their funds in securities.

We noted the meaning of intermediation as the service of connecting lenders and borrowers. The term, however, is broader in the sense that intermediation can connect different types of lenders with different borrowers. Thus, SPVs intermediate mainly between the lenders that made the loans or those who purchased the loans from the lenders in order to securitize them, and the new lenders—the investors, who bought securities backed by these loans. In fact, SPVs are "second tier" intermediaries. Banks intermediate between lenders—the depositors or holders of the banks' bonds and stocks, and borrowers to whom the banks lend money. SPVs acquire loans rather than make loans and then intermediate between the lenders (e.g.,

[64] 1 TAMAR FRANKEL, SECURITIZATION §2.5.3 (Ann Taylor Schwing ed., 2d ed. 2005).

[65] 1 TAMAR FRANKEL, SECURITIZATION § 1.2 (Ann Taylor Schwing ed., 2d ed. 2005); *id.* §3.3.

banks) and the investors. Nonetheless, SPVs can affect the volume of initial lending. While traditionally lending Institutions held loans to maturity, securitization enables lenders to recycle funds by selling loans before maturity and relending the proceeds. The SPV buys loans, sells SPV securities to ultimate investors (or to another SPV that issues securities), and buys more loans with the proceeds. Buyers of SPV securities can be intermediaries, such as banks, with long-term obligations, such as long-term loans. Such buyers raise their funds by issuing their own obligations to individual investors, such as depositors. Therefore, funds available for lending (deposit money) may increase by recycling (lending and selling the loans and lending the proceeds again).

The design of SPV financial structure reflects the conflicting objectives of all Institutional intermediaries. One purpose of these Institutions is to intermediate between savers and borrowers with different needs (as to amount, risk, return, and maturity of the loans). Institutions borrow from savers on terms acceptable to them and lend the proceeds on terms acceptable to borrowers. The more diverse the desires of investors and borrowers are, the more useful an Institution is.

Yet this very benefit of Institutions often poses a threat to their safety and soundness. The greater the difference between the terms of an Institution's assets and liabilities, the more risky the financial structure of the Institution becomes. The challenge in designing an Institution's financial structure is to satisfy the diverse desires of investors and borrowers and, at the same time, to narrow, if not eliminate, the mismatch between the Institution's assets and liabilities (in terms of risks, returns, and maturity).

For example, the Savings and Loan Associations problems arose when the holders of their seven day savings accounts demanded their money (in light of inflation and offering of higher interest rates somewhere else). Because the Savings and Loan Associations lent the money from the savings accounts to borrowers for 15 to 30 years, they could not meet the demand of the savings account holders. The time mismatch between the Savings and Loan liabilities (savings accounts) and assets (mortgage loans) was very great, and created a risk which they could not overcome. The evolution of SPVs' financial structures reflects various attempts to meet this challenge. In the case of Savings and Loan Associations, the 30 year loans they held in their assets were packaged and produced securities backed by the loans. These securities could be sold and helped meet the demands of the holders of the savings accounts. The securities matched the seven-day accounts in terms of the time necessary to produce cash and repay the account holders-depositors.

With some exceptions SPVs' structures are less risky and less likely to fail than banks and S&Ls. Their assets and liabilities do represent a risk of mismatch. However, this risk posed by SPV's assets is usually shifted among the classes of obligations that it issues—the tranches[66]. As a crude example, if the SPV issues four tranches, each representing $100,000, and if the assets of the SPV amounted to $250,000, the first tranche will be entitled to receive $100,000, the second tranche will be entitled to $100,000, the third tranche $50,000 and the fourth tranche -- nothing. The design of the rights of each tranche, however, is more sophisticated and complex, but the priorities are the same.

The risk of mismatching liabilities and assets that Institutions are designed to accommodate are also reduced in the case of SPVs. Institutions such as banks are bound by their clients' needs. In contrast, SPVs can select and diversify their loan portfolios. That is because SPVs do not make loans and do not compete for borrowers. For example, SPVs can hold long term and short-term loans backed by mortgages; more risky and less risky borrowers. The buyers of loans for securitization have a universe of loans from which to choose the ones to package and create the most diversified portfolio and most predictable cash flow. But some conflicting purpose exists in the design of SPVs as well. That is because SPVs should usually hold loans of the same type to reduce the information costs to investors in SPVs' securities. Similarly, the buyers of the loans that organize the SPVs tend to choose the same type of loans. In addition, SPVs reduce the investors' information costs by offering investors credit and liquidity enhancement. Some SPVs reduce the investors' information costs by obtaining ratings.

b. Protection of the SPV Structure from Bankruptcy

The SPV buys loans from various sources. If the sellers of the loans become insolvent, the investors, who paid fully for the SPVs' assets, may be faced with the unpleasant claim of the seller's creditors for the SPVs assets. One such claim may be based on the structure of the SPV. If, for example, the SPV is a subsidiary of the seller of the loans or if the seller of the loan is in fact controlling the SPV, the bankruptcy court may view the SPV as part of the seller and consolidate the two. In such a case the investors in the SPV may become creditors (unsecured creditors) of the seller of the loans. To avoid such a situation, care is taken to ensure that the relationship between the SPV and the seller of the loan does not reach the possibility of consolidation.

c. SPVs Structure and Liquidity Risk for Investors

Like banks, SPVs can hold illiquid loans. But unlike banks, SPVs do not promise to repurchase and redeem their securities on demand or on short notice. Instead, SPVs provide investors with liquidity through secondary Markets for SPV securities or

[66] A tranche is "a piece, portion or slice of a deal or structured financing. This portion is one of several related securities that are offered at the same time but have different risks, rewards and/or maturities." *Tranches,* http://www.investopedia.com/terms/t/tranches.asp (last visited Sept. 9, 2009).

through third-party promises (such as bank letters of credit) to purchase the securities at face value on demand or on short notice. For example, if an investor in a security issued by an SPV which promises payment in one year needs the money immediately, the investors cannot demand the value of the security from the SPV, as the holders of a bank deposit, or an investor in a mutual fund -- open end investment company -- can. The investor in the SPV securities may seek an investor in the Market who would be interested to buy the securities. Therefore, compared to banks and open-end investment companies, the maturity of SPVs' long-term assets (e.g., 30-year mortgages) can be designed to better match with the maturity of their liabilities. The promises of the SPV that holds such long-term obligations will be as long as the term of these obligations. This design reduces the risk of the SPVs structures.

d. Operation and Structure of SPVs That Hold Receivables[67]

There are cases in which the assets and obligations of the SPVs do not match in terms of timing. In that case, the structure of the SPV is adjusted to resolve the problem. For example, an SPV that holds receivables presents a unique problem because the entire SPV portfolio matures much earlier than investors' desire. In other words, the investors do not wish to receive payment in very short intervals but rather long-term, for example, in six months or a year. The Markets developed a unique structure, a "feeder structure," to address the problem. Securities issued by the SPV state fixed amounts and have a payment schedule. The originator, which is in the business of generating such receivables, keeps an account that holds additional receivables. Since receivables are usually paid off before maturity of the SPV securities, the sponsor continues to transfer similar receivables to the SPV to maintain the SPV's fixed balance. In fact, the sponsor adjusts the discrepancy between the maturities of the SPV portfolio and the maturity dates of the SPV's securities. The sponsor's account fluctuates, while the SPV investors' accounts remain stable, reflecting the terms of the securities. This feeder structure also reduces the security holders' risk from prepayments of the receivables. Prepayment might be made when interest rates fall. This is the time when the investors would prefer not to receive their money, because they cannot reinvest it at the same interest rate. The sponsor covers the risk from prepayments by transferring a substantial amount of receivables to the sponsor's own account at the outset for continuous sale to the SPV.

e. Structure of SPVs as a Subsidiary [68]

Often the sellers of loans, especially banks, are motivated by conflicting desires to reduce their assets on the one hand, and to lower the credit risk for investors on the

---

[67] 1 TAMAR FRANKEL, SECURITIZATION § 5.3.6 (Ann Taylor Schwing ed., 2d ed. 2005).

[68] 1 TAMAR FRANKEL, SECURITIZATION § 2.5.6 (Ann Taylor Schwing ed., 2d ed. 2005).

loans they sell on the other hand. By lowering the investors' risks, sellers can reduce the return that investors demand and make the loan-backed securities attractive to large regulated Institutions. For the sellers, especially banks, the least expensive ways to reduce investors' credit risks are to sell the loans with recourse or to provide loan collateral in excess of the face amount of the sold loans. However, these methods can conflict with the bank regulators' view of what a "sale" of loans means and may lead to imposition of heavier regulatory costs on the banks.

Banks rarely borrow short-term directly, except by issuing bonds. Banks usually sell their loan portfolios or use the loans as collateral for obligations of their subsidiaries. In one example, the bank establishes a wholly-owned subsidiary that is an SPV. This SPV subsidiary acquires credit card receivables (from an unrelated source or from the bank). The subsidiary issues commercial paper or other short-term obligations backed by these receivables and supported by an insurance company's guarantee or a letter of credit issued by another bank. Another bank distributes the securities issued by the SPV, and makes a secondary market in these securities. If the commercial paper issued by the SPV subsidiary holding the credit card receivables, receives a higher rating than the bank's rating, the bank would pay investors in the subsidiary SPV's commercial paper less than if it issued commercial paper directly. It should be noted that this structure will be feasible if there is in fact no chance that the bank will fail and that the investors in the subsidiary will share the SPVs' assets.

f. Secondary SPVs[69]

Like all SPVs, secondary SPVs issue securities. Their distinctive feature is that they hold a *portfolio of securities issued by other SPVs.* Secondary SPVs can provide investors with liquidity, not only through secondary markets in the secondary SPV's securities, but also by redemptions, if the secondary SPVs' *portfolio securities* are traded actively. The benefits from secondary SPVs for investors are similar to the benefits from investment companies: the SPVs can diversify the risk posed by SPV securities, for example, by mixing short-term and long-term, or issuing debt securities collateralized by bonds, or both.

GNMA II, which was launched in 1983, allowed for numerous Originators' pools of single family home mortgages. GNMA also introduced the Multiclass Securities Program "to increase liquidity in the secondary mortgage market and to attract new sources of capital for federally insured or guaranteed residential loans."[70]

Benefits from this diversification are reduced by higher management and transaction fees and by the risks that such secondary SPVs, like any intermediary, pose for

[69] 1 TAMAR FRANKEL, SECURITIZATION § 2.7 (Ann Taylor Schwing ed., 2d ed. 2005).

[70] GINNIE MAE, ANNUAL REPORT 2007, at 3, http://www.ginniemae.gov/about/ann_rep/annual_report07.pdf (last visited Sept. 9, 2009).

investors. The financial structure of SPVs and secondary SPVs that invest in SPV securities partly resembles that of banks and partly resembles that of investment companies.

The structure of these SPVs poses to investors the dangers that any financial intermediary with this structure poses for investors. A sample of these dangers appears in the preamble to the Investment Company Act of 1940 ("the 1940 Act") and is worth listing. First, in contrast to most real assets, financial assets can be easily embezzled. Second, since managers of the SPVs have opportunities for self-dealing, the greater the managers' discretion to deal with in the SPVs' portfolio is, the greater the danger investors might suffer losses from self-dealing. Third, when the financial structure and the portfolio of SPVs are very complex, it is difficult to value the securities that the SPVs issue. A complex financial structure also makes disclosure to investors more difficult, and hinders their ability to gauge the risks accompanying senior and junior securities. Fourth, complex structures may be so unfair to investors as to raise the presumption of fraud. Fifth, if the SPVs cater to small unsophisticated investors, commissions charged on purchases of SPV shares may be very high, and unethical sales practices could develop. Finally, SPVs are also subject to the risk that servicers and trustees will not fulfill their obligations properly.

"Re-securitizing" outstanding mortgage backed securities by transferring them to SPVs that issue their own securities has been popular with underwriters especially when the securities issued by the original structure did not sell well. Subordinate securities and senior securities that were not sold in one issuance or in unrelated transactions can be pooled, transferred to another SPV and offered to investors.

Discussion Topics:

One of the features of an Institution is the ability to create a pyramid. A pyramid means an entity that holds part of the *obligations* of another entity that holds part of the obligations of still another entity. For example, assume a SPV1 has issued four classes of securities, each for $100,000, rated AAA, AA, A and B respectively, Assume that another SPV, SPV2 is organized with the same class structure and that SPV1 transfers to SPV2 the fourth tranche, rated B. Now that tranche becomes the first one to receive payments due, and the others stand in line after each higher rated tranche was paid. The assets in SPV2 are backed not by the assets of SPV1 but by the securities it issued marked tranche B. The second SPV2 does not have the mortgage obligations but the securities which are backed by these mortgage obligations. The same process can be performed again with any of the tranches of SPV2, to create SPV3. SPV3 will hold assets consisting of securities issued by SPV2 which holds securities issued by SPV1, which holds mortgage loans.

In fact, pyramids exist in sales organizations as well. The head of the department may reward the salesperson with a percentage of the commissions that the salesperson received from customers. Most of the commission would be paid to the salesperson, and some of it—to the head of the department. However, the head of the department must receive a fixed amount, regardless of whether the salesperson sells anything. The salesperson may then recruit two or three or more salespersons to sell the products, reward them with part of the commission, retain for himself part of the commission and pay the rest to the head of the department. However, this salesperson, like the head of the department, may charge a fixed amount to the recruited salespersons. They, in turn may do the sale thing: recruit other salespersons and charge them a fixed amount for the advertising materials and coaching.

1. What, in your opinion is the value of this scheme?
2. Under what conditions and terms does this scheme pose a problem?
3. How would you avoid the problems but retain the benefits of the structure?
4. Securitization consists of making loans, transferring loans to an SPV, and causing the SPV to distribute securities backed by the income stream from the loans. Which areas of the law do these activities touch?
5. What legal risks does securitization pose for the investors?
6. Is the U.C.C. relevant in this case? Is the bankruptcy law relevant? Is securities regulation or taxation?
7. In terms of disseminating information about mortgage-backed securities (MBS), should the rules governing disclosure concerning securities be different in this case from the rules governing disclosure about securities issued by an industrial or financial corporation?
8. Mortgage backed securities have been evaluated by rating agencies. There are three or four such agencies in the United States. Does this fact make a difference to your evaluation of the securities acts?
9. Should the investors be assured of a secure status, as bank deposits are? If so, who should be regulated to ensure a fairly secure investment in MBS?
10. Where would you look for the regulation of the Institutions that are engaged in the securitization process?

C. Operations of SPVs[71]

Once an SPV is established and its securities are distributed, the SPV continues to operate until all its debt securities have been paid and, often, until the SPV has been liquidated and the residue, if any, paid to its equity security holders. Regardless of how they are legally organized, SPVs serve merely as receptacles for financial assets and as managers of the one-time or continuous receipt and distribution of funds from the SPVs' assets. Management and servicing of SPVs are performed under contracts with outsiders rather than by an internal management of the SPVs. In this respect, among

[71] 1 TAMAR FRANKEL, SECURITIZATION § 14.1 A (Ann Taylor Schwing ed., 2d ed. 2005).

others, SPVs resemble investment companies, most of which are operated by outside advisers.

The management and servicing of SPVs differ depending on SPVs' structure and the nature of the assets that SPVs hold. Some generalizations, however, can be made, focusing on the functions that SPVs must perform. The duties and liabilities of SPV operators are based both on the contracts under which they perform their functions, and on legal rules that are superimposed on these contractual arrangements, such as fiduciary duties.

SPVs must (i) receive and examine the documentation for the financial assets that the SPVs buy; (ii) hold their assets and funds in safe custody; (iii) collect payments from borrowers and distribute payments to SPV security holders and others; (iv) exercise lender's rights to enforce the borrowers' obligations when borrowers are delinquent or insolvent and to liquidate the collateral, if any; (v) perform other duties with respect to the borrowers, such as giving them notices as to where they should send their payments; (vi) report to SPV security holders on the status of their portfolios and on other matters relevant to security holders' accounts, and provide other persons, such as the SPVs' accountants, with needed information; (vii) invest money received from borrowers that is to be distributed to SPV security holders later, including borrowers' prepayments; (viii) enforce obligations of the transferors of assets to the SPVs (e.g., to substitute other loans for loans in default, or continue to transfer to the SPVs additional assets, such as receivables); and (ix) enforce obligations of guarantors and insurers if borrowers fail to pay, and enforce obligations of guarantors of timely payments by the issuer.[72]

These functions can be grouped as related to (i) custody of assets, (ii) service of loans, and (iii) limited portfolio management. These functions need not necessarily be performed by the same Institution. Most Originators establish SPVs in order to serve and receive income from one or more continuous functions that they perform for the SPVs (e.g., servicing the loan portfolio). Originators also establish SPVs to make a secondary Market for SPV securities as broker-dealers. Originators select the continuous functions according to their own specializations and "farm out" the rest of the functions to other specialized Institutions. Some functions such as custody and servicing of the loans are closely related and conveniently performed by the same Institution, although for legal reasons the functions may be vested in different Institutions.

When the SPV are organized as trusts, as many are, they engage outside servicers to manage the cash flows from the financial assets they hold. For example, with respect

[72] Some guarantees are called Guaranteed Investment Contracts (GICs). These are guarantees issued by insurance companies and some banks that cover certain risks of pooled investment assets. They appeared in the 1980s, and then were allowed to banks as well.

to mortgages, "[m]ost loan servicing agreements have been structured under the assumption that loan modifications are rare and would be pursued on a case-by-case basis. Generally, delinquent loans can be modified under this approach if the borrower demonstrates a willingness and ability to repay the loan under modified terms and it was in the best interest of the investors to modify the loan rather than foreclose. However, a loan-by-loan evaluation is very time consuming. With the rate of delinquencies [during the 2008 financial crisis,] in the mortgage market and the impending payment resets of various ARM [subprime mortgages that pose high risk for lenders and investors mortgages] products, there is little time for this type of in-depth loan-by-loan analysis."[73] A number of initiatives have been proposed to streamline the process, including those suggested by the American Securitization Forum and the HOPE NOW alliance.[74]

Originators of SPVs[75] expect most of their rewards from future services to the SPVs, such as servicing the financial assets or loans in the SPV's portfolio or managing the SPV's portfolio, or acting as servicers of borrowers' payments. Originators who are broker-dealers expect benefits from future sales of SPV securities and from making a secondary Market in them. Originators who are loan originators expect benefits from future sales of financial assets to the SPVs. Originators generally act for the SPVs in more than one capacity. Institutions can sponsor SPVs and continuously sell financial assets to these SPVs and, at the same time, serve as trustees or in another fiduciary capacity to the SPVs and their security holders. In addition, banks offer SPVs commercial loan and deposit services and insurance companies offer them insurance services. These differing capacities can create conflicts of interest and are of constant concern to regulators.

In general, a fiduciary may not personally engage in transactions with trust assets, on the ground that the trustee may use his discretion for personal benefit, in violation of obligations to the beneficiaries. However, the extent of this prohibition and the conditions under which the fiduciary is released from this prohibition vary, depending on the nature and circumstances of the relationship. The laws governing the contours of this prohibition may be exclusively federal law, such as the Employee Retirement Income Security Act of 1974, or federal regulations, such as those of the Office of the Comptroller of the Currency, or state statutes governing trusts and state pension funds, or principles of common law.

[73] *State of the Banking Industry: hearing on H.R. 3915 Before the S. Comm. On Banking, Housing, and Urban Affairs* (2008), LEXIS, News Library, Curnws File (statement of John M. Reich, Director, Office of Thrift Supervision).

[74] *Id.*

[75] 2 TAMAR FRANKEL, SECURITIZATION § 14.11 (Ann Taylor Schwing ed., 2d ed. 2005).

The securitization process lends itself to conflict of interest transactions because it is a continuous process of recycling, in which Institutions make or purchase loans, sell the loans to SPVs, distribute securities to investors, and service the loans. As mentioned, not all these functions are necessarily performed by one Institution, but seldom is each function performed by an unrelated separate Institution. If some functions are performed by the same Institution, a conflict may arise. A sponsor, such as a bank, an insurance company, or a large securities firm, may make or buy loans, sell them to an SPV, and serve as the SPV's trustee or investment adviser. Yet, once the sponsor becomes the SPV fiduciary, further sales of loans by it to the SPV are made in conflict of interest. A requirement to assign each function to an unrelated Institution may result in inefficiencies and additional expense.

Further, the success of securitization may depend on allowing Originators to play a continuous role in the process. Most SPV Originators invest in the loans to be securitized and take risks in the hope of reaping benefits from future services. Therefore, the law is designed to balance the two conflicting policies: to encourage efficient concentration of functions, thereby promoting loan securitization, and at the same time to prevent or mitigate problematic conflicts of interest.

a. Custodians[76]

The initial custodian in a securitization process is an escrow agent.[77] Before transferring assets to the SPV, the sponsor or Originator may be required to place the assets in the hands of an escrow agent, whose duty together with the independent trustee is to examine the assets before paying the price to the transferor. The escrow agent and the trustee are expected to examine the documentation of the loans and ensure that they comply with the pooling and servicing agreement or with the trust indenture.

Once the transfer of assets to the SPV has been completed, the SPV will issue its securities or other obligations to investors. SPVs issue their securities to investors pursuant to pooling and servicing agreements, or pursuant to trust indentures. A bank will serve as an indenture trustee for the security holders. The SPV will issue certificates evidencing beneficial ownership in a specified percentage of future interest payments after deducting servicing fees and a specified percentage of future principal payments.

---

[76] 2 TAMAR FRANKEL, SECURITIZATION § 14.2 B (Ann Taylor Schwing ed., 2d ed. 2005).

[77] An escrow agent is "a person or entity holding documents and funds in a transfer of real property, acting for both parties pursuant to instructions. Typically the agent is a person (commonly an attorney), escrow company or title company, depending on local practice." *Escrow Agent,* http://legal-dictionary.thefreedictionary.com/escrow+agent (last visited Sept. 10, 2009).

The trustee need not necessarily hold the SPV's assets. They may be held by a custodian. The function of the two differs. An independent trustee may supervise the actions of the custodian in accordance with the directives of the trust indenture.

Documents pertaining to the SPV assets given to an escrow agent are released to the SPV-designated representative (usually a trustee) upon consummation of the transfer to the SPV. If the documents are handed to a trustee, the trustee will maintain custody of the documents in accordance with the trust agreement with the SPV. Usually, if the trustee also performs the servicing functions, the documents will be in the trustee's name to facilitate performance of trust functions; for example, to release the documents to the borrowers upon full payment of the amounts they owe, or to transfer the documents in accordance with appropriate directives from SPV representatives.

When SPV assets consist of receivables, the SPV managers rather than the custodian or trustee collect on the receivables and purchase new receivables. The structure of the relationships among the actors and their functions is more complex. For example, the Originators-managers purchase new receivables. The money collected on the outstanding receivables is paid to a designated bank and is available to the Originators to buy new receivables. The same bank or another bank may hold the security interest on the receivables. Another bank or the same bank may record the transactions and verify the signatures of the Originators that are authorized to purchase new receivables.

Nature and Extent of the Custodian's and Trustee's Fiduciary Duties.[78] Institutions that hold SPV assets or assets designed to be transferred to the SPVs are fiduciaries; they hold and deal with other people's money. The parties call these Institutions by different names and the Institutions-fiduciaries may perform different duties. For example, escrow agents hold financial assets until the representatives of the SPVs and the sellers of the financial assets to the SPVs close the transfer transactions. For example, an Originator may purchase loans from different sources and combine them into a portfolio of loans. It takes time to assemble the loans and transfer them to the SPV. During that time, the payment for the loans and the loans themselves may be transferred to an escrow agent. At the closing of the transaction, the escrow agent transfers the money to the seller and the loans to the buyer. These escrow agents are fiduciaries. The money and assets they receive are given in trust. Similarly, the securitization transaction may involve agents for the various parties, who are fiduciaries. Custodians that hold the SPVs' assets, and trustees, who may be custodians or trustees of SPVs organized as trusts, are also fiduciaries. Legally, these actors' names denote the extent of control they have over entrusted assets and the commensurate fiduciary duties to which they are subject.

---

[78] 2 TAMAR FRANKEL, SECURITIZATION §14.3 (Ann Taylor Schwing ed., 2d ed. 2005).

For example, as the discretion and power of a custodian increases, so will the concomitant fiduciary duties. If a custodian has mere physical control over SPV assets, but the SPV is the named payor in the documents, and if the custodian must transfer and deal with SPV assets without discretion, by the orders of others, then the custodian's fiduciary duties are not very strict. Subject to statute and regulation, the duties may be similar to those of a bailee. If SPV assets are held in the custodian's own name, the fiduciary duties will probably be the stricter duties imposed on an agent. If SPV assets are in the custodian's name and the custodian has discretion to perform service functions, subject to the terms of the agreement with the SPV, the custodian's duties may be as strict as those of a trustee.

Fiduciary Duty of Care.[79] Like any trustee, a trustee-custodian who receives documentation as guardian for the SPV is required to review the property given in trust, such as the documentation that the sponsor of the SPV provides regarding each loan, to ensure that the documentation complies with all applicable standards set out in the pooling and servicing agreements. A similar duty of care is imposed on an escrow agent who holds funds on behalf of an SPV and is charged with releasing the funds to the seller upon receipt of the assets that the SPV buys. Thus, when Bank of America, acting as trustee, did not perform due diligence with respect to the quality of the loans it received, it voluntarily assumed a loss of $133 million to investors as detailed in the next section. This may be what other institutions did in response to the sub-prime losses. They wrote off the losses to keep investors happy. But there comes a point when writing off losses cannot solve the problem.

An SPV trustee must perform all responsibilities to the SPVs and their security holders with care but there is not any duty to the underlying borrower. The degree of care to which SPV trustees will be held liable depends in part on the type of financial assets that the SPVs hold. If the SPVs hold credit card receivables, the degree of care by the SPV trustee may be higher than if the SPVs held mortgage-backed securities issued by government agencies' SPVs. The reason for a higher duty of care is that credit card receivables consist of a very large number of loan accounts and the primary documentation for these loans is not based on manually signed documents as is the case with other types of loans. Therefore, an SPV trustee that holds such assets must perform with stricter due diligence. Industry practice includes in due diligence obtaining a "comfort letter" from an accountant or another independent party with respect to the legality and enforceability of the assets.

The trustee should evaluate the SPV's portfolio. If the portfolio is composed of credit card receivables or other account receivables, the trustee should evaluate the loan originator and sponsor on a long list of items: (i) the origination and underwriting procedures; (ii) the level of reliance by the loan originator and sponsor on prescreened promotional mailings, their use of credit scoring systems, their borrower

[79] 2 TAMAR FRANKEL, SECURITIZATION § 14.3.1 (Ann Taylor Schwing ed., 2d ed. 2005).

applications and verification procedures of these applications, their level of reliance on bulk portfolio purchases and their history of delinquency write-offs; (iii) the borrowers' historical rates of payments and reborrowing, if available, and (iv) other factors that may influence the return on SPV securities. When the securitized assets are receivables (e.g. short-term accounts payable), the cost of the trustee's verification of each transaction would be prohibitive. In such a case, a separate trust may hold the assets while a separate bank holds the cash receipts. The trust indenture trustee may hold the security interest on these assets and be required to verify the signature of the promoters who pay for assets received.

Cautious fiduciaries sometimes seek a verification of numerical data and account information by sampling the borrowers' accounts. The evaluation may also focus on possible personal liabilities of SPV security holders.

Duty of Loyalty.[80] A trustee owes a duty of loyalty to the trust beneficiaries. In dealing with trust property, the trustee may not act in conflict of interest. In addition to trust law, specific laws impose such a duty on a trustee. For example, a trustee who is also a "plan fiduciary" subject to the Employee Retirement Income Security Act of 1974 may not engage in transactions in conflict of interest with the trust. Such specific laws may impose different or more stringent requirements or may provide additional remedies for those harmed by a breach of the trust.

Rights of the Trustee and Escrow Agent to Indemnification.[81] A fraud committed in connection with mortgage SPVs in the mid-1980s yielded several judicial decisions concerning the rights and duties of the trustee and escrow agent. In one case, the trustee was alerted to irregularities in mortgage documentation in particular SPVs and, upon investigation, found that the Originator had defrauded investors in the SPV. The trustee also discovered that some of its own employees had been grossly negligent in performing their functions and that the investors might lose all or most of their investments as a result of the fraud.

To discharge its duties, one of the trustees, Bank of America, purchased some of the investors' SPV securities and replaced the defunct mortgages in the SPVs at a cost of \$133 million, incurring a \$95 million loss to itself. The trustee received an assignment from investors, whom it made whole. The investors assigned all their claims against the SPV Originators and others to Bank of America. Wells Fargo Bank, which also served as trustee for four SPVs, declined to settle with the investors, and was sued by the investors. Thereafter, Bank of America brought an action against its own employees for indemnity, negligence, gross negligence, breach of fiduciary duty, equitable subrogation, breach of insurance contracts, and

[80] 2 TAMAR FRANKEL, SECURITIZATION § 14.4 (Ann Taylor Schwing ed., 2d ed. 2005).

[81] 2 TAMAR FRANKEL, SECURITIZATION § 14.6 (Ann Taylor Schwing ed., 2d ed. 2005).

declaratory relief as to the fraudulent insurance agreements involved in the case. In addition, the Bank, as assignee of the investors' claims, sued the SPV Originators, charging violations of numerous laws.

The district court dismissed all of Bank of America's claims against the SPV Originators, except the claim based on RICO. The basis for the dismissal was the "one-satisfaction rule." Under this rule, Bank of America's payments to the investors constituted full satisfaction of the claims against the Originators-tortfeasors. This payment operated to discharge the Originators fully from liability to the investors. The court did grant Bank of America leave to amend the complaint to seek contribution and indemnification from the Originators-defendants.

The amended complaint was based on violations of the securities acts and on common law theories of fraud and negligence. On each claim, Bank of America sought total or partial indemnity under the doctrine of comparative equitable indemnity, available in California. This doctrine, a modified version of the equitable indemnity doctrine, permits "the apportionment of liability among multiple tortfeasors whose tortious conduct combined to cause an indivisible injury."[82] Comparative equitable indemnity is available in California not only among concurrent tortfeasors, but also among successive tortfeasors, and not only in personal injury but also in commercial transactions.

However, the district court held that the theory is not applicable to intentional tortfeasors. Thus, if the tortfeasor's employees have committed an intentional fraud, rather than a negligent or reckless negligent act, the tortfeasor is barred from invoking the comparative equity indemnification or any equity indemnification. Further, the doctrine of comparative equitable indemnity applies to corporate tortfeasors that are liable through employees, as it applies to tortfeasors who committed the tort themselves. Therefore, a corporate employer whose employees acted negligently can claim only partial indemnity, not total indemnity. Moreover, the doctrine applies to the federal securities acts violations, provided it does not conflict with the policies underlying the securities acts. This holding is consistent with Supreme Court decisions upholding the availability of contribution in actions under the federal securities acts.

Thus, when a custodian or a trustee purchases the investors' claims, including claims grounded in the securities acts, and sues the Originators for indemnity, the trustee

---

[82] *In re* Nat'l Mortg. Equity Corp. Mortg. Pool Certificates Sec. Litig., 682 F. Supp. 1073, 1088 (C.D. Cal. 1987), *decision after trial,* 723 F. Supp. 497 (C.D. Cal. 1989) (citing Am. Motorcycle Ass'n v. Superior Court, 578 P.2d 899, 911 (1978)). For other cases applying comparative equitable indemnity under California law in a securities context, see Employers Ins. v. Musick, Peeler & Garrett, 954 F.2d 575, 578 (9th Cir. 1992), *aff'd*, 508 U.S. 286 (1993); Riverhead Sav. Bank v. Nat'l Mortg. Equity Corp., 893 F.2d 1109, 1116-17 (9th Cir. 1990).

must show that the Originators violated their duties to the investors, not to the trustee. The trustee's claim is or includes the assigned breach of duties. While the violations are based on federal law, the trustee's claim is based on an assignment under state law. Therefore, even though the trustee is neither a seller nor a buyer of SPV securities, and cannot sue on Rule 10b-5 under the Securities Exchange Act of 1934, a violation of Rule 10b-5 can be established because the investors are buyers (and the defendant does not have to be a buyer or a seller). Furthermore, the district court held that the statute of limitations on the investors' claims is irrelevant to the trustee's claim in state law; the state statute of limitations starts running from the time in which the trustee settled with, and purchased the claims from the investors and its right to indemnity accrued.

b. Servicers[83]

If the SPV trustee is charged with choosing and monitoring the SPV servicer, industry practice includes in due diligence an evaluation of the servicer's collection procedures and write-off policy. The trustee should obtain a "comfort letter" providing assurances that data processing procedures employed by the servicer for the SPV are adequate to serve as a reliable basis for servicing the loans, identifying investors' interests in the loans or credit card receivables, and remitting funds to investors in a timely fashion. The letter should also provide assurances that adequate arrangements are made to transfer the servicing function, if necessary. Moreover, the letter should provide assurances that computerized information and SPV assets are segregated from those of the servicer. Prudent servicers should know their customers and check the reliability of a third-party loan originator. Servicers that do not may be exposed to the claims of the loan buyers.

The Role of the Servicer.[84] The securitization process allows for separating different intermediation functions among various actors, such as making loans, holding them, and servicing them. Servicing includes collecting and distributing payments from the borrowers to the SPVs and their security holders, enforcing delinquent loans, and foreclosing the collateral, if any. Servicing of receivables and small loans requires a substantial expertise and investment in automated information systems. Negligent servicing can create havoc. When all works well, computers do not make mistakes. When they malfunction or their programs are faulty, the results can be disastrous, since reconstructing thousands of small payments and distributions may be impossible. SPV security holders may lose substantial amounts if the computer numbers are erroneous. Bank of America was sued by nine banks in 1989 in just such a circumstance. Given these risks, the Department of Housing and Urban Development requires operators to install a quality control program for loan

---

[83] 2 TAMAR FRANKEL, SECURITIZATION § 14.3.2 (Ann Taylor Schwing ed., 2d ed. 2005).

[84] 2 TAMAR FRANKEL, SECURITIZATION § 14.7 C (Ann Taylor Schwing ed., 2d ed. 2005).

servicing activities. Prudent mortgagees who are not subject to the regulation might be wise to adopt such a program as well.

Because servicing involves handling large amounts of money and negotiable instruments, the servicer should be financially sound and strictly regulated as a fiduciary. Further, because effective servicing of the loans is crucial to investors in SPV securities, some investors require that the trustee holding the loans should be capable of performing the service functions as a servicer of last resort if the primary servicer ceases to act.

Generally, the Originator of the loans sells the loans to the SPV that they organize. The Originator is likely to continue to perform the servicing functions. If the SPV contains loans from one Originator, the Originator may continue to be the servicer. If the SPV holds loans from several sources, each Originator may retain servicing rights as a subservicer. In the latter case, a single "master" servicer will regulate the activities of all subservicers on behalf of the trustee. However, a loan Originator that is unqualified, unequipped, or too small to perform the servicing for the large number of loans in the SPV may sell the servicing rights, subject to approval of the buyer of the loans. Thus, securitization allows the allocation of servicing to Institutions that are suited to perform the service by developing a Market for servicing rights. This Market has been recognized by the bank and thrift regulators; they count servicing rights that have been purchased toward the tangible capital requirements of these Institutions.

When financial assets are sold, the sale may be accompanied by the sale of the servicing rights. The sale is often effectuated in three stages, especially if it involves the approval of government agencies and the financing Institution. The stages are contract, sale, and transfer.

Servicers' Duty of Loyalty Toward the Owner of the Loans.[85] Toward the owner of the loans, the servicer is a fiduciary and owes the owner the duty of loyalty. If funds that the servicer collects from borrowers for disbursement to the loan owner are segregated and placed in a deposit, these funds should be deemed trust funds protected from creditors and from setoff, even if the servicer is described as an agent in the agreement between the parties. Further, for purposes of section 541(d) of the Bankruptcy Code, a servicer of mortgage loans is deemed to be a trustee who holds the legal title to the mortgages while the loan owner is deemed the beneficial owner of the mortgages.

In performing collection and enforcement functions, the status of the servicer is that of an agent for the financial assets' owner because the servicer is usually subject to the owner's control and acting for the owner's benefit. If the servicer's discretion is

[85] 2 TAMAR FRANKEL, SECURITIZATION § 14.9 (Ann Taylor Schwing ed., 2d ed. 2005).

limited only by the agreement between the parties and the owner cannot interfere in the exercise of that discretion, the status of the servicer may be that of a trustee. Lenders who make loans for securitization take into account the programs for which the loans are made, either the lenders' own programs or those established by other Originators. If the programs are sponsored by a government corporation such as GNMA, the Originators design their lending accordingly.

In some cases, lenders who join Ginnie Mae's program sponsor the issuance of mortgage-backed securities; that is, they make loans secured by mortgages to qualified borrowers and obtain GNMA guarantees. Then they sometimes pool the mortgage loans in a SPV and either cause distribution of the securities issued by the SPV or issue their own obligations backed by the particular loans and guaranteed by GNMA. In such cases, the lenders become issuers. These lenders then continue to service the loans. In some cases, for example, if a servicer is terminated, GNMA enters into a servicing contract with an institution that did not lend, issue, or sponsor the issuance of the securities backed by the loans.

Transfer of Servicing Functions and Termination of Servicing Agreements. Servicing includes collecting payments from borrowers, transferring the payments due to the securities holder-investors, and, if borrowers default, initiating collection and foreclosure procedures by claiming from the U.S. Government payments on the defaulted loans on behalf of investors and making such payments to the investors. Originators and servicers for GNMA programs must be qualified and approved by GNMA.

Servicing agreements commonly contain a termination clause. Termination on notice without cause usually requires payment by the terminating party. Termination for cause, for example, for fraud or breach of contract, does not require a penalty payment.

Duty of Care Toward Owners of Financial Assets and Loans and Towards Third Parties.[86] The duties of the servicer towards the owner of the financial assets and loans as well as towards assignees are discussed above. In performing their functions, servicers must comply with the laws applicable to lenders toward borrowers. Thus, the servicers must notify certain mortgagors who are delinquent or about to become delinquent that home ownership counseling is available to them, and they must give notices to recipients of student loans. Certain Rules apply to servicers directly.

If SPV securities are privately placed and Rule 144A applies to them, the holder of the securities has the right to demand certain information from the issuer. For purposes of this duty, the servicer is deemed to be the issuer. Normally, the servicer

---

[86] 2 TAMAR FRANKEL, SECURITIZATION § 14.10 (Ann Taylor Schwing ed., 2d ed. 2005).

possesses the information and is the party on whom the burden of supplying the information is the least costly.

c. Attorneys [87]

Liability of the Originators' Attorney. [88] The Originators' attorney may be vulnerable to legal claims by SPV security holders in connection with a fraud committed by SPV Originators on these investors. Such a suit may be based on the attorney's violations of the securities acts, RICO, and common law fraud. Furthermore, if the attorney continues to serve the sponsor after the securities are assigned to new buyers, the attorney may be liable to the buyers for such violations. Under California law, an attorney may be liable for nondisclosure to the new buyers if that nondisclosure amounts to "active concealment or suppression of facts by a nonfiduciary."[89] Such concealment can amount to misrepresentation and actual fraud.

A. Formation and marketing of the pools.[90] "Defendant David A. Feldman ('Feldman'), promoted, organized and managed defendant National Mortgage Equity Corporation ('NMEC'). Beginning in 1981, NMEC organized pools of real estate loans secured by first or second deeds of trust on residential real property, located primarily in California and Texas. Riverhead, Missouri and First Federal allege that defendants Wells Fargo Bank ('Wells Fargo') and Advance Mortgage Corporation ('Advance') also played a role in promoting the formation of certain of the pools during 1981 and 1982. In connection with these mortgage pools, NMEC marketed 'Mortgage Pass-Through Certificates' (the 'Certificates') to various financial institutions, *i.e.*, the Investor Institutions. Each Certificate represented an undivided interest in an individual pool. The Certificate holder was entitled to receive interest at a fixed 'pass-through' rate, regardless of the rates paid by individual mortgagors. NMEC solicited buyers of Certificates, *i.e.*, Investor Institutions, through various means, including, as alleged by B of A, through Private Placement Memoranda ('PPM'). The PPM were prepared by defendant law firm Lord, Bissell and Brook ('Lord Bissell'). Defendant Leslie W. Michael ('Michael'), is a partner in Lord Bissell and was also a part owner and officer of NMEC.

NMEC was responsible for the initial selection of loans to be included in the pools. B of A was to act as escrow agent for each pool. Advance was to act as servicer on

---

[87] 2 TAMAR FRANKEL, SECURITIZATION § 14.3.3 (Ann Taylor Schwing ed., 2d ed. 2005).

[88] 2 TAMAR FRANKEL, SECURITIZATION § 14.14 (Ann Taylor Schwing ed., 2d ed. 2005).

[89] *In re* Nat'l Mortg. Equity Corp. Mortg. Pool Certificates Sec. Litig., 636 F. Supp. 1138, 1164 (C.D. Cal. 1986).

[90] *In re* Nat'l Mortg. Equity Corp. Mortg. Pool Certificates Sec. Litig., 636 F. Supp. 1138 (C.D. Cal. 1986) (footnotes and authorities omitted).

the mortgages for at least some of the pools, and did so act until March, 1983, when it resigned and was replaced by NMEC. NMEC apparently at all times acted as servicer for all the loans in the pools that form the basis of B of A's complaint. A trustee was appointed for each pool. B of A was trustee for most of the pools, but with respect to four pools, Wells Fargo acted as trustee. In their respective roles as trustees, Wells Fargo and B of A were to review the documentation NMEC provided regarding each mortgage in order to determine whether it complied with all the applicable standards set out in the pooling and service agreements.

NMEC, Feldman, Lord Bissell and Michael made numerous representations to the Investor Institutions regarding the nature of the mortgages selected for the pools. Defendants represented that the underlying loans were made in arms-length transactions, the borrowers were capable of servicing their debts on the loans, the values of the residential properties involved were determined by independent appraisals, each loan was fully protected by mortgage insurance and that Glacier General Assurance Company ('Glacier') and Pacific American Insurance Company ('Pacific American'), the primary insurers, had the financial resources to cover any likely defaults and had also secured reinsurance.

B. The fraud. The essence of the fraud allegations is that despite defendants' representations respecting the high standards used to select mortgages for the pools, defendants actually were engaged in a widespread series of sham mortgage transactions between various related entities that diverted the Investor Institutions' funds for defendants' personal benefit. Entities and individuals related to or controlled by NMEC, including Michael, Glacier, Energy Resources Financial Inc. ('Energy Resources'), Marvin Weiss ('Weiss'), West Pac Corporation ('West Pac'), and Kent B. Rogers ('Rogers') would obtain funds from NMEC. These entities or individuals would then use these funds to purchase properties through still other related entities. After obtaining a fraudulently inflated appraisal of the property, the related entities would arrange a 'loan' between themselves, secured by a note and deed of trust on the overvalued property. The 'loan' would then be transferred to NMEC's mortgage pools in exchange for cash the Investor Institutions had entrusted to NMEC.

B of A alleges that Glacier and Pacific American were an integral part of this scheme. It is alleged that these insurance companies were selected to insure the mortgages not because of their ability to provide adequate coverage but because they were related, through common principals, to one or more of the other participants in the scheme. It also is alleged that the insurance companies actively participated in the scheme by recycling properties on which borrowers had defaulted back into the NMEC pools.

This scheme began to unravel in late 1984 and early 1985. In October, 1984, the Seaman's Bank for Savings, one of the Investor Institutions for which B of A acted as trustee, advised the Bank of 'certain irregularities in the processing and documentation' of the mortgages comprising Seaman's pool. B of A responded by conducting an investigation into NMEC pools. Through this investigation, the Bank learned not only of the NMEC-managed fraud, but also that its own employees had not, in the Bank's words, 'adequately discharged the Bank's responsibilities' as escrow agent and trustee. As a result of its investigation, B of A filed an action in California state court against several of its own employees for their roles in the handling of the NMEC pools.

B of A's investigation also led it to conclude that as a result of the fraud, the Investor Institutions for which it had acted as trustee stood to lose all or most of their investments in the NMEC pools. The Bank, therefore, decided to 'resolve its liability' to those Investor Institutions by repurchasing their Certificates or by replacing the mortgages in the pools represented by the Certificates. The Bank paid in cash and replacement collateral to the Investor Institutions a total of $133 million (which apparently was 100 percent of the funds invested in Certificates by them). It expects to realize $38 million on liquidation of the collateral and from the mortgage guarantee insurance claims assigned to it, leaving a net loss of $95 million from its resolving its liability to the Investor Institutions. In return, the Investor Institutions assigned to B of A any claims they might have against any of the defendants.[10] B of A then filed this action, both for damages sustained in its own right and as assignee of the Investor Institutions' claims."[91]

The complaint also contains multi-paragraph sections that identify the role of each defendant in the alleged fraud in a manner sufficient to allow defendants to prepare a responsive pleading. Nonetheless, Lord Bissell argues that the complaint contains only collective allegations of misrepresentations and omissions by all defendants, and does not attribute any specific misrepresentations to Lord Bissell and Michael. Those defendants argue that, as lawyers, they simply drafted the language of the PPM and cannot be responsible for the misrepresentations of other defendants found in those documents. However, the complaint does allege that Lord Bissell and Michael continued to prepare misleading PPM even after they received notice of the fraud in the form of a letter from Advance in December 1982 that outlined many of the deficiencies in the NMEC pools.

---

[91] *Id.* at 1144-46.

Discussion Topic

Prepare the judgment in the case. To what extent is the lawyer responsible for checking the information it receives from the clients and from people who are arguing that they were defrauded by the Originator?

In addition, the attorney of the SPV's trustee bears a duty of diligence that covers a careful examination of legal issues. These issues include various consumer protection laws; for example, (i) the Truth in Lending Act, which limits the liability of credit card holders for unauthorized use of the card and imposes liability for payment on the bank; (ii) the Equal Credit Opportunity Act, which makes it unlawful for lenders to discriminate against prospective borrowers; (iii) the Fair Credit Billing Act, under which the issuer of a credit card is '"subject to all claims (other than tort claims) and defenses arising out of any transaction in which the credit card is used as a method of payment or extension of credit" if the debtor has made a "good faith attempt to obtain satisfactory resolution of a disagreement or problem relative to the transaction from the person honoring the credit card";[92] (iv) the Fair Credit Reporting Act; (v) the Fair Debt Collection Practices Act, and other federal and state consumer protection laws.

Due diligence may require the attorney to consider the issues presented by the specific types of debtors significantly represented in the assets, the effect of varying remedies for default, and any other legal ramifications peculiar to the circumstances. Due diligence also includes consideration of pending legislation and proposed Rules that might affect the Originators' and investors' risks and costs in the future.

D. Case Study: The Dark Side of SPVs – Masking and Manipulating Enron's Financial Performance

"The Examiner has concluded that, through pervasive use of structured finance techniques involving SPEs [special purpose entities] and aggressive accounting practices, Enron so engineered its reported financial position and results of operations that its financial statements bore little resemblance to its actual financial condition and performance."[93] With these words, Neal Batson (the bankruptcy court authorized special investigator) summarized how Enron, the 7th largest company in the world with $100 billion in revenues in 2000, could completely implode only 11 months later. The data provided by the Examiner brings the magnitude of the financial engineering into sharp focus. At year-end 2000 Enron reported net income of $979 million but after correction, predominantly for misuse of SPE related

---

[92] 15 U.S.C. § 1666*i*(a) (2006).

[93] SECOND INTERIM REPORT OF NEAL BATSON, COURT-APPOINTED EXAMINER 15 (2003), http://www.enron.com/media/2nd_Examiners_Report.pdf (last visited Oct. 10, 2009)..

transactions, the actual income was only $42 million. Funds flow from operations was adjusted downward from a positive $3 billion to a negative $154 million. Finally, debt was reported as $10.2 billion; however, it was actually over $22 billion.[94] (See Exhibit 1)

The special purpose entity (SPE) also known as a special purpose vehicle (SPV) is central to the process of structured finance and securitization. Through a true sale of assets from an originator to the SPV, the securities issued by the SPV are "bankruptcy remote" and shielded from the claims of the creditors of the Originator, in the event of the Originator's failure. Thus, investors in securities issued by the SPV are protected from creditors' claims to these assets. When properly done, structured finance and securitization, using an SPV, generate benefits for both the Originator and investors. The investors are insulated from the risks of Originator bankruptcy, thus reducing possible losses. The lower risk to the investors, often reflected in higher credit ratings, in turn reduces the cost of capital for the Originator. Structured finance and securitization via an SPV also allows an Originator to convert future cash flows into immediately available funds to tap additional investment opportunities. Moreover, the SPV's structure allows the Originator to remove the debt liability to the ultimate investor from its balance sheet. "Off-balance sheet" transactions can increase the overall capital available to the Originator.[95]

However, the use of the SPV to facilitate structured financing can also mask or manipulate the originator's financial performance as was the case at Enron. At the time of its bankruptcy Enron had created more than 3000 SPVs.[96] The Examiner honed in on six accounting techniques associated with the SPV transactions which enabled Enron to present itself as the financial success story of the 21st century when in reality the company was headed for a dramatic bankruptcy. The use and misuse of SPVs at Enron provides insights into the risks associated with SPE transactions and the "red flags" that indicate potential problems.

---

[94] *Id.* at 48.

[95] Conceptually, debt on and off the sponsors balance sheet would be combined in determining its cost of capital and thus off-balance sheet transactions would not lower the sponsor's cost of capital; however, the lower cost of capital and/or availability of funds might still be realized because the unified version might not be undertaken as a result of information availability and cost. At a minimum the creation of an off-balance sheet SPV reduces the sponsor's cost of capital by reducing expected bankruptcy costs. *See* Gary Gorton & Nicholas S. Souleles, *Special Purpose Vehicles and Securitization* (rev. Sept. 2005), http://fic.wharton.upenn.edu/fic/papers/05/0503.pdf (last visited Oct. 10, 2009).

[96] *Id.* at 2.

Enron Profile[97]

In 1985, the gas pipeline company InterNorth acquired Houston Natural Gas and shortly after renamed the combined company "Enteron." The name, created by a high profile branding consulting firm, was meant to signify the company's intended broad energy focus and international scope. Perhaps foreshadowing the future, the name was short lived because enteron is also a part of the human digestive system! Within a week the name became Enron.

The pipeline business in 1980s was particularly challenging. The industry was in the midst of moving from a regulated monopoly to a competitive market. Under the old regulatory model, pipeline companies provided a bundled product offering. They bought gas from producers and sold it to gas distribution companies on a delivered basis. The pipeline business had been a state of flux since the 1970s when low regulated interstate gas prices led to a reduction in production. Therefore, the gas that was produced was sold in intrastate markets which allowed for higher prices. The problem came to a head in the winter of 1976 and 1977 when 22 states faced gas shortages resulting in the closings of schools and factories. Congress and the regulators responded to the crisis by passing the Natural Gas Policy Act of 1978 and the Power Plant and Industrial Fuel Use Act. The former raised price ceilings for interstate and intrastate gas, brought into production after the Act (old gas prices were grandfathered at the lower regulated rates) and the latter restricted the use of gas as a fuel for new industrial and power plant facilities. The pipeline companies responded to the shortage by committing to long term "take or pay" contracts with suppliers to assure supplies and accepting escalating prices during the contract term.

The new incentives worked very well, perhaps too well. On the supply side, gas exploration and production expanded dramatically anticipating greater profits. The higher prices and restrictions on new users caused demand to fall. The net result was a glut of gas and falling prices. The pipeline companies were caught in the unenviable position of having high cost take or pay contracts in a declining price market. End-users facing high bundled prices offered by the pipelines (who were left to mix expensive take or pay gas with new low price gas) lobbied regulators for the freedom to negotiate directly with producers for gas. The users won a partial victory in 1985 when the Federal Energy Regulatory Commission issued Order 436, which began the move toward unbundling of gas, that is, the purchase of the gas could be completed independently of its transportation. Transportation rates were market based within a floor and ceiling established by the regulators. The order also encouraged pipelines to buy out their take or pay contracts. (By 1992, pipelines were limited to only transporting gas; although arms' length affiliates could buy and sell the gas.)

---

[97] Text extracted from MARK FAGAN & TAMAR FRANKEL, TRUST AND HONESTY IN THE REAL WORLD 157-62 (2007).

It is against this background of turbulent market conditions and changing regulatory environment that Enron came into being. Moreover, the company was loaded with debt. InterNorth paid about $70 per share for HNG -- a company whose stock had been trading at $45 prior to the acquisition. The company's future during the first few years was tenuous at best.

In 1990, a management consultant to Enron, Jeff Skilling, had an idea that would enable Enron not only to survive but also to thrive during these challenging times. He envisioned that the company would be "purveyors not of products but of ideas, of what Jeff Skilling called 'intellectual capital.' A company didn't need bricks and mortar to triumph in the new age. It needed smarts . . . [and those smarts] would propel Enron from its role as the World's Leading Energy company to its destiny as the World's Leading Company."[98] Skilling's first "idea" was a gas bank. Skilling realized that the new regulatory environment created more uncertainty for producers and consumers. The deregulation of the industry begged for someone to make the market and address uncertainty – enter his gas bank. The gas bank would accept gas from producers at a fixed price and sell it to consumers at known prices for the long term; Enron would profit from the spread between buy and sell prices. The key to success was insuring long term supply at a known price. Skilling was able to do this by buying the future production of wells for cash up front.

A second innovation that Skilling brought to Enron was mark-to-market accounting. In traditional accounting, revenues are recognized as sales take place, even when there is a long term contract in place. Under mark-to-market accounting the revenues for the entire contract period can be recorded in the first year. In time, Enron also extended the mark-to-market concept to recognize the future value of assets it acquired (e.g., power plant or barges) as initial year revenues. To the extent that the underlying value of the contracts or assets changed during their life, an adjustment would be made to Enron's financial statements. Skilling believed firmly that mark-to-market was the best portrayal of Enron's value creation. "[Trading] creates value and completes its earning process when the transactions are finalized" and "other commodity trading businesses which are analogous used market-to market accounting."[99] Enron's outside auditors, Arthur Andersen, agreed. The Securities and Exchange Commission's chief accountant "informed Enron that, based upon Enron's representations, the SEC accounting staff would not object to Enron's use of MTM [mark-to-market] accounting for its natural gas trading activities beginning in 1992."[100] The new accounting methodology enabled Enron to report substantial revenues from long term gas sale contracts in the first year of the

---

[98] MIMI SWARTZ & SHERRON WATKINS, POWER FAILURE 75 (2003).

[99] BETHANY MCLEAN & PETER ELKIND, THE SMARTEST GUYS IN THE ROOM 41 (paperback ed. 2004).

[100] SECOND INTERIM REPORT OF NEAL BATSON, COURT-APPOINTED EXAMINER 23 (2003), http://www.enron.com/media/2nd_Examiners_Report.pdf (last visited Oct. 10, 2009).

deal thus putting itself on the growth fast track. (Ultimately, Enron expanded the mark-to-market concept to other commodities and other instruments without explicit SEC approval.)[101]

This regulator-approved business and accounting methodology had two side effects. First, because Enron booked the future value of assets as revenue when it acquired the assets, it had a strong incentive to assure that the value of those assets did not fall. If the value of these asset fell, the company would be required to report a loss on its income statement. Second, since all the revenue from a long term contract or asset was recognized in the first year, new and larger deals would be needed each year to demonstrate sustained growth. While Enron was able to record all future cash flows in the first year for financial reporting purposes, the actual cash would flow in year by year. In Enron's model, cash from operations was not large enough to support growth. Debt was not an alternative either since Enron was already leveraged. Thus, finding sources of cash to fund Enron's expansion was management's next challenge. Where would the cash come from?

Use and Misuse of SPVs at Enron

Andy Fastow, the corporation's CFO, had the solution – special purpose vehicles. This process enabled Enron to raise investment funds but keep the liability for these funds off its own books. The starting point was Enron's creation of an SPV, often a limited partnership, which purchased an asset from Enron in exchange for cash. The SPV raised the cash to buy the asset from two sources. A small amount of cash was raised through non-Enron equity investors who took a direct stake in the SPV. This amount was typically only 3 percent of the funds raised, the minimum necessary for the transaction to be off-balance sheet for Enron. The majority of the SPVs funds came from other, non-equity investors who purchased securities from the SPV that were supported by the cash flows from the assets of the SPV. (In some cases Enron itself was an investor in the SPV typically contributing its stock while other investors provided cash.) Two additional features were common in the Enron SPV transactions. First, Enron often directly guaranteed the cash flow to the SPV investors with Enron stock. Second, a set fixed yield was provided to the equity investor.

Enron's outside accountants and lawyers established the requirements to create these SPVs which were consistent with the Financial Accounting Standards Board's guidance.[102] First, ownership of the assets had to shift to the independent investors

[101] *Id.* at 24.

[102] EMERGING ISSUES TASK FORCE, ISSUE 90-15, *described in* J. Paul Forrester & Benjamin S. Neuhausen, *Is My SPE a VIE Under FIN46R and, If So, So What?*, http://www.mayerbrown.com/publications/article.asp?id=1300&nid=6 (last visited May 5, 2009).

and losses could not be made whole by Enron.[103] Second, at least three percent of the SPV's capital had to come from investors that were independent of Enron. These investors, not Enron, had to control strategic decisions. The first SPV (Jedi) was created in conjunction with the California Public Employees Retirement System (CalPERS). CalPERS made up to $500 million available for Enron investments. Enron's capital contribution was in the form of its own stock.

The Jedi deal worked very well. Enron bought gas with the cash provided by Jedi and in turn sold the gas to customers generally under long term contracts. For Enron the combination of Jedi cash and mark-to-market accounting produced rapid revenue growth. (Exhibit 2 shows Enron's revenue growth.) CalPERS also liked the arrangement. It received an attractive rate of return on its investment. After the initial commitment of cash was invested, Enron sought to establish another SPV modeled on Jedi. CalPERS was interested in participating but wanted its initial investment repaid first. Enron agreed, and Jedi II was born. There was one sticking point. How would Enron buy out the CalPERS portion of Jedi? If Enron itself purchased CalPERS' share, Jedi would no longer be an SPV and would need to return to Enron's financial statements. That was not desirable. Fastow's solution to this dilemma was the creation of another SPV known as Chewco. Because he was unable to find new independent investors to meet the three percent requirement, Fastow "manufactured an outside investor known as 'Big River.' In reality, the money for Big River's investment came from a thinly disguised loan from Barclays Bank, who demanded that Enron put up $6.6 million in cash collateral and guarantee repayment."[104] In fact, the outside investor was Enron. The general partner of Chewco was Michael Kopper, an Enron finance department employee reporting to Fastow. Through Big River and Chewco the buyout of CalPERS was accomplished and new CalPERS capital from Jedi II flowed into Enron enabling the company to make additional investments.

The need to find "3%" investors to make Enron's SPVs "legal" was proving difficult and time consuming. Therefore, Fastow proposed a new fund to provide the independent equity. He would create an entity, LJM (named for his wife and children), that would provide the outside funding (his own money and that of others) needed when Enron wanted to create a new SPV to move a transaction off the books. The Enron board recognized the potential conflict of interest – Fastow might be negotiating on behalf of LJM to buy an Enron asset that was the property of his employer – but the board granted a waiver of the company's code of ethics and LJM was born. Enron's sale of its electricity barges off the coast of Nigeria illustrates how LJM was used to "manufacture" profits. The *Houston Chronicle* described the

---

[103] Some of the guarantees that Enron provided to SPVs appear to have violated this requirement.

[104] *The Fall of Enron*, CHRON.COM (HOUSTON CHRONICLE), http://www.chron.com/news/specials/enron/glossary.html (last visited May 11, 2007).

arrangement. "With 1999 year-end financial reports looming and attempts to sell off its interest in the barges going nowhere, Enron executives who were determined to collect bonus for meeting projected profits presented an enticing offer to Merrill Lynch."[105] If Merrill Lynch bought the barges Enron or another buyer would buy them back after six months leaving Merrill Lynch with a 22% profit. Enron provided Merrill Lynch with a $22 million loan and Merrill Lynch paid $28 million for the barges. "The 'sale' allowed Enron to improperly record a $12 million profit. . . . Enron met its earnings targets, and its executives got their bonuses."[106] LJM funds enabled this transaction.

Yet another use of SPVs was to hedge Enron profits. These SPVs, named the Raptors, were "established to shield [Enron] from mark-to-market losses in its growing equity investment business."[107] As Sherron Watkins, the Enron whistleblower, testified before Congress "A number of assets were hedged with an entity called Raptor. Any asset that was hedged should, for the most part, have a locked-in sales value for Enron, meaning despite current market prices, Enron should realize the hedged price of the Raptor."[108] The concept of hedging is a common business practice. However at Enron the Raptors were generally backed with Enron stock. "In effect, Enron was hedging risk with itself."[109] The combination of declining asset values and lower Enron stock price doomed Enron.

The Raptor III (also known as Porcupine) arrangement illustrates the mechanics. Enron created a new entity called The New Power Company (TNPC) to deliver power to residential and commercial customers. Enron contributed its investment in TNPC to Porcupine at $10.75 per share. TNPC went public a month later in October 2000. The stock opened at $21 per share which left Porcupine and thus Enron with a $370 million gain which Porcupine hedged for Enron. However, the hedge was

---

[105] *Special Report: Enron: Nigerian Barge Trial,* CHRON.COM (HOUSTON CHRONICLE), http://www.chron.com/content/chronicle/special/01/enron/skillinglay/barge.html (last visited May 11, 2007).

[106] *Id.*

[107] Mark P. Holtzman et al., *Enron and the Raptors,* CPA J., Apr. 2003, at 24, 24, *available at* http://www.nysscpa.org/cpajournal/2003/0403/features/f042403.htm (last visited Oct. 10, 2009).

[108] *Financial Collapse of Enron: Hearing of the Oversight and Investigations Subcomm. of the H. Comm. on Energy and Finance,* 107th Cong. (2002), LEXIS, News Library, Arcnws File (statement of Sherron Watkins, Vice President, Enron).

[109] WILMER, CUTLER & PICKERING, REPORT OF THE INVESTIGATION BY THE SPECIAL INVESTIGATIVE COMMITTEE OF THE BOARD OF DIRECTORS OF ENRON CORP. 97 (2002), http://fl1.findlaw.com/news.findlaw.com/hdocs/docs/enron/sicreport/sicreport020102.pdf (last visited May 6, 2009).

accomplished with TNPC stock. "Consequently, Enron's transaction with Porcupine was not a true economic hedge."[110] Enron's interest in locking in the gain was well founded; within two months TNPC stock price fell below $10 per share. "Raptor III's assets had therefore declined substantially in value, and its obligation to Enron had increased. As a result, Raptor III also had negative credit capacity."[111]

The loss position of Raptor III was similar to that of Raptor I. By the first quarter of 2001 "it appeared that Enron would have to take a pre-tax charge against earnings of more than $500 million."[112] Enron sought to improve the financial position of Raptors I and III with the capital capacity that remained in Raptor II and IV through cross-collateralization and an infusion of Enron stock. "Restructuring the Raptors allowed Enron to avoid reflecting the $504 million reserve loss in its first quarter [2001] financial statements."[113] However, the continual slide in Enron's share price, related to concerns about the company's profitability, made it impossible to keep the Raptors afloat. "As of September 28, 2001, Enron calculated that the Raptors' combined assets were approximately $2.5 billion, and their combined liabilities were approximately $3.2 billion."[114] The Achilles Heel that actually triggered Enron to restate its financials was an unrelated accounting error associated with the Raptors when the company entered a notes receivable as an increase to shareholder equity rather than a decrease. When investors read the footnote in Enron's quarterly financials the death spiral began.

Enron Epilogue[115]

The media, not the financial community or regulators, finally brought Enron down. Reporters for the *Wall Street Journal* learned about Fastow's relationship with the SPVs. They wrote that "[w]hile the company says that this arrangement was proper, some corporate governance watchdogs have questioned whether the chief financial officer . . . should have been involved in such a partnership that was, among other things, looking to purchase assets from Enron."[116] A story the next day revealed that

---

[110] *Id.* at 118.

[111] *Id.* at 120.

[112] *Id.* at 121.

[113] *Id.* at 125.

[114] *Id.* at 127 (footnote omitted).

[115] Text extracted from MARK FAGAN & TAMAR FRANKEL, TRUST AND HONESTY IN THE REAL WORLD 163-64 (2007).

[116] John Emshwiller & Rebecca Smith, *Enron Jolt: Investments, Assets Generate Big Loss --- Part of Charge Tied to 2 Partnerships Interests Wall Street,* WALL ST. J., Oct. 17, 2001, at C1, LEXIS, Meganw Library, Wsj File.

Fastow had made millions from the questionable arrangement.[117] Not surprisingly the negative media attention led to a decline in Enron's share price. Not well known outside the Enron inner financial circle, the lower stock price was driving many of the SPVs into covenant violations. (Exhibit 3 shows the Enron's declining share price.)

On November 8, 2001, Enron issued a financial restatement. The *Wall Street Journal* would not let Enron off the hook, noting that the stock price sank below $9.[118] An online journal ran an article headlined "Enron Restatements Don't Go Far Enough."[119] Enron management sought a white knight – Dynergy, a major player in the energy market. While a deal looked promising for a short time and Dynergy infused $1.5 billion into Enron, the cash hemorrhaging at Enron and sliding price led Moody's to downgrade Enron to junk bond status. That was too much for Dynergy which ended the merger discussion. The downgrade also triggered $3.9 billion in off-balance sheet debt to be repaid in 30 days. Enron's share price dropped to 27 cents and the company filed for bankruptcy.

The collapse of Enron led to a non-stop set of investigations, political and legal. As of March 2007, 16 people have pled guilty in conjunction with the Enron affair.[120] Fastow entered into a bargain with prosecutors pleading guilty to conspiracy to commit wire and securities fraud. He forfeited more than $20 million and agreed to cooperate with the prosecution before his sentencing.[121] Fastow was sentenced to only six years in prison compared to the expected 10 year term. The lesser sentence reflected his cooperation with prosecutors in building their case against Skilling and Lay. Skilling was tried and convicted for insider trading, securities fraud and conspiracy. He was sentenced to more than 20 years in prison. Ken Lay was also found guilty "on all six counts that relate to Enron fraud, including conspiracy to

---

[117] Rebecca Smith & John R. Emshwiller & Rebecca Smith, *Partnership Spurs Enron Equity Cut --- Vehicle Is Connected to Financial Officer,* WALL ST. J., Oct. 18, 2001, at C1, LEXIS, Meganw Library, Wsj File.

[118] John R. Emshwiller et al., *Enron Slashes Profits Since 1997 by 20% --- Partnership Dealings Cited as Dynegy Talks Go On; Debt Ratings an Issue,* WALL ST. J., Nov. 9, 2001, at A3, LEXIS, Meganw Library, Wsj File.

[119] Peter Eavis, *Enron Restatements Don't Go Far Enough,* THESTREET.COM, Nov. 8, 2001, http://www.thestreet.com/markets/detox/10003703.html (last visited May 6, 2009).

[120] *Special Report: Enron: Ken Lay,* CHRON.COM (HOUSTON CHRONICLE), http://www.chron.com/content/news/photos/02/10/21/players/photo1.html (last visited May 11, 2007).

[121] Plea Agreement, United States v. Fastow, Cr. No. H-02-0665 (S.D. Tex. filed Jan. 14, 2004), http://www.usdoj.gov/enron/exhibit/03-07/BBC-0001/OCR/EXH025-01745.TXT (last visited Oct. 10, 2009).

commit wire fraud, perpetrating wire fraud, and making false and misleading statements to employees at a company meeting, as well as to banks, securities analysts and corporate credit agencies."[122] Lay was never sentenced. He died of a heart attack six weeks after the verdict.

Post bankruptcy, Enron's debtors filed complaints against other institutions that supported Enron's SPV transactions. The debtors sought recovery of Enron's payments to banks, investment banks, and other investment groups that participated and profited from many of Enron's SPVs. The defendants included Citigroup, Salomon Brothers, JP Morgan Chase, Barclays, and Deutsche Bank. The complaint alleged that the defendants "participated with a small group of senior officers and managers of Enron (the 'Insiders') in a multi-year scheme to manipulate and misstate Enron's financial condition. . . . The Bank Defendants principally assisted the scheme by designing, implementing, and often financing structured finance transactions with Enron, *knowing* that the Insiders were improperly recording the financial effects of these transactions. . . . For the Bank Defendants, the scheme offered the irresistible temptation of enormous fees . . . ."[123]

The suit sought to recover more than $3 billion in payments made to the banks "in connection with the structured finance transactions as preferential transfers under section 547(b), improper postpetition payments under section 549 of the Bankruptcy Code, and/or as fraudulent transfers under sections 544 and 548 of the Bankruptcy Code and applicable state law."[124] The plaintiffs also sought to "disallow the Bank Defendants' claims filed against the plaintiff's estates [and] recover the enormous damages it suffered as a result of the Bank Defendants' knowing participation in the scheme with the Insiders to manipulate and misstate Enron's financial condition."[125] The litigation arising from this suit ended on March 26, 2008, when Citigroup agreed

---

[122] *Special Report: Enron: Ken Lay,* CHRON.COM (HOUSTON CHRONICLE), www.chron.com/content/news/photos/02/10/21/players/photo1.html/enron (last visited May 11, 2007)

[123] Complaint, Enron Corp. v. Citigroup Inc. (*In re* Enron Corp.), No. 01-16034 (AJG), at 1, 3 (Bankr. S.D.N.Y. Sept. 24, 2003), http://news.corporatecounselcentre.ca/hdocs/docs/enron/eciti92403advprcd.pdf (last visited Oct. 10, 2009).

[124] *Id.* at 4.

[125] *Id.* at 4-5.

to pay the Enron creditors $1.66 billion.[126] In total the Defendant Banks paid $5 billion to the Enron creditors.[127]

Beyond the monetary examples provided above the fallout from Enron included calls for new regulations of SPV transactions. "For example, shortly after the Enron controversy, and as a result thereof, Congress deleted from pending bankruptcy-reform legislation a long-awaited legislative 'safe harbor' for determining what constitutes a sale in securitization transactions."[128] Thus, proponents of securitization worried that weakening the clarity about what constitutes a true sale could hamper the use of securitization. "In sum, Enron has made both regulators and investors wary. Indeed, investors are fleeing, not to 'quality' as in typical crises, but to simplicity and transparency. Both investors and regulators may react with what is arguably an excess of caution, tarring much financial innovation with the Enron brush."[129]

The Enron Examiner evaluated the role of the SPVs in the bankruptcy of the company and found a strong relationship. The Examiner determined that Enron's expansion oriented business model "made Enron a voracious consumer of cash."[130] In order to maintain the flow of cash for investment and to avoid trading without posting collateral, Enron needed to maintain an investment-grade debt rating. The SPVs were critical for Enron to maintain its investment-grade rating which was predicated on meeting target levels for five key financial ratios – funds flow from operations to total obligations, funds flow interest coverage, pre-tax interest coverage, total obligations to total obligations plus shareholder's equity, and debt to total capital. Shifting debt from Enron's balance sheet to SPVs made several of those measures easier to achieve. The SPVs in conjunction with mark-to-market accounting also enabled Enron to report higher funds flow from operations positively impacting several of the measures. Exhibit 4 shows the magnitude of false success Enron reported at year-end 2000. For example, funds flow from operations to total

---

126 Madlen Read, *Citi Settlement Ends Enron's Creditors 'Mega Claims' Suit,* WASH. POST, Mar. 27, 2008, at D04, LEXIS, News Library, Curnws File, *available at* http://www.washingtonpost.com/wp-dyn/content/article/2008/03/26/AR2008032603046.html (last visited Oct. 10, 2009).

127 *Id.*

128 Steven L. Schwarcz, *Securitization Post-Enron,* 25 CARDOZO L. REV. 1539, 1541 (2004).

129 Claire A. Hill, *The Future of Synthetic Securitization, A Comment on Bell & Dawson,* 12 DUKE J. COMP. & INT'L L. 563, 566 (2002).

130 SECOND INTERIM REPORT OF NEAL BATSON, COURT-APPOINTED EXAMINER 17 (2003), http://www.enron.com/media/2nd_Examiners_Report.pdf (last visited Oct. 10, 2009).

obligations was overstated by 102 percent and debt to total capital was understated by 67 percent.[131]

Warning Signs and Risk Mitigation

The SPV structure can be a powerful tool to enable Originators to lower their cost of capital and monetize future cash flows as well as provide bankruptcy protection for investors. In addition, Enron demonstrates the misuse of structured financing. In retrospect there were numerous warnings that Enron's financial success came from financial engineering not business results. The first sign was the complexity of the financial transactions Enron was using. The arrangements rapidly became incomprehensible even with footnote disclosure. "Enron's structured finance transactions were so complex that disclosure is necessarily imperfect – either oversimplifying the transactions or providing detail and sophistication beyond the level of an ordinary investor in Enron's securities."[132] For investors, the strategy for mitigating risk is simple -- If you can not understand the deal, stay away.

A second warning sign was the conflicts of interest between the Enron and its SPVs. Senior Enron managers were investors and/or managers of related SPVs from the outset of Enron's structured financing efforts. Perhaps the most egregious conflict was with LJM where Fastow was simultaneously responsible to Enron shareholders and LJM investors when negotiating over the terms for assets being sold by Enron to LJM. Nevertheless, Enron's board permitted the conflict. The risk of such conflicts can be reduced by enforcing existing codes of ethics. Had that been done at Enron, LJM, Raptors and other flawed SPV arrangements would not have taken place.

The use of Originator's stock to finance the SPV transaction is a third warning sign. "In a typical transaction, for example, Enron would transfer its own stock to an SPE in exchange for a note or cash, and also directly or indirectly guarantee the SPE's value. The SPE, in turn, would hedge the value of a particular investment on Enron's balance sheet, using the transferred Enron stock as the principal source of payment."[133] If the value of an investment being hedged falls at the same time originator's own stock declines, a vicious cycle of reinforcing declines can take place. This is in fact what happened at Enron during 2001. This risk can be protected by guarantees with independence from the originator's financial condition such as over-collateralization or letters of credit.

---

[131] SECOND INTERIM REPORT OF NEAL BATSON, COURT-APPOINTED EXAMINER 48 (2003), http://www.enron.com/media/2nd_Examiners_Report.pdf (last visited Oct. 10, 2009).

[132] Steven L. Schwarcz, *Enron and the Use and Abuse of Special Purpose Entities in Corporate Structures,* 70 U. CIN. L. REV. 1309, 1316-17.

[133] *Id.* at 1310 (footnotes omitted).

An overall risk mitigation strategy is to obtain a legal opinion letter. Third party attorneys can provide opinions as to legal status of an SPV vis-à-vis true sale and nonconsolidation. Typically the opinion letters only address bankruptcy law issues not accounting analysis. The letters do have limitations even in the legal arena as "[s]uch opinions typically are given at a time when bankruptcy is perceived merely as a theoretical possibility, not as a likely risk"[134] and thus may not cover all eventualities. Moreover, "[l]egal opinions are merely informed judgments."[135] The opinions do help to reduce the information imbalance between the SPV and investors in its securities but they do not comment on the soundness of the business decision. Those who rely on such letters need to recognize that the letters provide reasoned opinions rather than black-letter answers and the lawyer's opinion letter does not replace an accounting analysis of the SPV arrangement in the context of GAAP.

Exhibit 1
Impact of Enron 's Financial Engineering
(as of 12/31/2000, millions of dollars)

Financial Measure	Reported	Adjusted	% Change
Funds flow from operations	$3,010	($154)	(105%)
Debt	$10,229	$22,060	116%
Total obligations	$10,466	$22,297	113%
Shareholders equity/other items	$14,788	$10,342	(31%)
Earnings for credit analysis	$2,492	$1,793	(28%)
Interest	$944	$1,567	66%

Source: Second Interim Report of Neal Batson, Court -Appointed Examiner 48 (2003), http://www.enron.com/media/2nd_Examiners_Report.pdf (last visited Oct. 10, 2009).

---

[134] Steven L. Schwarcz, *The Limits of Lawyering: Legal Opinions in Structured Finance,* 84 TEX. L. REV. 1, 6 (2005).

[135] *Id.* at 9.

Exhibit 2
Enron Revenue Growth

(Billions of Dollars)

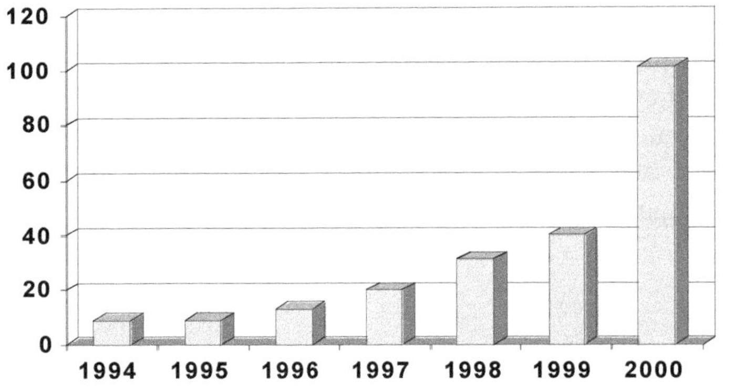

Source: Enron Annual Report 1998, at 1, http://picker.uchicago.edu/Enron/EnronAnnualReport1998.pdf (last visited Oct. 10, 2009); Enron Annual Report 2000, at 1, http://picker.uchicago.edu/Enron/EnronAnnualReport2000.pdf (last visited Oct. 10, 2009).

Exhibit 3
2001 Enron Stock Price
(Approximate Dollars per Share)

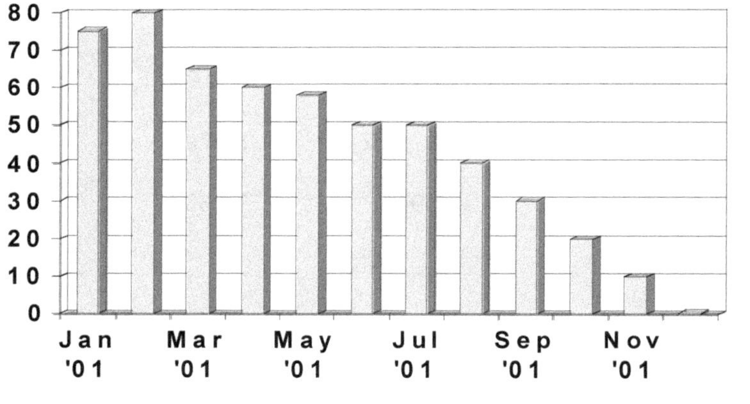

Source: BBC News, *Enron: The Rise and Fall*, http://news.bbc.co.uk/hi/english/static/in_depth/business/2002/enron/timeline/12.stm (last visited May 5, 2009).

Exhibit 4
Restatement of Enron Key Ratios
(as of 12/31/2000, millions of dollars)

Financial Measure	**Reported**	**Adjusted**	**% Change**
Funds flow interest coverage	4.07	0.90	(78%)
Pretax interest coverage	2.54	1.11	(56%)
Funds flow from operations/ Total obligations	28.8%	(0.7%)	(102%)
Debt/total capital	40.9%	68.1%	67%

Source: Second Interim Report of Neal Batson, Court -Appointed Examiner 49 (2003), http://www.enron.com/media/2nd_Examiners_Report.pdf (last visited Oct. 10, 2009).

Discussion Questions
Law

- What is the role of internal legal counsel in assessing the legality of structured finance transactions?
- What are the duties and obligations of a third party lawyer who writes an opinion letter?
- Under what circumstances is it appropriate for the board to suspend its conflict of interest policies?
- What is the obligation of outside financiers to assure that SPV transactions meet the spirit as well as the letter of the law?

Business

- Why is the SPV essential to the structured finance transaction?
- What options does a company have to reduce its cost of capital beyond structured finance/securitization?
- Why did even sophisticated investors fail to understand that Enron's success was the result of financial engineering?
- If disclosed, in what ways do off-balance sheet transactions change the debt carrying capacity of a public corporation?
- What actions can the board take to minimize the risk of the SPV being misused?

Public Policy

- Do Enron's SPV related misdeeds justify additional regulation of the use of SPVs for structured finance in general and securitization in particular?
- Is greater disclosure of SPV transactions required?
- What skills and competencies do regulators need to effectively oversee structured finance/securitization transactions?

Chapter 5: The Creation of the Assets SPVs Acquire

This chapter focuses on the type of assets that SPVs acquire. These assets serve as the basis for the securities that the SPV's issues; hence the term "asset-backed securities." However, the nature of the assets depends on the creators of these assets and the regulation to which they are subject. Therefore, we start by examining the main creators of SPV assets and their regulation addressing loans first and then turning to debt. In each area, case studies are provided to illustrate the asset creation process in practice. The chapter concludes with a discussion of borrowers' rights highlighting the decisions in *Washington Steel* and *United Jersey Bank.*

A. Loans

a. The Lenders and Originators[136]

Any legal entity can lend money. However, historically, most significant lenders were regulated Institutions. Now, the number and kind of lenders has increased; governmental entities and non-banks act as intermediaries in competition with banks. In the past, the cost of the funds for banks was lower than for other potential lenders. Now, since banks must raise funds in the Markets, lenders with good credit can compete as intermediaries. In fact, non-bank lenders have an advantage over banks, to the extent that these lenders do not bear the regulatory costs that banks bear. As banks fail to serve particular borrowers (e.g., students, homebuyers), federal, state, and local governments increasingly act in the place of banks as intermediaries. In addition, governments intermediate to subsidize particular borrowers to advance public policies, while other non-bank lenders, such as manufacturers, intermediate to increase the sale of their products. The most recent large lenders were unregulated mortgage bankers and construction firms that made sub-prime loans to borrowers. The banks engaged mortgage brokers who offered borrowers these loans.

Most Originators are intermediaries, interested in expanding their primary business and/or entering new business sectors. Thus, banks sponsor SPVs to extend their lending, while members of the securities industry sponsor SPVs to extend their securities distribution and market-making activities. However specialized lenders have entered the field, as they learned other aspects of the business, and may venture into other phases of the securitization process.

Securities brokers have also developed expertise in assembling portfolios of financial assets for sale. Loans that banks have charged off their books as bad debt have been securitized, mostly by debt collection agencies. While the sale price of the debt is set

[136] 1 TAMAR FRANKEL, SECURITIZATION § 2.5 (Ann Taylor Schwing ed., 2d ed. 2005).

at a deep discount of its face value, the sellers benefit by receiving cash immediately rather than at an uncertain future date.

b. Applicable Regulation

As mentioned, not all lenders and Originators of securitization are regulated, and those that are regulated to a different extent and for different purposes. Regulators have been concerned with securitization largely to the extent that it increases the risk of the regulated lenders, or the risk to investors, when Originators are induced to sell to the public more risky instruments without disclosing the extent of the risk. Thus, bank regulators are concerned about the risks banks may take in making loans intended for sale. First, a bank might take on implicit obligations to repurchase nonperforming securitized loans. While repurchase obligations are covered by capital requirements, these implicit obligations or understandings are not.

Second, banks might lower their credit standards in making loans intended for sale. This concern can be addressed through the banks' internal organization by requiring that decisions to approve loans be made independently from decisions to securitize loans. "Banks . . . should have well-defined procedures for handling problem credits and a diversified investor base as well as a diversified geographic base for securitized loans."[137] Third, a bank might be selling only its best assets. This concern is partially addressed by the capital requirements. Fourth, a bank might provide credit enhancement for securities backed by loans of low credit quality. This problem is addressed by imposing the same standard of prudence for providing credit enhancement as for making loans directly. These concerns are reflected in the examination guidelines that the regulators have adopted with respect to securitization. In contrast, private entrepreneurs who put together securitization deals are not regulated except to the extent of protecting vulnerable public investors.

c. Bank Regulation [138]

Bank regulation can affect securitization. For example, in the opinion of the Comptroller and the FDIC, what banks are permitted to do directly, they may do through subsidiaries. The Comptroller has allowed banks to pledge portfolio loans to subsidiaries that hold the loans and engage in banking activities through subsidiaries.

In 1970, the Comptroller recognized the power of national banks to service loans held by, and act as custodians for, SPVs that hold GNMA pass-through certificates. Banks may (1) service securitized loans, that is, collect the money owed to the SPV

---

[137] *Regulators Explain Supervisory Efforts to Oversee Securitization Activities,* 57 Banking Rep. (BNA) 217 (Aug. 5, 1991).

[138] 1 TAMAR FRANKEL, SECURITIZATION §§ 4.2-.3 (Ann Taylor Schwing ed., 2d ed. 2005).

and distribute the payments to the investors in the SPV's obligations (2) act as custodians for SPV's assets and cash and (3) act in accordance with the directives of the operators of the SPVs, while creating and keeping the records of the transactions. In this capacity, the banks are responsible only for the integrity of the assets but not the quality of the transactions, or for monitoring the operators of the securitization process because they have no responsibility or power to determine the transactions they are ordered to perform. The only exception appears if the bank is responsible for the wrongdoing by its involvement or the involvement of the employees. In some cases the banks may be subject to the Trust Indenture Act of 1939, depending on their activities and the type of securities that they hold under the Indenture.[139]

Banks may invest funds in a fiduciary capacity both in accounts and in collective investment funds. In addition, under the Secondary Mortgage Market Enhancement Act of 1984, state and federal banks, thrifts, and credit unions may invest in qualified privately sponsored mortgage-backed securities (MBS).

The National Bank Act authorizes banks to purchase, hold, or sell real property only under limited circumstances, in order "'to keep the capital of the banks flowing in the daily channels of commerce; to deter them [banks] from embarking in hazardous real-estate speculations; and to prevent the accumulation of large masses of such property in their hands, to be held as it were, in mortmain.'"[140]

These developments raise a number of implications. First, banks have been allowed to act as market intermediaries. Second, banks have been increasingly permitted to act in the commercial area. This movement is in contrast to the basic views of banking in the 1930s on which most of our laws were based. The traditional policy aimed at (1) keeping banks small, (2) avoiding the rise of concentrated financial and market power, and (3) separating banking from investment banking. Thus, in our review we pay attention to the dichotomy between the developments in the Markets

---

[139] Until its repeal in 1999, section 16 of the Glass-Steagall Act applied to banks and state chartered banks that are members of the Federal Reserve System. Subject to exceptions, and the Comptroller's regulations, the Act prohibited banks from purchasing and selling certain securities for their own account ("investing"). Even though banks may engage in the business of securitizing loans, whether the loans that they originated or those originated by others, the banks may invest in securitized loans subject to the Rules regulating their investments. Securitization raises a number of questions under these regulations.

Banks may not invest more than 10 percent of their capital and surplus in the investment securities of any one issuer, nor lend more than 15 percent. Therefore, whether asset-backed securities ("ABS") are loans or investment securities is important, in the context of bank powers. In 1970, the Comptroller recognized the power of national banks to invest in GNMA pass-through certificates, on the same grounds on which permission to sell GNMAs was based. Thus, for purposes of determining eligible investments, the Comptroller ignored the interpositioned SPV and looked through it to the assets that the SPV was holding.

[140] First Nat'l Bank v. Comptroller of Currency, 697 F.2d 674, 681 (5th Cir. 1983) (quoting National Bank v. Matthews, 98 U.S. 621, 626 (1878)) (describing purposes of 12 U.S.C. § 29).

and the image of the financial system on which the policies and fundamental rules of regulatory law are based.

The regulation designed to protect investors may conflict with protection of borrowers. In such a conflict, the interests of the borrowers might take precedence. For example, laws that protect borrowers, especially small borrowers, can become inoperative unless they apply to loan buyers as well. The explicit recognition of the pervasiveness of the Market in mortgage loans and its effect on homebuyers is expressed in the 1988 amendments to the Fair Housing Act. The House Report states that "the provisions of the Act extend to the secondary mortgage market."[141] Thus, the prohibition on lenders from discriminating against persons who seek to finance home purchases was extended to the purchasers of such loans. By and large however, the transfer of loans among lenders is free of constraints. The assumption is that the borrowers are in no worse position if they pay one lender or another.

Safe and Sound Banking Practices.[142] Banks should follow "safe and sound banking practices" in making their investment decisions.[143] A bank should consider such factors as "the interest rate, credit, liquidity, price, foreign exchange, transaction, compliance, strategic, and reputation risks presented by a proposed activity" and its appropriateness for the bank.[144] With respect to all securities investments, banks must "maintain records available for examination purposes adequate to demonstrate" compliance with the Comptroller's regulations.[145] Specifically, the Comptroller provides that the bank shall determine that there is adequate evidence that an obligor possesses resources sufficient to provide for all required payments on its obligations, or, in the case of securities deemed to be investment securities on the basis of reliable estimates of an obligor's performance, that the bank reasonably believes that the obligor will be able to satisfy the obligation.

A bank may treat a debt security as an investment security if it "concludes, on the basis of estimates that the bank reasonably believes are reliable, that the obligor will be able to satisfy its obligations under that security, and the bank believes that the security may be sold with reasonable promptness at a price that corresponds reasonably to its fair value."[146] However, a bank may not invest more than five

---

[141] H.R. Rep. No. 711, 100th Cong., 2d Sess. 30 (1988), *reprinted in* 1988 U.S.C.C.A.N. 2173, 2191.

[142] 1 TAMAR FRANKEL, SECURITIZATION § 7.5.1 (Ann Taylor Schwing ed., 2d ed. 2005).

[143] 12 C.F.R. § 1.5(a) (2005).

[144] 12 C.F.R. § 1.5(a) (2005).

[145] 12 C.F.R. § 1.5(c) (2005) (information may be stored "in any manner that can be readily retrieved and reproduced in a readable form").

[146] 12 C.F.R. §1.3(*i*)(1) (2005).

percent of its capital and surplus in securities with respect to which it must rely on such estimates.

Federal bank regulators issued a 1998 statement of policy regarding sound risk management practices for investment securities and end-user derivatives. The release discusses the oversight by the board of directors and senior management and the elements of an effective risk management process, including (i) policies, procedures, and limits; (ii) risk identification, measurement, and reporting; and (iii) internal controls. The release also discusses practices for managing specific risks, including market risk, credit risk, liquidity risk, operational (transaction) risk, and legal risk. Sound practice requires national banks to perform quantitative tests on mortgage-derivative securities to ascertain cash flow and interest rate risks, and purchases of such securities are subject to the other sound practices guidelines in the statement.

Valuation of Loans and Securitized Loans in the Bank Portfolio.[147] The valuation of loans and securitized loans may also affect a bank's capital level, soundness, or even solvency. The valuation of asset-backed securities can be based on a number of methods, such as market basics, actuarial, default and eclectic methods. The lawyer need not become an expert in these methods but should know enough to ask the relevant questions.

Transactions between Banks and Their Affiliates.[148] Banks must be organized as corporations. Therefore, the fiduciary duties of corporate managements apply to bank managements. In addition, banks and their holding companies are subject to sections 23A and 23B of the Federal Reserve Act. These sections limit the transactions between banks and affiliates to protect the safety and soundness of banks. Section 23A of the Federal Reserve Act prohibits a bank from making any loan or extension of credit to an affiliate, except under certain conditions. One condition is that the loan must be secured by collateral. The limitations apply to transactions involving securitization of loans. In a June 30, 1993 opinion, the Chief Counsel's office addressed the sale of an affiliate's mutual fund shares. The Chief Counsel held that a service corporation of a federal savings association may purchase shares of an affiliated mutual fund on a "riskless principal" basis without regard to limitations and prohibitions imposed by sections 23A and 23B of the Federal Reserve Act and section 11(a)(1)(B) of the Home Owners' Loan Act ("HOLA").

Similarly, in a September 9, 1993, ruling, the Chief Counsel's office held that, while a savings association's purchases from affiliates of mortgage-backed securities guaranteed by Ginnie Mae, Freddie Mac, and Fannie Mae are permitted under HOLA section 11(a), they are still under the auspices of sections 23A and 23B of the Federal Reserve Act. The Chief Counsel concluded that these types of government-

---

[147] 1 TAMAR FRANKEL, SECURITIZATION §7.5.2 (Ann Taylor Schwing ed., 2d ed. 2005).

[148] 1 TAMAR FRANKEL, SECURITIZATION § 4 (Ann Taylor Schwing ed., 2d ed. 2005).

backed securities should not be construed as securities issued by an affiliate under section 11(a), as the mortgage-backed securities issued by the government entities are not traditional equity or debt securities that succeed or fail based on the affiliate's business fortunes.

E. Case Study: The Rise of Mortgage Brokers

For the first 70 years of the 20th century the vast majority of Americans had one path to securing a home mortgage, their local bank. The process was straightforward although bureaucratic. You (often with assistance of your real estate agent) met with the bank's loan officer and received a mortgage application, a daunting stack of forms, to complete. One set focused on your creditworthiness where your income, assets, and liabilities were detailed. Another set of forms addressed the home that would secure the mortgage centering on its appraised value and physical condition. The paperwork continued with the financial details of the transaction: the amount of your down payment, the expected monthly payments (including interest, principal repayment, taxes and insurance) and the portion of your income required to service the mortgage. The completed application then was reviewed by the bank's loan committee to determine if you represented a good "investment" for the bank. Some of the decision criteria were objective; for example a 20% down payment and the monthly mortgage payment representing less than 1/3 of your monthly income were desirable. Other decision criteria were subjective – the neighborhood where the house was located and who you knew at the bank among others. A "yes" vote led to a mortgage offer from the bank based on a rarely negotiable standard interest rate sheet. If you were turned down, your only option was to begin the process anew with another local bank.

There were significant advantages to this process. First, the bank carefully selected customers who had a very high probability of meeting the terms of the mortgage by asking the question: Can the borrower afford this house? The loan officer asked the question to the benefit of the borrower, preventing the mortgagee from drowning in debt, and to the benefit of the bank, which would hold the mortgage for several decades and did not want to incur the high costs of a non-performing loan. Second, the bank relied on a local professional appraiser to assess the value of the home. This was someone whose credentials the bank knew it could rely upon. Moreover the bank's lending officer lived in the community, knew the neighborhoods, and could even drive by the property for a first hand inspection. Third, if a problem arose with repayment during the life of the mortgage, the borrower could meet with the banker, explain the problem and work out a mutually acceptable solution.

Banks as the dominant source of mortgages also had a downside. The banks provided very little flexibility in the review process. If you did not meet the objective standards, it was unlikely that the subjective measures would lead to a loan approval. Once you were turned down for a loan the likelihood of finding a mortgage was low as the banks generally used the same acceptance criteria. Another concern was that the interest rates were largely fixed with little opportunity to negotiate. The funds available for lending were also limited as the banks relied predominantly on deposits to fund mortgages. Given the limited geographic reach of the banks at this time there was a constrained supply of mortgage money allowing the banks to lend very selectively, freezing out of the market borrowers who would have been less qualified yet still responsible mortgagors. Finally, there was strong evidence that banks were not lending to potential homeowners in low income and minority neighborhoods. Banks were accused of "redlining," drawing a red line around areas where they would not offer loans regardless of the qualifications of the potential borrower.

In addition, before the rise of mortgage brokers there were a number of such brokers who worked closely with real estate brokers in arranging financing for clients who wished to buy a house. The link was mainly between the mortgage and real estate broker rather than the mortgage broker and the customer. As the demand for mortgage loans increased, mortgage brokers began to touch base directly with potential borrowers. The brokers were also encouraged to do so by builders who sought buyers for new homes.

Thus, mortgage brokers are a relatively new phenomenon. As the pressure to acquire mortgage loans grew, both by home builders and mortgage bankers, banks and other lenders as well as real estate brokers began to rely on mortgage brokers to bring the borrowers (and the buyers) to the banks. Thus, during the years of 2004 to 2008 there arose a cadre of brokers that offered loans on behalf of lenders, mainly those who made loans for sale by securitization.

With the growth of the mortgage broker community, mortgage brokers began to negotiate the terms of the loans with the borrowers and captured market share. They thus "became an essential component of the subprime mortgage origination."[149] Some of the brokers did not prepare the financial and registration forms correctly. Some of the brokers did not fill in the true information which potential borrowers gave them, including inflationary numbers concerning the earning abilities of these borrowers. There arose an aggressive cadre of lenders and brokers in search of borrowers. Some argue that this was the beginning of the crisis of sub-prime mortgage loans. One commentator argued that mortgage brokers should be regulated to avoid the practices that they develop in inducing unqualified borrowers to apply for loans they could not possibly afford on terms that more sophisticated and less speculating borrowers would not accept.[150]

---

[149] Cassandra Jones Havard, *"Goin' Round in Circles" . . . and Letting the Bad Loans Win: When Subprime Lending Fails Borrowers: The Need for Uniform Broker Regulation,* 86 NEB. L. REV. 746 (2008).

[150] *Id.* at 738-41..

From humble beginnings, the mortgage broker industry ended up employing more than 400,000 employees in all 50 states and originated more than half of all residential mortgages in 2004.[151] According to the National Association of Mortgage Brokers, "The rise of the mortgage broker has been accompanied by a decline in mortgage interest rates and closing costs and an increase in the home ownership rate. Mortgage brokers have dramatically increased competition in almost every region and community in the country. While the number of mortgage lenders is continually declining through mergers and consolidation, the number of mortgage brokers is growing."[152]

The mortgage broker serves two masters, the borrower and the lender. The broker adds value to the borrower by finding the lender offering the lowest total cost mortgage. The broker also assists the borrower in completing the documents necessary to close the loan. An industry consultant summarized the broker's offering this way: "Brokers know all the lending programs from one end of the spectrum to the other, from affordable housing to jumbo finance. They command over 50 percent market share because they know their stuff and they are willing to meet with you at your office in the afternoon or to make a home visit in the evening."[153] "Good service plus good price equals a good deal in the eyes of most mortgagors [borrowers]."[154] Value is also created for the lender community as brokers provide a new channel to reach borrowers, not just those around the corner but also around the world. The brokers serve as a huge commission sales force that do all the legwork for the lenders and are only paid if a mortgage is closed.

The mortgage brokerage sector grew rapidly throughout the last three decades. The growth was attributable to several factors. First, the broker offered a customer-centric service as described above. Second, the broker's economics were favorable. Brokers search the market to find attractive interest rates for their clients. Also, their low overhead compared to banks (1.5% of loan value versus 3.0%) enabled them to offer a lower total cost mortgage to the borrower. Third, they were better able to find nonstandard product offerings for borrowers who did not meet bank standards. For example, a retired Navy veteran and single mother was unable to find work in her field after leaving the military. She supported her family as a checkout clerk at a

---

151 Nat'l Ass'n of Mortg. Brokers, *NAMB Mission,* http://www.namb.org/namb/Mission.asp?SnID=727146017 (last visited Sept. 9, 2009).

152 *The Role of Mortgage Brokers in the Mortgage Finance Market: Hearing before the Subcomm. on Housing and Community Opportunity of the H. Comm. on Banking and Financial Services,* 105th Cong. 28, 30 (1998) (statement of Janet Hix, President, National Association of Mortgage Brokers), http://commdocs.house.gov/committees/bank/hba47579.000/hba47579_0f.htm (last visited Sept. 10, 2009).

153 *Id.* at 41, 43 (statement of Thomas S. LaMalfa, Partner, Wholesale Access).

154 *Id.*

grocery store until she found a higher paying job in the computer industry. Her period of low wage employment made her unable to meet institutional standards. Nevertheless, she did become a homeowner because of the efforts a brokerage broker who "took on my loan and amazed me with his dedication. Nowhere else would anyone really consider the tough times I had gone through."[155] His efforts paid off and the woman realized her dream of homeownership. Fourth, the broker helps the borrower plow through the mound of paperwork required to secure a mortgage. "The sheer amount of paperwork that I have seen is enough to confuse and frustrate anyone. I know all these disclosures are supposed to help me, but how am I supposed to digest all that material about a subject as foreign to me as a mortgage?"[156] The broker provides the role of interpreter.

The brokers viewed themselves as independent contractors who worked for a fee. The fees often amount to 1% to 3% of the loan value.[157] The borrower typically pays 1% of the loan value plus additional fees for obtaining mortgage information and assisting in the completion of the loan application for the broker's services. However, the payment does not imply that the broker works for the borrower since a portion of the fees may also be funded from the originator of the loan. The originator payments are usually yield-spread premiums (YSP), "a cash bonus that a broker receives from a lender for placing borrowers in a loan with a higher interest than the lender would accept."[158] The YSP amounts to $1,850 for the average loan making this usually the largest portion of the broker's compensation.[159]

The rationale for YSP is that it can allow borrowers to avoid paying the brokers fees upfront; rather the fees are built into the life of the mortgage through a higher interest rate. By law the broker's receipt of YSP must be disclosed to the borrower but "[t]here is no legal requirement to inform borrowers about the connection between YSP and the interest charged on a loan."[160] Moreover the magnitude of the YSP need not be revealed.[161] The Center for Responsible Lending among others raised

---

[155] *Id.* at 33, 36 (statement of Terri R. Cook)..

[156] *Id.* at 33.

[157] James R. Hagerty, *Mortgage Brokers: Are They Friends or Foes?,* WALL ST. J. (May 2, 2007), at D1, LEXIS, News Library, Wsj File.

[158] Center for Responsible Lending, *Yield Spread Premiums: A Powerful Incentive for Equity Theft* ((June 18, 2004) (CRL Issue Brief #11), http://www.hiddenmysteries.org/money/aids/Equity_Theft-0604.pdf (last visited Sept. 15, 2009).

[159] *Id.*

[160] *Id.*

[161] Howell E. Jackson & Jeremy Berry, *Kickbacks or Compensation: The Case of Yield Spread Premiums* 6 (Jan. 8, 2002), http://www.law.harvard.edu/faculty/hjackson/pdfs/january_draft.pdf (last visited Sept. 15, 2009).

questions about the broker's incentives associated with YSP: "These kickbacks provide brokers a strong incentive to charge borrowers a higher interest rate when they could quality for a less expensive loan. The effect of YSPs is to steal equity from struggling families."[162] An analytical analysis of YSP mortgages shows "With the highest degree of statistical confidence and using multiple formulations, we can reject the notion that consumers fully recoup the cost of yield spread premiums. Our best estimate is the consumers get only twenty-five cents of value for every dollar of yield spread premiums. …This price dispersion strongly suggests that yield spread premiums are not simply another form of mortgage broker compensation, but rather that the payments constitute a deceptive device that the mortgage broker industry employs to extract unnecessary and excessive payments from unsuspecting borrowers."[163]

The concerns about YPS and broader issues of broker motivations and integrity stem from the lack of regulation of the mortgage brokerage industry. In contrast to banks which owe a duty to the borrower, mortgage brokers do not have a fiduciary responsibility to the borrower at the federal or state level with the expectation of California where a 1979 court decision led to brokers having such an obligation to the borrowers they serve.[164] There is state-level regulation of brokers which often involves only registration/licensing and an explicit prohibition on predatory lending.

There have been numerous efforts to increase regulatory oversight at the federal level over the past decade. For example in 1998, the U.S. House of Representatives Subcommittee on Housing and Community Opportunity held a hearing on the role of mortgage brokers. One focus was on whether regulation was required to increase the transparency of broker compensation, especially the use of YPS. While there was a push to increase disclosure that the broker works for both the buyer and the lender, the faith in the market prevailed. "Again, I am going to go back to Adam Smith and say the invisible hand is going to be the protector, and I mean that in a very serious way. The market governs itself. There is plenty of competition out there, and [a broker] can't charge too much, because I am going to undercut her."[165] No federal oversight was enacted.

---

[162] Center for Responsible Lending, *Yield Spread Premiums: A Powerful Incentive for Equity Theft*(June 18, 2004) (CRL Issue Brief #11), http://www.hiddenmysteries.org/money/aids/Equity_Theft-0604.pdf (last visited Sept. 15, 2009)..

[163] Howell E. Jackson & Jeremy Berry, *Kickbacks or Compensation: The Case of Yield Spread Premiums* 8-9 (Jan. 8, 2002), http://www.law.harvard.edu/faculty/hjackson/pdfs/january_draft.pdf (last visited Sept. 15, 2009).

[164] James R. Hagerty, *Mortgage Brokers: Are They Friends or Foes?,* WALL ST. J., May 2, 2007, at D1, LEXIS, News Library, Wsj File.

[165] *The Role of Mortgage Brokers in the Mortgage Finance Market: Hearing before the Subcomm. on Housing and Community Opportunity of the H. Comm. on Banking and Financial Services,* 105th Cong. 41, 55 (1998) (statement of Thomas S. LaMalfa, Partner, Wholesale Access),

A decade later in 2007, hearings were held before the U.S. House Committee on Financial Services to again consider proposals on reforming mortgage practices. The hearings were motivated by the growing failure of subprime mortgages as the rise in housing prices slowed and reversed. At issue was the balancing of preventing predatory lending with allowing the market to innovate new product offerings. Representative Bachus of Alabama summarized one goal of the proceeding: "The testimony of the witnesses will be helpful to us as we consider measures to curtail predatory practices, going forward to ensure that mortgage credit remains available for those . . . subprime borrowers who are worthy of [it] and have the ability to repay [it]."[166] The proposed legislation would have provided federal regulation of mortgage brokers through the establishment of national standards for mortgage lending. Key provisions included licensing and registration of all mortgage brokers and a "bright line" test for affordability. More controversial topics were creating a duty of care for brokers and assignee liability. The importance of eliminating predatory lending practices was highlighted by the FDIC witness: "Poor lending standards and weak consumer protection are the root cause of the current problems, resulting in serious consequences for consumers, lenders, and the United States economy."[167]

The mortgage brokerage industry responded with support for "the implementation and enforcement of minimum standards for all mortgage originators; the creation of a national registry to track and remove bad actors from the industry; improved prohibitions against deceptive and misleading advertising of mortgage products, [and] reformed mortgage disclosures."[168] The brokerage industry, however, took exception to the anti-steering provisions for the proposed legislation. Under this provision, originators would be barred from compensation that is based on the terms of the loan including YPS. The industry argued that this would confound the legislation's objective of providing affordable credit to all, especially those with low and middle incomes, since YPS is what enables borrowers to close without having to pay broker fees. Such a "zero point" mortgage "is the 'typical loan' that represents somewhere between 85 and 90% of the market because is has clear benefits to the consumer: (1) it lowers the amount of cash needed to bring to closing; and (2) may

---

http://commdocs.house.gov/committees/bank/hba47579.000/hba47579_0f.htm (last visited Sept. 10, 2009)..

[166] *Legislative Proposals on Reforming Mortgage Practices Including Consideration of the "The Mortgage Reform and Anti-Predatory Lending Act of 2007": Hearing Before the H. Comm. on Financial Services* , 110th Cong. (2007), LEXIS, News Library, Curnws File (statement of Rep. Bachus)..

[167] *Id.* (statement of Martin J. Gruenberg, Chair, FDIC).

[168] *Revising Mortgage Practices: Hearing Before the H. Comm. On Financial Services.* 110th Cong. (2007), LEXIS, News Library, Curnws File (statement of Marc Savitt, President-Elect, National Association of Mortgage Brokers).

actually decrease the total origination fee paid on the loan if a borrower remains in the home only 5 to 7 years, or refinances within that time period."[169]

The mortgage brokerage industry also argued that industry self-regulation is a powerful compliment to national standards. The National Association of Mortgage Brokers (NAMB) is the industry's trade organization with more than 25,000 members across the country. "NAMB promotes the industry through programs and services such as education, professional certification and government affairs representation. NAMB members subscribe to a code of ethics and best lending practices that foster integrity, professionalism and confidentiality when working with consumers."[170] The code of ethics calls for honesty and integrity, professional conduct, honesty in advertising, confidentiality, compliance with law and disclosure of financial interests. NAMB also provides best lending practice guidelines. Highlights of the best practices are "[o]ffer rates and fees to all equally . . . [c]harge only those fees disclosed . . . [p]rovide a written agreement, which explains the nature of the business and how I am compensated . . . explain all programs and pricing options."[171] NAMB has introduced several programs to increase the professionalism for the industry and provide consumers with greater confidence. One program is broker certification. Another is the Lending Integrity Seal of Approval launched in late 2007. The goal of the seal is to "help consumers identify mortgage brokers and loan officers who meet the industry's highest standards for knowledge, professionalism, ethics and integrity."[172] Brokers earn the seal through continuing education, a criminal background check, and a pledge to abide by the code of ethics, best lending practices, and an ethics grievance process.

The mortgage brokerage industry has received substantial criticism in conjunction with its role in the 2008 financial crisis. Of particular concern are the subprime loans originated by mortgage brokers. The primary charge against the industry is its direct responsibility for predatory lending. The Center for Responsible Lending estimates that 70% of subprime loans were originated by independent mortgage brokers.[173] The Center suggests that "The demand from Wall Street was so intense that it encouraged subprime lenders to abandon reasonable qualifying standards . . . and to

---

169 *Id.*

170 Nat'l Ass'n of Mortg. Brokers, *NAMB Mission,* http://www.namb.org/namb/Mission.asp?SnID=727146017 (last visited Sept.15, 2009).

171 Nat'l Ass'n of Mortg. Brokers, *Professional Standards & Best Lending Practices,* http://www.namb.org/images/namb/Ethics/Best_Lending_Practices.pdf (last visited Sept. 15, 2009).

172 Nat'l Ass'n of Mortg. Brokers, *2007-2008 Year in Review* 2. https://www.namb.org/images/namb/Membership/Year%20in%20Review%20Final.pdf

173 *Revising Mortgage Practices: Hearing Before the H. Comm. On Financial Services.* 110th Cong. (2007), LEXIS, News Library, Curnws File (statement of Michael D. Calhoun, President and Chief Operating Officer, Center for Responsible Lending).

ignore whether borrowers could actually afford the loan."[174] A second tie between the financial crisis and mortgage brokerage is the "moral hazard" that resulted from the securitization of mortgage loans. The *Economist* defines problem of the moral hazard as "people with insurance may take greater risks than they would do without it because they know they are protected, so the insurer may get more claims than it bargained for."[175] In the case of securitized loans the moral hazard is that once the loan originator sells the mortgage it is free of repayment risk. The Massachusetts Commission of Banks articulated the linkage between securitization and the moral hazard as follows: "The evolution of the securitized mortgage market has also, however, created moral hazard by redistributing the risk of loan defaults thought contractual agreements that begin with the local broker, and end with a Wall Street investor. This dispersal of risk has created opportunities and incentives for some actors to engage in weak underwriting or fraud."[176]

As policy makers search for solutions they will undoubtedly return to proposals offered in conjunction with more than a decade of hearings on appropriate mortgage lending. Three actions in particular appear likely to move from proposal to legislation/regulation. The first is the creation of a national licensing and registration (including competency tests and background checks) for all mortgage originators including mortgage brokers. This is viewed as a barrier to unscrupulous originators entering and/or remaining in the business. Second is requiring mortgage brokers to meet the same standards on consumer protection as bank lenders. This is viewed as a way to increase the use of existing regulations rather than create new requirements. A third proposal is for greater disclosure of mortgage broker compensation. This information would help borrowers understand the brokers' incentives.

Several other interesting proposals have been made but have less chance of implementation. One is the creation of a federal duty of care for mortgage brokers in their relationship with borrowers. This is a fiduciary obligation that bank lenders carry; however, brokers argue that they are independent intermediaries who work on behalf of both borrowers and lenders. A second proposal is "modifying compensation incentives to mortgage originators, to consider a longer term payout on loan origination, to protect the borrower or a customer's economic best interest."[177] The supporters of this approach point to the compensation system for life

---

[174] *Id.*

[175] *Moral Hazard,* http://www.economist.com/research/Economics/alphabetic.cfm?letter=M#moralhazard (last visited Sept. 15, 2009).

[176] *Revising Mortgage Practices: Hearing Before the H. Comm. On Financial Services.* 110th Cong. (2007), LEXIS, News Library, Curnws File (statement of Steven L. Antonakes, Commissioner of Banks, Commonwealth of Massachusetts).

[177] *Legislative Proposals on Reforming Mortgage Practices Including Consideration of the "The Mortgage Reform and Anti-Predatory Lending Act of 2007": Hearing Bef. the H. Comm. on Financial*

insurance sales. A third idea is a "bright line" test of affordability where there is a negative presumption if debt-to-income ratio is greater than 50%. While there is logic to such a test, a rigid threshold faces significant opposition. A final proposal has been to eliminate the YSP from broker compensation to better align broker and borrower interests. Given the economic model of mortgage brokerage this proposal is unlikely to be adopted.

Are mortgage brokers fiduciaries, and if so, to whom do they owe the duty? The legal status of mortgage brokers as fiduciaries is unclear, and not uniform. Under California law, a mortgage broker is a fiduciary.[178] "This duty obligates brokers to 'make a full and accurate disclosure of the terms of a loan to borrowers and to act always in the utmost good faith toward their principals.'"[179] Further, if the borrower has "'modest means and limited experience in financial affairs,' a mortgage broker also has 'duties of oral disclosure and counseling,' which require the broker to 'disclose orally the true rate of interest, the penalty for late payments or [other material terms of the loan] . . . .'"[180]

In another California case, allegations by a borrower of conduct by a mortgage broker in violation of the broker's fiduciary duty were held sufficient to allege the existence of such duty.[181] Two other California cases suggest that there is a duty to the lender under certain circumstances. In the first, the court first stated that a mortgage loan broker owes a fiduciary duty,[182] stating, "The broker owes this duty to the lender-investor as well as to the borrower."[183] In this case, the lender-investor was told that the borrower was seeking a new loan secured by her residential property, and invested in the loan based on an allegedly inaccurate appraisal. "In addition to the general fiduciary duty imposed on mortgage loan brokers," a state statute imposes on mortgage loan brokers an additional duty, "to provide an estimate of the fair market value of the property."[184]

In a second case, following the above case, an investment counselor for an investment broker/real estate broker firm sought investments from the

Services (2007), LEXIS, News Library, Curnws File (statement of John M. Reich, Director, Office of Thrift Supervision).

[178] Zimmer v. Nawabi, 566 F. Supp. 2d 1025, 1031 (E.D. Cal. 2008).

[179] *Id.* at 1031-32 (citation omitted).

[180] *Id.* at 1032 (citation omitted).

[181] Magnallez v. Hiltop Lending Corp., 505 F. Supp. 2d 594, 608 (N.D. Cal. 2007).

[182] Barry v. Raskov, 283 Cal. Rptr. 463, 467 (Ct. App. 1991).

[183] *Id.*

[184] *Id.* at 468.

investors for a loan. While the counselor was paid by a broker for the firm, and not by the investors, the court found an agency relationship with the investors based on her conduct, which included "soliciting investors and brokering loans," more than merely "introducing" the broker and lender. [185] The court then found this duty to be a fiduciary duty.[186] Another California case stated that mortgage brokers are customarily agents of borrowers; therefore, a fiduciary relationship is created.[187]

Under Illinois law, a court denied a motion to dismiss a cause of action for breach of fiduciary duty by a borrower against a mortgage broker, implying that such a duty may exist. [188] Another court found sufficient allegations that another company induced breach of mortgage broker's fiduciary duty, implying that such a duty exists.[189]

A Washington court held that the mortgage broker relationship itself does not create a fiduciary duty, but the borrower established facts sufficient to support a finding of such duty (illness, reliance on the other party, the relative positions of the parties). [190] Further, a Washington state statute provided that a mortgage broker has a duty to disclose the borrower's fees and costs in connection with obtaining the loan; however, there is no duty to negotiate a loan for the borrower at the best rate. [191] Yet another Washington court held that a mortgage broker is an "agent," therefore a fiduciary; and a court upheld a trial court finding of breach of fiduciary duty, finding "ample" findings to support the breach. [192]

Under Minnesota law, "[w]hether a fiduciary relationship exists between a mortgage broker and a borrower depends on their conduct." [193] In Pennsylvania, a mortgage broker is an agent of the borrower and therefore a fiduciary.[194]

---

[185] Montoya v. McLeod, 221 Cal. Rptr. 353, 356-58 (Ct. App. 1985).

[186] *Id.* at 358.

[187] UMET Trust v. Santa Monica Medical Investment Co., 189 Cal. Rptr. 922, 927 (Ct. App. 1983).

[188] Ware v. Indymac Bank, F.S.B., 534 F. Supp. 2d 835, 836 (N.D. Ill. 2008).

[189] Cunningham v. Equicredit Corp., 256 F. Supp. 2d 785, 796 (N.D. Ill. 2003).

[190] Anderson v. Wells Fargo Home Mortgage, Inc., 259 F. Supp. 2d 1143, 1150-51 (W.D. Wash. 2003).

[191] Brazier v. Sec. Pac. Mortg., Inc., 245 F. Supp. 2d 1136, 1143 (W.D. Wash. 2003).

[192] Rushing v. Stephanus, 393 P.2d 281, 283-84 (Wash. 1964).

[193] Brancheau v. Residential Mortgage & Mercantile Bank, 182 F.R.D. 579, 588 n.6 (D. Minn. 1998).

[194] Barker v. Altegra Credit Co. (*In re* Barker), 251 B.R. 250, 259 (Bankr. E.D. Pa. 2000); *see also* McGlawn v. Pa. Human Relations Comm'n, 891 A.2d 757, 769 (Pa.Commw. Ct. 2006) (following *Barker*).

The relationships between the broker and the lender have received different treatment. An Alabama court upheld a trial court finding that based on the facts the mortgage broker had no fiduciary duty to the lender, as the broker introduced an uncontroverted deposition that it had no employment relationship with the borrower; rather, it had one with another party.[195] However, the court found that there was still a factual dispute whether the broker owed the borrower a duty to disclose certain material facts.[196] The court found that the alleged facts "properly state a claim of actionable fraud based upon a duty to disclose or to communicate."[197] New York decisions imply that a mortgage broker has no per se fiduciary duty to the borrower.[198] While in Ohio, a court held that a mortgage broker is an agent and therefore a fiduciary of the borrower.[199]

Discussion Questions

Legal

- Under what circumstances should mortgage brokers owe a duty to the borrower? Should mortgage brokers owe fiduciary duties to the borrowers, the lenders, or to both borrower and lender?
- Are yield spread premiums kickbacks, and violations of the brokers' fiduciary duties?
- Is a bright-line affordability test required by law? Is such a test possible? Note that FNMA had imposed certain criteria on eligible borrowers and eligible homes, and that these criteria were relaxed in the course of time. What drove FNMA to relax the criteria? Did it have any duty to the borrowers or investors?

---

195 Shades Ridge Holding Co., Inc. v. Cobbs, Allen & Hall Mortgage Co., Inc., 390 So. 2d 601, 615-16 (Ala. 1980).

196 *Id.* at 616.

197 *Id.* (citing Washington v. Ford Motor Credit Co., Inc., 384 So. 2d 83 (Ala. 1980) ("where the defendant has special knowledge or means of knowledge not open to the plaintiff and is aware that the plaintiff is acting under a misapprehension as to facts which would be of importance to him and would probably affect his decision")).

198 *See* Lum v. New Century Mortgage Corp., 19 A.D.3d 558, 559 (N.Y. App. Div. 2005) (upholding dismissal of action for damages for inducement of breach of fiduciary duty because borrower failed to show fiduciary duty between her and nonparty mortgage broker); Shovak v. Long Island Commercial Bank, 50 A.D.3d 1118, 1120 (N.Y. App. Div. 2008) (stating that court should have granted dismissal of cause of action for breach of fiduciary duty, as borrower failed to show fiduciary duty between him and mortgage broker; following *Lum*).

199 Swayne v. Beebles Investments, Inc., 891 N.E.2d 1216, 1226 (Ohio Ct. App. 2008); *see also* Myer v. Preferred Credit, Inc., 766 N.E.2d 612, 622 (Ohio Ct. Com. Pl. 2001) (similar).

- How can the link between borrower and investor be maintained when loans are securitized?

Business

- Can Brokers effectively serve two masters (borrowers and lenders)?
- What is the evidence that brokers are generating competition-based consumer benefits?
- Will the market discipline unethical brokers?
- What actions can reduce the impact of the mortgage broker's moral hazard when loans are securitized?
- How can the link between borrower and investor be maintained when loans are securitized?

Public Policy

- Why has federal regulation of mortgage brokers not been enacted?
- Why should federal rather than state regulation be adopted?
- What information beyond current disclosures is necessary?
- Should mortgage brokers owe a duty to borrowers?
- Should yield spread premiums be barred?

C. Simulation Exercise: The Community Reinvestment Act – Is "Encouragement" to Lend Still Needed?

July 1967 and the inner city of Detroit was burning. "[T]he Detroit police raided an after-hours bar at the corner of 12th and Clairmount streets, in a poor black section of the city's west side. . . . A few onlookers started tossing insults at the officers, followed by bottles and stones…On the edge of the crowd, a teenager launched a trash can through the window of Hardy's drugstore, while someone else set a shoe shop ablaze. Within an hour, the melee had escalated into a riot. . . . [It began] a week-long conflagration so fierce it killed 43 people, injured hundreds and destroyed huge swaths of the city's most impoverished neighborhoods."[200] The same stories were written about urban centers around the country from Newark to Chicago to Los Angeles. Numerous root causes were offered to explain the urban unrest. There was high unemployment in the inner cities as better paying manufacturing jobs moved south, race relations in the country were tense as minorities felt trapped and oppressed in urban ghettos, "white flight" led to rapid growth of the suburbs further reducing investment and jobs in the urban areas, and urban infrastructure crumbled, schools decayed and policing eroded as the tax base in the cities declined. These individual factors combined to cause a vicious cycle of disinvestment in urban centers.

---

[200] Kevin Boyle, *The Fire Last Time,* WASH. POST, July 29, 2007, at B01, LEXIS, News Library, Arcnws File..

The riots took place despite President Johnson's 1960s war on poverty. The weapons he employed were a set of bills passed by Congress aimed at improving conditions in the inner cities. One of the first was the Economic Opportunity Act of 1964 which focused on skills training for urban youth. Another was the Elementary and Secondary Education School Act of 1965 which provided funds for schools that served low income populations. The Fair Housing Act of 1968 (Title VIII of the Civil Rights Act) prohibited discrimination in housing based on race and other factors. It also provided funding for subsidized housing. These and other acts were not sufficient to diffuse the anger and resentment that led to the riots described above. After the riots, a variety of new initiatives were launched to combat the economic and social crisis facing the country's major cities ranging from programs to improve inner city education to increased funding for low income housing.

One focus for policy makers was increasing the level of investment in urban centers. Their logic was that investment would both increase economic opportunities for the residents of the urban core and reduce the blight which perpetuated the vicious cycle of decline. The role of banks in providing the investment funds came into question as concerns mounted that bank deposits from inner city customers were flowing to the suburbs rather than supporting community investment opportunities. There was also increasing evidence that banks were automatically refusing to lend mortgage money in certain communities independent of the financial qualifications of the prospective borrowers. This practice, known as "redlining," became a focus for urban activists in the 1960s. The origins of redlining date back to the 1930s when the Home Owners' Loan Corporation drew residential security maps indicating the comparative risk of lending in different neighborhoods. By the 1960s banks were drawing red lines around areas where they would not offer mortgage loans, based solely on geography rather than the ability of individuals to repay the loan. The discrimination resulting from this practice was viewed as a root cause of urban decay. One objective of the Fair Housing Act of 1968 was to eliminate redlining.

The elimination of redlining was viewed as only a partial solution to the lack of capital available in the urban core. Policy analysts argued that inner cities needed greater investment. Congress responded with the Community Reinvestment Act of 1977 (CRA) which was signed into law by President Carter. "The Community Reinvestment Act is intended to encourage depository institutions to help meet the credit needs of the communities in which they operate, including low- and moderate-income neighborhoods. . . ."[201] The logic for the legislation was that "regulated financial institutions are required by law to demonstrate that their [deposits] serve the convenience and needs of the communit[y] . . . [which] include the need for credit services as well as deposit services . . . regulated financial institutions have continuing and affirmative obligation to help meet the credit needs of the local

[201] Fed. Reserve Board, *Community Reinvestment Act,* http://www. Federalreserve.gov/dcca/cra/ (last visited Sept. 15, 2009).

communities in which they are chartered."[202] Federal agencies responsible for the supervision of these agencies were directed to "use [their] authority . . . to encourage such institutions to help meet the credit needs of the local communities."[203] It is important to note that the "encouragement" needed to be consistent with "safe and sound operation[s]."[204] The Act applied to federally chartered and insured banks and thrift institutions; other lenders including non-bank affiliates of regulated banks were not subject to the Act.

CRA required regulators to evaluate the performance of banks in supporting community investment and assign a performance rating – outstanding, satisfactory, needs to improve, and substantial noncompliance. However, the legislation was not prescriptive in the criteria for the assessment. The Act's enforcement mechanisms were limited to making the results of the assessment public and "tak[ing] such record into account in its evaluation of an application for a deposit facility by such institution."[205]

The Act has undergone several important revisions over its 30-year history. In conjunction with the Financial Institutions Reform, Recovery, and Enforcement Act of 1989, which followed the savings and loan crisis, the CRA assessment became a written, fact-based determination of performance. CRA considerations were explicitly added to the criteria for evaluating out-of-state mergers and acquisitions. The Gramm-Leach-Bliley Act of 1999, which allowed banks to broaden their financial services offerings, included a provision requiring regulators to not approve service expansions "where any of the holding company's banks or thrifts has a CRA rating of less than satisfactory."[206] The assessment process has become more objective with regulators considering the amount of lending, investment in community development and retail depository services in rating a bank.

There is no explicit regulatory tie between CRA and securitization. However, the Federal Housing Enterprises Financial Safety and Soundness Act of 1992 connected CRA with mortgage-backed securities. The 1992 act required Fannie Mae and Freddie Mac, government sponsored enterprises[207] empowered to facilitate a well functioning secondary market for home mortgages, to support financing of affordable housing. Fannie Mae developed the My Community Mortgage program to

---

[202] Housing and Community Development Act of 1977, 12 U.S.C. § 2901(a) (2006).

[203] *Id.* § 2901(b).

[204] *Id.*

[205] *Id.* § 2903(a)(2).

[206] Kathleen C. Engel & Patricia A. McCoy, *The CRA Implications of Predatory Lending,* 29 FORDHAM URBAN L.J. 1571, 1575 (2002) (citing 12 U.S.C. §§ 1843(*l*), 2903(a)(2) (2006)).

[207] In 2008 both entities were brought into federal conservatorship.

provide mortgages to low- and moderate-income families. Between 1997 and 2001, Fannie Mae acquired more than $10 billion in CRA targeted loans. The loans were in turn securitized by Fannie Mae. In 2001 Fannie Mae announced a goal of supporting a cumulative $500 billion in CRA loans by 2010.[208]

On the occasion of CRA's 30th anniversary, the U.S. House Committee on Financial Services held hearings on the accomplishments of CRA. The chairman of the Citizens Financial Group, a regional bank focused on emerging domestic markets, testified that "the CRA helped right a previous wrong by addressing . . . redlining . . . . Redlining was racist, sexist, deeply unfair . . . . The CRA ended this practice."[209] His testimony also cited the dramatic increases in lending attributable to CRA. "Since 1977, more that $1.5 trillion has been lent for community development."[210] He further referenced Federal Reserve research which found that 98 percent of large residential lenders viewed their CRA loans as profitable.[211] At the same hearing, Michael Barr, a professor of law at the University of Michigan, stated that CRA helped overcome information asymmetries and other market failures. He also cited quantitative evidence of CRA's success. "The number of CRA-eligible mortgage loans increased by 39 percent between 1993 and 1998, while other loans increased by only 17 percent."[212] Speaking before the Community Affairs Research Conference, Federal Reserve Chairman Ben Bernanke stated "It appears that, at least in some instances, the CRA has served as a catalyst, inducing banks to enter the underserved markets that they might otherwise have ignored. At its most successful, the CRA may have had a multiplier effect, supplementing its direct impact by stimulating new market-based, profit-driven economic activity in lower-income neighborhoods."[213]

---

[208] See Right View Wisconsin, *Economy,* "Fannie and Freddie came into the game in 1992 and had to dedicate a certain percentage of their lending to support CRA. It hit $10 billion in CRA loans in 2001, with the goal of $500 billion by 2010.", http://www.rightviewwi.com/the_right_view_wisconsin/economy/ (Aug. 27, 2009) (last visited Sept. 15, 2009)..

[209] *Community Reinvestment Act; Hearings Before the H. Comm. on Financial Services,* 110th Cong. (2008), LEXIS, News Library, Curnws File (statement of Larry Fish, Chairman, Citizens Financial Group).

[210] *Id.*.

[211] *Id.*

[212] *Id.* (testimony of Michael Barr, Professor, University of Michigan Law School).

[213] Ben S. Bernanke, Chairman, Bd. Of Governors of the Fed. Reserve Sys., The Community Reinvestment Act: Its Evolution and New Challenges, Speech at the Community Affairs Research Conference, Washington, D.C., (Mar. 30, 2007), http://www.federalreserve.gov/newsevents/speech/Bernanke20070330a.htm (last visited Sept. 15, 2009).

Bernanke went on to highlight evidence that CRA has not met its objectives citing studies that conclude "the CRA has been ineffective in addressing discrimination and market failures and that its social costs outweigh its benefits."[214] He also noted a study by the Joint Center of Housing Studies at Harvard that finds the impact of CRA has diminished as non-bank lending organizations have expanded their share of mortgage originations. Questions about the effectiveness of CRA, especially in light of the changing financial services landscape (e.g., the growth of interstate banking, innovations such as securitization of mortgages, and the rise of mortgage brokers), are not new. In 1995 as proposals to redesign CRA were being debated, the Cato Institute called for the repeal of CRA arguing: "The primary effect of the current regulations is to increase the cost of operation, especially for small banks and in low income areas, without any significant effect on the allocation of new credit. . . . Congress should be most critical of proposals to use regulatory powers to reallocate credit, either across neighborhoods or among groups. The primary long term effect of such measures would be to further contract the banking system, increasing the number of neighborhoods dependent on check cashing outlets and pawnshops."[215] The calls for repeal were also heard at the 30th anniversary hearing in 2008. Professor Lawrence White testified: "I believe that, despite the good intentions and worthwhile goals of the CRA's advocates, the CRA is an inappropriate instrument for achieving those goals. Fundamentally, the CRA is a regulatory effort to 'lean on' banks and savings institutions, in vague and subjective ways, to make loans and investments that . . . those depository institutions would otherwise not make. . . . At base, the CRA is an anachronistic and protectionist effort to force artificially a local focus for finance in an increasingly competitive, increasingly electronic, and ever-widening realm of financial services."[216]

Some commentators have been more strident in their criticism of CRA, blaming the program for the 2008 financial crisis. A September 2008 column in the *Boston Globe* by Jeff Jacoby suggested that the current financial crisis had its roots in the establishment of the CRA. "The pressure to make more loans to minorities (read: to borrowers with weak credit histories) became relentless. . . . Lenders responded by loosening their underwriting standards and making increasingly shoddy loans. . . . Affirmative action policies trumped sound business practices."[217] *Investors Business*

---

[214] *Id.*

[215] *Community Reinvestment Act: Hearing Before the H. Comm. on Banking, Financial Institutions, and Consumer Credit,* 104th Cong. (1995), LEXIS, News Library, Arcnws File (testimony of William A. Niskanen, Chairman, Cato Institute).

[216] *Community Reinvestment Revision: Hearing Before the H. Comm. on Financial Services,* 110th Cong. (2008), LEXIS, News Library, Curnws File (statement of Lawrence J. White, Professor, Economics, New York University Stern School of Business).

[217] Jeff Jacoby, *Frank's Fingerprints Are All Over the Financial Fiasco,* BOSTON GLOBE, Sept. 28, 2008, at D9, LEXIS, News Library, Curnws File..

Daily echoed this sentiment in a September 2008 editorial: "While President Carter in 1977 signed the Community Reinvestment Act, which pushed Fannie and Freddie to aggressively lend to minorities communities, it was Clinton who supercharged the process. . . . In so doing, he turned the two quasi-private, mortgage-funding firms into a semi-nationalized monopoly that dispensed cash to markets, made loans to large Democratic voting blocs and handed favors, jobs, and money to political allies. This potent mix led . . . to corruption and the Fannie-Freddie collapse."[218]

CRA supporters responded with counterarguments. First, CRA only applies to federally regulated depository lenders. The portion of high cost mortgages made by CRA banks was significantly lower than those made by mortgage bankers and brokers not subject to CRA.. The share of high cost loans in the 15 most populous metropolitan areas made by CRA banks in 2006 was 9.2 percent compared to 22.8 percent for other lenders.[219] Moreover, when high cost loans were provided by CRA banks they were on average priced 68 basis points lower than comparable other lenders.[220] Second, the CRA loans were more than twice as likely to be retained by the lender as those provided by other originators.[221] Retention positioned lenders and borrowers to negotiate alterative repayment terms if necessary in contrast to loans that were securitized and then "sliced and diced." Third, CRA had significantly increased the credit ability for low and moderate income borrowers. "Between 1993 and 1999, depository institutions covered by the CRA and their affiliates made over $800 billion in home mortgage, small business, and community development loans to low- and moderate-income borrowers and communities."[222] Finally, the expansion of subprime loans took place after 2001 when "CRA enforcement became a lower priority for bank regulators."[223]

Assignment:

1. Was the original passage of CRA "good" public policy?
2. What role did CRA play in the 2008 housing crisis?
3. Take a position and provide supporting rationale for either:

---

[218] Terry Jones, *How A Clinton-Era Rule Rewrite Made Subprime Crisis Inevitable,* INVESTOR'S BUS. DAILY, Sept. 25, 2008, at A01, LEXIS, News Library, Curnws File..

[219] Warren W. Traiger, *The CRA: A Welcome Anomaly in the Foreclosure Crisis,* 53 N.Y.L. SCH. L. REV. 227, 231 (2008/2009).

[220] *Id.* at 234.

[221] *Id.* at 237.

[222] *Community Reinvestment Act; Hearings Before the H. Comm. on Financial Services,* 110th Cong. (2008), LEXIS, News Library, Curnws File (testimony of Michael Barr, Professor, University of Michigan Law School)..

[223] Ellen Seidman, *It's Still Not CRA* (Sept. 22, 2008), http://www.newamerica.net/blog/asset-building/2008/its-still-not-cra-7222 (last visited Sept. 15, 2009).

- Repeal CRA: What, if anything, would you replace it with?
- Retain CRA: What, if anything, would you do to enhance it?

D. Debt

a. The Lenders and Originators

By and large, banks, thrifts, and mortgage bankers are the main lenders of loans for sale and securitization or originators who purchase loans for securitization. With the expansion of structured financing, corporations were added to the producers of the loan originators. Another group of lenders are manufacturers and retailers that sell the credit (receivables) they give their customers. Underwriters may help corporations to sell their receivables. In addition, there are promoters of securitization that are purchasing receivables, such as healthcare receivables, and collection agencies that buy failed loans at very low cost and manage to collect and gain significant returns, even as they collect around 15 percent of the face amounts of the loans.

Securitized debts are of various kinds, such as credit card, health care, and leases receivables.

b. Applicable Regulation

A variety of financial assets that can be securitized. We usually view them as debt or loans. However, the following example is the securitization of something akin to risk, which is in fact the other aspect of any investment. This example also demonstrates the legal adjustments that are necessary for such securitization.

c. Securitizing Insurance Risks[224]

Disaster/ Catastrophe Bonds. "Innovations can consist of new lenses for viewing the state of the world. Securitizing risks is such an innovation."[225] Insurance securitization uses securitization to strip risk and transfer it to investors for compensation. Thus, the aggregate investor group takes on some of the insurance risk for profit.[226] Catastrophe bond offerings appeared in the 1990s.[227] The insurance

---

[224] Most of the text and source of this section is drawn from the following article: Tamar Frankel & Joseph W. La Plume, *Securitizing Insurance Risks,* 19 ANN. REV. BANKING L. 203 (2000).

[225] Tamar Frankel & Joseph W. LaPlume, *Securitizing Insurance Risks,* 19 ANN. REV. BANKING L. 203 (2000).

[226] Most of the text and sources cited in this section are drawn from the following article: Tamar Frankel & Joseph W. LaPlume, *Securitizing Insurance Risks,* 19 ANN. REV. BANKING L. 203 (2000).

securitization process is as follows: creating an SPV, and causing the SPV to issue bonds to investors and enter into reinsurance contracts with ceding insurers or other beneficiaries for annual payments ("premiums"); investing the proceeds from the bond distribution and the premiums; ensuring the safety and soundness of the SPV and its investments; and servicing by reliable collection and distribution of the SPV's net earnings and premiums payments (after paying the claims under the reinsurance contracts, and management and other expenses).

This insurance risk can be taken either directly or constitute an added layer over traditional insurance. The risk transfer differs from usual insurance because the insurance companies remain secondary risk bearers and the new risk underwriters are investors, not other insurance companies. The payment of claims is conditioned on payment of premiums. While some issues in this area are resolved by the others, other legal issues must be resolved by law. The first issue relates to the classification of insurance risk securitization (the SPVs and the bonds): is it insurance or reinsurance? Law treats these categories differently. The National Association of Insurance Commissioners ("NAIC") as well as a number of states addressed the issues.[228] The following are some of the legal issues.

Insurance presents a special relationship between state and federal laws. Under the federal McCarran-Ferguson Act [229] the "business of insurance" is to be governed by state laws, unless federal laws expressly apply to insurance business.[230] If a state adopts a clear law applicable to insurance securitization and classifies it as the business of insurance, federal courts might concede jurisdiction.[231] Even though each

---

[227] *See* Investors Guar. Fund, Ltd. v. Morgan Stanley & Co., Inc., No. 96 Civ. 3520 (RPP), 1998 U.S. Dist. LEXIS 20225 (S.D.N.Y. Dec. 23, 1998), *aff'd,* 199 F.3d 1322 (2d Cir. 1999), *cert. denied,* 529 U.S 1062 (2000). For a proposal that insurance-based securitization be used to address the catastrophic risk auditing firms face from audit failure, see Lawrence A. Cunningham, *Securitizing Audit Failure Risk: An Alternative to Caps on Damages,* 49 WM. & MARY L. REV. 711, 763-79 (2007).

[228] *See* PROTECTED CELL COMPANY MODEL ACT (NAIC 2002), *reprinted in Catastrophe Bonds: Spreading Risk: Hearing before the Subcomm. on Oversight and Investigations of the H. Comm. on Financial Services,* 107th Cong. 89 (2002); Protected Cell Companies Act, 1999 R.I. PUB. LAWS ch. 22 (codified as amended at R.I. GEN. LAWS, §§ 27-64-1 to 27-64-12 (2008)); Protected Cell Company Law, 1999 Ill. Laws 278 (1999) (codified as amended at 215 ILL. COMP. STAT. ANN. §§ 5/107.06a, /179A-1 to -40 (West Supp. 2000 & Supp. 2008)).

[229] 15 U.S.C. §§ 1011-1015 (2006).

[230] For a discussion of what constitutes the "business of insurance" see, e.g., Group Life & Health Ins. Co. v. Royal Drug Co., 440 U.S. 205 (1979); Union Labor Life Ins. Co. v. Pireno, 458 U.S. 119 (1982); Metropolitan Life Ins. Co. v. Massachusetts, 471 U.S. 724 (1985); Pilot Life Ins. Co. v. Dedeaux, 481 U.S. 41 (1987).

[231] *See In re* Estate of Medicare HMO, 998 F.2d 436, 441 (7th Cir. 1993) (stating that "when Congress has not provided an explicit alternative to state law, we are mindful that the Bankruptcy Code was written in the shadow of state law and conclude that Congress intended state law to fill the interstices"); *see also* Butner v. United States, 440 U.S. 48, 54 (1979); *In re* Roach, 824 F.2d 1370, 1373-74 (3d Cir. 1987). *But see* SEC v. Variable Annuity Life Ins. Co. of Am., 359 U.S. 65 (1959)

state can define the "business of insurance" under the McCarran-Ferguson Act differently, SPVs are likely to be defined as the "business of insurance."[232]

In traditional securitization investors are concerned about the SPV's exposure to the claims of the transferors' creditors. In insurance securitization, however, the assets that investors may lose to the creditors of the ceding insurance company are the premiums due to the SPV under reinsurance contracts. The SPV's other assets derive from the bondholders' payments, which are not paid to anyone, but remain in the SPV and the policies remain with the SPV. As to premiums, the SPV is the obligor. If premiums remain unpaid, no claims will be paid either. The policies are canceled before the covered period. Under this scenario investors will not stand in line with other creditors of the ceding company, and they need not perfect a security interest in the assets of the insurance company.[233]

In addition, under bankruptcy laws, the status of insurance risk securitization is complex. In light of the McCarran-Ferguson Act and Section 109(b)(2) of the Bankruptcy Code they are likely to be subject to insurance laws rather than to the Federal Bankruptcy Code, provided they are classified as insurance companies. Alternatively, the courts may classify SPVs independently, presumably applying a federal common law analysis.[234] Under this approach, a reviewing court would look only to the language and legislative history of section 109(b)(2) and make a determination using traditional techniques of statutory construction, or examine the policy question whether federal bankruptcy relief would be a satisfactory alternative to the state proceedings. In addition the courts may resort to the state of incorporation, subject to the policies of the Bankruptcy Code.[235]

The main test seems to be whether state law classifies the SPV as an insurance

---

(variable annuities are subject to the Securities Act of 1933); SEC v. Nat'l Sec., Inc., 393 U.S. 453 (1969) (mergers among insurance companies may be subject to securities regulation); 1 TAMAR FRANKEL & ANN TAYLOR SCHWING, THE REGULATION OF MONEY MANAGERS § 1.05[A][1]-[4], at 1-92 to -99 (2d ed. 2001).

[232] To avoid such regulation, SPVs were established and operated offshore in Bermuda and the Cayman Islands. See Alex Maurice, *NAIC Poised to Adopt Securitization Models,* NAT'L UNDERWRITER, PROP. & CASUALTY/RISK & BENEFITS MGMT. EDITION, July 12, 1999, at S28, LEXIS, News Library, Arcnws File; Jeany Haggerty, *U.S. Regulators to Bust Open Insurer Securitization,* DERIVATIVES WK., Aug. 16, 1999, at 1.

[233] *See* Chapter 8.

[234] *See* Cash Currency Exch., Inc. v. Shine (*In re* Cash Currency Exch., Inc.), 762 F.2d 542, 548, 551-52 (7th Cir. 1985).

[235] *See id.* (using statutory construction approach); *In re* Republic Trust & Sav. Co., 59 B.R. 606, 614 (Bankr. N.D. Okla.1986) (using policy approach); *In re* Estate of Medicare HMO, 998 F.2d 436, 440-42 (7th Cir. 1993) (using law of state of incorporation; determining that an HMO was a "domestic insurance company" under the Bankruptcy Code and thus excluded from federal Bankruptcy Code relief) (citing Sec. Bldg. & Loan v. Spurlock, 65 F.2d 768, 771 (9th Cir.), *cert. denied,* 290 U.S. 678 (1933)).

company: Does the insurance company assume risk of a third party for a premium, is it desirable to split laws and jurisdiction over the SPVs' bankruptcy issues? Unlike insurance companies that are likely to be anchored in one state, investors in catastrophic events bonds can be located all over the world. For them, uniformity of the law and jurisdiction are very important.[236]

Insurance Risk Securitization and its SPVs Pose Regulatory Issues. Are the SPVs that issue catastrophic event bonds insurance companies or reinsurance companies?[237] If SPVs underwrite insurance risks by undertaking to pay policyholders upon the occurrence of catastrophic events, then the SPVs seem to pose the same problems as any insurance company does.[238] But, if the main insurers remain regulated insurance companies, then the SPVs might be sufficiently regulated as reinsurance companies.[239]

Are the SPVs and the catastrophic event bonds subject to the securities acts? If the assets that the SPVs hold and the bonds that they issue are securities, they will fall

---

[236] International transactions may raise choice of law and choice of forum considerations. *See* Richards v. Lloyd's of London, 135 F.2d 1289 (9th Cir. 1997), *cert. denied,* 525 U.S. 943 (1998). U.S. citizens became members of an English insurance market, signing agreements with choice of forum and choice of law clauses providing that rights and obligations under the agreement would be governed by English law and that English courts would have exclusive jurisdiction of disputes under the agreement. The U.S. parties argued that the clauses were void under the antiwaiver provisions of the U.S. securities laws. The court held that the *Bremen* standard applies even though there is a conflict with a statute. *Id.* at 1292-94 (citing United States v. Bremen, 407 U.S. 1, 12-13, 15 (1972)). Applying the standard, the court found the provisions valid as not in violation of a strong U.S. public policy. *Id.* at 1294-96. The court also found that English law would not deprive the U.S. parties of appropriate recourse. *Id.* at 1296. In a dissenting opinion, three judges said first that the *Bremen* standard should not apply in view of the statutory language. *Id.* at 1297-99. The dissent also said that the clauses should be void as they preclude certain remedies and English law provides weaker protections, *id.* at 1299-1300, and violate public policy, *id.* at 1300.

[237] See Michael P. Goldman et al., *Legal and Regulatory Issues Affecting Insurance Derivatives and Securitization, in* SWAPS AND OTHER DERIVATIVES IN 1999, at 433, 441 (PLI).

[238] Tamar Frankel & Joseph W. La Plume, *Securitizing Insurance Risks,* 19 ANN. REV. BANKING L. 203, 213 (2000) "The SPVs may not have sufficient assets to cover the losses under the policies because they would distribute funds to the holders of the securities that they issue without keeping sufficient funds for reserves, or because they invest the reserves in speculative investments. These were some of the problems that led to the passage of state laws. These were the problems that led to the mutualization of insurance companies, since the managements of the companies at that time were more concerned with the safety and soundness of the companies (and the longevity of the managements' positions) than the controlling shareholders, who desired to spend, or speculate in, the reserves."

[239] *See* Michael P. Goldman et al., *Legal and Regulatory Issues Affecting Insurance Derivatives and Securitization, in* SWAPS AND OTHER DERIVATIVES IN 1999, at 433, 441, 446 (PLI).

within the definition of an investment company.[240] If the bonds they issue are securities, they will be subject to the Securities Act of 1933 and the Securities Exchange Act of 1934.

Are the Bonds Issued by SPVs Insurance Obligations? Arguably, the bonds are insurance obligations because they cover all or part of the damages caused by catastrophic events, and receive compensation for underwriting the risk. In fact, the bondholders indirectly pay the policyholders all or part of the proceeds under their policies if such events occur. However, the bondholders do not underwrite the risks and do not undertake to pay policyholders directly; they do so through the SPV (or through insurance or reinsurance companies). In that respect the bonds are similar to financiers of the insurer or, better still, its partners. Presumably, investors have no control over the SPVs investment decisions and business practices. Therefore, even though the bonds are linked to underwriting of insurance, their holders are not engaged in the insurance business and are not insurers. The key difference would seem to be control. To the extent that the bondholders do not control, they are not insurers. On the insurance side, insurance commissions should issue interpretative statements exempting the parties to insurance securitization transactions from licensing requirements. It is likely that most, but not necessarily all,[241] state insurance commissioners do so and issue such exemptions. The proposed Model Act described below would exclude the bonds from the definition of "insurance contract," and thus would make it clear that federal law applies to the SPV issuers of catastrophic events bonds. This does not mean that insurance companies engaged in insurance risk securitization will not be regulated by the states if they are permitted to engage in that activity which will then be classified as "insurance business."

Are the Bonds Issued by the SPVs Securities? The bonds also may fall within the definition of a "security" in the securities acts,[242] under the rubric of investment contracts. The bonds meet most of the elements of the *SEC v. W. J. Howey Co.*[243] test, since the investors' money is invested in a common enterprise (the SPV) with the expectation of receiving profits from the efforts of others. However, this last factor may be debatable because the efforts of others have occurred before the bonds

---

[240] *See* Investment Company Act of 1940, § 3, 15 U.S.C. § 80a-3 (2006).

[241] For example, the New York-based Catastrophe Risk Exchange (CATEX), established in 1996 to promote trading in property and casualty insurance risks, was licensed by the New York Insurance Department as a reinsurance intermediary. *See* Susanne Sclafane, *Insurers Can Soon Swap CAT Exposure,* NAT'L UNDERWRITER, PROP. & CASUALTY/RISK & BENEFITS MGMT. EDITION, July 31, 1995, at 1, LEXIS, News Library, Arcnws File (noting that department licensed CATEX as "neutral" reinsurance intermediary, with "no contractual affiliation to negotiate for either side of a risk-swapping transaction").

[242] Securities Act of 1933, § 2(a)(1), 15 U.S.C. § 77b(a)(1) (2006) (defining a "security" to include bond and evidence of indebtedness).

[243] 328 U.S. 293 (1946).

were distributed to the public. Although they may have insurance features, catastrophic event bonds are distinguished from "pure" insurance contracts. In fact, these bonds are similar to variable insurance contracts (variable annuities and variable life insurance). They are securities with insurance features, and may be subject to the securities acts and to some insurance regulation as well. If the catastrophic events bonds are securities, they are subject to the Securities Act of 1933. The SPV and any sales and secondary trading in the bonds will be regulated by the Securities Exchange Act of 1934, ensuring investors of information and regulated secondary markets in the bonds. SPVs are investment companies, exempt from the Investment Company Act of 1940 by Rule 3a-7, subject to a number of important conditions.[244]

For SPVs of risk securitization there is another avenue of escaping the 1940 Act. If SPVs are deemed insurance companies subject to regulation under state laws, then they are excepted from the definition of an investment company under section 3(c)(1) of the 1940 Act. Although the proposed Model Act would exclude the bonds issued by the SPVs from the definition of an investment contract, if the Model Act regulates the SPV in other ways, the SPV may be excluded from the definition of an investment company as an insurance company. Barring such state regulation, however, the better argument seems to be that SPVs are investment companies, unless an exemption or rule 3a-7 applies to them.

The rule requires SPVs to hold static portfolios and does not permit trading in the portfolios. SPVs issuing catastrophic event bonds are in a somewhat different position. If they engage in active trading in their investment, and if their portfolio does not conform to the conditions of the rule, they may have to seek a special exemption from the SEC.

The Status of SPVs and the Bonds They Issue Under the Commodity Exchange Act of 1934. The Commodity Exchange Act of 1934 ("CEA") regulates a "futures contract" or a "commodity option," which it defines as a security in which principal and or interest payments are dependent on changes in the value of a commodity.[245] The definition of a commodity is broad, and includes financial instruments and intangibles such as interest rates and indexes. Consequently, there is a question whether the sale of bonds, which provide for payments based on an index (combined damages from possible events), is regulated under the CEA.

Arguably the bonds are not included in the definition and escape the regulation of the CEA. However, this is unlikely since all instruments, including all Chicago Board of

---

[244] 17 C.F. R. § 270.3a-7 (2008).

[245] Section 1a(4) of the Commodity Exchange Act defines the term commodity as "all . . . goods and articles . . . and all services, rights, and interests in which contracts for future delivery are presently or in the future dealt in." 7 U.S.C. § 1a(4) (2006). It should be noted that this term is defined broadly.

Trade insurance options and over-the-counter insurance derivatives, defined as "futures contracts" will be subject to the Commodity Futures Trading Commission regulation and the CEA's exchange trading requirement. Alternatively, narrow exemptions in the CFTC's rules may cover securities issued by the SPV.[246]

The Cell Structure. To attract insurance risk securitization business, states such as Rhode Island and Illinois passed comprehensive legislation ("Protected Cell Acts") in 1999 aimed at promoting insurance securitization onshore. These Acts offer not only reduced burdens on SPVs but marketing advantages to SPV sponsors. In December 1999, the NAIC adopted a Protected Cell Company Model Act, similar to the Illinois act.[247]

The Protected Cell Acts passed in Rhode Island and Illinois allow insurers to tap the capital markets directly by selling catastrophic event bonds using a Protected Cell within the insurance company. Protected Cells offer a number of advantages. First, a Protected Cell would retain the accounting advantages offered to insurers. Second, the Cell would protect investors from any liabilities incurred by the insurance company of which it is a part.

Third, under the Rhode Island and Illinois laws, the Cell's assets are separate from those of the insurance company. Therefore, a domestic insurer can protect the assets in the Cell from its own creditors or its receiver, should the insurer become insolvent. For investors, the new laws' features offer a number of advantages. Investors seem to have their cake and eat it. The Cell's assets are part of the insurance company's assets. Therefore, they are not subject to state or federal bankruptcy acts, but rather to state laws regulating insurance companies' insolvency. Moreover, if the host insurance companies become insolvent, policyholders (including the bondholders) can resort to state funds that support insurance companies' obligations.

Additionally, the law relieves the insurance company issuing catastrophic event bonds of the need to show a "true sale" of assets to an SPV that would normally

---

[246] See, for example, the CEA's cash forward contracts under section 1a(19) of the CEA, 7 U.S.C. § 1a(19) (2006), may apply; the CFTC's Statutory Interpretation Concerning Forward Transactions (Sept. 25, 1990); the "Treasury Amendment" generally excluding transactions in foreign currency and other instruments such as government securities, security warrants, security rights, resales of installment loan contracts, repurchase transactions in an excluded commodity, or mortgage and mortgage purchase commitments not traded on an exchange (Section 2(c) of the CEA, 7 U.S.C. § 2(c) (2006)); a limited exception from the exchange-trading requirement for "trade options" (CFTC Regulation 32.4(a), 17 C.F.R. § 32.4(a) (2008)).

[247] PROTECTED CELL COMPANY MODEL ACT (NAIC 2002), *reprinted in Catastrophe Bonds: Spreading Risk: Hearing before the Subcomm. on Oversight and Investigations of the H. Comm. on Financial Services,* 107th Cong. 89 (2002); *NAIC Adopts Catastrophe Bond Protected-Cell Model,* BESTWIRE, Dec. 7, 1999, LEXIS, News Library, Curnws File (noting that Act is similar to the Illinois act).

issue the bonds. These assets include insurance policies, if any, and cash and investments that are due from the insurance company to an SPV. Thus, the Protected Cell solves the difficulty of rendering an SPV "bankruptcy remote." Finally, the Protected Cell is likely to solve the problem of double taxation. Absent an SPV there is no entity to be taxed from the insurance company.

Arguably, the Protected Cell is specially designed for insurance securitization, and is more efficient than the traditional SPVs that are currently situated offshore. The offshore SPVs involve administrative and office costs while the Protected Cell is held domestically, and is created within a domestic insurance company involving no additional administrative costs.

A number of issues remain. The Protected Cell structure within a U.S. domiciled reinsurer raises an accounting question of whether the ceding insurer could take credit for the transaction using reinsurance.[248] In the 1980s, the NAIC changed the accounting rules for ceded reinsurance.[249] If reinsurance accounting is followed, FASB 113 requires that prepaid insurance premiums and reinsurance receivables be reported as assets, while it recognized estimated reinsurance receivables in a manner consistent with the liabilities relating to the underlying reinsured contracts. Thus, the precise accounting treatment for insurance securitization must be resolved in all 50 states before these transactions can come onshore.

Presumably, the treatment of a Protected Cell under these Protected Cell Acts would be analogous to the treatment of a separate account used by a life insurer. That may reduce tax-related problems with federal and state authorities.[250] Whether the Cells are investment companies remains to be seen. They may follow the model of separate accounts, or be excluded from the definition of the Act under rule 3a-7.

---

[248] *See* ACCOUNTING AND REPORTING FOR REINSURANCE OF SHORT-DURATION AND LONG-DURATION CONTRACTS, Statement of Financial Accounting Standards No. 113, § 33 (Financial Accounting Standards Bd. 1992); NAIC, ACCOUNTING PRACTICES AND PROCEDURES MANUAL ch. 22 (as of Mar. 2009).

[249] Douglas McLeod, *New Reinsurance Regs May be Needed: GAO,* BUS. INS., June 4, 1990, at 4, LEXIS, News Library, Arcnws File (stating that in 1989 "the NAIC amended a model law . . . to toughen standards that reinsurers must meet for ceding insurers to be allowed credit for reinsurance on their financial statements"; "an unlicensed reinsurer must allow a state to examine its records, submit an annual statement consistent with the NAIC's convention blank for insurers and have at least $ 20 million in surplus"); CREDIT FOR REINSURANCE MODEL LAW § 2 (NAIC 1996), *reprinted in Catastrophe Bonds: Spreading Risk: Hearing before the Subcomm. on Oversight and Investigations of the H. Comm. on Financial Services,* 107th Cong. 98, 98 (2002).

[250] *See* Subcomm. on Ann. Rev. of the Fed. Regulation of Sec. Comm. of the Am. Bar Ass'n, *Significant 1993 Legislative and Regulatory Developments,* 49 BUS. LAW. 948, 983-84 (1994); *NAIC Delays Catastrophe Reserve Action,* INS. ACCT., June 14, 1999, at 1, LEXIS, News Library, Arcnws File. *See generally* Gerald Kaplan et al., *Taxation of Insurance Companies: Annual Survey,* 26 TORT & INS L.J. 402 (1991).

Arguably, the bonds issued by the insurance company will be subject to the Securities Act of 1933 and the Securities Exchange Act of 1934, perhaps with future exemptions as to sales load limitations. In sum, Cells constitute bondholders as secured creditors to the insurance companies, avoiding bankruptcy, tax, and regulatory problems that arise when SPVs are viewed as separate entities. Of course, the Cell Acts subject Cells to safety and soundness of insurance regulation and to prudence requirements for reserves.

The Cell Acts allow insurance companies to set aside certain assets and subject them to the bondholders' priority claims. These holders will then have a first claim on the assets, and perhaps on reserves supporting the obligations, as secured creditors do. However, the claims will not be subject to the Uniform Commercial Code requirements, or to burdens usually designed to protect the creditors of the transferor of the financial assets to the SPVs. Instead, state insurance commissions would determine the priorities due to the bondholders under the terms of the bonds and the Acts.

The main problem of Cells, however, seems to be a business problem for insurance companies. The cell structure creates a preferred class of bondholders at the expense of other policyholders. If policyholders constitute the bulk of the insurance companies' business, the priority may not help their business. Further, the structure is unique and new. It goes beyond what insurance companies were allowed to do in the past. Insurance companies were allowed to offer segregated assets to policyholders as security, but in most cases the insurance companies did not guarantee payments from their general accounts.[251] In the Protected Cell case they will. The question is whether insurance companies will take advantage of the structure at the risk of losing other insurance business.

The NAIC Model Act. A second solution to the insurance risk securitization is the Special Purpose Reinsurance Vehicle Model Act of the Insurance Securitization Working Group of the NAIC, an Act designed to facilitate the issuance of catastrophic event bonds. The Model Act's structure differs from that of the Illinois and Rhode Island acts. The Act was adopted by the NAIC in 2001.[252]

---

[251] Pro forma, insurance companies have segregated assets as separate accounts that funded variable insurance products, but guaranteed only the insurance component of the securities issued by these accounts. *See* Travelers Ins. Co., SEC No-Action Letter, 1990 SEC No-Act. LEXIS 1006 (Aug. 6, 1990) (stating that insurance regulators required full funding of the insurance obligations, and that the investment risks and benefits are transferred to the contract holders); 1 TAMAR FRANKEL & ANN TAYLOR SCHWING, THE REGULATION OF MONEY MANAGERS § 5.06, at 5-86 to -100 (2d ed. 2001).

[252] Special Purpose Reinsurance Vehicle Model Act (NAIC 2002), *reprinted in Catastrophe Bonds: Spreading Risk: Hearing before the Subcomm. on Oversight and Investigations of the H. Comm. on Financial Services,* 107th Cong. 138 (2002); *NAIC Approves Special Purpose Reinsurance Vehicle Model Act*, BESTWIRE, Oct. 31, 2001, LEXIS, News Library, Arcnws File; *see NAIC Addresses Reinsurance Regulatory Issues at Winter National Meeting,* INT'L REINSURANCE DISP. REP., Dec. 27, 1999, at 9, LEXIS, News Library, Arcnws File.

Unlike the Cell structure, in the Model Act, the SPV is established as a separate entity (SPRV). One reason for a separate SPRV is to capitalize on the investors' familiarity with the structure. This structure is also doctrinally clearer, and politically more feasible. The choice of insurance state laws will bring predictability. But there is no free lunch. The choice of state laws will bring forum shopping as well.

The Model Act states that catastrophic event bonds are not insurance contracts. The Act does allow insurance companies to engage in issuing such bonds through a subsidiary by classifying the business as "insurance business." The distinction between insurance contract and insurance business is important. While insurance companies have an exclusive power to issue insurance contracts, they do not have a monopoly over insurance business, although they may engage in that business. That business includes broker dealer transactions, investment advisory services and many other functions. Therefore, other entities may organize SPVs, buy and transfer policies to them, and engage in sponsoring and distributing catastrophic event bonds without encroaching on the exclusive territory of insurance companies and running afoul of insurance laws.

The Model Act requires SPVs to organize as a corporation, domiciled under state law. Corporate form, however, may present problems under tax laws, as discussed above. SPVs will not be able to organize limited partnerships or grantor trusts or other organizational forms that allow pass-through tax treatment. Thus, the question of whether an SPV under the Model Act is still feasible without congressional actions remains open, and unless that issue is resolved, there is little use for the Model Act.

The Model Act has addressed the bankruptcy issue by providing that the SPV enter into a reinsurance contract with the ceding insurance company, thus insulating SPVs from insolvency of the ceding insurance company, provided the SPV meets its obligations under the reinsurance contract, under normal conditions.

The Future of Insurance (and Generally, Risk) Securitization is Quite Promising. So long as markets function, securitization makes sense. Insurance risk securitization is less likely to fail, given the size of potential catastrophe losses to the relative size of capital available in the securities markets, and the insurance industry. As catastrophic event bonds become more standardized, a public market is likely to develop, reducing transaction costs. Insurance securitization grew rapidly from one deal of $84 million in 1994 to 18 deals involving $2.5 billion in 1998.[253] Operating enterprises that are exposed to catastrophic event risks or other risks may expand insurance securitization by issuing catastrophic event bonds directly to the capital

[253] See Alex Maurice, *NAIC Poised to Adopt Securitization Models,* NAT'L UNDERWRITER, PROP. & CASUALTY/RISK & BENEFITS MGMT. EDITION, July 12, 1999, at S28, LEXIS, News Library, Arcnws File.

markets. These issues add depth and liquidity to the markets in such bonds. Indeed, the first issue of a catastrophe bond by a non-insurer (Oriental Land Company) took place in May 1999.[254]

Such direct issuances, however, will by-pass insurance companies and reinsurers altogether, thus dramatically affecting the industry. While in the past, reinsurers have usually played the role of underwriters and ultimate risk bearers for the industry, in the future, reinsurers will continue to use their expertise to select portfolios of reinsurance contracts. However, they will bear a lesser part of the risk directly, and distribute a higher proportion of risk to the securities markets by buying and selling catastrophic event bonds.

Securitization of catastrophic events risks may result in broader coverage of the risks, and lower insurance costs. It may save taxpayers money. If the net costs of insurance exceed the net benefits, bondholders will limit their obligations to their investments and the premiums (unless investors forego limited liability and agree to assessments). Policyholders will also be covered by state insurance funds (in which the SPV must participate). Further, the calculation of the contingent liabilities of the SPVs and the reserves covering the liabilities should be regulated to prevent the problems that insurance companies have faced in the past, when long-term liabilities remained uncovered and reserves were spent on current (sometimes extravagant) expenses. Who should regulate these functions, however, is another issue. There is no reason why bank regulators should not monitor the activities of banks in this area.

Risk securitization can radically alter risk management. If insurance risks can be securitized so can other risks. So long as the markets function as they should, and so long as investors are ready to bear risk for a return, risk securitization may offer great benefits that can be shared among the many. Innovative lawmaking must address the attendant problems by accommodating the issuers and other actors in the new process, and ensuring investors' confidence. Most importantly, the problems and challenges that new hybrid financial innovations pose can be addressed by analyzing the existing laws as to their underlying policies and ensuring that the hybrids meet the objectives of these policies.

E. Case Study: The "Cats" – Protecting Against Catastrophic Loss

Insurance developed to manage and transfer risk from a party that is vulnerable to a loss to a party more able and willing to accept the exposure in exchange for payment. The roots of the modern day insurance industry trace back thousands of years. Greek and Phoenician traders used a rudimentary form of insurance to protect against cargo losses at sea. Historians tell us that the first insurance contract was written in 14th Century Genoa. Three hundred years later the first insurance company, Lloyd's of

---

[254] See J. David Cummins, *The Insurance Link To Securities,* RISK MGMT., Aug. 1, 1999, at 17, LEXIS, News Library, Arcnws File.

London, was formed to protect the owners of ships and their cargos from losses in transit. From these modest beginnings the insurance has grown to a multi-billion dollar financial industry insuring not only property but also life and health.

The principles of insurance have remained largely the same since its inception. First, the loss covered is the result of chance and is largely beyond the control of the party seeking insurance, and the probability of a triggering event is low, such as an insurance policy against the fire damage or theft of the contents of a home. Second, there must be a large number of similar parties that desire similar protection. The statistical "law of large numbers" suggests that the larger the pool of insured parties, the greater the convergence between predicted and actual loss as long as the likelihood of one party incurring a loss is largely independent of other parties' losses. Third, losses can be accurately estimated. Two additional principles are that the loss must be large enough to warrant the administrative costs of the insurance and that the premium must be affordable.

If any of these principles is not met, insurers can face significant financial losses. When multiple principles are not met, the very viability of the insurance financial industry can be at stake. Such is the case of catastrophic loss resulting from natural disasters or terrorist actions (where the ability to predict the likelihood of the triggering event and the lack of independence of loss principles are violated). Hurricane Andrew struck Florida in 1992 causing $15.5 billion in insurance claims and led to the failure of 11 insurance companies.[255] Hurricane Katrina provides a more recent powerful illustration of the financial impacts of a natural disaster. In August 2005, Katrina made landfall in southeast Louisiana as a Category 3 hurricane causing wind and flooding damage from Louisiana to Florida. In New Orleans failure of the levees resulted in flooding of 80 percent of the city forcing the extended evaluation of hundreds of thousands of residents. More than 1800 people lost their lives as a result of Katrina. The financial losses from the hurricane were staggering: "Total damages are expected to exceed $200 billion" [256] including government aid and reconstruction expenditures.[257] The insured portion of the loss was estimated between $40 and $60 billion. Exhibit 1 shows that these examples are only two of many catastrophic events for both the insurance industry which must

---

[255] Michael Lewis, *In Nature's Casino,* N.Y. TIMES, Aug. 26, 2007, § 6, at 26, LEXIS, News Library, Nyt File..

[256] CONG. RESEARCH SERV., HURRICANE KATRINA: INSURANCE LOSSES AND NATIONAL CAPACITY FOR FINANCING DISASTER RISK 4 (2005), http://fpc.state.gov/documents/organization/53683.pdf (last visited Oct. 11, 2009).

[257] The direct costs of the storm were subsequently estimated at $70-135 billion. Peter N. Spotts, *Storm Season Ends: Are Potent Hurricanes Linked to Global Warning?,* CHRISTIAN SCIENCE MONITOR, Nov. 30, 2005, at 3, LEXIS, News Library, Arcnws File.

compensate their customers for losses, and for governments which often cover a portion of the uninsured losses.

The insurance industry understands the threat that catastrophic events present and has worked to mitigate the risk primarily by reinsurance--insurance for the insurance companies. The basic logic of reinsurance is the same as insurance – diversify the loss of an individual (in this case insurance company) by pooling the risk of losses of many insurance companies. The reinsurance market has successfully enabled the insurance industry to weather catastrophic losses although the costs for the protection swing significantly, based on proximate loss history. For example, reinsurance rates more than doubled after Hurricane Andrew (1992) and the Northridge earthquake (1994) and did not return to 1990 levels until the end of the decade. (See Exhibit 2) Cost increases also followed the 2001 terrorist attacks and Hurricane Katrina. Most agree that the reinsurance market will continue to be the primary source of insurance provider risk mitigation but the costs are likely to rise further as the frequency and magnitude of losses from natural disasters increase which is likely as more people move to geographically desirable yet high risk areas such as California and Florida. Both states have experienced population growth per square mile that has been more than double the national average.[258] Not only is the population growing in these vulnerable locations, but also the homes being built are expensive. Since 9/11 the insurance financial industry faces a new risk--losses from another terrorist attack. The combination of natural disasters and terrorist actions since 2000 is cause for concern in the insurance companies. It is not difficult to envision two or three catastrophic events happening 2 years in a row totaling more than $200 billion in losses which could threaten the solvency of these companies.

While $200 billion represents a huge loss for insurance companies, that amount is small in the context of the capital markets. The daily value of equities traded on the New York Stock exchange alone averaged $157 billion in 2008.[259] When the United States Congress failed to pass a bailout bill in September 2008, "$1.2 trillion in market value was erased from American equities."[260] An important question for insurers is how to tap the broader capital market to help protect against catastrophic loss. One promising solution is Catastrophe Bonds or "Cats" as they are known in the industry.

---

[258] Kenneth A. Froot, *The Limited Financing of Catastrophe Risk: An Overview* 2 (NBER, Working Paper No. 6025, 1997), http://www.nber.org/papers/w6025.pdf (last visited Oct. 11, 2009).

[259] *Claymore/Raymond James SB-1 Equity ETF Lists on NYSE Arca,* ISTOCKANALYST, Sept. 4, 2008, http://www.istockanalyst.com/article/viewiStockNews/articleid/2579468 (last visited Oct. 11, 2009).

[260] Eric Martin, *U.S. Stocks Plunge After House Votes Against Bailout Plan,* BLOOMBERG.COM, Sept. 29, 2008, http://www.bloomberg.com/apps/news?pid=20601087&refer=home&sid=aFVo3p8GzeWk (last visited Oct. 11, 2009).

Catastrophe bonds are event-linked securities sold by sponsors who are exposed to the risk of catastrophe loss to investors who accept the risk in exchange for a coupon return. If the catastrophe does not occur, the investor gains the coupon and the entire principal is returned. However, if the event takes place the coupon, and a portion or the entire principal which is used to pay claims against the sponsor, will not be paid. Exhibit 3 illustrates the process of creating catastrophe bonds. Sponsors, often reinsurance companies, enter into a reinsurance contract with a special purpose vehicle (SPV). The SPV may be created by the sponsor or by a third party, such as an investment bank. The sponsor pays the SPV premiums covering a specified catastrophic loss. The SPV uses the premiums to cover coupon bonds, which it issues to investors. The investors in turn provide the SPV with a principal payment that covers the protected event. The SPV may enter into a counter party arrangement to invest the principal and premium in very low risk instruments. The SPV makes scheduled coupon payments to the investors and returns the investors' principal on due dates, as long as the catastrophe does not occur. If the catastrophe takes place, the SPV pays the sponsor the agreed upon amount.

Each bond specifies the "trigger" that initiates a payout. The trigger typically relates to the actual or modeled loss that has been incurred resulting from the occurrence of the insured event. Several mechanisms have been used use to determine the amount of the payout. One mechanism is indemnity recovery which is based on the actual losses incurred by the sponsor. While this method avoids the need to estimate losses, it often takes months to determine and it can "create a moral hazard from the investor's point of view, as the sponsor could become less vigilant in settling claims."[261] Another mechanism is an industry loss index where the insurance industry loss, as measured by a Property Claims Services, is used to determine the payout. The notional portfolio mechanism models losses based on the actual parameters of the catastrophe. A third mechanism is parametric-based recovery where "objective measurements, such as a hurricane's maximum wind speed and landfall location, or the ground motion measured by . . . seismometers"[262] are used to determine the amount of investor principal that is paid to the catastrophe bond sponsor.

Cats with indemnity triggers were the most common in 2007, reflecting their advantage of being based on actual losses, similar to other types of insurance coverage. (See Exhibit 4) However, practical constraints may reduce the insurance companies' use of this trigger mechanism in the future. First, investors have required a premium for indemnity triggers because of uncertainty "in the sponsor's

---

[261] David A. Lalonde & Pascal Karsenti, *So You Want to Issue a Cat Bond,* AIRCURRENTS, Feb. 2008, at 4, http://www.air-worldwide.com/_public/NewsData/001410/AIRCurrents_CatBond.pdf (last visited Oct. 11, 2009).

[262] *Id.*

underwriting, risk management, loss and claims adjustment processes, among other factors."[263] Second, the risk is a function not only of the catastrophe occurrence but also on the sponsor's actions. Consequently, investors may require "substantial disclosure of internal, often sensitive or proprietary, information."[264] The ability of the investors to sue sponsors for failure to disclose represents further risk to the sponsors. Third, the time and administrative costs of providing information and modeling outcomes impose higher costs on the sponsor.

Insurers conduct extensive modeling to understand the degree of risk that Cat bonds impose on investors. For example, the characteristics of past catastrophes (e.g. Hurricane Katrina, the Kobe earthquake) are used to model the losses that would be incurred if they happened under the bond that is being evaluated. Probabilities of some loss and total exhaustion of resources are the outputs of the analytical analyses. In modeling the risks specialists rely not only on statisticians but also meteorologists and seismologists. While models have been built, the difficulty in calculating risk has been a barrier to the more extensive use of this investment vehicle. As one industry expert observed, "It's too much like throwing dice. You can say how many times you can expect to get a double-six out of one hundred throws, but it is impossible to know when they'll turn up."[265]

The first issues of catastrophe bonds took place in the mid-1990s. Since then the number and value of catastrophe bonds has increased substantially. Exhibit 5 shows that while the growth in Cats was modest between 1997 and 2005, the value increased markedly in 2006 and 2007. During 2007 twenty-seven Cat transactions were completed and at year-end the risk capital outstanding on Cats was $13.8 billion.[266] The bonds have been primarily used to cover hurricanes/typhoons, earthquakes, wind storms and heat waves. Coverage for hurricanes/typhoons accounted for half of the catastrophe bonds issued in 2007. Almost 2/3 of the catastrophe bonds issued in that year covered events in the United States. (See

---

[263] GC SECURITIES, THE CATASTROPHE BOND MARKET AT YEAR-END 2007, at 16 (2008), http://www.guycarp.com/portal/extranet/insights/reportsPDF/2008/Cat%20Bond%202%2027.pdf;jsessionid=JpXZyrvxFKhLmCwzPNypYVrgbQwP4Mc1xngbvGv72wfl rp0csB1T!1688904587?vid=6&vid=4 (last visited Oct. 11, 2009).

[264] *Id.*

[265] Digby Larner, *Bonds from Insurers Thrive if Nature Is Kind,* INT'L HERALD TRIB., Jan. 11, 1997, at 17, LEXIS, News Library, Arcnws File.

[266] GC SECURITIES, THE CATASTROPHE BOND MARKET AT YEAR-END 2007, at 4 (2008), http://www.guycarp.com/portal/extranet/insights/reportsPDF/2008/Cat%20Bond%202%2027.pdf;jsessionid=JpXZyrvxFKhLmCwzPNypYVrgbQwP4Mc1xngbvGv72wfl rp0csB1T!1688904587?vid=6&vid=4 (last visited Oct. 11, 2009).

Exhibit 6) While Cats have grown rapidly since 2005, they still account for a small percentage of the global reinsurance market.

One of the earliest catastrophe bonds was a $44.5 million issue of 10-year notes offered by Goldman, Sachs on behalf of St. Paul Companies' reinsurance subsidiary, St. Paul Re. The bonds provided a yield almost 1/3 higher than comparable Treasury notes; yet, both Moody's and Standard and Poor's rated the bonds triple-A.[267] While this early offering carried a very high rating Cats are more typically BBB or lower, making most catastrophe bonds non-investment grade as shown in Exhibit 7. Bonds that carry investment grade ratings typically require multiple events to trigger a payout. Cats are often written for multiple years of coverage. While most were two year bonds (in 2007), some were written for up to 10 years. (See Exhibit 8.)

The sponsors in Cats have generally been reinsurance companies, companies facing extreme risks, or governments seeking to tap capital market funds beyond the insurance industry. For the reinsurance companies Cats provide a new source of outside capital. Governments have used catastrophe bonds to insure against losses that could undermine the country's financial stability. In 2005 Mexico proposed an issue of $450 million in catastrophe bonds to protect against major earthquakes in three highly populated regions of Mexico. The bonds covering Mexico City would trigger with an earthquake of 7.5 or higher on the Richter scale.

The SPVs created by the sponsors have generally been located in tax havens such as the Cayman Islands and Bermuda. The rationale for offshoring is the legal uncertainties involved in securitizing insurance risk in the United States. "Underlying these issues is the difficulty in classifying insurance risk securitization as insurance or securities or futures contracts."[268] The classification, however, is critical since it dictates the relevant laws and regulations covering issues from taxation to creditors' rights. Rather than untangle the classification, sponsors have placed the SPVs in countries that do not tax and provide greater protection to creditors if the sponsor is bankrupt. The offshore SPVs must limit their activities in the United States because "[i]f the SPRV were determined to be engaged in a U.S. trade or business, it could be subject to U.S. income tax at a rate of up to 35 percent, and to a 30 percent branch profits tax on its income, resulting in an effective U.S. federal tax rate of up to 54.5 percent."[269]

---

[267] Digby Larner, *Bonds from Insurers Thrive if Nature Is Kind,* INT'L HERALD TRIB., Jan. 11, 1997, at 17, LEXIS, News Library, Arcnws File.

[268] Tamar Frankel & Joseph W. LaPlume, *Securitizing Insurance Risks,* 2000 ANN. REV. BANKING L.,20?, 207.

[269] GAO, CATASTROPHE INSURANCE RISKS 26 n.36 (2002).

Some United States insurance companies have sought to issue catastrophe bonds onshore to improve the efficiency of the transaction and provide regulatory oversight. The National Association of Insurance Commissioners, representing the state insurance regulators, has developed a model law to allow limited purpose SPVs to be domiciled domestically. However, the federal tax issue still requires resolution. There have been proposals to extend the REMIC concept, which allows for mortgage-backed securities to pass through SPVs without taxation, but this remains only a proposal. An alternative solution is "if catastrophic event bonds are viewed as debt for tax purposes. In such a case, SPVs can deduct from the income they receive through investments and premiums the payments they make to investors (as return on debt)."[270]

Several states have created acts that permit "protected cells," essentially SPVs within a company, as a way to develop specialized United States insurance companies that issue Cats. Under these structures, an insurance company sponsored cell's assets remain part of the insurance company and thus fall under state insurance law not federal law. (There is no need for a true sale.) In the case of the company's bankruptcy the investors would be viewed as secured creditors. Moreover, bankruptcy could also trigger a payout of state funds that support the insurance industry which would provide greater protection for investors. The cell also avoids double taxation since "[a]bsent an SPV there is no entity to be tax[ed] from the insurance company."[271]

Investors are attracted to Cats by their comparatively high returns; notwithstanding the fact that, if the catastrophe takes place, their entire investment will likely be lost. A second rationale for investors to purchase Cats is that Cats are not correlated with other financial market movements. The triggering event of a Cat is dictated by nature, not events in financial markets. Initially, Cat investors were associated with reinsurance but since 2006 high income hedge funds and other institutional investors who value the diversification Cats offer have become buyers as well. These investors have done well thus far in the 2008 financial crisis. "Swiss Re's index of BB-rated catastrophe bonds had returned 7.96 percent since January 2007, compared with a loss of about 10.31 percent over the same period for similarly-rated corporate bonds."[272] Moreover the ownership of a Cat bond is irrelevant from the sponsor's perspective because the bond is fully collateralized, the entire amount of the coverage is held by the SPV. This feature of Cats contrasts with typical reinsurance

[270] Tamar Frankel & Joseph W. La Plume, *Securitizing Insurance Risks,* 19 ANN. REV. BANKING L. 203, 218 (2000).

[271] *Id.* at 221.

[272] Catherine Evans, *Disaster Bond Sales on Hold Despite Robust Returns,* Reuters UK, Nov. 11, 2008, http://uk.reuters.com/article/reutersEdge/idUKLNE4AK08Z20081121 (last visited Oct. 11, 2009).

contacts, which are not typically fully collateralized and thus "cedants may find themselves in competition for the reinsurer's surplus when collecting recoveries after a catastrophic event."[273]

Investors must also understand the downside of Cat bonds. First, even the risk modeling companies recognize that "[t]here are frequently sharp differences between simulated performance results and the actual results subsequently achieved by any particular account, product, or strategy."[274] Second, the Cats, when triggered, represent a "credit cliff" where the entire invested principal can be lost. Third, catastrophe bonds offer little liquidity. Finding parties interested in such bonds and pricing for these securities can be problematic.

Looking to the future, the growth of catastrophe bonds is likely to continue because of (1) the combination of more frequent and higher costs catastrophes; (2) the desire for additional sources of capital to protect against catastrophic claims; and (3) investors' attraction to high return securities that are not correlated with other financial instruments.

Exhibit 1
Losses from Catastrophes

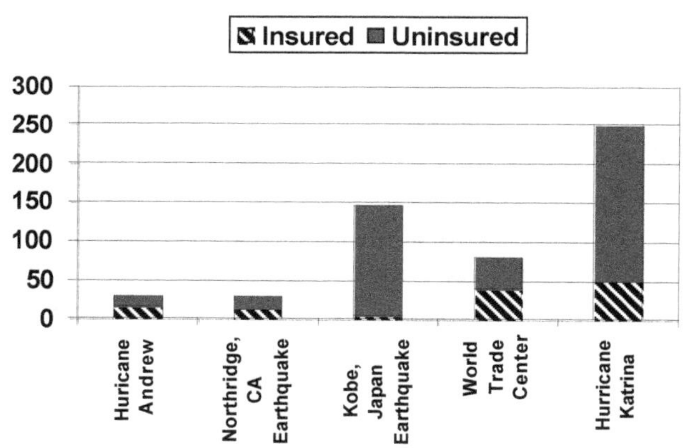

Source: GAO, Catastrophe Insurance Risks 12, Figure 2 (2002), http://www.gao.gov/new.items/d02941.pdf ; Cong. Research Serv., Hurricane Katrina: Insurance Losses and National Capacity for Financing Disaster Risk 4 (2005), http://fpc.state.gov/documents/organization/53683.pdf.

---

[273] David A. Lalonde & Pascal Karsenti, *So You Want to Issue a Cat Bond,* AIRCURRENTS, Feb. 2008, at 3, http://www.air-worldwide.com/_public/NewsData/001410/AIRCurrents_CatBond.pdf (last visited Oct. 11, 2009).

[274] FINRA, *Catastrophe Bonds and Other Event-Linked Securities,* http://www.finra.org/Investors/ProtectYourself/InvestorAlerts/Bonds/P038367 (last updated Apr. 4, 2008) (last visited Oct. 11, 2009).

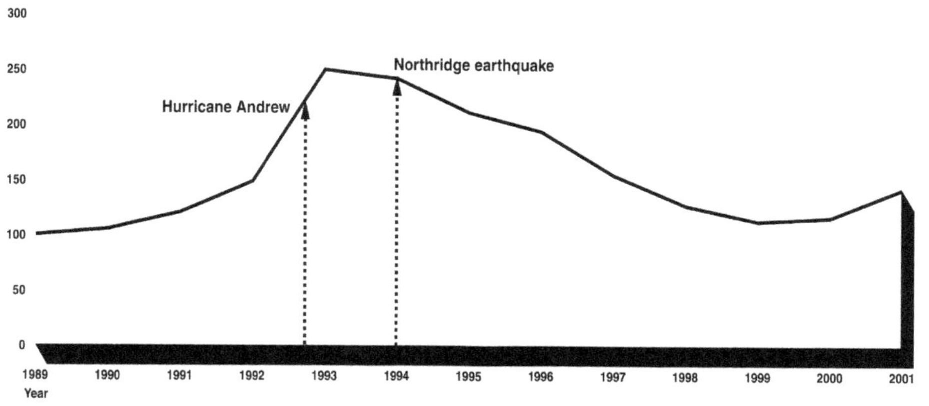

Source: GAO, Catastrophe Insurance Risks 14, Figure 4 (2002), http://www.gao.gov/new.items/d02941.pdf.

Exhibit 3
Cat Bond Structure and Financial Flows

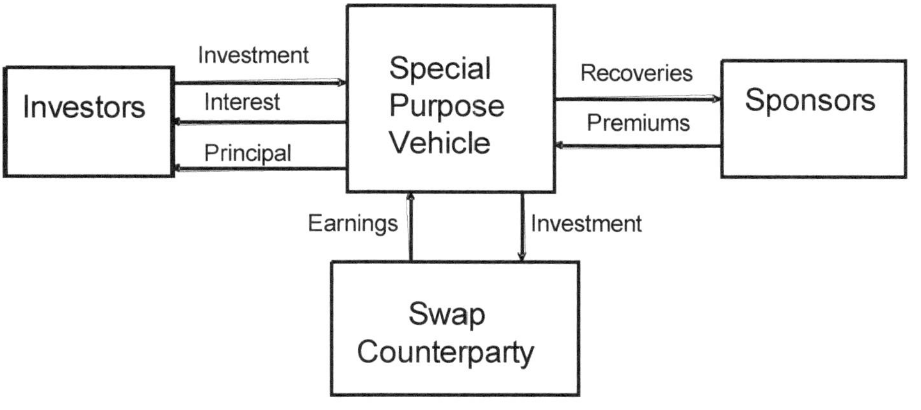

Source: David A. Lalonde & Pascal Karsenti, *So You Want to Issue a Cat Bond,* AIRCurrents, Feb. 2008, at 3, Figure 2, http://www.air-worldwide.com/_public/NewsData/001410/AIRCurrents_CatBond.pdf.

Exhibit 4:
Catastrophe Bond by Trigger Type

(2007)

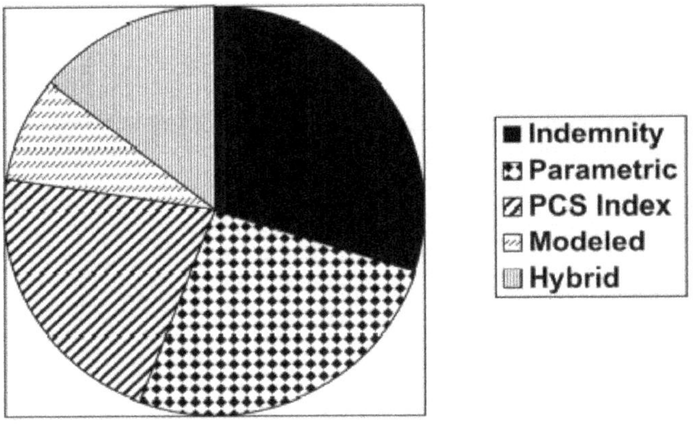

Source: Author estimates from data presented in GC Securities,
The Catastrophe Bond Market at Year-End 2007, at 23, Table 3 (2008), http://www.guycarp.com.

Exhibit 5
Catastrophe Bond Market Annual Risk Capital Issuance

(Millions of Dollars)

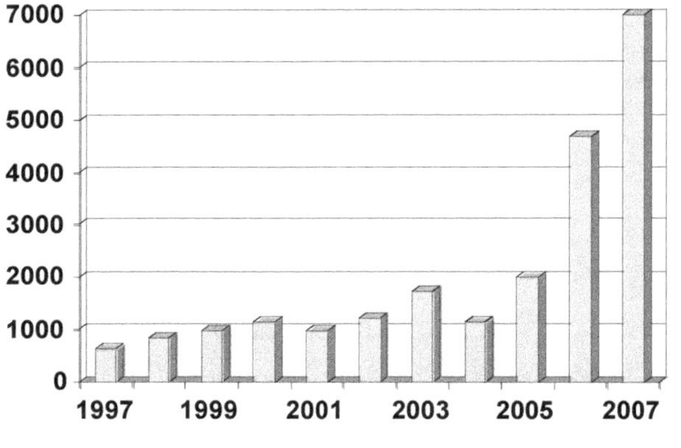

Source: Author estimates from data presented in GC Securities,
The Catastrophe Bond Market at Year -End 2007, at 5, Figure 1 (2008), http://www.guycarp.com .

Exhibit 6:
Risk Capital by Type of Catastrophe

(2007)

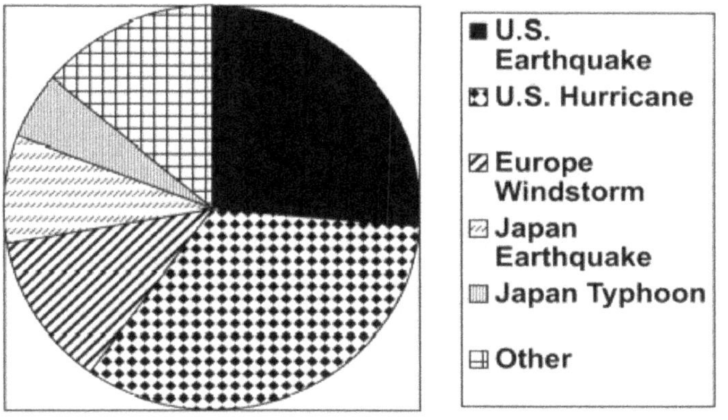

Source: Author estimates from data presented in GC Securities,
The Catastrophe Bond Market at Year-End 2007, at 22, Table 2 (2008), http://www.guycarp.com.

Exhibit 7:
Catastrophe Bond by Rating

(2007)

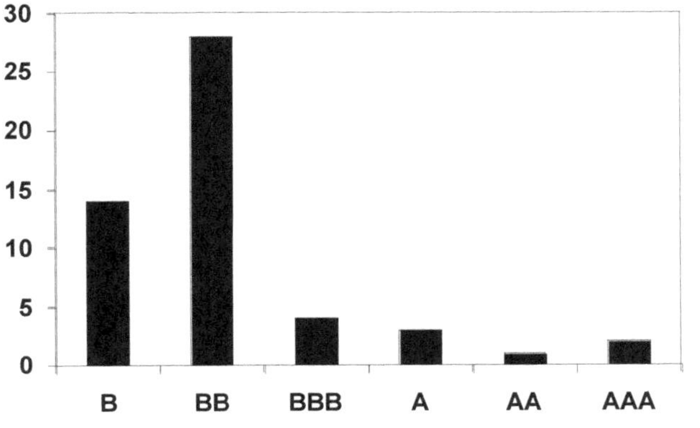

Source: Author estimates from data presented in GC Securities,
The Catastrophe Bond Market at Year-End 2007, at 28, Table 8 (2008), http://www.guycarp.com.

Exhibit 8:
Catastrophe Bond by Tenor
(2007)

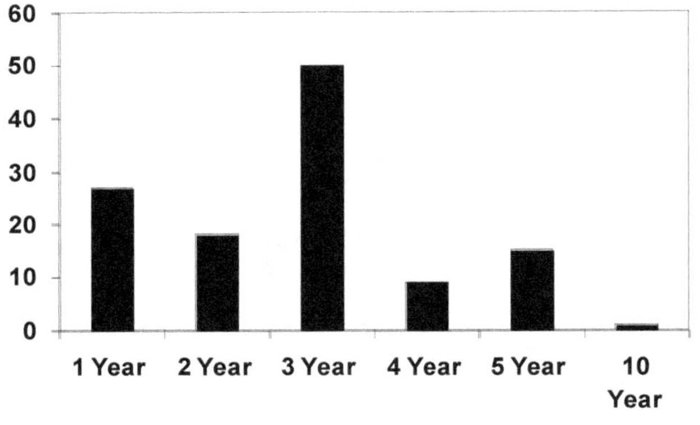

Source: GC Securities, The Catastrophe Bond Market at Year-End 2007, at 25, Table 5 (2008), http://www.guycarp.com.

Discussion Questions

Legal

- Are catastrophe bonds insurance or securities? Why? What are the implications of each classification?
- What are the barriers to creating a REMIC-like exemption for catastrophe bonds?
- How can an investor gain a secured creditor status in a protected cell structure?
- How should the risk modelers protect themselves from liability to the investors?

Business

- Are buyers of catastrophe bonds investing or gambling?
- Why would reinsurers invest in catastrophe bonds?
- Is the attractiveness of catastrophe bonds different for natural disasters versus terrorism?
- Do catastrophe bonds represent a useful diversification vehicle for investors?

Public Policy

- What are the roles of private insurance and the government in indemnifying losses from catastrophes?
- Does a government bailout of those who suffer an uninsured loss from a catastrophe create a moral hazard?
- The GAO recommends actions that will bring the issuance of catastrophe bonds from offshore to onshore; what is the rationale for a domestic market?

F. Borrowers Rights

a. Borrowers' Protection. Usury Laws[275]

SPVs are used to securitize small loans, many of which are consumer loans to individuals. Therefore, consumer protection laws apply to these loans. Notably, usury laws apply to consumer loans. In approximately one third of the states, usury laws do not apply to corporate loans under some or all circumstances by statute or by public policy enforced in the courts.

Typically, a party can invoke usury laws only as a personal defense that may be asserted only against the party in privity with the borrower and by a bankruptcy trustee, receiver, a corporation formed by the debtor, an alter ego of debtor, and sometimes a guarantor. Furthermore, federal law has preempted state usury laws with respect to some business and agricultural loans and loans by national banks.

Consumer protection laws can apply not only to the lenders but also to the buyers of loans. SPVs holding loans from several jurisdictions may become subject to multiple state consumer protection laws, perhaps with conflicting provisions. For example, in November 1995, the Supreme Court of Alabama held that nonexempt out-of-state holders of loans secured by mortgages on property located in Alabama or made to Alabama residents must be licensed under Alabama's Consumer Finance Law (the "Alabama Mini-Code") even though a 1973 Alabama attorney general opinion had reached a contrary conclusion. In response to the high probability that the Alabama decision would apply to entities formed to hold loans for securitization purposes, several subsequent securitized offerings explicitly excluded Alabama loans. Three months later, on rehearing, the court withdrew its earlier opinion and held that out-of-state holders of Alabama loans were not required to register under the Alabama Mini-Code. In that opinion, the court relied on an interpretation of the Alabama Mini-Code by the State Banking Department and, contrary to its earlier opinion, the attorney general's advisory opinion, reasoning that reenactment of the relevant sections of the Alabama Mini-Code without material change indicated the legislature's approval of the agency's interpretation. The application of widely different state laws such as this can have a serious impact on the mortgage origination business in the relevant state and on the interstate origination business.

Discussion Topic:

One author argued that "Market incentives encourage lenders to use unfair and deceptive practices and racial discrimination when making loans to subprime borrowers, or those who do not qualify for credit at lower rates."[276] Do you agree?

---

[275] 1 TAMAR FRANKEL, SECURITIZATION §4.9.2 (Ann Taylor Schwing ed., 2d ed. 2005).

b. Borrowers' Rights to Confidentiality[277]

As compared to the laws of other countries, such as Switzerland, American law affords relatively little protection to borrowers in terms of privacy, except as against the United States Government, although there is variation among the different States within the United States. This different treatment in the various countries and States may be due to differences in individual mobility and to differences in the availability of lenders and the competition among them. These differences may vest more bargaining power in borrowers as against the Institutions in these countries.

While historically the Swiss population usually used one source of financing, Americans have available more than one source, such as credit card short-term borrowing. And because Americans are more mobile and their country is larger, Americans change banks more often, even as the regulators allow banks to move their business interstate. Further, because historically American Institutions were specialized, no one type of institution can satisfy all the financing needs of its customers. Therefore, at least in the past, when securitization began to flourish in the United States, the information costs regarding borrowers for American Institutions far exceeded, for example, those for Swiss Institutions.

c. Incentives to Use Nonpublic Information

Securitization has increased the incentive of lenders to use confidential information about borrowers in aid of other functions that lenders now perform, including those in the securitization process. Use of nonpublic information also involves policy issues under the securities laws. Banks engaged both in securities activities and in commercial lending have incentives to use information acquired confidentially in commercial lending to aid their securities activities. Regardless of the consent of the borrowers, this use may conflict with the policy underlying the securities laws to prohibit securities trades on the basis of nonpublic information. Nonetheless, banks are entitled to use the borrowers' information to some extent.

Discussion Topics

1. How strong, do you think, are the borrowers' rights? Do the laws present a balanced view of these rights?
2. Evaluate a single-source financing as against a multi-source financing available to Americans.

---

[276] Cassandra Jones Havard , *Invisible Markets Netting Visible Results: When Sub-Prime Lending Becomes Predatory,* 26 OKLA. CITY U.L. REV. 1057, 1059 (2001).

[277] 2 TAMAR FRANKEL, SECURITIZATION § 21.1 (Ann Taylor Schwing ed., 2d ed. 2005).

d. Borrowers' Protection against Government Intrusion[278]

Customers of financial Institutions are protected from invasion of their privacy by the Government. The Comptroller and its employees are generally prohibited from disclosing confidential information except to authorized persons. The Right to Financial Privacy Act of 1978 prohibits banks from disclosing information about customers to government authorities, unless the customers authorize the disclosure. A number of states provide their citizens with similar protection. These prohibitions are subject to statutory and judicially created exceptions.

e. Borrowers' Common Law Rights: A Bank's Duty of Confidentiality to Borrowers[279]

Unlike depositors, borrowers are not entitled to confidentiality in some jurisdictions, unless a fiduciary relationship exists between the borrower and the lending bank or the bank has undertaken a contractual obligation to maintain privacy involving the borrowers' facts or documents.

The relation between a bank and a borrower is that of a creditor and debtor. Attempts to impose on banks significant additional duties to the borrowers with respect to confidential information have rarely been successful. Thus, in *Washington Steel Corp. v. TW Corp.,* the Third Circuit held that a bank is not a fiduciary of the borrower with respect to confidential information merely by virtue of holding confidential information received from the borrower in connection with a credit evaluation or monitoring of the borrower. This holding, however, was limited to (i) the use of confidential information by the bank's loan department (ii) for the purpose of making another credit decision. Thus, disclosure of borrowers' information to the bank's trust department is prohibited. To that end, a more detailed discussion of the *Washington Steel* case is necessary.

In the case of *Washington Steel* a borrower developed close relations with the bank and gave the bank confidential information about its cash flow and projected earnings. Later, using the confidential information, the bank considered participation in the financing of a hostile takeover of the borrower. The borrower sought to enjoin the bank from doing so on the basis of two theories. The first was a *per se* fiduciary duty theory that, by virtue of making the loan, the bank became a fiduciary of the borrower with respect to the confidential information. The second theory was that the bank misused the confidential information.

It can be argued in support of the *per se* fiduciary duty rule that the rule would give borrowers incentive to provide lending banks with all material information for

---

[278] 2 TAMAR FRANKEL, SECURITIZATION § 21.2 (Ann Taylor Schwing ed., 2d ed. 2005).

[279] 2 TAMAR FRANKEL, SECURITIZATION § 21.3.2 (Ann Taylor Schwing ed., 2d ed. 2005).

making a credit decision. Otherwise, the rule may reduce the flow of information to banks. However, the need for credit may be sufficiently strong to ensure that banks receive adequate information from borrowers. In addition, borrowers with bargaining power can bar banks by contract from using the information for other credit decisions, especially if the decisions affect the borrowers adversely. Another argument for the *per se* rule is grounded in morality and fairness. A bank that encourages the confidence and trust of its customers should not be allowed to benefit from their trust to the customers' detriment. The argument is less convincing today, when the loyalty of customers is weaker than in the past.

There are also serious arguments against the *per se* fiduciary rule. By taking loans from major banks, borrowers could exclude competitors or raiders from getting credit. Further, restricting banks' lending may have serious adverse effects on the economy and the banks, by giving unregulated lenders an unfair advantage over banks. Also, banks owe a fiduciary duty to their shareholders to invest their money prudently. The soundness of bank business is regulated to protect depositors and the FDIC. The interests of a bank's source of capital, the shareholders and depositors, should have priority over the borrowers' right to privacy. This preference militates toward protecting the depositors' privacy but not that of the borrowers.

In addition, legal rules should allow banks to operate efficiently in determining credit and encourage efficient credit markets. Both policies require a free flow of credit information. A fiduciary duty that prevents banks and other lenders from using information received in connection with one credit decision in making another credit decision would reduce efficiencies both in the lenders' own operations and in the credit markets. In fact, this argument embraces transactions other than lending. Lessors, buyers of property, and those seeking to engage in a transaction that involves their creditworthiness also benefit from the ability of the other party to evaluate their credit. Lower credit evaluation costs expand the availability of transactions and reduce the costs to both parties.

Balancing these conflicting arguments, the Third Circuit concluded that the mere making of loans does not impose fiduciary duties on lending banks to borrowers and does not prevent lenders from using confidential information received in connection with loan transactions for purposes of making credit decisions with respect to other loans.[280]

The courts' posture, however, is far from clear. On the one hand, courts have reserved their jurisdiction to impose fiduciary duties on banks toward their customers and have purposely left the boundaries of this jurisdiction undefined. On the other hand, some courts have suggested that courts should adopt a hands-off attitude with

---

[280] Washington Steel v. TW Corp., 602 F.2d 594 (3d Cir. 1979).

respect to use of confidential information among banks' departments and leave this issue to legislation and the regulatory agencies.

Further, the court in *Washington Steel* left open the question whether banks may provide one customer with confidential information about another customer generally, or for the purpose of financing the first customer's takeover by the second customer. The court also did not determine whether banks may transfer information from their commercial department to other departments (e.g., the trust department in a trustee or other fiduciary capacity). The court noted that such a disclosure may be in violation of Rule 10b-5 under the Securities Exchange Act of 1934, presumably in a transaction involving securities.

The plaintiff in *Washington Steel* also attacked the bank's use of confidential information on the ground that the bank breached its duty not to misuse such information. The Third Circuit held that misuse of information will not be presumed but must be proved. In addition, it noted the following facts that militated against holding the bank liable: the confidential information was of secondary importance to the raider of the customer, since the loan was to a raider, rather than the target-borrower; the bank officers did not give the information to the raider but merely kept silent, although they mentioned that the target was the bank's borrower; a "wall" was created between the loan officers of the borrower and those working on the loan to the raider. The latter were instructed not to talk to anyone who worked on the borrower's account, nor to look at the target's files, which were kept out of their reach. Such a procedure would go far toward sheltering a bank from claims of misuse of confidential information.[281]

f. The Borrowers Rights Against the Lender Based on Fiduciary Law

The relationship between borrowers and lenders is generally regulated by contract law. However, as usual, there are exceptions in which a lender would be liable as a fiduciary of the borrower. The following is an opinion on the issues.[282] In this case the Plaintiff Bank [United Jersey Bank (UJB)] sought to foreclose mortgages on three properties owned by defendants Kenneth and Michelle Kensey (Defendants). The couple bought "several properties from Gerald Katzoff, a bank customer. Katzoff had suffered severe financial losses and was attempting to reduce the substantial debt he owed UJB. [The] Defendants contended that UJB fraudulently induced them to enter into the loan transaction in order to substitute a healthy debtor for the financially ailing Katzoff."[283] The issue was "whether UJB had a duty to disclose an internal appraisal which indicated that the properties [which the Defendant bought]

[281] *Id.*

[282] United Jersey Bank v. Kensey, 704 A.2d 38 (N.J. Super. App. Div. 1997).

[283] *Id.* at 40.

were worth substantially less than the selling price and mortgage amounts, as well as information relating to Katzoff's precarious financial condition." "Although Defendants were highly experienced commercial real estate investors and were urged by the bank to perform a due diligence investigation of the . . . properties," they did not make an independent inquiry concerning the value of the properties. The Chancery Division entered summary judgment for the Bank and the appeals court affirmed.

The Defendant was "a highly sophisticated businessman . . . [with] substantial experience in real estate" and bank financing. He bought a summer home from Katzoff and negotiated the purchase of a golf course. The Defendant "knew that Katzoff's financial condition was deteriorating[,] that Katzoff had defaulted on his loans and that [the bank] had 'take[n] back' several of his properties." Also, the defendant distrusted the seller because the seller "had misrepresented the condition of the [house] and had taken various fixtures prior to the sale."[284] Nonetheless, the defendant did not seem to have exercised reasonable due diligence.

To be sure the bank was interested in recouping the loans it made to the property seller, Katzoff. In fact, the loan on the property was higher than the value of the property. The Defendants claimed fraud arguing that the bank was bound to inform them about the relationship of the seller and other parties and to "disclose the appraisal which indicated that the properties were worth significantly less than the purchase price and the mortgage amount."[285] The court held that "'Every fraud in its most fundamental conception consists of 'the obtaining of an undue advantage by means of some act or omission that is unconscientious or a violation of good faith.' . . . Legal fraud consists of 'a material representation of a presently existing or past fact, made with knowledge of its falsity and with the intention that the other party rely [on the misstatement], resulting in reliance by that party to his detriment.'"[286] . . . The elements of scienter, *i.e.*, knowledge of the falsity and an intention to obtain an advantage by deceit, "'are not essential if [the] plaintiff seeks to prove that a misrepresentation constituted only equitable fraud.' . . . Silence in the face of a duty to disclose may constitute a fraudulent concealment. . . . The question of whether a duty exists is a matter of law. . . . The question is one of fairness and policy that 'involves identifying, weighing, and balancing several factors -- the relationship of the parties, the nature of the attendant risk, the opportunity and ability to exercise care, and the public interest in the proposed solution.'"[287]

---

[284] *Id.* at 40-42.

[285] *Id.* at 43.

[286] *Id.*

[287] *Id.* at 43-44.

The court noted three classes of transactions triggering a duty to disclose arises: (1) fiduciary relationships, (2) situations in which """"either one or each of the parties, in entering . . . [the] transaction, expressly reposes . . . a trust and confidence in the other . . . or [because of the] circumstances of the case, the nature of their dealings, or their position towards each other, such a trust and confidence . . . is necessarily implied,'" . . . and (3) "contracts or transactions which in their essential nature, are 'intrinsically fiduciary,' and 'necessarily call[] for perfect good faith and full disclosure, without regard to any particular intention of the parties.'"[288]

Applying these three classes to the facts of the case the Court found that none applies. The relationship is creditor and debtor is very rarely fiduciary. "There is . . . general presumption that the 'relationship between lenders and borrowers is conducted at arms-length, and the parties are each acting in their own interest.'"[289]

As to the second category, the court recognized "the growing trend to impose a duty to disclose in many circumstances in which silence historically sufficed. . . . This trend is reflected in the *Restatement (Second) of Torts § 551* (1977 & Supp.1997). Subsection (1) sets out the traditional rule requiring disclosure of a fact which the individual knows may justifiably induce another to act, or refrain from acting, in a business transaction only if the individual is under a duty to disclose the matter. Subsection (2) sets out the conditions under which an individual has a duty to disclose certain information. Subsection 2(e) imposes a duty upon a party to disclose to another 'facts basic to the transaction, if he knows that the other is about to enter into it under a mistake . . . and that the other, because of the relationship between them, the customs of the trade or other objective circumstances, would reasonably expect a disclosure of those facts.' Comment 1 to *§ 551*, subsection (2), recognizes the difficulty in determining or identifying the factors that would give rise to an expectation of disclosure. The comment observes that the situation envisioned is one in which the advantage taken of the plaintiff's ignorance is ''so shocking to the ethical sense of the community, and is so extreme and unfair, as to amount to a form of swindling . . . .'''[290] . . .

Thus, in one case a bank loan officer told the plaintiff-bank customer that another bank customer [customer B] was financially sound and "encouraged the plaintiff to borrow $ 90,000 from the bank and place it with [customer B]'s account as a tax shelter investment." The bank loan officer knew that customer B "was involved in a 'check kiting' scheme and that its checking account was substantially overdrawn." The bank then applied the amount to "'zero out the [debtor's] account." "While 'reluctant to formulate a rule of disclosure . . . at tension with the general [principle of confidentiality],' the Supreme Court of Florida found the existence of 'special

---

[288] *Id.* at 44.

[289] *Id.* at 44-45.

[290] *Id.* at 45.

circumstances' that required the bank to apprise the plaintiff of [customer B's] perfidious scheme. . . . '[W]here a bank having actual knowledge of fraud being perpetrated upon a customer, enters into a transaction with that customer in furtherance of the fraud,' it could be held liable for the resulting loss."[291]

Similarly, a bank was held to be a fiduciary when the bank "continuously promised and pressured [a customer] to enter into transactions with [another customer]" for the bank's benefit: The customer was told: "'[d]o it for us. . . . [Y]ou are part of [the] Capital Bank family. You help the bank, we are going to help you.'"[292] "In finding that a fiduciary relationship existed, the court stated that 'special circumstances transformed this lender/borrower relationship into a fiduciary one.' . . . It found that the loan officer's actions advising, reassuring and urging" the client posited the bank as "financial advisor.""[293]

Another bank assured the plaintiff that, "although the customer was somewhat undercapitalized, it had 'maintain[ed]' its financial commitments. . . . In fact, the customer was heavily indebted to the bank, which had assumed a supervisory role over its day-to-day management. Immediately after the plaintiff made a substantial payment to the customer, the equipment company went out of business. The payment was used by the bank to reduce the defunct customer's debt. . . . [T]he Court of Appeals for the Sixth Circuit held that the bank was guilty of fraudulent concealment. . . . The court reasoned that once the bank undertook to advise the plaintiff with respect to the bank customer's financial condition it 'had a duty to disclose information in [its] possession which would reasonably be considered material to the decision [it] knew [the plaintiff] was in the process of making.' . . . [All three cases] involved egregious breaches of the lender's duty of good faith and fair dealing. . . In less egregious circumstances, however, the courts have found no duty on the part of lenders to disclose information they may have concerning the financial viability of the transactions the borrowers were about to enter.."[294]

In *United Jersey Bank* the court found no special circumstances that required the bank to disclose the seller's details or the fact that the property was worth less than the loan which it constituted the collateral.

"[A] bank generally owes no duty to disclose an internal appraisal to a prospective borrower. Here, for example, the appraisal was done for [the bank's] benefit, not for the benefit of the borrower. It is axiomatic that estimating the value of commercial property is a difficult task, a task which is dependent upon numerous factors. Where,

[291] *Id.* at 45-46.

[292] *Id.* at 46.

[293] *Id.*

[294] *Id.*

as here, the underlying information is readily accessible to the borrower, we perceive no sound basis to impose on the bank the duty to investigate the value of the property and supply that information to the borrower. . . . We discern no basis to impose liability on UJB. To be sure, banks are not popular institutions. Only bankers and bank robbers love banks. But, we perceive no sound reason to impose upon a bank the responsibility to supply a potential borrower with its estimate of the value of the subject property, at least where, as here, the borrower has the ability to make that determination. The principal factors shaping the duty to disclose 'have been the difference in bargaining power' between the parties 'and the difference in access to information.' . . . Neither factor is present in this case. Defendants were not neophytes to real estate transactions. They saw advantage and profit in Katzoff's failing financial condition. The Kenseys gambled and lost. The loss should remain where lack of success in the marketplace has put it."[295]

G. Prohibition on Referral Fees[296]

Real estate transactions depend on the financing available to the purchasers. Therefore, real estate agents are under great pressure to secure financing for potential buyers. This pressure may lead to problems. Section 8(a) of the Real Estate Settlement Procedures Act of 1974 ("RESPA") prohibits the gift or receipt of benefits in return for real estate settlement services involving federally related mortgage loans. Both Fannie Mae and Freddie Mac have adopted automated procedures to streamline the origination and securitization of mortgage loans. In their efforts, however, both entities risk adopting practices that conflict with the requirements of RESPA. In 1983, the Department of Housing and Urban Development attempted to enforce the prohibition on the payment of referral fees, but the regulation was overruled as too vague by the Sixth Circuit. Thereafter, the Department issued a definition of "settlement service" that would appear to include charging interest on mortgage loans.

Use of referral fees from lenders to real estate brokers may be expanding, as mortgage bankers, banks, and other lenders compete for real estate loans. They promise referral fees to brokers who bring them customers. For big lenders in the securitization business, these fees help increase the amount of loans that they can securitize. These fees create a conflict of interest between the brokers and their customers because the fees provide an incentive for the brokers to recommend to the purchasers those lenders who pay the highest fees rather than those lenders that offer the best loan terms. If the broker does not disclose the fee, the conflict of interest constitutes a violation of the broker's common law fiduciary duty of the broker to give disinterested advice. If the broker gives advice for compensation and the transaction involves securities, the broker's receipt of referral fees without disclosure to the customer may constitute a violation of the antifraud provisions of the

[295] *Id.* at 48-49. *See also* Wiener v. Lazard Freres & Co., 672 N.Y.S.2d 8 (App. Div. 1998).

[296] 1 TAMAR FRANKEL, SECURITIZATION § 7.18 (Ann Taylor Schwing ed., 2d ed. 2005).

Investment Advisers Act of 1940. However, if fees are paid to brokers for other services and charged to the borrowers, there is a question whether such fees are referral fees that should be prohibited.

Predatory Lending. Commentators argue that the firms that securitize sub-prime loans did not examine whether the loans were obtained in a predatory fashion. They were concerned to protect the investors from the defenses of the borrowers. "[S]ecuritization solves the lemons problem for investors without requiring the capital markets to screen out predatory loans from securitized offerings."[297] Thus, securitization shields investors from all credit and litigation risks, such as the protection of a "holder in due course." Securitization, in contrast, "inflicts negative externalities on subprime borrowers" by enabling "small, thinly capitalized lenders and brokers," who are more likely to use predatory techniques to enter the markets, and dilutes the incentives of lenders and brokers to make loans to more creditworthy borrowers and those that can protect themselves from predatory terms.[298] "One recent study estimated that lengthy prepayment penalties in securitized subprime loans boosted borrowers' risk of foreclosure by sixteen to twenty percent." [299]

Another commentator[300] blamed predatory lending on the rating agencies. This commentator argued that because the rating agencies required "a borrower's remedies . . . be limited to rescission of the loan contract and/or recoupment of any damages from the loan amount owed"[301] and "Standard & Poor's required credit enhancements would impose unacceptable costs on the New Jersey mortgage market, the New Jersey legislature was forced to acquiesce and amend its predatory lending law on July 6, 2004."[302]

"The task of cleaning up falls to cities, yet predatory lending reduces the resources available for this clean up. . . . I conclude by arguing that broad grants of standing to cities to pursue claims against predatory lenders are necessary to enable cities to protect residents from lender wrongdoing, to recover damages for the injuries predatory lenders impose on cities, and to force abusive lenders to internalize the externalities of their lending practices. . . . Whether a municipality has standing as a

---

297 Kathleen C. Engel & Patricia A. McCoy, *Turning a Blind Eye: Wall Street Finance of Predatory Lending*, 75 FORDHAM L. REV. 2041, 2041 (2007).

298 *Id.*

299 *Id.* at 2039. .

300 David Reiss, *Subprime Standardization: How Rating Agencies Allow Predatory Lending to Flourish in the Secondary Mortgage Market*, 33 FLA. ST. U.L. REV. 985 (2006).

301 *Id.* at 1030-31.

302 *Id.* at 1052.

quasi-sovereign turns on its jurisdiction's statutory and constitutional home rule provisions. . . . Even when aggrieved borrowers have the financial and emotional resources to litigate claims against predatory lenders, the remedies they obtain are personal to them, e.g. damages or loan rescission or reformation, and have little or no impact on lenders' practices and do not redress the externalities that predatory lending imposes on cities."[303]

Consider the Following Section Applicable to Mortgages:

15 USCS § 1641. Liability of assignees

(d) Rights upon assignment of certain mortgages.

(1) In general. Any person who purchases or is otherwise assigned a mortgage referred to in section 103(aa) [15 USCS § 1602(aa)] shall be subject to all claims and defenses with respect to that mortgage that the consumer could assert against the creditor of the mortgage, unless the purchaser or assignee demonstrates, by a preponderance of the evidence, that a reasonable person exercising ordinary due diligence, could not determine, based on the documentation required by this title [15 USCS §§ 1601 et seq.], the itemization of the amount financed, and other disclosure of disbursements that the mortgage was a mortgage referred to in section 103(aa) [15 USCS § 1602(aa)]. . . .

(2) Limitation on damages. Notwithstanding any other provision of law, relief provided as a result of any action made permissible by paragraph (1) may not exceed--

(A) with respect to actions based upon a violation of this title, the amount specified in section 130 [15 USCS § 1640]; and

(B) with respect to all other causes of action, the sum of--

(i) the amount of all remaining indebtedness; and

(ii) the total amount paid by the consumer in connection with the transaction.

(3) Offset. The amount of damages that may be awarded under paragraph (2)(B) shall be reduced by the amount of any damages awarded under paragraph (2)(A).

(4) Notice. Any person who sells or otherwise assigns a mortgage referred to in section 103(aa) [15 USCS § 1602(aa)] shall include a prominent notice of the potential liability under this subsection as determined by the Board.

[303] Kathleen C. Engel, *Do Cities Have Standing? Redressing the Externalities of Predatory Lending,* 38 CONN. L. REV. 355, 355-56, 366, 391 (2006) (footnote omitted).

Chapter 6. The SPV's Asset Portfolio

This chapter provides a more detailed consideration of the assets that comprise the SPV's portfolio. First the risks associated with the portfolio are described in terms of the level of risk, the impact of law on risk, and how the terms of the loans affect risk including the impact of sub-prime loans. Next, a key risk mitigation strategy, credit enhancement, is explained and a simulation exercise is provided. The chapter concludes with an introduction to the credit rating process in the context of evaluating the assets that the SPVs acquire.

A. Portfolio Risk

Standards and risks are interactive. The very existence of Markets in asset-backed securities and the efficiency of the Markets depend in part on minimum standards or requirements that (i) the documents involved are essentially similar; (ii) underwriting standards guiding the making of the loans and evaluating loan risks are known and followed; and (iii) operations and financial structures of the loan makers and other parties, such as guarantors, comply with minimal standards. Standards may be a necessary condition to creation of a Market because, at some point, if information costs of pricing loan portfolios held by the SPVs are too high, no Market in SPV securities is possible. Standards help make Markets efficient because they reduce information costs and risks for investors.

a. The Level of Portfolio Risk

The lower the risk involved in the SPVs' securities, the lower will be the cost of the SPVs' funds, because investors will accept lower return when there is lower risk. Usually, an SPV has no assets other than its loans, and no obligations other than its securities. Therefore, the risk of an SPV's securities is determined by the quality of the loans in the SPV's portfolio and its promises under its securities. The SPV's asset risk can be reduced in different ways. For example, the Originator of the loans can reassure investors by retaining a junior security to back up the more senior securities. Investors can be assured by the Originator's guarantee or the guarantees of a third party, or by agreeing to repurchase any defaulting loans, or by offering any combination of these assurances. The Originator may thus obtain a higher rating for the SPV securities than the quality of the portfolio loans might otherwise warrant.

Initial Standards Are Determined by Loan Originators. Investors and regulators may impose additional or stricter standards on loan originators because makers of loans for sale may be less interested in insuring the quality of the loans and disclosing risks involved in the loans than those who make loans for investment. Therefore, notwithstanding their conflicts of interest, Originators of loans for sale may have incentive to reduce information costs to buyers and facilitate efficient

Markets in asset-backed securities. In addition, they have incentives to increase the number of loans they make. After all, this is the source of their profits.

b. Impact of the Law

The impact of the law on the loan standards is substantial, because many if not most originating lenders, insurers of the loans, and investors in asset-backed securities are regulated Institutions. The main laws governing standards are the federal and state laws regulating Institutions that act as loan originators, state laws regulating insurance companies, ERISA regulating pension funds; state laws regulating state and local pension funds, and the Rules of the government insurance agencies, such as the FDIC, regulating insured Institutions.

Standards are also imposed by the Markets. Investors demand that asset-backed securities will be rated and are willing to accept a lower return on rated securities because rating reduces their information costs. The securities laws provide issuers with an incentive to bear the cost of rating by exempting from regulation securities that are rated at a specified level by nationally recognized rating agencies. To reduce their own cost of evaluating numerous small loans, rating agencies impose underwriting and other standards on loan Originators.

Needless to say, the laws and regulations are not uniform. They differ depending on the nature of the securitized loans. For example, mortgages receive far more attention than car loans. The laws differ depending on the identity of the borrower. Thus, consumer loans are regulated by specific federal and state legislation and usury laws, while commercial loans are not. These legal differences stem in part from the different purposes of the laws. While the purpose of some laws is to encourage Markets in particular loans, such as mortgages, other laws are aimed at ensuring the safety and soundness of particular Institutional lenders and investors, while the purpose of other laws, such as usury laws, is to protect the borrowers. Clearly, the broader the regulation, the more standardized the loans will be, and the more efficient the Markets for asset-backed securities are likely to be.

Mortgage-backed securities ("MBS") are substantially standardized, and Market forces are pushing toward standardization of other loans as well. Private sector operators have entered the Markets, selling securities in SPVs holding individual mortgages that exceed limits imposed by statute on FHLMC and FNMA.

Many areas of the law that impact MBS have evaded standardization. Bankruptcy (both of loan originators and borrowers) is one area in which substantial variations remain. Variations also depend on whether the bankrupt is an Institution or an individual. Thus, when one party to the arrangement becomes insolvent, the outcome for all parties involved is uncertain. Property law governing the effect and foreclosure of mortgages has remained within the domain of state laws, and it varies greatly. Nonetheless, a federal uniform law is emerging, and it serves as a model to the states and the private sector.

c. Terms of the Loans[304]

Although loan terms depend initially on parties to the loans, lenders are constrained by various consumer and usury laws with respect to these terms. In addition, loan terms may have to be structured in accordance with the regulation of the Institutional buyers, such as pension funds, insurance companies, and investment companies. The laws that protect borrowers, especially small borrowers, can become inoperative unless they apply to loan buyers as well. National banks may be precluded from applying to the transactions any law other than the law of the state in which they are located. The magnitude of the problem was explicitly recognized in the 1988 amendments to the Fair Housing Act that, as the House Report states, extend "the provisions of the Act. . . to the secondary mortgage market."[305] As a result, provisions prohibiting discrimination apply to the purchase of loans too.

d. Terms of Subprime Loans

Things have changed since the sub-prime mortgage-backed securities crisis. "Sub-prime mortgage loans" are loans, secured by real estate, generally by private homes, that were made to highly risky borrowers at less than the usual prime rate. Names can mislead. Traditional "mortgage loans" that are considered relatively secure carry a relatively low interest rate. That is because borrowers who mortgage their homes are expected to take care of the real estate, and make every effort to pay their mortgage loans for fear of losing their homes. In addition the amount of such loans is lower than the value of the real estate when the loans are made. Therefore, if the value of the real estate fell, the lenders can still recoup the loan mount or close to that amount.

Historically, and often today "prime interest rate" is the interest rate offered by banks to low-risk – prime borrowers. "The Prime Interest Rate is the interest rate charged by banks to their most creditworthy customers (usually the most prominent and stable business customers). The rate [was] almost always the same amongst major banks. Adjustments to the prime lending rate are made by banks at the same time; although, the prime rate does not adjust on any regular basis. The rates reported below are based upon the prime rates on the first day of each respective month."[306] Thus, these prime rates are adjusted periodically, but served usually as low interest basis for "prime" borrowers. Borrowers that pose higher risks were usually charged prime rate plus an

---

304 1 TAMAR FRANKEL, SECURITIZATION § 7.13 (Ann Taylor Schwing ed., 2d ed. 2005).

305 H.R. Rep. No. 711, 100th Cong., 2d Sess. 30 (1988), reprinted in 1988 U.S.C.C.A.N. 2173, 2191.

306 Huliq News. *Vachovia (sic) Lowers Prime Rate* (Jan. 22, 2008), ,http://www.huliq.com/47986/vachovia-lowers-prime-rate (last visited Sept. 15, 2009).

additional percentage. In some cases the definition of "prime rate" may be flexible and subject to different interpretations. Thus, in a 1984 case, a bank promised the plaintiff borrowers "prime rate." They sued the bank when they discovered that other borrowers paid lower than the plaintiffs' rate. The Court denied the plaintiffs' petition for a partial summary judgment. The court reasoned that the parties "never intended that the bank would undertake an impractical categorization of its borrowers in order to establish its prime rate. . . . [the] bank's practice of charging below prime rate interest to certain customers was not a per se breach of a contractual duty owed to the borrowers."[307]

The term "sub-prime mortgages" is even more ambiguous than the term "prime rate" and could be misleading. While it indicates to the borrowers that they pay less than the prime rate, it suggests that the borrowers represent an even lower risk than borrowers that pay prime rate. Yet, in fact the borrowers of sub-prime mortgages presented far greater risk to lenders than the borrowers that paid prime rate. In addition, the terms of the loans were far more risky to the borrowers, thus enhancing the possibility of their default. In sum, what looked like safe investments was far from it. How did this development come about?

Early in 2000, mortgage interest rates increased in the United States. Consequently, there were fewer borrowers and fewer loan origination activities. But the demand for loan products had not diminished. Lenders sought new ways to market their loan products and satisfy the demand in the secondary market. Not surprisingly, there appeared Nontraditional Mortgage Loans (NTMs). Unlike prime rate mortgages, sub-prime mortgages carried interest that was below prime rates. And in contrast to prime-rate mortgage-borrowers, the borrowers of sub-prime mortgages were high-risk borrowers. Paradoxically, the lower the rate of sub-prime loans carried, the higher the risk posed by these borrowers seemed to be.

NTMs included "Adjustable Rate Mortgages" (ARMs), "stated income loans," "2/28 or 3/27 loans" and "80% loan to value loans." ARMs combined "negative amortization features and graduated payments."[308] In plain English, they posed future higher risk for the borrowers.

"Stated income loans" made it possible for borrowers who could not, or did not want to, provide documentation necessary to prove their income and/or cash flow to borrow.[309] Such borrowers might not be able to sustain the payments on the loans. These loans posed higher risk for the lenders.

---

[307] Kleiner v. First Nat'l Bank, 581 F. Supp. 955, 1984 U.S. Dist. LEXIS 19065 (N.D. Ga. 1984) (citing the LEXIS overview).

[308] Doyle v. Trinity Sav. & Loan Ass'n., 869 F.2d 558, 559 n.2 (10th Cir. 1989) (describing features of an ARM).

[309] McCloskey v. NovaStar Mortg., Inc., No. 06-00542, 2007 U.S. Dist. LEXIS 62297 (E.D. Pa. Aug. 21, 2007); *In re* Marriage of Chakko (Chakko v. Chakko), 8 Cal. Rptr. 3d 699 (Ct. App. 2004).

"2/28 or 3/27 loans" meant loans with an initial 2- or 3- year period of fixed interest. "2/28 or 3/27" loans attracted borrowers who wanted to borrow with an initial 2- or 3- year period of fixed interest. This term offered more predictable payments to the borrowers and postponed their risk of higher payments. It postponed the risk of default for the lenders.

"Loan to value" refers to loans amounting to up to 125% of the value of the collateral[310] Needless to say, these terms reduced the value of the collateral and posed higher risk to the lender. The rationale for these loans was that the value of the home would increase with time. This was true for a period of time but when housing prices stalled and then declined these loans became problematic.

Thus, the broad range of new loan terms drew borrowers who could not afford to borrow under traditional terms. Most were low-income people or borrowers who could not provide information on their cash flow. Borrowers began to fail, especially those who signed for option adjustable rate, providing low payments in the first, usually five years. The standards of the "prime borrower" definition were lowered as the need for increased loan origination rose.

UBS research shows that 3.55% of these option ARMs originated by Countrywide in 2006 and sold in the secondary market have defaulted. The rising defaults are linked to increasingly difficult refinancing, and the loans were higher than the homes were worth. Although Countrywide alleged that part of the losses have been covered by its insurance policy, 96% of its option ARMs had little or no documentation, and the down payments on the loans were as little as 5%. These mortgages were considered prime, and were bought in higher prices, making their origination more lucrative. Countrywide's employees were offered incentives such as Hawaii trips in order to increase their production of such mortgages. In 2008, Countrywide was sold in a fire sale.

B. Credit Enhancement

Credit enhancement is a mechanism designed to reduce the risk of investors in SPVs' securities. Thus, insurance, letters of credit and other guarantees enhance the credit of the securities. Credit enhancement can take three forms. One form supports the level of credit of each asset that the SPVs holds. Thus, the credit of loans supported by mortgages provide credit enhancement of each loan. The second form of credit enhancement supports the aggregate assets held by the SPVs. For example, when the amount of the aggregate issued of SPVs securities constitutes 80% of the value of the SPVs' assets. The 20% of the assets back up any shortfall in the assets. The third form of credit enhancement covers the securities issued by the SPVs rather than the

[310] *In re* Cmty. Bank of N. Va. Second Mortg. Loan Litig., 418 F.3d 277 (3d Cir. 2005).

assets that they hold. The form of this credit enhancement can be a guarantee of the obligations that the securities constitute. For example, an insurance company may guarantee the payment of the amount specified in a bond issued by the SPV. The distinctions may be important from both a financial and a legal point of view.

C. Simulation Exercise: Credit Enhancement - What is the Right Recipe?

TFMF Partners[311] had built a reputation for low risk mortgage-backed securities (MBS). While Fannie Mae and Freddie Mac were the dominate players in securitizing conventional or conforming loans, there was still a sizable market for securities comprised of mortgages that did not conform to standard loan requirements because of the size of the mortgage, the loan-to-value ratio, or the earnings history of the borrower. TFMF focused on a subset of the non-conforming loans known as "jumbo" mortgages. These loans exceeded that maximum amount for conventional loans established by Fannie Mae and Freddie Mac which at the beginning of 2008 was $417,000.[312] This mortgage cap was well above the U.S. median house sale price of $196,300 at that time[313] but in portions of the Northeast and in California the median house prices were substantially higher. The median house price in the New York/Northern New Jersey area was $445,000.[314] In San Diego and San Francisco the median prices exceeded $700,000.[315] Borrowers in these geographies turn to jumbo loans to buy homes. The origination of jumbo loans grew rapidly with the value of these mortgages more than doubling from $252 billion in 2000 to $570 billion in 2005.[316] The dollar value of jumbo loans accounted for 18 percent of total mortgage originations in 2005.[317]

The rationale for securitizing conventional loans applied equally to jumbo loans. New mortgage capital was drawn into the market through the sale of securitized

---

[311] TFMF is a fictitious entity as are the descriptions of its transactions.

[312] FannieMae, Loan Limits, http://www.fanniemae.com/aboutfm/loanlimits.jhtml?p=About+Fannie+Mae&s=Loan+Limits (last revised Aug. 4, 2009) (last visited Sept. 15, 2009) ("not[ing] that the 2009 general conforming loan limits are identical to the . . . 2008 conforming loan limits".

[313] Stephanie Armour, *Median Home Price Falls 7.7%; Slump Spreads in 1st Quarter,* USA TODA

Y, May 14, 2008, at 4B, LEXIS, News Library, Curnws File..

[314] .Sam Ali, *Bucking the Trend Jersey's Housing Market Is Doing Better than Most Other States',* TIMES OF TRENTON, May 14, 2008, at C08, LEXIS, News Library, Curnws File.

[315] *Mixed Home Price Performance Continues in Metro Areas, One-Third Show Gains,* PR Newswire, May 3, 2008, LEXIS, News Library, Curnws File.

[316] Everson W. Hull, *Securitized Jumbo Mortgages: 1986-2005,* at 6 (OFHEO Working Paper No. 07-1, 2007) http://www.fhfa.gov/webfiles/1272/workingpaper071.pdf (last visited Sept. 15, 2009)..

[317] *Id.*

jumbo loans which increased opportunities for competitively priced mortgages. Moreover, many of the prospective large loan borrowers had excellent credit scores. More than half of the borrowers who took jumbo loans that were securitized between 1996 and 2005, had very strong credit ratings (Fair, Isaac and Co. [FICO] scores in the 700-800 range).[318] The loan-to-valuation ratios of these more expensive properties often met or were even better than those required for conventional loans. As the value of jumbo mortgages grew so did the amount of those loans that were securitized. By 2005, securitization of jumbo mortgages reached over $200 billion, nearly three-quarters of which were collateralized by houses in California.[319] TFMF was one of the first investment firms to offer securitized jumbo loans. From 1986 through 2005 the firm underwrote more than 20 securities issues. In all cases the senior holders of the securities were paid in full and on time. Only in three issues did junior security holders experience delays in receiving their interest payments. Compared with other mortgage-backed security offerings TFMF's performance was impressive.

TFMF's great track record was in part due to the credit enhancement offered on TFMF's securities. Credit enhancement is "[t]he process of reducing credit risk by requiring collateral, insurance, or other agreements to provide the lender with reassurance that it will be compensated if the borrower defaulted."[320] TFMF utilized three credit enhancement techniques to reduce the risk for their investors in securitized jumbo mortgages.

The first technique was creating senior and subordinate ownership classes of each security pool. The ownership structure protected the senior owners by putting them first in line for interest and principal payments. Thus if borrowers did default the senior investors would likely receive their anticipated cash flow. The subordinated owners would bear the costs of default. These junior owners would, however, earn a greater rate of return for taking on the default risk. TFMF carefully designed the split between senior and subordinated ownership to cover the default risk for senior owners without paying an excessive risk premium by having too much of the issue in subordinated shares. Based on the historical default rate on jumbo mortgages TFMF determined that an 85% senior and 15% junior ownership structure was optimal.

The second credit enhancement technique TFMF used was the creation of an excess spread account. The interest rate paid by the borrowers on TFMF's jumbo loan securities was higher than the rate paid to investors. This spread was retained in a special account that could be used to cover borrowers' defaults. The funds in the

---

[318] *Id.* at 22.

[319] *Id.* at 10.

[320] *Credit Enhancement*, INVESTORWORDS.COM, http://www.investorwords.com/5489/credit_enhancement.html (last visited Sept. 15, 2009).

account were invested in a treasury bills which further increased the money available to fund defaults. The third technique was overcollateralization. Each time TFMF bundled a pool of mortgages into a security, it only issued 95% of the face value of the mortgages in securities. Thus, the value of the collateral backing the securities exceeded the amount of the securities issued. In the unlikely event of erosion in the value of underlying assets or payment defaults, investors had a cushion before they faced a repayment shortfall.

The financial crisis in 2008 changed TFMF's business model. The collapse of the mortgage market meant that fewer mortgage loans were made and almost none were being securitized. Thus, the company needed to replace its bread and butter product with a new kind of offering. The answer was entering the market for asset-backed securities; in particular, securities that were backed by hospital accounts receivables. Hospitals pay for the medical services provided to patients (e.g., doctors, nurses, medical supplies) at the time services are provided. The patients' payments are usually funded by healthcare insurers, however. The payments of these insurers are often made weeks or months later. In order to have sufficient operating cash to continue providing medical services, hospitals often "sell" their accounts receivable. For decades hospitals had sold their receivables to factors that provided immediate cash for the receivables and then took on the responsibility of collecting payment. The advantage to the hospitals was both immediate cash and the transfer of credit risk to the factors. The downside to this arrangement was the cost. Factoring fees could be in the 15-20 percent of the value of the receivables.[321] Also, the hospitals received 50 percent of the cash value in advance. The remainder was remitted to the hospitals upon the factors' receipt of the payment from the receivables.[322]

Securitization of the hospital's receivables represented a cost-effective alternative to factoring. The hospital could securitize 80-90 percent of its receivables and thus receive far more cash upon the transfer of the receivables. Also, the transaction would be off-balance sheet and thus did not affect the ability of the hospital to obtain further capital. There was, however, a downside to securitization. First, the hospital remained responsible for collecting its accounts receivable. Second, these securities, much like mortgage-backed securities, are subject to repayment risk. If a patient or an insurance company defaults, the cash streams cannot be as anticipated.

The risk associated with hospital receivables-based securities is different from the risks associated with mortgage-backed securities. The securities backed by mortgages have a real asset, the house, which serves as collateral. In the case of payments owed to the hospital there is no underlying real asset but only a contractual obligation of the patient to pay for the services rendered by the medical facility.

---

[321] Sandra Ferconio & Michael R. Lane, *Financing Maneuvers: Two Opportunities to Boost a Hospital's Working Capital,* HEALTHCARE FIN. MGMT., Oct. 1991, at 74, 76.

[322] *Id.* at 78.

Consequently, credit enhancement of hospital receivables typically involves not only the techniques described above for the jumbo loan-backed securities but also other methods of reducing default risk. The senior-junior structure, excess spread account, and over-collateralization are part of the design of TFMF's offerings. For asset-backed securities such as hospital receivables internal design techniques are supplanted with external sources of credit enhancement.

The dominant approach to external credit enhancement is insurance, broadly defined. Bond insurance provided by mono-line companies including Financial Guaranty Assurance Company and Capital Markets Assurance Corporation is one of the most common forms of credit enhancement. The insurers protect investors, up to a predefined limit, not only against default but also against fraud and bankruptcy. The underwriter provides an upfront and/or ongoing fee for the insurance. The coverage can apply to the entire issue or be reserved for specific investor classes. Often these insurance providers will not be the initial source of funds for credit support. Rather they provide a backup to other credit enhancement vehicles. Corporate guarantees can also reduce credit risk although they are subject to reevaluation as the credit rating of the guarantying corporation changes and thus have had limited application. A third source of external credit enhancement is a letter of credit in which a financial institution, under contract with the underwriter, is obligated to reimburse investors for losses. Because the guarantee is no better than the credit rating of the financial institution that provides the letter, this technique is used infrequently.

Assignment:

You recently took a position at TFMF. You have been asked to design the credit enhancement program for the firm's foray into securitization of hospital receivables. Specifically:

1. Document the pros and cons of the alterative internal and external credit enhancement techniques.
2. Propose a credit enhancement strategy for hospital receivable-backed securities.
3. Explain the rationale for this design vis-à-vis the credit enhancement strategy used by TFMF for its jumbo mortgage-backed securities.
4. What questions would you ask and what legal documents would you check in the case of mortgage-backed securities as compared to securities backed by healthcare receivables?

D. The Rating Agencies

Rating agencies have played a major role in securitization. Like appraisals, the rating of borrowers or SPV assets or securities can reduce the cost for investors of information and expert evaluation of the borrowers' credit risk. Consequently, rating agencies have substantial impact on the pricing of asset-backed securities and can lower the cost of capital for the SPVs. Five nationally recognized rating agencies operate in the United States: Standard & Poor's Ratings Services, a division of McGraw-Hill; Moody's Investors Service, Inc.; Fitch, Inc.; and, most recently, Dominion Bond Rating Service Limited, and in March 2005 A.M. Best Company, Inc. Their four highest rating categories are considered investment grade securities.

Initially, the SEC made limited use of rating in its regulation. Because rating reduces information costs and credit evaluation risks to investors, and thereby provides greater market liquidity, the SEC has increasingly used rating by "nationally recognized statistical rating organizations" or "NRSROs" to gauge the level of its regulatory requirements in an increasing number of instances. The SEC has used rating in Rules 134 and 436 under the 1933 Act, Rules 101 and 15c3-1 under the 1934 Act, and Rules 2a-7, 3a-7, and 10f-3 under the 1940 Act. The Board of Governors of the Federal Reserve has also resorted to rating in regulations. These regulations have provided rating agencies with a partial monopoly, similar to that of lawyers and accountants. The regulated entities had to resort to rating. Rating agencies are not numerous because it takes a long time to create a reputation as a "nationally recognized statistical organization." Thus, the rating agencies' monopoly power cannot be underestimated.

Rating agencies have substantial power to affect the pricing of asset-backed securities; they do not merely rate the securities that are presented to them. They can impose conditions on the issuers. The agencies can demand changes in the making of the securitized loans and the design of the securitization process. For example, rating agencies usually require that a mortgage SPV will be a single-purpose entity (whether a corporation or a trust) or that the debtor will be limited to a single purpose, that is, a debtor that holds only one significant asset. These requirements help limit the classes of creditors that may claim the assets of the SPVs, thus minimizing the potential for bankruptcy that might affect the holders of the securitized debt adversely.

Traditional rating involves one borrower and one type of loan, usually in terms that the borrower or similar borrowers have offered to lenders in the past. SPV portfolios involve numerous small borrowers with loans on different terms. In addition, the terms of the securities issued by the SPVs differ from the terms of the portfolio loans and (in collateralized mortgage obligations) the terms differ from the terms of other classes of debt securities held by the SPVs. Therefore, historical default experience takes a long time to acquire and is hard to build.

While bonds have been rated for generations, credit ratings of commercial loans were initiated by Standard & Poor's in July 1987. Ratings of securities backed by pools of corporate loans appeared in January 1988; the Market for such securities continues to expand, though it is yet unclear how large it will become. Rating for small corporations may be too expensive, especially for debtors who use ratings only for special financing that requires expertise. It is also unclear to what extent investors value the rating of securitized corporate loans. Nevertheless, information regarding debt of medium-size corporations has become more standardized and available. Statistical methods for valuation are also being developed.

Following the collapse of Enron, Congress and the SEC held hearings and devoted substantial effort to determining how the ratings agencies failed so badly. Enron's debt was rated investment grade until four days before its bankruptcy. Many institutional investors do not rely heavily on the ratings, distrusting their accuracy or timeliness.[323] The failure of securitized mortgage-backed securities in 2008 has raised more questions about the robustness of the rating process.

a. The Process of Rating[324]

Rating securitized corporate bonds or collateralized bond obligations ("CBOs") utilizes the credit analysis of corporate bonds. In small SPVs, for which actuarial analysis is less reliable, each obligor may be rated. The process of rating securitized small consumer loans does not involve rating each obligor; but the rating agency focuses in both cases on the cash flows as a basic element of the credit evaluation. The agency analyzes the expected cash flow of the SPV loans as compared to the promised cash flow under the SPV securities (pass-through and pay-through securities).

In rating securitized small loans, the agency examines the financial condition of the originator of the securitized loans, since its failure may result in claims for the loans by its creditors (depending on how the transfer of the loans is effected legally). Rather than evaluate each loan in the portfolio, the agency examines the originator's processes of credit approval, loan documentation, and collection, and its internal controls designed to enforce these processes. The rating agency examines the criteria used by the originators for selecting the loans in the SPV: the underwriting and delinquency criteria, other relevant risk factors, and previous pool selections from the same loan portfolio. The agency also examines the loan terms and the profile of the borrowers.

---

[323] *See* Credit Rating Agency Reform Act of 2006, Pub. L. No. 109-201, sec. 4(a), §15E, 120 Stat. 1327, 1329-37 (codified at 15 U.S.C. § 78*o*-7 (2006)). The SEC's implementation appears in rules 17 C.F.R. §§ 240.17g1-.17g1-6 (2008).

[324] 1 TAMAR FRANKEL, SECURITIZATION §§ 9.15-.16 (Ann Taylor Schwing ed., 2d ed. 2005).

Rating of small commercial loans posed difficulties for rating agencies because the agencies were less familiar with such loans. In addition, it is costly to evaluate these loans when no standardized profile of the borrowers exists, requiring each loan to be examined separately. A publication such as the Loan Pricing Corporation may help reduce the cost of rating such loans, but, in the short run, Institutions may be better evaluators of these loans.

Regardless of the nature of the SPV assets, rating agencies also examine relevant objective and subjective risk concentrations in the portfolios (e.g., industry, geographic, obligor concentration) and the record of loan delinquency and default, including recovery value, and impact of excessive or too slow prepayments by the borrowers. A rating agency also evaluates the servicer of the loans, its service capability, and its capacity to make payments to investors in advance of the anticipated cash flow. In addition, the agency evaluates the value of the collateral and any credit enhancement. This review includes the methods of valuation of the collateral and valuation assumption, the value and certainty of excess cash flow or over-collateralization provided by the SPV, such as excess reinvestment income for investments yielding rates higher than those assumed, discounting at highest rate when determining note value, interest income from premium collateral, and recapture of discount if discount collateral pays before maturity. If the SPV portfolio is partially or fully insured, the rating agency evaluates the insurer or other providers of credit enhancement.

In contrast to appraisals, rating is a continuous rather than one-time evaluation in most cases. The agencies grade and re-grade the securities periodically. The rating focuses on several aspects of risk in a transaction in addition to the collateral. However, although rating reflects a measure of the risks associated with rated securities, ratings do not take into account all variables that investors face. For example, when evaluating mortgage-backed securities, the rating addresses the likelihood that mortgage-backed securities holders will receive payments to which they are entitled, including distributions of all principal. In grading residential mortgage-backed and asset-backed securities issued by SPVs, rating agencies do not evaluate the credit risk of the specific or individual loans that constitute the SPVs' portfolio; rather they evaluate the reliability of the originators of the loans as prudent lenders and the servicers. With commercial mortgage-backed securities, the rating takes into consideration the credit quality of the SPV, structural and legal aspects associated with the certificates, and the extent to which the payment stream from the SPV is adequate to make payments required under the certificates.

Ratings on all mortgage-backed securities do not, however, constitute a statement regarding the likelihood or frequency of prepayments (whether voluntary or involuntary) on the related mortgage loans. With an SPV comprised of residential mortgage loans, the loans will prepay at a rate that is affected by prevailing interest rates. For instance, if a loan is secured by a mortgage on a residence at a high interest rate, a rational borrower will refinance the loan when rates fall, if the property value has not declined significantly. Assumptions about such prepayments will be the primary factor in pricing an offering of residential mortgage-backed securities. Unlike residential mortgage loans, commercial mortgage loans may contain prohibitions on prepayments or yield maintenance charges or prepayment premiums in connection with prepayments. Investors in commercial mortgage-backed securities must consider these features when they determine the prepayment characteristics of the underlying pool of loans to calculate the anticipated yield to final payment on the securities. In addition, a rating does not address the likelihood or frequency of voluntary or mandatory prepayments of mortgage loans, payments of any prepayment premiums or yield maintenance charges or the corresponding effect on yield to investors. For example, if the monthly interest on an interest-only certificate is based on a fixed interest rate plus a notional principal amount equal to the aggregate outstanding principal of the SPV, the notional amount will be reduced as the loans are prepaid.

Further, the rating of SPV certificates will take into account the timing or magnitude of the reduction of the notional amount. It will only address the obligation to pay interest on the notional amount, as reduced from time to time. Taking the extreme case, if the entire mortgage SPV were to prepay in the first month, so that holders of interest-only certificates receive only a single month's interest and thus suffer a near complete loss of their investment, all amounts "due" to such holders will nevertheless have been paid, consistent with an investment grade rating on such certificates. Therefore, investors must separately assess the characteristics of a mortgage SPV and the manner in which proceeds and losses are allocated among various classes of certificates to determine the expected yield for a particular class of securities. While sophisticated investors understand the process of rating of asset-backed securities, small investors often do not.

Examining Legal Issues.[325] Rating agencies also perform a legal analysis. They evaluate the risk that the borrower's or transferor's bankruptcy could impair payments on the securities and the risk that the SPV could become insolvent. As to the first risk, the agencies require that, for entities subject to the Uniform Commercial Code, the transfer of the loans be a sale rather than a pledge of the loans as collateral. If the transfer is a pledge, the automatic stay provision of section 362 of the Bankruptcy Code could impair the rights of the security holders, and a court may allow the trustee in bankruptcy to substitute other financial assets for the collateral under section 363 of the Code.

To assure that the transaction is a true sale of the loans (and not a secured lending, which would put the SPV and its investors in a weaker position vis-à-vis the creditors of the transferor if the transferor became bankrupt), and to ensure that in the

[325] 1 TAMAR FRANKEL, SECURITIZATION § 9.17 (Ann Taylor Schwing ed., 2d ed. 2005).

case of the transferor's bankruptcy the SPV will not be consolidated with the transferor, rating agencies usually requires an opinion from the transferor's counsel stating that (i) the transfer of the loans to the SPV is sufficient to remove the loans from the seller's estate for the purpose of section 541 of the Bankruptcy Code; (ii) section 362 of the Code would not apply to the loans if the transferor becomes bankrupt; (iii) collection of payments from the borrowers under the loans is not commingled with the transferor's account; (iv) recourse back to the transferor for defaulted loans is not excessive relative to the historical losses and other risk factors, and (v) transfer of the loans is accounted as a sale in the transferor's books. In addition to the opinion, the agency reviews the economic incentives and intent of the transaction to determine whether they comport with the classification of the transaction as a sale.

If the SPV that issues the securities is a subsidiary of another corporation, the assets of the subsidiary might be consolidated with those of the bankrupt parent, and the loans might be viewed as assets of the parent. Therefore, rating agencies generally require an unqualified "nonconsolidation opinion" by the parent's counsel. Counsel's opinion must state that the attorney knows of no theory of law under which the loans would be made available to the bankrupt transferor or its creditors or under which the transferor's bankruptcy would impair the timely flow of the proceeds of the loans to the security holders. The agency attempts to establish that the subsidiaries have a separate corporate existence, with independent officers and directors and separate books and records.

The "true sale/nonconsolidation opinion" letters often contain a recharacterization portion opinion dealing with whether the bankruptcy court could recharacterize a loan as an equity investment. In such a case the security holders will be placed in the position of shareholders rather than secured lenders. Why do the parties insert such a provision?

Note that in a consolidation case, the parties-in-interest try to view the SPVs as consolidated with the bankrupt. But if the SPV security holders are properly secured in the *underlying assets* held by the SPV, then even if the transferor and the SPV were consolidated the SPV security holders would still have priority over all the parties-in-interest.

Since commingling of proceeds of receivables with the funds of the transferor may eliminate perfection of the buyer's rights as a secured creditor (and render the SPV an unsecured creditor of the transferor with respect to funds in the commingled account on the date of the transferor's bankruptcy), the rating agency reviews the steps taken to avoid this result. For example, most issues are structured so that the funds on receivables are collected directly by the SPV, or are collected by a bank acting as agent for both the seller and the SPV, or are commingled with the seller's general funds for only 48 hours.

The parent of the SPV may be required to include in the prospectus accompanying the securities (i) a statement that the parent intends to keep the issuing subsidiary separate, (ii) a nonconsolidation opinion, (iii) a statement that the transfer is a true sale, and (iv) a statement that the parent and the SPV have no intent to file a petition that the SPV is bankrupt so long as the SPV is solvent. SPVs that are eligible to become debtors under the Bankruptcy Code must satisfy "special purpose bankruptcy remote" criteria: (i) the SPVs' business must be restricted to the purchase of financial assets and the issuance of rated debt securities; and (ii) the SPV may not incur any debt (other than debt that is rated) at the same level as the rated debt securities, unless the additional debt is fully subordinated to the rated securities. The subordinated debt must be issued with no recourse, other than with respect to the proceeds of the SPV portfolio in excess of the proceeds necessary to pay the rated securities. To the extent that the excess proceeds are insufficient to pay the subordinated debt, there must be no claim against the SPV.

The transfer of receivables by sellers of financial assets that are not subject to the Bankruptcy Code (e.g., banks, thrifts), may not meet the "true sale" or "special purpose, bankruptcy-remote criteria." However, because of assurances of the FDIC, rating agency would agree to rate the issues that are only pledges as opposed to sales. In these cases, the rating agencies may require a legal opinion that the security holders' rights with respect to the receivables held by the SPVs and proceeds thereon would be valid, binding, and enforceable, notwithstanding the bankruptcy of the transferor of the receivables. In addition, the rating agencies would seek a legal opinion that the SPV or the security holders have a perfected security interest in the receivables held by the SPVs. The security interest may be held by an indenture trustee for the benefit of the security holders.

b. The Problem of Misleading Ratings [326]

The interests of rating agencies may conflict in part with those of investors because issuers of securities, interested in higher ratings, pay the agencies, not the investors. In addition, rating agencies have few competitors because entry into the rating business requires a long-term investment in developing a national reputation. This investment, however, gives the agencies an incentive to incur what economists call "bonding costs": substantial self-limitation to maintain their reputation. If the public doubts the impartiality, diligence, or expertise of rating agencies, their business could evaporate. Consequently, agencies take care to be impartial and especially to be correct in their rating, even though they are paid by the issuers. Nonetheless, as the impact of these agencies on the asset-backed securities Markets increases, they should be monitored to determine whether market pressures are sufficient to ensure their accountability or whether it is desirable to regulate them by law. (In 2009,

[326] 1 TAMAR FRANKEL, SECURITIZATION § 9.19 (Ann Taylor Schwing ed., 2d ed. 2005).

concerns about conflicts of interest between the rating agencies and the issuers led the SEC to issue new regulations to minimize conflicts.)

When a rating agency published a faulty description of certain bonds that had been prepared negligently, the Second Circuit held in 1989 under New York and Florida law that the agency was not liable for contract or most tort damages to subscribing investors who had relied on the description. These subscribers could sue only if they could show that the agency intended to defraud them. The court noted that liability in negligence would expose the agency to numerous claims and that the publication contained express disclaimers against any guarantee of accuracy or completeness. Further, since the publications consisted of summaries, the subscribers could not expect all the details. In addition, the details were publicly available, and the subscribers could have examined the full original documents. Therefore, the risk of failing to verify the accuracy of the summaries should be borne by the investors.

It is unclear whether investors in rated securities should also be limited to claims in fraud. Arguably, if an agency (1) prepared the rating negligently, in violation of its own standards (or industry standards), (2) the investors knew of the standards and relied on them to their detriment, (3) if the agency acted in clear conflict of interest without disclosing the conflict publicly, for example, if it received pay after it established a rating and upgraded the rating as a result of the pay, and (4) if the subscribers-investors suffered losses as a result of the negligent rating, then perhaps the investors should have a claim against the agency. Unlike mere errors in published summaries, claims such as these may be less numerous because they are hard to prove or because the facts rarely occur. The basis for the ratings is not necessarily readily verifiable by the investors. Rating agencies are concerned to preserve their most important asset, that is, their reputation. They can be expected to take great pains to avoid or terminate claims against them. To date, reported claims against the agencies have been few; and fewer have been successful.

Chapter 7: The Securities and Obligations That SPVs Issue

Because SPVs are Institutional intermediaries, they both invest in financial assets and also issue financial assets. This Chapter deals with the kind of financial assets that SPVs issue. The variety of offerings is described as is an overview of the process for setting the price of the securities. The role of the credit rating agencies and appraisers in providing information providers to investors is then explained with case studies providing real world context. The chapter concludes with a description of financial derivatives.

To meet the financial obligations that the SPV issues, it draws on the financial assets that the SPV owns. Therefore, to a certain extent the issued obligations may depend on the nature of the assets that the SPV would draw upon to pay for its obligations. For example, if the SPV holds short-term financial assets, such as receivables, its Originator will not acquire for the SPV's obligations that are very long-term, unless the Originator provides investors with assurance that the long-term obligations will be sufficient to pay for the short-term SPV obligations. Otherwise investors would be reluctant to buy the SPV's obligations or will demand very high return for such obligations. In addition, to reduce the investors' risks and thereby reduce the return they would demand, SPVs could offer credit enhancement for the entire SPVs' portfolios or credit enhancement directly related to the securities that the investors hold, such as insurance appended to the securities or a letter of credit backing a security.

In addition, the law regulates SPVs with respect to the securities it issues. The regulation does not require the SPV to reduce the risk or increase the return of, or change the proposed terms of, the securities. The law does, however, require the SPV to provide extensive disclosure to the investors, and the disclosure is backed by sanctions in case of misinformation. Thus, securities offered to the public must be registered with the SEC and the staff of the SEC, representing the investors, may demand further clarifications of the information in the disclosure documents.

For sophisticated investors it is sufficient for the SPV to offer the investors the information and send a copy of that information to the SEC. It is assumed that instead of the SEC staff, the sophisticated investors can inquire sufficiently for additional information and clarifications. We start with the various kinds of securities that SPVs issue. The list is far from exhaustive. In fact, the design of the securities is in the hands of the promoters of the securitization; the government only requires disclosure of the design.

A. The obligations issued by SPVs

The securities issued by SPVs that hold a large number of small illiquid loans pose a variety of risks for investors. First, SPV assets have maturities that do not accommodate investors. For example, the maturities of credit card receivables are too short for some investors, such as pension funds. Second, SPV assets present uncertain dates on which they mature-must be paid. Since by law consumer loans (e.g., mortgages and car loans) can be fully prepaid without penalty, investors may receive their money back when they least desire it, that is, when interest rates fall. Third, SPVs can be subject to double taxation. If SPVs are conduits for investment and are taxed on the SPV level, investors will be taxed twice, when the SPV receives income and when it distributes the income to investors. Such securities are undesirable, as compared to direct investments in the SPV assets, or as compared to securities of SPVs that are treated as conduits for tax purposes. Fourth, insolvency of the seller of loans to the SPVs may threaten the rights of the SPV and its security holders to the loan portfolio. The SPV's "corporate veil may be pierced" or the ownership or interest of the SPV in the portfolio loans may be flawed. Fraudulent transfer laws may apply. Fifth, SPV Originators and sellers of loans have their own motivations for engaging in securitization. These motivations may affect the financial structure of the SPVs and the securities they issue and conflict with interests of investors. Sixth, information about the credit risk of SPV portfolios is costly to obtain and evaluate. Seventh, SPVs have been used to securitize bonds of low quality ("junk bonds"). By transferring to SPVs a much higher amount of junk bonds, the holders of the bonds can obtain a higher rating for SPV securities and liquidate part of their junk bond holdings without selling the bonds at a loss. SPV designs are aimed at reducing drawbacks for investors and satisfying the desires of loan sellers and SPV Originators. A number of these drawbacks and desires have been addressed by legislation and regulation, either generally or with respect to particular types of preferred loans, such as mortgages.

B. The Variety of SPV Obligations

SPVs raise funds by issuing obligations of various kinds. The following are some of the type of obligations that the SPVs issue.

a. Pass-throughs[327]

The first type of securities that were issued by SPVs were the so-called "pass-throughs." If an SPV issues only pass-through securities, the buyers of the securities receive (pro rata) all the benefits and take (pro rata) all the risks from the SPV's loan portfolio. The SPV itself exposes these security holders only to the risk of mismanagement, since the SPV's assets and liabilities are matched and logically the

---

[327] 1 TAMAR FRANKEL, SECURITIZATION § 2.6.1 (Ann Taylor Schwing ed., 2d ed. 2005).

SPV cannot fail. An SPV that issues pass-throughs usually purchases loans outright; the seller of the loans receives the price and exits the scene, although the seller may continue to service the loans. For the buyers, pass-throughs pose a disadvantage. The buyers may wish to receive their money on terms and at times that differ from those of the borrowers. Even if the pass-throughs are traded in the markets, they are at a disadvantage because it is unclear when they will be paid and how much they will pay. Under these conditions the pricing of such securities is difficult and uncertain.

b. Pay-throughs[328]

A second type of SPV securities is "pay-throughs." Pay-throughs are bond-like obligations, but not actually bonds. They are collateralized solely by the assets of the SPV. Pay-throughs enable banks to make an outright sale of loans and reduce their assets and capital requirements. Loans are sold to the SPV, and the lending bank disappears from the picture—the sale is complete.

Pay-throughs are designed to protect the SPV's structural financial integrity and simultaneously provide the desirable terms for investors. The SPV issues bonds in terms acceptable to investors and manipulates the cash flow from the loan portfolio to produce different streams of payments. For example, the SPV separates principal and interest payments from loans and issues a class of bonds that promises only periodic payments of principal and another that entitles holders only to periodic payments of interest. Each type of security has a different maturity and payment schedule. The class of bonds paying "interest only" bears a lower market risk from prepayment of principal. That risk is shifted to "principal-only" bonds. But for principal-only bonds, the prepayment risk is lower because their maturity is longer, and borrowers' prepayments are distributed over a longer period of time. Pay-throughs may be issued in classes of bonds with different maturities and provide that all prepayments of principal will be first applied to the short-term bonds, then to the next class, and so on. This arrangement redistributes the market risk among the various classes of bonds.

Arguably, SPVs that issue bonds may be more prone to failure than SPVs that issue pass-throughs because SPVs with bond obligations may miscalculate their cash flow from the loans. But by and large, pay-throughs have worked well; SPV managers have generally succeeded in manipulating cash flows from loans with one set of terms to match liabilities with another set of terms. In fact, the risk from miscalculation is borne by the various classes of security holders rather than the SPVs. If the assumptions on which the cash flow manipulations are based prove wrong, the bondholders of a particular class bear the loss, and other classes gain, since the structure distributes market and prepayment risks among the different

[328] 1 TAMAR FRANKEL, SECURITIZATION § 2.6.3 (Ann Taylor Schwing ed., 2d ed. 2005).

classes of bonds. The SPV remains unaffected, because the aggregate payments on all classes are always equal to the aggregate cash flow from its loan portfolio.

c. Callable Trust Obligations

These obligations were designed by GNMA II. They "allow[ed] investors the flexibility of [redemption or of "calling"] a security prior to its maturity date under certain conditions. This feature enabled investors to "hedge against fluctuating rate environments."[329]

d. Stripped Securities

SPVs may hold mortgage-backed securities issued by Government agencies as collateral and issue CMOs that "strip" the cash flow from the collateral. The CMOs promise the periodic payments of the principal to one class of securities and the periodic payments of the interest to another class. Some stripped CMOs representing the principal only (POs) or interest only (IOs) are very risky. Therefore, SPVs that issue such securities must be excepted or exempted from the 1940 Act. The SEC noted the existence of stripped securities in its proposal to Rule 3a-7, discussed below, and did not exclude them in its discussion of the final Rule.

GNMA II also issued a new investment vehicle -- SMBS. This obligations "are custom-designed securities that redirect MBS cash flows to meet investors' specific income needs around interest and principal payments."[330]

e. Commercial Paper[331]

SPVs issue commercial paper collateralized by SPV portfolio loans. SPVs are also used to hold collateral for commercial paper obligations of third-party issuers that pledge the collateral and segregate it in the SPV. Commercial paper has the advantage for the issuer of lower cost as compared to long-term obligations. Yet, there is a good chance that a percentage of the commercial paper holders will roll over their investments. In addition, although commercial paper promises fixed amounts, it reduces the mismatch between liabilities and assets that poses a risk to the SPV's structure.

---

[329] GINNIE MAE, ANNUAL REPORT 2007, at 3-4..

[330] *Id.* at 4.

[331] 1 TAMAR FRANKEL, SECURITIZATION § 2.6.4 (Ann Taylor Schwing ed., 2d ed. 2005).

f. Preferred Stock[332]

SPVs can issue preferred stock for corporate investors so that these investors can take the advantage of excluding 70 to 80 percent of the dividends from taxation. These tax benefits reduce the dividend rate on the preferred stock and thereby reduce the funding costs.

g. Bonds[333]

A second prototype of SPV securities is bonds. The objective of this type of obligation is to remedy some of the disadvantages of pass-throughs. The cash flows generated by the loans in the SPV usually do not suit investors' needs. For example, mortgages produce a constant flow of monthly payments, but Institutional investors prefer quarterly or semiannual payments. The bond prototype can provide investors with terms preferable to them, such as fixed payments and amounts, even as the SPV holds loans on different terms.

Further, structurally, bonds carry lower risk than equity. While pass-throughs are considered equity, because there are no other classes of securities that the SPVs issue that provide a back-up to the pass-through, bonds can be collateralized by a portfolio of loans (or by pass-throughs, loan-backed securities) that the SPV holds or by recourse obligations, insurance or guarantees, or a combination of such risk-reducing instruments. In the early bond versions, the initial transferor (usually a bank) transferred unsecured loans to the SPV in an amount exceeding the face amount of the bonds. If the value of the loans depreciated, the initial transferor undertook to transfer additional collateral to the SPV periodically. After the bonds were paid off, the transferor recouped the remaining collateral. Nonbank lenders-sellers still use such a bond structure.

The collateral supporting bonds can be increased by setting aside portions of payments from the portfolio loans as additional collateral. For example, during a first designated period, say 18 months, investors receive interest payments only. Payments of principal and prepayments on the loans are added to the collateral. These amounts cover future credit risks.

Bonds have disadvantages. They render the structure of the SPV more risky for the investors. After all, if the obligations of the SPVs do not match their liabilities, for example, if the assets of the SPVs are long-term and their liabilities are short-term, the SPVs can fail. However, the risk of the faulty assets will then be divided among the investors in the case of failure, and that risk can be distributed among the investors and be accompanied by suitable compensation, that is, a higher rate of

---

[332] 1 TAMAR FRANKEL, SECURITIZATION § 2.6.5 (Ann Taylor Schwing ed., 2d ed. 2005).

[333] 1 TAMAR FRANKEL, SECURITIZATION § 2.6.2 (Ann Taylor Schwing ed., 2d ed. 2005).

return. In the last analysis, the difference may depend on timing. When the SPV issues bonds and fails, the investors will bear the losses equally or in accordance with their security interests, if any. However, in bankruptcy proceedings, the investors' rights will change. In contrast, when the chances of the SPV's failure are very low, the pre-established relative rights of the investors are more likely to survive. In short, the bond structure negates the benefits of pass-throughs. In addition, for banks, regulation discourages the use of bonds mainly because bank regulators do not recognize the transfer of the loans to the SPV as a sale of assets and a corresponding increase of bank capital. When loans are put up merely as collateral, and the bank retains some credit risk, the Comptroller views the transaction as "financing" or "borrowing" by the bank. This view then introduces limits on the amount and terms that the bank can raise by using such obligations. The main point is that if the bank, in one fashion or another, remains holding the loans or remains responsible for some amount of their default, the regulators may demand backup for these obligations. The backup in turn reduces the amount that the bank can lend and the profits that it might declare to its investors, which in turn might raise the cost of the banks' capital and its profitability.

"Builder bonds" are bonds that help finance builders.[334] These bonds are issued in series by wholly owned subsidiaries of home builders or thrifts. The proceeds of the bonds are used to purchase mortgages from mortgage originators (usually small thrifts), or mortgage collateral, or notes secured by a mortgage collateral. The SPVs may issue CMOs. Portfolios held by the SPVs are fixed when the series are issued and cannot be changed by the SPVs' managers. The proceeds of the mortgage collateral are used to service each series.

SPVs can also issue floating rate bonds. The interest rate on these bonds changes periodically in accordance with a predetermined formula, such as a fixed percentage above prime rate.[335]

Discussion Topic

What are the pros and cons of each of these forms of securities?

B. Setting the Price

In terms of dollars, the largest segment of the securitization Market involves whole mortgage loans traded among Institutions and Government agencies for the purpose of securitizing. Insurance companies and pension funds also buy whole mortgages for their portfolios.

---

334 1 TAMAR FRANKEL, SECURITIZATION § 11.25 (Ann Taylor Schwing ed., 2d ed. 2005).

335 1 TAMAR FRANKEL, SECURITIZATION § 11.26 (Ann Taylor Schwing ed., 2d ed. 2005).

The pricing of SPV loans can follow an agreed upon model. In one sample loan purchase agreement, the price is determined by pricing standards in the purchaser's "Seller's Manual." The purchaser delivers a confirmation to the seller with the terms, including the price. Another loan purchase agreement references the buyer's "Seller's Guide," and also notes that the price is determined by reference to "the applicable Rate Sheet issued by Buyer to Seller."[336]

The valuation of a large number of small loans owed by individuals is too complex for the public investors to evaluate. Arguably, a group of loans poses lower risk to the buyer than single loans because the risk is diversified. The models differ however.[337] In addition, mortgage loans are supposed to be less risky because people are likely to pay their loans rather than lose their homes. The price is determined by the sponsor or Originator with the help of an expert.

The FDIC generally sells bulk loans from failed institutions "in pools through sealed bid sale or English outcry auction."[338] The FDIC allows potential purchasers to review the loan files after executing a confidentiality agreement.[339] Through its Asset Sales program, the Small Business Administration sells loans and other assets through "[p]ublic auction, sealed bid, sealed bidders auction, listing with brokers or dealers, and private negotiation."[340] The SBA advertises sales through sources including newspapers and trade and industry journals, and bulk loan sale information is placed on the SBA website and advertised through other sources including the *Wall Street Journal* and other newspapers.[341]

Two parties that are critical to setting appropriate prices are the rating agencies and the appraisers. The rating agencies evaluate the probability that the borrower will repay the loan in full and on time. Appraisers certify the value of the underlying asset that serves as collateral for the loan.

---

[336] United Pan Am. Financial Corp., *Continuing Master Loan Repurchase Agreement* 3 (Aug. 21, 1996), http://www.secinfo.com/dsBqn.6gv.7.htm#1stPage (last visited Sept. 16, 2009).

[337] Xudong An et al., *Value Creation Through Securitization: Evidence from the CMBS Market* (Feb 2008) (abstract), http://ssrn.com/abstract=1095645 (last visited Sept. 15, 2009) ("Despite recent volatility and constraints in secondary market funding, analysts have ascribed substantial value creation to the securitization of commercial mortgages," estimated at 11 basis point reduced mortgage interest rates); Andreas A. Jobst *Tranche Pricing in Subordinated Loan Securitization,* J. STRUCTURED FIN., Summer 2005., at 64.

[338] Mortgage Banking Solutions, *Bulk Loan Sales,* http://www.mortgagebankingsolutions.com/bulk_loan_sales.html (last visited Sept. 16, 2009).

[339] *Id.*

[340] Small Business Administration, *What Is Sold,* http://www.pueblo.gsa.gov/cic_text/fed_prog/fedsales/sba.htm (last visited Sept. 16, 2009).

[341] *Id.*

C. Case Study and Simulation: Regulating the Credit Rating Agencies

Those trying to explain the subprime meltdown often point to a failure of the credit rating agencies (CRAs). The CRAs evaluate for investors the quality of debt and structured finance offerings. Moody's Corporation, the first credit rating agency in the world, began rating bonds in the U.S. in 1909. Since that time Moody's and other CRAs have provided ratings on most government and private debt offerings and more recently on asset backed securities. The ratings are intended to provide potential investors with "forward-looking opinions that seek to measure relative credit loss"; i.e., forecast the likelihood of default on a bond and the estimated severity of loss in the event of that bond's default.[342] Investors, in turn, use the ratings to assess the risk and return of alternative investments. In the language of economics, ratings help reduce the information asymmetry between borrowers, issuers and investors. Less uncertainty increases liquidity and reduces the costs of borrowing money. Ratings are also used in private contracts where a decline in rating can trigger demand for increased collateral or even repayment of an outstanding loan.

The CRAs establish ratings by gathering a broad array of public and private information, applying analytical models to the relevant data, and reaching conclusions about the level of risks posed by the offered securities. As Moody's CEO wrote in his 2007 letter to the shareholders: "The Company's long-term success depends critically on the confidence of our stakeholders – debt issuers, the investment community, employees, government authorities and shareholders – in Moody's ethics, objectivity and credit judgments."[343] Understanding credit ratings also requires knowledge of what credit ratings are not: "Credit Ratings do not constitute investment or financial advice, and Credit Ratings are not recommendations to purchase, sell, or hold particular securities. Credit Ratings do not comment on the suitability of an investment for any particular investor."[344] Moreover, the CRAs acknowledge that their ratings are based on the best available information but that their rating analysts do not necessarily perform due diligence to assure the accuracy of the information they use.

---

342 MOODY'S INVESTORS SERVICE, CODE OF PROFESSIONAL CONDUCT 2 (2008), http://www.moodys.com/cust/content/Content.ashx?source=StaticContent/Free%20Pages/Regulatory%20Affairs/Documents/professional_conduct.pdf (last visited Sept. 16, 2009).

343 MOODY'S CORP., ANNUAL REPORT 2007, at 2, http://files.shareholder.com/downloads/MOOD/727105136x0x181773/F099885F-F1B2-4861-A5A0-4BA8FCF109BB/2007_Annual_Report.pdf (last visited Sept. 16, 2009)..

344 MOODY'S INVESTORS SERVICE, CODE OF PROFESSIONAL CONDUCT 6 (2008), http://www.moodys.com/cust/content/Content.ashx?source=StaticContent/Free%20Pages/Regulatory%20Affairs/Documents/professional_conduct.pdf (last visited Sept. 16, 2009).

Ratings are used by all issuers of debt instruments. Bond issuers use ratings to both confirm their internal risk assessments and communicate the grade of the investment they are selling to investors. The CRA may also help the issuer design the offering to maximize the attractiveness of the issue for investors. These ancillary services have become more important with the growth of securitization and structured finance. Investment banks and broker-dealers use the ratings for the "buy" and "sell" sides of their businesses. The ratings enable the sell side to communicate effectively with investors about the risk of a particular offering. The CRA ratings are used by the buy-side analysts to confirm internal assessments of portfolio risk. Ratings have historically provided peace of mind to investors; and an understanding of risk without the work that it requires.

Rating is also used by financial regulators. Regulators have relied on ratings since the 1970s to determine the Net Capital Rule which regulates the capital of brokers.[345] To assure the accuracy and truthfulness of ratings the government established certain CRAs as Nationally Recognized Statistical Rating Organizations (NRSROs) based on a national reputation for credible evaluations. Attaining the NRSRO designation is based on organizational structure, financial resources, size and quality of staff, independence from those being rated, and rating methodologies and procedures. NRSRO ratings are also used in the regulation of "money market funds." Rule 2a-7 under the Investment Company Act of 1940 limits the designation "money market funds" to short-term obligations that receive the highest two ratings from NRSROs.[346]

There were three major NRSROs at the end of 2007[347] – Moody's Investor Services, Standard and Poor's (S&P) and Fitch. Together these firms account for 95 percent of all NRSRO revenues in the U.S. Moody's and S&P share 80 percent of the market.[348] Moody's "invented" the rating industry in the early 1900s.[349] By 2007, the

[345] 17 C.F.R. § 240.15c3-1 (2007).

[346] *See* 17 C.F.R. § 270.2a-7(b)(2) (2007) (limiting designation to funds meeting portfolio quality requirement); *id.* § 270.2a-7(c)(3) (portfolio quality requirement, limiting portfolio to "Eligible Securities"); *id.* § 270.2a-7(a)(10)(i), (ii) (generally defining "Eligible Security" as security rated in one of two highest rating categories by NRSRO or unrated security of comparable quality).

[347] Four additional credit rating agencies, A.M. Best Co, Inc., DBRS Ltd., Japan Credit Rating A, Ltd., and Rating and Investment Information, Inc., have been designated as NRSROs; however, their market share is very small. *See* Press Release, U.S. Sec. & Exch. Comm'n, *Seven Credit Rating Agencies Register with SEC as Nationally Recognized Statistical Rating Organizations* (Sept. 24, 2007), http://www.sec.gov/news/press/2007/2007-199.htm(last visited Sept. 16, 2009) (listing agencies registered with SEC as NRSROs).

[348] Alex J. Pollock, *End the Government-Sponsored Cartel in Credit Ratings,* Jan. 2005, at 1 (American Enterprise Institute for Public Policy Research) (citing Alec Klein, *Borrowers Find System Open to Conflicts, Manipulation,* WASH. POST, Nov. 22, 2004, at A1).

company provided ratings for 29,000 public finance issuers, 12,000 corporate issuers and 96,000 asset-backed securities offerings. Moody's revenues in 2007 were $2.26 billion and its net income was $701 million.[350] Its ratings and associated services "help investors analyze the credit risks associated with fixed-income securities. Such independent credit ratings and research also contribute to efficiencies in fixed-income markets and other obligations . . . by providing credible and independent assessments of credit risk."[351] The company's basic principles in establishing ratings are to emphasize quantitative and qualitative factors as well as a long-term focus on the risks of "receiving full and timely repayment of principal and interest . . . and how [that risk compares] with that of all other debt obligations[.]"[352]

S&P's homepage begins with the following words: "Every day investors and financial professionals the world over look to one firm for financial market intelligence that is authoritative, objective and credible. Standard and Poor's credit ratings, indices, investment research and data provide financial decision-makers with the information and opinions they need to feel confident about their decisions."[353] S&P also dates back to the beginning of the 20th century when Standard Statistics and Poor's Publishing began providing investors with financial information about U.S. corporations. The two companies merged in 1941 and subsequently were acquired by McGraw-Hill in 1966.[354] Evidence of S&P's importance to the financial community includes: "Over $1.7 trillion in investment assets is directly tied to S&P indexes and more than $4.85 trillion is benchmarked to S&P indices – more than all other index providers combined. The total amount of outstanding debt rated by S&P globally is approximately US$32 trillion, in 100 countries. In 2008 alone, Standard

[349] Moody's Investors Service, *Moody's History,* http://www.moodys.com/moodys/cust/AboutMoodys/AboutMoodys.aspx?topic=history (last visited Sept. 16, 2009).

[350] MOODY'S CORP., ANNUAL REPORT 2007, at 67, http://files.shareholder.com/downloads/MOOD/727105136x0x181773/F099885F-F1B2-4861-A5A0-4BA48FCF109BB/2007_Annual_Report.pdf (last visited Sept. 16, 2009)..

[351] Moody's Investors Service, *Introduction to Moody's,* http://www.moodys.com/moodys/cust/AboutMoodys/AboutMoodys.aspx?topic=intro (last visited Sept. 16, 2009).

[352] Moody's Investors Service, *Rating Approach,* http://www.moodys.com/moodys/cust/aboutmoodys/aboutmoodys.aspx?topic=rapproach (last visited Sept. 16, 2009).

[353] Standard & Poor's, http://www2.standardandpoors.com/portal/site/sp/en/us/page.home/home/0,0,0,0,0,0,0,0,0,0,0,0,0,0,0,0.html (last visited Sept. 16, 2009).

[354] Standard & Poor's, *Company History,* http://www2.standardandpoors.com/portal/site/sp/en/us/page.topic/aboutsp_ch/4,2,2,0,0,0,0,0,0,0,0,0,0,0,0,0.html?lid=us_topnav_comphistory (last visited Sept. 16, 2009).

& Poor's Ratings Services published more than 1,150,000 ratings, including new and revised ratings."[355]

Fitch Ratings dates back to the early 1900s as well. John Knowles Fitch, the company's founder, introduced the rating scale "AAA" to "D" which has been broadly adopted.[356] Today, "Fitch Ratings is a global rating agency committed to providing the world's credit markets with independent and prospective credit opinions, research, and data."[357] The CEO's message on Fitch's website highlights why his company's ratings are used: "Issuers choose Fitch Ratings because our independent research and ratings heighten investor awareness, raise the liquidity of the issuer's securities and reduce the cost of funds."[358] Fitch differentiates itself from the other rating agencies by offering a prospective orientation. "The firm consistently demonstrates leadership by developing innovative approaches to rating new and highly complex securities, as well as through its market-leading product launches."[359] The company emphasizes its leadership in creating effective rating criteria for structured finance. Also, "Fitch was the first agency to offer surveillance for every Fitch-rated transaction in the [structured finance] market."[360]

The process for ratings varies somewhat across the firms; however, the SEC's description in its 2003 investigation of the industry is representative. The ratings activities are segmented by industry and type of instrument. "At the core of the rating process is the rating committee. Rating committees are generally formed *ad hoc* to initiate, withdraw, or change a rating. They typically are composed of a lead credit analyst, managing directors or other area supervisors, and junior analytical staff. Rating decisions are made upon a simple majority vote of the committee and are, at their most basic level, an opinion regarding the likelihood the issuer will repay its

---

[355] Standard & Poor's, *About S&P*, http://www2.standardandpoors.com/portal/site/sp/en/us/page.topic/aboutsp_overview/4,1,1,0,0,0,0,0,0,0,0,0,0,0,0,0.html (last visited Sept. 16, 2009).

[356] FitchRatings, *The History of Fitch Ratings*, http://www.fitchratings.com/jsp/corporate/AboutFitch.faces?context=1&detail=3 (last visited Sept. 16, 2008).

[357] FitchRatings, *Overview*, http://www.fitchratings.com/jsp/corporate/AboutFitch.faces?context=1&detail=1 (last visited Sept. 16, 2009).

[358] FitchRatings, *A Message from the President and CEO*, http://www.fitchratings.com.tw/en/about/ceo_message.html (last visited Sept. 16, 2009).

[359] FitchRatings, *Culture & Values*, http://www.fitchgraduates.com/culture.html (last visited Sept. 16, 2009).

[360] FitchRatings, *Structured Finance*, http://www.fitchgraduates.com/sfin.html (last visited Sept. 16, 2009).

financial obligation."[361] The rating recommendations presented to the committee are based on detailed modeling of public information (e.g., filings, news reports, industry information, market trends) and private data (e.g., credit agreements, private placement memoranda, off-balance sheet liabilities, and internal projections).[362] The analytical techniques include linear regression and ordered probit models.[363] In 2006 Moody's introduced a new credit rating prediction model that "has better in-and out-of-sample performance by every measure considered. It converts individual credit metrics to implied ratings, takes an appropriate weighted average of them, and then apples small notching adjustments for time and industry to obtain the final credit rating. This model is easier to interpret and leads to straightforward analysis and counterfactual testing."[364]

The advent of securitization has added a new dimension to the rating process. The evaluation of a traditional debt offering involves a relatively straightforward assessment of whether a projected cash stream, generally from a single activity, will likely be sufficient to repay the loan. For example, will highway toll collections cover the financing of its construction? In the case of securitization such as collateralized debt obligations (CDOs), multiple obligations are pooled to create the financial instrument. Each obligation may carry its own risk of default. Moreover there may be correlations between the obligations that can exacerbate or dampen risk levels. Thus, the risk assessment on such investments is far more complex and the traditional tools may not be sufficient. As Moody's describes: "[W]ith the development of loan pooling and risk transfer via securitization, the 'originate-to-distribute' model altered many lenders' behaviors. As a result, rating agencies no longer serve just as information intermediaries between entities with like-minded investment orientations. Instead, we may also have to assess information gaps that arise from the changed behaviors of market participants and discover alternative sources of information, or accommodate and more completely capture such gaps in our ratings."[365]

---

[361] U.S. SEC. & EXCH. COMM'N, SEC REPORT ON THE ROLE AND FUNCTION OF CREDIT RATING AGENCIES IN THE OPERATION OF THE SECURITIES MARKETS 25 (2003), http://www.sec.gov/news/studies/credratingreport0103.pdf (last visited Sept. 16, 2009).

[362] *Id.* at 26.

[363] Moody's Investors Service, *Moody's Credit Rating Prediction Model* 1 (Nov. 2006) (Special Comment), http://www.moodys.com/cust/content/content.ashx?source=StaticContent/Free+pages/Credit+Policy+Research/documents/current/2006200000425644.pdf (last visited. Sept. 16, 2009).

[364] *Id.* at 18.

[365] MOODY'S CORP., ANNUAL REPORT 2007, at 3, http://files.shareholder.com/downloads/MOOD/317224853x0x181773/F099885F-F1B2-4861-A5A0-4BA8FCF109BB/2007_Annual_Report.pdf.

Concerns about the reliability of ratings surfaced in the 1980s when the Washington Public Power Supply System could not repay its debts which amounted to more than $2 billion. Those obligations were rated highly by the CRAs.[366] The questions intensified at the outset of the 21st century especially with the failure of Enron. Guardians of public trust from Congress to the SEC in the U.S. and their counterparts globally began investigating the function and role of rating agencies in the financial marketplace. The Senate Committee on Governmental Affairs held a hearing in 2002 "to elicit information on why the credit rating agencies continued to rate Enron Corporation a good credit risk until four days before the firm declared bankruptcy."[367] The staff report section concerning the role of the credit rating agencies opens with: "Like the analysts, another outside watchdog failed the public with respect to Enron: the credit rating agencies."[368] The report goes on to indicate that the role of the rating agencies has increased "with investors trusting that a good credit rating reflects the results of a careful, unbiased and accurate assessment by the credit rating agencies of the rated company."[369] The staff acknowledges that the rating agencies "generally get it right: bonds rated AAA have a less that one percent default rate over ten years or more, and S&P has found that there is almost an 88 percent likelihood that companies with ratings of A or above will still have that rating one year later."[370] However, they also highlighted the significant negative impacts when they are wrong such as in the rating of Enron.

Why did the rating agencies "miss" the deteriorating financial position of Enron, even a week before its implosion? The staff identified four failures in the Enron rating process. First, the raters failed to provide a comprehensive review of company disclosure materials. For example, disclosures about special purpose entities operated by Enron insiders could have been more fully understood by reviewing Enron's proxy statement.[371] Second, the raters focused on Enron's short-term issues such as access to cash and merger activity rather than on long-term issues of financial viability.[372] Third, the staff report criticized the credit rating industry's "lack of

[366] *See* U.S. SEC. & EXCH. COMM'N, SEC REPORT ON THE ROLE AND FUNCTION OF CREDIT RATING AGENCIES IN THE OPERATION OF THE SECURITIES MARKETS 10 (2003), http://www.sec.gov/news/studies/credratingreport0103.pdf (last visited Sept. 16, 2009) (noting that SEC and Congress "reviewed the regulatory treatment of credit rating agencies" at the time of the Washington Public Power Supply System's "large scale credit default").

[367] *Id.* at 16.

[368] U.S. SEC. & EXCH. COMM'N, FINANCIAL OVERSIGHT OF ENRON: THE SEC AND PRIVATE-SECTOR WATCHDOGS: REPORT OF THE STAFF TO THE SENATE COMMITTEE ON GOVERNMENTAL AFFAIRS 97 (2002), http://hsgac.senate.gov/100702watchdogsreport.pdf (last visited Sept. 16, 2009).

[369] *Id.*

[370] *Id.* at 99 (footnote omitted).

[371] *Id.* at 116-17.

[372] *Id.* at 117-18.

inquisitiveness."[373] A rating agency representative testified that the raters rely on the information provided by management since management has an incentive to maintain the integrity of the rating system. Senator Thompson raised an alternative view: "corporate executives might instead view it in their best interests 'to minimize bad news and stretch the truth.'"[374] The staff was critical of the lack of investigation of Enron even as issues of concern were raised in the press. The fourth issue, raised as a result of the Senate hearing, was a lack of accountability of the rating agencies. "Committee staff concluded that the credit analysts do not view themselves as accountable for their actions."[375] The agencies responded by asserting that they are accountable for their opinions and that their ratings are just that – opinions. They argued that their need to maintain their reputation is their incentive for accountability. They also pointed out that their ratings are protected by the First Amendment.[376] The staff concluded "Although the credit rating agencies' ratings are generally right, when they are wrong, the consequences can be serious. . . . [W]hen company officials are not honest, and their auditors are too entrenched or conflicted to call management out on problems, investors need someone to raise a red flag. Credit raters, with their special access, strong market power, and lack of conflicts, are in a perfect position to do this."[377]

The SEC also conducted an investigation into the role of the CRAs in response to a requirement under the Sarbanes-Oxley Act of 2002. The report acknowledged the importance of reliable credit ratings to the functioning of the securities market. The SEC highlighted the areas that might inhibit the development of accurate, independent credit ratings. It suggested a need for more disclosure of information by the issuers (such as ratings-based triggers in financial agreements) and the need for rating agencies to take a broader perspective on verifying data provided to them. The SEC highlighted its concern over conflicts of interest between the raters and the issuers, especially with the expanded offering of ancillary services that has grown with the advent of structured finance. The SEC also detailed concerns about the current oligopoly in the rating industry. While technical barriers to entry are lower, "the dominance of a few highly-regarded, well-capitalized rating agencies that pioneered the industry many decades ago"[378] inhibits new providers. They further acknowledged that the NRSRO designation itself may be a significant barrier.

---

[373] *Id.* at 114.

[374] *Id.* at 118.

[375] *Id.* at 122.

[376] *Id.* at 123.

[377] *Id.* at 125.

[378] U.S. SEC. & EXCH. COMM'N, SEC REPORT ON THE ROLE AND FUNCTION OF CREDIT RATING AGENCIES IN THE OPERATION OF THE SECURITIES MARKETS 36 (2003), http://www.sec.gov/news/studies/credratingreport0103.pdf (last visited Sept. 16, 2009).

Congress responded to the calls for improving the rating agencies' performance by enacting the Credit Rating Agency Reform Act of 2006.[379] The Act seeks to prevent abusive practices, address conflicts of interest, and introduce more competition among rating agencies.[380] The Act formalizes the process for attaining NRSRO status. A registration process, administered by the SEC, was established allowing agencies that provide credible ratings, to implement procedures for the protection of non-public information and adopting measures to avoid conflicts of interest in order to gain the NRSRO designation.[381] The implementing rules, adopted by the SEC, require NRSRO agencies to publicly disclose their rating methodologies as well as their past downgrades and defaults of rated securities and their issuers.[382] In addition, the Act requires the NRSROs to disclose their conflicts of interest.[383] While the SEC is assigned responsibility for rating agencies' oversight, "the Commission is ever mindful of the explicit intent of Congress that we not substitute the Commission's judgment for that of the rating agencies."[384]

There has also been international action on the credit rating front. The International Organization of Securities Commissions (IOSCO) adopted the Code of Conduct Fundamentals for Credit Rating Agencies in 2004. The Code Fundamentals provide rating agencies with a pragmatic set of actions that are intended to improve their performance. The Code addresses the quality and integrity of the rating process, the avoidance of conflicts of interest and the CRAs' responsibilities to the public and issuers. Quality of ratings is heightened by requiring that all available and relevant information should be applied to models that are "rigorous, systematic, and, where possible, result in ratings that can be subjected to some form of objective validation based on historical experience."[385] The code also calls for CRAs to monitor their

---

[379] Credit Rating Agency Reform Act of 2006, Pub. L. No. 109-291, 120 Stat. 1327 (codified in scattered sections of 12, 15, 20, 23 U.S.C. (2006)).

[380] Oversight of Credit Rating Agencies Registered as Nationally Recognized Statistical Rating Organizations, Exchange Act Release No. 55,231 (Feb. 2, 2007), 72 Fed. Reg. 33,564, 33,634 (Feb. 9, 2007).

[381] 15 U.S.C. § 78*o*-7 (2006).

[382] Oversight of Credit Rating Agencies Registered as Nationally Recognized Statistical Rating Organizations, Exchange Act Release No. 55,857 (June 5, 2007), 72 Fed. Reg. 33,564, 33,634 (June 18, 2007) (instructions to Form NRSRO Exhibit 1).

[383] 15 U.S.C. § 78*o*-7(a)(1)(B)(vi) (2006).

[384] *Testimony Concerning Credit Rating Agencies: Hearing Before the S. Comm. on Banking, Housing and Urban Affairs,* 110th Cong. (2007) (statement of Christopher Cox, Chairman, United States Securities and Exchange Commission), http://banking.senate.gov/public/_files/ACF75B3.pdf (last visited Sept, 16, 2009)..

[385] TECHNICAL COMM., INT'L ORG. OF SEC. COMM'NS, CODE OF CONDUCT FUNDAMENTALS FOR CREDIT RATING AGENCIES 4 (2004), http://www.iosco.org/library/pubdocs/pdf/IOSCOPD180.pdf (last visited Sept. 16, 2009).

ratings on an ongoing basis. Integrity is a key component of quality. For example, the Code details that "[t]he CRA and its employees should not, either implicitly or explicitly, give any assurance or guarantee of a particular rating prior to a rating assessment."[386] The code also addresses the potential for conflicts of interest. Beyond the typical pronouncements of the need for independence, the Code details specific actions and prohibitions. First, "[t]he CRA should separate, operationally and legally, its credit rating business and CRA analysts from any other business of the CRA, including consulting businesses, that may present a conflict of interest."[387] Second, actual and even potential conflicts should be disclosed.[388] Third, analysts should be compensated independently of the rating provided – higher pay for more accurate ratings, not for revenue generation.[389] Fourth, the CRA personnel are prohibited from trading in issues that they have involvement in rating.[390] Finally, the Code includes actions that improve the disseminating of information to the issuers and the investing public. For example, details of the rating methodology and assumptions are made public in a timely fashion.[391] The IOSCO also requires publication of the historical default rates of the CRA rating categories.[392]

The failure of credit rating agencies to send a warning of the subprime crisis rekindled congressional interest in the role of the CRAs. Chair of the Senate Committee on Banking, Senator Dodd, opened a September 2007 hearing on the role of the credit agencies in the subprime market stating: "Families all across this nation continue to struggle to hold on to their homes . . . because of abusive and predatory subprime lending. These loans were facilitated by Wall Street with the support of credit rating agencies."[393] The CRA representatives testified that they appropriately fulfilled their responsibility in the debt rating process. They explained that their "ratings represent our opinion of the likelihood that a particular obligor or financial obligation will timely repay owed principal and interest. . . . [W]e assess the

[386] *Id.* at 5.

[387] *Id.* at 6.

[388] *Id.* at 7.

[389] *Id.*

[390] *Id.* at 8.

[391] *Id.* at 9.

[392] *Id.*

[393] Press Release, Sen. Chris Dodd, Statement of Senator Dodd, Chairman of the Senate Committee on Banking, Housing and Urban Affairs, on Hearing Entitled "The Role and Impact of Credit Rating Agencies on the Subprime Credit Markets." (Sept. 26, 2007), http://banking.senate.gov/public/_files/dodd.pdf (last visited Sept. 16, 2009)..

likelihood . . . of default – nothing more or less."[394] The industry witnesses explicitly detailed what messages their ratings are not including, such as whether an investor should buy or sell a rated security, or whether the investment is appropriate for an individual, or whether the risk-return relationship in the particular rated security is appropriate. The testimony went on to detail the accuracy of their ratings in the subprime market. Exhibit 1 shows that the default rate on A or greater residential mortgage backed securities (RMBS) as rated by S&P, for example, was less that 1/3 of 1 percent. Moody's presented evidence that the subprime loans issued in 2002-2005 performed quite well. (Exhibit 2) The rating agencies acknowledged that in 2006 they became concerned about the rating of newer issued RMBS and provided numerous examples of alerting the marketplace to credit problems in this arena. S&P for example wrote in January 2006: "Standard & Poor's believes that there are increasing risks that may contribute to determining credit quality in the U.S. RMBS transactions; it is probable that these risks will be triggered in 2006."[395]

The CRAs also addressed the Committee's concerns about conflicts of interest. Both S&P and Moody's stressed the benefits of the "issuer-pays" model that the industry uses. The model's primary benefit is that it allows for the public disclosure of rating, leveling the information playing field for all investors. The rating agencies also detailed the ways that potential conflicts are mitigated. Examples include the facts that the rating committees are fully independent of the companies they rate; that analysts are not compensated on the basis of the ratings they provide or the revenues generated through the rating process, and that they operate separate surveillance teams to assess ratings quality. S&P offered evidence of their independence from the companies they rate. They showed that they are 3 times more likely to upgrade an initial rating than downgrade it. (Exhibit 3)

Notwithstanding the strong defense of their actions, S&P's representative acknowledged that "we have learned hard lessons from the recent difficulties in the subprime mortgage area."[396] Consequently, rating agencies have responded by improving analytical methodologies. The agencies' representatives spoke of increasing the incorporation of delinquency and loss expectations into the rating models. They also have addressed enhancements to their surveillance processes. Moreover, the CRAs committed to better understanding the processes of the loan originators especially with regard to data quality.

---

[394] *Hearing Before the S. Comm. on Banking, Housing and Urban Affairs,* 110th Cong. 3 (2007), http://banking.senate.gov/public/_files/ACF75B8.pdf (last visited Sept. 16, 2009) (testimony of Vickie A. Tillman, Executive Vice President, Standard and Poor's Credit Market Services).

[395] *Id.* at 21.

[396] *Id.* at 1.

Concerns over the accuracy of the CRAs ratings persisted into 2008. At a Senate Banking Committee hearing Senator Shelby "compared the rating agencies to doctors. 'If they're incompetent, they jerk their licenses,' Shelby said, adding that by being 'consistently wrong' on mortgage investment risks, credit rating agencies have contributed greatly to the financial crisis."[397] Worries over potential conflicts of interest also continued. SEC Chair Cox indicated he had 40 staff members examining the practices of the rating agencies. "'[S]taff members have found several cases in which rating agencies failed to disclose conflicts of interest, some as recently as this year,' Cox said."[398] Moreover the *Baltimore Sun* reported: "SEC Chairman Christopher Cox said yesterday at a hearing of the Senate Banking Committee that the government might soon create rules to ban credit-rating agencies from doing consulting work for issuers of debt."[399]

In early 2009, the SEC issued new rules for the nationally recognized statistical credit rating agencies in an attempt to rectify the shortcomings of the ratings process, especially with respect to the rating of structured finance products.[400] The first change increased the disclosure of performance measurement statistics and rating methodologies. A key feature of this requirement is the disclosure of whether and how the verification of the underlying assets in an asset-backed security and the quality of the originators of assets were used in establishing the credit rating. The second change required the public posting of a sample of issuer-paid rating actions. The third change required the nationally recognized rating firms to expand their recordkeeping. An example of the type of records required is rationale for any material differences between the rating suggested by the firm's statistical models and the rating action taken. Of note, the SEC did not define "material difference." A final set of rule changes addressed the concerns about conflict of interest. Under the new rules the rating agencies are not permitted to provide a rating for securities where the firm has also provided recommendations about how securities should be structured. The new rules also bar an individual in the rating agencies from participating in fee discussions if the person was also involved in the rating process for that issuer.

---

397 *SEC Weighs Credit Rating Rules,* BALTIMORESUN.COM, Apr. 23, 2008, http://www.baltimoresun.com/business/investing/bal-bz.sec23apr23001520,0,6896322.story (last visited Sept. 16, 2009) .

398 *Id.*

399 *Id.*

400 Amendments to Rules for Nationally Recognized Statistical Rating Agencies, Exchange Act Release No. 59,342 (Feb. 2, 2009), 74 Fed. Reg. 6456 (Feb. 9, 2009) (effective Apr. 10, 2009). 17 C.F.R. §§ 240.17g-1 to -6 (2008), *as amended by* Amendments to Rules for Nationally Recognized Statistical Rating Agencies, Exchange Act Release No. 59,342 (Feb. 2, 2009), 74 Fed. Reg. 6456 (Feb. 9, 2009) (effective Apr. 10, 2009).

Exhibit 1
S&P's Cumulative Default Rate by Originating Class
(Through September 2007)

Initial Rating	Percent of Default
AAA	0.04
AA	0.24
A	0.33
BBB	1.09
BB	2.11
B	3.34

Source: Testimony of Vickie A. Tillman, Executive Vice President, Standard and Poor's' Credit Market Services, Before the Committee on Banking, Housing, and Urban Affairs, United States Senate, at 6 (Sept. 26, 2007), http://banking.senate.gov/public/_files/ACF75B8.pdf (last visited Oct. 11, 2009).

Exhibit 2
Moody's Rating Changes of Subprime Mortgages by Vintage

	Percent of Ratings	
Vintage	Upgraded	Down Graded
2002	2.0	2.3
2003	2.7	1.1
2004	0.2	0.3
2005	0.3	0.5
2006	-	5.4

Source: Testimony of Michael Kanef, Group Managing Executive, Moody's Investors Service, Before the United States Senate Committee on Banking, Housing, and Urban Affairs, at 16 (Sept. 26, 2007) http://v3.moodys.com/researchdocumentcontentpage.aspx?docid=PBC_104935 (last visited Oct. 11, 2009)

Exhibit 3
S&P's Rating Changes

	Percent of Ratings	
	Upgraded	Down Graded
1994	6.81	2.21
1995	2.54	1.70
1996	1.38	1.18
1997	2.54	1.25
1998	2.20	1.28
1999	2.78	0.54
2000	10.08	1.93
2001	10.21	1.05
2002	9.24	0.98
2003	12.82	0.85
2004	10.74	0.45
2005	7.91	0.64
2006	3.79	1.04

Source: Testimony of Vickie A. Tillman, Executive Vice President, Standard and Poor's Credit Market Services, Before the Committee on Banking, Housing, and Urban Affairs, United States Senate, at 6 (Sept. 26, 2007), http://banking.senate.gov/public/_files/ACF75B8.pdf (last visited Oct. 11, 2009).

Assignment:

1. How effectively do the new SEC rules address the limitations and concerns about the credit rating process?
2. What additional actions should have been taken to improvement the value of the rating agencies?
3. What public policy or political considerations inhibit more comprehensive actions?
4. Who beyond the SEC should influence the rating agencies?

D. Appraisers and Appraisals[401]

Appraisers play a crucial role in the process of securitizing collateralized loans in general and mortgage loans in particular. The price of mortgage-backed securities, both when issued initially and in the secondary Markets, depends in part on the value of the underlying collateral. If the collateral for securitized mortgages is overvalued, investors could suffer losses. In recent years, fraudulent and negligent appraisals of collateral for securitized loans have occurred, and the number of these appraisals increased. While the Fair Credit Reporting Act and similar state laws attempt to protect the borrowers from unfair practices of credit agencies, no similar legislation exists for investors who rely on third-party appraisals.

[401] 1 TAMAR FRANKEL, SECURITIZATION § 9.8 (Ann Taylor Schwing ed., 2d ed. 2005).

The law does not require appraisals of mortgage-backed securities. Rather, the issuers and distributers of these securities offer appraisals to reduce the information risks for the investors, and hence the price of the securities which the investors would be willing to pay. After all, appraisal costs are higher for investors than for loan originators, SPV Originators, and distributors of SPV securities ("issuers"). If investors had to appraise, they would deduct these costs from the price they are willing to pay for the securities. By assuming the costs, issuers can raise the price of the securities, reduce their cost of capital, and increase the success of the distribution of the SPVs' securities. Therefore, if the public comes to distrust appraisals generally, when some appraisals prove unreliable, the cost of the securities to the issuers will rise as the securities' price will fall. Hence, significant policy grounds for regulating appraisers are to reduce the number of unreliable appraisals that may cause losses to investors and institutional lenders and to prevent the deterioration of public trust in appraisals.

For many years, the law regulating appraisers lagged behind the needs of the lending institutions and investors in asset-backed securities. Judicial regulation of appraisers under the common law and certification by trade associations was limited for many years. Generally, until relatively recently, appraisers have not been strictly regulated, perhaps because appraising real estate and other unique assets is not a developed art, let alone an exact science; appraisals can be inconsistent and unreliable. Since courts usually enforce rather than create industry practices and the appraisal industry lacked set standards for many years, the courts found little to enforce, and the primitive state of the art shielded appraisers from liability. More recently, associations of appraisers have developed codes of conduct and professional standards governing their work. These standards offer a basis for courts to assess the conduct of appraisers. The extent to which courts look to these codes of conduct varies from state to state.

The historical standard of appraisers' legal duties was developed primarily by the courts, based on the common law of contract, negligence, and fraud. Appraisals have been used in the past mostly for valuing real estate, and reliance on them in that context is widespread. Substantial legal literature and judicial decisions exist defining the duties and liabilities of real estate appraisers, and claims are brought not only against disloyal or negligent appraisers but also against lenders that order and use such appraisals. Common law principles of contract, agency, tort, and even public policy have been applied to impose liability on real estate appraisers and lenders. These theories are suited for arm's length, face-to-face transactions in the marketplace. They are less suitable for information and advice on which many thousands of investors rely in transacting anonymously in the marketplace. The common law was inadequate to protect investors in asset-backed securities who relied on faulty appraisals because the common law evolved in the context of claims by clients with direct relationships to the appraisers. Consequently, it imposed substantial burdens of proof on the plaintiffs and restricted their standing to sue based on notions of privity (contract relationship). These requirements are too onerous when applied to investors in mortgage-backed securities with no direct relationship to the appraisers but who nevertheless have a right to rely on the appraisals based on the market prices. Over time, the burdens on investors have been loosened in various states for various circumstances, expanding the right to sue to a greater or lesser degree.

Congressional hearings on the crisis in the thrift industry in the late 1980s revealed that "poor quality and, in some cases, fraudulent appraisals have been associated with enormous losses at failed thrifts and contributed measurably to the thrift crisis."[402] Consequently, the Financial Institutions Reform, Recovery, and Enforcement Act ("FIRREA") was enacted to require federal agencies regulating depository Institutions to establish standards for performing real estate appraisals and use state certified and licensed appraisers on federally related transactions. In addition, the Act established an Appraisal Subcommittee within the existing Federal Financial Institutions Examination Council ("FFIEC") to deal with real estate appraisals. FIRREA granted significant authority to the Appraisal Subcommittee and to the Appraisal Foundation. The Subcommittee monitors state certifying and licensing agencies and monitors the appraisal regulations adopted by federal regulators. The Subcommittee also maintains a national registry of state certified and licensed appraisers eligible to perform appraisals.

a. Appraisers' Duties to Their Clients[403]

The liability of an appraiser to a direct client for a faulty appraisal can be based on a number of legal bases. The first ground is breach of the appraisal contract and implied provisions in the appraisal contract warranting that the appraiser has the necessary skill and will perform the service with care and loyalty. A second basis for appraisers' liability is in tort law remedies for fraud and negligence. If privity of contract exists between an appraiser and the plaintiff, actions in contract and tort may be similar, although the difference may be important in states in which the statutes of limitations or the measure of damages on tort and contract claims differ. Some states recognize only the contract action and do not permit suits on a tort theory or permit an action for negligence but not for fraud. A third ground for appraisers' liability is tort claims for breach of fiduciary duties.

[402] S. Rep. No. 19, 101st Cong., 1st Sess. 36 (1989).

[403] 1 TAMAR FRANKEL, SECURITIZATION § 9.9 (Ann Taylor Schwing ed., 2d ed. 2005).

b. Appraisers' Duties to Parties without Privity Relation[404]

The historical tort law requirement of privity between the defendant and plaintiff has largely ceded to a looser concept. A plaintiff who belongs to a class of persons who would rely on the defendant-appraiser's actions to their detriment can sue in most states if the defendant knew or could reasonably have foreseen that reliance. Thus, even when an appraiser has no privity of contract with the plaintiff, tort law in fraud and negligence may provide the plaintiff with a remedy in some states. In New York, for example, there are three prerequisites for a finding of professional liability to persons with whom the professionals are not in privity: " '(1) the [professional] must have been aware that the financial reports were to be used for a particular purpose or purposes; (2) in furtherance of which a known party or parties was intended to rely; and (3) there must have been some conduct on the part of the [professionals] linking them to that party or parties, which evinces the [professionals'] understanding of that party or parties' reliance.' "[405]

To succeed on a claim in fraud, the plaintiff must meet a clear and convincing standard in some states, but only a preponderance in others, and show that (i) the appraiser intended to prepare an untrue appraisal; (ii) the appraiser intended to defraud the plaintiff or a class of persons to whom the plaintiff belongs; (iii) the plaintiff justifiably or reasonably relied on the fraudulent appraisal; and (iv) the plaintiff suffered damages as a result of the fraudulent appraisal and reliance on it.

To succeed on a claim in negligence or negligent misrepresentation, the plaintiff must prove by a preponderance of the evidence that (i) preparation of the appraisal was negligent; (ii) the plaintiff justifiably and reasonably relied on the appraisal; (iii) the appraiser knew, or in some states should have known, that the plaintiff, or the class of persons to whom the plaintiff belongs, would reasonably rely on the appraisal; and (iv) the plaintiff suffered damages as a result of the fraudulent appraisal and reliance on it. An appraiser who did not know of an unanticipated intended use for the appraisal and had no notice of the intended use will not be liable to the plaintiff.

c. Liability of Persons That Use Faulty Appraisals[406]

A defendant, other than an appraiser, who uses a faulty appraisal (prepared in breach of a legal duty) may be liable to a contracting party for breach of implied duties to choose a skillful, careful, and loyal appraiser and not to use a faulty appraisal in connection with the transaction. In addition, depending on the circumstances, the

---

[404] 1 TAMAR FRANKEL, SECURITIZATION § 9.10 (Ann Taylor Schwing ed., 2d ed. 2005).

[405] *LaSalle Nat'l Bank v. Duff & Phelps Credit Rating Co.*, 951 F. Supp. 1071, 1092-93 & n.17 (S.D.N.Y. 1996) (quoting *Credit Alliance Corp. v. Arthur Andersen & Co.*, 65 N.Y.2d 536, 551),

[406] 1 TAMAR FRANKEL, SECURITIZATION § 9.11 (Ann Taylor Schwing ed., 2d ed. 2005).

defendant may be deemed to have breached an implied contract warranty guaranteeing the quality of the appraisal.

Another basis for the liability of a defendant other than the appraiser is fraud or negligence in tort. In such a suit, the plaintiff may be required to show fraud or negligence by the appraiser, including plaintiff's reliance on the appraisal for a reasonable purpose, coupled with fraud or negligence on the part of the defendant in obtaining, providing or using the appraisal.

A defendant may also be liable for negligent selection of the appraiser when the defendant had notice of the appraiser's poor performance in other circumstances. To be liable for a faulty appraisal prepared by a person other than the defendant, the plaintiff must show that the defendant is vicariously liable for the appraiser's wrong or breach. If the appraiser is the defendant's employee, the defendant may be liable even if the faulty appraisal was produced for the defendant's own use, provided the appraiser or the defendant knew or should have known that the plaintiff would rely on the appraisal.

The greater the defendant's control over the appraiser, the appraisal process, and the product, the greater should be the defendant's liability for a faulty appraisal. Therefore, liability for faulty appraisals prepared by a defendant's employees is more easily established than liability for an independent appraiser's product.

If the user of a faulty appraisal received it from an independent appraiser hired by another person, there is no privity of contract between the appraiser and the plaintiff who relied on the appraisal. Therefore, the plaintiff/user cannot sue the appraiser on a traditional breach of contract theory. Privity would exist if the plaintiff hired the independent appraiser to conduct the appraisal for the plaintiff's own benefit. However, the plaintiff may sue either or both the user and the appraiser on a third-party beneficiary that the *contract between them* was made for the benefit of the plaintiff. The right of a third-party beneficiary is usually based on the terms of the contract expressly or impliedly referring to the beneficiary, but a number of courts have allowed extrinsic evidence of the parties' intent. Moreover, some courts extend possible liability beyond contractual privity and third party beneficiary relations to circumstances that amount to "the legal equivalent of contractual privity" that arise when there is an "intimate nexus" between the plaintiff and appraiser. Usually, to be liable to a third-party beneficiary, the appraiser must know how the appraisal will be used and for whom it is prepared, either specifically or by category or general classification. In at least one case, the court imposed on the appraiser the duty to inquire for whom the appraisal was made, and another court held that an appraiser cannot limit liability to a third-party beneficiary by naming the persons for whom the appraisal is intended.

Presumably the theory of third-party beneficiary can expose the Institution that engages an appraiser to possible suits from a very large class, which may include prospective buyers and all persons who would usually be shown the appraisal in connection with the business of the Institution. Such a possibility, however, seems very remote. A third party beneficiary theory is irrelevant as between the Institution and an actual buyer to whom the Institution showed the appraisal. As to the actual buyer, there is a direct privity between Institution and buyer. The Institution that shows a buyer an appraisal and causes the buyer to rely on it is potentially liable for breach of contract and various torts including negligence and fraud, based on the nature of the relationship and the communications between Institution and buyer. The appraiser may face liability on a third party beneficiary theory, depending on the circumstances. Unless the Institution lacks funds or is otherwise an unattractive defendant, the prospective plaintiff may elect not to sue the appraiser.

Federal and state governmental entities that hire and use appraisers may enjoy immunity from suit for errors and omissions in the appraisals even if a third party has relied on them. The Supreme Court ruled on this issue in *United States v. Neustadt* in 1961, holding that an appraiser for the Federal Housing Administration owes a duty only to the federal agency and not a borrower who relied on the appraisal. The decision was grounded in part in the Federal Tort Claims Act, which grants immunity to government agencies in certain cases. Since the question before the Supreme Court involved an interpretation of a federal statute, the Court did not resort to state law dealing with the appraiser's duties under similar circumstances involving private parties. In another case, the defendant was an appraiser for the Veterans Administration. The Administration used the appraisal in connection with its lending. A California court interpreted the federal statutes that required appraisals as designed to protect the VA, not the borrowers. The court barred suit on the ground that the borrower had no right to rely on the appraisal. However, the immunity does not extend without limit. Liability can still be founded on breach of contract or negligence. But claims that are essentially founded in misrepresentation, including negligent supervision, and the like are barred.

Absent an amendment of the Federal Tort Claims Act expanding the right to sue, the bar of *Neustadt* and the Act on suits based on a misrepresentation theory will apply to protect government entities. These entities include GNMA, FNMA, the Office of Thrift Supervision, the Resolution Trust Corporation, the FDIC, the Federal Housing Finance Board and similar federal agencies and their employees. These agencies should not be held liable to borrowers on a misrepresentation theory for faulty appraisals of the collateral, although the agencies may be held liable on a contract theory or if they fail to assert the statutory immunity. No similar immunity applies to claims against appraisers involving private sector transactions when no federal or state agency is involved.

d. Applicability of Appraisers' Issues to Asset-Backed Securities[407]

Investors in asset-backed securities who rely on faulty appraisals face difficulties in seeking redress. Investors may sue the banks or Originators of loans for selling the loans to the SPVs in reliance on the faulty real estate appraisals, or investors could sue the SPVs that bought the loans in reliance on the appraised value of the collateral for the loans. Investors can base their claims by analogy on the rights of borrowers or insured who relied on faulty appraisals. These borrowers and insured may sue lenders and insurers who, as a matter of practice, use appraisals before entering into a loan agreement or issuing insurance policies. Similarly, the SPVs may be liable to investors of their securities for faulty appraisals. Perhaps, on the basis of the theories discussed above and by analogy to accountants' liabilities, third parties and appraisers may be liable to buyers of mortgage-backed SPV securities on the theory that the buyers are third-party beneficiaries.

e. The Regulation of Appraisals[408]

In the mid-1980s, Congress has determined, as a matter of policy, that appraisals affect real estate-related transactions. Congress found that faulty appraisals had become a recurrent phenomenon in part because appraisers are hard pressed by parties involved in real estate transactions to put artificially high market values on real estate collateral especially in light of the great competition among appraisers. Therefore, Congress determined to (i) establish federal appraisal standards to assure realistic appraisals; (ii) require that appraisers who service federally related real estate transactions be certified to assure that they are qualified and reliable; (iii) enforce the standards and requirements by state certifying agencies, and (iv) establish a federal supervising organization.

After extensive hearings in 1985 and 1986, the House Committee on Government Operations and its subcommittee identified many of the practices and policies that facilitated fraudulent appraisals. The committee's report found that the appraisal industry was fragmented and that many appraisers were unskilled or too willing to comply with clients' directives. Lenders treated appraisals as obstacles to the goal of closing as many loans as quickly as possible. Even those lenders who reviewed appraisals in-house lacked internal controls to ensure effective reviews.

The report criticized federal agencies that have supervising authority or leverage for failing to focus on appraisals. The FHLBB was found to be the only federal agency with a comprehensive system detailing appraisal policies and practices. Other agencies had not established adequate standards for recordkeeping, and their examiners were not trained to evaluate written appraisals. Bank examiners

---

[407] 1 TAMAR FRANKEL, SECURITIZATION § 9.12 (Ann Taylor Schwing ed., 2d ed. 2005).

[408] 1 TAMAR FRANKEL, SECURITIZATION § 9.13 (Ann Taylor Schwing ed., 2d ed. 2005).

emphasized the credit-worthiness of the borrowers and ignored the appraised value of the collateral. The agencies also failed to set minimum qualifications for appraisers, were lax in pursuing civil penalties against negligent appraisers, and perpetuated the problems by failing to cooperate with other agencies. Government and private mortgage insurers and Institutions engaged in secondary market operations delegated too much responsibility to other parties. The VA failed to monitor appraisals and its internal controls were easy to circumvent.

The assumption that a lender's self-interest will result in closer monitoring of the appraisal process rests on two often erroneous presumptions: (i) the lender will continue to hold the loans in its portfolio and be forced to bear the losses caused by mistakes of its appraisers, and (ii) the lender has adequate internal controls to ensure that performance of those individuals who solicit loans will reflect the ultimate performance of the solicited loans. Insurers and other Institutions incorrectly assumed that the lenders were sufficiently self-interested to exercise caution and observe the appraisal process and participants carefully.

The report found that states were lax in regulating real estate appraisers and failed to promote meaningful exchange of market information on appraisers. In 1986, only 12 states licensed or certified appraisers and then typically as an adjunct concern of a real estate commission rather than to regulate them as a profession.

Even before enactment of legislation to regulate appraisers, government agencies acted to strengthen their policies and practices. The VA, FHA, FNMA, and FHLMC developed a standard appraisal form, and the VA, FHA, FNMA, and private mortgage insurers tightened their appraisal-related procedures. The FDIC, the Comptroller, and the Fed cooperated on uniform guidelines for real estate appraisals. Appraisers' professional organizations moved to create a self-regulatory group. A few states took steps in the same direction, and Congressman Barnard introduced legislation in Congress.

f. Congressional Acts[409]

In 1989, Congress passed the Financial Institutions Reform, Recovery, and Enforcement Act ("FIRREA"). Sections 1101-1122 of Title XI of that Act address the issue of appraisals, much along the lines of the House Committee Report and Congressman Barnard's legislative proposals. The Act requires each federal financial Institution's regulatory agency to establish standards for the performance of real estate appraisals and for utilization of State certified and licensed appraisers on federally related transactions. The rules would, at a minimum, have to meet generally accepted real estate appraisal and certification standards as evidenced by those promulgated by the Appraisal Foundation. . . .

[409] 1 TAMAR FRANKEL, SECURITIZATION § 9.14 (Ann Taylor Schwing ed., 2d ed. 2005).

In order to monitor the Federal appraisal standards and the State certification and licensing standards, the [Act] creates an Appraisal Subcommittee within the existing Federal Financial Institutions Examination Council. In addition to its monitoring functions, the Appraisal Subcommittee will maintain a national registry of State certified and licensed appraisers and submit annual reports to the Congress on how the law is being enforced.

FIRREA establishes an elaborate program for upgrading the qualification of appraisers. The Act requires that "[e]ach Federal financial institutions regulatory agency and the Resolution Trust Corporation ["agencies"] shall prescribe appropriate standards for the performance of real estate appraisals in connection with federally related transactions under [their] jurisdiction . . . ."[410] The standards require at a minimum that real estate appraisals be in writing and performed in accordance with generally accepted appraisal standards as promulgated by the Appraisal Standards Board of the Appraisal Foundation. Agencies may establish stricter standards.

In addition, the Act requires the agencies to prescribe "which categories of federally related transactions should be appraised by a State certified appraiser and which by a State licensed appraiser" ("qualified appraiser").[411] The Act itself sets forth certain federally related transactions that require the services of a state-certified appraiser. FNMA, FHLMC, and the Resolution Trust Corporation are required to use certified or licensed appraisers.

Thus, the Act creates a demand for appraisals, and limits appraisers' access to this business unless they qualify as required by the states. The Act further provides for states to establish a mechanism for qualifying and supervising appraisers through a "State appraiser certifying and licensing agency."[412] The activities of state agencies are monitored and supervised by the Appraisal Subcommittee of the Federal Financial Institutions Examination Council. Finally, the Act provides that Institutions may make exceptions to the standards prescribed by the Act in certain circumstances "with respect to real property located within a disaster area" if timing, safety and necessity requirements are satisfied.[413]

These provisions are enforced by civil penalties In addition, FNMA, FHLMC, or the Resolution Trust Corporation may not "knowingly contract for the performance of any appraisal by a person who is not a . . . [qualified] appraiser in connection with a

[410] 12 U.S.C. §3339. "Federally related transactions" are defined in 12 U.S.C. §3350.

[411] 12 U.S.C. §3341(a).

[412] 12 U.S.C. §3346.

[413] 12 U.S.C. §3352(a).

real estate related financial transaction . . . to which such association or corporation is a party."[414] In addition, section 907 expands and increases civil money penalties and criminal penalties for institutions and institution-affiliated parties. The Act allows recourse against appraisers by authorizing the agencies to impose on "institution-affiliated parties" the sanctions to which institutions are subject.[415] Institution-affiliated parties include not only directors, officers, and employees but also agents, appraisers and other persons who participate in the wrongful activities. Thus the Act vests in the regulatory agencies power to sanction appraisers to protect Institutions that make or purchase loans. Since these loans are securitized, this provision indirectly protects the buyers of asset-backed securities. However, the Act does not affirmatively establish a private right of action by the buyers of securitized loans against the appraisers or the institutions for damages caused to the buyers. Presumably, the Act leaves intact the common law remedies available to persons injured by faulty appraisals.

In 1990, all of the federal depository institution regulators—the Board of Governors of the Federal Reserve ("Fed"), the Office of Thrift Supervision ("OTS"), the Office of the Comptroller of the Currency (OCC), the National Credit Union Administration (NCUA), the Resolution Trust Corporation ("RTC"), and the Federal Deposit Insurance Corporation ("FDIC")—promulgated nearly identical regulations governing the use of appraisers by their supervisees "to implement revised standards to enhance the performance of real estate appraisals," for the purpose of protecting "federal financial and public policy interests in real estate related financial transactions requiring the services of an appraiser."[416] In 1994, the OCC, the Fed, the FDIC, and the OTS amended the regulations "to further federal financial and public policy interests by reducing regulatory burden, while requiring Title XI appraisals when necessary to protect the safety and soundness of financial institutions or otherwise advance public policy."[417] Under these Rules, appraisals by state-certified or licensed appraisers are required for all "real estate-related transactions" except for transactions (i) with a value of $250,000 or less, (ii) in which a lien is placed on the property through "an abundance of caution," (iii) that are not secured by real estate, (iv) in which a lien "has been taken for purposes other than the real estate's value," (v) that are business loans with a value of $1 million or less and are "not dependent on the sale of, or rental income derived from, real estate as the primary source of

[414] 12 U.S.C. §3349(a)(2).

[415] FIRREA, Pub. L. No. 101-73, §901, 1989 U.S.C.C.A.N. (103 Stat.) 446-450 (codified in scattered sections of 12 U.S.C.).

[416] 12 C.F.R. Part 34 (subpt. C) (July 2005), *adopted,* 55 Fed. Reg. 34,696 (Aug. 24, 1990) (OCC regulation).

[417] 59 Fed. Reg. 29,482, 29,499 (June 7, 1994), *codified at* 12 C.F.R. Part 34 (subpt. C) (July 2005) (OCC regulation).

repayment," (vi) involving a lease "unless the lease is the economic equivalent of a purchase or sale of the leased real estate," and (vii) involving an existing extension of credit at the lending institution, under certain conditions.[418]

The Rules also exempt transactions that involve[] "the purchase, sale, investment in, exchange of, or extension of credit secured by, a loan or interest in a loan, pooled loans, or interests in real property, including mortgage-backed securities, [when] each loan or interest in a loan, pooled loan, or real property interest met [agency] regulatory requirements for appraisals at the time of origination . . . .Also exempt are transactions that are "wholly or partially insured or guaranteed by a United States Government agency or United States Government sponsored agency,"[419] and transactions that

> (i) qualif[y] for sale to a United States government agency or United States government sponsored agency; or
>
> (ii) involve[] a residential real estate transaction in which the appraisal conforms to the Federal National Mortgage Association or Federal Home Loan Mortgage Corporation appraisal standards applicable to that category of real estate.[420]

These provisions reduce the cost of transferring pooled loans and mortgage-backed securities to federal agencies. The Rules affect Originators of SPVs and mortgage-backed securities in the private sector, giving them incentives to comply with the requirements if the Originators expect to sell these financial assets to federal agencies in the future. The Rules also exempt transactions in which the "institution is acting in a fiduciary capacity and is not required to obtain an appraisal under other law" or the agency determines that the appraiser's services "are not necessary in order to protect Federal financial and public policy interests in real estate-related financial transactions or to protect the safety and soundness of the institution."[421] The Fed's Rules exempt a transaction that "involves underwriting or dealing in mortgage-backed securities."[422]

If a state-certified or state-licensed appraiser is not required because the transaction is a business loan, involves an existing extension of credit, or is for $250,000 or less, then the agency must "obtain an appropriate evaluation of real property collateral

---

[418] 12 C.F.R. §§34.43(a), 225.63(a), 323.3(a), 564.3(a) (July 2005).

[419] 12 C.F.R. §§34.43(a)(9), 225.63(a)(9), 323.3(a)(9), 564.3(a)(9) (July 2005).

[420] 12 C.F.R. §§34.43(a)(10), 225.63(a)(10), 323.3(a)(10), 564.3(a)(10) (July 2005).

[421] 12 C.F.R. §§34.43(a)(12), 225.63(a)(13), 323.3(a)(12), 564.3(a)(12) (July 2005).

[422] 12 C.F.R. §225.63(a)(12) (July 2005).

that is consistent with sale and sound banking practices."[423] The agency may also require an appraisal to address safety and soundness concerns.

In addition, the Rules require the use of state-certified appraisers in all appraisals performed in connection with (i) federally related transactions with a value of $1 million or more, (ii) federally related transactions with a value of $250,000 or more "other than those involving appraisals of 1-to-4 family residential properties,"[424] and "complex 1-4 family residential property appraisals rendered in connection with federally related transactions" with a value of $250,000 or more.[425]

If a federally related transaction does not require a state-certified appraiser, the appraisal can be performed by either a state-certified or state-licensed appraiser. The regulators have also established standards for appraisals in connection with federally related transactions. Excerpts from the Uniform Standards of Professional Appraisal Practice Applicable to Federally Related Transactions are printed as appendix A to each regulation, parenthetically described as "based upon the Uniform Standards of Professional Appraisal Practice as promulgated by the Appraisal Standards Board of the Appraisal Foundation."[426]

E. Case Study: You Need a Higher Appraisal – No Worries!

The initial real estate appraisal came in at $535,000; it was revised to $556,000 upon review. The initial real estate appraisal came in at $825,000; it was revised to $850,000 upon review. The initial real estate appraisal came in at $1.55 million; it was revised to $2.27 million upon review.[427] Was it a coincidence that these and other appraisals were increased after a review? New York Attorney General Andrew Cuomo thought not. On November 1, 2007 he filed suit on behalf of the people of New York against First American Corporation (and its eAppraiseIT unit) alleging that they "have abdicated their role in providing 'third-party, unbiased valuations'" by allowing eAppraiseIT's customer's "loan production staff to hand-pick appraisers who bring in appraisal values high enough to permit [customer] loans to close. . . . This wrongful conduct constitutes a deceptive, fraudulent, and illegal business practice. It violates New York law as well as federal law and regulations."[428]

---

[423] 12 C.F.R. §§34.43(b), 225.63(b), 323.3(b), 564.3(b) (July 2005).

[424] 12 C.F.R. §§34.43(d)(2), 225.63(d)(2), 323.3(d)(2), 564.3(d)(2) (July 2005).

[425] 12 C.F.R. §§34.43(d)(3), 225.63(d)(3), 323.3(d)(3), 564.3(d)(3) (July 2005).

[426] 12 C.F.R. pt. 34 app. A (2005).

[427] Complaint, People v. First Am. Corp., at 29 (N.Y. Sup. Ct. Nov. 1, 2007), http://www.oag.state.ny.us/press/2007/nov/EA%20Complaint.pdf.

[428] *Id.* at 3.

Accurate real estate appraisals are essential for the integrity of the mortgage process. From an economic perspective accurate valuations are required to assure efficient allocation of mortgage capital. If appraisals are too low then the aggregate amount of the loans could be higher. And although borrowers might not need to borrow more, they should know about the opportunity to borrow more. On the other hand if the valuations are too high the amounts of the loans will exceed the appropriate value of the collateral, allowing the making of a higher amount of less secure loans. From a more pragmatic viewpoint, accurate valuations are required to reduce the risks to those who hold the loans, or the loan backed securities. After all, it is the value of property that provides the collateral for the loan holder in the case of default. The Appraisal Foundation, the congressionally authorized source of standards for appraisers, created the Uniform Standards of Professional Appraisal Practice (USPAP) to guide the industry's provision of appraisal services. The goal of the USPAP is "to promote and maintain a high level of public trust in appraisal practice by establishing requirements for appraisers."[429] The appraiser owes a duty to those served and thus has a responsibility "to protect the overall public trust."[430] Moreover, the importance of the integrity of the appraisal system "places ethical obligations on those who serve in this capacity."[431] The USPAP details the ethical requirements of appraisers. For example, "An appraiser must perform assignments with impartiality, objectivity, and independence, and without accommodation of personal interests."[432] The appraiser must also "advocate the cause or interest of any party or issue."[433] The USPAP explicitly defines what is unethical: to "accept an assignment that includes the reporting of predetermined opinions and conclusions."[434]

The importance of accurate appraisals increases with the securitization of mortgages since the investors are not legally connected with the borrowers and lenders. One of the few risk reduction strategies for investors is knowing the true value of the collateral that secures the loan. While accurate valuations are more important, the incentives of the appraisal firms are moving in the opposite direction. Lenders, who hire the appraisers, have one dominant objective – close loans, sell and securitize mortgages, collect fees and start the process again. Appraisals that support the loan

---

429 USPAP, *Preamble*, http://209.190.242.26/html/USPAP2008/USPAP_folder/uspap_foreword/Preamble.htm (last visited Sept. 16, 2009).

430 *Id.*

431 *Id.*

432 USPAP, *Conduct (Ethics Rule)*, http://209.190.242.26/html/USPAP2008/USPAP_folder/uspap_foreword/er_conduct_.htm (last visited Sept. 16, 2009).

433 *Id.*

434 *Id.*

approvals are a crucial input into this process. "Successful" appraisers, from the perspective of some loan originators, are those who consistently provide valuations that allow for mortgage approval. These loan originator and appraiser incentives are evident in the relationship between First American and Washington Mutual (WuMu).

WaMu is the "bank for everyday people."[435] Its vision is "[t]o be the nation's leading retailer of financial services for consumers and small business."[436] To support the achievement of this mission, WaMu established core values which focus on treating customers and employees with fairness, caring and humanity and being dynamic and driven. The first of the core values is that "[e]thics of absolute fairness, honesty, and integrity guide everything we do."[437] With more than $200 billion in deposits, WaMu is the fifth largest bank in the US. Through 2,180 offices the bank offers retail banking, home loans, credit cards and commercial services. The composition of its loan portfolio is heavily weighted to single family residential mortgages which accounted for approximately half of the bank's $254.5 billion outstanding loans in 2007.[438] (Exhibit 1) The value of WaMu's mortgage loans increased substantially during the early years of the 21st century from $137 million in 2002 to $218 million in 2005. (Exhibit 2) The growth, in part, was spurred by offering mortgages to subprime borrowers. The bank's subprime portfolio doubled during the 2002 to 2005 period from $10 to $21 million. (Exhibit 3)

In order to make its mortgage loans, WaMu required an appraisal of the property. WaMu operated an internal department of bank appraisers to perform this function. According to the Cuomo complaint filed against First American, WaMu decided in 2006 to outsource this function to assure that the appraisals it received were independent and unbiased. Most of the appraisal work was transferred to two appraisal management companies, Lender's Services Inc. (LSI) and First America's eAppraiseIT unit. First America "[p]rovide[s] [b]usiness [i]nformation . . . [d]eveloped with [i]nsight . . . [a]nd [d]elivered with [i]ntegrity."[439] It is a Fortune 500 company with revenues of $8.5 billion in 2006, employing 40,000 people. The firm provides an array of business information focused on title insurance and

---

[435] WaMu, *Corporate Profile,* www.wamu.com/about/corporateprofile/default.asp (last visited May 21, 2008).

[436] WaMu, *Vision, Mission & Values,* http://www.wamu.com/about/corporateprofile/valuesandmission/default.asp (last visited May 21, 2008).

[437] *Id.*

[438] Ron Cathcart, EVP and Chief Enterprise Risk Officer, WaMu, *Risk Management and Credit, in* WAMU, INVESTOR DAY 15, 20 (Nov. 7, 2007), http://investors.wamu.com/Cache/1001138248.PDF?FID=1001138248&O=PDF&T=&D=&IID=102028&Y=.

[439] FIRST AM. CORP., 2006 ANNUAL REPORT (page inside cover), http://thomson.mobular.net/thomson/7/2346/2577/ (last visited Sept. 16, 2009).

property valuations. Mortgage information, provided by the eAppraiseIT unit, accounted for 6 percent of its revenues in 2006. Although a small revenue base, this segment accounted for 16 percent of its operating income.[440] Shortly after being awarded the outsource appraisal work for WaMu, WaMu's account became a $50 million account for eAppraiseIT.[441]

First American stresses the importance of its impartiality and integrity in the provision of its services. In the 2006 Letter to Shareholders its CEO wrote "[I]t goes without saying that our Company and our people must operate with the highest values and integrity, or we certainly won't succeed in the long run."[442] With respect to accurate appraisals, First American identifies the value it creates for consumers. "Homeowners, who place a large investment in their property, can be particularly victimized by appraisal fraud. First American's warranted valuations, which are supported by our third-party perspective and backed by more than a century of integrity, virtually eliminate risk from this type of fraud."[443] For business customers: "Inaccurately appraised properties that make their way into lender portfolios increase the opportunity for foreclosures. Our national services provide our mortgage lender customers with a welcomed resource for unbiased appraisals that satisfy increased regulatory concerns, help to accurately determine value, and mitigate default risk."[444] First American supports this value creation with a Code of Ethics and Conduct. Section D deals with fair dealing. "As an employee, officer or director you must endeavor to deal fairly and in good faith with Company customers, suppliers, competitors and employees. You should not take unfair advantage of anyone through manipulation, concealment, abuse of privileged or confidential information, misrepresentation of material facts, or any other unfair dealing practice."[445] The Code also defines fraud as "deliberately practiced deception, whether by words, conduct, false or misleading allegations, or by concealment, to secure unfair or unlawful gain. Fraud covers both express and implied representations of fact, and may be written or oral."[446] The Code concludes noting: "The Company has provided

---

440 *Id.* at 1.

441 Complaint, People v. First Am. Corp., at 9 (N.Y. Sup. Ct. Nov. 1, 2007), http://www.oag.state.ny.us/press/2007/nov/EA%20Complaint.pdf.

442 FIRST AM. CORP., 2006 ANNUAL REPORT 5, http://thomson.mobular.net/thomson/7/2346/2577/ (last visited Sept. 16, 2009).

443 *Id.* at 13.

444 *Id.*

445 FIRST AM. CORP., CODE OF ETHICS AND CONDUCT 1, http://media.corporate-ir.net/media_files/irol/11/118425/corpgov/FAF-codeofethics.pdf (last visited May 21, 2008).

446 *Id.* at 2.

this Code as a guide and expects that each employee, officer and director will use its principles of ethical conduct as a foundation for behavior."[447]

The New York Attorney General's complaint against First American details a relationship with WaMu that appears inconsistent with the company's process for value-creation and its code of ethics. The overarching concern is lack of independence between WaMu's loan-originating staff and eAppraiseIT's appraisers, which is in direct conflict with USPAP as detailed above. The complaint identifies several examples of the lack of independence between the parties. The first example is the staff composition of First American's eAppraiseIT unit. The unit hired 50 former WaMu appraisers when it began its appraisal work for WaMu as a complement to its existing staff in-house and third-party staff. On the surface this does not appear problematic; however, at the request of WaMu, a subset of the former WaMu employees was designated as Appraisal Business Managers with authority to "override and revise the values reached by third-party appraisers."[448] A second example is that under a contract WaMu can "challenge an appraiser's conclusions by requesting a 'reconsideration of value' ('ROV') when WaMu disagrees with an appraised home value set forth in an appraisal report."[449] The complaint suggests that this process sought to "ensure that appraisal did not come in lower than WaMu wanted."[450]

A third and more direct example detailed in the complaint is the use of a select panel of appraisers. "In February 2007, WaMu directed eAppraiseIT to stop using its usual panels of staff and fee appraisers to perform WaMu appraisals. Instead, WaMu's loan origination staff demanded that eAppraiseIT use a Proven Panel of appraisers selected by the loan origination staff, who were chosen because they provided high values."[451] The President of eAppraiseIT allegedly acknowledged the rationale for the proven panel in an email to WaMu management writing: "Said differently, WaMu proven appraisers bring the value in a greater majority of the time with minimal involvement of the vendor, sales and Appraisal Oversight."[452] The proven list of appraisers was developed by mortgage lenders for use by eAppraiseIT and other appraisal vendors on a priority basis.

---

447 *Id.* at 4.

448 Complaint, People v. First Am. Corp., at 9 (N.Y. Sup. Ct. Nov. 1, 2007), http://www.oag.state.ny.us/press/2007/nov/EA%20Complaint.pdf.

449 *Id.* at 10.

450 *Id.*

451 *Id.* at 13.

452 *Id.* at 15.

Yet another example of the lack of independence between eAppraiseIT and WaMu was that WaMu's loan origination staff was able to remove individual appraisers from the Proven Panel. The Attorney General's complaint details an example of an approved appraiser who conducted five appraisals for WaMu after being included in the Proven Panel. In each case, WaMu requested he reconsider his valuations. He did not increase the values upon review. However, "[s]hortly thereafter, Appraiser A was removed from the Proven List and placed in the WaMu inactive list. He was then told by a WaMu sales assistant that he was removed from the panel because he did not increase values in response to these reconsiderations of value."[453] Another appraiser actually removed herself from conducting appraisals for WaMu after: "I was pressured for 2 weeks to change both my value and the conditions of my appraisal report . . . both of which were violations of UAPAP, FANNIE MAE and the Supplemental Standards I am required to observe and am bound by my license to complete."[454]

Numerous emails and other communications cited in the complaint demonstrate that eAppraiseIT management knew about the lack of independence with WaMu. Shortly after commencing appraisal services for WaMu in August 2006, an executive vice president informed eAppraiseIT's president "that WaMu's loan officers would often pressure WaMu's internal appraisal field managers for an 'extra few thousand.'" The executive noted that eAppraiseIT did not do that for any customers without supporting information. One month later the executive noted that: "[W]e are studying [the possibility of] allowing [the manager's] group a little flexibility to raise the value 5% with a cap of $50K if it is fully justified."[455] With regard to the Proven Panel, eAppraiseIT's president wrote to First American management: "We had a joint call with WaMu and LSI today. The attached document outlines the new appraiser assigning process. In short, we will now assign all WaMu's work to WaMu's 'Proven Appraisers' . . . . Performance ratings to retain position as a WaMu Proven Appraiser will be based on how many come in on value, negating a need for an ROV."[456]

There appears to have been concern within eAppraiseIT about the legal issues surrounding the relationship with WaMu. "eAppraiseIT's Executive Vice President analyzed the federal guidelines and regulations on appraiser independence and selection of appraisers by loan production staff, and advised eAppraiseIT's president that 'Based on this, I think WAMU's new initiative is way over the line.'"[457] In an

---

[453] *Id.* at 25.

[454] *Id.* at 27.

[455] *Id.* at 11-12.

[456] *Id.* at 13-14.

[457] *Id.* at 16.

April 2007 email the Executive Vice President noted that appraiser independence is the responsibility of the lender. The executive goes on to explain: "However, we as an AMC need to retain our independence from the lender or it will look like collusion. Imagine a simple mortgage broker saying he will give us the work if we use his 'proven' appraiser. We say no. This is very similar to that except they are very big."[458] In another memo the Executive Vice President wrote: "However, there is the legal concern about collusion. . . . Then we are liable I would say because we have gone along with it. . . . In addition, I think it will tarnish our reputation in the appraisal community because we are allowing WAMU to pick appraisers based on their loan officers. It makes us look complicit."[459] By the end of April the concerns about independence were significant enough for eAppraiseIT to tell WaMu it would stop warranting the bank's appraisals, a warranty that "presents a much simpler way to recover losses due to appraisal fraud or gross negligence."[460] The complaint alleges: "eAppraiseIT threatened to stop warranting WaMu appraisals because eAppraiseIT's management knew it had compromised its appraiser independence by using the WaMu Proven Appraiser List."[461]

In May 2007, eAppraiseIT management communicated to their parent company concerns about independence; however, "First American's Chief Operating Officer instructed eAppraiseIT's President and Executive Vice President to continue the relationship with WaMu and to 'design a model that predominantly leverages their panel but doesn't violate our independence which is probably easier said than done but there should be a way to figure it out.'"[462] On June 7, 2007, WaMu instructed eAppraiseIT to change the name of the Proven Panel to "WaMu Select." Why? "We are utilizing a more generic term acceptable w/in regulatory guidelines and industry standards."[463]

---

[458] *Id.* at 16-17.

[459] *Id.* at 19.

[460] *Id.* at 21-22.

[461] *Id.* at 22.

[462] *Id.* at 23.

[463] *Id.* at 24.

Exhibit 1
Composition of WaMu Loan Portfolio

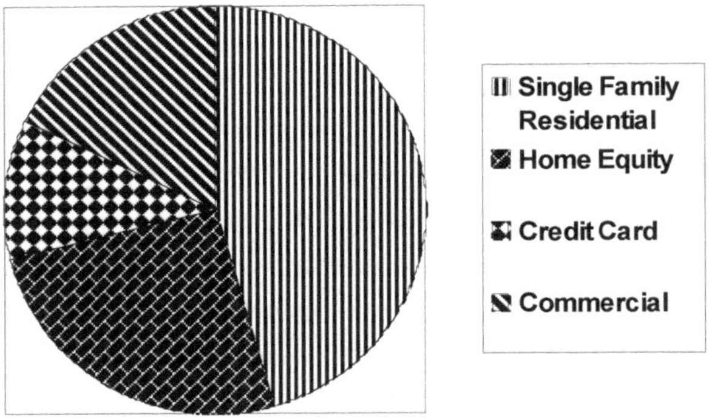

Source: Ron Cathcart, EVP and Chief Enterprise Risk Officer, WaMu, *Risk Management and Credit, in* WaMu, Investor Day 15, 20 (Nov. 7, 2007), http://investors.wamu.com/Cache/1001138248.PDF?FID=1001138248&O= PDF&T=&D=&IID=102028&Y =.

Exhibit 2
Value of WaMu Outstanding Mortgages
(millions of dollars)

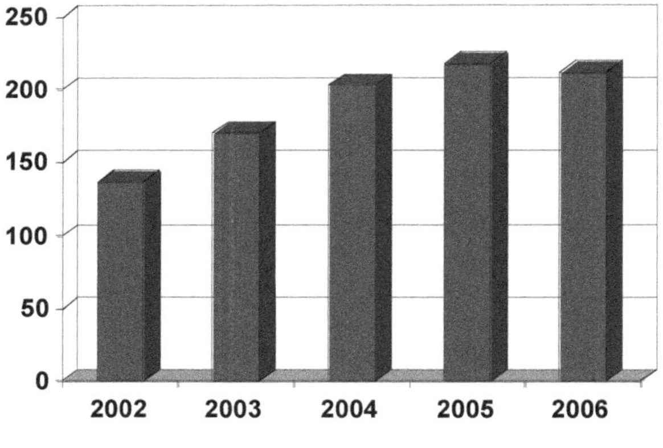

Source: Washington Mutual, Inc. 2006 Annual Report Form 10K, p. 34.

Exhibit 3
Value of WaMu Outstanding Subprime Mortgages
(millions of dollars)

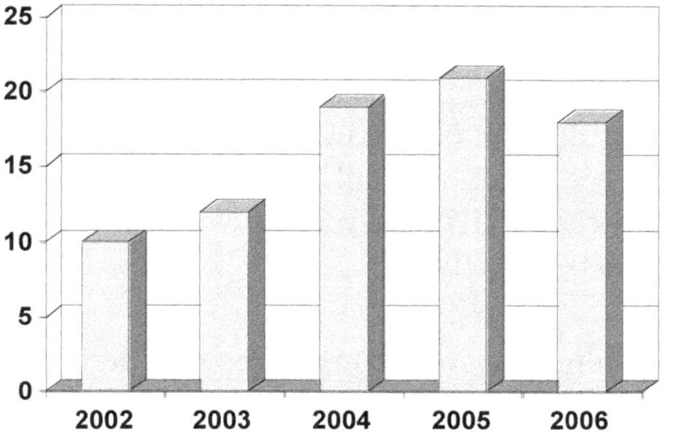

Source: Washington Mutual, Inc. 2006 Annual Report Form 10K, p. 34.

Discussion Questions

Legal

- What are the remedies against appraisers and who can assert them?
- Are there legal barriers to reviewing and revising appraisals?
- Is the "abdication of their role in proving unbiased valuations" an appraisers' violation of law?
- What is the recourse of an appraiser who is pressured to increase ratings or one who is blacklisted?
- Why did New York's Attorney General file a complaint only against First American but did not include WaMu?
- As internal counsel for the appraisal company, how would you have addressed the concerns about lack of the appraisers' independence?

Business

- What guidelines should appraisers follow in establishing their valuations?
- How can the potential conflict of interest between the loan originator and appraiser be managed?
- How could concerns about appraisal independence be more effectively communicated within First American?
- What inhibited a stronger and faster response to concerns about independence within the appraiser's organization?

Public Policy

- Should appraisers be directly regulated by the government?

F. Derivatives

a. What are Derivatives?

Frank Partnoy & David A. Skeel defined derivatives as "financial instruments whose payoffs are linked in some way to a change in credit quality of an issuer or issuers."[464] Credit default swaps (CDSs) are "private contract[s] in which private parties bet on a debt issuer's bankruptcy, default, or restructuring."[465] For example, John bets that the Market price company A's bonds will fall by 10% while Betty bets that these Bonds will either not fall at all or will fall only by 1% or will gain 12%. Whoever wins the bet gets paid the bet's results by the other.

"A collateralized debt obligation" (CDO) is a type of a derivative, defined by Partnoy and Skeel as a "pool of debt contracts housed within a [SPV] whose capital structure is sliced and resold based on differences in credit quality."[466] In a "cash flow" CDO, the SPV buys a portfolio of debt obligations issued by various companies, and "finances its purchase by issuing its own financial instruments, including primarily debt but also equity. Credit rating agencies rate the various tranches of the [SPV's] debt, whose terms vary depending on seniority."[467]

A "synthetic" CDO means an arrangement under which a SPV "enters into several credit default swaps with a third party . . . to create synthetic exposure to the outstanding debt issued by a range of companies." The SPV finances its purchase by issuing financial instruments to investors, but these instruments "are backed by credit default swaps rather than any actual bonds."[468]

CDOs offer opportunities for additional hedging,[469] more liquidity, and access to capital.[470] Being standardized, they can reduce the cost of contracting,[471] create a

---

[464] Frank Partnoy & David A. Skeel, Jr., *The Promise and Perils of Credit Derivatives*, 75 U. CIN. L. REV. 1019, 1021 (2007).

[465] *Id. See also* Kathleen C. Engel & Patricia A. McCoy, *Turning a Blind Eye: Wall Street Finance of Predatory Lending*, 75 FORDHAM L. REV. 2039, 2049 (2007).

[466] Frank Partnoy & David A. Skeel, Jr., *The Promise and Perils of Credit Derivatives*, 75 U. CIN. L. REV. 1019, 1022 (2007).

[467] *Id.*

[468] *Id.*

[469] Frank Partnoy & David A. Skeel, Jr., *The Promise and Perils of Credit Derivatives*, 75 U. CIN. L. REV. 1019, 1024 (2007) (CDOs can create a risk profile specific to one borrower or can be combined with other derivatives to create another risk profile; for example, a lender may bear a borrower's specific risk but exclude industry risk by purchasing derivatives linked to industry stock prices).

deeper and potentially more efficient market for trading credit risks,[472] and a balance of risk levels.[473] CDOs offer benefits by generating hard to get investment opportunities.[474] CDOs can be considered innovative, offering mathematical sophistication in the pricing methods[475] and new diversification opportunities.[476]

b. Derivatives Pose Risks and Benefits

First, there is risk that the other party does not intend to, or later cannot, meet its obligations. These instruments reduce banks' incentives to monitor the other party.[477] Parties may have incentives to destroy value, if, as they hedge one way, they also hedge the other way. In such a case they may benefit more from losing the bet.[478] The instruments pose a potential systemic risk by industry self-regulation and monopoly of regulation.[479] Similarly, CDOs pose the danger of reduced monitoring

---

[470] Frank Partnoy & David A. Skeel, Jr., *The Promise and Perils of Credit Derivatives*, 75 U. CIN. L. REV. 1019, 1025 (2007) (swaps encourage bank lending by limiting banks' downside risk).

[471] Frank Partnoy & David A. Skeel, Jr., *The Promise and Perils of Credit Derivatives*, 75 U. CIN. L. REV. 1019, 1025 (2007) (standardization has reduced transaction costs); *id.* at 1026 (market oversight by ISDA and derivatives firms has further reduced contracting costs).

[472] Frank Partnoy & David A. Skeel, Jr., *The Promise and Perils of Credit Derivatives*, 75 U. CIN. L. REV. 1019, 1025 (2007) (credit default swaps' pricing information may be available to the market, providing information about a company)..

[473] Aaron Unterman, *Exporting Risk: Global Implications of the Securitization of U.S. Housing Debt*, 4 HASTINGS BUS. L.J. 77, 82 (2008).

[474] Frank Partnoy & David A. Skeel, Jr., *The Promise and Perils of Credit Derivatives*, 75 U. CIN. L. REV. 1019, 1028-29 (2007) (cash flow CDOs may be available at lower cost because they have higher credit ratings than the underlying bonds; synthetic CDOs, because they do not use assets on balance sheets, are not motivated by reducing the cost of regulatory requirements).

[475] Frank Partnoy & David A. Skeel, Jr., *The Promise and Perils of Credit Derivatives*, 75 U. CIN. L. REV. 1019, 1030 (2007) (CDO technology is similar to other mathematical developments including a more accurate pricing model that added value for investors and created new instruments).

[476] Frank Partnoy & David A. Skeel, Jr., *The Promise and Perils of Credit Derivatives*, 75 U. CIN. L. REV. 1019, 1030-31 (2007) (CDOs enhance diversification by allowing investors to own divided interest in bond portfolios; synthetic CDOs allow investors to invest in diversified credit default swap portfolios).

[477] Frank Partnoy & David A. Skeel, Jr., *The Promise and Perils of Credit Derivatives*, 75 U. CIN. L. REV. 1019, 1032-33 (2007) (credit default swaps reduce banks' risk exposure, reducing incentive to monitor; pension funds and insurance companies that accept risk have less knowledge of borrowers and are less effective monitors).

[478] Frank Partnoy & David A. Skeel, Jr., *The Promise and Perils of Credit Derivatives*, 75 U. CIN. L. REV. 1019, 1035 (2007) (lender that also owns credit default swaps may benefit more from default).

[479] Frank Partnoy & David A. Skeel, Jr., *The Promise and Perils of Credit Derivatives*, 75 U. CIN. L. REV. 1019, 1040 (2007) (because "[m]any investors place highly leveraged . . . bets on credit default

by banks and investors' incentives to manipulate the pricing and structuring of CDOs. CDOs managers might manipulate the collateral in order to shift risks among the various SPVs' tranches.[480] The risks increase because there is a limited disclosure[481] and opaqueness,[482] about these instruments, involving high transaction costs, and the mispricing of credit. This is especially so because the investment bank structures the CDOs rather than the rating agency that performs the mathematical calculations measuring the correlation of pricing and the underlying assets.[483]

The International Swaps and Derivatives Association (ISDA) is the body that sets terms and conditions for derivative trades.[484] The organization has a "virtual monopoly" in creating "legal rules". "If a few major dealers control ISDA [agreement forms], those [forms] might be [used for] dealer-to-dealer contracts, . . . or . . . to advantage dealers in dealer-to-end-user contracts."[485]

In *Caiola v. Citibank,*[486] Citibank proposed "synthetic" trading based on stocks and options to a major client, Caiola. The synthetic transactions were documented through an ISDA Master Agreement and each transaction was governed by a confirmation. Citibank promised Caiola that it would control its risks through "delta hedging" but later changed to physical trades in stock and options that mirrored Caiola's synthetic transactions, exposing him to risks. Later, Citibank ceased synthetic trading, preventing Caiola from profiting on options he wrote on a stock expected to rise in

---

swaps, . . . a relatively small market change could trigger a crisis")." Frank Partnoy & David A. Skeel, Jr., *The Promise and Perils of Credit Derivatives*, 75 U. CIN. L. REV. 1019, 1040 (2007).

480 *See* Kendran Garrison, Manager Incentives in Collateralized Debt Obligations 6 (Aug. 15, 2005) (unpublished manuscript), *available at* http://papers.ssrn.com/sol3/papers.cfm?abstract_id=72048.

481 Frank Partnoy & David A. Skeel, Jr., *The Promise and Perils of Credit Derivatives*, 75 U. CIN. L. REV. 1019, 1036-37 (2007) (because swaps are generally not regulated, disclosure is limited).

482 FRANK PARTNOY, INFECTIOUS GREED: HOW DECEIT AND RISK CORRUPTED THE FINANCIAL MARKET 390-91 (2003).

483 Frank Partnoy & David A. Skeel, Jr., *The Promise and Perils of Credit Derivatives*, 75 U. CIN. L. REV. 1019, 1041-42 (2007) (arguably, after the rating agencies determine the rating formulas and variables, market participants could select a set of assets to create a CDO with tranches more valuable than its assets; this may be due to errors in : (1) rating the assets, (2) calculating the relationship between them and the tranche payouts, or (3) rating the tranches).

484 ForexTips, *Forex Terms,* http://www.forextips.com/forex-terms-ghijkl.htm (last visited Sept. 18, 2009).

485 Frank Partnoy & David A. Skeel, Jr., *The Promise and Perils of Credit Derivatives,* 75 U. CIN. L. REV. 1019, 1039 (2007).

486 Caiola v. Citibank, N.A., 295 F.3d 312 (2d Cir. 2002). *See* Frank Partnoy & David A. Skeel, Jr., *The Promise and Perils of Credit Derivatives*, 75 U. CIN. L. REV. 1019, 1037-38 (2007) (discussing case).

value that in fact did. Caiola sued under the securities laws and state law, alleging that he suffered losses relying on Citibank's misrepresentations that it would continue synthetic trading.

The district court stated that apparently no court had yet addressed whether synthetic transactions of these types are securities. The court held that the transactions were not securities and that there were no material representations, noting that the alleged oral misrepresentations conflict with language in the confirmation that neither party is relying on advice or statements of the other.[487] The Second Circuit reversed, holding that the options were securities. The court also said that the disclaimers relate to the element of reliance rather than materiality and found that the complaint adequately alleged materiality. In addition, the court held that the disclaimers did not bar reliance as they did not track the alleged misrepresentations.[488]

The Commodity Futures Modernization Act of 2000[489] did not impose restrictions respecting the underlying commodities trading of futures and options on contract (not personal) markets.[490] "[T]here are no restrictions on the types of market participants that may enter into transactions on a designated contract market.[491] Contract markets are no longer required to obtain separate designation for each futures contract.[492] Instead, contract markets are to be designated to trade all commodities, though there are special requirements applicable to securities futures."[493]

For a new entrant to qualify as a contract market, the exchange (if not previously registered), must meet seven criteria for designation and seventeen "core principles" set forth in the Act. The basic criteria include installing mechanisms designed to prevent market manipulations, assuring fair trading practices, operating an effective trading system, ensuring the financial integrity of transactions, disciplining offenders,

---

[487] Caiola v. Citibank, N.A., 137 F. Supp. 2d 362 (S.D.N.Y. 2001), *rev'd,* 295 F.3d 312 (2d Cir. 2002).

[488] Caiola v. Citibank, N.A., 295 F.3d 312 (2d Cir. 2002).

[489] Commodity Futures Modernization Act of 2000, Pub. L. No. 106-554, 114 Stat. 2763 (codified as amended at 7 U.S.C. §§ 1-27f (2006)).

[490] 1 PHILIP MCBRIDE JOHNSON & THOMAS LEE HAZEN, DERIVATIVES REGULATION § 2.03 (2004). *See also* Thomas Lee Hazen, *Disparate Regulatory Schemes for Parallel Activities: Securities Regulation, Derivatives Regulation, Gambling, and Insurance*, 24 ANN. REV. BANKING & FIN. L. 375, 381 (2005).

[491] 1 PHILIP MCBRIDE JOHNSON & THOMAS LEE HAZEN, DERIVATIVES REGULATION § 2.03 (2004) (citing 1 PHILIP MCBRIDE JOHNSON & THOMAS LEE HAZEN, DERIVATIVES REGULATION § 2.03 (2004)).

[492] *Id.* (citing 1 PHILIP MCBRIDE JOHNSON & THOMAS LEE HAZEN, DERIVATIVES REGULATION § 2.03 (2004)).

[493] *Id.;* 7 U.S.C. § 7 (2006).

making its rules and contract specifications available to the public, and having public access to all relevant information.[494] In order to qualify for designation as a contract market, the trading facility applying for Commodity Futures Trading Commission (CFTC) designation must demonstrate to the CFTC in its application that seven specified standards are satisfied.

The Modernization Act allows the use of certain trading facilities with lower regulatory oversight than designated contract markets.[495] These trading facilities are defined by the Commodity Exchange Act as derivatives transaction execution facilities ("DTEFs"). There are restrictions on both categories of the futures and options contracts that may be traded, and the types of investors that may participate in transactions on DTEFs.[496] A DTEF that is a national securities exchange, and thus subject to SEC regulation, may trade security futures contracts.[497]

In addition to contract markets and DTEFs, the Modernization Act recognized a new category of marketplace ("exempt board of trade"), which can offer certain types of futures contracts (except securities futures products) free of CFTC oversight. To qualify as an exempt board of trade, the trading facility must limit trading to contracts

---

494 7 U.S.C. § 7 (2006); *see also* CFTC Designates Brokerage Futures Exchange as a Contract Market and Brokered Clearing Corporation as a Resister Derivatives Organization, CTFC Rel. No. 4526-01 (June 19, 2001); Thomas Lee Hazen, *Disparate Regulatory Schemes for Parallel Activities: Securities Regulation, Derivatives Regulation, Gambling, and Insurance*, 24 ANN. REV. BANKING & FIN. L. 375, 381.(2006).

495 7 U.S.C. § 1a(33)(A) (2006).

496 The Commodity Exchange Act currently permits two types of DTEFs: those serving the retail market and those serving the commercial market. A DTEF that operates as a retail market must limit its participants to those who trade through a futures commission merchant that (1) is a member of a futures self-regulatory organization (or if trading a security futures product, a national securities association); (2) is a clearing member of a derivatives clearing organization; and (3) has net capital of at least $ 20 million. Retail customers trading through derivatives transaction execution facilities are permitted to trade only in instruments based on commodities that meet certain requirements designed to make the contracts particularly unsusceptible to manipulation, and to security futures products if the DTEF is registered as a national securities exchange. The Act further authorizes the CFTC to approve on a case-by-case basis additional contracts that can be traded on a retail DTEF. *Id.* § 7a(b)(2).

Derivatives transaction execution facilities that operate as commercial markets are required to restrict its participants to those who qualify as "eligible commercial entities." Commercial DTEFs are not limited to the same extent as retail DTEFs with respect to the contracts that may be traded. A commercial derivatives transaction execution facility may trade futures on any non-agricultural commodity if trade is limited to eligible commercial entities trading for their own account. *Id.* § 7a(b). *See also* Thomas Lee Hazen, *Disparate Regulatory Schemes for Parallel Activities: Securities Regulation, Derivatives Regulation, Gambling, and Insurance*, 24 ANN. REV. BANKING & FIN. L. 375, 381 (2006).

497 7 U.S.C. § 7a(d)(2)-(9), (b)(2)(D) (2006).

that are not susceptible to manipulation or have no cash market.[498] Participation in an exempt board of trade is limited to eligible contract participants,[499] and an exempt board of trade may not trade securities futures products.

c. Problems and Proposed Solutions

The notional value of derivatives contracts was estimated to exceed $100 trillion dollars in 2008. The sheer size of these financial instruments and the lack of transparency in their trading have caused concern. The first proposal to address the potential risks of the derivatives market is to require greater disclosure. ISDA should disclose all credit derivatives documentation for free on the Internet.[500] Market participants should publish credit derivatives transactions, e.g., through the Securities and Exchange Commission's (SEC) EDGAR service.[501] A central pricing service should be offered for credit derivatives .[502] Reporting companies should be required to disclose the effects of credit derivatives.[503] As to credit ratings, proposals include (1) increasing competition among rating agencies,[504] and (2) requiring companies to "explain their investment policy with respect to credit rating."[505]

There are proposals concerning bankruptcy situations, such as a requirement for automatic stay and termination rights in bankruptcy. The non-debtor participants in derivatives contracts are allowed to enforce their claims without regard to the bankruptcy process of automatic stay of payments. Otherwise, the participant could collapse and create a "run."[506] However, it is unclear that this exception reduces the

---

[498] 7 U.S.C. §ß 7a-3(b) (2006).

[499] 7 U.S.C. §ß 7a-3(b)(2) (2006).

[500] Frank Partnoy & David A. Skeel, Jr., *The Promise and Perils of Credit Derivatives*, 75 U. CIN. L. REV. 1019, 1047 (2009).

[501] *Id.*

[502] *Id.*

[503] *Id.* at 1047-48.

[504] *Id.* at 1048. *See also* Frank Partnoy, *How and Why Credit Rating Agencies are Not Like Other Gatekeepers, in Financial Gatekeepers: Can They Protect Investors*? 59 (2006).

[505] Frank Partnoy & David A. Skeel, Jr., *The Promise and Perils of Credit Derivatives*, 75 U. CIN. L. REV. 1019, 1048 (2007).

[506] H.R. Rep. No. 97-420, at 1 (1982) (exception needed to prevent the "insolvency of one commodity or security firm from spreading to other firms and possibly threatening the collapse of the affected market"). *See also* Frank Partnoy & David A. Skeel, Jr., *The Promise and Perils of Credit Derivatives*, 75 U. CIN. L. REV. 1019, 1048-50 (2007).

risk. In fact, it might increase the risk, as it permits counter-parties' "rush to close out their contracts" in case of failures.[507]

Derivatives induced banks to raise the risk of the instruments that they produced, and enhanced liquidity by being standardized and more efficient. However, the trades remained increasingly unconfirmed, and highly complex.[508] They used financial engineering for new investment opportunities, and using mathematical finance. Arguably CDO technology "leads to new, higher value financial instruments" as is similar to other mathematical developments including a more accurate pricing model that added value for investors and created new instruments.[509]

Finally, CDOs benefit investors by permitting them to pool their resources to invest in a diversified bond portfolio, selected by a manager. The various participants benefit from the diversification.[510] Synthetic CDOs allow additional diversification through credit default swaps. They are expected to resemble credit default swap indices, instruments based on credit default swaps.[511]

Investors in a synthetic CDO, like investors in a mutual fund, pay for the underlying assets' cash flows. Those assets might be fixed or actively managed funds. In contrast, the value of a credit default swap index, like that of a commodity product, is determined by another asset. This suggests that the credit default swap index may become more popular than the synthetic CDO, as commodity products such as exchange-traded funds (ETFs) and index funds have lower transaction costs.[512]

Like all good things these derivatives have a "dark side." First, banks have less incentive to monitor and supervise them. Large banks "lent billions of dollars to Enron," but hardly supervised it, and their purchased protection was not enough. Counter-parties to swaps can fail. And some lenders that hedged their bets by selling short or buying credit protection may benefit (and perhaps benefit more) from the borrowers' bankruptcy. These lenders may enhance the borrower's demise.[513]

---

[507] Franklin R. Edwards & Edward R. Morrison, *Derivatives and the Bankruptcy Code: Why the Special Treatment?*, 22 YALE J. ON REG. 101, 107-09 (2005).

[508] Frank Partnoy & David A. Skeel, Jr., *The Promise and Perils of Credit Derivatives*, 75 U. CIN. L. REV. 1019, 1023-26 (2007).

[509] *Id.* at 1029-30.

[510] *Id.* at 1030-31.

[511] *Id.* at 1031.

[512] *Id.*

[513] *Id.* at 1032-35.

Further, the credit default swaps market is "opaque" as "the swaps are structured as over-the-counter (OTC) derivatives" and are "largely unregulated."[514] It is also unclear to what extent a bank's general disclaimer of risks and liabilities can protect the bank when there is a significant asymmetry between the bank and its client.[515] These instruments pose a systemic risk as well. "Because many investors - particularly hedge fund investors - place highly leveraged bets on credit default swaps, even a relatively small market change could trigger a crisis of the sort that Long Term Capital Management threatened to unleash when it collapsed in 1998."[516] CDOs pose similar problems. CDOs present not only the numerous risks associated with credit default swaps, but also the risk that parties are spending billions of dollars in fees to buy mispriced debt. The question remains: How do we retain the good of these innovations but reduce if not eliminate their bad effects?"

In addition, securities investments, non-securities derivative investments, insurance and gambling may be similar, but are subject to different regulations and government intervention. Insurance and gambling were subject to regulation that was stricter, and the approach was different, than the regulation and approach of investments in securities—regulated mostly by disclosure.

On August 6, 2008 the *Financial Times* disclosed[517] that "[b]ig banks seek to limit their own risks" by proposing to "limit the size and scope of their businesses" relating to the "number of investors who can buy complex financial products," inform the regulators about "large swathes of the derivatives" and "call on banks to spend more on technology and risk management." This might affect and reduce the securitization businesses. It shows the seriousness of the crisis. The banks concede that the regulatory costs would be miniscule as compared to the losses of the financial institutions and the economies. Under the proposed plan large institutional investors "would no longer be automatically allowed to buy bonds backed by assets such as subprime mortgages," and "[a]ll but the wealthiest retail investors" would not be able to buy structured products (e.g., auction rate securities). The banks criticized the complexity of the instruments and trading. But the spokesman for the banks did not see the proposal as the "death of securiti[z]ation."

---

[514] *Id.* at 1036.

[515] Caiola v. Citibank, N.A., 295 F.3d 312 (2d Cir. 2002).

[516] Frank Partnoy & David A. Skeel, Jr., *The Promise and Perils of Credit Derivatives*, 75 U. CIN. L. REV. 1019, 1040 (2007).

[517] Aline van Duyn, *Big Banks Seek to Limit Their Own Risks,* FIN. TIMES, Aug. 6, 2008, *available at* http://www.ft.com/cms/s/0/94dc3528-63c6-11dd-844f-0000779fd18c,dwp_uuid=e8477cc4-c820-11db-b0dc-000b5df10621.html (last visited Sept. 21, 2009).

Discussion Topics

1. What are the differences between derivatives, insurance, and gambling?
2. Why should banks that deal in these instruments ask for a law to limit their business? Could they not limit their business themselves?
3. If securities trading, insurance, derivatives, and synthetic derivatives are so similar, what is the rational basis for their different regulatory schemes? And why do we not have a consistent approach to this question?[518]

d. Derivatives Status Under Bankruptcy Law

The non-debtor participants in derivatives contracts are allowed to enforce their claims without regard to the bankruptcy process of automatic stay of payments. Otherwise, the participant could collapse and create a "run."[519] However, it is unclear that this exception reduces the risk. In fact, it might increase the risk, as it permits counter-parties' "rush to close out their contracts" in case of failures. The participants in derivatives contracts that are not debtors are permitted to enforce their rights without interference from the bankruptcy process. This is due to a perception that if enforcement of their rights were delayed, the collapse of an important player in the derivatives markets could have a contagious effect throughout the financial markets.[520] It is far from clear that the exception reduces systemic risk; it may even increase this risk because it eliminates a possible curb on counter-parties' rush to close out their contracts in the event of a wave of failures.[521] It is unnecessary to impose the automatic stay on, and delay enforcement of, derivatives contracts. The stay, as traditionally conceived, enables the debtor to keep assets together in order to preserve their going concern value for a reorganization or sale. Because derivatives are fungible financial instruments - more like cash than essential equipment or property - preventing a counter-party from exercising its rights is unnecessary.[522]

---

[518] Thomas Lee Hazen, *Disparate Regulatory Schemes for Parallel Activities: Securities Regulation, Derivatives Regulation, Gambling, and Insurance,* 24 ANN. REV BANKING & FIN. L. 375 (2005) (footnote omitted).

[519] H.R. Rep. No. 97-420, at 1 (1982) (exception needed to prevent the "insolvency of one commodity or security firm from spreading to other firms and possibly threatening the collapse of the affected market"). *See also* Frank Partnoy & David A. Skeel, Jr., *The Promise and Perils of Credit Derivatives*, 75 U. CIN. L. REV. 1019, 1048-50 (2007).

[520] H.R. Rep. No. 97-420, at 1 (1982) (exception needed to prevent the "insolvency of one commodity or security firm from spreading to other firms and possibly threatening the collapse of the affected market"). *See also* Frank Partnoy & David A. Skeel, Jr., *The Promise and Perils of Credit Derivatives*, 75 U. CIN. L. REV. 1019, 1048-50 (2007).

[521] Edwards R. Franklin R.& Edward R. Morrison, *Derivatives and the Bankruptcy Code: Why the Special Treatment*?, 22 YALE J. ON REG. 101, 107-09 (2005).

[522] *Id.*

Chapter 8: The Transfer of Assets to the SPV – True Sale

This Chapter focuses on the legal issues concerning the transfer financial assets, such as loans, or loan collateral such as mortgages, to the SPV. The law requires the parties to take formal steps in order to transfer some type of assets but not for other types. For example, to be binding against any claimant the transfer of real estate requires a formal public registration of the transfer in a registry open to the public. Real estate transfers in ancient times required the presence of witnesses on the particular land to witness the transaction. The publicity necessary for the transfer of land is related to the importance of land. Similarly, wills require the authentication by witnesses and sometimes verification of the signatures by a public notary. That is because the date in which the transfer will actually occur can be years later, the transferor will not be alive, the transfer can cover significant property.

Public notice is required in connection with the transfer of financial assets to notify the creditors of the transferor that the financial assets are no longer part of the transferor's assets. Such notice would bind parties to the transfer and give notice to the public that the property has been sold or used as collateral. If such public notice is not made then transfers of the property would be binding only on the third party to the agreement, but not on other parties without knowledge of the transfer. A required formality helps avoid or reduce ambiguities and offers clear evidence of the transfer. A required publication helps protect a market in the particular property by sheltering buyers without notice of a previous transfer who paid reasonable value for the property.

This chapter focuses on the transfer of financial assets that consist of promises by one party to pay another. Therefore, in addition to formality, a number of questions arise. First, what is the extent to which the obligor--the borrower or debtor--whose obligation is being transferred--must be involved in the transaction? Is it necessary for the obligor to consent to the transfer? Is it sufficient to notify the obligor of the new owner of the obligation and require the obligor to send the payments due to the new owner? Second, how can the investors in the asset-backed securities be protected? As pointed out before, the transfer of the assets to the SPV must be complete and certain, in order to prevent the creditors of the transferor from later claiming the assets. Thus, the next two sections will deal with these subjects. The first section deals with the borrowers' defenses against the lenders and assignees. The second section covers the difference between a transfer of a loan and a secure loan.

A. Borrowers Defenses Against the Lenders and Assignees[523]

Historically creditors had quite a bit of power over the debtors. In England, debtors who did not pay could end in the debtors' prison. Therefore, debtors had an interest in the identity of their creditors. But as time went by, creditors' powers were eliminated, and bankruptcy may have protected debtors more than punished them. Not surprisingly, the rights of the creditors to transfer the debtors owed to them became stronger. After all there are efficiencies in allowing and facilitating the transfer of debts. Nonetheless, there is a balance between the rights of the debtors the rights of the buyers and the interests in protecting the debtors and maintaining an efficient market in the debtors' obligations. The search for this balance is reflected in the law.

Securitization converts loans (personal contract relations) into securities (transferable property). To facilitate transferability, some of the borrower's defenses and setoff rights against their lender may be eroded similarly to the way that the rule of *bona fide* purchaser for value has eroded the borrowers' rights against such a holder. The more tradable loans become, the more likely it is that the borrower's defenses and rights against the lender will not be enforceable against the buyers of the loan.

a. General Rule and Exceptions[524]

Borrowers' rights v. market efficiency. Securitization exposes borrowers to possible loss of their rights to assert defenses against the original lender. One example is the debtor who took a loan from the bank and has deposited cash in its bank account. If the bank failed, the debtor may reduce (set-off) the amount it owes the bank by the amount of the debtor's bank account. But if the debtor's obligation was sold to an SPV, the debtor cannot reduce the amount of the debt it owes by the amount of its bank account. This difference in situation may result in losses to the debtor, in terms of time, and perhaps even the amount due.

The borrowers and lenders, who wish to transfer the obligations, have conflicting interests. The law provides borrowers with legal protection when they are assumed to be the weaker party in need of money. If the lenders sell and transfer the borrowers' obligations to third parties the question arises: Will the borrowers' protections be effective against the transferee of the obligations? On this issue two public policies clash. The policy of protecting the borrowers, especially if the transfers were made without the borrowers' consent clashes with the policy of encouraging a market in the borrowers' obligations. Hence, the law strives for a balance between these two interests.

---

[523] 1 TAMAR FRANKEL, SECURITIZATION § 7.11 (Ann Taylor Schwing ed., 2d ed. 2005).

[524] 1 TAMAR FRANKEL, SECURITIZATION § 5.5 (Ann Taylor Schwing ed., 2d ed. 2005).

A balance between the rights of the borrower and the rights of the buyers of borrowers' obligations is sometimes achieved piecemeal. For example, the Home Ownership and Equity Protection Act of 1994 preserves the claims and defenses of a consumer-borrower against a purchaser or assignee of the loans with respect to certain mortgages, unless the assignee demonstrates that "a reasonable person exercising ordinary due diligence . . . could not determine" that the mortgage qualifies for coverage under the statute.[525] Some States have passed legislation against predatory lending, and these affect the buyers of loans containing predatory terms. Also, a lender-seller of the loans may be required to guarantee or indemnify the "SPV borrower," that is, the borrower whose obligations were transferred to an SPV, for certain losses caused to the borrower.

Uniform Commercial Code. A main source of the law for both the relationships between the lenders and borrowers as well as between the buyers and sellers of financial assets is the Uniform Commercial Code (Code or UCC). The Uniform Commercial Code was conceived as a replacement for a former series of uniform acts, to reflect changes in "patterns of commercial activity" and to promote uniformity among states.[526] The Code is derived from the common law, is based on principles of law, equity, and an underlying obligation of good faith.[527] The Code supplements rather than replaces the common law except where specifically provided.[528]

NetBank, FSB v. Kipperman (*In re* Commercial Money Center, Inc.)[529]

350 B.R. 465 (B.A.P. 9th Cir. 2006), *summary judgment granted,* FDIC v. Kipperman (*In re* Commer. Money Ctr., Inc.), 2008 Bankr. LEXIS 2189 (B.A.P. 9th Cir., Aug. 4, 2008)

DISPOSITION: AFFIRMED IN PART, REVERSED IN PART, AND REMANDED.

---

[525] Home Ownership and Equity Protection Act of 1994, 15 U.S.C. § 1641(d) (2006).

[526] JAMES J. WHITE & ROBERT S. SUMMERS, UNIFORM COMMERCIAL CODE § 1, at 2-3 (5th ed. 2000).

[527] *Id.* § 6, at 20.

[528] *Id.* § 3, at 8; § 6, at 19-20.

[529] 350 B.R. 465 (B.A.P. 9th Cir. 2006), *summary judgment granted,* FDIC v. Kipperman (*In re* Commer. Money Ctr., Inc.), 2008 Bankr. LEXIS 2189 (B.A.P. 9th Cir., Aug. 4, 2008). Some citations and footnotes omitted.

***

JUDGES: Before: MONTALI, TCHAIKOVSKY,[2] and BRANDT, Bankruptcy Judges.

OPINION BY: MONTALI

OPINION

AMENDED

OPINION

MONTALI, Bankruptcy Judge:

The principal issue in this case appears to be one of first impression for us or any court of appeals. We are told that the multi-billion dollar securitization industry depends on being able to fractionalize financial assets, and specifically on stripping payment streams from underlying transactions such as the equipment leases in this case. The issue is whether those payment streams are chattel paper or payment intangibles. On cross-motions for partial summary judgment the bankruptcy court held that the payment streams are chattel paper. We disagree. The underlying equipment leases are chattel paper but the payment streams stripped from the leases are payment intangibles.

This means that the assignment of the payment streams could be automatically perfected under Revised Uniform Commercial Code ("UCC") Article 9, Revised Uniform Commercial Code ("UCC") Article 9, Section 9-309(3), but only if the assignment is a sale. We agree with the bankruptcy court that the transactions in this case are loans, not sales, so there is no automatic perfection. However, there are unresolved factual and legal issues as to whether perfection was accomplished by taking possession of the underlying leases through a third party agent.

Accordingly, we AFFIRM IN PART, REVERSE IN PART, AND REMAND.

I. FACTS

Commercial Money Center, Inc. ("Debtor") leased equipment to lessees with sub-prime credit. It packaged groups of leases together and assigned its contractual rights to future lease payments to entities such as Net.Bnk, Inc., FSB ("NetBank"). To enhance the marketability of these payment streams Debtor obtained surety bonds guaranteeing the payments and it assigned its rights under the surety bonds to NetBank. As security for NetBank's receipt of the lease payments and any surety bond payments, Debtor granted NetBank a security interest in the underlying leases and other property. In other words, Debtor assigned NetBank both an interest in the payment streams and an interest in the underlying leases, but it separated the two interests.

A. *Transaction terms*

In 1999 and 2000 NetBank transferred over $ 47 million to Debtor in transactions involving 17 pools of leases. Seven lease pools remain at issue. Each transaction involved (1) a Sale and Servicing Agreement ("SSA") among NetBank, Debtor, and a surety company ("Surety"), (2) surety bonds issued by Surety to Debtor, which Debtor assigned to NetBank under the SSA and was supposed to deliver to NetBank, and (3) an indemnity agreement between Surety and Debtor. A typical lease involved 62 payments of which two had been paid at the inception, leaving 60 payments assigned by Debtor NetBank. Debtor paid Surety a premium equal to approximately two percent of the total of all payments due under each lease.

A representative SSA in the excerpts of record states in one part that Debtor and NetBank intend a sale, not a loan:

> (c) The execution and delivery of this Agreement shall constitute an acknowledgment by each of [Debtor as] Seller and [NetBank as] Purchaser that they intend that each assignment and transfer herein contemplated *constitute a sale and assignment outright, and not for security,* of the [Transferred Assets, defined in Section 2.1(a) to include the payment streams due or on deposit, the surety bonds, and proceeds of those things], conveying good title thereto free and clear of any Liens, from [Debtor] to [NetBank], *and that all such property shall not be part of the estate of [Debtor] in the event of bankruptcy* . . . . In the event that such conveyance is determined to be made as security for a loan made by [NetBank] to [Debtor], [Debtor] hereby grants to [NetBank] a first priority security interest in all of [Debtor's] right, title and interest in and to the [Transferred Assets] . . . . [Emphasis added.]

On the other hand, Section 2.10 of the SSA characterizes the transaction as a loan, not a sale, for tax purposes:

> SECTION 2.10 *Income Tax Characterization.* This Agreement has been structured with the intention that the [amounts payable to NetBank] will qualify under applicable federal, state, local and foreign tax law as *indebtedness* of [Debtor] secured by the Leases and other assets described in Section 2.1. The parties hereto agree to treat and to take no action inconsistent with the treatment of [such amounts] as such indebtedness for purposes of federal, state, local and foreign income or franchise taxes and any other tax imposed on or measured by income.
>
> [Emphasis added.]

Other provisions of the SSA also use both sale and loan terminology. The sample SSA provides for NetBank to wire an "Original Principal Amount" of $ 11,610,558.80 to Debtor "[a]s the purchase price," "being the Present Value of the payment stream discounted to effect Interest Rate yield" applying an "Interest Rate" of 12% per annum (later amended to 11.22876% per annum). In exchange Debtor assigns the Transferred Assets to NetBank "without recourse" and Debtor "shall have no interest in [the] Lease Assets which it may be permitted to sell, pledge, assign or transfer to any Person."

Debtor was required to perfect its own security interests in the leased equipment. It was also supposed to list NetBank in financing statements and lease documents as the "assignee" of those security interests, stamp the original lease, documents with an "appropriate legend . . .indicating [NetBank's] ownership interest and security interest in the Lease and Transferred Assets", and deliver to NetBank (A) evidence of the filing of financing statements, (B) a letter from Surety "acknowledging the valid issuance and delivery of the Surety Bonds," and (C) "the original of each executed Surety Bond with Power of Attorney and Notary attached . . . ." Debtor's Chapter 7 trustee, Richard M. Kipperman ("Trustee"), alleges that in fact Debtor did not fulfill all of these obligations and NetBank's interests were never perfected.

The SSA appoints Surety as "Servicer" of the leases and Debtor as "Sub-Servicer" to assume all responsibilities and perform all duties of the Servicer. Despite the extensive financial and other obligations of the Servicer and Sub-Servicer, further described below, NetBank has "no obligation to pay any Servicing Fee."

Duties of the Servicer/Sub-Servicer include paying all taxes and insurance on the leased equipment, collecting the payment streams from the lessees, and holding the leases and associated files on NetBank's behalf. Surety/Debtor have the option to commence legal proceedings to enforce the leases "at [their] own expense," but regardless of the amounts collected they must pay a fixed "Monthly Base Distribution Amount," which is $ 258,270.47 in the sample SSA, plus other sums including an initial payment of "Interest" and a final payment of any remaining "Principal Balance" and "Interest." They are permitted to grant some extensions to lessees but "in no event shall such extension change the Monthly Base Distribution Amount [$ 258,270.47] to be received by [NetBank]." If a lessee falls behind then Surety/Debtor shall "as [their] first recourse . . . realize upon and collect the proceeds in respect of the Surety Bond," but if Surety/Debtor wish to avoid whatever costs and consequences would flow from that choice, they can elect to make a "Servicer Advance" to NetBank to cover the shortfall. When all "Principal" and "Interest" payments have been made Section 2.8 of the SSA provides for any residual Transferred Assets to be transferred back to Debtor:

> *Termination of this Agreement.* This agreement shall terminate upon the receipt by [NetBank] of the Original *Principal* Amount plus all *Interest* Distributable Amounts [i.e., any remaining unpaid monthly "interest" payments, equal to one-twelfth of the product of the Interest Rate and the Principal Balance of all outstanding Leases] and, if the Monthly Total Distribution Amount is not paid in full on the Stated Maturity Date, *interest* accrued at the Interest Rate on such unpaid portion from and after the Stated Maturity Date. Upon such termination, [Surety/Debtor] shall be entitled to any amounts payable to it as provided herein. *Any remaining Transferred Assets shall thence be conveyed to [Debtor] without recourse.* [Emphasis added.]

A sample indemnity agreement between Debtor and Surety, included in the excerpts of record, obligates Debtor and its principals to indemnify Surety and hold it harmless "against all demands, claims, loss, costs, damages, expenses and attorneys' fees whatever, and any and all liability therefore, sustained or incurred by the Surety" under any surety bonds. NetBank is not a party to the indemnity agreement or the bonds.

Section 10.3 of the SSA provides: *"Governing law.* This agreement shall be governed by and construed in accordance with the laws of the state of Nevada without regard to the principles of conflicts of laws thereof and the obligations, rights and remedies of the parties under this agreement shall be determined in accordance with such laws." (Original entirely in capital letters.)

***

II. ISSUES

A. Are the payment streams "chattel paper" within the meaning of Revised UCC Article 9

B. Alternatively, were the transactions at issue loans, rather than sales?

C. If the answer to either question is affirmative, is there a genuine issue of material fact whether NetBank perfected its interests in the payment streams, or regarding NetBank's alleged equitable defenses?

III. STANDARDS OF REVIEW

***

***

For the reasons discussed below, we agree with the bankruptcy court's finding that the transactions at issue were loans rather than sales.

IV. DISCUSSION

Trustee's strong-arm powers generally enable him to avoid a pre-petition unperfected transfer by Debtor of an interest in its property. 11 U.S.C. § 544. Trustee argues that NetBank's interests were not perfected.

***

Like other courts we recognize the usefulness of the Official Comments in interpreting the UCC. We also recognize that some of the decisions cited below predate Revised UCC Article 9, but they are still useful on the issues discussed.

The perfection rules of Revised UCC Article 9 apply not just to security interests for *loans* but also to *sales* of chattel paper and payment intangibles. [UCC § 9-101(a)(3)] (with inapplicable exceptions, "this article applies to . . . (c) a *sale* of accounts, chattel paper, payment intangibles, or promissory notes") (emphasis added). Somewhat confusingly, the UCC uses lending terminology in provisions that are applicable to sales. *See* [UCC § 1-201(b)(35)] ("'Security interest' means' an interest in personal property or fixtures which secures payment or performance of an obligation. 'Security interest' includes any interest of a consignor and a *buyer* of accounts, *chattel paper, a payment intangible* or a promissory note in a transaction that is subject to Article 9.") (emphasis added). *See also* Rev. UCC § 9-109, Official Comment 5 ("Use of terminology such as 'security interest,' 'debtor,' and collateral' is merely a drafting convention adopted to reach [the] end [of applying 'this Article's perfection and priority rules' to sales transactions], and it's use has no relevance to distinguishing sales from other transactions. *See* PEB [Permanent Editorial Board] Commentary No. 14.").

Most perfection is not automatic. One exception is a sale of payment intangibles (referred to as a security interest), which is perfected automatically: "The following *security interests* are perfected when they attach: . . . 3. a *sale* of a payment intangible[.]" [UCC § 9-309(3)] (emphasis added).

NetBank claims that its transactions with Debtor come within this exception and are automatically perfected. NetBank argues in the alternative that its interests were perfected by possession of the chattel paper or perhaps by filed financing statements. *See* [UCC §§ 9-310(a)] (filed financing statement generally required for perfection), [9-312(a)] (chattel paper, perfection by filing), [9-313(a)] (tangible chattel paper, perfection by possession).

A. The payment streams are payment intangibles, not chattel paper

NetBank claims that the payment streams are payment intangibles, which is one of the requirements for automatic perfection under [UCC § 9-309(3)] -- the other principal requirement is that the transactions be sales, which we address in the next section of this discussion. The bankruptcy court held that the payment streams are chattel paper.

The UCC distinguishes between the monetary obligation *evidenced* by chattel paper and the chattel paper itself:

> 1. In this article:
>
> * * *
>
> (k) "Chattel paper" means a *record or records* that *evidence* both a monetary obligation and a security interest in or a lease of specific goods . . . . [I]n this paragraph, "monetary obligation" means a monetary obligation secured by the goods or owed under a lease of the goods . . . . [Emphasis added.]

[UCC § 9-102(a)(11)] (emphasis added).

This language on its face defines chattel paper to mean the "records" that "evidence" certain things, including monetary obligations. Payment streams stripped from the underlying leases are not records that evidence monetary obligations -- they *are* monetary obligations. Therefore, we agree with NetBank that the payment streams are not chattel paper.

If they are not chattel paper, what are they? Most monetary obligations are "accounts" but the definition of account excludes "rights to payment evidenced by chattel paper." Therefore the monetary obligations in this case fall within the payment intangible subset of the catch-all definition of general intangibles. *See* [UCC §§ 9-102(a)(2)] ("Account" means "a right to payment of a monetary obligation . . . for property that has been or is to be . . . leased . . . [but the term] does not include rights to payment evidenced by chattel paper . . ."); [9-102(a)(42)] ("General intangible" means any personal property other than accounts, chattel paper, and various other specified types of property, and specifically "includes payment intangibles"); [7] [9-102(a)(61)] ("Payment intangible" means "a general intangible under which the account debtor's principal obligation [is a monetary obligation]").

> 7 We recognize that the definition of general intangibles excludes chattel paper, but because the monetary obligations are not chattel paper they are not excluded from the definition of general intangibles.

As stated by one publication, the "carved-out payment streams seem to fit the definition of 'payment intangible' like a glove." That publication specifically disagrees with the bankruptcy court's decision in this case that the payment streams are chattel paper.

Our analysis might stop here. As the bankruptcy court noted, the plain language of the statute is usually conclusive.

Nevertheless, the bankruptcy court interpreted the plain words of the statute in a manner with which we do not agree:

> The definition [of chattel paper] states three requirements before collateral is characterized as chattel paper: 1) a record; 2) that evidences both a monetary obligation; and 3) a security in or a lease of specific goods. A monetary obligation is defined as a monetary obligation secured by the goods or owed under a lease of the goods. The parties do not dispute that all three elements for chattel paper are met with respect to the underlying equipment leases, but NetBank seeks to characterize the "monetary obligation" owed under the lease as a "payment intangible." This proposition does not follow from the plain language of the statutory definition of chattel paper and *such a reading would essentially delete the monetary obligation requirement from the definition.* (A canon of statutory construction is that a definition which declares what a term "means" excludes any meaning that is not stated). The court finds that the monetary obligation (i.e., the payment streams) constitute chattel paper. [Emphasis added.]

We do not understand how NetBank's reading "would essentially delete the monetary obligation requirement from the definition" of chattel paper. That requirement simply describes the *type* of records involved they must be records that "evidence" a monetary obligation, among other characteristics. [UCC § 9-102(a)(11)]. The leases do that, so they are chattel paper, but the payment streams do not. As stated above, they are not "records" that "evidence" monetary obligations, they *are* the monetary obligations.

The bankruptcy court's memorandum decision also comments, a footnote, that "The Court views NetBank's argument that [Debtor] transferred only the payment streams, and not the underlying leases, immaterial to the legal issue involved." We disagree, for the reasons just stated.

As an alternative basis for its ruling, the bankruptcy court considered the policies behind the statute. We agree with the bankruptcy court that the UCC aims to provide certainty in financial transactions and some means for third parties to discover competing interests in property, at least when that property is collateral or some types of purchased property. We are not persuaded that the plain meaning of the statute conflicts with such policies, or alternatively that it is our role to rewrite the statute if there is any such conflict.

The principal decision cited by the bankruptcy court involved an assignee ("Jefferson") that had been assigned only the payment streams and not the underlying equipment leases. *In re Commer. Mgmt. Serv., Inc.* A critical difference is that Jefferson had also taken possession of the leases. Here the possession of the leases is a disputed issue.

The Chapter 7 trustee in that case argued that the payment streams were general intangibles and that Jefferson had not perfected its interest in those payment streams because it had not filed any financing statements. The *Commercial Management* court rejected this argument, holding that "Jefferson perfected its security interest [in the payment streams] by possession" of the leases. The *Commercial Management* court acknowledged that the UCC does not "specifically provide" for this result:

> The [UCC] does not specifically provide that the transfer of chattel paper transfers the obligation it represents; nor does it specifically provide that perfection of a security interest in the written paper, for example, by possession, perfects a security interest in those obligations. It merely provides in Section 9-305 that "[a] security interest in chattel paper may be perfected by the secured party's taking possession of the collateral."

Nevertheless,

> [t]aking possession of the collateral, the chattel paper itself, would be meaningless unless the paper represented the underlying rights which were transferred by a transfer of the paper. Therefore, the necessary implication of [former UCC] Section 9-305 [permitting perfection by possession] is that delivery of chattel paper operates to transfer the claim that the paper represents . . . .

Commercial Management is not binding precedent but we assume for purposes of this discussion that it is correct. [8] Nevertheless, it is distinguishable. As NetBank's attorney argued before the bankruptcy court:

> Certainly if you sell a piece of chattel paper, it does come with all the rights that are thereunder. But the flip side of that is not true. If you buy some of the pieces under the chattel paper (i.e. the payment streams], it doesn't mean that you're getting the chattel paper as well.

8 *See generally* Rev. UCC § 9-109 Official Comment 5 (stating that a "'sale' of chattel paper" includes "a sale of a right in the receivable"); Rev. UCC § 9-313 Official Comment 2 (implying that delivery of a writing, such as tangible chattel paper, "operates to transfer the right to payment"); *Commercial Management* (quoting authority that the advantages of chattel paper would be lost if possession of the records does not perfect an interest in the payment

streams, and such perfection prevents a dishonest pledgor from "misleading a potential subsequent lender into believing that [the pledgor] is free to pledge that same property again . . .") (citations and footnotes omitted).

In other words, delivery of the chattel paper may "operate[] to transfer" a perfected interest in the associated payment streams, as *Commercial Management* holds, but that does not mean that payment streams *are* chattel paper. When stripped from the chattel paper they are payment intangibles.

Trustee argues that the automatic perfection of payment intangibles in Revised UCC § 9-309(3) was only intended to address loan participations, not the payment streams in this case. We are not persuaded. Nothing in the statute limits its application to loan participations. *See* [UCC § 9-309(a)] (stating simply, "The following security interests are perfected when they attach: . . . (3) a sale of a payment intangible," without mentioning loan participations). The official comments imply that a participation is just one type of interest that a party can assign in the monetary obligation. *See* Rev. UCC § 9-109, Official Comment 5 (a sale of chattel paper or certain other things, such as an account, "includes a sale of a right in the receivable, *such as* a sale of a participation interest") (emphasis added).

Trustee argues that our interpretation of the statute will lead to endless, debates over whether particular assignments are actually sales or secured loans. Again, we are not persuaded. Many transactions fall clearly on one side or the other of the sale versus loan dichotomy. When the answer is not clear the UCC contemplates that courts will need to decide the issue. *See, e.g.,* Rev. UCC § 9-109, Official Comment 5 ("[N]either this Article nor the definition of 'security interest' in [Rev. UCC] Section 1-201 provides rules for distinguishing sales transactions from those that create a security interest . . . ."). If such decisions are too burdensome on the commercial markets or on litigants then the remedy is with the legislature and not the courts.

Trustee also argues that if Revised UCC Article 9 permits purchases of payment streams to be automatically perfected, as we have held, then this permits secret interests and will wreak havoc on the financing markets. According to Trustee, there is no way for a hypothetical financier to protect itself against the possibility that an entity such as Debtor will transfer interests in the same payment streams more than once. NetBank responds that payment stripping is a bedrock principle of the securitization industry and that Trustee's concerns are misplaced.

NetBank argues persuasively that, if the hypothetical financier is the first to perfect, then generally it will be first in priority. *See* [UCC § 9-322(a)(1)]. [9] For these purposes it does not matter if the transaction was a sale or a secured loan because the UCC covers both, as we have discussed. Nor does it matter if the financier's interest is in the payment streams alone or in the underlying chattel paper leases, because a perfected interest in chattel paper includes the associated payment streams, at least if the reasoning in *Commercial Management* applies.

9 "1. Except as otherwise provided in this section, . . . (a) Conflicting perfected security interests and agricultural liens rank according to priority in time of filing or perfection." [UCC § 9-322(a)(1)].

A more difficult example is if the financier purchased an interest in the chattel paper leases *after* Debtor had already sold the payment streams to someone else. The financier might have no way to know of that prior "security interest."[10] The holder of that secret interest might not have filed any financing statements, or taken possession of the leases, or given any other notice because, under our holding, its interest would be automatically perfected under Revised UCC § 9-309(3).

10 As noted at the start of this discussion, the term "security interest" includes sales, not just collateral for loans.

NetBank taking argues that the financier could protect itself by possession of the leases, which allegedly would give it priority over the secret interest under the special rule of Revised UCC § 9-330(b). . . .

[9-330]. Priority of purchaser of chattel paper or instrument.

* * *

[(b)] A purchaser [i.e., financier] has priority over a security interest [i.e. the secret interest] in the chattel paper which is claimed other than merely as proceeds of inventory subject to a security interest if the purchaser [financier] gives new value and takes possession of the chattel paper under [Section 9-105] in good faith, in the ordinary course of [the financier's] business, and without knowledge that the purchase violates the rights of the secured party [i.e., the holder of the prior but secret interest].

[UCC § 9-330(b)].[11]

11 In the above hypothetical the chattel paper leases are sold to the financier, rather than assigned as security for a loan, but NetBank's argument is not limited to sales because the term "purchaser" includes not only a buyer but also a secured lender. *See* [UCC § 1-201(b)(29)] ("'Purchase' means taking by sale, lease, discount, negotiation, mortgage, pledge, *lien, security interest,* issue or reissue, gift or any other voluntary transaction creating an interest in property.") (emphasis added) and [(30)] ("'Purchaser' means a person that takes by purchase.").

We note that this special priority rule only applies by its terms to an interest "in the chattel paper." We have just held that the payment streams stripped from the leases are not chattel paper, so arguably this special priority rule is inapplicable, although Trustee has not argued the point. On the other hand, from the financier's point of view the assignment of an interest in chattel paper includes the associated payment streams, under the reasoning in *Commercial Management.* Therefore, for purposes of competing priorities under Revised UCC Section 9-330(b), the secret interest may be an interest in the financier's "chattel paper." We explicitly decline to resolve this ambiguity in Revised UCC Section 9-330(b), because neither that statute nor the hypothetical situations posed by the parties are before us on this appeal. It is sufficient for our purposes that the plain meaning of the "chattel paper" definition in [UCC § 9-102(a)(11)] does not lead to a result that is demonstrably counter to the legislative intent. If it turns out that the plain meaning of the "chattel paper" definition could cause problems under statutory provisions that are not at issue on this appeal, such as Revised UCC Section 9-330(b), then the answer lies either in the courts' interpretation of those provisions to harmonize the statute or in legislative amendment to the statute, not in disregarding the plain meaning of unambiguous provisions.

For all of these reasons we must apply the plain meaning of the statute: the payment streams separated from the underlying leases do not fall within the definition of chattel paper. [UCC § 9-102(a)(11)]. Rather, these monetary obligations fall within the payment intangible subset of the catch-all definition of general intangibles.

Because the payment streams are payment intangibles, NetBank's interest in them would be automatically perfected upon attachment under [UCC § 9-309(a)(3)] if its transactions with Debtor were sales rather than loans. We now turn to that issue.

B. *Debtor's transactions with NetBank were loans, not sales*

***

Whether a transaction is a sale or a loan is based on the intentions of the parties as "determined from all the facts and circumstances surrounding the transactions at issue." . . .

***

We must read the executives' declarations in the light most favorable to NetBank, as the non-moving party. Nevertheless, we conclude that they either contradict the documents or add nothing to the documents and the undisputed facts.

***

Turning to the documents, NetBank points out that in *Golden Plan* the Ninth Circuit reversed a finding that the transactions at issue were loans rather than sales, and did so despite the fact that the debtor or its agent retained physical possession of the property being sold and had a similar servicer "advance" provision. NetBank also notes that the courts do not give controlling weight to any one factor and not all factors need to point in the same direction.

NetBank cites numerous alleged characteristics of sales in the documents:

* sale terminology in the SSAs and other documents and the lack of "typical loan provisions" (presumably meaning guarantees, extensive foreclosure rights, and similar provisions);

* Debtor's assignment of the payment streams to NetBank "without recourse";

* the fact that Debtor was permitted but not required to make Servicer Advances;

* NetBank's ability to assign its rights in certain circumstances which it characterizes as treating the payment streams as its own property; [13]

* Debtor's lack of such rights;

* NetBank's purported inability to accelerate payments under the SSAs, and Debtor's purported lack of rights to repurchase or receive a reconveyance of the payment streams;

* the fact that the interest rate is fixed, which NetBank characterizes as evidence that the "Interest Rate" is simply a mechanism to compute the present discounted value of the Transferred Property; and

* that Debtor allegedly "retained no residual interest in the payment streams upon their sale to NetBank."

13 The SSA provides that NetBank "may assign or transfer the Transferred Assets and related security interests . . . in whole but not in part to another financial institution," and if NetBank assigns a part interest then the conveyance "shall be exclusively between the [NetBank] and such assignees or transferees, and other parties [to the SSA] shall not in any respect be obligated to, nor shall they be required to deal or communicate with, such assignees or transferees."

In our view this provision is entirely consistent with NetBank's role as a lender. It can sell participations in the loan, but unless it sells the entire loan the borrower (Debtor) and Sureties are entitled to deal solely with NetBank.

On this last point NetBank argues that the reconveyance of the Transferred Assets at the end of the SSAs' 60-month Collection Period would not actually convey any payment streams because those payment streams will be exhausted when NetBank is paid the full "Original Principal Amount" plus all "Interest" amounts. Trustee acknowledges that typically there were 62 payments under each lease and the lessee made two payments to Debtor upon signing the lease so there were 60 remaining payments. The exception, NetBank concedes, is that if Debtor made an "optional" Servicer Advance because a lessee failed to make a lease payment then

Debtor would retain any lease payments that it received after termination of the SSAs along with any late fees. According to NetBank, these latter circumstances do not evidence that Debtor retained any interest in the payment streams. Trustee posits a situation in which the last 10 of 60 lease payments were not paid by the lessee and were advanced by Debtor to illustrate that Debtor could receive a substantial residual interest upon termination of the SSA.

Despite NetBank's arguments, the transactions bear far more hallmarks of a loan than a sale. Each month Debtor as Sub-Servicer is required to pay NetBank a minimum fixed amount ($ 258,270.47 in the sample SSA) plus any additional "interest" and "principal" amounts owing to NetBank, regardless of what is or is not paid by the lessees. Debtor's assignment of the Transferred Assets to NetBank is non-recourse but just like many non-recourse loans it is secured by Debtor's property, including the underlying leases and equipment. Debtor as Sub-Servicer bears all costs of collection, from lessees, NetBank pays no fees for this expense or any other costs of servicing the leases, and if there is a shortfall at the end of the 60-month Collection Period then Debtor as Sub-Servicer is required to make up the shortfall and pay ongoing "interest" until all "principal" is repaid in full. At that point any residual value in the Transferred Assets is returned to Debtor with no possibility of NetBank receiving more than repayment of the "principal" and "interest" *(id.)* whereas Debtor can retain any subsequent payments and late fees paid by the lessees. SSA § 4.6. In other words, NetBank (1) has none of the potential benefits of ownership and (2) is contractually allocated none of the risk of loss.

These are strong indicia of a loan rather than a sale. The absence of risk "seems to result in a finding of a debtor-creditor relationship in most cases."

NetBank argues that it now has a "real risk" of loss, as evidenced by the bankruptcy court's Judgment. NetBank misstates the issue. In determining whether parties intended a sale or a loan the issue is how risks are contractually allocated when the transactions were entered into. In this case the risk was allocated to Debtor. The fact that Debtor later became insolvent is irrelevant. In *Woodson* the debtor had not paid its investors and was in bankruptcy but the contractual risk was allocated to the debtor. Primarily for that reason the transaction was determined to be a loan rather than a sale. NetBank argues that the issue on this appeal is "not whether [Debtor] was relieved of the risks of owning the Leases" but "whether [Debtor] continued at risk *with regard to NetBank.*" (Emphasis added.) This is too narrow a reading of the transactions and of *Woodson* and the other cases cited above. For purposes of determining whether a transaction is a sale or a loan, one useful factor is who is economically at risk. Under the transaction terms described above, it is Debtor, not NetBank, which is contractually allocated the risk of loss if, for example, a larger number of lessees default than expected.

***

We agree with the bankruptcy court that the transactions were loans, not sales. Therefore, NetBank does not satisfy one of the criteria under [UCC § 9-309(a)(3)] ("The following security interests are perfected when they attach: . . . 3) a *sale* of a payment intangible[.]") (emphasis added). NetBank's interest was not automatically perfected.

***

V. CONCLUSION

NetBank entered into transactions with Debtor that were intentionally structured to have characteristics of both a loan and a sale. It relied on Debtor and others to file UCC-1 financing statements, or otherwise assure that its interests in the payment streams from Debtor's leases were perfected, if they were not automatically perfected.

We hold, contrary to the bankruptcy court, that the payment streams are payment intangibles under Revised UCC Article 9 and therefore could have been automatically perfected if the payment streams had been sold to NetBank. We agree with the bankruptcy court, however, that the transactions between NetBank and Debtor are not sales but are secured, non-recourse loans instead. Therefore, NetBank's interests were not automatically perfected. There remain genuine issues of fact and law as to whether NetBank's interests were perfected by possession through an agent . . . . . Trustee did not meet his burden on the factual issue by submitting uncontested evidence regarding who held the leases at the relevant times, nor did Trustee establish entitlement to a judgment as a matter of law by establishing that, contrary to *Commercial Management,* possession of the leases could not perfect an interest in the payment streams. These unresolved issues preclude summary judgment for Trustee.

Accordingly, we AFFIRM IN PART, REVERSE IN PART, AND REMAND.

In re Kang Jin Hwang

396 B.R. 757 (Bankr. C.D. Cal. 2008)[530]

***

JUDGES: Hon. Samuel L. Bufford, United States Bankruptcy Judge.

OPINION BY: Samuel L. Bufford

---

[530] Some citations and footnotes omitted.

OPINION

AMENDED OPINION DENYING RELIEF FROM AUTOMATIC STAY

I Introduction

IndyMac Federal Bank ("IndyMac Federal") brings this motion, which the court grants, to reconsider its denial of relief from the § 362 [1] automatic stay to foreclose on real property belonging to debtor Kang Jin Hwang in Las Vegas. The property is security for a promissory note that was sold to the Federal Home Loan Mortgage Corp. ("Freddie Mac"), which has not joined and is not a party to this motion. Freddie Mac, in turn, has most likely sold the note to unknown third parties for securitization.

1 Unless otherwise indicated, all chapter, section and rule references are to the Bankruptcy Code, 11 U.S.C.A. §§ 101-1532 (West 2008) and to the Federal Rules of Bankruptcy Procedure, Rules 1001-9036.

After trial on the motion for relief from stay, and several rounds of briefing, the question remains: to whom is the debt owed (i.e., who owns the promissory note)? *See In re Gavin*, 319 B.R. 27, 31 (B.A.P. 1st Cir. 2004) (same). The court denies the motion on two procedural grounds: IndyMac Federal is not the real party in interest pursuant to Rule 17 of the Federal Rules of Civil Procedure, and the joinder of the owner of the note is required by Rule 19.

Subject to these procedural infirmities, the court finds that IndyMac Federal is entitled to enforce the note under California law (and the Uniform Commercial Code ("UCC")): IndyMac Federal remains the holder of the note, notwithstanding the sale, because it has possession of the note and the note is payable to its predecessor IndyMac Bank, F.S.E. ("IndyMac Bank").

II. RELEVANT FACTS

Kang Jin Hwang filed this chapter 7 case on April 22, 2008. Hwang's residence in Las Vegas, Nevada is encumbered by a first deed of trust recorded on February 1, 2007, supporting a promissory note in the amount of $ 376,000. The original payee on the promissory note, as well as the beneficiary of the deed of trust, is Mortgageit, Inc. ("Mortgageit"). Apparently, at some time before this case was filed, Mortgageit transferred the note to IndyMac Bank. After this motion was filed, IndyMac Bank was taken over by the Federal Deposit Insurance Corporation ("FDIC") and put into a conservatorship that now operates under the name IndyMac Federal, which has substituted into this motion. (Because IndyMac Bank, IndyMac Federal and the conservatorship have an identity of interests, they are referred to collectively here as "IndyMac.")

The deed of trust names MERS as "the beneficiary under the Security Instrument as a separate corporation that is acting solely as a nominee for Lender and Lender's successors and assigns." By Assignment of Deed of Trust dated January 29, 2008, which is attached to the motion, MERS transferred the deed of trust to IndyMac. Thus, MERS is no longer a party in interest as to this loan.

IndyMac sold the note to unidentified "investors" through Freddie Mac, apparently at some time prior to the filing of this bankruptcy case. Most likely, Freddie Mac sold the note into a securitization trust. [3] IndyMac does not know who owns the note today, although it still has possession of the note and there is nothing on the note to indicate that it has been transferred. Neither Freddie Mac nor any of the investors has joined in this motion. In addition, IndyMac has failed to provide any documents showing its sale of the note or its status as a servicing agent for the note's new owner.

IndyMac filed this motion for relief from the automatic stay on May 23, 2008, and set it for hearing on June 24. The motion included a declaration by Erica A. Johnson-Sect, an IndyMac vice president, providing the factual grounds for the motion. Copies of the promissory note and the deed of trust are attached to her declaration. Pursuant to Local Rule 9013-1(a)(13)(A), the court issued an order on June 10 requiring that IndyMac bring to court each declarant for whom a declaration had been submitted in support of its motion, for the purpose of presenting testimony to support the declaration.

Erica A. Johnson-Sect, a Vice President of IndyMac, testified at the trial on this motion on July 15, 2008, and brought the original note to court. While the court was satisfied with the declarant's testimony on the accuracy of the payment records, she testified that IndyMac no longer owned the note, but had sold it to investors through Freddie Mac. The court finds her testimony credible on this point.

Ms. Johnson-Sect also testified that IndyMac has brought this motion as the duly authorized servicing agent for the new owner of the note. The court disbelieves this testimony, particularly in view of (a) her testimony that she does not know who owns the note at the present time, and (b) the failure to offer in evidence any servicing agreement with the new owner.

III. DISCUSSION

IndyMac argues that it is entitled to enforce the note because it possesses the note and the note shows it as transferee and no endorsement transferring it to any other party. IndyMac also argues that the court may not raise *sua sponte* any deficiencies in the evidence it has presented to the court.

A motion for relief from the automatic stay must satisfy both substantive and procedural requirements. The substantive requirements are provided by § 362(d). The procedural requirements are imposed by the United States Constitution (due process) and the Federal Rules of Bankruptcy Procedure (which mostly incorporate the Federal Rules of Civil Procedure). The applicable rules here are the "real party in interest" rule and the "required joinder" rule.

The court finds that IndyMac is entitled to enforce the note, notwithstanding the sale to Freddie Mac. However, in coming to federal court, IndyMac must comply with the applicable procedures in this court. Two of these rules, the real party in interest rule and the required joinder rule, each requires IndyMac to join the present owner of the note in this motion for relief from stay, which it has refused to do.

A. Right to Enforce the Note

Since a party (such as IndyMac in this case) that seeks relief under § 362(d) does so in order to enforce rights that have been stayed by § 362(a), it is necessary to consider who is entitled to enforce the note under the substantive law that governs those rights. Thus, for a relief from stay motion based on a promissory note, the court must look to the substantive law that governs promissory notes.

Bankruptcy law does not provide for the enforcement of promissory notes generally. In the absence of bankruptcy law, the legal obligations of the parties are determined by the applicable non-bankruptcy law, which is usually state law.

In the United States, the law of promissory notes is not unified at the federal level. Instead, each state has its own law on promissory notes. However, every state has adopted a version of the UCC to govern negotiable promissory notes. Thus, we turn to the California Commercial Code ("CComC"), the California version of the UCC.

1. Relevant Law of Negotiable Instruments

The substantive California law that governs negotiable instruments is CComC Division 3 (the California version of UCC Article 3). *See* CComC § 3102(a). A negotiable instrument [6] (or more briefly, for Division 3 purposes, an "instrument") [7] typically takes one of two forms: a promissory note (designated as a "note"), or a draft (such as a check), [8] This case involves a note secured by a deed of trust.

6 "Negotiable instrument" is defined in § 3104(a) (UCC § 3-104) as follows (with certain exceptions not relevant in this case):

> (a) "[Ne]gotiable instrument" means an unconditional promise or order to pay a fixed amount of money, with or without interest or other charges described in the promise or order, if it is all of the following:
>
> (1) Is payable to bearer or to order at the time it is issued or first comes into possession of a holder.
>
> (2) Is payable on demand or at a definite time.
>
> (3) Does not state any other undertaking or instruction by the person promising or ordering payment to do any act in addition to the payment of money, but the promise or order may contain (i) an

undertaking or power to give, maintain, or protect collateral to secure payment, (ii) an authorization or power to the holder to confess judgment or realize on or dispose of collateral, or (Hi) a waiver of the benefit of any law intended for the advantage or protection of an obligor.

7 For the purposes of Division 3, "[i]nstrument means a negotiable instrument." *Id.* § 3104(b) (internal quotations omitted).
8 *See id.* § 3104(e); *see also* cmt. 4: "Instruments are divided into two general categories: drafts and notes." Negotiable instruments also include cashiers checks, teller's checks, money orders, travelers checks and certificates of deposit.

An instrument (including a secured note) may only be enforced by the "holder" of the note (with minor exceptions not relevant to this case). *See* CComC § 3301(a); UCC § 3-301. For an instrument payable to an identified person (such as the note in this case), there are two requirements for a person to qualify as a holder: (a) the person must be in possession of the instrument, and (b) the instrument must be payable to that person. *See* CComC § 1201(20); UCC § 1-201(20).

The payee of an instrument may negotiate it by indorsing it and delivering it to another person, who then becomes its holder [9] (and entitled to enforce it). Commercial Code § 3201 (UCC § 3-201) defines "negotiation" as follows:

> (a) "Negotiation" means a transfer of possession ... of an instrument by a person other than the issuer to a person who thereby becomes its holder.
>
> (b) . . . [I]f an instrument is payable to an identified person, negotiation requires transfer of possession of the instrument and its indorsement by the holder. If an instrument is payable to bearer, it may be negotiated by transfer of possession alone.

A fundamental feature of negotiable instruments is that they are transferred by the delivery of possession, not by contract or assignment. The transfer of an instrument "vests in the transferee any right of the transferor to enforce the instrument . . . ." CComC § 3203(b); UCC § 3-203(b). Thus, the right to enforce a negotiable instrument is only transferable by delivery of the instrument itself. CComC § 3203; UCC § 3-203.

9 In some circumstances, the transferee may obtain better rights than the transferor, by virtue of being a holder in due course. *See* CComC § 3305(b); UCC § 3-305(b). No such issue arises in this case.

The transfer of a negotiable instrument has an additional requirement: the transferor must indorse the instrument to make it payable to the transferee. *See* CComC § 3205(a); UCC § 3-205(a). Alternatively, the transferor may indorse the instrument in blank, and thereby make it enforceable by anyone in its possession (much like paper currency). *See* CComC § 3205(b); UCC § 3-205(b). If the transferor makes a transfer without indorsing the instrument, the transferee has a right to demand indorsement by the transferor. *See* CComC § 3203(c); UCC § 3-203(c).

2. Who May Enforce the Note in this Case

IndyMac contends, and the court assumes without deciding, that the note here at issue is a negotiable instrument, as defined in the CComC § 3104(a), (b) and (e). The note is on a standard printed form that is used in the finance industry for notes that are freely bought and sold in a manner inconsistent with treating it as a non-negotiable note. Thus IndyMac must be the holder of the note to entitle it to enforce the note (including bringing this relief from stay motion).

In this case, the note is payable to IndyMac (pursuant to its negotiation from Mortgageit to IndyMac), and IndyMac had possession of the note at the time that the motion was filed. Under these facts, IndyMac qualifies as the holder of the note.

There is a second scenario, not supported by the evidence in this case, in which IndyMac would have a right to enforce the note. If IndyMac held the note on behalf of the new owner (Freddie Mac or its subsequent transferee), this would constitute possession by the new owner, and IndyMac would be entitled to seek relief from stay on the new owner's behalf (provided that it joined the new owner in the motion).

Notably, however, IndyMac does not contend that it holds the note as an agent on behalf of Freddie Mac or its transferee. Indeed, it is doubtful that IndyMac could make such a claim, because IndyMac does not know who owns the note. Thus, this argument is not available.

3. Sale of the Note to Freddie Mac

In this case IndyMac sold the note to Freddie Mac, which in turn most likely sold it again as part of a securitization transaction. Insofar as the record before the court discloses, the owner of the note today is unknown.

In this case, IndyMac has not delivered the note to Freddie Mac (or its successor): IndyMac still possesses the note. In addition, the note bears no indication of a transfer: it still shows IndyMac as the payee (pursuant to the indorsement from Mortgageit). In consequence, IndyMac remains the holder of the note and is entitled to enforce it under CComC § 3301(a) (UCC § 3-301): the right to enforce the note has not yet passed to Freddie Mac or its successor owner of the note. This interpretation of § 3203 is supported by Note 1, which states in relevant part:

> [A] person who has an ownership right in an instrument might not be a person entitled to enforce the instrument. For example, suppose X is the owner and holder of an instrument payable to X. X sells the instrument to Y but is unable to deliver immediate possession to Y. Instead, X signs a document conveying all of X's right, title, and interest in the instrument to Y. Although the document may be effective to give Y a claim to ownership of the instrument, Y is not a person entitled to enforce the instrument until Y obtains possession of the instrument. No transfer of the instrument occurs under Section 3203(a) until it is delivered to Y.
>
> An instrument is a reified right to payment. The right is represented by the instrument itself. The right to payment is transferred by delivery of possession of the instrument "by a person other than its issuer for the purpose of giving to the person receiving delivery the right to enforce the instrument."

The foregoing makes it clear that no successor to IndyMac presently has a right to enforce the note, because IndyMac still has possession of the note.

This raises the question of who, if anybody, is presently entitled to enforce the note in these circumstances. Two alternatives are available. First, there may be no entity that is entitled to enforce the note until its delivery to its new rightful owner is accomplished. Second, because IndyMac continues to possess the note, it may be entitled to enforce the note, even though the note is owned by another entity.

There are good policy reasons for adopting the first alternative. Disabling the transferor from enforcing the note upon its sale to a new owner encourages the parties to complete the transaction by delivery of the instrument to the new owner. In the present configuration of the home mortgage industry, this policy can be important: it would discourage an apparently common practice in the secondary mortgage market of failure to deliver notes when they are sold, often numerous times, so that the possessor of the note may be far removed from the real owner of the note.

The second alternative also has substantial policy support. A note supporting a home mortgage ought to be enforceable, and the homeowner should be required to make the payments owing. If the owner fails to pay, the markets rely on the ability of the noteholder to bring foreclosure proceedings to realize the value of the note. As the court in *In re Foreclosure Cases* stated: "This Court is well aware that entities who hold valid notes are entitled to receive timely payments in accordance with the notes. And, if they do not receive timely payments, the entities have the right to seek foreclosure on the accompanying mortgages."

Interposing a hiatus on the right to foreclose (apart from the automatic stay resulting from the filing of a bankruptcy case) interferes with the security of lenders in the home mortgage market. In addition, the noteholder is in position to cancel the note upon payment and to deliver the canceled note to the obligor.

IndyMac cites no case holding that, after selling (but not delivering) a secured note to an unrelated third party, the seller is entitled to enforce the note for its own account. The court's independent research has discovered two such cases, both involving transfers to corporations wholly owned by the sellers. Both cases involved transfers to corporations owned by the sellers . . . . The sale of a note to an unrelated third party, as in this case, is a very different situation.

In the court's view, the second alternative is the better view: the holder of a note is entitled to enforce it, notwithstanding sale of the note to another party, until the note is delivered to the purchaser (after indorsement, if appropriate). This assures that, notwithstanding the sale of the note and the failure to deliver the note pursuant to the sale, a holder exists that may enforce the note against the obligor. Thus, the court holds that, notwithstanding the sale of the note, IndyMac remains the holder of the note and is entitled to enforce it.

The debtor is not at risk in making payments on the note to IndyMac instead of the owner of the note. CComC § 3602 (UCC § 3-602) provides that any payment to a "person entitled to enforce the instrument" must be credited against the note, even if the debtor knows that a different party is claiming ownership of or an interest in the note.

B. Real Party in Interest

IndyMac's substantive right to enforce the note, as the holder, does not dispose of the motion before the court. In coming to federal court to enforce this right, IndyMac must comply with the applicable procedures of federal court. Two such procedures stand in the way of granting the motion for relief from stay in this case. The first procedural problem arises from the real party in interest rule.

Rule 17 of the Federal Rules of Civil Procedure provides: "An action must be prosecuted in the name of the real party in interest." The purpose of this rule is to require that an action be brought "in the name of the party who possesses the substantive right being asserted under the applicable law . . . ."

***

1. Real Party in Interest After Securitization

If a loan has been securitized, the real party in interest is the trustee of the securitization trust, not the servicing agent. *See LaSalle Bank N.A. v. Nomura Asset Capital Corp.* ("*LaSalle-Nomura*"); *accord, LaSalle Bank N.A. v. Lehman Bros. Holdings, Inc.* ("*LaSalle-Lehman*"). This rule does not turn on who is in possession of the note.

In the *LaSalle-Nomura* case, the bank brought an action against Nomura Asset Capital Corp., the asset securitization trustee, "as Trustee for Certificate Holders of Asset Securitization Corporation Commercial Mortgage Pass-Through Certificates, Series 1997- D5." Defendants moved to dismiss, in part on the grounds that the real party in interest, pursuant to Rule 17, was the mortgage servicer. In denying the motion, the court found that the real party in interest was the trustee of the trust (the plaintiff in the case), and not its loan servicer (which had not been joined in the litigation).

***

In this case, although it is most likely that the note here at issue has been included in a securitization, IndyMac has refused to provide any information about the present owner of the note, to join the owner as a moving party, or to provide copies of any of the relevant contracts. Because IndyMac has not provided the relevant documents, the court cannot determine the identity of the real party in interest.

If the note is part of a securitization, the burden of joining the owner of the note is not substantial. A securitization typically involves the creation of a trust, the appointment of a trustee, a transfer to the trust of some ten thousand secured real estate notes (such as the one involved in this case) and the sale of interests in the trust to a substantial number of investors. The trustee of the trust is authorized, pursuant to trust law, to act on behalf of the trust. Thus only the trustee, and not the investors, should be joined as the owner of the note at issue. Indeed, this is exactly what happened in both *LaSalle-Nomura and LaSalle-Lehman.*

The right to enforce a note on behalf of a noteholder does not convert the noteholder's agent into a real party in interest. "As a general rule, a person who is an attorney-in-fact or an agent solely for the purpose of bringing suit is viewed as a nominal rather than a real party in interest and will be required to litigate in the name of his principal rather than in his own name." Consequently, even if the court had found that a proper agency relationship exists between the holder of the note and the party seeking to enforce its security, this does not excuse the agent from the requirement that an action be prosecuted in the name of the noteholder, who is the real party in interest. Thus, even if IndyMac is the loan servicer for the unidentified owner of the note here at issue (a fact that IndyMac has failed to prove), it is not the real party in interest that is required to bring the motion before the court.

The court concludes that the real party in interest has not joined in the motion before the court. Indeed, neither the court nor IndyMac even knows who the real party in interest is. Pursuant to Rule 17(a)(3), the court must give IndyMac a reasonable amount of time to accomplish this joinder. Despite two continuances (totaling more than two months) to accomplish this joinder, IndyMac has refused to join the owner of the note in this motion. Thus, the motion must be denied on these grounds.

***

IV. CONCLUSION

In conclusion, the court finds upon reconsideration that IndyMac is entitled to enforce the secured note here at issue. However, it must satisfy the procedural requirements of federal law in seeking relief from the automatic stay for this purpose. These requirements include joining the owner of the note on two separate grounds: it is the real party in interest under Rule 17, and it is a required party under Rule 19.

Because IndyMac has failed and refused to join the owner of the secured note, the motion for relief from stay is denied.

Rights of the purchaser-assignee. The general rule is found in Article 9 of the UCC. Under this Article, the rights of the purchaser (assignee) of certain financial assets (accounts, chattel paper, or payment intangibles)[531] are subject to:

(1) terms of the agreement between the borrower ("account debtor") and lender (assignor) and to any defense or claim in recoupment arising from the transaction, and

(2) any other defense or claim of the borrower against the lender occurring before the borrower receives notice of the assignment authenticated by the lender or purchaser.

However, the general rule does not apply if the borrower "made an enforceable agreement not to assert defenses or claims."[532] The borrower's claim against the lender may be asserted against the purchaser under subsection (1) only to reduce the debt.[533] This general rule is subject to exceptions, based on (1) other laws applicable to certain transactions by individual debtors, (2) consumer transactions and (3) health-care-insurance receivables.[534]

---

[531] See definition below.

[532] U.C.C. §9-404(a) (2005).

[533] U.C.C. §9-404(b) (2005). Section 9-102(a)(3) defines an "account debtor" [to mean] a person obligated on an account, chattel paper, or general intangible. The term does not include persons obligated to pay a negotiable instrument, even if the instrument constitutes part of chattel paper. Section 9-102(a)(42) defines "general intangible" as "any personal property, including things in action, other than accounts, chattel paper, commercial tort claims, deposit accounts, documents, goods, instruments, investment property, letter-of-credit rights, letters of credit, money, and oil, gas, or other minerals before extraction. The term includes payment intangibles and software. " This general rule is subject to exceptions, based on (1) other laws applicable to certain transactions by individual debtors, (2) consumer transactions and (3) health-care-insurance receivables. U.C.C. § 9-102(a)(3), (42) (2009).

[534] U.C.C. § 9-404(c)-(e) (2009).

But not all financial assets are covered by Article 9. Excluded from the Article are negotiable instruments and securities.

If the purchased assets are negotiable instruments, Article 3 of the UCC applies.[535] And if the financial assets are securities, Article 8 of the UCC governs instead.

Article 3 applies to "negotiable instruments."[536] A negotiable instrument is generally defined as "an unconditional promise or order to pay a fixed amount of money" that is "payable to bearer or to order" provided that certain conditions are met.[537] A negotiable instrument that is a promise is a "note"; a negotiable instrument that is an order is a "draft," which includes a "check."[538] In a note, the "issuer" (or "maker") makes a promise to pay "to a person entitled to enforce the instrument";[539] in a draft, the "drawer" orders another party, the "drawee" (commonly a bank), to make payment to another party, and is "secondarily" liable, *e.g.,* liable if the drawee does

[535] A negotiable instrument (NI) is a special type of contract for the payment of money that is unconditional and capable of transfer by negotiation (e.g., checks, commercial paper). A negotiable instrument is different from a contract. Unlike a contract: (1) formation of a NI does not require offer, acceptance and consideration, but (2) the right to the performance is linked possession of the document (except, e.g., loss or theft). The Payee's rights are not subject to set-off, and are not conditioned on the validity of the underlying contract giving rise to the debt (e.g., sale of goods). A prior party liable on the NI need not receive notice of the transfer of the rights under the NI. Finally, the transfer is free of equities. The title of a holder in due course of NI is better than title of the transferor from whom the holder obtained it. Negotiation enables the transferee to become the party to the contract, and to enforce it in his own name. One can negotiate the instrument by endorsement or its delivery alone. Promissory notes and bills of exchange are two main types of negotiable instruments. A promissory note is a written promise by the *maker* to pay money to the *payee*. A maker or a drawer of a promissory note promises to unconditionally pay the payee (beneficiary) a specific amount on a specified date. A promissory note is an unconditional order to pay a specific amount to the order of a person on demand or on a specified date. Articles 3 and 4 of the U.C.C. govern the issuance and negotiation of negotiable instruments. For a writing to be a negotiable instrument under Article 3: 1) The promise or order to pay must be unconditional; 2) The payment must be a specific sum of money, although interest may be added to the sum; 3) The payment must be made on demand or at a definite time; 4) The instrument must not require the person promising payment to perform any act other than paying the money specified; 5) The instrument must be payable to bearer or to order ("words of negotiability"). U.C.C. § 3-104(a) (2009). The following are not NI: letters of credit (governed by Article 5 of the Code); bills of lading and other documents of title (governed by Article 7 of the Code); securities (governed by Article 8 of the Code); deeds and other documents conveying interests in real estate, although a mortgage may secure a promissory note which is governed by Article 3.

[536] U.C.C. § 3-102(a) (2009).

[537] *Id.* § 3-104(a).

[538] *Id.* § 3-104 cmt. 4.

[539] JAMES J. WHITE & ROBERT S. SUMMERS, UNIFORM COMMERCIAL CODE § 13-6, at 476 (5th ed. 2000) (quoting U.C.C. § 3-104(e)).

not pay.[540] A negotiable instrument may be transferred or "negotiated" to another person.[541]

Article 8 applies to securities.[542] The definition of "security" includes "[a] share or similar equity interest issued by a corporation, business trust, joint stock company, or similar entity."[543]

The purchaser's rights are subject to the borrower's rights against the lender, unless the purchaser is a "holder in due course"[544] or "protected purchaser" (if the purchaser

---

540 JAMES J. WHITE & ROBERT S. SUMMERS, UNIFORM COMMERCIAL CODE § 13-6, at 477 (5th ed. 2000).

541 *See* U.C.C. § 3-201(a) (2009) ("'Negotiation' means a transfer of possession, whether voluntary or involuntary, of an instrument by a person other than the issuer to a person who thereby becomes its holder."); *id.* § 3-104(b) ("Instrument" means a negotiable instrument.").

542 *Id.* § 8-104 cmt. 1 ("This section lists the ways in which interests in securities and other financial assets are acquired under Article 8. In that sense, it describes the scope of Article 8.")..

543 *Id.* § 8-103(a); *see id.* § 8-102(a)(15) (defining "security").

544 Section 3-302 of the UCC defines a holder in due course. "(a) Subject to subsection (c) and Section 3-106(d), '"holder in due course' means the holder of an instrument if: (1) the instrument when issued or negotiated to the holder does not bear such apparent evidence of forgery or alteration or is not otherwise so irregular or incomplete as to call into question its authenticity; and (2) the holder took the instrument (i) for value, (ii) in good faith, (iii) without notice that the instrument is overdue or has been dishonored or that there is an uncured default with respect to payment of another instrument issued as part of the same series, (iv) without notice that the instrument contains an unauthorized signature or has been altered, (v) without notice of any claim to the instrument described in Section 3-306, and (vi) without notice that any party has a defense or claim in recoupment described in Section 3-305(a). (b) Notice of discharge of a party, other than discharge in an insolvency proceeding, is not notice of a defense under subsection (a), but discharge is effective against a person who became a holder in due course with notice of the discharge. Public filing or recording of a document does not of itself constitute notice of a defense, claim in recoupment, or claim to the instrument. (c) Except to the extent a transferor or predecessor in interest has rights as a holder in due course, a person does not acquire rights of a holder in due course of an instrument taken (i) by legal process or by purchase in an execution, bankruptcy, or creditor's sale or similar proceeding, (ii) by purchase as part of a bulk transaction not in ordinary course of business of the transferor, or (iii) as the successor in interest to an estate or other organization. (d) If, under Section 3-303(a)(1), the promise of performance that is the consideration for an instrument has been partially performed, the holder may assert rights as a holder in due course of the instrument only to the fraction of the amount payable under the instrument equal to the value of the partial performance divided by the value of the promised performance. (e) If (i) the person entitled to enforce an instrument has only a security interest in the instrument and (ii) the person obliged to pay the instrument has a defense, claim in recoupment, or claim to the instrument that may be asserted against the person who granted the security interest, the person entitled to enforce the instrument may assert rights as a holder in due course only to an amount payable under the instrument which, at the time of enforcement of the instrument, does not exceed the amount of the unpaid obligation secured. (f) To be effective, notice must be received at a time and in a manner that gives a reasonable opportunity to act on it. (g) This

of a security).[545] In that case the purchaser takes the assets free of most defenses and claims. The holder in due course doctrine protects qualifying purchasers who purchase an instrument without notice of certain defenses.[546] The doctrine, in theory, facilitates commerce by encouraging purchase of instruments.[547]

The difference between Article 9 and Articles 3 and 8 of the U.C.C. suggests that, as markets develop in financial instruments, the pressure to erode the defensive rights of the borrowers rises. In such a case lenders would more likely insist on the borrowers' consent in their agreements not to enforce their rights, or rely on rules that protect lenders from the borrowers' defensive rights.

B. Distinguishing a Sale from a Secured Loan[548]

After a loan is made, or a debt is created, it is transferred to a SPV (directly or through the Originator). In most cases, the loan documents (including the note) remain in the seller's possession, and the seller or another party, other than the buyer SPV, continues to service the loan. The servicer receives the payments from the borrowers and transfers the money to the investors, in accordance with the terms of the investors' securities. Furthermore, the note accompanying the loan is rarely indorsed to the buyer, be it the Originator or the SPV, because the holder of the note is usually the one that collects the payments in court, and the servicer would be the one to perform the function to suing borrowers and collecting the proceedings.[549]

The main question in connection with the transfer of the loan to the SPV is: how to categorize the transfer legally? From that category, we can derive the rules that govern the form of the transfer, the rights of the SPV to the loan and accompanying note and collateral, if any, and the extent of these rights against the seller, borrower, and third parties, especially when the borrower or the seller become insolvent.

---

section is subject to any law limiting status as a holder in due course in particular classes of transactions. U.C.C. § 3-302 (2009).

[545] Section 8-303 of the UCC deals with protected purchasers. (a) "Protected purchaser" means a purchaser of a certificated or uncertificated security, or of an interest therein, who: (1) gives value; (2) does not have notice of any adverse claim to the security; and (3) obtains control of the certificated or uncertificated security. (b) In addition to acquiring the rights of a purchaser, a protected purchaser also acquires its interest in the security free of any adverse claim. U.C.C. § 8-303 (2009).

[546] JAMES J. WHITE & ROBERT S. SUMMERS, UNIFORM COMMERCIAL CODE § 14-2, at 509 (5th ed. 2000).

[547] *Id.* § 14-1, at 507-08.

[548] 1 TAMAR FRANKEL, SECURITIZATION § 7.11 (Ann Taylor Schwing ed., 2d ed. 2005).

[549] For a discussion of "security interest" see B.c. below.

a. Categorizing a Sale from a Secured Loan[550]

Like other instruments that do not bear clear "class earmarks," the transfer of loans to SPVs can point to both secured loans to the transferor or an assignment of beneficial ownership in the loans. Courts do not follow a uniform analysis in choosing and weighing the earmarks of these transactions. Circumstances may make the analysis even more difficult. For example, if the transferor sells the loan and undertakes to repurchase it from the buyers, the transaction can be categorized by form, as a sale of the loan, or by substance, as a loan to the transferor, secured by the transferred loan. To classify a loan transfer, courts turn to the terms of the agreement between the parties. Courts take into account the parties' categorization of the transaction, although this categorization is not conclusive. Courts also examine the intent of the parties and how they allocated the benefits and risks from the loan, that is, the economic reality of the transaction. A party may be estopped from arguing for a different classification if the other party to the agreement relied on that classification and the change in the legal category works to its detriment.

b. What Law Applies to the Issue?

In bankruptcy cases, courts usually apply state law to classify the transaction, and most states resort to Article 9 of the U.C.C., with its modifications in the specific state. Article 9 generally applies to "a transaction, regardless of its form, that creates a security interest in personal property or fixtures by contract."

A "security interest" is defined as "an interest in personal property or fixtures which secures performance of an obligation."[551] A security interest generally arises as part of a loan transaction, when the debtor signs a "security agreement" granting the creditor a security interest in some property of the debtor (collateral).[552] The security interest provides the creditor an alternate remedy upon the debtor's default by taking possession of the collateral and disposing of it to satisfy the debt.[553]

Therefore, the intent of the parties is the principal test to classifying the transaction. Courts derive the parties' intent from the way in which the parties characterized the

---

[550] 1 TAMAR FRANKEL, SECURITIZATION § 7.11.1 (Ann Taylor Schwing ed., 2d ed. 2005).

[551] U.C.C. § 1-201(b)(35) (2009).

[552] JAMES J. WHITE & ROBERT S. SUMMERS, UNIFORM COMMERCIAL CODE § 21-1, at 711 (5th ed. 2000)

[553] *Id.* § 25-1, at 885; *see* U.C.C. §§ 9-601 to -628 (2009) (governing default and enforcement of security interest).

transaction and from the terms of transaction itself, taking into account the risks allocated among the parties. These risks include recourse provisions, and whether the repurchase is at the option of the transferor (a sale) or the transferee (a grant of security). Courts also give weight to whether the borrower and the transferor's creditors received notice of the transaction and whether the transferor retained the loan documents. The terms of the transaction may point to its classification: the rate of interest paid by the borrower as compared to that received by the buyers, excess servicing fees received by the transferor, the maturity date of the transferred loan, tax and accounting treatment of the transaction, who controls the lender's rights, and whether the seller has the right to substitute the loan for another.

The history of the transaction can also be informative: whether the seller has a preexisting obligation to the buyers, whether the full price for the loan was paid at the transfer, whether the buyer gave a note to the seller for the amount of the loan, and whether the transferee performed a credit check on the transferor. The courts may examine whether the assets held by the seller for servicing are commingled with the seller's assets, although this factor may not be accorded much weight. Similarly, the fact that the service function was retained by the transferor is not a decisive factor. There are efficiency reasons for these arrangements. Finally, public policy issues, such as usury, are taken into account to determine whether the transaction is a loan or sale. A transaction should not be recognized as a sale if it is a subterfuge for a usurious loan. For example, if the ratio of the price paid for the loan to its fair market value is high, the transaction may be a usurious loan.

In *Octagon Gas Systems, Inc. v. Rimmer (In re Meridian Reserve, Inc.)*, the Tenth Circuit held that if the subject matter of the transaction is an account, Article 9 applies whether a transaction is a sale or a loan (secured or unsecured). Under Article 9 at that date, the transaction created a security interest. Even if the account is assigned before the transferor's bankruptcy petition, the account remains the estate of the transferor upon the transferor's bankruptcy pursuant to section 541 of the Bankruptcy Code. However, Article 9 was amended, and the decision no longer has this impact.

c. The Creation and Perfection of a Security Interest

Article 9 distinguishes between two concepts concerning a security of interest. One is the attachment of the security interest. When the interest is created and attached, the secured party can realize the interest as against the debtor. However, if the secured party is to realize the interest as against third parties, the interest must also be perfected (after the attachment). With perfection, the security interest is enforceable against third parties as well as the debtor. There are different methods of perfection. Among them are the secured party taking possession of the collateral, as well as the filing of a financing statement in one or more public filing offices, which is the most common method of perfection.[554] The secured creditor must give notice that it may have a security interest, giving its own name and the name of the debtor. Persons who are interested in the details may have to inquire about them. The filing, however, must be at a central location. The filing is designed to protect future creditors from assuming that the financial assets belong freely to the debtor, and protect the secured creditors from the debtor's creditors. Filing is in fact protective disclosure, perhaps similar to the trust law requirement to earmark trust property.

d The Role of Recourse in the Sale of Financial Assets

When a buyer of a financial asset retains recourse to the seller so that only some risks are transferred, is the transaction a sale or a secured loan? The question often arises when the buyer attempts to enforce or has to defend its ownership rights to an asset in the seller's later bankruptcy case. Authors noted that "true sale" is the "holy grail" of the securitization Market. Assuming an arm's-length transaction in which the buyer has taken all requisite steps to perfect its interest in the asset, some scholars concluded that a distinction can be made between two types of recourse.

The First is Recourse for Collectability. Recourse to a seller who warrants performance of the asset being sold (collectability) should not turn the sale into a loan. In a typical case of receivables sold with recourse for collectability: (i) the buyer's return is tied directly to the payment terms of the underlying asset; (ii) upon liquidation, the buyer's interest in proceeds is not limited to this investment plus a predetermined rate of return that is unrelated to the underlying asset; (iii) only the buyer's interest, not the seller's, is affected by post purchase changes in the asset's Market value; and (iv) normally, the seller would not have a right to substitute the asset purchased with a new asset.

The Other Type of Recourse that Buyers may have Toward Sellers is Economic Recourse. An absolute promise by the seller to repay the purchase price, with an agreed upon rate of return unrelated to the payment terms of the underlying asset, clearly risks turning a sale into a loan. This, in some fashion, guarantees the return to the purchaser without any regard to the economic characteristics of the transferred asset. In sum, the writers distinguish between a situation in which the seller retains the collection costs on the loans, which remains a true sale, and a situation in which the seller retains the losses from nonpayment of the loans, which is not a true sale but a secured loan to the seller. Therefore, the focus should be on the nature of the recourse rather than on the extent of the risks. Arguably bankruptcy courts should accept the definition of a true sale under state law: A sale of financial assets, with or without recourse for collectability, does not offend the policy of equitable distribution because such a sale should not be a fraudulent conveyance and, as a practical matter, recharacterizing a sale with recourse as a loan will not result in any

[554] U.C.C. § 9-310(a) (2009)..

significant increased distribution to unsecured creditors. Besides the law governing the securitization transactions would thereby be more certain.

Recognizing sales with recourse for collectability may promote several important policies. Among these are transactional efficiency and predictability, allowing sellers to better assess the risk of assets they originate and minimize the amount by which they discount the asset's sale price. Buyers would also benefit because they would not have to wonder how much recourse is "too much" and become involved in expensive and complicated two-tiered structures to accomplish a true sale. Even though the sellers may be able to collect on the loans more effectively than the buyers, there are reasons for questioning this approach. Collection costs and ultimate losses are not separate, and are open to interpretation. The distinction offers a way to "sell" and "retain" the sold loans, and that is precisely what should be avoided. If the seller is a better collection agent, let the buyer appoint the seller a collection agent and pay the seller for its services. That would create a clearer distinction.

e. Chattel Paper and Accounts[555]

If Article 9 of the U.C.C. applies to the transfer, that is, if the transfer is of a "chattel paper" or an "account," as defined in the U.C.C., the transfer is categorized as creating a security interest (rather than the transfer of beneficial ownership interests), and the transaction will be deemed to create a security for a borrowing by the transferor.

The definition provides: "Account", except as used in "account for", means a right to payment of a monetary obligation, whether or not earned by performance, (i) for property that has been or is to be sold, leased, licensed, assigned, or otherwise disposed of, (ii) for services rendered or to be rendered, (iii) for a policy of insurance issued or to be issued, (iv) for a secondary obligation incurred or to be incurred, (v) for energy provided or to be provided, (vi) for the use or hire of a vessel under a charter or other contract, (vii) arising out of the use of a credit or charge card or information contained on or for use with the card, or (viii) as winnings in a lottery or other game of chance operated or sponsored by a State, governmental unit of a State, or person licensed or authorized to operate the game by a State or governmental unit of a State. The term includes health-care-insurance receivables. The term does not include (i) rights to payment evidenced by chattel paper or an instrument, (ii) commercial tort claims, (iii) deposit accounts, (iv) investment property, (v) letter-of-credit rights or letters of credit, or (vi) rights to payment for money or funds advanced or sold, other than rights arising out of the use of a credit or charge card or information contained on or for use with the card.

---

[555] 1 TAMAR FRANKEL, SECURITIZATION § 7.11.2 (Ann Taylor Schwing ed., 2d ed. 2005).

The U.C.C. defines "chattel paper" to mean "a record or records that evidence both a monetary obligation and a security interest in specific goods. . . . If a transaction is evidenced by records that include an instrument or series of instruments, the group of records taken together constitutes chattel paper." [556]

In the opinion of some, Article 9 application of sales of accounts and chattel paper provided an approach that generally has been successful in avoiding the problem of sale v. security interest. Therefore, transfers of chattel paper and accounts are subject to Article 9 even when they involve an undisputed sale of the interests to buyers. Further, it may be argued that the parties should follow the form set forth in Article 9 even if the parties intended to create an assignment of title—a sale. Article 9 applies to "a transaction, regardless of its form, that creates a security interest in personal property" except as otherwise provided. This interpretation of Article 9 has been disputed on several grounds. First, for at least 100 years, the assignment of portions of mortgage loans (mortgage participations) has been recognized as a transfer of ownership rights. Numerous decisions upheld the buyers' ownership rights by holding that such assignments pass the beneficial rights in notes that accompany mortgages. Second, to effect an assignment of a security interest, the U.C.C. does not require any action, apart from an agreement; buyers may purchase interests in notes and thereby receive legal title to these interests. Third, an assignment providing that the buyer receives a security interest and a share in the proceeds of the assigned note may be ineffective as an attempt to create "floating secured parties."

The better opinion, optimistically supported by bank counsel, seems to be that Article 9 was intended to apply only to transfers in which the parties intended to create a security interest in personal property. When the parties intended to create an assignment of beneficial ownership rights rather than a security interest, the transaction is outside the intent and language of the Article. Interests in accounts and chattel paper can be assigned, and legal ownership can be transferred in them.

Receivables-backed Securities.[557] When an SPV holds receivables, investors in the SPV's securities are vulnerable to the claims of the transferor's creditors. That is

---

[556] Section 9-102(a)(11) defines "Chattel paper" [as] a record or records that evidence both a monetary obligation and a security interest in specific goods, a security interest in specific goods and software used in the goods, a security interest in specific goods and license of software used in the goods, a lease of specific goods, or a lease of specific goods and license of software used in the goods. In this paragraph, "monetary obligation" means a monetary obligation secured by the goods or owed under a lease of the goods and includes a monetary obligation with respect to software used in the goods. The term does not include (i) charters or other contracts involving the use or hire of a vessel or (ii) records that evidence a right to payment arising out of the use of a credit or charge card or information contained on or for use with the card. If a transaction is evidenced by records that include an instrument or series of instruments, the group of records taken together constitutes chattel paper. U.C.C. § 9-102(a)(11) (2009).

[557] 1 TAMAR FRANKEL, SECURITIZATION § 10.10.5 (Ann Taylor Schwing ed., 2d ed. 2005).

because it is difficult to classify the transfer of the receivables to the SPV as an assignment. The difficulty arises from the fact that the transferor retains an interest in the SPV's assets, and because the payment-features of the securities are conditioned on future transfers of receivables by the Originator. If the transaction is deemed a borrowing by the transferor, the security interest of the SPV in the receivables must be perfected before the Originator's insolvency.

Under the U.C.C., receivables can be classified either as accounts or as general intangibles. A sale of accounts is subject to Article 9 of the U.C.C. Pledges of receivables and accounts are governed by Article 9 of the U.C.C., and a security interest in them must be perfected by filing, except in specific stated circumstances. Furthermore, to avoid the liabilities of the transferor to the borrowers of the transferred loans, if the transferor becomes insolvent, the SPV should assume only the rights, not the obligations, of the transferor towards the borrowers. Therefore, the transferee should not be deemed to have extended credit to the borrower, nor engage in any activity that could produce a potential liability. However, the SPV-transferee should secure from the transferor the right to proceed directly against the borrowers, without having to enforce an executory contract against the transferor.

f. Regulation of the Process of Sale and Purchase[558]

Some of the problems posed by loan securitization stem from the initial making of the securitized loans. For example, the lender may fail to exercise prudence in making the loans or may perpetrate a fraud. If the lender is a bank, the loans might have been made in violation of banking laws. For example Penn Square Bank produced billions of dollars of loans that became worthless, brought down the bank, and damaged hundreds of Institutions, including Continental Illinois in Chicago, which was bailed out by the FDIC. In the indictment of the two top officials of that bank, the FDIC alleged violations of the duty of care, skill and diligence, as well as violations of the duties of officers and directors. These officials were also charged with violating banking laws and regulations by routinely exceeding the lending limits, and by repeatedly making loans to affiliates, executive officers, directors, and principal shareholders. Similar problems arise for buyers of loans that overextend their purchases, lack experience and information with respect to the loans they buy, and fail to maintain adequate controls commensurate with the growth of their loan portfolios.

Problems may also arise in the purchase and sale of securitized debt, a largely unregulated Market. The government-sponsored corporations, such as Freddie Mac and Fannie Mae, sell their debt by auction to obtain the highest price possible (under similar conditions) and establish fairness among the bidding dealers. However, to avoid possible "cornering" of the Market, which may lead to Market manipulation,

[558] 1 TAMAR FRANKEL, SECURITIZATION § 7.17 F (Ann Taylor Schwing ed., 2d ed. 2005).

such sellers usually limit the amount of debt for which a dealer may bid. During the summer of 1991, a number of dealers confessed to bidding for more debt than they were allowed and to making inaccurate reports to various agencies. Rather than resolve the issue in court, the dealers and the agencies involved settled; the dealers agreed to pay penalties.

Agreements concerning the sale of mortgage loans have been interpreted in the context of the use of these loans. Thus, a mortgage buyer sued a mortgage seller for breach of contract, among other claims, on the ground that the seller sold the buyer a loan that was not of investment quality. The district court granted the buyer's motion for a summary judgment, holding that the agreement between the parties placed responsibility for the non-investment quality loans with the seller. The requirement that the seller should provide the buyer with investment quality loans applied no matter which party was the underwriter for the mortgage loans. Similarly, problems regarding securitization may stem from usual contract conflicts between the buyer and seller of the financial assets that are securitized.

C. Case Study: Transforming Healthcare Receivables Into Cash

"Imagine that you or your loved one has just been involved in a serious auto accident. You feel fortunate because you know that one of the best trauma centers in the city is close by. But the ambulance ride is taking longer than expected. With the chances of survival lessening every minute, you hear the ambulance driver tell the paramedics that they have been asked to divert to another emergency room across town. The trauma center that was so critical to your future has been temporarily forced to close its doors to new patients because it is short-staffed and under-funded."[559]

The scenario described has become a reality for trauma victims across the country and especially in less affluent areas. The closing of the trauma unit at the Martin Luther King Jr./Drew Medical Center provides a case in point. King/Drew is located in South Los Angeles in one of the City's poorest and most violent neighborhoods. Prior to closing the trauma unit was serving 2150 patients per year. That is an average of treating almost 6 life-threatening injuries per day. The closing was not for lack of caregiver and community support. "County supervisors heard more than six hours of testimony from community members and local political leaders last week, all of it opposed the closure."[560] However, "despite impassioned protests, Los

---

[559] Kimberly Easter Zirkle, *Not So Perfect: The Disconnect Between Medicare and the Uniform Commercial Code Regarding Health-Care-Insurance Receivables,* 9 N.C. BANKING INST. 373, 373 (2005).

[560] Mitchell Landsberg & Jack Leonard, *King/Drew's Trauma Unit Ordered Shut,* L.A. TIMES, Nov. 24, 2004, at A1, LEXIS, News Library, Arcfile.

Angeles County supervisors voted . . . to close the trauma center."[561] Even an appeal to the federal courts alleging that the closure was a civil rights violation failed to keep the trauma unit open. The King/Drew trauma unit closure was not an isolated event. During the 1980s and 1990s, the county saw 10 trauma units close.[562]

The County supervisors understood the life-saving mission of the trauma unit and reluctantly closed it with a broader goal in mind – sacrificing trauma care in order to save the hospital itself and its emergency room that treats 45,000 patients per year.[563] How did King/Drew and hundreds of other health care facilities get to the point where such undesirable choices had to be made? The answers date back to World War II when employer offered health care benefits were used in lieu of wage increases to attract employees. Once in place, health care became an institutional benefit with very deep roots as the economy expanded during the 1950s and 1960s. Moreover, as part of President Johnson's Great Society those without employer provided health insurance were provided care through Medicare (primarily for people over 65) and Medicaid (for low income individuals). Concerns over the U.S. model emerged in the 1970s as health care costs skyrocketed. The rapid growth in these costs resulted from an increase in the number of people covered and greater patient demands for service. "By 1982, the nation had endured double-digit increases in health care spending for seventeen consecutive years. Health care inflation outpaced GDP growth, and wages no longer kept pace with rising health care costs."[564] President Reagan's effort to substitute the private market for government involvement in the health care system led the shift of public facilities to private, non-profit operations. To control costs the industry adopted the managed-care model. Under this approach providers were compensated based on pre-established reimbursement schedules for care rather than costs incurred. Moreover, the patient was offered a limited set of providers, those who agreed to the reimbursement plans.

These changes did dampen the health care cost escalation but the increases continued to outpace general inflation and even wages. The recession in the early 1990s brought concerns about the health care system center stage again. Health care insurance was increasing, becoming unaffordable for employers and employees. Also, as unemployment rose during the downturn, more families lost their coverage. Newly elected President Clinton tried his hand at a solution, national health care

---

[561] *Id.*

[562] Tracy Weber et al., *King/Drew Trauma Unit Faces Closure,* L.A. TIMES, Sept. 14, 2004, at A1, LEXIS, News Library, Arcnws File.

[563] *Id.*

[564] Stephanie Kelton, An Introduction to the Health Care Crisis in America: How Did We Get Here?, (Ctr. For Full Time Employment & Price Stability, Special Series on Health Care, Sept. 2007), http://www.cfeps.org/health/chapters/html/ch1.htm (last visited Sept. 22, 2009).

reform. "Mr. Clintons' effort to restructure health care, which became a target for an army of interest groups, failed to pass either the House or the Senate, and is widely considered a major reason that his party lost Congress in the 1994 election."[565] In the aftermath of Clinton's debacle, health care policy was left adrift.

At the end of the 1990s, the Balanced Budget Act of 1997 had a profound impact of the health care sector. The goal of the Act was to balance the federal budget by 2002. One important feature of the legislation, intended to improve the probability of meeting the balanced budget target, was a set of reforms to Medicare. For hospital services, the Act "froze base payments in fiscal year 1998 and reduced updates in subsequent years, instituted a new policy for transfer cases, lowered the adjustment for indirect medical education (IME) to teaching hospitals, lowered the adjustment received by hospitals that treat a disproportionate share of (DSH) of low-income patients, and reduced capital payment rates."[566] Similar reductions were implemented for outpatient hospital services, as well as home health care and physician services. One outcome of the Act was a spate of hospital defaults and bankruptcies.[567] Before the House Subcommittee on Health and Environment of the Committee on Commerce, the chair of the Medicare Payment Advisory Commission stated: "Hospitals' financial status deteriorated significantly in 1998 and 1999. . . . Medicare margins dropped from 9.8 percent in 1997 to 6.5 percent in 1998. . . . [W]e estimate the aggregate total margin for hospitals covered by Medicare's inpatient prospective payment system to have been 2.7 percent in 1999, less that half its 1997 level."[568]

The dawn of the new millennium saw a continuing heath care concern. The economic slowdown that followed the end of the dot-com bubble led to more changes in the health care system. To stem the financial impact of rising health care costs, employers increased the portion of expenses covered by employees. Costs also continued to increase and premiums outstripped wage increases by a wide margin. The current iteration of the crisis is compounded by the spate of medical innovations. There has been an explosion in new diagnostics, treatments, and pharmaceuticals that

---

[565] Robin Toner & Sheryl Gay Stolgerb, *Decade After Health Care Crisis, Soaring Costs Bring New Strains,* N.Y. TIMES, Aug. 11, 2002, sec. 1, at 1, LEXIS, News Library, Arcnws file.

[566] *The Balanced Budget Act of 1997: A Current Look at Its Impact on Patients and Providers: Hearing Bef. the Subcomm. on Health and Environment of the H. Comm. On Commerce,* 106th Cong. 19 (2000) (statement of Gail Wilensky, Chair, Medicare Payment Advisory Council).

[567] CTRS. FOR MEDICARE & MEDICAID SERVS., HEALTH CARE INDUSTRY MARKET UPDATE, ACUTE CARE HOSPITALS 13 (2003), http://www.cms.hhs.gov/CapMarketUpdates/Downloads/hcimu71403.pdf (last visited Sept. 19, 2009).

[568] *The Balanced Budget Act of 1997: A Current Look at Its Impact on Patients and Providers: Hearing Bef. the Subcomm. on Health and Environment of the H. Comm. On Commerce,* 106th Cong. 6 (2000) (statement of Gail Wilensky, Chair, Medicare Payment Advisory Council).

offer improved health outcomes but at a cost. For health care providers there has been a race to the top, equipping facilities with the latest technology. The race, however, is for the financially strong which have access to the capital needed to compete for health care dollars in the 21st century. At the other end of the scale are the facilities like King/Drew which after being squeezed by government programs must choose to close an important trauma clinic in order to preserve broader neighborhood medical care.

Remaining competitive or in some cases just operational required health care providers to have access to investment capital. The sources of capital for the health care industry were similar to those for other sectors – self-generated free cash flow, short-term bank loans, long-term debt, and equity. The equity option was only available to the for-profit health care providers. While Wall Street has invested in this segment of the industry, interest and therefore availability of capital has ebbed and flowed. Clearly this is not a stable source of funds and for those non-profit providers this is not an option at all. Short and long term loans are available but costly sources of capital. The majority of providers are not viewed as prime borrowers. Funding capital investments from free cash flow (i.e. revenues less all expenses), has not been a strong option either as most providers operate on thin margins and thus generate limited free cash. A last and more promising option is turning the provider's accounts receivables into cash for investment.

Americans spent $2.2 trillion for healthcare in 2007.[569] The vast majority of this amount was paid to doctors, hospitals, and other medical providers by private insurers and government agencies. Payment process seeks to meet a number of objectives. First, it must be efficient to handle the millions of payment requests handled in the U.S. each year. The efficiency is achieved through standardization, fee pre-determination, and automation. Two other goals are to control reimbursement costs and prevent fraud. These goals are achieved by referencing the majority of payments to pre-established fee schedules; the days of cost based repayment which is subject to interpretation and potentially manipulation are largely over. While the process is reasonably streamlined, payment time for providers still averages 42 days and for more than 25% exceeding 60 days.[570] Thus, providers need a sizable amount of working capital.

---

569 KAISER FAMILY FOUNDATION, TRENDS IN HEALTH CARE COSTS AND SPENDING (2007), , http://www.kff.org/insurance/7692.cfm (last visited Sept. 19, 2009).

570 Stephanie Wasek, *From the VMG Health 2008 Intellimarker: Accounts Receivable Analysis for ASCs by Revenues,* BECKER'S ASC REV., Dec. 2, 2008, http://www.beckersasc.com/news-analysis-asc/coding-billing-reimbursement-issues/from-the-vmg-health-2008-intellimarker-accounts-receivable-analysis-for-ascs-by-revenues.html (last visited Sept. 19, 2009).

Providers have long understood that turning receivables into cash would reduce the need for working capital and potentially free funds for capital investment. One technique for making receivables more liquid is selling the receivables to factors, collection agencies that pay cash to the provider upfront for the receivables. The factor also assumed responsibility for the collection of the receivables. These benefits to the provider, however, came at a cost to the provider - factoring fees were approximately 15-20 percent of the value of the receivables.[571] Also, the hospital only received 50 percent of the cash value up front; the remainder was remitted to the hospital upon collection by the factor.[572]

Aside from the costs of factoring receivables, there were concerns that the factors were inflating the required payments. The concern arose before pre-establishment of fees was widely used. This led the government to prohibit the assignment of Medicare and Medicaid receivables as a way to reduce the potential for fraud. Although almost all payments are now made based on pre-established fee schedules, the law remains in force.

An alternative to factoring the receivables was to use the future payment as a basis for offering bonds to outside investors – the securitization of health care receivables. Under this approach the provider would "sell" the receivables to a related entity (known as a special purpose vehicle [SPV]) for the vast majority of their cash value. The entity would in turn sell securities based on the cash flow from the receivables to outside investors. The investors' cash would provide the entity with the capital to buy the receivables. Health care receivables are a particularly effective source of collateral for health care providers because the creditworthiness of health care receivables' securities is based on the highly rated government or large private insurance payers not the often lower rated providers.

The pressure on providers to rapidly monetize receivables increased in the mid-1980s as accounts receivable increased owing to changes in Medicare. The first change was the 1983 introduction of the Prospective Payment System. Under this program hospitals received payments from Medicare only after the patient was discharged. A second change came in 1987 when Congress eliminated biweekly payments to providers. Payment cycles also lengthened with private providers as rising health care costs led the insurers to increase scrutiny of providers' bills.

From a financial perspective securitization of receivables is significantly more attractive than factoring. First, the factor's fees are avoided and almost full value is

---

[571] Sandra Ferconio & Michael R. Lane, *Financing Maneuvers: Two Opportunities to Bboost a Hospital's Working Capital – Factoring and Asset-Backed Securities,* HEALTHCARE FIN. MGMT.t, Oct. 1991, at 74, 74-76.

[572] *Id.* at 78.

received immediately. Second, the cost of capital for securitized receivables are 50-150 basis points below prime rate compared with borrowing costs above prime rate for most health care institutions.[573] Securitization also helped the provider's financial position more broadly because "[a]ccounting standards allow the removal of accounts receivable from a hospital's balance sheet when the accounts are sold as an asset."[574]

The securitization of health care receivables was first undertaken in 1988 with an $80 million commercial paper offering for Healthcare International.[575] The securitization of Jersey City Medical Center's receivables illustrates the type of transactions that took place. Jersey City was not a hospital short on cash when it sought to securitize its receivables. Rather it was looking for low cost capital for expansion. The Center was able to raise $19 million. The securities backed by the receivables were 5.2 year floating rate securities priced with a coupon of 90 basis points above the London Interbank Lending Rate. Prudential Securities handled the private placement.[576] In the early 1990s analysts expected a robust market for the securitization of health care receivables. Off a base of $50-$60 billion in net receivables,[577] even a small percentage could have generated a large market for these securities.

However, over the next decade only a handful of deals took place accounting for about 10 percent of third-party health care receivables.[578] Several barriers prevented more extensive use of securitization. Many of these barriers were legal. First, in response to concerns about "abuses of Medicare and Medicaid systems attributable

---

[573] Gregory Salathe, Note, *Reducing Health Care Costs Through Hospital Accounts Receivable Securitization,* 80 VA. L. REV. 549, 556 (1994).

[574] *Id.* at 566-67..

[575] Yvette Kantrow, *Asset-Backed Specialists Eye Healthcare Receivables Market; The Stars Are Aligning for a New Market,* INV. DEALER'S DIG., June 12, 1995, at 30, LEXIS, News Library, Arcnws File.

[576] *Single Seller Health Care Deal Gives NJ Hospitals Added Liquidity,* ASSET SALES REP., Jan. 17, 1994, at 6, LEXIS, News Library, Arcnws File.

[577] Sandra Ferconio & Michael R. Lane, *Financing Maneuvers: Two Opportunities to Boost a Hospital's Working Capital – Factoring and Asset-Backed Securities,* HEALTHCARE FIN. MGMT., Oct. 1991, at 74, 74.

[578] Charles E. Harrell & Mark D. Folk, *Financing American Health Security: The Securitization of Healthcare Receivables,* 50 BUS. LAW. 47, 48 n.5 (1994) (citing STANDARD & POOR'S RATINGS GROUP, STRUCTURED FIN. 11 (1993)).

to factoring"[579] Congress in 1972 enacted legislation that prevented the transfer or reassignment of Medicaid and Medicare payments. "The [amendment to the] statute stops [the factoring] practice by *prohibiting* payment to those who are *not* providers. . . . Payment to a collection agency with no accountability for the nature and costs of the services rendered is quite different from payment to a hospital which is required to furnish the services and which has itself been determined to be eligible to participate as a provider in the Medicaid program."[580] A key requirement for securitization was for the assets of the special purpose vehicle to be unreachable by creditors of the SPV's parent in the case of bankruptcy. If the government receivables were not assignable, a true sale to the SPV could not take place. The result was to remove approximately 50 percent of receivables from the potential securitization pool.[581]

A second barrier was that the Uniform Commercial Code prevented insurance proceeds from being used as primary collateral.[582] Yet another barrier, this one financial, was the variability around the actual cash flow from the receivables. The potential for dilution of receivables stemmed from (1) the federal government's right to offset health care receivables against other liabilities of the provider such as unpaid taxes; (2) reductions in payment due to patient or provider violations of procedures; or (3) exhaustion of benefits.[583]

The fundamental desirability of securitizing health care receivables has encouraged providers and the financial community to overcome or at least mitigated the barriers. The UCC barrier was overcome in 2001 when Article 9 was revised so that health care insurance receivables could be used as primary collateral.[584] The dilution of

---

[579] Mark Spradling, *Issues in the Securitization of Health Care Receivables,* 11 HEALTH L. REP. (BNA) 1703 (Dec. 5, 2002), http://healthcenter.bna.com/pic2/hc.nsf/id/BNAP-5GRL8Z?OpenDocument (last visited Sept. 23, 2009).

[580] Charles E. Harrell & Mark D. Folk, *Financing American Health Security: The Securitization of Healthcare Receivables,* 50 BUS. LAW. 47, 56 n.34 (1994) (quoting Danvers Pathology Assocs., Inc. v. Atkins, 757 F.2d 427, 430 (1st Cir. 1985)).

[581] Gregory Salathe, Note, *Reducing Health Care Costs Through Hospital Accounts Receivable Securitization,* 80 VA. L. REV. 549, 550 (1994).

[582] C Scott Pryor, *Revised Uniform Commercial Code Article 9: Impact in Bankruptcy,* 7 AM. BANKR. INST. L. REV. 465, 487 (1999).

[583] NOMURA FIXED INCOME RESEARCH, HEALTHCARE ABS PRIMER 3 (2002), http://www.securitization.net/pdf/nomura_abs_101802.pdf (last visited Sept. 22, 2009).

[584] Kimberly Easter Zirkle, *Not So Perfect: The Disconnect Between Medicare and the Uniform Commercial Code Regarding Health-Care-Insurance Receivables,* 9 N.C. BANKING INST. 373, 375 & n.13 (2005).

receivables remains an issue but through greater experience the securitization participants are learning the bounds of the problem.

The anti-assignment issue remains a concern but there has been some progress. The foundation for the progress was a 1986 Fifth Circuit United States Court of Appeals decision in *Wilson v. First National Bank (In re Mission Baptist Foundation of America, Inc.)* In *Mission Baptist* the "Court noted that the federal anti-assignment statute on its face provides that it shall not 'be construed . . . to preclude an agent of the person or institution providing medical care or services from receiving any such payment' so long as a 'factoring' arrangement is not used.;'"[585] The Health Care Finance Administration which oversaw Medicare and Medicaid issued a 1990 policy memorandum that "addressed a scenario in which a financing entity would issue securities to advance funds to healthcare providers based on their pledge or sale of accounts receivable to the financing entity."[586] The memo concludes that financing in this manner is "consistent with Medicaid law and regulations if certain conditions exist." "Medicaid payments must be sent directly to provider at its own address, not that of a bank, and negotiated by and in control of the provider before being turned over to the financing institution. Direct payment to the financing institutions is not permitted."[587] Thus, while the pledge of receivables was acceptable, payment to the provider and no one else was a requirement.

The Double Lock Box has emerged as the solution to the direct payment dilemma. This technique allows for government payments to be made directly to a bank lock box exclusively owned and controlled by the service provider. The provider in turn instructs the depository institution to sweep the funds from this lock box into a second lock box on a daily basis. The second box is owned and controlled by the purchaser of the receivables, typically the SPV. "In policy statements and private decisions, the Centers for Medicare & Medicaid Services ("*CMS*), formerly known as the Health Care Financing Administration ("*HCFA*), has approved the double lock box technique, stating that the key issue is whether the health care provider has actual control over the funds and thus discretion about the funds' transfer to a private

---

[585] Charles E. Harrell & Mark D. Folk, *Financing American Health Security: The Securitization of Healthcare Receivables,* 50 BUS. LAW. 47, 56 n.34 (1994) (quoting Wilson v. First Nat'l Bank (*In re* Mission Baptist Foundation of Am., Inc.), 796 F.2d 752, 758 (5th Cir. 1986)).

[586] *Id.* at 63.

[587] *Id.* (quoting Memorandum from Christine Nye, Director, Medicaid Bureau, to All Associate Regional Administrators for Medicaid (Dec. 11, 1990) (on file with Health Care Financing Administration)).

financing entity."[588] While the technique is not, a priori, bankruptcy proof, it was a major step in that direction.

The safest strategy is for a health care provider to only securitize private insurance receivables which are not subject to anti-assignment. Although this strategy significantly reduces the pool of available receivables for securitizing, there would still be billions of dollars in receivables for these transactions. This option, however, does raise questions of equity. Providers with a higher share of Medicare and Medicaid patients would not get the financing benefits of securitized receivables. These providers disproportionally serve poorer areas and thus these communicates would be at a disadvantage vis-à-vis providers with a larger private insurance patient pool. It is also possible that providers, to avoid the financial penalty associated with Medicare and Medicaid receivables, would opt to serve fewer of these patients.

The improved conditions for securitization have lead to a consistent growth in receivables backed securities offerings. While only a small fraction of the estimated more than $400 billion in health care receivables have been securitized,[589] the potential exists for securitization to be an important source of capital for the health industry for years to come.

---

[588] Mark Spradling, *Issues in the Securitization of Health Care Receivables,* 11 HEALTH L. REP. (BNA) 1708 (Dec. 5, 2002), http://healthcenter.bna.com/pic2/hc.nsf/id/BNAP-5GRL8Z?OpenDocument (last visited Sept. 22, 2009).

[589] Delilah Brummet Flaum & Marc L. Klyman, *Health Care Receivables Securitization: Structuring Issues and Future Trends,* http://www.securitization.net/knowledge/transactions/flaum_healthcare_clr.asp (last visited Sept. 23, 2009).

Chapter 9: Protection of SPV and Its Investors - Bankruptcy Issues

A key feature of the SPV is its protection from the bankruptcy of the transferor of the financial assets that the SPV bought and hold. This transferor may have been the Originator or the sponsor. If the transferor fails, its creditors might attempt to claim the assets that were transferred to the SPV. If they succeed, the investors, who paid the full price for the assets, will stand in line in the bankruptcy proceedings of the transferor as unsecured creditors, and may receive far less than the amount they paid for the securities. Therefore, the lawyer designing the securitization process must be aware of the bankruptcy dangers and prepared to protect the investors from these dangers. This chapter provides an overview of the main issues concerning bankruptcy. At the end of this overview the risks of bankruptcy are linked to the legal steps of protecting the investors from those risks. We note that in bankruptcy proceedings the rights of the parties can be rearranged. A trustee is appointed to either sell the business of the bankrupt as a going concern or liquidate it, and, with a committee of creditors, propose a plan either to divide the remaining property subject to the court's approval.

Bankruptcy law is concerned with distributing the assets of a debtor in a bankruptcy case among its creditors.[590] Bankruptcy law is primarily the federal Bankruptcy Code.[591] Most bankruptcy cases fall under Chapter 7 of the Bankruptcy Code[592] and are "liquidation" cases in which a trustee, as representative of the creditors, collects the debtor's property (except for certain exempt property), converts it to cash, and distributes it.[593] After the liquidation, the debtor is generally discharged from further liability on the debts.[594]

A. The Risk to Investors in the Case of the Transferor's Bankruptcy

As mentioned, the SPV and its investors may incur losses if the Transferor of financial assets to the SPV becomes bankrupt. The transferor may have been the

---

[590] DAVID G. EPSTEIN, STEVE H. NICKLES, & JAMES J. WHITE, BANKRUPTCY § 1-2, at 2 (1993).

[591] *Id.* § 1-3, at 3-4; 11 U.S.C. §§ 101-1532 (2006) (Bankruptcy Code).

[592] DAVID G. EPSTEIN, STEVE H. NICKLES, & JAMES J. WHITE, BANKRUPTCY § 1-6, at 9 (1993); 11 U.S.C. §§ 701-784 (2006) (Chapter 7).

[593] DAVID G. EPSTEIN, STEVE H. NICKLES, & JAMES J. WHITE, BANKRUPTCY § 1-5, at 8 (1993).

[594] *Id.* § 1-3, at 6. Under certain circumstances, such as involving debtor's debts as a fiduciary, the debtor is not discharged, and certain debts are not discharged. *Id.* § 1-7, at 11.

Originator of any other party (Transferor). We noted in Chapter 8 the importance of a "true sale" by the Transferor to the SPV.

If the Transferor fails, its creditors might claim the assets that were transferred to the SPV from the Transferor. If the creditors succeed, the investors, who paid the full price for the assets will stand in line in the bankruptcy proceedings as unsecured creditors, and may receive far less than the amount they paid for the SPV's securities. Therefore, even if the loans themselves are of the highest quality, investors in these loans are vulnerable if the transferor's financial position is weak.

Discussion Topic
Compare the following Delaware Statute with that of Texas. Which one of the statutes would you choose to use as a lawyer concerned with protecting the investors in securitized financial assets. Would you preference differ if you advised the legislators?

Title 6, Delaware Statutes [595]

Section 2701A Title
This title may be referred to as the "Asset Backed Securities Facilitation Act.

Section 2702A Intent

It is intended by the general Assembly that the term "securitization transaction" shall be construed broadly.

Section 2703A Securitization transaction

(a) Notwithstanding any other provision of law, including, but not limited to, Section 9-506 of this title 'Debtor's rights to redeem collateral' as said section existed in July 1, 2001, and 9-623 of the title, 'Right to redeem collateral' that became effective July 1, 2001, to the extent set forth in the transaction documents relating to a securitization transaction:

(1) Any property, assets or rights purported to be transferred, in whole or in part, in the securitization transaction shall be deemed to no longer be the property, assets or rights of the transferor.

(2) A transferor in the securitization transaction, its creditors or, in any insolvency proceedings with respect to the transferor or the transferor's property, a bankruptcy trustee, received, debtor, debtor in possession or similar person, to the extent the issue is governed by Delaware law, shall

[595] DEL. CODE ANN. tit. 6, §§ 2701A-2703A (2005).

have no rights, legal or equitable, whatsoever to reacquire, reclaim, recover, repudiate, disaffirm, redeem or recharacterize as property of the transferor any property, assets or rights purported to be transferred, in whole or in part, by the transferor; and

(3) In the event of a bankruptcy, receivership or other insolvency proceedings with respect to the transferor or the transferor's property, to the extent the issue is governed by Delaware law, such property, asset and rights shall not be deemed to be part of the transferor's property, assets, rights or estate.

(b) Nothing contained in this chapter shall be deemed to require any securitization transaction to be treated as a sale for federal or state tax purposes or to preclude the treatment of any applicable laws relating to the perfection and priority of security or ownership interests of persons other than the transferor, hypothetical lien creditor or, in the event of a bankruptcy, receivership or its property, a bankruptcy trustee, receiver, debtor, debtor in possession or similar person.

It is not the purpose of this Chapter to change the tax treatment of securitizations that take place pursuant to this Chapter.

The Texas Statute:[596]

Section 9.109(e), Texas Business and Commercial Code:

(3) The application of this chapter to the sale of accounts, chattel paper, payment intangibles, or promissory notes is not to recharacterize that sale as a transaction to secure indebtedness but to protect purchasers of these assets by providing a notice filing system. For all purposes, in the absence of fraud or intentional misrepresentation, the parties' characterization of a transaction as a sale of such assets shall be conclusive that the transaction is a sale and not a secured transaction and that title, legal and equitable, has passed to the party characterized as the purchaser of those assets regardless of whether the secured party has any recourse against the debtor, whether the debtor is entitled to any surplus, or any other term of the parties' agreement.

a. Possible Effects of Bankruptcy Law on the SPV

The major effects of bankruptcy are (i) an automatic stay on all creditors' actions (including the claims of the SPV); (ii) a prohibition on preferences among creditors; (iii) the power of the trustee in bankruptcy to avoid certain transactions; (iv) the

[596] TEX. BUS. & COM. CODE § 9.109(e) (2002).

power of the court to subordinate the creditors' claims to those of others; and (v) the right of the debtor and some of the debtor's creditors to set off their mutual claims.

Automatic Stay.[597] When an entity files for bankruptcy, be it the Transferor of the loans to the SPV, or the borrowers, or the SPV, an automatic stay is imposed on all the creditors' actions against the bankrupt, including actions related to the collateral that the bankrupt offered for its loans. A stay causes delay in payments to the creditors of the debtor-bankrupt and prevents them from liquidating the collateral in their possession. Furthermore, the debtor may use the collateral if the secured creditors' interests are otherwise protected.

If the Transferor fails, a stay may adversely affect the SPV and its investors in other ways as well. Usually, the Transferor continues to service the loans, receiving payments from the borrowers for transfer to the SPV; sometimes the Transferor is obligated to transfer more financial assets (e.g., receivables) to the SPV. In these cases, the stay may prevent the Transferor from making transfers to the SPV.

The Bankruptcy Code provides for possible relief from the automatic stay provisions. Section 362(c)(1) requires the bankruptcy court to dissolve the stay if the property in question is no longer the property of the bankrupt's estate, and section 362(d) grants the court discretion to terminate, annul, or modify the stay on a number of grounds for the purpose of relieving a party in interest of undue harm. The Code provides that the court "shall grant relief from the stay . . . for cause, including the lack of adequate protection of an interest in property . . . or . . . if—(A) the debtor does not have an equity in such property . . . ." Thus, judicial relief from the stay can be granted if the investors in the SPV can show that the SPV is not "adequately protected" unless it continues to receive payments from the collateral or unless the collateral is liquidated. However, what is "adequate protection" is subject to conflicting decisions.

Under section 362(b) (11) of the Bankruptcy Code, the automatic stay provisions do not apply to "the presentment of a negotiable instrument [or][598] the giving of notice

---

[597] 1 TAMAR FRANKEL, SECURITIZATION § 10.2 (Ann Taylor Schwing ed., 2d ed. 2005).

[598] A negotiable instrument (NI) is a special type of contract for the payment of money that is unconditional and capable of transfer by negotiation (e.g., checks, commercial paper). A negotiable instrument is different from contract. Unlike a contract: (1) formation of a NI does not require offer, acceptance and consideration, but (2) the right to the performance is linked to possession of the document (except, e.g., loss or theft). The Payee's rights are not subject to set-off, and are not conditioned on the validity of the underlying contract giving rise to the debt (e.g., sale of goods). A prior party liable on the NI need not receive notice of the transfer of the rights under the NI. Finally, the transfer is free of equities. The title of a holder in due course of NI is better than title of the transferor from whom the holder obtained it. Negotiation enables the transferee to become the party to the contract, and to enforce it in his own name. One can negotiate the instrument by endorsement or its delivery alone. Promissory notes and bills of exchange are two main types of negotiable instruments. A promissory note is a written promise by the *maker* to pay money to the *payee*. A maker or a drawer of a

of and protesting dishonor of such an instrument."[599] There are different requirements for the physical presentation of a negotiable instrument, such as for payment or acceptance by the person liable for payment. Even though these activities improve the creditors' rights, preventing the activities may detract from the creditors' rights. Presentation and notice relate to the creditors' duties required in order to preserve their rights.

Prohibition on Preferences.[600] Section 547(b) of the Bankruptcy Code is designed to prevent a debtor on the brink of insolvency from preferring some creditors over others. Section 547(b) lists six factors, which together constitute an avoidable preferred transfer: (i) the debtor must transfer an interest that the debtor has in property, (ii) for the benefit of a creditor, (iii) for or on account of an antecedent debt owed by the debtor before the transfer is made, (iv) while the debtor is insolvent, (v) the transfer must be made during 90 days immediately before the petition for bankruptcy or, if the transfer is made to an "insider" of the bankrupt, during one year immediately preceding the petition, and (vi) the transfer must result in the creditor's receipt of more than the creditor would otherwise receive under the liquidation and distribution in the bankruptcy. Unlike the prohibition on fraudulent transfers, the debtor's intent is not an element in determining whether a payment is a preferred payment.

For an avoidable preference to arise, section 547(b) requires that the creditor receive more than the creditor would have received under liquidation and distribution in the bankruptcy proceedings. The determination of this factor depends not on the date of the transfer but on the results in the bankruptcy proceedings. If the creditor would receive less in the bankruptcy proceedings, a higher payment will be preferential. Therefore, if the SPVs and security holders are fully secured creditors and the value of the collateral is equal to or greater than the balance due to the SPV under bankruptcy proceedings, then a transfer will not be avoided as preferential. That is

---

promissory note promises to unconditionally pay the payee (beneficiary) a specific amount on a specified date. A promissory note is an unconditional order to pay a specific amount to the order of a person on demand or on a specified date. Articles 3 and 4 of the U.C.C. govern the issuance and negotiation of negotiable instruments. For a writing to be a negotiable instrument under Article 3: 1) The promise or order to pay must be unconditional; 2) The payment must be a specific sum of money, although interest may be added to the sum; 3) The payment must be made on demand or at a definite time; 4) The instrument must not require the person promising payment to perform any act other than paying the money specified; 5) The instrument must be payable to bearer or to order ("words of negotiability"). The following are not NI: Letters of credit (governed by Article 5 of the Code) Bills of lading and other documents of title (governed by Article 7 of the Code) securities (governed by Article 8 of the Code); Deeds and other documents conveying interests in real estate, although a mortgage may secure a promissory note which is governed by Article 3.

[599] When a negotiable instrument has not been paid or accepted the holder must give notice to all the parties that signed the instrument. U.C.C. § 3-503 (2009).

[600] 1 TAMAR FRANKEL, SECURITIZATION § 10.3.1 (Ann Taylor Schwing ed., 2d ed. 2005).\

because the security holders cannot have received more than they are entitled to on bankruptcy liquidation. The issue of preference is especially acute if the securitization process involves the bankrupt's obligation to make future transfers of financial assets to the SPV.

Exceptions.[601] Under section 547(c) of the Bankruptcy Code, the trustee in bankruptcy may not avoid certain transfers. For example, the trustee may not avoid a transfer to the extent that the transfer was intended to be a contemporaneous exchange of property for new value. Further, the trustee may not avoid transfers "in payment of a debt incurred by the debtor in the ordinary course of business or financial affairs of the debtor and the transferee, and such transfer was—(A) made in the ordinary course of business or financial affairs of the debtor and the transferee; or (B) made according to ordinary business terms."[602]

To determine the meaning of "ordinary course of business" and "ordinary business terms," left undefined in the Code, courts have examined a number of factors for the "ordinary course of business" test and have used an objective industry practice test for the "ordinary business terms" test.[603] Arguably, this exception applies to SPVs and their Originators. For example, it is necessary for the Originator of an SPV holding receivables to continuously transfer receivables to the SPV. It is just as important for the transfers to be consistent with the practice of the industry. These transfers may therefore be deemed to be made in the ordinary course of business. The exclusion in section 547(c)(2) depends on the identity of the debtor and the nature of the debt. Debts incurred by the debtor in the ordinary course of business, such as trade debts, are excluded. If the debtor is the SPV or the Transferor of a traded mortgage, the transfer is excluded; if the debtor is the mortgagee, then arguably only his trade debt secured by the mortgage will be excluded.

Discussion Topics:

1. Why is the trustee prohibited from avoiding transfers in payment of a debt incurred by the debtor in the ordinary course of business or financial affairs? Can the trustee be prevented from avoiding transfers to the SPV of the borrowers' payments after the filing of the Transferor's petition for bankruptcy?

2. Our SPV holds 10,000 loans of $50,000 each. Monthly payments due from the borrowers are $25,000. The loans are accompanied by notes. The notes

---

601 1 TAMAR FRANKEL, SECURITIZATION § 10.3.2 (Ann Taylor Schwing ed., 2d ed. 2005).§10.3.2

602 11 U.S.C. § 547(c)(2) (2006); 5 COLLIER ON BANKRUPTCY ¶ 547.04[2] (Alan N. Resnick et al. eds., 15th ed. rev. 1996 & Supp. 2003).

603 5 COLLIER ON BANKRUPTCY ¶ 547.02[2][a][ii][A], at 547-59 (Alan N. Resnicket al.. eds., 15th ed. rev. 1996 & Supp. 2003).

are held by the Transferor that is also the Servicer. The Transferor has filed for bankruptcy. After that date, two borrowers failed to pay. How will the SPV be affected by a stay?

3. Section 362(c)(1) requires the bankruptcy court to dissolve the stay if the property in question is no longer the property of the bankrupt's estate. How can you show that the Transferor no longer has ownership of the assets held by the SPV? What proof would you have to bring to court?

4. Section 362(d) grants the court discretion to terminate, annul, or modify the stay on a number of grounds for the purpose of relieving a party in interest of undue harm. How can you show "undue harm?"

Protecting Perfected Security Interests. Section 547(c)(5) of the Bankruptcy Code protects a perfected security interest in a loan from the trustee's power of avoidance. The section provides that:

The trustee may not avoid under this section a transfer—. . .

(5) that creates a perfected security interest in inventory or a receivable or the proceeds of either, except to the extent that the aggregate of all such transfers to the transferee caused a reduction, as of the date of the filing of the petition and to the prejudice of other creditors holding unsecured claims, of any amount by which the debt secured by such security interest exceeded the value of all security interests for such debt on the later of—

(A)(i) with respect to a transfer to which subsection (b)(4)(A) of this section applies, 90 days before the date of the filing of the petition; or

(ii) with respect to a transfer to which subsection (b)(4)(B) of this section applies, one year before the date of the filing of the petition; or

(B) the date on which new value was first given under the security agreement creating such security.

Thus, section 547(c)(5) protects the holder of a security interest in a receivable if the value of the secured loan is not lower than the face amount of the assets that serve as collateral (e.g., receivables), as of the later of the date the new value was first given under the security agreement or the start of a 90-day to one-year preference period before the petition for bankruptcy.

However, future transfers (usually of receivables) by the Originator to the SPV or the investors can constitute an avoidable preference or transfer when the Transferor-servicer fails. Money that the Transferor-servicer received from the borrower under the loan may constitute a preferential transfer unless the SPV perfected a security interest in the borrower's payments.

Nonetheless, section 547(c)(5) can protect a transfer of a loan characterized as a perfected secured lending to the transferor. Under section 9-306 of the U.C.C., cash proceeds are deemed unperfected unless segregated within ten days after receipt by the debtor. Therefore, loan proceeds received before insolvency of the transferor-servicer should be deposited in a segregated trust account for the benefit of the SPV within ten days of receipt. Because the Code provides for a thirty-day grace period, previously ten days, if proceeds from the loans are transferred within that period to a trust account for the SPV, the transfer will date as of thirty days before the receipt of the funds by the debtor. Otherwise, the transfer will be deemed perfected on the actual date of perfection.

b. The Bankruptcy Trustee's Power to Avoid the Transfer[604]

Section 544(a) of the Bankruptcy Code grants the trustee in bankruptcy, as of the date of commencement of the bankruptcy case, (i) the rights and powers of a judicial lien creditor, (ii) the rights of a creditor with an unsatisfied writ of execution, and (iii) the rights of a bona fide purchaser of real property. These powers and rights may have precedence over the rights of secured creditors with unperfected security interest and creditors with unexecuted transactions.

c. Subordination of SPV Interests in the Financial Assets[605]

Under section 510(c) of the Bankruptcy Code, the court has power in equity to subordinate the rights of secured creditors to the rights of unsecured creditors. When loans are transferred to an SPV and the transferor continues to service the loans, there is a danger that the transferor may act inequitably, so as to trigger the court's powers to subordinate the interests in the loans to the interests of the borrower's unsecured creditors. If the SPV and the transferor have joint interests in the loans, the transferor's interests in the loans can be subordinated. The question arises whether the interests of the transferee SPV in the loan should be subordinated as well.

d. The Issue of Lender Liability

This question has assumed importance in light of some cases that have held lenders liable for damages to the borrowers ("lender liability" cases). Most cases on lender liability have arisen in connection with commercial, rather than individual consumer, loans, probably because the cost of litigation is so high that individual loans usually will not support a lender liability lawsuit beyond the early stages.

---

[604] 1 TAMAR FRANKEL, SECURITIZATION § 10.4.1 (Ann Taylor Schwing ed., 2d ed. 2005).

[605] 1 TAMAR FRANKEL, SECURITIZATION § 10.5 (Ann Taylor Schwing ed., 2d ed. 2005).

For an SPV that will securitize commercial loans, the issue of subordination will arise when the servicer of the loans behaves in an inequitable fashion or, being the lender as well, incurs a lender's liability towards the borrowers whose loan the servicer-lender transferred to the SPV. In such a case, the rights of the SPV are pitted against the rights of the other creditors of the borrowers whose loan the SPV holds. Enough money would probably be at stake in such a case to support lender liability litigation through trial and appeal.

In the usual circumstance, subordination is proper only if it is required to redress inequity. A court should not exercise its power in equity to subordinate the interests of innocent assignees, that is, in most cases, the SPV and its security holders. However, equitable subordination should apply to the *interests issued by the SPV* if the SPV was used to aid and abet the servicer's misconduct. Such subordination would apply to the servicer's claims if the servicer was negligent in exercising its control over the SPV's operations.

It should be noted that equitable subordination applies not only to the SPV, but through the SPV to the securities that the SPV issues. It is difficult to protect SPVs against the dangers of subordination. A guarantee from the Transferor may be one solution. However, when the Transferors are banks, guarantees by the banks might destroy the benefits to the banks from the sale of assets without recourse: the banks may not be able to reduce their capital requirements. A similar disadvantage to the banks may result even from a weaker provision in the transfer agreement. For example, the transfer agreements may prohibit the banks from acting in a way that might result in avoidance of an otherwise valid loan. Or the agreements may prohibit the banks from acting in a way that would invalidate an equitable subordination. The agreements may entitle the SPV in these cases to rescind the transfer and receive the price it paid for the loan, as if the loan were paid in full. Even if the agreements are binding, however, these provisions are unlikely to protect the SPVs from losses if the transferor banks failed.

e. Avoidance of Fraudulent Conveyances[606]

The idea of fraudulent transfer by debtors is ancient. In 1571 England's Statute of Elizabeth contained a provision making it a crime to effect such transfers "with intent to delay, hinder or defraud creditors and others of their just and lawful actions."[607] A total prohibition on conveyance would allow creditors to follow conveyed property in the hands of anyone. It would freeze the property in the hands of a debtor who is in trouble and render the debtor unable to convey property,

[606] 1 TAMAR FRANKEL, SECURITIZATION § 10.4.2 (Ann Taylor Schwing ed., 2d ed. 2005).

[607] An Act Touching Orders for Bankrupts, 13 Eliz., ch. 5 (1571), *repealed by* The Law of Property Act, 15 Geo. 5, ch. 20, § 172 (1925).

whether fraudulent or not. Even though fraudulent intent was required the very transfer close to the date of the bankruptcy might be enough to show intent. Gifts could signify such intent.

Section 548(a) of the Bankruptcy Code provides:

(1) The trustee may avoid any transfer (including any transfer to or for the benefit of an insider under an employment contract) of an interest of the debtor in property, or any obligation (including any obligation to or for the benefit of an insider under an employment contract) incurred by the debtor, that was made or incurred on or within two years before the date of the filing of the petition, if the debtor voluntarily or involuntarily—

(A) made such transfer or incurred such obligation with actual intent to hinder, delay, or defraud any entity to which the debtor was or became, on or after the date that such transfer was made or such obligation was incurred, indebted; or

(B)(i) received less than a reasonably equivalent value in exchange for such transfer or obligation; and

(ii)(I) was insolvent on the date that such transfer was made or such obligation was incurred, or became insolvent as a result of such transfer or obligation;

(II) was engaged in business or a transaction, or was about to engage in business or a transaction, for which any property remaining with the debtor was an unreasonably small capital;

(III) intended to incur, or believed that the debtor would incur, debts that would be beyond the debtor's ability to pay as such debts matured; or

(IV) made such transfer to or for the benefit of an insider, or incurred such obligation to or for the benefit of an insider, under an employment contract and not in the ordinary course of business.

(2) A transfer of a charitable contribution to a qualified religious or charitable entity or organization shall not be considered to be a transfer covered under paragraph (1)(B) in any case in which—

(A) the amount of that contribution does not exceed 15 percent of the gross annual income of the debtor for the year in which the transfer or contribution was made; or

(B) the contribution made by a debtor exceeded the percentage amount of gross annual income specified in subparagraph (A), if the transfer was consistent with the practices of the debtor in making charitable contributions.

Section 548(c) makes an exception for a transferee that took for value in good faith, to the extent that the transferee gave such value to the debtor.

Leveraged buyouts. Some corporations have increased their debt as compared to equity and sold their assets using the proceeds to buy out their voting shares or help their managements transfer or retain control of the corporations. These transactions reduce the corporate assets and cash flow for corporate operations and may increase the likelihood of corporate failure. When such corporations failed, their trustees in bankruptcy attempted to avoid, as fraudulent transfers, the obligations that financed the acquisitions of the voting shares. If loans to finance buyouts of voting shares are sold and the borrowing corporations fail, their trustees in bankruptcy may attack the loans as fraudulent transfers and attempt to avoid the loans. Loans to finance such buyouts are particularly vulnerable to the trustees' attack when borrowers cannot service their existing debts under the terms of these later loans.

To succeed under section 548, the trustee often must show that the debtor had an intent to defraud other creditors. The trustee need not show actual knowledge of the relevant facts, however, as it is sufficient for the trustee to show that the debtor had notice of facts that should have led to an inquiry or that recognized indicia of fraud were present. The debtor's intent can be proved by an objective standard, for example, when the loan proceeds are used to acquire the debtor's voting shares rather than used for the debtor's operations, or when assets viewed as available to satisfy the current creditors' claims are transferred beyond the creditors' reach. Furthermore, in these buyouts, the corporation's assets are depleted because its assets are transferred without consideration. In fact, the transactions result in liquidation of part of the assets and distribution of the proceeds to the equity shareholders. Even if the target corporation obtains some benefits from the buyout, such as efficiencies, these benefits hardly constitute fair consideration under section 548.

Fraudulent Transfers May Distinguish Between Intentional Fraudulent Transfer and Constructive Fraudulent Transfer. In both cases the trustee in bankruptcy can follow the property so transferred. If the transfers were intentional fraudulent transfers the Trustee has the power and obligation to avoid and recover fraudulent transfers. An example of an intentional fraudulent transfer is a situation in which a husband and wife quitclaim their house to their children just before the couple files for bankruptcy protection.

In order to prove intentional fraudulent transfer, the trustee must prove that "the debtor made such transfer with actual intent to 'hinder, delay, or defraud'" any entity to which the debtor was or became, on or after the date that such transfer was made, indebted."[608]

Note that the trustee must show only one of these intentions: "hinder, delay, or defraud." Thus, in our example, the husband and wife could argue that they did not intend to defraud creditors, but "preserve the home for their children." Nonetheless, their action would fall within "hindering" their creditors. Because the actual intent of a debtor is difficult to prove, the trustee often uses the constructive fraudulent

---

[608] 11 U.S.C. § 548(a) (2006).

transfer provisions. This is where the fraudulent nature of the transfer is shown through circumstantial evidence. Proving a constructive fraudulent transfer is based on the adequacy of the consideration and the debtor's financial position at the time of the transfer, rather than the debtor's actual intent. In such a case the trustee has to prove that the debtor received less than a reasonably equivalent value in exchange for such transfer, and that the debtor was insolvent on the date that such transfer was made, or became insolvent as a result of such transfer.

Consider the previous example. Assume the trustee has difficulty showing the husband and wife's actual intent, but the couple state that they transferred the house as a gift (so no value given) and the couple was insolvent, or the house was their only real asset. Therefore, when they gave it away they became insolvent.

The trustee can avoid and recover fraudulent transfers made within two years of the bankruptcy filing under Section 548. Section 544 allows the trustee to use the Massachusetts fraudulent conveyance act, which enables the trustee to avoid transfers made within four years of the petition date.[609]

In *Wieboldt Stores, Inc. v. Schottenstein,* the lenders, who financed a leveraged buyout, knew that the purpose of the loan was to buy out most of the public equity shareholders. They also knew that, after the buyout, the corporation would have substantial additional debt but no additional working capital. The court applied the fraudulent conveyance prohibition to the loan, holding that the defendants intended to hinder, delay, or defraud other creditors and that the corporation was insolvent immediately after transaction.

In *Wolf & Vine ("Wolf"),*[610] a company was owned by Morris Wolf and the Marmon Group, Inc ("Marmon"). David Adashek bought Wolf's shares. The company's management bought the investors' shares by borrowing and pledging the company's assets in a leveraged buyout transaction (LBO).[611] However, after Wolf filed for bankruptcy Adashek made installment payments to the selling shareholders of Wolf. Wolf's trustee in bankruptcy filed a complaint alleging that the manner in which the sale was financed constituted fraudulent conveyances to Morris Wolf and Marmon under state law and bankruptcy law, as well as improper distributions to shareholders. The court held that: 1) the LBO is not a fraudulent conveyance where the sellers did not know that the transactions was being financed by a LBO and there

[609] These materials derived from the notes of Colin Darke, former LL.M. graduate of Boston University Law School, when assistant to Professor Tamar Frankel.

[610] Kupetz v. Wolf, 845 F.2d 842 (9th Cir. 1988).

[611] The LBO transactions were: Adashek formed a corporation with little equity and bought all the outstanding shares of Wolf with the loan from the Bank. Then the corporation merged into Wolf and Wolf assumed all the obligations and pledged its assets to the Bank to secure the loan.

is no evidence of any intention on the part of the selling shareholders to defraud the corporation's creditors; 2) installment payments that were made to the selling shareholders following the leveraged buyout were not "distributions" to shareholders.

Discussion Topics

1. Why was the loan to finance a buyout vulnerable to the trustee's attack?
2. What must a trustee in bankruptcy show in order to attack the LBO transaction as a fraudulent conveyance?
3. What principle guides the power of trustee's avoidance? Whose interest should have priority of protection in this transaction?
4. How can this issue be relevant to transactions of securitization involving bankruptcy procedure?
5. How would the filing of bankruptcy adversely affect an inevitable transfer from the transfer to the SPV? Under what circumstances will the filing of bankruptcy have an effect on the transfer? Please list as many situations as possible in which bankruptcy filing of the transferor of the financial assets to the SPV can affect investors in asset-backed securities.
6. What is the effect of the automatic stay? Note, however, the exceptions under section 547(c) of the Bankruptcy Code, such as the trustee may not avoid transfers "in payment of a debt incurred by the debtor in the ordinary course of business or financial affairs of the debtor and the transferee."

B. The Problem of SPVs Organized as Subsidiaries of the Transferor[612]

a. When the Insolvent Transferor is the Parent Corporation of the SPV[613]

In some cases, an Originator-Transferor may choose to hold the SPV's equity, thereby causing the SPV to become the Originator-Transferor's subsidiary. One reason for the sponsor's equity holding is that the Transferor-sponsor receives the SPV's equity in exchange for the financial assets it transfers to the SPV. In such a case the problem of preference under Bankruptcy Code may not arise if the Originator-Transferor fails later. An SPV issuing Collateral Mortgage Obligations is usually organized as a subsidiary of the Originator that holds the residual interests in the SPV. In addition, Originators usually continue to service the transferred loans and hold the loan documents.

If the SPV is a subsidiary of the Transferor of the loans, the trustee in bankruptcy can claim the loans by seeking to pierce the subsidiary's corporate veil and consolidate the assets of the SPV with those of the insolvent parent. Regardless of whether the SPV is

[612] 1 TAMAR FRANKEL, SECURITIZATION § 10.8 (Ann Taylor Schwing ed., 2d ed. 2005).

[613] 1 TAMAR FRANKEL, SECURITIZATION §§ 10.6-.7 (Ann Taylor Schwing ed., 2d ed. 2005).

an independent entity or a subsidiary of the transferor, the trustee may claim the assets of the SPV by attacking the loan transfer transaction and attempting to classify the transaction as an unsecured loan to the transferor or a secured loan with an unperfected security interest. Thus, the trustee can attack the priority rights of the SPV to the loans. If the SPV is deemed an unsecured creditor of the insolvent transferor, the SPV and its security holders will receive less than the full amounts of the loans. This discussion focuses on the general bankruptcy law. Banks, thrifts, and insurance companies are not subject to this law. However, the principles discussed here are likely to be applied to these entities, unless specifically excluded.

If the transferor continues to control the SPV by retaining the equity interest, the SPV's are at risk because the transferor's creditors may seek the SPV's assets to satisfy their claims against the transferor. If the transferor is not insolvent, the creditors may resort to the doctrine of "piercing the corporate veil" of the SPV under corporate law. If the transferor becomes insolvent, its creditors and the trustee in bankruptcy may seek to consolidate the SPV assets with those of the insolvent transferor under a similar, though not identical, doctrine.

Bankruptcy courts have consolidated the assets of subsidiaries with those of the insolvent parents on a case-by-case basis, considering a number of factors. Among these factors are the following: the extent, to which the assets of the two entities are commingled, or transferred without formalities, or difficult to segregate; the existence of consolidated financial statements of the parent and subsidiary; the profitability of consolidation of operation of the parent and subsidiary at a single location; the unity of interest and ownership among the two entities; and the existence of interoperate guarantees on their loans. Courts have also weighed the competing creditors' interests in determining whether to consolidate.

b. The Markets Are Aware of the Risk that the Transferor's Equity-Holding in the SPV May Pose for Investors

If the separate existence of the corporation and the transferor is not maintained, SPV securities will obtain a lower rating. Therefore, attorneys and rating agencies have taken certain precautions against these dangers in the belief that these steps help insulate the SPV from the failure of its parent.

First, the SPVs are organized as legal entities, whether corporations, limited partnerships, or trusts, separate from the Originator-Transferor. Each SPV has its own board of directors or its trustees and maintains its records separately from that of the parent company. These conditions may reduce the problem of "piercing the corporate veil." Whether the steps listed here protect SPV investors if the loan transferors fail is an open question.

Second, the SPV's equity can be transferred to parties other than the Originator or Transferor of the SPV assets. If the SPV is organized as a corporation whose equity is held by a nonprofit organization, which is virtually bankruptcy-proof, that ownership may protect the SPV from claims of the creditors of the transferor. Equity in the SPV is sometimes initially held by the underwriter of the SPV's securities or is publicly distributed.

Third, the rights of SPV creditors to petition for involuntary bankruptcy may be restricted in the SPVs' constitutional documents.

Fourth, a transferor that controls the SPV may cause the SPV to file a voluntary petition for bankruptcy. Therefore, the SPV and the transferor usually agree that they will not petition for each other's bankruptcy. Whether such an agreement is valid is far from clear. However, the constitutional documents of a corporate SPV may be drafted to restrict its own ability to place itself in bankruptcy. If SPV's assets are not consolidated with those of its insolvent parent, it is likely that the SPV will be bankruptcy-proof.

Fifth, an SPV may be organized as a true trust to avoid the other application of the federal bankruptcy law. However, a business trust may be subject to the federal Bankruptcy Code.

Sixth, the transfer of assets to the SPV should be structured as a "true sale" so that the assets will not be considered assets of the transferor and the transfer can not be revoked as a fraudulent conveyance.

Seventh, the SPV should have no prior business activities that could have given rise to preexisting creditors or other claimants. Its activities should be limited to those related to the financing. It should have no debts other than the asset-backed securities and obligations to credit enhancers and liquidity providers, and the securitized assets should be free of liens or security interests in favor of anyone other than the security holders, credit enhancers, or liquidity providers.

Discussion Topics:

1. What legal form of organization helps protect SPVs from the claims of the Originator's creditors, if the Originator-Transferor is bankrupt? Assume that an Originator-Transferor bank holds the mortgage loans which it made through a subsidiary of the bank that then issues its securities backed by the mortgage loans.
2. If the Originator-Transferor exchanges the financial assets it wishes to securitize with the SPV's equity (which would become its subsidiary) how does this process help in the case of alleged preference? If it does help, is it because the exchange is "contemporaneous exchange for new value?" Or is it because the transfer of the loan can be classified more readily as a sale rather than borrowing by the bank? Other reasons?

C. The Exception for Mortgage-Backed Securities

a. Section 541(d) of the Bankruptcy Code[614]

In 1976, Hamilton Mortgage Company, a mortgage broker, engaged in selling mortgage loan participations, became bankrupt. Hamilton's trustee retained unendorsed notes that accompanied the mortgages, and alleged that the buyers of the participations in the mortgages had merely an unsecured interest in the mortgages, because they failed to perfect a security interest in the notes and mortgages. Uncertainty about the effectiveness of assignments of interests in mortgages and mortgage notes threatened the stability of the $600 billion mortgage-backed securities Market. Consequently, Congress enacted section 541(d) of the Bankruptcy Code. The purpose of the section is to ensure that secondary mortgage-market sales, as they are currently structured, will not be challenged by bankruptcy trustees, and that purchasers of the mortgages will be able to obtain from the trustees the mortgages or interests in the mortgages which they have purchased, barring the trustees from asserting that a sale of mortgages was a loan from the purchaser to the seller.

Amended section 541(d) of the Code provides that, if a debtor (e.g., an insolvent servicer of the mortgage loans) holds only the legal title to, but not the equitable interest in, property, "such as a mortgage secured by real property, or an interest in such a mortgage, sold by the debtor but as to which the debtor retains legal title to service or supervise the servicing of such mortgage or interest, [the property] becomes property of the [bankrupt's] estate . . . only to the extent of the debtor's legal title to such property, and not to the extent of any equitable interest in such property that the debtor does not hold."[615]

Section 541(d) protects the holders of mortgage-backed securities that were unperfected. In addition, section 541(d) may protect the holders against the common law doctrine of "fraud in law" followed in some states.[616] This doctrine incorporates a presumption of fraud against other creditors of a seller if the purchased property remains in the hands of the seller. By statute, this presumption is conclusive in some states. Section 541(d) of the Bankruptcy Code affords the holders of mortgage-backed securities protection against such allegations and presumptions.

Whether Section 541(s) protects against attacks by the bankruptcy trustee based on other fact situations is doubtful. Arguably, if a mortgage is not the property of the

---

[614] 1 TAMAR FRANKEL, SECURITIZATION § 10.10.2 (Ann Taylor Schwing ed., 2d ed. 2005).

[615] 11 U.S.C. § 541(d) (2006).

[616] *E.g.*, Regan v. Ivanelli, 617 N.E.2d 808, 814 (Ill. App. Ct. 1993); Berland v. Mussa (*In re* Mussa), 215 B.R. 158 (Bankr. N.D. Ill. 1997), *motion denied*, 218 B.R. 428 (Bankr. N.D. Ill. 1998).

bankrupt's estate, it seems unlikely that the mortgage becomes the property of the estate after the bankruptcy trustee has exercised his power to avoid certain prebankruptcy transfers by the debtor-assignor. Nonetheless, if attacks on the entitlement to the mortgage loan or mortgage-backed security are based on fraud or fraudulent conveyance or preferences, courts might sustain the attacks. Although Congress desired to provide certainty of title for mortgage-backed security holders there is no indication that it intended to allow Section 541(d) to be used as a cover for fraud.

Most courts hold that Section 541(d) does not impose a general limitation on the trustee's power of avoidance in section 544. When the creditors' claims are grounded in a constructive trust, the trustee may avoid the transaction. In *Belisle v. Plunkett (In re Plunkett)*, former partners of the debtor claimed a leasehold that the debtor held, contending he was holding the leasehold as a constructive trustee, because the leasehold had been purchased with partnership money. The court held that the debtor's obligations as a constructive trustee could be avoided by the trustee in bankruptcy. Section 541(d) applies only if the debtor holds the bare legal title, not when he is subject to a claim based on unjust enrichment (constructive trust). In enacting Section 541(d), Congress was concerned solely with secondary mortgage market transactions. Therefore, the *Plunkett* court agreed with the majority of other courts that Section 541(d) does not constitute a general limitation on the trustee's powers under section 544(a).

At least one commentator has argued that Section 541(d) does not protect the holders of mortgage-backed securities against the claims of creditors with a perfected security interest, since the section is addressed to conflicts between the security holders and the trustee in bankruptcy. In addition, the protection will probably not apply to chattel paper. Thus, the precise contours of Section 541(d) remain uncertain.

Chapter 10: The Distribution and Trading of SPV Obligations and Securities[617]

The focus of this chapter is on the distribution and trading of the obligations and securities that SPVs issue. The chapter begins with a discussion of the "securities" status of asset-backed securities. Next, registration requirements under the Securities Act of 1933 are detailed. This is followed by an explanation of the trading of SPV obligations in the secondary markets. With this material as context, the issuers' registration as broker-dealers under the Securities Exchange Act of 1934 is outlined. The chapter concludes with a simulation exercise which considers the appropriateness of investing in Fannie Mae mortgage-backed securities.

The Markets in SPV securities consist of various financial assets, the largest portion of which is backed by mortgages. The Market for mortgage-backed securities ("MBS") consists mostly of mortgages securitized by Government agencies, but private sector Originators have been taking an increasingly greater share in this Market, especially with respect to mortgages that do not qualify for securitization by Government agencies.

The initial Markets in asset-backed securities except MBS were, and largely still are, the wholesale Markets, populated by Institutions, and most issues of these securities are privately placed. MBS are retailed to small investors, usually through open-end investment companies (mutual funds). Banks began to distribute receivable-backed securities to small investors in the mid-1980s, and this trend is continuing. This development, which may introduce highly risky securities to investors, may affect the applicability of the securities acts to these instruments.

Registration of asset-backed securities under the Securities Act of 1933 may raise problems that apply to all securities. These problems are not discussed in this book. This section focuses on issues unique to asset-backed securities. The special structure of asset-backed securities raises a number of issues under the 1933 Act and state securities acts, including:

(i) Are asset-backed securities "securities"?

(ii) If so, who is the issuer of these securities?

(iii) What exemptions are available to these securities?

(iv) Is "shelf registration" available for these securities?

(v) What is the status of the securities under state blue sky laws?

[617] 2 TAMAR FRANKEL, SECURITIZATION § 12.1 (Ann Taylor Schwing ed., 2d ed. 2005).

(vi)If the 1933 Act applies to them, how should conflicts between the unique way these securities are created and the provisions of the 1933 Act be reconciled?

(vii) What kind of information and expertise do investors need to evaluate these securities?

The securities of SPVs that hold numerous illiquid loans present substantial information costs. It is costly to evaluate the credit risk of illiquid SPV portfolios. It is costly to evaluate the risk presented by receivables. They are short-term, issued by numerous issuers whose circumstances may change. Unlike a bank, the SPV does not have the information about the borrowers or debtors that is reflected in their bank account transactions. Certain types of portfolio loans (mortgages) involve cumbersome and un-standardized documents while other types of loans (credit card debt) can involve unreliable documentation, since the borrowers do not sign all the documents and multiple documents created at many locations may suffer loss or damage. The performance of SPV portfolios is difficult to predict, since historical data is not always helpful; such SPVs may not have existed in the past.

There are modern methods by which such securities can be evaluated, such as those analyzed and proposed by Sylvain Raynes and Ann Rutledge.[618] Nonetheless, this evaluation requires sophistication. In addition, there is limited certainty about the underwriting standards that the loan Originators will use. It is likely that the credit risk of the loans will be higher when the Originating lenders make loans for sale rather than investment, since lenders tend to relax their underwriting standards when they will not bear the ultimate risk.

Furthermore, by and large, the terms of asset-backed securities, such as maturity and market risk, cannot be easily ascertained, because sometime the borrowers have a right to prepay the loans at any time, and most SPV securities offer returns based on anticipated cash flows from the borrowers. Therefore, investors in these securities must master special expertise to evaluate the assumptions underlying the returns and maturities of the securities; in addition, investors need special information different from that needed to evaluate traditional securities (corporate securities, mutual funds). Notwithstanding these difficulties, the benefits of requiring registration of mortgage-backed securities and other debt securities sold to Institutions are limited as Institutions have become familiar with the instruments and standards have been developed in the industry. This conclusion, however, may be open to question in light of the sub-prime mortgage securitization crisis in 2006-8.

---

[618] SYLVAIN RAYNES & ANN RUTLEDGE, THE ANALYSIS OF STRUCTURED SECURITIES: PRECISE RISK MEASUREMENT AND CAPITAL ALLOCATION (2003).

A. The "Security" Status of Asset-Backed Securities under the 1933 Act[619]

The term "asset-backed securities" includes securities issued by SPVs and securities issued by someone else that are collateralized by financial assets held by SPVs. In their attempt to determine the status of asset-backed securities, the courts and the SEC have tried to fit the instruments into one of the terms in the definition of a security in section 2(a)(1) of the 1933 Act. In addition, the test that the Supreme Court established in *SEC v. W.J. Howey Co.* and *United Housing Foundation, Inc. v. Forman* has served as a guide.

a. The *Howey* Test

This test focused on "investment contracts" similar to equity securities, however, and is not entirely applicable to asset-backed securities. The distinction between debt securities and commercial loans has been problematic because debt instruments may represent one-to-one contracts or mass-produced obligations that are distributed to the public.

The one-to-one contracts are not securities, and the mass-produced obligations are, even though the two may look alike. Courts have struggled with this problem in the securities area, including the area of securities that are produced in the securitization process. The problem is greater in connection with asset-backed securities. At their inception, asset-backed securities are commercial loans; therefore, they cannot be distinguished by risk. Rather, they are distinguishable by their features that may make them amenable to market trading and liquidity, such as standardized form.

One may also distinguish the instruments by how the SPV is treated. If the SPV's existence is ignored, and the value of the securities is based on the holdings of the SPV, the status of the SPV's portfolio as commercial loans determines the status of the instruments that the SPV issues. If the SPV's existence is not ignored, either because it is a legal entity or because its portfolio represents additional risk to investors as compared to the aggregate assets that it holds, then the instruments that the SPV issues are not commercial loans but securities.

b. The Status of MBS as Investment Contracts

In the SEC's view, the status of MBS depends on whether they are "investment contracts" within the definition of security in section 2(a)(1) of the 1933 Act. In *In re EPIC Mortgage Insurance Litigation,* a federal district court held that MBS are not investment contracts because they do not meet the tests established in *SEC v. W.J. Howey Co.* However, there are authorities to the contrary.

---

[619] 2 TAMAR FRANKEL, SECURITIZATION § 12.2 (Ann Taylor Schwing ed., 2d ed. 2005).

In a California case, involving allegations of massive fraud by SPV Originators and their attorneys, the court held, on a motion to dismiss, that pass-through certificates issued by SPVs that held mortgages are securities within section 2(a)(1) of the 1933 Act. The court declined to follow the Second Circuit "literalist" interpretation of the section and resorted to the three tests set forth in *SEC v. W.J. Howey Co.* and the "risk capital" test, which is incorporated into the Supreme Court's "economic realities" test.

These tests focus on whether investors provide risk capital and whether investors expect profits from the entrepreneurial or managerial efforts of others. The district court applied the "risk capital" test to distinguish securities from commercial loans and concluded that the complaint allegations were sufficient to "meet the *Howey* test, as amplified by the *Kotz* six-factor analysis."[620] In denying the motion to dismiss, the court emphasized the heavy factual component involved in this issue, such as documentation of the loans and the nature of the negotiations between the parties. However, when the case came to trial, the district court held that mortgage-backed certificates are not securities within the definition in the 1933 Act, following the tests established by the Ninth Circuit. The court followed a number of tests.

Under the first test, whether the particular investors needed the protection of the securities acts, the court concluded that the facts of the case showed that the investors did not need such protection.

Second, the court tested the certificates under the definition in *SEC v. W.J. Howey Co.* and concluded that the certificates were not investment contracts: there was no investment of risk capital, especially since the investment was in loans, not in the business of the issuer; there was no common enterprise; and the investors did not expect profits from the entrepreneurial efforts of others. The efforts of the sponsor preceded the transaction. The efforts of the servicer and the trustee were administrative rather than "managerial or entrepreneurial."[621] Since the investors negotiated the deal and had a right to reject loans that did not conform to the standards set forth in the agreement, the investors had only themselves to blame; they should not have relied on the seller as to the quality of the loans.

Arguably, the certificates in the California case are securities, even if the transaction was negotiated directly with the seller. Perhaps the very fact of this fraud, the ease in which it was perpetrated, and the difficulty of discovering it show the similarity of this sale to a securities sale. The distinction between a loan and a security may be based on whether the transferee was actively involved in negotiating the loan and

---

[620] *In re* Nat'l Mortg. Equity Corp. Mortg. Pool Certificates Sec. Litig., 636 F. Supp. 1138, 1163-64 (C.D. Cal. 1986).

[621] *In re* Nat'l Mortg. Pool Certificates Sec. Litig., 723 F. Supp. 497, 505 (C.D. Cal. 1989).

acted as a lender or whether the transferee was purchasing the loan for investment, as a passive investor. In the past, this distinction could depend on whether the transferee was a financial institution. With securitization, that distinction is being eroded since lending institutions also purchase loans made by others.

Thus, even though the buyers numbered some 85 thrift institutions each received an undivided equity right in loans made by others as investment. These transferees need the protection of the securities acts because the cost of discovering the fraud is so high for them. After all, even if they were sophisticated, they had limited access to the relevant information. Further, asset-backed securities, especially in mortgage-backed securities, are viewed as securities by the market players. To determine whether these instruments are subject to the securities acts on the basis of the nature of the transfer negotiations would undermine the securities act protections for passive investors and involve the courts in substantial litigation. In addition, the reliance on judicial decisions with respect to loan participations is inappropriate. These participations historically represented interbank loans and are securities when standardized and sold as investments. Therefore, the better view is that asset-backed securities are generally securities in the context of the securities acts. The party that argues that these instruments are not securities should have the burden to show that they are loans in the sense that the transferees were active lenders rather than passive investors.

This analysis also follows the approach of the Supreme Court in classifying notes as securities. In February 1990, the Supreme Court adopted the approach of the Second Circuit holding that a demand note issued by a farmers' cooperative was a security for the purposes of the 1934 Act. Under this approach, it is presumed that any note with a term of more than nine months is a security, unless it is included on a judicially-developed list of notes that have been determined not to be securities. The Court found that the notes at issue did not resemble any recognized exception. In addition, after analyzing four factors that it determined were pertinent (purpose of issuance, plan of distribution, reasonable expectations of the investing public, and existence of another regulatory scheme governing the investments), the Court held there was no reason to exclude the notes from the definition of a security.

c. Persistent Difficult Issues

Two cases illustrate the continuing difficulties of classifying mortgage notes. Both cases arose from the sale of mortgage notes originated by First American Mortgage Corporation ("FAMCO"). In both cases, FAMCO continued to service the mortgages after the sale and engaged in fraudulent sales until it became insolvent. Both cases were decided on the defendants' motion to dismiss.

In *First Financial Federal Savings & Loan Association v. E.F. Hutton Mortgage Corp.*, a presumably sophisticated thrift bought from a broker in the secondary

Market a large number of the mortgage notes amounting to over $2 million. The court held that the notes did not constitute securities. In *Zolfaghari v. Sheikholeslami*, small unsophisticated investors bought the notes from the originator FAMCO. The Fourth Circuit held that the notes could constitute securities and remanded for trial. Although the results seem intuitively correct, the rationale of the cases is hard to understand and harder to reconcile.

In *Hutton,* the court held that the mortgage notes were not securities under Arkansas blue sky law. Because Arkansas law and federal law definitions are similar, the court applied the *Howey* test. The court held that the arrangement between the parties failed the test because the plaintiffs did not expect profits from the efforts of others. Alone, the seller's continued servicing of the loans did not constitute such efforts, especially when the buyers retained control of the servicing under the sale agreement, having reserved the power to replace the servicer. In addition, "neither party relied on any representations made by the other concerning the loans purchased."[622] The buyers waived their right to seek information from the sellers, were offered an opportunity to check the notes, and had the sophistication to understand the information.

The *Zolfaghari* court held the mortgage notes were securities, distinguishing *Hutton* on a number of grounds. First, while the buyers in *Hutton* bought specific individual FAMCO-originated mortgage loans through a dealer, the buyers in *Zolfaghari* bought "combined mortgages operating as security for a mutual fund investment."[623] Second, the *Howey* test was met because the seller was expected not only to service the mortgages but also to manage the SPV of mortgages. Thus, the buyers might have expected "the success of the investments [to depend] upon FAMCO's skill in managing mortgage based investments."[624]

However, it was unclear whether the buyers bought notes or participations in an SPV of notes. While FAMCO represented that it was selling participations in an SPV, FAMCO's "internal paperwork was structured so as to appear to regulators that individual loans were 'sold' to plaintiffs, but the misleading paperwork apparently was done only to avoid reporting requirements."[625] It could be shown at trial that neither buyer nor seller believed that the transactions were sales of individual notes and that the plaintiffs bought instruments described in FAMCO's presentations, not those described "internally" in writings designed to avoid regulation. On a motion

---

[622] First Financial Fed. Sav. & Loan Ass'n v. E.F. Hutton Mortg. Corp., 652 F. Supp. 471, 476 (D. Ark.), *aff'd,* 834 F.2d 685 (8th Cir. 1987).

[623] Zolfaghari v. Sheikholeslami, 943 F.2d 451, 454 (4th Cir. 1991).

[624] *Id.* at 455.

[625] Zolfaghari v. Sheikholeslami, 943 F.2d 451, 456 (4th Cir. 1991).

for summary judgment, these speculations were sufficient to sustain continuation of the case.

In the opinion of the dissenting judge, the securities laws are designed to protect only those who intend to buy securities, not those who intend to buy something else but are defrauded into buying securities. Whatever plaintiffs actually received, they did not intend to buy securities, but mortgage notes, as they admitted in their brief. Thus, if the nature of the instrument is misrepresented by the seller (as securities or not securities), it is unclear when and for what purpose the buyer may assert the misrepresented terms. Arguably, the agreement could be subject to rescission for lack of mutual intent or mistake. Presumably, the dissent agreed with the majority that shares in pooled and managed mortgage notes are securities, while mortgage notes are not. Therefore, the *Zolfaghari* and *Hutton* decisions are based on the distinction between mortgage notes that the buyer will manage and service (directly or through agents) and participations in an SPV of mortgage notes, managed and serviced by others.

d. Notes

The dual status of notes seems to reflect the historical two separate forms of intermediation through which the notes can pass from borrowers to savers: market intermediation (e.g., investment banking) and Institutional intermediation (e.g., commercial banking). Some notes (e.g., commercial paper) can constitute securities, and some (e.g., bank loans) can constitute lending contracts. Secondary market transactions can involve notes that are securities and notes that are not (sale by discount). Pooling notes that are securities can produce an investment company; pooling notes that are not securities can produce an Institution that is not an investment company (e.g., a bank, a factor, or a finance company). Notes were usually classified by the type of intermediary that dealt with them. Since our financial system is allocating to market intermediaries an increasing part, the role of securities regulation will probably increase.

e. Mortgage Loans

As a matter of policy, Markets in mortgage loans would be encouraged if the cost of obtaining information on the status of the traded instruments and the obligors is reduced. To reduce these costs, the instruments can be classified by form, transaction, buyers, or sellers, among others; classification by form seems to be the least costly. Further, as compared to securities issues, the cost of ascertaining the credit-worthiness of mortgage notes of relatively small denominations is far greater because the number of issuers (borrowers) of mortgage notes is usually higher. To impose a duty of verifying credit-worthiness on either the broker or the buyer might hinder the development of the Market in such notes. Even rating agencies focus on the practices of the loan originator, rather than on those of the individual borrowers.

It seems that only the originators and perhaps the trustees of SPVs containing such notes are sufficiently compensated to bear the costs.

f. Viatical Settlements

In *SEC v. Life Partners, Inc.*, the D.C. Circuit held that the following arrangements were not securities. Promoters sold to investors participations in viatical settlements (life insurance policies purchased from terminally ill insureds), acquired by the promoters in negotiations with terminally ill insureds at a discount. Then these participations were serviced by a trust company with little discretionary powers. The court applied the *Howey* test to the participations. It held that two of the three basic *Howey* formulas were met. The investors parted with their money, and the money was pooled into a common enterprise (purchase of the group life insurance contracts or pool of such contracts). However, the court held that, although the investors expected profits, their profits did not come from the efforts of the promoters *after the sale of the participations.* To be sure, the promoters did make efforts that led to profits before sale of the participations. The court stated that these profits were incorporated into the price of the participations or the service fees of the promoters. Hence, no additional information would affect the buyers' investment decisions, and none was required. In addition, the court held that the profits of the investors did not stem from the efforts of the promoters nor from the Markets, but from the death of the insureds and such events did not cause the participations to be securities. More importantly, the court held that there is no investment contract if the investors' profits do not stem from the promoters' services *after sale of the participations.* Only such post-purchase managerial efforts would constitute the participations securities. Judge Wald, dissenting, pointed to numerous arrangements that held participations in financial assets to be securities such as mortgage-backed securities. In fact, the viatical settlements constitute the beginning steps in the securitization of these policies, no different from the securitization of other financial assets.

In denying rehearing, the D.C. Circuit responded to the SEC's assertion that the court "placed in question the applicability of the federal securities laws to . . . certain asset-backed securities" including mortgage-backed securities. The court noted that "a mortgage pool must be managed on a continuing basis" and listed post-purchase services that should meet the "efforts of others" test.[626] The decision is not binding outside circuit boundaries, and the SEC has established that it will continue to investigate possible securities laws violations in viatical settlement transactions. The SEC succeeded in fining a viatical settlement company for engaging in activities that could be construed as selling securities. The value of a viatical settlement security may reflect various expenses associated with the assignation of life insurance proceeds. For example, proceeds from such sale may be subject to federal income taxation; in addition, receipt of a large lump sum by the terminally ill assignor can

[626] SEC v. Life Partners, Inc., 102 F.3d 587, 588-89 (D.C. Cir. 1996).

affect that individual's eligibility for Medicaid or other Government-sponsored assistance programs. There are those who argue that *SEC v. Life Partners, Inc.* is erroneous and contravenes congressional mandates in implementing securities laws. Others contend that the D.C. Circuit decision was an affront to accepted investment contract principles and was largely motivated out of a belief that viatical settlement agreements are socially beneficial and useful to terminally ill patients.

Discussion Topic

In 2009 a number of insurance companies had a plan. They would offer to buy elderly persons' life insurance at a discount for cash. The insurance policies would be then pooled into an SPV and the SPV will offer securities backed by the life insurance policies. The SPV holding the policies would issue securities for this aggregate amount. Assume that the SPV issues only two tranches, one, to be paid the amount of policies cashed at the death of the insured after one year, and the other, paid the amount of the policies any time thereafter. Evaluate this transaction as (1) an insurance company, (2) an investor, and (3) a regulator.

g. Equipment Leases

A problem similar to that of the classification of viatical settlements arises in the case of equipment leases issued by municipal governments that are securitized or slated for securitization. In general, such equipment leases are viewed as securities under the heading of investment contracts, although there are dissenters as well. If the leases are pooled and vested in trustees who issue "equipment-trust certificates or like securities," then the certificates are securities and the issuer of such securities is deemed to be "the person by whom the equipment or property is or is to be used."[627] The trustees for such equipment leases usually are subject to the provisions of the Trust Indenture Act of 1939 and are charged with collecting and distributing the rent, and enforcing the certificate holders' rights in the case of default. Traditionally, such equipment leases issued by municipal governments were exempt from registration under section 3(a)(2) of the 1933 Act, as securities issued or guaranteed by a political subdivision of a state. Equipment leases increasingly have been securitized. The leases are pooled and vested in a trustee or a legal entity that publicly issues trust participations or shares or debt obligations. One issue arising out of these arrangements involves the status of the equipment leases' pre-securitization stage. Some leases may never be securitized, some may be securitized immediately, and some may be securitized after time. The second issue concerning securitized leases involves their status as municipal securities and whether they are exempt from registration under the 1933 Act.

---

[627] Section 2(a)(4), 1933 Act, 15 U.S.C. §77b(a)(4) (2006).

h. Limited Partnerships

Limited partnerships' participations in a securitization scheme were held not to be securities following the interpretation of the 1933 Act. Thus, the Third Circuit held that a securitization transaction between defendant Citicorp and an investor in a limited partnership did not constitute an investment contract as defined in *Howey*. The *Howey* test requirements for an investment contract are (i) "an investment of money," (ii) "in a common enterprise," (iii) "with profits to come solely from the efforts of others." Examination of the partnership agreement convinced the court that the control over the management of the partnership given to the plaintiff was significant and directly affected the profits it received from the partnership. Therefore, the court determined that the transaction failed to meet the third prong of the *Howey* test.[628]

i. Securities, Contracts, Financing and Other Elements

In *Realtek v. Nomura* a transaction raised the issue of classifying securitization.[629] Realtek owned a number of apartment buildings. Realtek had borrowed and mortgaged these buildings. It aimed at refinancing its loans and entered into an agreement with Nomura. Nomura agreed to help refinance the properties by structured financing. Realtek later sued Nomura (defendants) alleging securities violations under section 10(b) of the Securities and Exchange Act of 1934,[630] and SEC Rule 10(b)-5.[631] The court denied the defendants' motion to dismiss.[632]

The court wrote: "In economic reality, this structured financing was designed to enable Realtek to raise $165 million from investors and to repay its existing, purportedly then-overpriced, mortgage loans. The basic outlines of this structured financing transaction were as follows. First the parties would establish an entity that would qualify as a 'real estate mortgage investment conduit" ('REMIC'), which could provide investors pass-through tax treatment under the Internal Revenue Code. Realtek would then give to this REMIC entity mortgages on about 60 of its buildings, in exchange for the $165 million from Nomura. Realtek would execute mortgage notes promising to repay these loans, the notes to be cross-collateralized by the buildings. Realtek would assign to the REMIC entity the right to the lease incomes from the buildings, so that the monthly payments due under the mortgage

[628] Steinhardt Group, Inc. v. Citicorp, 126 F.3d 144, 151 (3d Cir. 1997) (quoting SEC v. W.J. Howey Co., 328 U.S. 293, 301 (1946)).

[629] Realtek Indus., Inc. v. Nomura Sec., 939 F. Supp. 572 (N.D. Ohio 1996).

[630] 15 U.S.C. § 78j (2006).

[631] 17 C.F.R. § 240.10b-5 (2008).

[632] Realtek Indus., Inc. v. Nomura Sec., 939 F. Supp. 572 (N.D. Ohio 1996).

notes could be paid out of the buildings' income rental streams. The 60 mortgage notes would be pooled to create 'certificates of undivided ownership'. . . ,[each representing] an ownership share in the pool containing the 60 mortgage notes; with the ownership share would come the right to receive a proportionate share of the income rental streams, secured by the buildings as underlying collateral. The REMIC entity would then issue the participation certificates, which Nomura would sell to private investors.

The result of this financing scheme was that the rental income streams from the 60 properties would 'pass-through' the mortgage pool and REMIC to the investors in the participation certificates, with beneficial 'pass-through' tax treatment. The rental income-streams would thus serve as a return on the investors' payment of the certificate price. In turn, the money paid by the private investors for their certificates would 'pass-through' the mortgage pool back to the original holder of the mortgage notes, Realtek. Realtek would then use the money generated by these investors to pay off its existing mortgage loans. Nomura, meanwhile, would receive a fee for its role in the process."[633]

"Grafted onto this general outline are details that made Nomura's proposed refinancing deal much more complex. First, the 'participation certificates' were to be divided into five classes. Each class of participation certificate would be assigned a rating by at least one credit rating agency. The ratings for the first four classes would be AAA, AA, A, and BBB. Essentially, these four classes of certificates were distinguished by the priority of the certificate-holder's claim to the properties' stream of rental income. The fifth class of certificates, known as 'R certificates,' would entitled the owners to the residual monies left after the holders of the first four classes of certificates were paid in full. Under the terms of the deal, Realtek was required to purchase the 'R certificates,' ensuring that: (1) the structure would qualify as a REMIC; and (2) Realtek would have an incentive to secure continued and increased rental income from its properties.

Second, the refinancing deal contemplated that Nomura would provide Realtek with 'Interim Loans' for a period of about six months, secured by the mortgages and income streams on Realtek's properties. The interest rate on the Interim Loans would float, changing monthly depending on a specified published interbank interest rate. Presumably, the Interim Loans would serve as an advance on the monies Realtek anticipated through the structured financing, although Nomura never promised Realtek permanent 'traditional' loans on its properties.

During the six month Interim Loan period, a process of due diligence was contemplated whereby Nomura would evaluate each of Realtek's properties to

[633] *Id.* at 575-76.

determine whether it qualified to be included in the securitization process. Only those properties which met certain criteria, including acceptable appraisals, minimum levels of rental income, and adequate debt/equity ratios, could be refinanced through the 'pass-through' structured financing. If a given property did not qualify, Realtek would simply pay off the Interim Loan on that particular property and seek permanent financing for it elsewhere. Qualified properties would eventually be financed through 'Permanent Loans' with new terms, rates, and principal amounts. The Interim Loans would be paid off with these new loan amounts. The notes and mortgages related to the Permanent Loans would then go into the ultimate mortgage pool for securitization. Also during the due diligence period, one or more credit rating agencies were to be engaged to evaluate the finances underlying each qualified property. These evaluations were to be used by the credit rating agencies to determine the size of each class of rated certificates. The better Realtek's operation of the properties, the larger Nomura's ultimate offering of AAA-rated participation certificates, and the smaller Nomura's offering of lower-rated certificates.

The credit rating agency evaluations impacted the interest rate Realtek would pay on the Permanent Loans. The rating agency evaluations and Realtek's Permanent Loan interest rate were linked (or had the potential to be linked). Shortly after signing the Commitment Letter, Realtek had to decide whether it or Nomura would bear the 'rating agency risk.' If Realtek decided that Nomura would bear the rating agency risk, then Realtek's Permanent Loan interest rate would be determined by reference to a pre-determined financial table. Under this option, the interest rate Realtek would pay on the Permanent Loans would not depend in any direct way on the rating agencies' assessments of the properties' finances or operations . . . . Under this option, each of the first four of the five classes of participation certificates would be assigned an interest rate commensurate with its rating. The higher-rated classes of participation certificates would be assigned lower interest rates, and the lower-rated classes assigned higher interest rates. The better the credit rating agencies' evaluation of Realtek's operations, the larger the classes of higher-rated certificates, and the lower Realtek's ultimate interest rate would be. As compared to the option under which Nomura bore the 'rating agency risk,' Realtek would pay a lower overall interest rate on its debt if the rating agencies' evaluations of its operations were sufficiently high. Realtek alleges that, between the two options, it elected to bear the rating agency risk in the hope of receiving high ratings on its properties from the credit rating agencies.

The parties disagreed on the impact that Realtek's assumption of the 'rating agency risk' had on its status as a seller of securities. Nomura insisted that *regardless* of which party bore the 'rating agency risk,' Nomura would be the *only* party that, at any point during the entire process, sold securities (the participation certificates) Realtek insisted that, because it was the holder of the mortgages, notes and leases to be transferred to the REMIC entity, if it chose to bear the 'rating agency risk,' it would also be the indirect seller of the participation certificates to be issued by the REMIC entity. Therefore, if it chose to bear this risk, it became obligated to issue *and* sell rated securities to the [SPV], and Nomura, as underwriter, would buy and resell the securities (possibly after repackaging) to investors. Realtek points to specific language in the exhibits to its second amended complaint to support its argument that Realtek, itself, was obligated to sell (and Nomura was obligated to buy and resell) securities under the 'Realtek bears rating agency risk' option."[634]

"[T]he parties also agreed that Realtek would pay certain of Nomura's due diligence costs, such as legal fees, printing fees, property appraisals, and so on, and would pay Nomura a 2% underwriting fee, or about $ 3.3 million. Realtek alleges the parties also agreed that: (1) all of the proceeds of Nomura's sale of participation certificates to the private investors, less specifically identified transaction costs, would go to Realtek, which would thereupon repay the Interim Loans; and (2) therefore, the overall interest rate earned by the investors would be equal to the interest rate on the Permanent Loans to be paid by Realtek. . . . Realtek alleges that Nomura breached dozens of other promises, for example, to meet certain deadlines, when it knew it could not meet them when it agreed to them, and that Nomura did not, and never intended to, provide the Interim Loans. . . ."

"[In addition,] Nomura intended all along to make additional profits on the refinancing deal by charging up to $14 million in trading fees to the private investors who would buy the participation certificates. Realtek asserted that this intention was inconsistent with its alleged agreement that all proceeds of Nomura's sale of the participation certificates to investors, less identified transaction costs, would be paid to Realtek and, therefore, the overall interest rate earned by investors would equal that paid by Realtek on the Permanent Loans."

Nomura argues that the Realtek deal was a very simple loan transaction—"Nomura would transfer money to Realtek in exchange for Realtek's existing mortgages, notes and assigned leases. Nomura would . . . pool those mortgages and sell them to investors to finance its own loans to Realtek. Hence, Nomura characterizes the deal as a two-step transaction: one involving a completed loan in return for collateral, and another involving an independent decision by Nomura to transfer the costs of, and some portion of the risk of, that loan to the open market by the sale of shares in the mortgage pool in the form of participation certificates. Under this scenario, Realtek would be uninvolved in any offer or sale of securities and the ultimate investors in securities would be unaffected by Realtek's negotiations with its lender, Nomura. The two ends of the transaction would operate independently and, as Nomura points

[634] *Id.* at 576-77.

out, would be treated independently under the securities laws. Indeed, at oral argument, counsel for Nomura argued that Nomura acted vis-à-vis Realtek much like Fannie Mae does vis-à-vis individual homeowners who finance their home purchase via a government mortgage." The court noted: "Nomura is correct that, when a lender takes mortgages as collateral in a traditional loan transaction, those mortgages are generally not deemed securities. And, Nomura is correct that, when lending institutions turn around and securitize their already-existing loans by selling interests in either the loans or the collateral, the original borrowers generally would not be deemed issuers or sellers of those end-product securities."[635] However, "[t]he transaction alleged in Realtek's complaint is neither as simple nor as divisible as Nomura asserts. Realtek describes a transaction in which Realtek contemplated all along the distribution of securities to the public (backed by its obligations and properties), and chose an investment banker to design for it a securities distribution through structured financing. Realtek alleges that it was, in fact, involved in the rating, design and distribution of the anticipated securities, through a REMIC entity designed for that purpose, *and* that it was Nomura who insisted that Realtek take on that role. In the deal Realtek describes, Nomura was to operate effectively as an underwriter whose payments to Realtek should really be described as advances on that activity, rather than as traditional lending transactions."[636]

On the issue of whether the notes were securities the court noted: "[E]ven under Nomura's characterization of the parties' agreement, the mortgage notes Realtek was to give to the REMIC entity are securities. Realtek has certainly alleged (and Nomura does not dispute) that, at the time it committed to make the Permanent Loans, Nomura intended to pool the Permanent Loan notes and distribute participation certificates to the public. Indeed, it made a commitment to Realtek that it would, in fact, do so. The sale of participation certificates to the public was an integral part of the transaction alleged and the transaction evidenced by the Commitment Letter.

Despite Nomura's contention to the contrary, the alleged transaction, though complex, was a fairly integrated one -- not a series of independent steps. Realtek's obligations under the Permanent Loans could ultimately depend on the price charged for the participation certificates to private investors, and the price and value of the interests purchased at the end of the deal were dependent upon the performance evaluations of Realtek's properties. The 'loan' piece of the transaction simply could not have been completed absent the rating of the participation certificates.

The participation certificates which Nomura and Realtek contemplated would be sold to investors almost certainly would have been securities . . . . [Therefore], the

[635] *Id.* at 578-79.

[636] *Id.* at 579-80.

mortgages and notes given by Realtek for the precise purpose of creating those certificates are, in the unique circumstances of this transaction, also securities. . . . .

Generally, only purchasers and sellers of securities have standing to bring a private cause of action under Rule 10b-5. . . . Nomura insists the parties' agreement contemplates that the only entity which would sell securities was Nomura, and those securities would be the participation certificates at the 'end' of the deal. Realtek responds that, under the 'retain rating agency risk' option, *it* was obligated to create a REMIC entity through which it would sell rated securities to Nomura in the 'middle' of the deal. The Court will not and should not resolve this factual dispute in the context of a motion to dismiss under Rule 12(b)(6). . . .

There is, again, an independent reason to find that the transaction included an agreement by Realtek to transfer securities to Nomura. If, by virtue of the integrated nature of this structured financing, the notes and mortgages which were pooled to form the source of the participation certificates can be deemed securities at the time of their transfer, Realtek must undoubtedly be considered a 'seller' of those securities. . . . This is true, even absent any obligation on Realtek's part to sell rated securities to Nomura. The structured financing Realtek and the Commitment Letter describe is one in which a transfer of mortgages and notes from Realtek was *only* to occur for purposes of facilitating their ultimate securitization. . . . Realtek would and should be deemed a seller of securities for purposes of Rule 10b-5. . . .

Realtek Has Alleged Fraud 'In Connection With' a Security. . . . The Supreme Court has made clear that the phrase 'in connection with' 'must be read flexibly, not technically and restrictively.' 'For the 'in connection with' requirement to be satisfied, it is enough that the fraud 'touch' the sale in some manner. The requirement is satisfied, for example, if the purchase or sale of a security and the proscribed conduct are part of the same fraudulent scheme.' . . .

Nomura focuses on the participation certificates as the relevant securities, and argues that any relationship between these certificates and the alleged fraud was 'incidental at best.' If the facts are as Nomura contends, and the sale of the participation certificates was contemplated as a distinct and separable phase of the transaction, Nomura's argument about the 'in connection with requirement' might be well-taken. As noted, however, Realtek's description of the transaction differs materially from Nomura's. Realtek alleges that: (1) Nomura intended to charge up to $ 14 million in trading fees to the private investors who bought the participation certificates; and (2) Nomura purposefully hid this fact from Realtek. . . . [T]hese fees would materially impact both the interest rate Realtek would ultimately be obligated to pay on the Permanent Loans and the end price of the participation certificates to the private investors, artificially increasing both. Thus, the 'cost' of the transaction both to Realtek and to the private investors would be increased by Nomura's trading fees, thereby decreasing the effective rate of return on, and the appeal of, the participation certificates. . . . [Therefore,] given the integrated nature of the transaction Realtek alleges, the 'in connection with' requirement would be sufficiently satisfied."[637]

Discussion Topics

1. In the Realtek case, how did the parties design the transaction? What was the role of each party?

2. What did "rating risk" mean and why was it important?

3. What impact did the different legal characterization of the transaction have and why were the differences important to the outcome of the case?

B. Registration Requirement Under the 1933 Act[638]

The 1933 Act requires the issuer to sign the registration statement. Dissemination of information to investors in asset-backed securities is affected by the process in which these securities are structured and created. The "structuring of [such] securities differs significantly from conventional offerings of corporate securities because of the variety of securities structures that can be issued based upon [an SPV] of underlying assets." "[A]lternative structures are developed by [the] underwriter[] . . . [in active] interaction [with prospective investors,]" extending to the printing date of the prospectus supplement. In contrast to offerings of traditional securities, the "'structuring' and 'offering' phases of [the] transaction" in mortgage-backed securities are closely related. "The interaction between underwriters and investors . . . involves . . . exchange of data and specification of assumptions [underlying] the payment priorities and [features] of the . . . securities . . . ."

"[Few] prospective investors have the computer resources and . . . sophistication to analyze data relating to the structure of, and the assets underlying, MBS/ABS Securities without [resorting to] the underwriters. [Most] prospective investors, however, require underwriters to furnish them, in writing, with computer generated tables and charts displaying for a proposed class of MBS/ABS Securities the yield, average life, duration[,] expected maturity, interest rate sensitivity and cash flow characteristics of the class under a variety of possible prepayment scenarios including, without limitation, such information as may be required to comply with the capital and reporting treatment recommendations of the Federal Financial Institutions Examination Council, as well as such background information concerning the underlying pool of assets and the proposed structure of the . . . Securities as may be

---

637 *Id.* at 581-83 (citations omitted).

638 2 TAMAR FRANKEL, SECURITIZATION § 12.3 (Ann Taylor Schwing ed., 2d ed. 2005).

necessary for an analysis of the comparative data . . . . This information is provided to a prospective investor, generally at such investor's request, in order to assist the prospective investor in determining whether the proposed structure will meet such investor's needs under varying assumptions."

Recognizing that asset and mortgage-backed securities involve complexities that are absent in other issuances, the Staff of the Division of Corporation Finance of the SEC indicated in 1994 that it would not recommend enforcement under section 5 of the 1933 Act against Kidder Peabody & Co. ("Kidder") for providing prospective investors with written "computational materials" after the effective date of a registration statement but before a final prospectus was available, in connection with the offer or sale of mortgage-backed securities, so long as certain procedures were followed.[639] In February 1995, the staff extended its no-action position in connection with a letter from the Public Securities Association ("PSA") to distribution of written "term sheets" under similar circumstances. The staff's no-action position was extended to cover marketing materials that consisted of combined computational materials and term sheets in 1996, subject to certain conditions.

a. Informational and Computational Material[640]

In December 2004, the SEC adopted Rule 167 under the 1933 Act codifying the exemption for informational and computational material regarding asset-backed securities ("ABS informational and computational material"). The SEC noted that the Rule's definition "is intended to include existing structural term sheets, collateral term sheets and computational materials and also to clarify that several additional items are permitted, such as static pool data and basic information about the offering process."[641] The Rule provides a conditional exemption from section 5(b)(1) of the 1933 Act for ABS informational and computational material. Rule 167 applies not only to the offeror of the securities but also to "any other participant that may need to rely on and complies with this section in communicating about the transaction." "Participant" is defined as "any person or entity that is a party to the asset-backed securities transaction and any persons authorized to act on their behalf."[642] Failure of one underwriter to cause the filing of a prospectus described in the Rule does not affect the ability of another underwriter to rely on the Rule. The Rule provides that "[a]n immaterial or unintentional failure to file or delay in filing a prospectus" described in the Rule "will not result in a violation of section 5(b)(1)" provided that (1) "[a] good faith and

---

[639] Mortgage & Asset-Backed Sec., Corres. (May 20, 1994).

[640] 2 TAMAR FRANKEL, SECURITIZATION § 12.4.1 (Ann Taylor Schwing ed., 2d ed. 2005).

[641] Asset-Backed Securities, 33-8518, 34-50905 (Dec. 22, 2004), 70 Fed. Reg. 1506, 1556 (Jan. 7, 2005).

[642] 17 C.F.R. § 230.167(c) (2009).

reasonable effort was made to comply with the filing requirement"; and (2) "[t]he prospectus is filed as soon as practicable after discovery of the failure to file."[643]

The ability of issuers to utilize computational materials and collateral as well as structural term sheets enables underwriters and issuers to make more information available to investors and structure transactions to take advantage of demand and prevailing economic conditions. However, there is also the risk that, by creating such a broad exception to the registration requirement in section 5 of the 1933 Act, investors will rarely read the material information in the prospectus as investors focus primarily on the quantitative information in the computational materials and collateral and structural term sheets. This risk is particularly great in transactions that lack sufficient diversification in the SPV, as in a commercial mortgage loan SPV in which certain loans contribute a significant percentage of the principal balance or overall cash flow. In such transactions, investors will be exposed to the business risks of the related properties, and understanding those risks is necessary to appreciate the overall risk of an investment in the resulting CMBS.

Although the SEC's position follows the policy of only requiring issuers and underwriters to make all material information available, it decreases the likelihood that the prospectus will actually be read by investors. At least when such materials were supposed to be included only in a prospectus, the investor had thorough descriptions of non-quantitative risk factors and special considerations. However, as a compromise position, allowing the use of term sheets and other materials is reasonable. Investors get earlier access to the information on which they primarily rely when pricing MBS, and the issuer has strict liability under the 1933 Act for information incorporated into the registration statement.

b. What Security is Being Distributed and Should be Registered?[644]

In the context of SPVs, the identity of the issuer of asset-backed securities is sometimes difficult to establish. The issuer could be the SPV, the Originator, or both. If the Originator or others are the issuers, or if the issuers are both the SPVs and their Originators, then all parties should sign the registration statement. If a nonexempt issuer establishes an SPV of nonexempt securities issued by another SPV ("Source SPV"), both the securities of the Source nonexempt SPV and the securities issued by the SPV must be registered. Rule 140 under the 1933 Act provides in effect that a conduit issuer, such as an SPV that raises funds by issuing its own securities and invests in the securities of another issuer, is deemed to be engaged in the distribution of its portfolio securities under section 2(a)(11) of the Act. As such it is subject to additional regulation.

---

[643] 17 C.F.R. § 230.167(e) (2009); 2 TAMAR FRANKEL, SECURITIZATION § 12.4.2 (Ann Taylor Schwing ed., 2d ed. 2005).

c. Information Required for Registration Post-2005 SEC Rule[645]

In 2005 the SEC provided a new Rule for registering SPVs. The SEC adjusted the usual disclosure requirements to the unique features of asset-backed securities, in terms of timing and information. The SEC has taken steps to standardize the information required of MBS issuers for whom no exemption is available and offers a number of special forms and guidelines for particular types of offerings, such as real estate investment trusts. The Task Force on Disclosure Simplification, an SEC working group, proposed that the SEC enact a "plain English" requirement for prospectuses, a proposal implemented through rules, staff bulletins and instructions. While seemingly benign, a thorough application of this standard in the ABS industry has sometimes been cumbersome. Describing the allocation of cash flows among ABS, the resulting effect on the weighted average lives of the securities and related quantitative information in "plain English" would be quite difficult. With respect to the financial statement accompanying registration of mortgage-backed securities, the staff has issued accounting bulletins regarding the properties securing mortgage loans.

In January 1997, the SEC adopted amendments to clarify and expand disclosure requirements for market risk-sensitive instruments, including mortgage-backed securities. The amendments require quantitative and qualitative information about market risk inherent in such instruments, and provide safe harbor protection for such information.

Asset-Backed Securities Registration and Disclosure.[646] In December 2004, the SEC adopted new and amended forms to "establish a separate framework for the registration and reporting of asset-backed securities."[647] In its release, the SEC noted that, with asset-backed securities, unlike corporate securities, "there is generally no business or management to describe" and that consequently investors are often more interested in "information about the transaction structure and the characteristics and quality of the asset pool and servicing."[648] New Regulation AB "is the source of various disclosure items and requirements for 'asset-backed securities' filings" under the 1933 and 1934 Acts.[649]

---

[645] 2 TAMAR FRANKEL, SECURITIZATION § 12.5 (Ann Taylor Schwing ed., 2d ed. 2005).

[646] 2 TAMAR FRANKEL, SECURITIZATION § 12.5.2 (Ann Taylor Schwing ed., 2d ed. 2005).

[647] Asset-Backed Securities, 33-8518, 34-50905 (Dec. 22, 2004), 70 Fed. Reg. 1506, 1507 (Jan. 7, 2005).

[648] *Id.* at 1508.

[649] 17 C.F.R. § 229.1100(a) (2009).

d. Applicability of Regulation AB to Asset-Backed Securities[650]

Regulation AB generally defines "asset-backed security" as a security that is primarily serviced by the cash flows of a discrete pool of receivables or other financial assets, either fixed or revolving, that by their terms convert into cash within a finite time period, plus any rights or other assets designed to assure the servicing or timely distributions of proceeds to the security holders; provided that in the case of financial assets that are leases, those assets may convert to cash partially by the cash proceeds from the disposition of the physical property underlying such leases. The following additional conditions apply in order to meet the definition:

(i) Neither the depositor nor the issuing entity is an investment company under the Investment Company Act of 1940 (15 U.S.C. 80a-1 et seq.) nor will become an investment company as a result of the asset-backed securities transaction.

(ii) The activities of the issuing entity for the asset-backed securities are limited to passively owning or holding the pool of assets, issuing the asset-backed securities supported or serviced by those assets, and other activities reasonably incidental thereto.

(iii) No non-performing assets are part of the asset pool as of the measurement date.

(iv) Delinquent assets do not constitute 50% or more, as measured by dollar volume, of the asset pool as of the measurement date.

(v) With respect to securities that are backed by leases, the portion of the securitized pool balance attributable to the residual value of the physical property underlying the leases, as determined in accordance with the transaction agreements for the securities, does not constitute:

(A) For motor vehicle leases, 65% or more, as measured by dollar volume, of the securitized pool balance as of the measurement date.

(B) For all other leases, 50% or more, as measured by dollar volume, of the securitized pool balance as of the measurement date.

e. The Meaning of "Discrete Pool of Assets"

(i) Master trusts. The offering related to the securities contemplates adding additional assets to the pool that backs such securities in connection with future issuances of asset-backed securities backed by such pool.

(ii) Prefunding periods. The offering related to the securities contemplates a prefunding account where a portion of the proceeds of that offering is to be used for the future acquisition of additional pool assets, if the duration of the prefunding period does not extend for more than one year from the date of

[650] 2 TAMAR FRANKEL, SECURITIZATION § 12.5.3 (Ann Taylor Schwing ed., 2d ed. 2005).

issuance of the securities and the portion of the proceeds for such prefunding account does not involve in excess of:

(A) For master trusts, 50% of the aggregate principal balance of the total asset pool whose cash flows support the securities; and

(B) For other offerings, 50% of the proceeds of the offering.

(iii) Revolving periods. The offering related to the securities contemplates a revolving period where cash flows from the pool assets may be used to acquire additional pool assets, provided, that, for securities backed by receivables or other financial assets that do not arise under revolving accounts, the revolving period does not extend for more than three years from the date of issuance of the securities and the additional pool assets are of the same general character as the original pool assets. Registration of asset-backed securities under the 1933 Act is limited to Forms S-1 and S-3.[651]

f. Exemptions from Registration Under the Securities Act of 1933 (1933 Act)[652]

To determine whether asset-backed securities are exempt from registration required in the 1933 Act, the identity of the issuer must be established. An SPV can be deemed the sole issuer of the securities if the SPV purchased the assets without recourse to the seller and issued the securities. However, a sponsor that issues securities and collateralizes them by an SPV of financial assets may be the sole issuer or a co-issuer with the SPV. If the sponsor is exempt from registration but the SPV is not, then the SPV might have to register its securities. If the exemption of the sponsor's securities extends to its guarantees, and the sponsor fully guarantees the obligations under the securities of the SPV, the SPV's securities might be exempt from registration.

g. SPVs Issuing Floating Rate Securities[653]

In 1986, SPVs issuing floating rate bonds applied to the SEC for exemptions from the 1940 Act. The interest rate on these bonds changes periodically in accordance with a predetermined formula, such as a fixed percentage above prime rate. The exemptions were granted subject to numerous conditions including: (i) the bonds must be registered under the 1933 Act, unless exempt under section 4(2) of the Act and "rated in one of the two highest categories by at least one nationally recognized statistical [unaffiliated] rating agency"; (ii) the SPVs must be audited at least annually by an independent public accountant; (iii) even if interest payments on the bonds go down, no part of the collateral for the bonds may be removed, and the

---

[651] 2 TAMAR FRANKEL, SECURITIZATION § 12.5.4 (Ann Taylor Schwing ed., 2d ed. 2005).§12.5.4

[652] 2 TAMAR FRANKEL, SECURITIZATION § 12.10 C (Ann Taylor Schwing ed., 2d ed. 2005).*§12.10 C.*

[653] 1 TAMAR FRANKEL, SECURITIZATION § 11.26 (Ann Taylor Schwing ed., 2d ed. 2005).

collateral initially pledged to secure a series of floating rate bonds should be sufficient to pay the maximum amount of principal and interest due on these bonds for the life of the bonds; (iv) "[e]ach class of adjustable interest rate Bonds will have a set maximum interest rate (an interest rate cap)."[654]

h. Government and Government-Agency Securities[655]

Section 3(a)(2) of the 1933 Act exempts securities issued by the Government and Government agencies from registration but not from the antifraud provisions in the Act. Securities issued by GNMA are Government securities, since the securities are guaranteed by the federal Government. Securities issued by FNMA and FHLMC were also exempt from registration because they were persons "controlled or supervised by and acting as an instrumentality of the Government of the United States pursuant to authority granted by the Congress of the United States," as stated in section 3(a)(2) of the 1933 Act. The section is less explicit with respect to securities issued by SPVs sponsored by these agencies that are within the exemption of section 3(a)(2). However, since the SPVs, the securities they issue, and their portfolios and operations are regulated under acts of Congress, it seems that the exemption would apply to them as well. This view has been adopted by the staff with respect to the status of SPVs under the 1940 Act. Although under section 3(a)(2) of the 1933 Act Government agencies are not required to register the securities issued by the SPVs that they establish and guarantee, the agencies provide buyers with an offering circular that contains substantial information regarding the securities.

i. Bank Letters of Credit and Guarantees[656]

Asset-backed securities are often guaranteed by a bank letter of credit. Section 3(a)(2) of the 1933 Act exempts from registration securities issued or guaranteed by banks and certain United States branches of foreign banks. In the opinion of the SEC, this exemption covers bank letters of credit. If a letter of credit guarantees the full payment of principal and interest of a security, the security (e.g., a security issued by an SPV) is exempt as a security guaranteed by a bank. Although the SEC recommended to Congress in the late 1980s that the statutory exemption for bank securities be replaced with exemptive powers by the SEC to exempt both banks and insurance securities, Congress has not adopted the recommendation.

j. Insurance Policies and Guarantees[657]

The 1933 Act does not accord insurance policies and guarantees the same treatment as bank letters of credit and guarantees. Insurance policies and annuities are exempt

---

[654] Drexel Burnham Lambert Mortg. Acceptance Corp., IC-15805/15850 (1987).

[655] 2 TAMAR FRANKEL, SECURITIZATION § 12.11 (Ann Taylor Schwing ed., 2d ed. 2005).

[656] 2 TAMAR FRANKEL, SECURITIZATION § 12.12 (Ann Taylor Schwing ed., 2d ed. 2005).

[657] 2 TAMAR FRANKEL, SECURITIZATION § 12.13 (Ann Taylor Schwing ed., 2d ed. 2005).

from registration under section 3(a)(8) of the 1933 Act. However, it is less clear whether securities backed by insurance polices and guarantees are exempt from registration. The staff has examined the disparate treatment of these two Institutions and concluded in 1987 that the exemption for bank-supported securities should be eliminated and that the SEC should be given discretion to grant exemptions to both types of Institutions in appropriate cases. Congress has not acted on these proposals.

k. Mortgage-backed Securities ("MBS") Traded Among Institutions[658]

MBS issued by the private sector must be registered under the 1933 Act, unless an exemption is available for them; for example, a private placement or a guarantee by a bank letter of credit. If mortgages are sold to SPVs without recourse, the SPVs are deemed the sole issuers of the securities. Therefore, even though the originators of the mortgages and the Originators of the SPVs may be exempt from registration, the securities issued by the SPVs are not exempt. This state of affairs limited the ability of the private sector to participate in the issuance of MBS; the private sector acted at a competitive disadvantage compared to Government agencies or the SPVs that they sponsor.

In 1975, Congress added section 4(5) to the 1933 Act, exempting from registration certain kinds of mortgage-backed securities offered and sold among Institutions that usually originate and invest in mortgage-backed securities. In 1984, Congress passed the Secondary Mortgage Market Enhancement Act of 1984 (the "Enhancement Act") to encourage private sector participation in the issuance of MBS and the secondary Markets in these securities. The initial proposed bill would have expanded the exemption in section 4(5) of the 1933 Act to other private sector-sponsored MBS. After the hearings on the bill, however, Congress concluded that the cost of registration would not substantially reduce the competitiveness of the private sector Originators. In addition, Congress considered it desirable to maintain a higher level of protection for investors in these securities. Therefore, the broader exemption was deleted from the final version of the Act. The Enhancement Act focused on the 1934 Act and other disadvantages that the private sector suffered vis-à-vis Government agencies and granted relief to private sector actors with respect to "mortgage related securities" defined in section 3(a)(41) of the 1934 Act. These securities must also meet the requirements of section 4(5) of the 1933 Act. Whether the Act or other causes were at work, the private sector in MBS has grown from $10 billion in 1984 to over $71 billion in 1988 and $1.76 trillion in 2004.

Dealers' Exemption: Section 4(3) of the 1933 Act.[659] Section 4(3) of the 1933 Act exempts dealers from the requirement to provide buyers a prospectus. Section 2(a)(12) of the 1933 Act includes in the definition of a dealer a person dealing in

---

[658] 2 TAMAR FRANKEL, SECURITIZATION § 12.15 (Ann Taylor Schwing ed., 2d ed. 2005).

[659] 2 TAMAR FRANKEL, SECURITIZATION § 12.16 (Ann Taylor Schwing ed., 2d ed. 2005).

"securities issued by another person." The staff interpreted this provision to exclude from the definition of a dealer a person that deals in the securities of its parent corporation. Therefore, a dealer who distributes asset-backed securities of the parent issuer must provide the buyers with a prospectus subject to the 1933 Act. However, in December 2004, the SEC determined that it would not require registration and prospectus delivery for market making transactions.

Commercial Paper.[660] Section 3(a)(3) of the 1933 Act exempts commercial paper from registration if the proceeds of commercial paper are used for "current transactions." A question arises whether lending money for certain transactions or for purchasing certain financial assets is considered "current transactions." The staff granted a no-action letter to a bank holding company that proposed to issue short-term paper and, without segregating the proceeds, lend an amount (not in excess of the proceeds) to its own bank subsidiary or to others for the purpose of making certain loans. It seems that the staff agreed to "see through" the issuing SPV and the bank and attribute to the commercial paper the "current transactions" of the borrowers from the SPV or the bank.

l. Rule 144A: Private Placement Market Among Institutions[661]

In April 1990, the SEC adopted Rule 144A, which clarifies the status of "qualified institutions" that may trade in unregistered securities. This Rule is important for Markets in asset-backed securities because the main players in these Markets are Institutional investors. These Institutions are not issuers or dealers, but their purchase and resale of unregistered securities could bring them within the definition of an "underwriter" under section 2(a)(11) of the 1933 Act if the resale of the unregistered securities involves a "distribution" as stated in the definition. If so, the exemption in section 4(1) of the Act for persons who are not issuers, dealers, and underwriters will not apply to these Institutions. Although other factors undoubtedly played a role, Rule 144A may have significantly encouraged expansion of the Market in securitized loans, by making debt on commercial real estate more liquid.

Rule 144A provides that a person, other than an issuer or dealer, who offers or sells securities in compliance with the Rule is deemed "not to be engaged in a distribution . . . and therefore not to be an underwriter."[662] Consequently, such a person is exempted under section 4(1) of the 1933 Act. The Rule also provides that a dealer who offers or sells securities in compliance with the Rule is deemed not "to be a participant in a distribution . . . and not to be an underwriter . . . , and such securities shall be deemed not to have been offered to the public."[663] Such a dealer will be

---

[660] 2 TAMAR FRANKEL, SECURITIZATION § 12.17 (Ann Taylor Schwing ed., 2d ed. 2005).

[661] 2 TAMAR FRANKEL, SECURITIZATION § 12.18 (Ann Taylor Schwing ed., 2d ed. 2005).-

[662] Rule 144A(b), 17 C.F.R. § 230.144A(b) (2009), *adopted*, 55 Fed. Reg. 17,945, 17,946 (1990).

[663] 17 C.F.R. § 230.144A(c) (2009).

exempted by section 4(3) of the 1933 Act which applies to dealers who are not participants in a distribution, unless the transaction takes place during a certain period after the securities have been "offered to the public."[664]

The Rule does not relieve sellers and others from liability under the antifraud provisions of the securities acts, nor does it limit the reach of state securities laws over the exempted transactions.

Accredited investors are defined in Rule 501(a) promulgated under the 1933 Act. SPVs that have received exemptions have issued mortgage-backed equity interests without registering the securities under the 1933 Act, provided that, with regard to non-Institutional investors, (i) the investors are sophisticated and experienced, (ii) their number does not exceed 15, (iii) the investors purchase at least $200,000 of the equity interests, and (iv) the investors' net worth exceeds $1 million exclusive of their primary residence. SPVs that agreed to comply with these conditions have received partial exemptions from the 1940 Act.

The concept of Institutional investors is also used in the recommendations of the staff for a new exemptive Rule covering issuers of all asset-backed securities that would otherwise be investment companies. Securities sold to persons other than affiliates of the issuer or "qualified institutional buyers" as defined in Rule 144A must comply with a number of conditions to enjoy the exemption. Rule 3a-7 excludes from the definition of an investment company SPVs subject to the following conditions: (i) management of the SPV's portfolios is restricted, (ii) SPV assets must be held by an independent trustee, (iii) the securities issued by the SPV must not be redeemable, (iv) securities issued publicly must be limited to debt or debt-like securities, and (v) securities issued publicly must be limited to those rated in the top two investment grades by a nationally recognized rating agency.

m. Regulation S: Offerings Outside the United States to Non-U.S. Persons[665]

As international Markets became receptive to SPV securities, U.S. SPV Originators have increasingly distributed these securities outside the United States, and foreign issuers distribute such securities in the United States. The internationalization of these securities has brought about conflicts between the securities acts and business practices and laws abroad.

For example, the traditional form for securities in the Eurodollar Markets is bearer bonds. Yet, mortgage-backed securities guaranteed by the United States Government or its agencies cannot be issued as bearer bonds. Before May 2, 1990, the law regarding international offerings was developed by SEC statements and no-action

[664] 15 U.S.C. § 77d(3)(A), (B) (2006).

[665] 2 TAMAR FRANKEL, SECURITIZATION §§ 12.19,1, 12.19.3 (Ann Taylor Schwing ed., 2d ed. 2005).

letters. On May 2, 1990, the SEC issued Regulation S, which became effective immediately and codified in part and changed in part its former positions.

On May 2, 1990, the SEC adopted Regulation S, which provides generally that the registration provisions of the 1933 Act do not apply to sale of securities outside the United States. The registration requirements in the 1933 Act apply literally to any sale of securities involving "interstate commerce." "Interstate commerce" includes "trade or commerce in securities . . . between any foreign country and any State, Territory, or the District of Columbia."[666] However, the SEC "has traditionally taken the position that the registration requirements of section 5 of the [1933] Act are primarily intended to protect American investors."[667] Consequently, the SEC stated in 1964 that it would not require registration for sales of securities to foreign purchasers, despite the use of "jurisdictional means,"[668] provided that "the distribution is to be effected in a manner which will result in the securities coming to rest abroad."[669] As trading in asset-backed securities began in international Markets; U.S. and foreign issuers sought relief from the reach of U.S. securities laws. Foreign buyers trust, and are familiar with, their own different securities regulations.

Thus, regardless of the strictness of the domestic regulation, sellers of U.S. issues in some foreign Markets are at a disadvantage. For foreign issuers, U.S. regulation may present substantial costs; this occurs, for example, if financial statements in the foreign country are structured differently from financial statements required in the United States. Regulation S is based on a territorial approach to section 5, under which "[t]he registration of securities is intended to protect the U.S. capital markets and investors purchasing in the U.S. market, whether U.S. or foreign nationals."[670] This approach "recognizes the primacy of the laws in which a market is located. As investors choose their markets, they choose the laws and regulations applicable in such markets."[671] In addition, "[p]rinciples of comity and the reasonable expectations of participants in the global markets justify reliance on laws applicable in jurisdictions outside the United States to define requirements for transactions effected offshore."[672]

---

[666] 15 U.S.C. § 77b(a)(7) (2006).

[667] 33-4708 (1964).

[668] *Id.*

[669] *Id. Cf.* ITT v. Vencap, Ltd., 519 F.2d 1001, 1016 (2d Cir. 1975).

[670] 33-6863 (1990).

[671] *Id.*

[672] *Id.*

Under Regulation S, section 5 of the 1933 Act does not apply to the sale of securities outside the United States. The regulation provides a safe harbor for sales by issuers and resales of securities. However, the regulation neither relieves issuers and others from the antifraud provisions of the securities acts, nor limits the reach of state securities laws. Furthermore, the regulation does not apply to open-end investment companies[673] or unit investment trusts. Closed-end investment companies can take advantage of the regulation, but they are generally placed in the category of issuers that must bear the heaviest burdens. Presumably, any SPV excepted from the definition of an investment company pursuant to section 3(c) of the 1940 Act may comply with Regulation S. Perhaps a company exempted by the SEC from registration pursuant to sections 6(c) or 6(e) of the 1940 Act may also become a reporting issuer by complying with the 1934 Act.

n. Sarbanes-Oxley Certifications[674]

The SEC amended Item 601 of Regulation S-K regarding the certifications required under section 302 of the Sarbanes-Oxley Act. The officer signing the report must certify that (1) he/she has reviewed the 1934 Act periodic reports; (2) based on his/her knowledge, the reports, "taken as a whole, do not contain any untrue statement of a material fact or omit to state a material fact necessary to make the statements made, in light of the circumstances under which such statements were made, not misleading with respect to the period covered by this report;" (3) based on his/her knowledge, "all of the distribution, servicing and other information required to be provided under Form 10-D" for the relevant period is included in the reports; (4) if the servicer is signing the report, the officer states that he/she is responsible for reviewing the servicer(s)' activities and based on his/her knowledge and the servicer compliance review, the servicer(s) fulfilled its/their obligations except as disclosed in the reports; if the depositor is signing the report, the officer makes a similar certification based on his/her knowledge and the servicer compliance statement; and (5) the required servicing compliance assessment reports and attestation reports have been included as an exhibit, unless otherwise disclosed, and material instances of noncompliance disclosed there have been disclosed."

The certification must be signed by either: (1) "[t]he senior officer in charge of securitization of the depositor if the depositor is signing the report on Form 10-K"; or (2) "[t]he senior officer in charge of the servicing function of the servicer if the servicer is signing the report on Form 10-K on behalf of the issuing entity." If a representative of the servicer is to sign, if multiple servicers are involved, "the senior

---

[673] Investment companies that have managed portfolios and offer redeemable securities. Unit investment trusts are non-managed companies that offer redeemable securities. *See* Investment Company Act of 1940 ,§ 80a-5 (2006). See chapter 12.

[674] 2 TAMAR FRANKEL, SECURITIZATION § 12.21.4 (Ann Taylor Schwing ed., 2d ed. 2005). There is also an amendment to Form 8-K.

officer in charge of the servicing function of the master servicer (or entity performing the equivalent function) must sign." If multiple servicers are involved, references to the servicer relate to the master servicer. "A natural person must sign the certification in his or her individual capacity, although the title of that person in the organization of which he or she is an officer may be included under the signature."[675] Thus, the Sarbanes-Oxley Act imposes on top management an explicit duty to ensure the truthfulness of the financial statements of its company.

Exercise: Find all the documents required to register asset backed securities

C Trading SPV Securities. The Secondary Markets[676]

a. The Securities Exchange Act of 1934 (The "1934 Act")

As noted at the beginning of this course, the secondary Market is a mechanism for moving funds from investors with surpluses to investors who wish to liquidate their investments. It provides investors with liquidity. In the past, secondary Markets in mortgage-backed securities helped dampen cyclical fluctuations in the housing industry. The most active and largest is the Market for mortgage-backed securities, issued by government agency-sponsored SPVs. However, the market portion of SPV securities sponsored by the private sector has increased greatly, and some attribute the increase to the Secondary Mortgage Market Enhancement Act of 1984. These attributions of course are largely speculative.

Like other areas concerning securitization, the Markets and new instruments in securitized loans grew faster than the infrastructure; they grew so fast that "neither the regulators nor the industry were able to respond."[677] Legal developments, however, show that the law is catching up. For example, in 1987 the Mortgage-Backed Securities Clearing Corporation was registered as the first clearing agency for mortgage-backed securities. Many others followed, including the Emerging Markets Clearing Corporation, the Options Clearing Corporation, and the Fixed Income Clearing Corporation.

Asset-based securities issued by SPVs sponsored by government agencies are usually carried in "book form." One entity maintains a book in which the securities owners are registered, without issuing certificates that represent the securities. The registered owners are usually large dealers in the securities. They, in turn, maintain books in which their customers are registered as owners. If the customers are dealers,

---

[675] 17 C.F.R. § 229.601(b)(31)(ii)(1) (2009).

[676] 2 TAMAR FRANKEL, SECURITIZATION § 13.1 (Ann Taylor Schwing ed., 2d ed. 2005).

[677] Edward L. Pittman, *Economic and Regulatory Developments Affecting Mortgage Related Securities,* 64 NOTRE DAME L. REV. 497, 544 (1989).

these dealers maintain similar books for their customers. The system eliminates the costs associated with physical transfer and loss or mutilation of the certificates. It also reduces greatly the cost of maintaining the owners' lists. Transfers among customers of the same dealers are not recorded on the higher level. Transfers among dealers are recorded by the entity that keeps their names as owners, at the end of the trading day, as the dealers settle their accounts. However, unless clear confirmations of trades are issued, the system may make it difficult to identify the owners of the securities and can facilitate fraud. Records in an electronic form are vulnerable to destruction, for example, by virus and terror, even if they are backed up. Therefore, security holders are wise to use paper confirmations as proof of ownership. Yet paper confirmations are expensive and cumbersome to create and mail.

The unique features of asset-backed securities raise a number of issues under the 1934 Act:

(i) are asset-backed securities "securities" under the Act?

(ii) do the antifraud provisions of the Act, including Rule 10b-5, apply to asset-backed securities?

(iii) should issuers of asset-backed securities register these securities under section 12 of the 1934 Act which renders them subject to reporting under section 13, proxy regulation under section 14, and prohibitions imposed on insiders from short-swing trading under section 16 of the Act?

(iv) should broker-dealers in asset-backed securities register as broker-dealers under section 15 of the 1934 Act?

(v) how does the margin credit regulation apply to trading in asset-backed securities?

Other applications of the 1934 Act to these securities do not break new ground but are discussed here because they relate to these securities.

b. Regulation of the Secondary Markets

Are asset-backed Securities "securities" under the 1934 Act?[678] The "security" status of asset-backed securities under the 1934 Act is as unclear as it is under the 1933 Act. Asset-backed securities issued by SPVs are generally treated as securities. Many offerings of such securities are registered under the 1933 Act. The fact that a substantial number of such securities are privately offered and placed does not exclude them from the definition of a security but only from the registration requirements in the 1933 Act. Even if the securities are government securities, they may still be deemed securities.

[678] 2 TAMAR FRANKEL, SECURITIZATION § 13.2 (Ann Taylor Schwing ed., 2d ed. 2005).

Do the Antifraud Provisions of the 1934 Act, Including Rule 10b-5, Apply to Asset-backed Securities?[679] Asset-backed securities do not raise unique issues under Rule 10b-5 of the 1934 Act. One case is notable for its facts. In that case, investors in SPV securities sued the SPV Originators and attorneys for fraud under Rule 10b-5, alleging failure to disclose material facts. The issue was whether the defendants had a duty to disclose. The court denied the defendants' motion to dismiss, and held that the alleged facts, if proved, could serve as a basis for a duty to disclose. The alleged facts were that the SPV attorneys had a close relationship with the SPV's Originators and that the attorneys not only prepared the documents but also participated in sale of the securities.

The court followed cases dealing generally with securities, listing the following factors as flexible tests for the duty to disclose under the Rule: the nature of the parties' relationship, the extent of the disparity between the parties' access to information, the benefits that the defendants derive from the relationship, the defendants' awareness of plaintiffs reliance on them, and the defendants' role in initiating the transaction. On full hearing, however, the district court dismissed the claims based on the 1934 Act on the ground that the certificates were not securities under the 1934 Act.

There is one context in which structured financing, and securitization in general, may raise unique issues under Rule 10b-5: an act of fraud involving two parties to the process, but not affecting other parties to the process. For example, fraud may be committed between the obligor in structured financing and the sponsor-underwriter, but the fraud may neither involve nor affect the investors in the entity's securities. In such a case, one question is whether the relationship between these two parties involves a security. A second question is whether fraud in the relationship between these parties (when the process, not the relationship, is a security) can be subject to Rule 10b-5 if no other parts of the transaction are tainted with fraud. Is a commitment letter issued by an underwriter to an obligor, describing the parties' future activities to create structured financing, a security? Are the parties sellers or buyers?

Broker-dealers who sell asset-backed securities at excessive markups could be liable under Rule 10b-5 under the 1934 Act, under section 12(2) of the 1933 Act, and under the Racketeer Influenced Corrupt Organizations Act (RICO). In *Elysian Federal Savings Bank v. First Interregional Equity Corp.*, the SEC argued as *amicus* that markups on CMOs and principal-only trust certificates were patently excessive because they were nearly double the usual markups on comparable Treasury bonds. Among the factors that the SEC considered were industry experiences with respect to the type of securities, the extent of the market activity in the securities, and the nature of the dealer's business. Excessive expenses or higher risks taken by the

[679] 2 TAMAR FRANKEL, SECURITIZATION § 13.3 (Ann Taylor Schwing ed., 2d ed. 2005).

dealer do not justify unreasonable markups. Neither can a dealer that sells short pass the risks to the investor in the form of an excessive markup.

The 1995 case of *United States v. York,*[680] which involved allegations of fiduciary duties, also raises issues concerning Rule 10b-5. The *York* district court examined two transactions in which York and its affiliates were engaged: one transaction relating to York's function as subservicer of assets guaranteed by the GNMA and one transaction relating to its functions as an issuer of securities guaranteed by GNMA. In the first transaction, York, which was at the time a subservicer for GNMA under an agreement, entered into an "understanding" or "arrangement" with an unaffiliated entity in another state, USGI, under which York would inform USGI about borrowers who were likely either to default or to prepay their loans. In both cases, holders of the securities backed by these loans would benefit if they bought their securities at a discount of the face value. That discount represents the Market's assessment of the loans' maturity date. Assuming that the market price does not reflect these imminent full payments of the face amount and that interest rates do not change drastically short-term, these security holders would collect the face amount of the securities either from the Government (if the borrowers default) or from the borrowers (if the borrowers prepay), and keep the difference between the discounted price they paid and the face value. Therefore, insider information about imminent prepayments or defaults covered by GNMA is extremely valuable.

Under the arrangement between York and USGI, USGI would purchase securities selling at a discount but that, according to York's information, would be shortly paid in full (because of imminent defaults or prepayments), and, upon collecting the face amount of these securities, USGI would pay York 75 percent of the gain and keep 25 percent. This arrangement was not disclosed to GNMA, and York did not inquire at GNMA whether the arrangement was appropriate. The district court held that, under the subservicing agreement between GNMA and York, York became an agent and a fiduciary of GNMA. York had custody of the assets and access to information regarding the assets. That information was given to York for the purpose of performing its functions and for no other purpose. When York used this information to benefit itself, it violated its fiduciary duties to GNMA.

The second transaction under the court's examination related to York's activities as issuer. York had refinanced an investor in certain real estate, as co-insuring lender, and issued a security guaranteed by GNMA. About a year later, the borrower notified York that he would default on the loan. The real estate project was refinanced again a year later. Instead of foreclosing, however, York took a deed on the property and sold bare legal title to a partnership required to act as an agent for York; provided the partnership indemnity and a $12.6 million loan co-insured by York and by GNMA;

---

[680] United States v. York 890 F. .Supp. 1117 (D.D.C.,1995), *rev'd, remanded,* 112 F.3d 1218, 1222 (D.C. Cir. 1997).

and issued securities backed by the loan. When York determined that the project would not be able to continue payment, it determined that it would discontinue advances and thereby caused default. About that time, York's affiliate purchased, from a religious order and (at a discount) from Salomon Brothers, the security backed by the loan. Neither seller knew the loan would soon default and the guarantee would kick in to pay the full face amount of the security. York made a claim for co-insurance benefits on the mortgage and collected over $700,000 more than it paid for the security.

The court held that York's position as an approved GNMA "issuer" of mortgage-backed GNMA securities triggered York's fiduciary duties as agent of GNMA because of GNMA's control over York's activities. York put itself in a conflict of interest by buying securities that it knew were likely to default, determining when the default would occur (by ceasing to pay advances), and then pocketing the difference between the face amount of the security and the price York paid for the security. York's fiduciary duties precluded it from putting itself in conflict of interest with GNMA—that is, acquiring claims against the Government and GNMA, especially by use of insider information gained through its relationship with GNMA. York also manipulated the dates at which it would cause a borrower to default so that York was assured of owning the security backed by the borrower's loan.

As York emphasized during the trial, GNMA did not suffer any losses from this arrangement. GNMA had to pay the security holders the face amount of defaulted loans regardless of who the security holders were. Therefore, York argued that it made no difference to GNMA whether GNMA paid York's partner, USGI, or someone else who did not know of the imminent payment and simply was lucky in obtaining the investment sooner. Similarly, if the borrower prepaid, it should make no difference to GNMA who the lucky security holders might be. The court disagreed. It recognized that the Government would have had to pay in the case of defaults and that prepayment by the borrowers did not cause the Government to pay additional amounts or incur losses in any other way. Nonetheless, the GNMA program could suffer from York's transactions. Use of insider information to purchase particular securities would undermine the trust of the GNMA securities holders and might reduce their participation in the Market. That would be very harmful to the GNMA program.

For both transactions, the court drew on the principles of fiduciary law established in connection with Government officials. The court held that, under fiduciary law, it had equitable powers to impose upon the disloyal fiduciary the remedy of disgorgement of all profits gained by fiduciary violations by means of a constructive trust. In addition, a disloyal agent is not entitled to any fees, even if the agent performed other functions satisfactorily. Thus, the court required York to repay its ill-gotten profits and fees collected under the subservicing contract and in connection with the issuance of GNMA securities back to GNMA.

The District of Columbia Circuit reversed. The court held that, even if York were GNMA's agent, it violated no duty. York's involvement in the transactions caused GNMA no direct financial loss, and the court found no other duty that York breached. The court found no duty of confidentiality under the agreement and no duty under GNMA rules or the securities laws.[681]

Discussion Topics:
1. What is your opinion about the court's analysis?
2. If you were a legal adviser to GNMA what advice would you give the agency to avoid situations such as the one that developed in York?
3. How would the advice indicate whether the court was correct in its decision?

The *York* case leaves open the question whether Salomon Brothers and the religious order from which York purchased the security using insider information could sue York under Rule 10b-5 for trading on the information without disclosure. It would seem that the sellers of securities who sell under these conditions should be able to sue the insiders and claim the difference between the price they received and the full face value of the securities that the insider received. However, as the district court noted, the insider should not be required to pay twice.

Material information concerning asset-backed securities may include loan payments by the borrower concerning prepayment, delinquency, or default; activities conducted on the mortgaged property, such as environmental risk, competition, or condemnation; and the financial status of the tenant, including bankruptcy or cash-flow problems.

What is the "Insider" Status of the Parties? Originators generally limit their involvement to lending money to borrowers and selling loans to an SPV. Bank originators may be further involved by servicing loans, directly or through affiliates, after the loans have been securitized. In both cases, banks so involved are more likely to be considered insiders, even though servicing through an affiliate may be a more removed activity.

Servicers of commercial mortgage-backed securities often are not related to the originators or the issuers of the securities. These servicers could be considered independent contractors if the other parties to the securitization process did not have the authority to control the servicer's performance. Nonetheless, such servicers may be subject to the prohibition on insider trading if they are considered "temporary insiders." A factual inquiry is necessary to determine the degree to which a servicer

[681] United States v. York, 112 F.3d 1218, 1222-25 (D.C. Cir. 1997).

"entered into a special confidential relationship in the conduct of the business of the enterprise and [was] given access to information solely for corporate purposes."[682]

c. Issuers' Registration Under Section 12 of the 1934 Act[683]

Many issuers of asset-backed securities fall under section 12 of the 1934 Act. If so, they are required to file periodic reports with the SEC under section 13 of the 1934 Act. In addition, section 15(d) requires issuers that filed registration statements that became effective under the 1933 Act to file periodic reports under section 13 of the 1934 Act.

The SEC is authorized under section 12(h) of the 1934 Act to grant exemptions from the reporting requirements if it finds that noncompliance with the Act would not reduce the protection of investors. Because parts of these reports are not relevant to MBS, the SEC was ready to grant partial exemptions, requiring instead reporting that is more suitable to these kinds of securities. However, since exemptions involve a lengthy procedure, and reporting requirements are rarely enforced by private parties, a process developed with respect to mortgage-backed securities by which the issuer applies for an exemption and agrees to receive a no-action letter by the staff. The reporting requirements concerning asset-backed securities were codified in 2005. To the extent that questions arise in connection with the codifications, it is likely that they will be resolved by no-action letters.

Issuers that are subject to section 12 of the 1934 Act become subject to section 14 of the Act, which regulate the issuers' proxy statement. In addition, the affiliates and fiduciaries of such issuers are subject to section 16 of the Act, which regulates such persons' "short swing" trading in the issuers' shares. The no-action letters that the staff issuers under section 12(h) in response to requests for exemption do not cover section 14 (relating to the proxy statements). However, asset-backed securities distributed to the public are rarely if ever accompanied by voting rights; issues of proxy regulation do not arise. In addition, these no-action letters also do not cover section 16 of the 1934 Act. There are, however a few letters in which the staff has taken a no-action position with respect to section 16(a) (which requires insiders to report their holdings of the issuer's securities). In this case, again, insiders of SPVs do not hold or trade in SPV securities. In addition, most asset-backed securities are structured as debt securities, which are not convertible into shares. Section 16 does not apply to such nonconvertible debt securities.

The staff has granted no-action letters to issuers whose securities are covered by an effective registration on the shelf, under Rule 415, but who have not yet made a

---

682 Dirks v. SEC, 463 U.S. 646, 655 n.14 (1983).

683 2 TAMAR FRANKEL, SECURITIZATION § 13.4 (Ann Taylor Schwing ed., 2d ed. 2005).

public offering of these securities. These issuers may postpone reporting until the public offering is made.

Relief from reporting is provided in section 15(d) of the 1934 Act for issuers as to any fiscal year after the fiscal year in which the registration statement was filed if, at the beginning of the new fiscal year, the class of registered securities is held of record by fewer than 300 persons (or fewer than 500 persons, if the issuer has less than $10 million in assets). In such a case, the issuer must file Form 15 within 30 days after the beginning of the new fiscal year.

D. Issuers' Registration as Broker-Dealers under the 1934 Act[684]

Issuers of asset-backed securities must register with the SEC as broker-dealers if they engage in sale and distribution of the securities, unless an exemption is available to them. Rule 3a4-1 promulgated under the 1934 Act exempts from registration as brokers persons who are associated with the issuer and engage in limited distribution activities. Distribution of securities in shelf registration is included among the exempt activities.

a. Exemption for Mortgage-backed Securities[685]

Section 15(a)(1) of the 1934 Act requires registration of broker-dealers under certain circumstances. Excluded from registration are brokers or dealers who deal in "exempted securities," as defined in section 3(a)(12) of the Act.

MBS are excluded from the application of section 15(a) of the 1934 Act by Rule 3a12-4. The Rule covers only MBS that (i) are not in default and (ii) have an unpaid principal of at least $50,000. In addition, the Rule covers only whole loan mortgages or an SPV of such mortgages or undivided interests in such mortgages (if the remaining interests are retained by the loan originator). The staff's interpretations exclude from the exemption MBS that are sold as investment contracts as defined by the SEC.

b. The Secondary Mortgage Market Enhancement Act of 1984[686]

Congress recognized that the secondary Market in MBS is a "forward trading Market," which requires a four- to six-month settlement period or delay between the date of the contract and date of payment and delivery. Therefore, Congress amended sections 7, 8(a) and 11(d)(1) to allow private sector issuers to hedge their interest rate risk by selling MBS under forward delivery contracts. Once sold in advance, mortgages that the SPV will hold are originated, loan commitments are issued at

---

[684] 2 TAMAR FRANKEL, SECURITIZATION § 13.4.1 (Ann Taylor Schwing ed., 2d ed. 2005).

[685] 2 TAMAR FRANKEL, SECURITIZATION § 13.4.5 (Ann Taylor Schwing ed., 2d ed. 2005).

[686] 2 TAMAR FRANKEL, SECURITIZATION § 13.5.1 (Ann Taylor Schwing ed., 2d ed. 2005).

current interest rates, and the mortgage loans become effective at the closing date. This procedure is used by the federal agencies engaged in securitizing mortgages.

The Secondary Mortgage Market Enhancement Act of 1984 removes the restrictions in section 11(d)(1) of the 1934 Act for private issuers of mortgage related securities by amending section 11(d)(1) to provide that broker-dealers will not be deemed to have extended credit "by reason of a bona fide delayed delivery of . . . any mortgage related security or any small business related security against full payment of the entire purchase price thereof upon such delivery within one hundred and eighty days after such purchase."[687]

Section 11(d)(1) authorizes the SEC to make Rules in the public interest and for the protection of investors, which shorten the forward trading period of 180 days specified in the Act, or to establish a minimum volume or a sales price requirement for forward trading. Section 7 and former section 8(a) of the 1934 Act were similarly amended. The Riegle Community Development and Regulatory Improvement Act of 1994 further amended sections 7(g), 8(a), and 11(d)(1) of the 1934 Act to make them applicable to small business related securities ("SBRS"), to mortgage related securities, and to commercial mortgage loans.

The SEC has taken the position that exceptions relating to broker-dealers in the Enhancement Act apply to the pooling process of securitization, but not to issuance of the mortgage-related securities. Therefore, a broker-dealer may not provide a longer payment period to a single buyer of mortgage related securities and may not undertake to repurchase mortgage related securities during the underwriting period of such securities. However, a "broker may extend credit against collateral that will be used for an offering."[688]

c. Definition of Mortgage Related Securities[689]

Section 3(a)(41) of the 1934 Act defines a "mortgage related security" as: a security that is rated in one of the two highest rating categories by at least one nationally recognized statistical rating organization, and either:

(A) represents ownership of one or more promissory notes or certificates of interest or participation in such notes . . . , which notes:

[687] 15 U.S.C. §78k(d)(1) (2006).

[688] 2 TAMAR FRANKEL, SECURITIZATION § 24.8, at 241-42 (Supp. 2004) (quoting Morley & Molenkamp, Structured Financing Under the Federal Securities Laws, paper presented at ABA Section of Bus. Law, Spring Meeting, Boston, Mass., at 13, 64 (Apr. 6, 1990)).

[689] 2 TAMAR FRANKEL, SECURITIZATION § 13.5.2 (Ann Taylor Schwing ed., 2d ed. 2005).

(i) are directly secured by a first lien on a single parcel of real estate, . . . upon which is located a dwelling or mixed residential and commercial structure, . . . ; and

(ii) were originated by a savings and loan association, savings bank, commercial bank, credit union, insurance company, or similar institution which is supervised and examined by a Federal or State authority, or by a mortgagee approved by the Secretary of Housing and Urban Development pursuant to sections 1709 and 1715(b) of Title 12, or, where such notes involve a lien on the manufactured home, by any such institution or by any financial institution approved for insurance by the Secretary of Housing and Urban Development pursuant to section 1703 of title 12 . . . .[690]

For manufactured homes, the section further provides that a "promissory note" includes "a loan, advance, or credit sale as evidence[d] by a retail installment sales contract or other instrument."[691] The Riegle Community Development and Regulatory Improvement Act of 1994 amended the definition of commercial mortgage related securities ("CMRS") provided in the Secondary Mortgage Market Enhancement Act of 1984 ("SMMEA") to include mortgages on real estate "upon which is located one or more commercial structures."[692] However, SMMEA premiums will apply to CMRS only after the OCC promulgates final regulations to implement these provisions. The 1994 Act also provides for a state opt-out statutorily within seven years.

Thus, the term "mortgage related security" includes an interest in a note secured by a first lien on a residential manufactured home if the related loan was made by certain Institutions, such as thrifts and banks, and in the case of manufactured homes includes a retail installment contract. Mortgages on nursing homes, mobile homes, and hospitals are probably outside the definition of a mortgage related security. Similarly, securities backed by a cash escrow to be paid to investors upon failure of the seller to deliver mortgages may not qualify because the securities are backed, at least temporarily, by mortgages and cash, and may never be funded by mortgages. However, if substantially all the mortgage collateral had been delivered and if there is no provision under which the investors or the seller can redeem the securities, a cash escrow for not more than 35 days to cover failed deliveries of additional mortgages would not disqualify the securities.

An issue arose whether "installment land contracts" are "mortgage related securities" within the meaning of section 3(a)(41). Some lenders, such as the Veterans Administration, use installment contracts instead of deeds of trust in states that

[690] 15 U.S.C. §78c(a)(41)(A) (2006).

[691] 15 U.S.C. §78c(a)(41) (2006).(footnote omitted).

[692] 15 U.S.C. §78c(a)(41)(A)(i) (2006).

impose protracted foreclosure procedures. In these contracts the ownership of the land is retained by the lender, and the borrower is entitled to a transfer of the ownership only after all payments due to the lender have been made. The staff granted a no-action letter on this issue because the contracts are utilized for the purpose of purchasing homes and represent a better security interest in land. The applicants cited congressional reports suggesting that the omission of the contracts was due to oversight.

Section 3(a)(41) limits mortgage related securities to first mortgages. In a unique case, however, the staff granted a no-action letter to securities backed by second mortgages, provided that the nonconforming mortgages in the SPV would be replaced by conforming mortgages within six months. In this case, a private-sector sponsor proposed to purchase mortgage loans from the Farmers Home Administration ("FmHA"). In 1986, the FmHA, which was authorized to make certain second mortgages under the Housing Act of 1949, was required to sell mortgages to the tune of $2.099 billion for fiscal years 1987 through 1989. FmHA lacked full information about the status of the mortgages it held; it had information only about amounts and other terms. To help FmHA meet its deadline, the lead underwriter proposed that the SPV purchase FmHA mortgages and make an offering based on available information about the mortgages; FmHA would offer warranties regarding the purchased mortgages, including a warranty about their first lien status. After the offering, the trustee would examine the loan documents, and FmHA would substitute mortgages that conformed to the definition in section 3(a)(41) for the nonconforming mortgages, including the second mortgages. This process could take up to six months. Following another no-action letter for GNMA SPVs that hold *de minimis* nonconforming assets, the staff agreed that the plan could be implemented under the unique circumstances of this case, especially the undertaking to replace nonconforming mortgages within six months.

Mortgage related securities need not require that all payments received by the SPV should be passed through to the securities holders immediately. Congress recognized the market practice of retaining some payments from the mortgages in the SPV to provide credit enhancement and the variations that exist among pass-through securities. The staff has granted a no-action letter for an arrangement under which principal payments on the mortgages were allowed to accumulate in a redemption fund for five years and then paid out to the security holders, unless they sought redemption. The staff also recognized limited partnership interests and commercial mortgage-based securities containing defeasance provisions as mortgage related securities.

The SMMEA does not apply to MBS traded as over-the-counter (OTC) bonds. These bonds are not usually traded on a national exchange.

E. Simulation Exercise: Should We Invest in Fannie Mae Mortgage-Backed Securities?

Ashley Peterson and Matt Brown graduated from law school in 2002. They both went to work at the New York office of a prestigious international law firm. Ashley was a litigator and Matt worked on environmental issues. On the occasion of their fifth anniversary at the firm, they dined together to celebrate. They had much to be excited about. Both had received exemplary reviews each year as well as sizable bonuses which they used to pay off their student loans. They had even accumulated some funds in their savings accounts. After discussing the office politics and their summer 2007 vacation plans their conversation turned to the future. They shared their dreams of making partner and then Ashley raised a more immediate and pragmatic issue: How should we invest our savings, just in case we do not make partner?

While neither were investment gurus they were able to quickly list the basic options – commodities, equities, bonds, or bank certificates of deposit (CDs). Commodities were a non-starter as both agreed in the absence of expertise, commodity trading was nothing more than gambling. The equities discussion was more robust. Matt recalled the conventional wisdom that over the long term equities outperformed highly-rated and therefore more secure bonds. He drew a risk and return curve on his napkin to illustrate the classic economic theory that with increased risk investors required greater returns. Both liked the idea of higher returns but Ashley raised three concerns. First, she had read that many stocks were at all time highs. While she was an investment neophyte she knew the saying "buy low and sell high" and given the market's conditions that summer buying equities at that time seemed at odds with the adage. Second, she had read some news stories about the potential for a slowing economy. Concerns about corporate profits were enough to make her wonder if the equities market might have peaked. Finally, she recalled the stories of Enron, WorldCom and HealthSouth from her ethics course in law school. It was very hard to know who was reporting facts and who fictions. Matt had heard enough, equities were off the list.

The bond discussion moved quickly to interest rates. In the summer of 2007 interest rates on government bonds were paying less than 4 percent. Ashley opened her copy of the newspaper and looked at bank advertisements that promoted the return on CDs. While slightly higher than government bonds, the CD returns were still unexciting. As Ashley was closing the paper, Matt noticed an article about Fannie Mae issuing new mortgage-backed securities. He read the article aloud and emphasized that the yield on these securities were higher than CDs, they were AAA rated, and that Fannie Mae was guaranteeing both interest and principal repayment. By the end of the story Ashley and Matt smiled at each other, perhaps this was the investment vehicle they were looking for. Their years of legal training ensured they would not make a decision without doing their homework. Ashley agreed to learn about Fannie Mae and its financial performance; Matt would evaluate the prospectus for the Fannie Mae Securities. Over coffee they agreed: "Next week, same time, same place to share our findings."

A week later they were at dinner discussing their respective research. Ashley presented her material on Fannie Mae first. Fannie Mae was formed as a government sponsored entity in the 1930s as part of the New Deal. Fannie Mae's goal was to increase the availability of funds for home mortgages through the creation of a secondary market for mortgage loans. Fannie Mae would buy loans from local originators who could use the funds to offer additional mortgages. Fannie Mae had fulfilled this mission and was feted as an enabler of Americans to fulfill their dream of home ownership. In the process it also amassed significant political power. A key to the company's success was its transformation of its loan portfolio into mortgage-backed securities. This process brought fresh capital into the mortgage market. Although the government privatized Fannie Mae in 1968 and the company was subsequently publicly traded on the New York Stock Exchange, Fannie Mae did retain some benefits of its government heritage including a line of credit with the United States Treasury and its securities were eligible for open-market purchase by Federal Reserve banks. Moreover, investors generally considered its securities backed by the U.S. government although it clearly stated in its materials that the company is not backed by the full faith and credit of the federal government.

Fannie Mae's financial performance in 2006 had been mixed. Net income was more than $4 billion which was consistent with performance over that past five years but down from $6.3 billion in 2005.[693] The company's credit book of business stood at $2.5 trillion having grown 7 percent in 2006, versus only 1 percent in 2005.[694] The firm's key indicator of risk, the credit loss ratio, had fallen from 2.2 basis points in 2005 to 0.5 basis points in 2006 for its multifamily portfolio; although the credit loss ratio increased from 1.9 basis points to 2.8 basis points for its single family holdings.[695] Looking toward the future, Fannie Mae's CEO in his Letter to Shareholders wrote that he was bullish about the market for securitized offerings. "Demand for loan securitization in our conventional 15- and 30-year products has increased dramatically, and we expect 2007 to be our single biggest year in history for growth in Fannie Mae MBS outstanding."[696] The letter went on in a positive vein: "The mortgage market is returning to tighter underwriting, more rational

[693] FANNIE MAE, 2006 ANNUAL REPORT 1, , http://www.fanniemae.com/ir/pdf/annualreport/2006/2006_annual_report.pdf;jsessionid=W0CPNELWK3BYJJ2FECISFGA (last visited Sept. 24, 2009).

[694] *Id.* at 2.

[695] *Id.* at 4.

[696] *Id.* at 5.

pricing, and more demand for traditional, fixed- and adjustable-rate products that have been our bread and butter. In other words, the market is returning to a place that Fannie Mae never left – safe, sensible, affordable mortgage lending. As it does, we see opportunities ahead for growth in our business and for gain in market share."[697] The investment community seemed to share the CEO's optimism – Fannie Mae's share price ended 2006 at $59 versus $49 a year earlier.

After this good news, she shared the bad – Fannie Mae management had smoothed its earnings between 1998 and 2003. She read from the Office of Federal Housing Enterprise Oversight's final report: "Fannie Mae senior management promoted an image of the Enterprise as one of the lowest-risk financial institutions in the world and as 'best–in–class' in term of risk management, financial reporting, internal controls and corporate governance. The findings in this report show that risks at Fannie Mae were greatly understated and that image was false."[698] Matt was stunned. She read on: "[From] 1998 to mid-2004 – Fannie Mae reported extremely smooth profit growth and hit announced targets for earnings per share precisely each quarter. Those achievements were illusions deliberately and systematically created by the Enterprise's senior management with the aid of inappropriate accounting and improper earnings management."[699] There was more- senior management also gained directly by the misrepresentation. "By deliberately and intentionally manipulating accounting to hit earnings targets, senior management maximized the bonuses and other executive compensation they received at the expense of shareholders." [700] The company was forced to restate its earnings downward by $6.3 billion and pay a multimillion dollar fine.[701] Much of the company's leadership including the CEO and CFO resigned or were terminated; 85 percent of the company's senior managers were now either new to the company or in new roles. Moreover, the federal government increased its oversight of Fannie Mae's operations. Ashley's closing comment was actually a question: "I think they are now trustworthy but how do you really know?!"

---

[697] *Id.* at 6.

[698] OFFICE OF FEDERAL HOUSING ENTERPRISE OVERSIGHT, REPORT OF THE SPECIAL EXAMINATION OF FANNIE MAE Summary of the Report (2006), http://online.wsj.com/public/resources/documents/ofheo20060523.pdf (last visited Sept. 24, 2009).

[699] *Id.*

[700] *Id.*

[701] Fannie Mae, *Fannie Mae Completes Restatement and Files 2004 Form 10-K,* News Release No. 3872-1 (Dec. 6, 2006), http://www.fanniemae.com/media/pdf/newsreleases/form10k_newsrelease_120606.pdf (last visited Sept. 24, 2009); Fannie Mae, *Fannie Mae Agrees to Comprehensive Settlements with OFHEO and SEC* (May 23, 2006), http://www.fanniemae.com/newsreleases/2006/3738.jhtml?p=Media&s=News+Releases (last visited Sept. 24, 2009).

Matt then shared his review of Fannie Mae's prospectus for Guaranteed Multifamily REMIC Pass-Through Certificates. He started with a caution that was boxed and in bold typeface on Page 1 of the prospectus. "The certificates are exempt from registration under the Securities and Exchange Act of 1933, as amended, and are 'exempted securities' under the Securities and Exchange Act of 1934, as amended. Neither the Securities and Exchange Commission nor any state securities commission has approved or disapproved these certificates or determined if this prospectus is truthful or complete."

That caveat duly noted he then described the securities. The certificates issued by Fannie Mae "represent beneficial ownership interests in the assets of [the] trust."[702] These assets are comprised of "underlying securities issued by Fannie Mae [as well as entities not affiliated with Fannie Mae] that represent the direct or indirect ownership of residential mortgage loans secured by multifamily properties . . . ; or . . . residential mortgage loans secured by multifamily properties."[703] The issuing trust "will elect to treat all or a portion of each series trust as at least one 'real estate mortgage investment conduit,' commonly referred to as a REMIC" for tax purposes.[704] Each series trust will have at least two classes; one is a residual interest in a REMIC and the other (or others) is a regular interest in a REMIC.

Ashley admitted that she had only a vague memory of REMIC from tax class and asked for more elaboration. Matt explained that Congress created REMICs as part of the Tax Reform Act of 1986. The goal was to facilitate the securitization of mortgages by eliminating the double taxation of both SPVs and investors. The REMIC designation provides the SPV with pass-through treatment; the tax obligation is passed to the securities holders. Congress established a set of requirements for REMIC status. First, REMIC status must be elected when the SPV is formed. Second, the SPV's financial structure must have two classes of securities – regular and residual interests. The regular interest is analogous to debt and typically has a fixed interest rate and specified principal amount. Senior and subordinate classes of regular interest are permitted. The residual interest is akin to equity. Residual interests "entitle the holders to all payments from the REMIC assets other than the payments to the holders of the regular interests and REMIC expenses.

702 FANNIE MAE, MULTIFAMILY REMIC PROSPECTUS 1 (Sept. 1, 2007), http://www.efanniemae.com/syndicated/documents/mbs/remicpros/MF_FM_September_1_2007.pdf (last visited Sept. 25, 2009).

703 *Id.*

704 *Id.*

Any distributions to the class of residual interests must be pro rata."[705] Only one class of residual interest is permitted. A third requirement is that the SPV hold only qualified assets, qualified mortgages on residential and commercial real estate and/or mortgage pass-through securities as well as permitted investments (including "any investment of amounts received under qualified mortgages for a temporary period before distribution to holders of interest in the REMIC").[706] Matt concluded his tutorial by enumerating the several advantages and sole concern of REMICs. On the positive side REMICs do not require minimum equity holdings, the SPV can opt for a range of legal forms, multiple classes of regular interests can be issued, and the single tax treatment is unambiguous. On the downside, if the SPV engages in prohibited transactions the associated income is taxed at 100 percent.[707]

Matt then turned his attention to explaining the section on the Fannie Mae guarantee. "We guarantee to each series trust that we will supplement amounts received by the series trust as required to permit payment of interest and principal on the certificates on each distribution date . . ."[708] Additionally, "[b]ecause we guarantee the payment of principal on the certificates, a default by a borrower does not reduce the amount of principal that will be paid to certificateholders."[709] As he read further he came to understand that the guarantee was exclusively the corporation's, not the federal government's. In bold typeface the prospectus declared "The certificates and payments of the principal and interest on the certificates are not guaranteed by the United States . . . ."[710] Elsewhere in the prospectus he found an important limitation. "If we were unable to perform our guaranty obligations, certificateholders would receive distributions only on the related underlying assets. . . . As a result, delinquencies and defaults on the mortgage loans could directly affect the amounts that certificateholders would receive each month."[711] Moreover, the guarantee "runs directly to each series trust and not directly to certificateholders. As a result, certificateholders do not have any rights to bring proceedings directly against Fannie Mae [except in certain limited circumstances]."[712]

---

[705] 1 TAMAR FRANKEL, SECURITIZATION § 8.15.3.2 (Ann Taylor Schwing ed., 2d ed. 2005) (footnote omitted).

[706] *Id.* § 8.15.4.2.

[707] *Id.* § 8.15.1.

[708] *Id.* at 7.

[709] *Id.* at 19.

[710] *Id.* at 1.

[711] *Id.* at 14.

[712] *Id.* at 7.

He then shared with Ashley a summary of the 16 pages describing the risk factors associated with these certificates. The first caution was the standard: "The certificates are complex financial instruments. They are not a suitable investment for every investor."[713] This was followed by a much more specific section detailing the reasons that the actual yield received by the investor might be lower than expected.[714] The dominant concern is prepayment of loans. Many of the mortgages that underlie the certificates can be prepaid by the borrower. The reasons for prepayment run the gamut from the borrower selling the home and therefore terminating the mortgage to declining interest rates that make refinancing attractive for the borrower. The latter is of particular concern for investors because if a high yield mortgage prepays because of lower interest rates it is unlikely that the investor will be able to replace the original yield. Mortgages can also be removed from the pool if the seller made "representations and warrantees [that] were not true when . . . made."[715] In this case Fannie Mae can force the seller to repurchase the security. One protection against prepayment is a prepayment penalty which is often included as a term of fixed rate multifamily mortgages (but was generally not incorporated into adjustable mortgages). However, even if there was a prepayment clause, it might be waived in the case of default or bankruptcy. Moreover, "[e]ven if borrowers pay prepayment premiums, certificateholders may not be entitled to receive a share of those payments."[716]

An additional concern was that the default rate on the loans would be higher than expected. Fannie Mae considers the underlying characteristics of the mortgage portfolio when establishing its expected yield but the company acknowledges that circumstances can change. For example, loss of employment, disability or other events can reduce the ability of the borrower to repay the loan. The prospectus also details the factors that are out of the control of Fannie Mae and the borrower. These include national or local economic conditions, location-specific real estate conditions, and even terrorism. Any of these factors individually can impact the default rate and taken together could have a sizable effect.[717]

Another important risk dealt with a potential lack of liquidity. If the investor wanted to sell the security prior to maturity the transaction could be made but "[w]e cannot be sure that new certificates, when issued, will have a ready market, or, if a market does develop, that the market will remain during the entire term for which the

---

713 *Id.* at 10.

714 *Id.* at 11-12.

715 *Id.* at 10.

716 *Id.* at 16.

717 *Id.* at 18-19.

certificates are outstanding."[718] Fannie Mae clearly stated that they were not required to create such a market and "it is possible that if you wish to sell your certificates in the future, you may have difficulty finding potential purchasers."[719] The prospectus listed nine factors that could affect the investor's ability to sell the certificates ranging from the amount of outstanding principal to the availability of comparable securities to the minimum denominations of the certificates.

The concern about liquidity was amplified by the caveats concerning Fannie Mae's credit status. "There could be an adverse change in our financial condition that would impair our credit rating or the perception of our credit."[720] In such circumstances "potential buyers may offer less for your certificates than they otherwise would offer if an adverse change in our financial condition were to remain unchanged."[721]

He finished his overview of the prospectus by explaining that Fannie Mae distributes the certificates through one or more securities dealers who in turn sell directly to investors or to other dealers. "We, the dealers or other parties may receive compensation, trading gain or other benefits in connection with these transactions. We typically receive a fee from the dealer or dealers for each offering."[722] He shared that the last line of the prospectus which again cautioned that there is no assured secondary market or benchmark price for the certificates.[723]

Ashley listened intently, digested the information and then realized the potential for a "perfect storm." What if we invested in the certificates and then (1) interest rates declined; (2) the overall economy slowed and with it housing prices slumped; and (3) the slowdown led to more delinquencies. The result would be significant prepayments reducing the effective yield of the investment and potentially defaults that Fannie Mae could not cover. Matt added that even if they were able to see the erosion of value coming, the lack of a secondary market for the certificates could make it difficult or even impossible to liquidate their position.

They both sat quietly thinking over the situation. While they were able to create a perfect storm in their minds, the reality was that Fannie Mae's 2006 financials were strong and to date the company's guarantee was as good as gold.

---

[718] *Id.* at 12.

[719] *Id.* at 12.

[720] *Id.* at 14.

[721] *Id.* at 14.

[722] *Id.* at 65.

[723] *Id.* at 65.

Assignment: What decision criteria should Ashley and Matt use to decide whether to invest in the Fannie Mae certificates? What is your assessment of those criteria? The bottom line: Would you invest in the mortgage-backed securities?

Chapter 11: Securitization in Light of the Investment Company Act of 1940, the Advisers Act of 1940, Accounting Issues and Taxation

This chapter explores a number of legal, regulatory and accounting issues that impact the overall securitization process. The first issue addresses the exemption of SPVs from the Investment Company Act of 1940 under Rule 3a-7. A second issue examines securitization in light of the Investment Advisers Act of 1940. The third issue deals with the accounting treatment of the securitization transactions. The fourth and last issue is the tax treatment of the securitization process, and in particular the avoidance of double taxation with a focus on real estate mortgage investment conduits or REMICs.

A. Exemption Under the Investment Company Act of 1940

The Investment Advisers Act of 1940[724] and the Investment Company Act of 1940[725] are enforced by the Securities and Exchange Commission (SEC). The two acts authorize the SEC to provide exemptions from the acts, subject to certain conditions. In addition, the staff of the SEC has been issuing "no-action" letters under the specified circumstances. These "no-action" letters notify the recipients that the staff will not recommend action to the SEC if the applicant-recipient acted as described in its request of the no-action letter. These letters have acquired significant precedential value throughout the years.

The Investment Company Act of 1940 defines among other types of investment companies two types that are mainly involved in the structure of SPVs. One is an open end investment company and the other is a unit investment trust. Open end companies offer redeemable securities and managed portfolios. Unit investment trusts offer redeemable securities but their portfolios are fixed at the outset and cannot be traded. Unit investment trusts, like open end companies, offer redeemable securities.

Even though SPVs are not called investment companies, which are regulated under the Investment Company Act of 1940 (the Act), SPVs can fall within the definition of an investment company.[726] Why can SPVs be defined as investment companies? It is because the definition of an investment company is very broad. In fact, it includes entities (and individuals) that issue securities and invest in securities. SPVs issue securities and invest in loans. If loans are defined as securities (because they are held for investment) then SPVs are investment companies.

---

[724] 15 U.S.C. § 80b-1 to -21 (2006)

[725] 15 U.S.C. § 80a-1 to -64 (2006)

[726] 15 U.S.C. § 80a-3 (2006)

However, had the Act applied to SPVs they could not operate, because of the various constraints of the Act. Even though arguably loans are not securities, the industry preferred to seek exemptions rather than to fight the Securities and Exchange Commission that enforces the Act.

One of the problems that SPVs posed for the Commission is the similarity of the SPVs to investment companies. Therefore, the SEC exempted SPVs from the Act subject to many conditions that apply with respect to the SPVs structure, assets, operations and management.

These conditions distinguish the SPVs from investment companies. The exemption from the Act is useful at this point because it offers a review of the nature and function of the SPVs and the limits imposed on their activities.

a. Rule 3a-7[727]

In November 1992, the SEC adopted Rule 3a-7, pursuant to its powers under sections 6(c) and 38(a) of the Act. The Rule implemented the Commission's staff's recommendations in its study of the 1940 Act. Rule 3a-7(a) provides: "Notwithstanding section 3(a) of the Act, any issuer who is engaged in the business of purchasing, or otherwise acquiring, and holding eligible assets (and in activities related or incidental thereto), and who does not issue redeemable securities will not be deemed to be an investment company" under certain conditions. Because section 3(a) covers all forms of investment companies, the Rule excepts those companies that meet its conditions from the full definition of an investment company, instead of exempting these companies from the provisions of the Act.

The conditions in Rule 3a-7 are detailed and complex. The exception relates to (i) the kind of securities the issuer SPV issues, (ii) the kind of assets the issuer SPV holds, (iii) the activities in which the issuer SPV is engaged, and (iv) various steps for the protection of investors.

The Rule's provisions highlight distinctions between investment companies and SPVs. These distinctions help avoid investors' confusion between regulated investment companies and SPVs, and in addition preclude regulated investment companies from finding in the Rule an escape from regulation. Therefore, these purposes ought to be kept in mind when interpreting the conditions of the Rule.

The Kind of Securities that the Issuer Issues. An issuer of redeemable securities, as defined in section 2(a)(32) of the Act, is not qualified under Rule 3a-7. Investors might confuse such an issuer that is an SPV with the popular open-end investment companies that offer redeemable securities. In addition, an issuer of redeemable

[727] 1 TAMAR FRANKEL, SECURITIZATION § 11.31 (Ann Taylor Schwing ed., 2d ed. 2005).

securities must be ready and able to redeem by holding liquid assets in its portfolio, whereas many of the SPVs hold illiquid assets, and cannot comply with the redemption requirement.

In the Commission's staff opinion, the following financing program (SPV) does not meet restrictions on redeemability of Rule 3a-7, if the SPV issues two classes of securities, one of which entitles the holder, absolutely or conditionally, to withdraw portfolio securities from the program upon acquisition and presentation of a specified amount of other securities of another class. Thus, if the SPV issues class A and Class B securities, and Class A holders acquire a specific amount of class B securities, then Class A could withdraw some securities which the investors hold. The staff disagreed with the assertion that "because the decision to combine [the two classes] is the investor's and is not dictated by the terms of the offering, . . . the program is [not] the 'issuer' of the combined security. . . . Although the decision to combine is the investor's, the structured financing program will define all of the rights attributable to the [two classes], and . . . the program, not the investor, is the obligor of the recombined security." The test of whether securities are not redeemable, wrote the staff, is "whether there are substantial enough restrictions on an investor's ability to withdraw portfolio securities," in light of eight factors:

"(1) whether an investor's . . . right is conditional or absolute, (2) whether the issuer offers the matching securities for sale to investors at the same time or only at different times, (3) whether and how often the issuer sponsors activities (such as auctions and mandatory tender features) designed to facilitate an investor's ability to acquire the matching security or securities and present them for withdrawal, (4) whether the amount of portfolio securities that an investor can withdraw from the program at any time is limited or unlimited, (5) how often an investor can withdraw portfolio securities from the program, (6) whether or not there is a holding period requirement, (7) the denomination of the securities and the minimum amount needed to withdraw portfolio securities, and (8) how the withdrawal right feature is presented to investors.[728] To qualify under the Rule, the issuer must issue "fixed-income securities or other securities which entitle their holders to receive payments that depend primarily on the cash flow from eligible assets."[729]

The Rule defines "fixed income securities" as any securities that entitle the holder to receive:

(i) A stated principal amount; or

(ii) Interest on a principal amount (which may be a notional principal amount) calculated by reference to a fixed rate or to a standard or formula

---

[728] Brown & Wood, Corres. (Feb. 24, 1994) (citing SuperTrust Trust for Capital Market Fund, Inc. Shares, IC-17613 (1990)) (footnotes omitted).

[729] 17 C.F.R. § 270.3a-7(a)(1) (2009).

which does not reference any change in the market value or fair value of eligible assets; or

(iii) Interest on a principal amount (which may be a notional principal amount) calculated by reference to auctions among holders and prospective holders, or through remarketing of the security; or

(iv) An amount equal to specified fixed or variable portions of the interest received on the assets held by the issuer; or

(v) Any combination of amounts described in paragraphs (b)(2) (i), (ii), (iii), and (iv) of this section;[730]

Provided, That substantially all of the payments to which the holders of such securities are entitled consist of the foregoing amounts.

This definition of the issued securities reflects the difference between these securities and debt securities on the one hand, and equity securities on the other. Fixed-income securities also include securities whose terms (mainly interest rate) are adjusted periodically by auction in which current and any interested new holders, including the issuer, participate. Further, the issuer's qualified securities include interest only and principal only securities and securities whose value does not depend on fixed income, such as the residual interests in the issuer, so long as the payment on the issued securities is "primarily" based on the cash flow from the assets that the issuer holds and not on market price fluctuations of the assets in the portfolio. Therefore, preferred stock does not qualify for the purpose of the Rule.

Further, the fixed-income securities "sold by the issuer or any underwriter thereof" must be "rated, at the time of initial sale, in one of the four highest categories assigned long-term debt or in an equivalent short-term category (within either of which there may be sub-categories or gradations indicating relative standing) by at least one nationally recognized statistical rating organization that is not an affiliated person of the issuer or of any person involved in the organization or operation of the issuer."[731] The rating requirements were designed to distinguish SPVs "from registered investment companies. The [SEC] wishes to emphasize that although ratings generally reflect evaluations of credit risk, the rating requirement is not intended to address investment risks associated with the credit quality of the financing."[732] The final Rule relaxed the rating requirement to qualify lower credit quality securities, and would presumably include securities backed by small business loans. Nonetheless, as compared to investment companies, this condition is costly and helps distinguish the SPV securities from those of investment companies.

---

[730] 17 C.F.R. § 270.3a-7(b)(2) (2009).

[731] 17 C.F.R. § 270.3a-7(a)(2) (2009).

[732] IC-19105 (1992).

Fixed-income securities that do not meet the rating requirements can be sold to "accredited investors." In addition, the issuers may sell any securities to institutional accredited buyers—"any entity in which all of the equity owners come within such paragraphs,"[733] and to affiliated persons of the issuer, except the rating agency involved. Individuals, however, are not qualified. In addition, the "issuer and any underwriter thereof affecting such sale" must "exercise reasonable care to ensure that such securities are sold and will be resold" only to these qualified persons, for example, by disclosing the limitations, putting legends on the certificates, and inquiring whether the securities are being purchased on behalf of or for others. Thus, presumably, the more sophisticated the investors are the more they can evaluate the securities and the less assurance they require from rating agencies....

The Kind of Assets that the Issuer Holds. The criteria for exemption under Rule 3a-7 relate to the issuer's assets as well. First, the issuer's business must consist of "purchasing, or otherwise acquiring, and holding eligible assets." Eligible assets are defined to mean "financial assets, either fixed or revolving, that by their terms convert into cash within a finite time period plus any rights or other assets designed to assure the servicing or timely distribution of proceeds to security holders."[734] Eligible assets include assets that would support liquidity and offer credit enhancement for the portfolio, such as guarantees. Qualified financial assets may also include securities that might be deemed equity such as pass-through securities representing a pro rata share in a pool of mortgages. Even though the definition is not clear, eligible assets would probably include also cumulative preferred stock.

The Issuer's Activities and Portfolio Management. To qualify for the exemption, the issuer's (SPV's) business must consist of "purchasing, or otherwise acquiring, and holding eligible assets." The issuer may not engage, even in part, in any other business. Unlike other exceptions from the definition of an investment company, the Rule does not qualify the type of business of the issuer by the word "primarily." That means that an SPV which engages primarily in purchasing and holding eligible securities, but also engages in another business will not be exempt. Further, the issuer is restricted from actively managing and trading in its portfolio—that is, acquiring additional assets or disposing of eligible assets that it holds. The Rule authorizes the qualified issuer to acquire[ ] additional eligible assets, or dispose[ ] of eligible assets, only if:

(i) The assets are acquired or disposed of in accordance with the terms and conditions set forth in the agreements, indentures, or other instruments pursuant to which the issuer's securities are issued;

---

733 17 C.F.R. § 270.3a-7(a)(2)(i) (2009).

734 17 C.F.R. § 270.3a-7(b)(1) (2009)

(ii) The acquisition or disposition of the assets does not result in a downgrading in the rating of the issuer's outstanding fixed-income securities; and

(iii) The assets are not acquired or disposed of for the primary purpose of recognizing gains or decreasing losses resulting from market value changes[735] . . .

Proposed Rule 3a-7 imposed on issuers far more restrictions. The final Rule relaxed these restrictions substantially. The issuer SPV under the Rule has more freedom to trade in the portfolio securities. This change came in response to arguments that the operation of SPVs and securitization requires more flexibility, and paragraph (a)(3) of the Rule appears to codify the industry practice. The limitations on trading are not fixed by statute or the Rule but by the instruments under which the securities are issued. But the Rule imposes two limitations. One limitation is objective and relates to the securities' rating. To protect investors, the instruments under which the securities are issued may not allow the SPV issuer to trade the portfolio if the trades *result* in the downgrading of the securities' rating. The second limitation is subjective: the issuer may not trade for the "primary purpose" of obtaining capital gains or avoiding capital losses. If the issuer purchases assets with cash that borrowers have prepaid or sells assets to cover obligations or expenses, then the fact that such activities generated capital gains or helped avoid capital losses would not be considered a "primary purpose." Similarly, an SPV issuer may engage in servicing the issuer's investors or in other activities incidental to the business of investing and holding eligible assets without falling outside the Rule. Because the issuer would be asserting an exemption, and because the facts are within its knowledge, the burden of showing a primary purpose should be on the issuer. In sum, Rule 3a-7(a)(3)(iii) excludes certain SPVs from the applicability of the 1940 Act, under certain conditions. Among these conditions, the Rule requires that the acquisition and disposition of eligible assets will not be "primarily" for "the purpose of recognizing gains or decreasing losses resulting from market value changes."[736]

In addition, the Release adopting the Rule notes that "the acquisition or disposition of assets in a structured financing generally does not occur for the 'sole purpose' of achieving gains or decreasing losses resulting in market value changes."[737] What is the difference between "primarily," in the Rule, and "sole," in the Release footnote? If the governing word is "solely" rather than "primarily," then any transaction can be interpreted as being solely for the purpose of gaining from trade. The word "primarily" is more appropriate in this context, both because it is used in the Act in other contexts, such as in section 3(a)(1), and because the word appears in the text of

[735] 17 C.F.R. § 270.3a-7(a)(3) (2009).

[736] 17 C.F.R. § 270.3a-7(a)(3)(iii) (2009).

[737] IC-19105 n.57 (1992).

the Rule rather than in a Release footnote, and because it leaves far more leeway to meet the particular situations.

Discussion Topics

1. To what extent does this provision precludes trading activities in the assets of the SPVs? For example, in some segments of the market the Originator is allowed to substitute the SPV's financial assets for other similar financial assets held by the issuer or repurchase an asset from the SPV issuer, subject to certain conditions. These conditions can include substitution and repurchase upon a breach of representation or warranty relating to an asset, or if the asset documentation is defective. Should such a transaction fall under the prohibition? Similarly, should the substitution and repurchase of SPV defaulted or charged-off assets fall under the prohibition? What if these conditions are specified in the transaction's documents? What if they are typical to structured financing or securitization and are not typical to mutual fund securities?

To interpret the provisions of the rule, one might look to its main purposes, that is, to distinguish between SPVs and mutual funds, to preclude SPV Originators and operators from competing with regulated investment companies, and to avoid opening a door for regulated investment companies to avoid regulation.

SPVs are a hybrid of mutual funds and debtors. Mutual funds must manage the assets in accordance with their investors' interests—as specified in the funds' investment policies. Debtors may manage the funds they borrow as they wish, subject to specific restrictions that the creditors impose on them in the transactions' documents. When SPVs offer investors guarantees, collateral, and equity that serves as collateral, the SPVs resemble debtors and their securities resemble debt securities. Hence they are less likely to be viewed as mutual funds.

Although SPVs are similar to unit investment trusts that must have a fixed portfolio, SPVs must exercise more flexibility in the management of their assets. Thus, the transactions that SPVs conduct should be tested in the light of this factor. The discretion of the SPV operators should be limited in various ways. First, the transaction documents should describe the permissible purchases and sales. The more discretion the description provides to the operators, the higher the legal risk that the SPV will not be covered by Rule 3a-7. The more detailed the description of the permissible purchases and sale is in the documents, the more likely the SPV will fall within the protection of the Rule. The following are a few examples of situations that arise in this area.

2. What if a provision in the document that establishes the SPV allows the management of the SPV's to follow a concentration criterion by substituting and repurchasing assets? This condition is more general, because it does not describe particular circumstances in which such transactions can occur. What legal risk is raised in this case?

3. Suppose the document that establishes the SPV impose quantitative limits on substitution and repurchases, such as a maximum of 20 percent of the collateral balance in the aggregate and 10 percent if the collateral balance for substitution and repurchase are credit related. What legal and other risks are raised in this case?

4. What about a document that establishes an SPV that allows the SPV to sell the SPV's assets either because the assets have deteriorated or because they have improved in credit quality, or as part of a discretionary sales "bucket"; for example, up to 15 percent of the value in a 12-month period?

5. Would the sale of "credit improved" assets be permitted under Rule 3a-7?

6. Is Rule 3a-7 important to securitization? If so, where does this importance lie?

b. Protection of Investors

To qualify for the exemption under Rule 3a-7, Rule 3a-7(a)(4) requires the following of several steps. First, it requires that issuers appoint unaffiliated trustees qualified under section 26(a)(1) of the Act and cause the SPV or its sponsor to enter with the trustees into agreements set forth in section 26(a)(3) of the Act. In the opinion of the SEC staff, the term "trustee" in Rule 3a-7(a)(4) does not include a custodian, because the Rule specifically requires the appointment of a trustee. The Rule does not prevent the trustee from acting as backup servicer if the primary servicer is unable to perform the functions. The requirement for appointing a trustee does not apply to securities backed by commercial paper. Because these securities are short-term, they do not involve the representation that long-term investors need. These short-term securities are not usually issued under a trust indenture.

The SEC granted an exemption from the requirement that the trustee would be unaffiliated where the trustee is affiliated with an underwriter involved with the organization of the issuer. Due to changes in the banking industry, most trustees providing services are affiliated with issuers through underwriters and that the requirement is disadvantageous to the asset-backed securities market and investors by requiring trustee selection by reasons other than market considerations. In addition the affiliation would not result in a conflict of interest, because of the timing and nature of the role of the trustee and the underwriter. The underwriter's role generally ends after the security distribution. Therefore there is no opportunity for the parties to act in concert. Further, the trustee has "virtually no discretion" in determining the choice of the securities to be held in the SPV.[738]

Second, the Rule requires that SPVs take "reasonable steps to cause the trustee to have a perfected security interest or ownership interest valid against third parties in those eligible assets that principally generate the cash flow needed to pay the fixed-income security holders, provided that such assets otherwise required to be held by the trustee may be released to the extent needed at the time for the operation of the issuer."[739] The Rule does not require that the security interest be taken in ancillary assets, such as the car bought by money from the securitized loan. The requirement applies only to the main assets that provide the cash flow for payment on the securities. The cash flows must be deposited periodically in a segregated account. However, the servicer may retain cash flows for some time, if a rating agency has determined that the risk to the assets is minimal.

The Rule does not require the Originator or sponsor of the issuer or the trustee to keep a list of the security holders of the issuer, as the proposed Rule did, because such a requirement would preclude the issuance of bearer securities, which are often issued in international transactions.

Finally, Rule 3a-7(a)(4) requires that SPVs take "actions necessary for the cash flows derived from eligible assets for the benefit of the holders of fixed-income securities to be deposited periodically in a segregated account that is maintained or controlled by the trustee consistent with the rating of the outstanding fixed-income securities."[740]

The Rule was expected to increase the volume of securitization of various financial assets, except stock, which is outside the Rule, and it did. Whether the Rule has caused these changes or met the expectations, however, is impossible to prove because any change may have occurred in the market for other causes or cumulative causes. The one effect that the Rule has had, however, is to reduce the requests for no-action letters and exemptions.

[738] Deutsche Bank Trust Co. Americas, IC-27644/27673 (2007).

[739] 17 C.F.R. § 270.3a-7(a)(4)(ii) (2009).

[740] 17 C.F.R. § 270.3a-7(a)(4)(iii) (2009).

c. Effect of SPV Exemptions on Third Parties[741]

SEC exemptive orders did not address the question of whether exempted SPVs remain investment companies for the purpose of determining the status and rights of third parties. The SEC's exemptions can be selective. The exemptions can cover the status of the SPVs as investment companies or only the activities of the SPVs. So the initial issue relates to the SPV being regulated as an entity, whether it is an investment company or not, and then the issue is whether the transactions that the SPV is involved in are exempted from the 1933 Act?

Two issues have arisen with respect to the SEC exemptions. One issue concerns the holding company of such an SPV. If 50% or more of the voting securities of the SPVs are held by another company ("holding company"), the securities of an exempted SPV that is an investment company will be "investment securities" within the meaning of section 3(a)(1)(C) of the Act. These securities will be counted in determining whether more than 40 percent of the value of the *assets of the holding company* consist of "investment securities." If they do, the holding company itself will become an investment company. A bank and an insurance company are excepted from the definition of an investment company, but other companies might not be.

The second issue that arises with respect to the status of exempted SPVs as investment companies is whether the SPVs' securities are subject to the provisions of section 12(d) of the 1940 Act. That section limits the holdings of investment companies in other investment companies' securities. Thus, if exempt SPVs are investment companies, the limitations of section 12(d) apply to investment companies that hold such SPV securities. Otherwise, they may hold investment companies' securities as well as create a pyramid of SPVs that hold *tranches* of other SPVs.

B. Exemption of SPVs Under the Advisers Act of 1940[742]

Advisers Act of 1940. With securitization and the development of Markets for loans came offers of advisory services to traders in loans and SPV securities. These activities may trigger application of the Investment Advisers Act of 1940 (the "Advisers Act"). A person who, for compensation, advises others with respect to SPV securities may be subject to the Advisers Act, unless the person is excepted from the definition of an investment adviser or exempted from the application of the Act. The Advisers Act requires investment advisers to register with the SEC. Registered advisers must file periodic reports with the SEC and comply with the

[741] 1 TAMAR FRANKEL, SECURITIZATION § 11.32 F (Ann Taylor Schwing ed., 2d ed. 2005).

[742] 1 TAMAR FRANKEL, SECURITIZATION § 13.7 B (Ann Taylor Schwing ed., 2d ed. 2005)..

Act's regulation of the measure of advisory fees, and the antifraud provisions of the Act.

In the context of SPVs and their securities, the main issue involving the Advisers Act concerns the applicability of the Act. Section 202(a)(11) of the Advisers Act defines an investment adviser as "any person who, for compensation, engages in the business of advising others, either directly or through publications or writings, as to the value of securities or as to the advisability of investing in, purchasing, or selling securities, or who, for compensation and as part of a regular business, issues or promulgates analyses or reports concerning securities."[743] In the opinion of the SEC staff, a person does not give advice and is not an adviser subject to the Advisers Act if the person only provides information about the availability of loans and their terms, without sponsoring, screening, analyzing, or recommending the loans, leaving those decisions to the investors or their representatives. Under the Act, an adviser is a person who gives advice with respect to securities. Investment advice on other kinds of property does not fall under the Advisers Act. If portfolio loans held by SPVs and SPV obligations are not securities, a person giving advice with respect to them is not an investment adviser under the Advisers Act.

The status of SPV portfolio loans and SPV securities under the Advisers Act has not been determined by the courts. The view of the SEC staff is that these instruments are securities. The definition of a security in the Advisers Act is identical to the definition of a security under the 1940 Act, and the staff has opined that SPV securities are securities in the context of the 1940 Act. The staff has granted a no-action letter to an SPV sponsor that organized limited partnerships that sold "convertible loans," based on the opinion of counsel that the loans were not securities. Similarly, in connection with loan participations, though there were no cases on point, the staff has granted no-action letters to non-bank advisers in unique cases, without conceding that the participations are not securities under the Advisers Act. With the elimination of the Glass-Steagall Act and the imposition of the Advisers Act on banks the issue has lost much of its importance.

Section 202(a)(11) of the Advisers Act contains a number of exceptions from the definition of an investment adviser. Effective May 2001, one exception is for a bank, or any bank holding company as defined in the Bank Holding Company Act of 1956 which is not an investment company. There is an exception to this definition. The term "investment adviser" includes any bank or bank holding company to the extent that the bank or bank holding company serves or acts as an investment adviser to a registered investment company. But if, in the case of a bank, such services are performed through a separately identifiable department or division, the department or division, and not the bank itself, shall be deemed to be the investment adviser.

---

[743] 15 U.S.C. § 80b-2(a)(11) (2006).

Before May 2001, the Act excepted any bank or bank holding company that was not an investment company. In addition, section 202(a)(11)(C) excepts from the definition of an investment adviser "any broker or dealer whose performance of such services is solely incidental to the conduct of his business . . . and who receives no special compensation therefor." Therefore, an SPV sponsor is not an investment adviser solely by engaging in the sale of SPV securities. The SPV sponsor is normally a broker or dealer, and the exemption in section 202(a)(11)(C) applies.

The staff of the SEC also took a no-action position with respect to the activities of a general partner in a limited partnership that issued "convertible loans." These loans were in fact composed of two transactions: a loan secured by real estate and an option to acquire a fee interest in the real estate. It was not contemplated that the loans and options would be transferred or that interests will be created in them. The efforts by a general or limited partner to sell partnership interests were not deemed advice, so long as advice was not given for compensation.

With respect to a general partner of an SPV organized as a limited partnership, the staff has followed its traditional position. In the staff's view, a general partner that merely manages the partnership is not an investment adviser to the limited partners. However, if "the general partner . . . offer[s] to provide advice for compensation about investing either in securities in general or in limited partnership interests offered by the limited partnerships, then the general partner would be an investment adviser."[744]

Another exception in section 202(a)(11) applies to "any person whose advice, analyses, or reports relate to no securities other than securities which are direct obligations of or obligations guaranteed as to principal or interest by the United States, or securities issued or guaranteed by corporations in which the United States has a direct or indirect interest which shall have been designated by the Secretary of the Treasury, pursuant to section 3(a)(12) of the Securities Exchange Act of 1934 . . . as exempted securities for the purposes of that Act."[745]

In contrast to the 1934 Act, which does not exempt from its definition of a broker-dealer any person who deals in exempt securities as defined in section 3(a)(12) of that Act, the Advisers Act excepts from the definition of an investment adviser any person who advises on exempt securities. However, exempt securities under the 1934 Act include securities exempt by the SEC Rules, whereas exempt securities in the Advisers Act are limited to "[i] direct obligations of or obligations guaranteed as to principal or interest by the United States, or [ii] guaranteed by corporations in which

---

[744] Coldwell Banker Comm. Group, Inc., Corres. (Jan. 12, 1982).

[745] 15 U.S.C. § 80b-2(a)(11)(E) (2006) (citing 15 U.S.C. § 78c(a)(12) (2006)).

the United States has a direct or indirect interest which shall have been designated by the Secretary of the Treasury" pursuant to section 3(a)(12) of the 1934 Act.[746]

Thus, persons who advise on mortgages loans guaranteed by GNMA, FNMA, and FHLMC are excepted from the definition of an investment adviser. Persons who advise on other securities exempt under the 1934 Act are not excluded from the definition of an investment adviser under section 202(a)(11)(E) of the Advisers Act.

C. Accounting Issues

a. Valuation of Assets

A company's balance sheet, which lists its assets and liabilities, reflect the company's financial position at a given time.[747] An income statement, in contrast, lists a company's revenues and expenses, measuring its performance "over a particular period of time." In a balance sheet items are "translated" into numbers. To determine the dollar amount indicated on the balance sheet for an item, one of several valuation bases is used.

Present value is used to value an asset that consists of predictable cash flows; i.e., a note receivable from another entity stating that the other entity will pay a specified amount at specified future points in time. Present value of this item is determined by discounting the amount expected in the future; i.e., determining what amount today would result in the future cash flows if invested at the stated interest rate for the stated time periods.[748] Market value is used to value items where such value is objectively determinable; i.e., equity securities listed on stock exchanges.[749]
Original cost is used to value other items.[750]

Why do we need valuations rules? First, valuation rules are important to establish standard values. Like all standards, the rules help compare assets and provide more accurate information. Thus, "[i]nformation about fair value better enables investors, creditors, and other users to assess the consequences of an entity's investment and financing strategies, that is, to assess its performance."[751]

---

[746] 15 U.S.C. § 80b-2(a)(11)(E) (2006).

[747] JAMIE PRATT, FINANCIAL ACCOUNTING IN AN ECONOMIC CONTEXT 11 (7th ed. 2009).

[748] *Id.* at 84-85; *see id.* app. A at 668-71 (illustrating computation of present value).

[749] JAMIE PRATT, FINANCIAL ACCOUNTING IN AN ECONOMIC CONTEXT 85 (7th ed. 2009).

[750] *Id.* at 86. Original cost may be modified by depreciation or amortization. *Id.*

[751] DISCLOSURES ABOUT FAIR VALUE OF FINANCIAL INSTRUMENTS, Statement of Fin. Accounting Standards No. 107. § 41 (Fin. Accounting Standards Bd. 1991) (superseded 2009).

Second, valuation offers transparency. "The [FASB] Board concluded that information about fair value of financial instruments meets the first objective of financial reporting stated in FASB Concepts Statement No. 1, Objectives of Financial Reporting by Business Enterprises, that is, to provide information that is useful to present and potential investors, creditors, and other users in making rational investment, credit, and similar decisions."[752] "Periodic information about the fair value of an entity's financial instruments under current conditions and expectations should help those users both in making their own predictions and in confirming or correcting their earlier expectations."[753]

Third, market value of financial instruments is useful as an indicator of the solvency of financial institutions. "For example, a report issued by the U.S. Department of the Treasury in February 1991: Modernizing the Financial System, discusses the possible advantages of market value information for regulatory supervision of financial institutions." [754] It is in the interest of government to tell banks how to value their financial assets for disclosure and regulation.

Fourth, valuation of banks' capital is crucial to ensuring the banks' ability to pay their depositors. Banks are institutional intermediaries. Their structure poses the risk of mismatch between their obligations to depositors and their cash on hand, which includes long-term loans. Bank depositors do not demand their money all at once. Nonetheless, to cover this mismatch regulation impose on banks capital requirements as a cushion to higher than expected depositors' demands, and ensures confidence in the banking system. In addition to capital reserves, confidence in banks is supported by Federal Reserve's short-term lending, and FDIC insurance for deposits.

Reg. D of the Federal Reserve Board's Regulation governs the banks' deposit reserve requirements.[755] Reserve requirements were originally adopted in State and national banking systems as a liquidity measure to counter deposit drains or note-conversions and thus protect bank depositors and investors. This objective, however, no longer receives much attention. Banks are provided emergency liquidity and public confidence though the Federal Reserve's monetary policy and lender of last resort roles and through the deposit insurance system. Moreover, by themselves, required reserves provide little support for depositors. Deposits are only partially backed by reserves under our fractional reserve system, and many types of deposits no longer carry reserve requirements. Consequently, reserve requirements are now

---

752 *Id.* § 39.

753 *Id.* § 40.

754 *Id.* § 42.

755 12 C.F.R. pt. 204 (2009).

viewed mainly as a tool of monetary policy.[756] Yet, they support investor confidence as well, although not as strongly as FDIC insurance.

Valuation Issues are Difficult. A simple fixed valuation rule would be the cost of an asset. However, the cost could be unrealistic if the valuation aims at determining how much money could be fetched by selling the asset at a later date. Land bought in the middle of the city 50 years ago could be worth far more today, unless the city has been abandoned, in which case the land would be worth far less. Thus, to create a more realistic valuation, regulation has moved from cost to market valuation. If the current market is irrelevant because there is no intention to sell the asset at the current market, then the valuation of an asset represents the current market valuation based on the probability of expected return to reach, discounted by time.[757]

There are Various Valuation Methods. For tradable securities and "marketable equity securities held for investment purposes," "fair values are based on quoted market prices or dealer quotes. For other securities held as investments, fair value equals quoted market price, if available. If a quoted market price is not available, fair value is estimated using quoted market prices for similar securities."[758] Securities must be valued in good faith.[759] A board of directors must establish adequate policies and procedures to determine the value of the corporation's assets.[760] Valuation by the board cannot be fully delegated. "While mutual fund directors are permitted to delegate some responsibility for pricing a fund's securities to a separate committee,

---

[756] KENNETH SPONG, BANKING REGULATION: ITS PURPOSES, IMPLEMENTATION, AND EFFECTS 105-06 (5th ed. 2000).

[757] See § 2(a)(41) of Investment Company Act of 1940, 15 U.S.C. § 80a-2(a)(41) (2006). Thus, if there is market price, directors of investment companies must follow the market price. If, however, there is no market price then the valuation, must follow a fair price..

[758] DISCLOSURES ABOUT FAIR VALUE OF FINANCIAL INSTRUMENTS, Statement of Fin. Accounting Standards No. 107. § 31 (Fin. Accounting Standards Bd. 1991) (superseded 2009), *codified at* Financial Accounting Standards Board, Accounting Standards Codification, topic 825, subtopic 10, § 55, ¶ 55-3, http://asc.fasb.org (last visited July 25, 2009).

[759] Accounting for Investment Securities by Registered Investment Companies, IC-6295, Accounting Series Release No. 118, 1970 SEC LEXIS 668, at *6 (Dec. 23, 1970).

[760] John N. Ake & Martha J. Hays, *Regulatory and Accounting Standards on the Valuation of Portfolio Securities by Investment Companies,* WALL ST. LAW., Jan. 2007, at 1, 7, http://www.ballardspahr.com/files/tbl_s11Newsletters/PDFFile142/913/01_2007_WSL%20Article%20-%20Ake_Hays.pdf (last accessed Sept. 28, 2009) (citing 17 C.F.R. § 270.38a-1 (2009); Compliance Programs of Investment Companies and Investment Advisers, IC-26299 (Dec. 17, 2003), 68 Fed. Reg. 74,714, 74,718 (Dec. 24, 2003)); *id.* (citing *In re* Parnassus Investments, Adm. Proc. Initial Decisions Rel. No. 131, 1998 SEC LEXIS 1877, at * (Sept. 3, 1998)) ("Administrative Law Judge found that the Board's valuation methods did not meet the standards required under ASR 113 and 118, and that the determinations made by the Board of the fair value of the Margaux convertible bond were not made in good faith"); *id.*at 8 (citing *In re* Western Asset Mgmt. Co., IA-1980, 2001 SEC LEXIS 2042 (Sept. 28, 2001)) ("The SEC found that Western failed to have adequate policies and procedures in place to ensure the funds in question were priced in compliance with the fund's offering documents").

each director retains responsibility to be involved in the valuation process and may not passively rely on securities valuations provided by such a committee"[761] The board of directors is responsible for valuing securities fairly but there is no single standard for making this determination.[762]

In the years 2008 and 2009 the market value of bank assets fell dramatically. William Isaac, former Chairman of the FDIC, noted that "mark-to-market accounting has destroyed $600 billion of capital in the banking industry, which is $6 trillion of lending capacity. And it's been a major, major cause of the crisis we're in."[763] Under the Emergency Economic Stabilization Act of 2008[764] (the "Bailout Act") the SEC was authorized to suspend mark-to-market valuation for any issuer or class of transaction and required to study the impact of mark-to-market's impact on the financial system.[765] In December of 2008 the SEC issued a report concluding that mark-to-market accounting did not cause the U.S. bank failures in 2008. The SEC recommended that the mark-to-market accounting should be maintained[766] as a mechanism that enhances transparency and facilitates good investments. In February 2009, FASB produced guidelines on mark-to-market valuations when the markets

---

761 *In re* Hammes, IC- 26290, 2003 SEC LEXIS 2918, at *22 (Dec. 11, 2003).

762 Factors identified that should be considered in a good faith evaluation include: "1) the fundamental analytical data relating to the investment, 2) the nature and duration of restrictions on disposition of the securities, and 3) an evaluation of the forces which influence the market in which these securities are purchased and sold." More specific factors include: "type of security, financial statements, cost at date of purchase, size of holding, discount from market value of unrestricted securities of the same class at time of purchase, special reports prepared by analysts, information as to any transactions or offers with respect to the security, existence of merger proposals or tender offers affecting the security, price and extent of public trading in similar securities of the issuer or comparable companies, and other relevant matters."Accounting for Investment Securities by Registered Investment Companies, IC-6295, Accounting Series Release No. 118, 1970 SEC LEXIS 668, at *12 (Dec. 23, 1970) (quoted in *In re* Parnassus Investments, Adm. Proc. Initial Decisions Rel. No. 31, 1998 SEC LEXIS 1877, at *40-41 (Sept. 3, 1998)).

763 *As Banking Woes Grow, Debate over Nationalization Increases,* Interview by Judy Woodruff with William Isaac, Chairman, Secura Group (Feb. 24, 2009), *available at* http://www.pbs.org/newshour/bb/business/jan-june09/banknational_02-24.html (last visited Sept. 28, 2009).

764 Pub. L. No. 110-343, 122 Stat. 3765 (2008) (to be codified as amended at 12 U.S.C. §§ 5201-5241).

765 Pub. L. No. 110-343, §§ 132-133, 122 Stat. 3765, 3798 (to be codified at 12 U.S.C. §§ 5237-5238).

766 OFFICE OF THE CHIEF ACCOUNTANT AND DIVISION OF CORPORATE FINANCE, U.S. SECURITIES AND EXCHANGE COMMISSION, REPORT AND RECOMMENDATIONS PURSUANT TO SECTION 133 OF THE EMERGENCY ECONOMIC STABILIZATION ACT OF 2008: STUDY ON MARK-TO-MARKET ACCOUNTING (2008), *available at* http://www.sec.gov/news/studies/2008/marktomarket123008.pdf (last visited Sept. 28, 2009).

are in disarray.[767] Congress, however, pressed the agencies to amend the FASB rule[768] notwithstanding the emphasis of SEC and FASB on transparency.[769] Congress threatened to act.[770] Thus, in April, 2009, FASB issued new staff positions,[771] which made three changes to mark-to-market accounting. First, FASB Staff Position FAS 157-4 requires companies to estimate fair value based on their "judgment" during inactive markets, but the judgments must incorporate market-based information.[772] This change gave banks some flexibility and avoided valuations based on other distressed transactions. It allowed factoring in historical data and cash flows, and controlled to some extent the continuing depreciating valuations.

---

[767] News Release, FASB, FASB Initiates Projects to Improve Measurement and Disclosure of Fair Value Estimates (Feb. 18, 2009), *available at* http://www.fasb.org/news/nr021809.shtml (last visited Sept. 28, 2009).

[768] *Mark-to-Market Accounting: Practices and Implications: Hearing Before the Subcomm. on Capital Markets, Insurance and Government Sponsored Enterprises of the H. Comm. on Financial Services* (.2009) (testimony by Robert H. Herz, Chairman, Financial Accounting Standards Board), noting Chairman Bernanke's prior testimony that "the basic idea of mark-to-market accounting is very attractive, the idea that wherever there are market values determined in free exchange, that those market values should be used in valuing assets so that investors would have a more accurate sense of what the institution is worth. So that's the principle and it's a good principle in general." [There are "some real challenges there and I think the accounting authorities have a great deal of work to do to try to figure out how to deal with some of these assets, which are not traded in liquid markets. But I don't see a suspension of the whole system as being constructive because there is a great deal of information in valuing many of these assets according to market principles."

[769] *Mark-to-Market Accounting: Practices and Implications: Hearing Before the Subcomm. on Capital Markets, Insurance and Government Sponsored Enterprises of the H. Comm. on Financial Services* (.2009) (testimony by Robert H. Herz, Chairman, Financial Accounting Standards Board).

[770] *Mark-to-Market Accounting: Practices and Implications: Hearing Before the Subcomm. on Capital Markets, Insurance and Government Sponsored Enterprises of the H. Comm. on Financial Services* (Mar.2009) (statement of Rep. Kanjorski, Chairman, Subcomm. on Capital Markets Insurance and Government Sponsored Enterprises).

[771] News Release, FASB, FASB Affirms Original Principles of Fair Value (aka Mark-to-Market) Accounting and Requires More Disclosures. Board Calls for Changes in Accounting Impairments (Apr. 9, 2009), *available at* http://www.fasb.org/news/040209_fv_and_otti_fsp.shtml (last visited Sept. 28, 2009).

[772] DETERMINING FAIR VALUE WHEN THE VOLUME AND LEVEL OF ACTIVITY FOR THE ASSET OR LIABILITY HAVE SIGNIFICANTLY DECREASED AND IDENTIFYING TRANSACTIONS THAT ARE NOT ORDERLY, FASB Staff Position No. FAS 157-4 § A1(Fin. Accounting Standards Bd. 2009) (amending FAIR VALUE MEASUREMENTS, Statement of Financial Accounting Standards No. 157, § ¶29D (Fin. Accounting Standards Bd. 2006) (superseded 2009)), *codified at* Financial Accounting Standards Board, Accounting Standards Codification, topic 820, subtopic 10, § 35, ¶ 35-51D, http://asc.fasb.org (last visited July 25, 2009).

Second, FASB Staff Position FAS 107-1 requires quarterly, instead of annual, disclosures of the fair values of all assets that are listed on an institution's balance sheet at non-market values.[773] Hopefully, this change balanced for investors the banks' increased flexibility, and offered investors more information in order to value an institution with greater precision, even as the investors do not fully trust its balance sheet.

Third, FASB Staff Position FAS 115-2 and FAS 124-2 expand the discretion of institutions in determining when an asset has permanently (not temporarily) depreciated,[774] and relieve financial institutions holding mortgage-backed securities. Institutions will not have to mark to market debt securities which they do not intend to sell and are likely to sell only after they recovered their cost basis. An institution is deemed unable to recover its basis if the present value of the cash flows expected from the securities is less than their basis, in which case the securities are marked down (i.e., the impairment is recognized).[775] In addition, the staff position changes the statement of earnings presentation for such impairments. In the instance above in which the impairment is recognized solely because of the credit loss, only the credit loss is recognized in earnings and any other amount of the impairment is recognized in 'other comprehensive income."[776]

---

[773] INTERIM DISCLOSURES ABOUT FAIR VALUE OF FINANCIAL INSTRUMENTS, FASB Staff Position No. FAS 107-1, §A1 b. (Fin. Accounting Standards Bd. 2009) (requiring fair value disclosure) (amending DISCLOSURES ABOUT FAIR VALUE OF FINANCIAL INSTRUMENTS, Statement of Fin.l Accounting Standards No. 107, § 10 (Fin. Accounting Standards Bd. 2006) (superseded 2009), *codified at* Financial Accounting Standards Board, Accounting Standards Codification, topic 825, subtopic 10, § 50, ¶ 50-10 (requiring fair value disclosure), http://asc.fasb.org (last visited July 25, 2009)); *id.* § A1 a. (amending Disclosures About Fair Value of Financial Instruments, Statement of Financial Accounting Standards No. 107, § 7 (Fin. Accounting Standards Bd. 2006) (superseded 2009)), *codified at* Financial Accounting Standards Board, Accounting Standards Codification, topic 820, subtopic 10, ¶¶ 50-2a, -3, -8 (applying requirement generally to publicly traded companies), http://asc.fasb.org (last visited July 25, 2009).

[774] RECOGNITION AND PRESENTATION OF OTHER-THAN-TEMPORARY IMPAIRMENTS, FASB Staff Position No. FAS 115-2, 124-2 (Fin. Accounting Standards Bd, 2009),

[775] *Id.* ¶¶ 19-26; Steve Burkholder, *Fair Value: Mainly Praise for FASB's Fair Value Guidance; Continued Doubts, Criticism of OTTI Changes*, 92 Banking Rep. (BNA) 862, 862 (Apr. 14, 2009).

[776] RECOGNITION AND PRESENTATION OF OTHER-THAN-TEMPORARY IMPAIRMENTS, FASB Staff Position No. FAS 115-2, 124-2, ¶¶ 27-31 (Fin. Accounting Standards Bd, 2009); Steve Burkholder, *Fair Value: Mainly Praise for FASB's Fair Value Guidance; Continued Doubts, Criticism of OTTI Changes*, 92 Banking Rep. (BNA) 862, 862 (Apr. 14, 2009).

The new rules offer a number of advantages. Accounting practices must reflect economic situation. Whether market prices reflect economic reality is a question either when the markets "bubble" or when they crash.[777] Hopefully the new staff interpretation allows valuation by fair value, and offers more disclosures. These help control possible bank manipulation of their financial statements. While the bubble allowed banks to show unrealistic values, a crash might require them to show unrealistic value as well. Banks might be unable to sell performing loans.[778] The asset values of loans include future cash flows. If they are not known, the market price of these loans may be lower than their actual future value. Low asset values may affect the trust in healthy banks. Market valuation may distort the value of banks in the case of bubbles as well as crashes, and induce liquidity when it should not be offered.[779]

The new rules are not without disadvantages. Arguably the rules might enable banks to manipulate their asset numbers.[780] Standard & Poor's was concerned that standardization will be undermined,[781] while a strict mark-to-market valuation may be more efficient, in predicting future price movements.[782] Two members of the FASB dissented from the rules changes, highlighting their concern that banks will fail to recognize their true financial losses.[783]

---

[777] Steve Burkholder, *Fair Value: FASB Clears Guidance on Fair Value, Securities Impairments; Effective 2nd Quarter*, 92 Banking Rep. (BNA) 781, 781 (Apr. 7, 2009).

[778] *Planet Money: Hear – Accounting Rules* (NPR radio broadcast Apr. 3, 2009), *available at* http://www.npr.org/blogs/money/2009/04/hear_accounting_rules.html (last visited Sept. 29, 2009).

[779] *Systemic Risk: Are Some Institutions Too Big to Fail and If So, What Should We Do About It?: Hearing Before the H. Comm. on Financial Services,* 111th Cong., LEXIS, News Library, Curnws File (statement of Peter J. Wallison, Arthur F. Burns Fellow in Financial Policy Studies, American Enterprise Institute).

[780] Heather Landy, *FASB Rules Changes: Weighing Who Gains*, AM. BANKER, Apr. 3, 2009, at 1, LEXIS, News Library, Curnws File (in the opinion of SEC Chairmen William H. Donaldson and Arthur Levitt Jr. the changes will cause "an increase in capital costs, erosion of investor confidence and ultimately a disruption of the markets").

[781] Matthew Monks, *S&P Cites Flaw in Fair-Value Changes*, AM. BANKER, Apr. 9, 2009. At 2, LEXIS, News Library, Curnws File. *See also* Malini Manickavasagam, *Economic Policy: Goldman's Blankfein Says More Companies Should Have Observed Fair Value Accounting*, 92 Banking Rep. (BNA) 868 (Apr. 14, 2009).

[782] *See, e.g.*, Peter Schiff, *Let's Play Pretend!*, LEWROCKWELL.COM, Apr. 5, 2009, http://www.lewrockwell.com/schiff/schiff13.html (last visited Sept. 29, 2009).

[783] Steve Burkholder, *Fair Value: Mainly Praise for FASB's Fair Value Guidance; Continued Doubts, Criticism of OTTI Changes*, 92 Banking Rep. (BNA) 862, 863 (Apr. 14, 2009) (delays in recognizing losses have induced length and cost of the savings and loan crisis).

Discussion Topics

1. What is the possible effect of the changes in valuation of bank assets?
2. When, do you think, institutions would use the freedom afforded them by the changes? Sooner as permitted or later when required?[784]
3. What effect will the changed rules have on conservative banks who will not take advantage of the change, or their conservative accountants?
4. What clarifications are necessary with respect to the new changes?[785] Other than that, it seems unlikely that the SEC will act to make further changes to mark-to-market accounting rules.
5. Do you think that the new changes will have an effect? Note that Chief Executive James Dimon asserted that JPMorgan Chase applied the new accounting rules in the first quarter, and "it had no impact. The whole thing was a big hullaboo about nothing, in my opinion." But Wells Fargo & Co. reported that the new rules reduced losses[786] FDIC's predictions were to the contrary.[787]
6. How would you propose to reform the system and counter both bubbles and crashes? Should we examine first the function of capital in banks? What is the function of bank capital?

---

[784] News Release, FASB, FASB Issues Final Staff Positions to Improve Guidance and Disclosures on Fair Value Measurement (Apr. 9, 2009), *available at* http://www.fasb.org/news/nr040909.shtml (last visited Sept. 29, 2009)..

[785] Malini Manickavasagam, *Economic Policy: Goldman's Blankfein Says More Companies Should Have Observed Fair Value Accounting*, 92 Banking Rep. (BNA) 868, 868 (Apr. 14, 2009) (the new SEC Chairman Mary Schapiro is contemplating how to go about clarifying what the new rules "mean[] and what [they don't] mean").

[786] Heather Landy, *Banks Claim Little Effect in Mark-to-Market Easing*, AM. BANKER, May 1, 2009, at 1, LEXIS, News Library, Curnws File.

[787] *See* News Release, FASB, FASB Affirms Original Principles of Fair Value (aka Mark-to-Market) Accounting and Requires More Disclosures. Board Calls for Changes in Accounting Impairments (Apr. 9, 2009), *available at* http://www.fasb.org/news/040209_fv_and_otti_fsp.shtml (last visited Sept. 29, 2009) (stating that objective of measuring fair value is the same, *i.e.,* to reflect sale price in orderly transaction; "[s]ome financial institutions . . . do not expect this proposal to significantly impact their financial statements"); Adam Lashinsky, *Why Warren Buffett's Berkshire Hathaway Owns Wells Fargo*, FORTUNE, Apr. 20, 2009.http://money.cnn.com/2009/04/19/news/companies/lashinsky_buffett.fortune/index.htm?postversion=2009042006 (last visited Sept. 29, 2009) (quoting Wells Fargo's largest shareholder Warren Buffett. stating that he does not think new Treasury capital requirements if imposed will hamper firm's earnings).

The revised FASB's staff position on determining fair value during a period of market inactivity suggests that federal regulators believe in the accuracy of alternative valuations of illiquid assets. If that is so, then the Federal Reserve Board can alleviate mark-to-market accounting's deleterious impact on banks by accepting those illiquid mortgage-backed assets as collateral against short-term window loans at the above-market values. Advantages of this plan include retaining the transparency of mark-to-market accounting and advancing the original goals of a capital cushion – it promotes confidence while simultaneously increasing liquidity.

Detractors may point to potential moral hazard, undesirable levels of government involvement in financing banks, and uncertainty over alternative methods of valuing illiquid assets. However, the same risks of moral hazard and government involvement adhere to deposit insurance and the knowledge that the FDIC will bail banks out by way of its depositors.

On a similar note, investor Warren Buffett recently referred to mark-to-market as "gasoline on the fire in terms of financial institutions," and proposed suspending mark-to-market accounting for regulatory capital purposes so that banks are not "forced to sell stock at ridiculously low prices."[788] Notably, Chairman Herz of FASB denied supporting the new staff positions for regulatory capital purposes, but rather emphasized that his job is to focus on the quality of financial reporting.[789] The recent FASB staff positions on mark-to-market valuation illustrate how the law responds to changes in the economic climate and how regulators seem to reflect congressional and banking industry signals, and investors' desire for transparency.

b. Accounting for a Sale of a Loan as Compared to Accounting for a Loan

The accounting treatment of a sale of a loan is fundamentally different from that of the lending --the creation of a loan. If the transaction is a sale of a loan or any other asset, the sold loan or asset is removed from the seller-transferor's balance sheet. Gain or loss of the seller is recorded if the fair value of the consideration the seller received for the sold asset differs from the carrying value of the asset. For example, if A has lent B $100, and sells B's loan to C for $100, then A, who carried B's loan for $100, will now carry the cash he received from C at $100, and record no gain or loss. If A sold the loan for $80, he will record a loss of $20 ($100-80). In contrast, if A borrowed $100 from C, and gave B's loan as a collateral, the transaction between A and C is not a sale of B's loan but a loan from C to A. B's loan which A offers as a collateral remains on the A—the borrower's--balance sheet, and the payment that A

[788] Holman W. Jenkins, Jr., Editorial, *Buffett's Unmentionable Bank Solution*, WALL ST. J., Mar. 11, 2009, at A13, LEXIS, News Library, Wsj File.

[789] Steve Burkholder, *Fair Value: FASB Clears Guidance on Fair Value, Securities Impairments; Effective 2nd Quarter*, 92 Banking Rep. (BNA) 781, 781 (Apr. 7, 2009).

received from C is recorded as a liability of A (with no loss or gain). C will remove $100 from his balance sheet as an asset and substitute for it the asset of A's IOU for $100. Thus, in some situations, the sale treatment may be more favorable to the seller of the loan, than if the seller borrowed the money and kept the loan.[790] The buyer of the loan, however, is unaffected by the different treatment because the entitlement created by the transaction (B's $100) and the cash transferred to A are treated the same in both situations. The entitlement to payment (either from B or from A) is added to the buyer's balance sheet and the payment to the seller or the borrower is deducted from the balance sheet.

In a clear and unambiguous sale, all rights and liabilities, benefits, risks, and control regarding the transferred asset are transferred from the seller to the buyer in exchange for consideration. There are, however, situations in which the seller retains some of these features and the classification of the transaction becomes an issue. The seller's retention of risks is usually represented as a right by the buyer to recourse from the seller. Thus, if A sold B's loan to C but promised C to repurchase B's loan under certain conditions, the seller may have some control over, or some obligation for, or other involvement with the asset (B's loan).

In securitization, the issue of classifying the transaction arises quite often because in many cases the sale is accompanied by a recourse provision. For example, a sale of loans can be accompanied by a collateral or other credit enhancement.[791] Yet, in a securitization transaction the seller often is interested in providing the buyers with a right of recourse. The right might reduce the interest that the buyer may demand and yet may be less expensive than credit enhancement (especially guarantee by a third party). Thus, as noted in connection with bankruptcy issues, the question of whether the transaction is a sale arises in the context of accounting as well.

c. The Two Accounting Systems

There are two closely related yet different accounting systems. One system is Generally Accepted Accounting Principles (GAAP). GAAP is disclosure-oriented, aimed at providing the readers with information about the reporting enterprise. The other system is Regulatory Accounting Principles (RAP). RAP is a regulatory tool and was formerly used, in addition to GAAP's reports for disclosure, in reporting to regulators. By classifying sales more restrictively through RAP, bank regulators could provide banks with incentive to act in certain ways (e.g., to refrain from

---

[790] *See* JAMES A. ROSENTHAL & JUAN M. OCAMPO, SECURITIZATION OF CREDIT 66 (1988); CHRISTINE A.. PAVEL, SECURITIZATION 167 n.4 (1989) (however, the loan treatment may be more favorable "[i]f it is important to the issuer to retain the tax benefits of the assets).

[791] Financial Accounting Standards Board, Accounting Standards Codification, topic 860, subtopic 10, § 05, para. 05-4, http://asc.fasb.org (last visited July 26, 2009).

retaining risks of loans that the banks transfer). GAAP accounting is used in preparing annual reports and other financial statements, Most loan transferors must use GAAP to determine whether a sale of receivables with recourse is treated as a sale or a loan.[792] By and large, compliance with RAP meets the requirements of GAAP. In the past, banks and certain regulated Institutions were required to comply with both RAP and GAAP in preparing their annual reports.[793]

GAAP. Under the Transfers and Servicing Topic of the Accounting Standards Codification (Topic 860),[794] which governs transfers of financial assets,[795] a transfer of financial assets, "in which the transferor surrenders control,"[796], is treated as a sale. The transferor surrenders control if three conditions are met. Generally, (1) the assets must be isolated from the transferor, i.e., put beyond its reach and that of its creditors; (2) the transferee must have the right to pledge or exchange the assets; and (3) the transferor may not maintain effective control over the assets, i.e., through an agreement that requires the transferor to repurchase or redeem them, or through the ability to require their return.

"Isolation" Test. First, the assets must be "isolated from the transferor—put presumptively beyond the reach of the transferor and its creditors, even in bankruptcy or other receivership."[797] This determination depends on facts and circumstances, including "whether the contract or circumstances permit the transferor to revoke the transfer" and "may include making judgments about the kind of bankruptcy or other receivership into which a transferor or SPE might be placed, whether a transfer of financial assets would likely be deemed a true sale at law, whether the transferor is affiliated with the transferee, and other factors pertinent under applicable." The transferor may derecognize the assets if there is "reasonable assurance" that they "would be beyond the reach of the powers of a bankruptcy

---

[792] If the transaction is a sale, the originator may enjoy cost savings and improve its financial ratios, such as the debt-equity ratio.

[793] Among other things, RAP differs from GAAP with respect to the treatment of the sale of receivables with recourse.

[794] Financial Accounting Standards Board, Accounting Standards Codification, topic 860, subtopic 10, § 05, ¶ 05-7, http://asc.fasb.org (last visited July 26, 2009) (sales of receivables with recourse are governed by Topic)..

[795] *Id.* ¶¶ 05-1, -3; ACCOUNTING FOR TRANSFERS AND SERVICING OF FINANCIAL ASSETS AND EXTINGUISHMENT OF LIABILITIES, Statement of Financial Accounting Standards No. 140, ¶ 73 (Fin. Accounting Standards Bd. 2000) (superseded 2009) (predecessor of Topic did not cover securitizations of nonfinancial assets).

[796] Financial Accounting Standards Board, Accounting Standards Codification, topic 860, subtopic 10, § 40, ¶ 40-4, http://asc.fasb.org (last visited July 26, 2009)

[797] *Id.* ¶ 40-5 a.

trustee or other receiver for the transferor or any consolidated affiliate of the transferor that is not a special-purpose corporation or other entity designed to make remote the possibility that it would enter bankruptcy or other receivership."[798]

In a securitization, isolation "may depend on such factors as whether the securitization is accomplished in one step or two steps."[799] Topic 860 provides guidance on how to implement isolation in securitizations. Isolation in securitization "depends on the structure of the securitization transaction taken as a whole, considering such factors as the type and extent of further involvement in arrangements to protect investors from credit and interest rate risks, the availability of other assets, and the powers of bankruptcy courts or other receivers."[800]

Isolation will usually be found in a securitization involving a transfer of "financial assets to a special-purpose trust in exchange for cash," which trust "raises that cash by issuing to investors beneficial interests that pass through all cash received from the financial assets, and the transferor has no further involvement with the trust or the transferred assets." [801]

Isolation is found in a "single-step" securitization in which the financial assets are transferred "to [an SPE] in exchange for cash and beneficial interests in the transferred assets." Here the SPE "raises the cash by issuing to investors commercial paper that gives them a senior interest in cash received from the financial assets." The transferor's beneficial interests "represent a junior interest to be reduced by any credit losses on the financial assets in trust." The commercial paper is "highly rated by credit rating agencies only if both (a) the credit enhancement from the junior interest is sufficient and (b) the transferor is highly rated." [802] "Depending on facts and circumstances," the transfer in such securitizations "often" may not meet the isolation requirement because the transferor's continuing involvement may prevent the assets from being beyond the reach of the creditor and its creditors for bankruptcy purposes.[803]

A "two-step" securitization is a process in which the assets are first transferred "to a special-purpose corporation that, although wholly owned, is so designed that the possibility that the transferor or its creditors could reclaim the assets is remote." This

---

[798] *Id.* ¶ 40-8.

[799] *Id.* ¶ 40-13.

[800] Topic 860. *Id.*

[801] *Id.* ¶ 55-19.

[802] *Id.* ¶ 55-20.

[803] *Id.* ¶ 55-21.

transfer is "likely" to meet the isolation requirement "in part because the transferor does not provide 'excessive' credit or yield protection to the special-purpose corporation."[804] In the second step, "the special-purpose corporation transfers the assets to a trust or other legal vehicle with a sufficient increase in the credit or yield protection on the second transfer (provided by a junior beneficial interest that continues to be held by the transferor or other means) to merit the high credit rating sought by third-party investors who buy senior beneficial interests in the trust." In theory, this step may not meet the isolation requirement.[805] However, "the special-purpose corporation is designed to make remote the possibility that it would enter bankruptcy, either by itself or by substantive consolidation into a bankruptcy of its parent." "For example, its charter forbids it from undertaking any other business or incurring any liabilities, so that there can be no creditors to petition to place it in bankruptcy," and further, "its dedication to a single purpose is intended to make it extremely unlikely, even if it somehow entered bankruptcy," that the transferred assets could be reclaimed by a receiver in bankruptcy "because [the special-purpose corporation] has no other assets to substitute for the transferred assets."[806] Such two-step securitizations, "taken as a whole," would generally meet the isolation requirement.[807]

Because the powers of receivers for entities not subject to the Bankruptcy Code (e.g., banks) vary, the powers of appropriate receivers, in the United States or other jurisdictions, must be considered in determining whether the isolation requirement is met. The requirement may be met "by only one transfer directly to [an SPE] that issues beneficial interests to investors and the transferor provides credit or yield protection" if a receiver could not reach the assets.[808]

"Pledge or Exchange" Test. The second requirement in determining if there is a surrender of control is:

> [e]ach transferee (or, if the transferee is a qualifying [SPE][809] . . . , each holder of its beneficial interests) has the right to pledge or exchange the assets (or beneficial interests) it received [, and] [n]o condition both constrains the transferee (or holder) from taking

---

[804] Topic 860. *Id.* ¶ 55-23 a.

[805] *Id.* ¶ 55-23 b.

[806] *Id.* ¶ 55-23 b.

[807] *Id.* ¶ 55-22.

[808] *Id.* ¶ 55-24.

[809] *See* Topic 860, *id.* subtopic 40, § 15, ¶ 15-3 (defining "qualifying SPE"); b. I. A. 1. of the text *infra* (discussing definition).

advantage of its right to pledge or exchange and provides more than a trivial benefit to the transferor . . . .[810]

Examples of conditions that negate the requirement include "[a] provision in the transfer contract that prohibits selling or pledging a transferred loan receivable" and "[t]ransferor-imposed contractual constraints that narrowly limit timing or terms, for example, allowing a transferee to pledge only on the day assets are obtained or only on terms agreed with the transferor."[811]

However, "[a] transferor's right of first refusal on the occurrence of a bona fide offer to the transferee from a third party" "presumptively would not constrain a transferee." Other examples that would not presumptively constrain a transferee include: (i) A requirement to obtain the transferor's permission to sell or pledge that is not to be unreasonably withheld; (ii) a prohibition on sale to the transferor's competitor if other potential willing buyers exist; (iii) a regulatory limitation such as on the number or nature of eligible transferees (as in the case of securities issued under Securities Act Rule 144A[812] or debt placed privately); (iv) illiquidity, for example, the absence of an active market[.][813] "Judgment is required to assess the significance of some conditions."[814]

"A condition imposed by a transferor that constrains the transferee presumptively provides more than a trivial benefit to the transferor. A condition not imposed by the transferor that constrains the transferee may or may not provide more than a trivial benefit to the transferor."[815] "However, the transferor cannot benefit from a constraint if it is unaware at the time of the transfer that the transferee is constrained."[816] Topic 860 also discusses the status of rights or obligations to reacquire transferred assets.[817]

---

[810] *Id.* subtopic 10, § 40, ¶ 40-5 b (footnote added).

[811] *Id.* ¶ 40-17 a., b.

[812] 17 C.F.R. § 230.144A (2008).

[813] Financial Accounting Standards Board, Accounting Standards Codification, topic 860, subtopic 10, § 40, ¶ 40-18, http://asc.fasb.org (last visited July 26, 2009) (footnote added).

[814] *Id.* ¶ 40-19.

[815] *Id.* ¶ 40-16. ("For example, if the transferor refrains from imposing its usual contractual constraint on a specific transfer because it knows an equivalent constraint is already imposed on the transferee by a third party, it presumptively benefits more than trivially from that constraint.").

[816] *Id.* ¶ 40-16.

[817] *Id.* ¶ 40-17 c. ("For example, a **freestanding call** option written by a transferee to the transferor . . . if the transferred assets are not readily obtainable in the marketplace" "is likely to" preclude sale status, as is "[a] freestanding forward purchase-sale contract between the transferor and the transferee on transferred assets not readily obtainable in the marketplace.") "Judgment is necessary to assess

The considerations discussed above regarding "conditions that may or may not constrain a transferee that is not a qualifying [SPE] from pledging or exchanging the transferred assets" also apply to "conditions that may or may not constrain a beneficial interest holder from pledging or exchanging its beneficial interests in assets transferred to a qualifying [SPE]."[818]

A qualifying SPE is defined as:

> a trust or other legal vehicle that meets all of the following criteria:
>
> a. . . . It is demonstrably distinct from the transferor. A qualifying [SPE] is demonstrably distinct from the transferor only if it cannot be unilaterally dissolved by any transferor, its affiliates, or its agents, and either
>
> (a) At least 10 percent of the fair value of its beneficial interests is held by parties other than any transferor, its affiliates, or its agents
>
> (b) The transfer is a guaranteed mortgage securitization.
>
> b. . . . Its permitted activities . . .
>
> (1) Are significantly limited
>
> (2) Were entirely specified in the legal documents that established the [SPE] or created the beneficial interests in the transferred assets that it holds [,and]
>
> (3) May be significantly changed only with the approval of the holders of at least a majority of the beneficial interests held by entities other than any transferor, its affiliates, and its agents . . . .
>
> c. . . . It may hold only . . . :
>
> (1) Financial assets transferred to it that are passive in nature . . .
>
> (2) Passive derivative financial instruments that pertain to beneficial interests issued or sold to parties other than the transferor, its affiliates, or its agents . . .
>
> (3) Financial assets (for example, guarantees or rights to collateral) that would reimburse it if others were to fail to

constraint and benefit." *Id.* ¶ 40-16. For example, "a put option on a not-readily-obtainable asset may benefit the transferor and effectively constrain the transferee if the option is sufficiently deep-in-the-money when it is written that it is probable that the transferee will exercise it and the transferor will reacquire the transferred asset." *Id.* ¶ 40-17 c. However, "[a] sufficiently out-of-the-money call option held by the transferor, if it is probable when the option is written that it will not be exercised [and] "[f]reestanding rights to reacquire transferred assets that are readily obtainable" "presumptively would not constrain a transferee." *Id.* ¶ 40-18.

[818] *Id.* ¶ 40-6. "For example, if beneficial interest holders agree to sell their beneficial interests in a qualifying [SPE] back to the transferor upon request at the price paid plus a stated return, . . . sale accounting for the transfer to the qualifying [SPE] would be precluded if that agreement constrained a beneficial interest holder from exchanging or pledging its beneficial interest." *Id.* ¶ 40-7.

adequately service financial assets transferred to it or to timely pay
obligations due to it and that it entered into when it was established, when assets were transferred to it, or when beneficial interests (other than derivative financial instruments) were issued by the [SPE]

(4) Servicing rights related to financial assets that it holds

(5) Temporarily, nonfinancial assets obtained in connection with the collection of financial assets that it holds . . .

(6) Cash collected from assets that it holds and investments purchased with that cash pending distribution to holders of beneficial interests that are appropriate for that purpose (that is, money-market or other relatively risk-free instruments without options and with maturities no later than the expected distribution date).

d. . . . If it can sell or otherwise dispose of noncash financial assets, it can do so only in automatic response to any one of the following conditions:

(1) Occurrence of an event or circumstance that has all of the following characteristics:

(i) is specified in the legal documents that established the [SPE] or created the beneficial interests in the transferred assets that it holds

(ii) is outside the control of the transferor, its affiliates, or its agents [and]

(iii) causes, or is expected at the date of transfer to cause, the fair value of those financial assets to decline by a specified degree below the fair value of those assets when the SPE obtained them . . .

(2) Exercise by a beneficial interest holder (other than the transferor, its affiliates, or its agents) of a right to put that holder's beneficial interest back to the [SPE] in exchange for any of the following:.

(i). A full or partial distribution of those assets

(ii) Cash (which may require that the [SPE] dispose of those assets or issue beneficial interests to generate cash to fund settlement of the put)

(iii). New beneficial interests in those assets.

(3) Exercise by the transferor of a call or ROAP [removal of accounts provision] specified in the legal documents that established the [SPE], transferred assets to the [SPE], or created the beneficial interests in the transferred assets that it holds . . .

> (4) Termination of the [SPE] or maturity of the beneficial interests in those financial assets on a fixed or determinable date that is specified at inception . . . .[819]

A qualifying SPE is not consolidated in the financial statements of the transferor or its affiliates, "unless the transferor holds more than 90 percent of the fair value of the beneficial interests or the transfer is a guaranteed mortgage securitization."[820]

"Demonstrably Distinct" Test. An SPE is "demonstrably distinct from the transferor" if: (1) "it cannot be unilaterally dissolved by any transferor, its affiliates, or its agents" and (2) either (a) "at least 10 percent of the fair value of its beneficial interests is held by parties other than any transferor, its affiliates, or its agents" or (b) "the transfer is a guaranteed mortgage securitization."[821] The ability to unilaterally dissolve an SPE may include "holding sufficient beneficial interests to demand that the trustee dissolve the [SPE], the right to call all the assets transferred to the [SPE], and a right to call or a prepayment privilege on the beneficial interests held by other parties."[822]

"Permitted Activities" Test. A "bank, insurance entity, pension plan, or investment company" cannot be a qualifying SPE as its powers cannot be limited to those allowed.[823] The beneficial interest holders (other than a transferor or its affiliates or agents) may have the ability to change the SPE's powers. If a qualifying SPE's powers change so that it is no longer qualifying, unless the SPE itself meets the pledge or exchange test and the other conditions for surrender of control are met, the transferred assets in the SPE return to the transferor's control.[824]

"Holdings" Test". "A financial asset or derivative financial instrument is passive only if holding the asset or instrument does not involve its holder in making

---

[819] *Id.* subtopic 40, § 15, ¶ 15-3.

[820] *Id.* § 45, ¶ 45-1.

[821] *Id.* § 15, ¶ 15-3. A "guaranteed mortgage securitization" is defined as "[a] securitization of mortgage loans that is within the scope of Topic 948 and includes a substantive guarantee by a third party." *Id.* § 20 Glossary. Consequently, "mortgage-backed securities that continue to be held by a transferor in a guaranteed mortgage securitization in which the [SPE] meets all conditions for being a qualifying [SPE] are classified in the financial statements of the transferor as securities that are subsequently measured under Topic 320." *Id.* § 45, ¶ 45-2.

[822] *Id.* § 15, ¶ 15-7.

[823] *Id.* ¶ 15-10.

[824] *Id.* § 25, ¶ 25-1.

decisions other than the decisions inherent in servicing. . . . Investments are not passive if through them, either in themselves or in combination with other investments or rights, the [SPE] or any related entity, such as the transferor, its affiliates, or its agents, is able to exercise control or significant influence (as defined in generally accepted accounting principles . . . for consolidation policy and for the equity method, respectively) over the investee. An equity instrument is not passive if the qualifying [SPE] can exercise the voting rights and is permitted to choose how to vote."[825]

> A derivative financial instrument pertains to beneficial interests issued only if it meets all of the following criteria:
>
> a. It is entered into in either of the following circumstances:
>
> 1. When the beneficial interests are issued by the qualifying [SPE] to parties other than the transferor, its affiliates, or its agents or sold to such other parties after being issued by the qualifying [SPE] to the transferor, its affiliates, or its agents
> 2. When a passive derivative financial instrument needs to be replaced upon occurrence of an event or circumstance (specified in the legal documents that established the [SPE] or created the beneficial interests in the transferred assets that it holds) outside the control of the transferor, its affiliates, or its agents, for example, when the counterparty to the derivative defaults or is downgraded below a specified threshold.
>
> b. It has a notional amount that does not initially exceed the amount of those beneficial interests and is not expected to exceed them subsequently.
>
> c. It has characteristics that relate to, and partly or fully but not excessively counteract, some risk associated with those beneficial interests or the related transferred assets.[826]

[825] *Id.* § 15, ¶ 15-14. For example, a derivative financial instrument is not passive if "it includes an option allowing the [SPE] to choose to call or put other financial instruments," but "interest rate caps and swaps and forward contracts" can be passive. "Derivative financial instruments that result in liabilities, like other liabilities of a qualifying [SPE], are a kind of beneficial interest in the qualifying [SPE's] assets." *Id.* ¶ 15-15.

[826] *Id.* ¶ 15-16. The category of nonfinancial assets held temporarily "obtained in connection with the collection of financial assets that it holds" may include "foreclosed nonfinancial collateral" but not "significant secured financial assets likely to default with the expectation that [the SPE] will foreclose on and profitably manage the securing nonfinancial assets." *Id.* ¶ 15-23. Iit may include "the residual value of a sales-type or a direct financing lease only to the extent that it is guaranteed at the inception of the lease either by the lessee or by a third party financially capable of discharging the obligations that may arise from the guarantee." *Id.* ¶ 15-24.

"Disposition" Test. Examples of permitted requirements to dispose of noncash assets "include requirements to dispose of transferred assets in response to:"

> a. A failure to properly service transferred assets that could result in the loss of a substantial third-party credit guarantee
> b. A default by the obligor
> c. A downgrade by a major rating agency of the transferred assets or of the underlying obligor to a rating below a specified minimum rating
> d. The involuntary insolvency of the transferor
> e. A decline in the fair value of the transferred assets to a specified value less than their fair value at the time they were transferred to the [SPE].[827]

Examples of prohibited powers or requirements to dispose of such assets include:

> a. A power that allows [an SPE] to choose to either dispose of transferred assets or hold them in response to a default, a downgrade, a decline in fair value, or a servicing failure
> b. A requirement to dispose of marketable equity securities upon a specified decline from their "highest fair value" if that power could result in disposing of the asset in exchange for an amount that is more than the fair value of those assets at the time they were transferred to the [SPE]
> c. A requirement to dispose of transferred assets in response to the violation of a nonsubstantive contractual provision (that is, a provision for which there is not a sufficiently large disincentive to ensure performance)
> d. Discretion by a transferor or servicer to select which loans to remove to reposition a portfolio.[828]

Permitted powers also include automatic disposal of noncash transferred assets in response to "the exercise by a beneficial interest holder (other than the transferor, its affiliates, or its agents) of a right to put [its] beneficial interests back to the [SPE] in exchange for:" (a) "[a] full or partial distribution of those assets"; (b) "[c]ash (which may require that the SPE dispose of those assets or issue beneficial interests to generate cash to fund settlement of the put)"; or (c) "[n]ew beneficial interests in those assets."[829]

---

[827] *Id.* ¶ 15-27.

[828] *Id.* ¶ 15-28.

[829] *Id.* ¶ 15-3.

In addition, the SPE "may have the power to dispose of assets to a party other than the transferor, its affiliate, or its agent on termination of the [SPE] or maturity of the beneficial interests, but only automatically on fixed or determinable dates that are specified at inception."[830]

"Effective Control" Test. The third requirement in determining if there is a surrender of control is that the transferor may not "maintain effective control over the transferred assets through either "[a]n agreement that both entitles and obligates the transferor to repurchase or redeem them before their maturity" or (2) [t]he ability to unilaterally cause the holder to return specific assets, other than through a cleanup call."[831]

An agreement maintains effective control (and causes the transaction to be accounted for as a secured borrowing) if: (a) "[t]he assets to be repurchased or redeemed are the same or substantially the same as those transferred"; (b) "[t]he transferor is able to repurchase or redeem them on substantially the agreed terms, even in the event of default by the transferee"; (c) "[t]he agreement is to repurchase or redeem them before maturity, at a fixed or determinable price"; and (d) "[t]he agreeement is entered into concurrently with the transfer."[832]

Assets are "substantially the same" if they have: (a) "[t]he same primary obligor (except for debt guaranteed by a sovereign government, central bank, government-sponsored enterprise or agency thereof, in which case the guarantor and the terms of the guarantee must be the same)"; (b) "[i]dentical form and type so as to provide the same risks and rights"; (c) "[t]he same maturity (or in the case of mortgage-backed pass-through and pay-through securities, similar remaining weighted-average maturities that result in approximately the same market yield); (d) "[i]dentical contractual interest rates"; (e) "[s]imilar assets as collateral"; and (f) "[t]he same aggregate unpaid principal amount or principal amounts within accepted good delivery standards for the type of security involved."[833]

The ability to repurchase or redeem the assets on substantially the agreed terms requires the transferor "at all times during the contract term" to "have obtained cash

---

[830] *Id.* § 55, ¶ 55-17 ("For example, if [an SPE] is required to dispose of long-term mortgage loans and terminate itself at the earlier of (a) the specified maturity of beneficial interests in those mortgage loans or (b) the date of prepayment of a specified amount of the transferred mortgage loans," the requirement is met; "if the [SPE] has the power to dispose of transferred assets on two specified dates and the [SPE] can decide which transferred assets to sell on each date," the requirement is not met).

[831] *Id.* subtopic 10, § 40, ¶ 40-5.

[832] *Id.* ¶ 40-24 a.

[833] *Id.*

or other collateral sufficient to fund substantially all of the cost of purchasing replacement assets from others."[834]

A change in law, qualifying SPE status, or other circumstance may result in the transferor's regaining control of assets previously accounted for as sold.[835] Such a change must be accounted for as a purchase from the former transferee in exchange for liabilities assumed, unless it results solely from a change in market prices.[836] A "[R]emoval-of-accounts" provisions (ROAPs) which "empower the transferor to reclaim assets subject to certain restrictions" may preclude sale accounting by allowing "effective control over specific transferred assets."[837]Examples of removal-of-accounts provisions that preclude sale accounting are (a) "[a]n unconditional removal-of- accounts provision or repurchase agreement that allows the transferor to specify the assets that may be removed" and (b) "a removal-of-accounts provision conditioned on a transferor's decision to exit some portion of its business." [838] Examples that do not preclude sale accounting are: (a) "[a] removal-of-accounts provision for random removal of excess assets, if the [provision] is sufficiently limited so that the transferor cannot remove specific transferred assets, for example, by limiting removals to the amount of the interests that continue to be held by the transferor and to one removal per month," (b) "[a] removal-of-accounts provision for defaulted receivables," and (c) "[a] removal-of-accounts provision conditioned on a third-party cancellation, or expiration without renewal, of an affinity or private-label arrangement."[839] "A removal-of-accounts provision that can be exercised only in response to a third party's action that has not yet occurred" does not preclude sale accounting;[840] however, when such action occurs (or does not occur) and allows exercise of the provision, the transfer must recognize the assets whether the provision is exercised.[841]

---

[834] *Id.* ¶ 40-24 b. *See also id.* subtopic 40, § 55, ¶ 55-25; *id.* subtopic 10, § 55, ¶ 55-40 (examples of rights to reacquire transferred assets (or acquire beneficial interests held by a qualifying SPE) that may or may not provide the unilateral ability to cause the return of specific transferred assets and thus preclude sale accounting)..

[835] *Id.* subtopic 10, § 40, ¶ 40-41; *id.* subtopic 20, § 25, ¶ 25-8.

[836] *Id.* subtopic 20, § 25, ¶ 25-9.

[837] *Id.* subtopic 10, § 40, ¶ 40-36.

[838] *Id.* ¶ 40-37..

[839] *Id.* ¶ 40-38.

[840] *Id.* ¶ 40-39.

[841] *Id.* subtopic 20, § 25, ¶ 25-11; *id.* ¶ 55-40. If it is exercised, the transferor has reclaimed the assets; if not, the effective control test is not met. *Id.* ¶ 55-40.

If these three requirements of mentioned are met, and the transaction is treated as a sale, a recourse provision by the transferor poses for the transferor a possible issue. The transferor must comply with the Contingencies Topic of the Accounting Standards Codification (Topic 450). According to Topic 450, the transferor must disclose the nature, and estimate the amount, of any loss relating to the transferred loan that is at least "reasonably estimated," but any loss that is 'probable' and can be reasonably estimated must be "accrued by a charge to income."[842]

RAP. Under RAP, a transfer of assets by a bank was a borrowing or "financing" by the transferring bank if, in economic terms, the transaction did not relieve the bank of credit risks that the loans posed.[843] Therefore, a bank that transferred assets with recourse could not reduce the reserve that it was required to keep had the assets been on the bank's books.

Currently, banks use GAAP in their call reports to regulatory agencies. The use of a single set of accounting standards for call reports and annual reports was requested by banks to reduce their regulatory burden. However, banks are required to report to regulators certain supplementary information not required to be disclosed by GAAP.[844]

---

[842] Financial Accounting Standards Board, Accounting Standards Codification, topic 450, subtopic 20, § 25, ¶ 25-2, http://asc.fasb.org (last visited Aug. 6, 2009). It may be necessary to disclose the nature and possibly the amount of the loss. *Id.* § 50, ¶ 50-1.

[843] FED. FIN. INSTS. EXAMINATION COUNCIL, INSTRUCTIONS FOR PREPARATION OF REPORTS OF CONDITION AND INCOME FOR A BANK WITH DOMESTIC AND FOREIGN OFFICES (FFIEC 031) A-48 to A-49 (1989) (superseded). There were two main exceptions to the rule that a transfer with recourse was deemed a borrowing and not a sale. One exception pertained to participations in Pools of residential mortgages. The transfer of privately sponsored or issued certificates of participation in such Pools was treated as borrowing by the issuing bank only if the bank retained a significant risk of loss from the underlying mortgages. Otherwise, the transfer was treated as a sale. Fed. Fin. Insts. Examination Council, Instructions for Preparation of Reports of Condition and Income for a Bank with Domestic and Foreign Offices (FFIEC 031) A-42 (1989) (superseded). The second exception pertained to spread accounts, which were not considered a retention of risk because the bank put at risk only its future income and not its current assets.

[844] Bloomberg Business News, *Feds Loosen Reporting Procedures for Banks, Move Expected to Cutwork (sic) Load, Confusion,* CHI. TRIB., Nov. 6, 1995, at 5, LEXIS, News Library, Arcnews File; *see also* Olaf de Senerpont Domis, *Regulators Ease Up with Move to GAAP for Call Reports,* AM. BANKER, Nov. 3, 1995, at 2, LEXIS, News Library, Arcnews File; FED. FIN. INSTS. EXAMINATION COUNCIL, INSTRUCTIONS FOR PREPARATION OF CONSOLIDATED REPORTS OF CONDITION AND INCOME (FFIEC 031 and 041) A-79 to A-82 (last revised June 2009), http://www.ffiec.gov/PDF/FFIEC_forms/FFIEC_031_FFIEC_041_200906_i.pdf (last visited Aug. 16, 2009) (providing that transfers of financial assets be reported according to GAAP).

d. Consolidation

Consolidation of the Transferor's Balance Sheet with a Controlled Transferee. The issue of consolidation arises when the transferor of the loans retains control of the transferee -- the SPV. If the transferor retains such control, it appears that the transferor should include the transferee Pool in its consolidated financial statements. According to the Consolidation Topic of the Accounting Standards Codification (Topic 810), consolidation is generally appropriate "if a reporting entity has a controlling financial interest in another entity."[845] "The usual condition for a controlling financial interest is ownership of a majority voting interest, and, therefore, as a general rule ownership by one reporting entity, directly or indirectly, of over 50 percent of the outstanding voting shares of another entity is a condition pointing toward consolidation."[846]

A number of types of entities are excluded from the scope of Topic 810. Neither a transferor of financial assets nor its affiliates consolidates a qualifying [SPE][847] or a "formerly qualifying [SPE]."[848] An enterprise with variable interests in a qualifying SPE or a formerly qualifying SPE does not consolidate the entity "unless that . . . enterprise has the unilateral ability to cause the [SPE] to liquidate or to change the [SPE] so that it no longer meets [the qualifying special-purpose entity or formerly qualifying SPE conditions]."[849]

Variable Interest Entity. FIN 46(R) provides that an entity is subject to consolidation under the interpretation if, "by design," one of three sets of conditions exists.[850] First, the entity is subject to consolidation under the interpretation if "[t]he total equity investment . . . at risk is not sufficient to permit the . . . entity to finance its activities without additional subordinated financial support provided by any parties."[851] The "total equity investment at risk":

---

845 Financial Accounting Standards Board, Accounting Standards Codification, topic 810, subtopic 10, § 25, ¶ 25-1, http://asc.fasb.org (last visited Aug. 7, 2009).

846 *Id.* § 15, ¶ 15-8.

847 *See id.* topic 860, subtopic 40, § 15, ¶ 15-12 b. (defining "qualifying [SPE]").

848 *Id.* topic 810, subtopic 10, § 15, ¶ 15-12 b.; *see id.* topic 860, subtopic 40, § 15, ¶ 15-12 b. (defining "qualifying [SPE]"); *id.* ¶ 15-29 (stating conditions under which "formerly qualifying [SPE] is considered qualifying SPE). .The transferor reports its rights and obligations relative to the entity according to Topic 860. *Id.* topic 810, subtopic 10, § 15, ¶ 15-12 b.

849 *Id.* topic 810, subtopic 10, ¶ 15-12 c. "If the [SPE] is not consolidated, the . . . enterprise reports its rights and obligations related to the entity." *Id.*

850 *Id.* ¶ 15-14.

851 *Id.* ¶ 15-14 a.

> (1) Includes only equity investments in the entity that participate significantly in profits and losses even if those investments do not carry voting rights
> (2) Does not include equity interests that the entity issued in exchange for subordinated interests in other [variable interest entities]
> (3) Does not include amounts provided to the equity investor directly or indirectly by the . . . entity or by other parties involved with the . . . entity (for example, by fees, charitable contributions, or other payments), unless the provider is a parent, subsidiary, or affiliate of the investor that is required to be included in the same set of consolidated financial statements as the investor
> (4) Does not include amounts financed for the equity investor (for example, by loans or guarantees of loans) directly by the entity or by other parties involved with the entity, unless that party is a parent, subsidiary, or affiliate of the investor that is required to be included in the same set of consolidated financial statements as the investor.[852]

There is a presumption that "[a]n equity investment at risk of less than 10 percent of the . . . entity's total assets shall not be considered sufficient to permit the . . . entity to finance its activities without subordinated financial support in addition to the equity investment unless the equity investment can be demonstrated to be sufficient."[853] In addition, some entities may require an equity investment at risk of greater than 10 percent.[854]

Second, the entity is subject to consolidation under the interpretation if "[a]s a group the holders of the equity investment at risk lack any one of the following three characteristics of a controlling financial interest":[855] (1) "[t]he direct or indirect ability through voting rights or similar rights to make decisions about a legal entity's activities that have a significant effect on the success of the entity";[856] (2) "[t]he

---

[852] *Id.*

[853] *Id.* § 25, ¶ 25-45 (stating that demonstration may be based on qualitative or quantitative analysis or both; elaborating on quantitative assessments and quantitative analyses to be made).

[854] *Id.* ¶ 25-46 (stating that entities may require greater equity at risk "especially if they engage in high-risk activities, hold high-risk assets, or have exposure to risks that are not reflected in the reported amounts of the legal entities' assets or liabilities").

[855] *Id.* § 15, ¶ 15-14 b.

[856] *Id.* ("The investors do not have that ability through voting rights or similar rights if no **owners** hold voting rights or similar rights (such as those of a common shareholder in a corporation or a general partner in a partnership).").

obligation to absorb the expected losses of the legal entity";[857] or (3) "[t]he right to receive the expected residual returns of the legal entity."[858]

Third, the investors are considered to lack "[t]he direct or indirect ability through voting rights or similar rights to make decisions about a legal entity's activities that have a significant effect on the success of the legal entity" in the test above if both:

> (1) The voting rights of some investors are not proportional to their obligations to absorb the expected losses of the legal entity, their rights to receive the expected residual returns of the legal entity, or both.
>
> (2) Substantially all of the legal entity's activities (for example, providing financing or buying assets) either involve or are conducted on behalf of an investor that has disproportionately few voting rights.[859]

If an entity is subject to consolidation under the interpretation, it is called a "variable interest entity"[860] and "[t]he investments or other interests that will absorb portions of a variable interest entity's (VIE's) expected losses or receive portions of the entity's expected residual returns are called variable interests."[861] The initial determination of variable interest entity status is made when an enterprise "becomes involved" with the entity, "based on the circumstances at that date including future changes that are required in existing governing documents and existing contractual arrangements."[862]

---

[857] *Id.* ("The investor or investors do not have that obligation if they are directly or indirectly protected from the expected losses or are guaranteed a return by the legal entity itself or by other parties involved with the legal entity."); *see id.* Master Glossary (defining "expected losses").

[858] *Id.* topic 810, subtopic 10, § 15, ¶ 15-14 b. ("The investors do not have that right if their return is capped by the legal entity's governing documents or arrangements with other variable interest holders or the entity."); *see id.* Master Glossary (defining "expected residual returns").

[859] *Id.* topic 810, subtopic 10, § 15, ¶ 15-14 ¶5 c. ("For purposes of applying this requirement, enterprises shall consider each party's obligations to absorb expected losses and rights to receive expected residual returns related to all of that party's interests in the legal entity and not only to its equity investment at risk.").

[860] *See id.* Master Glossary (defining "variable interest entity" as "[a] legal entity subject to consolidation according to the provisions of the Variable Interest Entities Subsections of Subtopic 810-10").

[861] *Id.*

[862] *Id.* topic 810, subtopic 10, § 25, ¶ 25-37 ("A reporting entity is not required to determine whether an entity with which it is involved is a [variable interest entity] if it is apparent that the enterprise's interest would not be a significant variable interest and if the reporting party, its related parties, and its de facto agents . . . did not participate significantly in the design or redesign of the legal entity.").

An initial determination that an entity is not a variable interest entity is not reconsidered after the initial determination "simply because of losses in excess of its expected losses that reduce the equity investment," but is reconsidered in any of the following circumstances:

> (1) The legal entity's governing documents or contractual arrangements are changed in a manner that changes the characteristics or adequacy of the legal entity's equity investment at risk.
> (2) The equity investment or some part thereof is returned to the equity investors, and other interests become exposed to expected losses of the legal entity.
> (3) The legal entity undertakes additional activities or acquires additional assets, beyond those that were anticipated at the later of the inception of the entity or the latest reconsideration event, that increase the entity's expected losses.
> (4) The legal entity receives an additional equity investment that is at risk, or the legal entity curtails or modifies its activities in a way that decreases its expected losses.[863]

"A variable interest in specified assets of a VIE (such as a guarantee or subordinated residual interest)" is "deemed to be a variable interest in the VIE" only (1) "if the fair value of the specified assets is more than half of the total fair value of the VIE's assets" or (2) "if the holder has another variable interest in the VIE as a whole (except interests that are insignificant or have little or no variability)."[864]

"An enterprise with a variable interest in specified assets of a variable interest entity shall treat a portion of the entity as a separate variable interest entity if the specified assets (and related credit enhancements, if any) are essentially the only source of payment for specified liabilities or specified other interests."[865]

---

[863] *Id.* § 35, ¶ 35-4. A "troubled debt restructuring" does not require reconsideration. *Id.* ¶ 35-5.

[864] *Id.* § 25, ¶ 25-55. "The expected losses and expected residual returns applicable to variable interests in specified assets of a VIE shall be deemed to be expected losses and expected residual returns of the entity only if that variable interest is deemed to be a variable interest in the VIE." *Id.* "The expected losses related to variable interests in specified assets are not considered part of the expected losses of the legal entity for purposes of determining the adequacy of the equity at risk in the legal entity or for identifying the primary beneficiary unless the specified assets constitute a majority of the assets of the legal entity." *Id.* ¶ 25-56.

[865] *Id.* ¶ 25-57. This requirement applies only if the entity has been determined to be a variable interest entity. "If one reporting entity is required to consolidate a discrete portion of a VIE, other variable interest holders shall not consider that portion to be part of the larger VIE." *Id.*

Consolidation. An enterprise must consolidate a variable interest entity if it "has a variable interest (or combination of variable interests) that will absorb a majority of the VIE's expected losses, receive a majority of the VIE's expected residual returns, or both." In making this determination, the enterprise must "consider the rights and obligations conveyed by its variable interests and the relationship of its variable interests with variable interests held by other parties."[866]

"The enterprise that consolidates a variable interest entity is called the primary beneficiary of that entity." Primary beneficiary status is determined "at the time the enterprise becomes involved with the entity." This status is reconsidered "if the entity's governing documents or contractual arrangements are changed in a manner that reallocates between the existing primary beneficiary and other unrelated parties": (a) "the obligation to absorb the expected losses of the variable interest entity" or (b) "the right to receive the expected residual returns of the variable interest entity." Consolidation status is also reconsidered "if the primary beneficiary sells or otherwise disposes of all or part of its variable interests to unrelated parties or if the variable interest entity issues new variable interests to parties other than the primary beneficiary or the primary beneficiary's related parties." In addition, "[a] holder of a variable interest that is not the primary beneficiary" must reconsider primary beneficiary status if it "acquires additional variable interests in the VIE."[867]

In determining primary beneficiary status, an enterprise with a variable interest must "treat variable interests in that same VIE held by its related parties as its own interests."[868] "Related parties" "includes those parties identified in Topic 850[869] and certain other parties that are acting as de facto agents or de facto principals of the variable interest holder."[870]

---

[866] *Id.* ¶ 25-38. "If one reporting entity will absorb a majority of a VIE's expected losses and another reporting entity will receive a majority of that VIE's expected residual returns, the reporting entity absorbing a majority of the losses shall consolidate the VIE." *Id.*

[867] *Id.* ¶ 25-40. A "troubled debt restructuring" does not require reconsideration of primary beneficiary status. *Id.* ¶ 25-41.

[868] *Id.* ¶ 25-42.

[869] *Id.* topic 850.

[870] *Id.* topic 810, subtopic 10, § 25, ¶ 25-43. The following are considered de facto agents: (a) "[a] party that cannot finance its operations without **subordinated financial support** from the reporting entity, for example, another VIE of which the enterprise is the primary beneficiary"; (b) "[a] party that received its interests as a contribution or a loan from the reporting entity"; (c) "[a]n officer, employee, or member of the governing board of the reporting entity"; (d) "[a] party that has . . . (1) [a]n agreement that it cannot sell, transfer, or encumber its interests in the VIE without the prior approval of the reporting entity [or] (2) [a] close business relationship like the relationship between a professional service provider and one of its significant clients." "The right of prior approval creates a de facto agency relationship only if that

"If two or more related parties . . . hold variable interests in the same VIE, and the aggregate variable interest held by those parties would, if held by a single party, identify that party as the primary beneficiary," the party within that group "most closely associated" with the variable interest entity is the primary beneficiary, determined by a facts and circumstances test.[871]

Measurement. "If the primary beneficiary . . . and the VIE are under common control, the primary beneficiary shall initially measure the assets, liabilities, and noncontrolling interests of the VIE at amounts at which they are carried in the accounts of reporting entity that controls the VIE (or would be carried if the enterprise issued financial statements prepared in conformity with generally accepted accounting principles)."[872]

If they are not under common control, if the entity is a *business,* the initial consolidation is accounted for as a business combination.[873] If they are not under common control and the entity is not a business, (a) the primary beneficiary initially shall measure and recognize the entity's assets and liabilities (except goodwill) "in accordance with Sections 805-20-25 and 805-20-30."[874] However, the primary beneficiary must measure assets and liabilities transferred to the entity "at, after, or shortly before the date that the reporting entity became the primary beneficiary" at the amounts at which they would have been measured if not been transferred. No gain or loss is recognized on the transfers.[875] In addition, the primary beneficiary must recognize a gain or loss for the difference between a.. "the sum of: 1. [t]he fair value of any consideration paid[,] 2. [t]he fair value of any noncontrolling interests [and] [t]he reported amount of any previously held interests" and b. "the net amount of the VIE's identifiable assets and liabilities recognized and measured in accordance with Topic 805." No goodwill is recognized if the entity is not a business.[876]

---

right could constrain the other party's ability to manage the economic risks or realize the economic rewards from its interests in a VIE through the sale, transfer, or encumbrance of those interests." *Id.*

[871] *Id.* ¶ 25-44 (such facts and circumstances include: (a) "[t]he existence of a principal-agency relationship between parties within the related party group"; (b) "[t]he relationship and significance of the activities of the VIE to the various parties within the related party group"; (c) "[a] party's exposure to the expected losses of the VIE"; and (d) "[t]he design of the VIE").

[872] *Id.* § 30, ¶ 30-1 (pending content, transition date Dec. 15, 2008). "Noncontrolling interest" is defined as "[t]he portion of equity (net assets) in a subsidiary not attributable, directly or indirectly, to a parent." *Id.* Master Glossary.

[873] *Id.* § 30, ¶ 30-2 (pending content, transition date Dec. 15, 2008) (citing *id.* topic 805).

[874] *Id.* topic 805, subtopic 20, §§ 25, 30.

[875] *Id.* topic 810, subtopic 10, § 30, ¶ 30-3 (pending content, transition date Dec. 15, 2008).

[876] *Id.* (pending content, transition date Dec. 15, 2008).

Accounting After Initial Measurement. For entities that prepare consolidated statements other than not-for-profit organizations, primary beneficiaries must follow the consolidated financial statements principles in Topic 810. The assets, liabilities, and noncontrolling interests must be accounted for in consolidated statements "as if the VIE were consolidated based on voting interests." Specialized accounting requirements applicable to the entity's type of business apply "as they would be applied to a consolidated subsidiary." The enterprise must "follow the requirements for elimination of intra-entity balances and transactions and other matters described in paragraphs 810-10-45-1 through 45-9 and existing practices for consolidated subsidiaries." "Fees or other sources of income or expense between a primary beneficiary and a consolidated VIE shall be eliminated against the related expense or income of the VIE." Its effect on the entity's net income or expense must be attributed to the primary beneficiary.[877]

Not-for-profit organizations that prepare consolidated statements follow similar requirements except that they follow the requirements of paragraphs 6-15 of ARB 51.[878]

Disclosure. The primary beneficiary of a variable interest entity that is a business must provide the disclosures required by Topic 805. The primary beneficiary of a variable interest entity that is not a business must disclose the gain or loss recognized on initial consolidation. In addition, the primary beneficiary of a variable interest entity must disclose (unless it holds a majority voting interest): (a) "[t]he nature, purpose, size, and activities of the VIE," (b) "[t]he carrying amount and classification of consolidated assets that are collateral for the VIE's obligations," and (c) "[l]ack of recourse if creditors (or beneficial interest holders) of a consolidated VIE have no recourse to the general credit of the primary beneficiary."[879]

An enterprise other than the primary beneficiary that holds a significant variable interest in a variable interest entity must disclose: (a) "[t]he nature of its involvement with the VIE and when that involvement began," (b) "[t]he nature, purpose, size, and activities of the VIE," and (c) "[t]he enterprise's maximum exposure to loss as a result of its involvement with the VIE."[880]

---

877 *Id.* § 35, ¶ 35-3 (pending content, transition date Dec. 15, 2008).

878 CONSOLIDATION OF VARIABLE INTEREST ENTITIES, FASB Interpretation No. 46(R), ¶ 22 note (Fin. Accounting Standards Bd. 2003) (as amended).

879 Financial Accounting Standards Board, Accounting Standards Codification, topic 810, subtopic 10, § 50, ¶ 50-3, http://asc.fasb.org (last visited Aug. 11, 2009). (pending content, transition date Dec. 15, 2008).

880 *Id.* ¶ 50-4.

The variable interest entity information required by Topic 860 must be included in the same note to the financial statements as the information required above. "Information about VIEs may be reported in the aggregate for similar entities if separate reporting would not add material information."[881]

For certain entities excluded from the scope of Topic 860, because the entity was created before December 31, 2003, and certain information regarding the entity is unavailable to the enterprise, additional disclosure is required.[882]

e. Recognition of Gain and Loss on Loan Transfer

Whether the transferor should recognize any profit or loss on the transfer depends on whether the transfer is treated as a sale or a loan. If the transaction is treated as a sale, the transferor recognizes any profit or loss.[883] If the transaction is treated as a loan, the transferor-borrower does not recognize a profit or a loss.[884] Gain or loss depends on whether the fair value of the consideration that the seller receives differs from the carrying value of the loan. The gains are "realized" when the buyer irrevocably transfers the consideration to the seller; losses are "realized" when they become probable, the seller has decided to sell, and the assets are susceptible to reasonable estimation.[885]

---

[881] *Id.* ¶ 50-5.

[882] *Id.* ¶ 50-6.

[883] *See* Financial Accounting Standards Board, Accounting Standards Codification, topic 860, subtopic 10, § 40, ¶ 40-5 50-3, http://asc.fasb.org (last visited Aug. 11, 2009).

[884] David M. Morris, *Accounting for Commercial Loan Sales, in* THE COMMERCIAL LOAN RESALE MARKET 99, 101 (Jess Lederman, Linda E. Feinne & Mark F. Dziagla eds., 1991) (sample accounting entry treating funds received as a liability).

[885] *See* 1 Tamar Frankel, Securitization § 24.8, at 242 (Supp. 1994) (citing Curley, *Accounting Considerations, in* SECURITIZATION, ASSET-BACKED AND MORTGAGE-BACKED SECURITIES § 3.02, at 3-6 to 3-8 (Ronald S. Borod ed.,1991)) (for example, if the fair value of the sold asset is less than its historical cost; timing is important, and sometimes losses might have to be recognized before gains could be allowed).

D. Taxation [886]

a. The Issue of Double Taxation[887]

If SPVs possess the characteristics of corporations, they will be taxed on their income, and, when they pay out funds to securityholders, securityholders will be taxed on this income as well. Some types of Institutions that hold financial assets and issue securities to the public conditionally receive a "pass-through" treatment, under which only the securityholders are taxed. One rationale for this special treatment is that, whereas large investors can create diversified portfolios for themselves, small investors, who must resort to Institutions for diversification, are penalized by double taxation. The pass-through status gives small investors equal treatment with large investors. Thus, regulated investment companies[888] and common trust funds maintained by banks[889] have a pass-through status under the Internal Revenue Code. Most other Institutions do not. For this reason, SPV securities are often structured as debt, since interest payments on debt, unlike dividends on equity, are deductible at the SPV level.[890] The issuance of debt therefore avoids double taxation.

In addition, entities that do not possess the features of corporations are not taxed separately from the recipients of their income. Grantor trusts do not have corporate characteristics. While the beneficiaries are taxed, the trust is not taxed on the income distributed to the beneficiaries. Certain partnerships and limited partnerships that do not possess corporate features also obtain such a treatment.[891]

It is difficult to find a niche for SPVs under the existing tax law. Subchapter M of the Internal Revenue Code grants a pass-through treatment only to "regulated investment companies" that is, investment companies that are registered under the 1940 Act.[892] Since most SPVs are not registered and in fact cannot function under the regime of that Act,[893] the SPVs cannot take advantage of the pass-through treatment.

886 1 TAMAR FRANKEL, SECURITIZATION § 8.15.1 (Ann Taylor Schwing ed., 2d ed. 2005).

887 1 TAMAR FRANKEL, SECURITIZATION § 8.12.1 (Ann Taylor Schwing ed., 2d ed. 2005).

888 I.R.C. § 852.

889 I.R.C. § 584.

890 I.R.C. § 163(a) (deduction for "all interest paid or accrued within the taxable year on indebtedness"). However, in certain circumstances, as when the issuer has tax loss carryforwards to shelter the SPV's income, an SPV may safely issue equity securities.

891 I.R.C. § 701.

892 I.R.C. § 852 (tax provisions do not apply to "a regulated investment company").

893 See Chapter 11 of the text.

The issue of double taxation is particularly serious in connection with mortgage SPVs since mortgage SPVs sponsored by government agencies received a pass-through treatment by virtue of their status. Therefore, the private sector was under a serious competitive disadvantage vis-à-vis these agencies. The markets have developed SPV structures to take advantage of the available arrangements under existing tax laws. In 1986, Congress provided pass-through tax treatment for SPVs that hold real estate interests and are structured in a particular way.[894]

"Check-the-Box" Regulations.[895] Historically, a trust that failed to qualify as a grantor trust (or a similar "pass-through" entity) would be subject to a four-factor corporate characteristic test to determine if the trust would be treated as a corporation for tax purposes. Usually, the trust would be characterized as a corporation and subject to an entity-level tax. In 1997, the Treasury adopted its so-called "check-the-box" regulations, under which most entities are allowed to choose to "check" either the "corporation" or "partnership" "box" on their tax returns.[896] This elective feature changed the default classification for most entities from "corporation" to "partnership," thereby allowing avoidance of an entity-level tax. In addition, the regulations eliminate the concern that the existence of only one equity owner will preclude treatment as a pass-through.

Check-the-box is not without limitations, however. The rules regarding the "publicly traded partnership" and the "taxable mortgage pool" are not affected by the regulations. Both of these entities are still potentially taxable as corporations. Also, some states have yet to adopt the check-the-box approach and, as a result, securitizations involving those states remain subject to the "corporate characteristics" test.

Trusts.[897] The legal form of trust does not secure a tax pass-through treatment because a trust can represent different economic arrangements. At one end of the spectrum a trust can represent a co-ownership of property by investors who will be taxed as the co-owners. At the other end of the spectrum, a trust can represent ownership of property by an entity that will be taxed as an association. Income distributed to the investors in trust certificates will then be taxed again. Therefore, whether a trust is taxed or ignored for tax purposes depends on whether the arrangement resembles an association, which is included in the definition of a "corporation" in section 7701 of the Internal Revenue Code (the "Code").[898]

---

[894] Tax Reform Act of 1986, Pub. L. No. 99-514, sec. 671, §§ 860A-860G,, 100 Stat. 2085, 2308-18 (codified as amended at 26 U.S.C. §§ 860A-860G.).

[895] 1 TAMAR FRANKEL, SECURITIZATION § 8.12.2 (Ann Taylor Schwing ed., 2d ed. 2005).

[896] Treas. Reg. § 301.7701-3; see Carden, *Tax Legislation and Proposed Regulations Offer New Structuring Options*, *in* NEW DEVELOPMENTS IN SECURITIZATION, 1996, at 75, 81 (PLI 1996).

[897] 1 TAMAR FRANKEL, SECURITIZATION § 8.13.1 (Ann Taylor Schwing ed., 2d ed. 2005).

[898] I.R.C. § 7701(a)(3).

Grantor Trusts.[899] The markets have developed a model of an SPV structured as a grantor trust, organized under sections 671 to 679 of the Internal Revenue Code.[900] Grantor trusts are self-liquidating state law trusts, but they are not statutory business trusts. The securities issued by a grantor trust are called "pass-through certificates" ("PCs").

Fixed Portfolio. To qualify as a grantor trust, the trust must hold a fixed portfolio and be managed as a passive investor for the protection and conservation of the portfolio. The Treasury Regulation providing the parameters for a grantor trust states: "An 'investment' trust will not be classified as a trust if there is a power under the trust agreement to vary the investment of the certificate holders."[901] Therefore, to qualify as a grantor trust, the trust property should be fixed at the outset, and the statement of trust filed with the IRS should avoid granting the trustee a general power to reinvest payments received from trust property. However, a trustee of a trust that makes quarterly distributions of all available cash to the certificateholders may temporarily invest the payments from the trust property in high-quality financial instruments if these instruments mature before the next distribution date and are held to maturity. In addition, defective financial instruments may be replaced under certain circumstances by nondefective instruments with similar material terms. Under a recent revenue ruling, trustees may consent to changes in the terms of the credit support for the trust's portfolio if the trustees deem these changes necessary to preserve the rating level of portfolio securities and maintain the value of trust assets.

Single Class of Securities. Further, a trust will be given a pass-through tax treatment of income only if it issues a single class of undivided, transferable interests in the trust's assets. "An investment trust with multiple classes of ownership interests will ordinarily be classified as a business entity under §301.7701-2"[902] with one exception: "an investment trust with multiple classes of ownership interests, in which there is no power under the trust agreement to vary the investment of the certificate holders, will be classified as a trust if the trust is formed to facilitate direct investment in the assets of the trust and the existence of multiple classes of ownership interests is incidental to that purpose."[903] In practice, the trust will issue certificates in one, two, or three classes—the second and third classes are usually subordinated (possibly strips) and represent 10 percent or less of the portfolio's total size. If multiple classes are issued, they cannot be time-tranched. It is unusual for

---

899 1 TAMAR FRANKEL, SECURITIZATION § 8.13.2 (Ann Taylor Schwing ed., 2d ed. 2005).

900 I.R.C. §§ 671-679.

901 Treas. Reg. § 301.7701-4(c)(1) (as amended in 1986 and 1996) ("Sears Regulations") (citing *Commissioner v. North Am. Bond Trust*, 122 F.2d 545 (2d Cir. 1941), *cert. denied,* 314 U.S. 701 (1942)).

902 Treas. Reg. § 301.7701-4(c)(1) (as amended in 1986).

903 *Id.*; see Mary Martell, *Taxation of the Mortgage Pool,* 11 J. REAL EST. TAXN. 347, 351 (1984).

more than two or three classes of certificates to be issued (even if they can be arranged so as not to invite re-characterization of the trust), "because collateral efficiency generally is not significantly improved thereby."[904]

When the trust is not deemed an entity subject to tax, the grantor is treated as the owner of the property and taxed accordingly. For tax purposes and accounting purposes, the sponsor is treated as having sold the collateral when the trust certificates are sold. The tax status of the trust certificates (as representing debt or some other type of asset) is determined by the nature of the trust collateral. Therefore, the practice is for the sponsor to establish a trust and transfer the financial assets to the trustee in exchange for trust certificates. The sponsor sells the certificates to investors, and the investors are treated as the beneficial owners of a pro rata share in the trust's assets and taxed accordingly.[905] Generally, the investors are also entitled to deductions of expenses attributable to the trust's assets.[906]

In sum, a trust that issues more than one class of securities may be excluded from the definition of a trust and taxed as an association (in addition to the certificateholders, who will be taxed upon payment by the trust).. If the trust issues one class of securities but is taxed as an association for other reasons, the securities will be deemed equity, and distribution of income on them will be treated as dividends (which the trust may not deduct from its income) rather than interest (which the trust may deduct from its income). The imposition of corporate tax on the SPV or the treatment of payments to investors as dividends rather than interest renders such trust securities uncompetitive and unmarketable.

Owner's Trusts.[907] A trust that issues equity and debt securities will be taxed as an association. However, if the trust is highly leveraged its income will suffice to cover only its expenses and payment of interest, and will not be taxed. Equity interests will receive no income. Since expenses and debt service are deductible, and no dividends (which are not deductible) are being paid, the trust's income receives an effective pass-through treatment. CMOs provide for a multiclass structure of classes of debt securities that investors prefer to pass-through securities.

However, classifying the CMOs as debt securities raises problems. The IRS imposes conditions on the treatment of CMOs as debt. SPVs that issued CMOs should comply with the following requirements: (i) the issuer retains significant control or discretion over the SPV's assets; (ii) the issuer meets minimum capitalization levels,

---

[904] 1 TAMAR FRANKEL, SECURITIZATION § 8.13.2, at 380 (Ann Taylor Schwing ed., 2d ed. 2005) (quoting.Johnson & Passage, *Auto Loan Securitization Getting to the Next Level, in* NEW DEVELOPMENTS IN SECURITIZATION 1997, at 269 (PLI 1997)).

[905] I.R.C. §§ 673-677, 679 (grantor is treated as owner of property).

[906] I.R.C. § 671.

[907] 1 TAMAR FRANKEL, SECURITIZATION § 8.13.3 (Ann Taylor Schwing ed., 2d ed. 2005).

apart from the pledged collateral—1½ percent to 2 percent of its total assets (this requirement can be met by over-collateralizing, leaving a "residual" value of the collateral pledged to secure the CMOs); (iii) the issuer has an option to call the debt securities, usually when 20 percent to 30 percent of the original principal amount of the CMOs is still outstanding; (iv) generally, no more than quarterly payments should be made on the debt securities (the CMOs). These conditions are burdensome, especially the condition that the issuer must be capitalized; that increases the sponsors' cost. In addition, issuers must account for the issue as their own debt; that may adversely affect their own balance sheets.

The burdens of these conditions were mitigated by the structure of a so-called owner's trust. The trust issues to the sponsor CMOs together with certificates of beneficial interest ("trust certificates"), and the sponsor sells the CMOs (if the sale is a permissible activity for the sponsor). If the sponsor continues to hold more than 5 percent of the reversionary interest in the trust, the sponsor will be taxed on that portion, while the remainder of the trust income will be taxed to the trust as an association.[908] In addition, a sponsor that holds more than 50 percent of the reversionary interest in the trust will have to consolidate the sponsor's balance sheet with that of the trust, and the trust's liabilities will appear on the sponsor's balance sheet.

Therefore, the sponsor-seller distributes the whole reversionary interests in the underlying assets. Consequently, (i) the sponsor is not taxed on the trust income, (ii) the sponsor can account for the transaction as a sale, and (iii) the sponsor's balance sheet need not be consolidated with the trust's balance sheet and can remain unaffected by the trust liabilities. If no single investor acquires more than 50 percent of the trust certificates, then, arguably, for accounting purposes, no investor will be required to report the trust liabilities on a balance sheet. For tax purposes, the grantor is deemed the owner of any portion of the trust where the grantor holds a reversionary interest in the corpus or income valued at more than 5 percent of the value of that portion "as of the inception of that portion of the trust."[909]

Limited Partnerships.[910] The result achieved by the structure of owner trusts issuing CMOs could be achieved by structuring SPVs as limited partnerships that issue CMOs to the sponsor, followed by a sale of limited partnership interests.[911] If it is desired that the certificates be treated as debt and the sponsor does not wish to undertake this debt, then the ownership of the assets must be vested in the SPV. Since certificates issued by a trust are usually treated as beneficial ownership interests, a trust that issues debt securities may be taxed as a corporation. In such a

908 I.R.C. § 673(a).

909 I.R.C. § 673(a).

910 1 TAMAR FRANKEL, SECURITIZATION § 8.14 (Ann Taylor Schwing ed., 2d ed. 2005).

911 I.R.C. § 701.

case it is imperative, in the opinion of one commentator, that the SPV be organized as a partnership.

b. Real Estate Mortgage Investment Conduits "REMICs"

The Tax Reform Act of 1986 provided pass-through treatment to certain mortgage SPVs: Real Estate Mortgage Investment Conduits ("REMICs"). REMICs were designed to assist the private sector to compete with government agencies in the mortgage-backed securities markets.

An SPV may elect the status of a REMIC. Even though Congress intended REMICs to be the exclusive structure for SPVs issuing multiclass mortgage-backed securities, Congress permitted the use of other vehicles (owner trusts, limited partnerships) for five years to allow the IRS and other regulatory agencies to adjust the current regulation regarding other forms of SPV structures. Since that date non-REMIC SPVs have been taxed as corporations.

REMICs operate very much like CMOs. An SPV that qualifies as a REMIC may issue more than one class of securities. The securities are deemed debt for purposes of computing SPV income, but the SPV securityholders are treated as equity owners of the SPV's assets. The securityholders receive pass-through treatment, and the SPV is not taxed.

For an SPV to achieve the status of a REMIC, a number of conditions must be met. The SPV must elect REMIC status on the tax return for its first taxable year and may not change its REMIC status later absent compliance with stated requirements. Once the SPV has elected, it will be treated as a REMIC, regardless of whether its organizational form is taxed differently (e.g., as a trust). However, if it ceases to fulfill the requirements for a REMIC, it will lose REMIC status and will not be able to regain it without a determination by the Secretary of the Treasury that the cessation was inadvertent, the deviations were corrected within a reasonable time, and the SPV and all investors agreed to make such adjustments as may be required by the Secretary.

The Act contains a self-enforcing provision designed to deter REMICs from violating the Act's conditions. If a REMIC engages in such "prohibited transactions," income from these transactions is taxed at 100 percent.[912] Subject to this penalty tax is income from (i) "disposition of any qualified mortgage . . . other than a disposition pursuant to . . . substitution of a qualified replacement mortgage for a qualified mortgage[,] . . . a disposition incident to the foreclosure, default, or imminent default of the mortgage, . . . the bankruptcy or insolvency of the REMIC,

[912] I.R.C. § 860F(a)(1).

or . . . a qualified liquidation"[913]; (ii) income from "any asset which is neither a qualified mortgage nor a permitted investment;"[914] (iii) compensation for services;[915] and (iv) "[g]ain from the disposition of any cash flow investment other than pursuant to any qualified liquidation."[916] The Internal Revenue Service issued regulations to clarify some of the Act's provisions.

Legal Form and Financial Structure. A REMIC offers substantial flexibility in designing the legal form of SPVs. SPVs may be organized as trusts, partnerships, corporations, associations, or as aggregate pools of mortgages. As a result, the legal form of the SPV is determined by business considerations without the constraining effects of tax conditions. However, the Act superimposes a financial structure on any legal form in which REMICs are organized. REMIC SPVs may issue only one or more classes of securities called "regular interests" and a single class of securities called "residual interests." No other financial structure is permitted to a REMIC.

Regular Interests. "Regular interests" can be designed in any form allowed by state law (debt, pass-throughs, trust interests, partnership interests, or common or preferred stock). However, these interests must have the following characteristics:

First, they must bear a fixed interest rate, although the Treasury may provide for a variable rate by regulation. Treasury regulations allow REMICs to issue securities with variable interest rates. The variable interest for this purpose may be a rate based on a current interest rate; i.e., a qualified floating rate as generally defined in Treasury Regulations, set at a current value, as defined. "For example, a rate based on the average cost of funds of one or more financial institutions is a variable rate."[917] The rate may also be a weighted average rate; *i.e.,* a rate based on a weighted average of the rates of some or all qualifying mortgages, all of which rates are fixed rates or qualifying variable rates.

Second, the securities must have a specified principal amount; they may vary only with respect to the maturity date. The terms of the regular interests must be fixed on or before the first day on which interests in the REMIC are sold, that is, the closing date. Generally, an accrual (compound interest) tranche for each class of regular interests would be permitted, regardless of the form of the offering. Presumably, a regular interest could be callable at the option of the holder of the residual interest (equity).

[913] I.R.C. § 860F(a)(2)(A).

[914] I.R.C. § 860F(a)(2)(B).

[915] I.R.C. § 860F(a)(2)(C).

[916] I.R.C. § 860F(a)(2)(D).

[917] Treas. Reg. § 1.860G-1(a)(3)(i).

Securities may not qualify as regular interests if payments on the securities are disproportionate to the amount of the principal. Such securities may be treated as residual interests or a combination of both regular and residual interests.

Subject to these conditions, the Act does not require either a debt or an equity form and does not dictate the economic terms of the security, unlike those that the Treasury regulation imposes (e.g., an initial equity investment or other protections for debt securities). Presumably, Congress relied on the markets to evaluate the risks and commensurate price. Furthermore, the Act does not require REMICs to characterize their securities as debt. Therefore, a REMIC can be structured "as a sale for accounting purposes," so that investors need not report the REMIC debt on their books as a liability (even if they do not own the residual interest).[918] In addition, the REMIC structure permits the issuance of a single class or multiple classes of regular interests. Thus, the REMIC may offer a single class of pass-throughs, or classes of senior and subordinate pass-throughs. Presumably, a REMIC may issue senior and subordinate pass-throughs, just as it may issue a subordinate regular interests class.

Residual Interests. REMICs must have one and only one class of residual interests. These interests must be "designated as . . . residual interest[s]" and entitle the holders to all payments from the REMIC assets other than the payments to the holders of the regular interests and REMIC expenses.[919] Any distributions to the class of residual interests must be pro rata. In short, REMICs must have one single class of equity.

In a REMIC organized as a trust, the trust certificates are deemed the residual interests. In a REMIC organized as a corporation, the common stock is treated as the residual interest. However, to qualify as a REMIC, the corporate SPV may issue only one class of residual interests "unless the other offerings of residual interests closed on the same day as the first offering."[920] When SPVs are organized as corporations and register the securities in a shelf registration, it may be desirable for each SPV, segregated under an indenture, to elect to be treated as a REMIC separately. That is because the terms of regular interests must be established on the first day on which any REMIC interests are issued. The residual interests for such a REMIC should be a contract (similar to a partnership agreement) and not the common stock of the corporation.

---

[918] 1 TAMAR FRANKEL, SECURITIZATION § 8.15.3.1, at 387 (Ann Taylor Schwing ed., 2d ed. 2005) (citing Rudnick, Adelman & Parise, *Real Estate Mortgage Investment Conduits: REMIC's,* Corp. L. & Prac. Course Handbook Series, 5 ANN. FIN. SERVS. INST. 613, 622 (PLI 1987)).

[919] I.R.C. § 860G(a)(2).

[920] 1 TAMAR FRANKEL, SECURITIZATION § 8.15.3.2, at 388 (Ann Taylor Schwing ed., 2d ed. 2005) (quoting Rudnick, Adelman & Parise, *Real Estate Mortgage Investment Conduits: REMIC's,* Corp. L. & Prac. Course Handbook Series, 5 ANN. FIN. SERVS. INST. 613, 624-25 (PLI 1987)).

When a REMIC issues a single class of senior and subordinate pass-throughs, the residual interests may be the contract to receive the difference between the interest rates paid under the mortgages and the interest paid on the pass-throughs, less reasonable fees for servicing the mortgages. Such fees should be subtracted because the Conference Report stated that the right to receive such payment from REMICs is not deemed an interest in the REMIC.

However, if the fees exceed the value of the goods or services rendered, the excess payment may constitute a residual interest. If such excess fees are paid, they may present a problem if another class of residual interest already exists (e.g., a multiclass pass-through), creating a second class of residual interest and disqualifying the REMIC.

Initially, residuals were retained by the issuer. Currently, they are sold to investors, usually in private placement with Institutions, which use the residuals as hedging devices. Residuals are fairly risky because their maturity is long-term and their value depends on relatively unpredictable future events such as the rates of prepayments by the borrowers. The value of the residuals may therefore experience extreme fluctuations.

REMICs may also issue floating rate tranches, that is, classes of securities that promise to pay interest measured by a generally accepted market index, such as the London Interbank Offered Rate ("LIBOR"). In addition, REMICs may issue a planned amortization class of securities ("PAC") or a targeted amortization class ("TAC") bond. Such a bond provides investors with a more stable maturity date. After a specified period, a PAC is entitled to receive before other classes all payments of principal from the mortgages in the SPV portfolio. Excess payments are paid to a class with an earlier maturity date while shortfalls are paid out to PACs at the next payment date.

Composition of Assets ("Qualified Assets"): Qualified Mortgages. To qualify, substantially all the assets of a REMIC must consist of either "qualified mortgages" or "permitted investments" as defined in the Act. The Conference Report stated that "substantially all assets" allows only de minimis nonqualified assets. The asset-qualifying test must be met as of the close of the third calendar month beginning after the "startup date" ("the day on which the REMIC issues all of its regular and residual interests"), and at all times thereafter.

"Qualified mortgages" include (i) mortgages on residential or commercial real property; (ii) mortgage pass-through securities; (iii) stripped mortgage-backed securities; (iv) other participations in mortgages transferred to the REMIC on or before the first day of issuance of REMIC interests or purchased within three months thereafter; (v) a regular interest in another REMIC transferred to the REMIC on or before the first day of issuance of REMIC interests; or (vi) qualified replacement mortgages, *i.e.,* qualified mortgages as defined above, substituted for defective obligations within two years, substituted for any other reason within three months of the first day of issuance of REMIC interests.[921]

A "defective obligation" is defined in regulations as a mortgage subject to any of the following defects. (i) The mortgage is in default, or a default with respect to the mortgage is reasonably foreseeable. (ii) The mortgage was fraudulently procured by the mortgagor. (iii) The mortgage was not in fact principally secured by an interest in real property within the meaning of paragraph (a)(1) of this section. (iv) The mortgage does not conform to a customary representation or warranty given by the sponsor or prior owner of the mortgage regarding the characteristics of the mortgage, or the characteristics of the pool of mortgages of which the mortgage is a part. A representation that payments on a qualified mortgage will be received at a rate no less than a specified minimum or no greater than a specified maximum is not customary for this purpose.

Assets that are not secured by real estate, directly or indirectly, do not constitute qualifying assets. Therefore, SPVs of car loans and credit card receivables do not qualify for a REMIC tax treatment. The Act is unclear as to the qualified mortgages status of buydown loans, partially secured by bank accounts, or liens on mobile homes. The Act is also unclear as to the qualified mortgage status of CMOs and notes issued in connection with funding agreements, secured exclusively by real property. Although CMOs seem to be qualified mortgages, if these instruments are backed by an additional different type of security, it is unclear what percentage of assets securing the CMOs or notes should be mortgages in order to qualify the CMOs as mortgages.

Regulations clarify the meaning of "secured by an interest in real property" in the definition of "qualified mortgage":[922] "Obligations secured by interests in real property include the following: mortgages, deeds of trust, and installment land contracts; mortgage pass-thru certificates guaranteed by GNMA, FNMA, FHLMC, or CMHC (Canada Mortgage and Housing Corporation); other investment trust interests that represent undivided beneficial ownership in a pool of obligations principally secured by interests in real property and related assets that would be considered to be permitted investments if the investment trust were a REMIC, and provided the investment trust is classified as a trust under [Treas. Reg. §301.7701-4(c)]; and obligations secured by manufactured housing treated as single family residences under [I.R.C. §25(e)(10)] (without regard to the treatment of the obligations or the properties under state law)."

---

[921] 1 TAMAR FRANKEL, SECURITIZATION § 8.15.4.1, at 391 (Ann Taylor Schwing ed., 2d ed. 2005) (citing Rudnick, Adelman & Parise, *Real Estate Mortgage Investment Conduits: REMIC's,* Corp. L. & Prac. Course Handbook Series, 5 ANN. FIN. SERVS. INST. 613, 626 (PLI 1987); I.R.C. § 860G(a)(3).

[922] See I.R.C. §860G(a)(3)(A).

"Obligations (other than regular interests in a REMIC) that are secured by other obligations are not principally secured by interests in real property even if the underlying obligations are secured by interests in real property. Thus, for example, a collateralized mortgage obligation issued by an issuer that is not a REMIC is not an obligation principally secured by an interest in real property. A residual interest (as defined in [I.R.C. §860G(a)(2)]) is not an obligation principally secured by an interest in real property."

Composition of Assets ("Qualified Assets"): Permitted Investments. "Permitted investments" are any "cash flow investment," "qualified reserve asset," or "foreclosure property." "Cash flow investments" are "any investment of amounts received under qualified mortgages for a temporary period before distribution to holders of interests in the REMIC."[923] These funds may be held in guaranteed investment contracts ("GICs") but only until the next payment date due on the REMIC securities.

"Qualified reserve assets" mean "any intangible property which is held for investment and as part of a qualified reserve fund."[924] A "qualified reserve fund" is "any reasonably required reserve to provide for full payment of expenses of the REMIC or amounts due on regular interests in the event of defaults on qualified mortgages or lower than expected returns on cash flow investments."[925] The status of reserve funds that serve other purposes is unclear. In addition, both the initial and continuing balance in reserve funds is limited to a reasonable amount, considering the credit-worthiness of the qualified mortgages and the extent and nature of any guarantee relating to these mortgages. Thus, reserve funds must be "promptly and appropriately reduced" as the REMIC receives payments of qualified mortgages.[926] The Treasury may prescribe regulations to prevent "unreasonable accumulations."[927] Up to 30 percent of the gross income from a reserve fund may be derived from the sale or other disposition of property held for less than three months; "gain on the disposition of a qualified reserve asset shall not be taken into account if the disposition giving rise to such gain is required to prevent default on a regular interest where the threatened default resulted from a default on 1 or more qualified mortgages."[928]

[923] I.R.C. § 860G(a)(6).

[924] I.R.C. § 860G(a)(7).

[925] I.R.C. § 860G(a)(7).

[926] I.R.C. § 860G(a)(7).

[927] I.R.C. § 860G(e)(1).

[928] I.R.C. § 860G(a)(7).

"Foreclosure property" is generally property acquired by the REMIC "in connection with the default or imminent default of a qualified mortgage" and held for less than two years.[929]

Tax Basis on Transfer of Mortgages to a REMIC. Upon the transfer of mortgages to a REMIC, the REMIC receives a tax basis in the mortgages equal to the fair market value immediately after the transfer, or at an earlier date, as may be provided in regulation, such as the date of pricing, reflecting in both cases current premium or discounted value. Presumably, "such fair market value . . . should include any enhanced arbitrage value of the [REMIC] so that the value of the assets would equal the combined value of the regular and residual REMIC interests."[930]

According to regulations, "the aggregate of the REMIC's bases in the assets contributed by the sponsor to the REMIC in [the formation of a REMIC] is equal to the aggregate of the issue prices . . . of all regular and residual interests in the REMIC."[931] "The issue price of any regular or residual interest in a REMIC shall be determined under [section 1273(b)] in the same manner as if such interest were a debt instrument; except that if the interest is issued for property, [section 1273(b)] shall apply whether or not the requirements of such paragraph are met."[932]

The seller of the mortgages receives a substituted basis in its REMIC interests; that is, the basis it had in the mortgages before the transfer, allocated in proportion to their fair market values, and will not recognize any gain or loss until the interests are sold. In short, "substantially all the gain or loss should be recognized when regular interests are issued by the REMIC for cash and the sponsor receives the residual interests plus the cash."[933]

Regulations provide that organizational expenses increase the basis of the interests received by the sponsor, while syndication expenses reduce the amount realized on sale of the interests. Any nonrecognized gain or loss on a residual interest is included in income or allowed as a deduction "ratably over the anticipated period during which the REMIC will be in existence."[934] Any nonrecognized gain on a regular interest is included in income in the same manner as market discount on bonds, under either a "ratable" or a "constant interest" method. Any nonrecognized loss on a

---

929 I.R.C. § 860G(a)(8).

930 1 TAMAR FRANKEL, SECURITIZATION § 8.15.5, at 394-95 (Ann Taylor Schwing ed., 2d ed. 2005) (quoting Rudnick, Adelman & Parise, *Real Estate Mortgage Investment Conduits: REMIC's,* Corp. L. & Prac. Course Handbook Series, ANN. FIN. SERVS. INST. 613, 629 (PLI 1987)).

931 Treas. Reg. § 1.860F-2(c).

932 I.R.C. § 860G(a)(10).

933 1 TAMAR FRANKEL, SECURITIZATION § 8.15.5, at 395 (Ann Taylor Schwing ed., 2d ed. 2005) (quoting Rudnick, Adelman & Parise, *Real Estate Mortgage Investment Conduits: REMIC's,* Corp. L. & Prac. Course Handbook Series, 5 ANN. FIN. SERVS. INST. 613, 629 (PLI 1987)).

934 I.R.C. § 860F(b)(1)(C)(ii), (D)(ii).

regular interest is allowed as a deduction in the same manner as an amortizable bond premium.

Taxation of Regular Interests as Debt. Regular interests are treated as debt for tax purposes regardless of the legal form of the interests. Holders must use the accrual method of accounting with respect to these interests. Original issue discount is included in income and is determined by accruing the discount at the original yield to maturity, under "a prepayment assumption determined in the manner prescribed by [anticipated] regulations."[935] The amount of income recognized will increase with faster prepayments and decrease (not below zero) with slower prepayments. Market discount is included in income under either a "ratable" or a "constant interest" method.

Partial principal payments are included in income to the extent they do not exceed accrued market discount and are recognized unless the interestholder makes an election under subsection 1278(b), in which case market discount is included as income "for the taxable years to which it is attributable."[936] "[H]olders of regular interests purchased at a premium should be entitled to amortize such premium using a constant interest method."[937]

When the regular interest is sold or exchanged, any gain on the disposition is treated as ordinary income to the extent that "the amount which would have been includible . . . if the yield on such interest were 110 percent of the applicable Federal rate . . . [exceeds] the amount actually includible."[938] A regular interest is excepted from the requirement that 30 percent of the interest income of foreign holders be withheld. A regular interest qualifies as a "portfolio interest" if it is in registered form and the party who would otherwise be required to withhold receives a statement from the holder or the organization holding its securities that the holder is a foreign holder. It also qualifies if it is not in registered form if arrangements are made to ensure that the interest is sold only to a foreign holder and other requirements are met.

A regular interest in a REMIC is considered "a qualifying real property loan" in determining the reasonable addition to the bad debt reserve for some banks, in the proportion that the REMIC assets consist of such loans. Similarly, a regular interest in a REMIC is considered a "real estate asset" when held by a real estate investment trust, in the proportion that the REMIC assets consist of real estate assets.

---

[935] I.R.C. § 1272(a)(6)(B)(iii).

[936] I.R.C. § 1278(b)(1)(B).

[937] 1 TAMAR FRANKEL, SECURITIZATION § 8.15.6, at 397 (Ann Taylor Schwing ed., 2d ed. 2005) (quoting Rudnick, Adelman & Parise, *Real Estate Mortgage Investment Conduits: REMIC's,* Corp. L. & Prac. Course Handbook Series, 5 ANN. FIN. SERVS. INST. 613, 631 (PLI 1987)); see I.R.C. §171.

[938] I.R.C. § 860B(c).

Taxation of Residual Interests. Although a REMIC is not generally taxed as an entity, its income is taxable to the holders of the residual interests in the same manner as a partnership or an owner's trust. Its taxable income is determined in the same manner as that of an individual, as gross income minus deductions. Gross income includes "interest, original issue discount income, and accrued market discount income on the qualified mortgages owned by the REMIC, plus income on reinvestment of cash flows and reserve assets."[939] Deductions include "interest and original issue discount expense on the regular interests, premium amortization and servicing fees on qualified mortgages, as well as bond administration expenses."[940]

"The ability to amortize premium on qualified mortgages could be particularly significant if such qualified mortgages are given a basis that reflects the enhanced arbitrage value represented by the combined value of the regular and residual interests. Any taxable loss would be limited to the residual holder's adjusted basis."[941] In addition, an interest holder may deduct section 212 deductions for expenses for production of income, such as servicing fees and perhaps administrative expenses of the REMIC, "only to the extent that the aggregate of such deductions exceeds 2 percent of [the holder's] adjusted gross income."[942]

The "taxable income of any holder of a residual interest in a REMIC for any taxable year shall in no event be less than the excess inclusion for such taxable year."[943] The excess inclusion may not be offset by net operating losses. The excess inclusion is considered "unrelated business taxable income" for exempt organizations and, if the holder is a nonresident alien, the 30 percent withholding of tax applies.

The "excess inclusion" of a residual interest for a calendar quarter is the excess of "the amount [of income] taken into account with respect to such interest by the holder . . . , over . . . the sum of the daily accruals with respect to such interest for days during such calendar quarter while held by such holder."[944] The "daily accrual" is "determined by allocating to each day in such quarter its ratable portion of the

---

939 1 TAMAR FRANKEL, SECURITIZATION § 8.15.7 (Ann Taylor Schwing ed., 2d ed. 2005) (citing Rudnick, Adelman & Parise, *Real Estate Mortgage Investment Conduits: REMIC's*, Corp. L. & Prac. Course Handbook Series, 5 ANN. FIN. SERVS. INST. 613, 634 (PLI 1987)).

940 *Id.* (quoting Rudnick, Adelman & Parise, *Real Estate Mortgage Investment Conduits: REMIC's*, Corp. L. & Prac. Course Handbook Series, 5 ANN. FIN. SERVS. INST. 613, 634 (PLI 1987)).

941 *Id.* (quoting Rudnick, Adelman & Parise, *Real Estate Mortgage Investment Conduits: REMIC's*, Corp. L. & Prac. Course Handbook Series, 5 ANN. FIN. SERVS. INST. 613, 634 (PLI 1987)).

942 I.R.C. § 67(a).

943 I.R.C. § 860E(a)(1).

944 I.R.C. § 860E(c)(1).

product of . . . the adjusted issue price of such interest at the beginning of each quarter, and . . . 120 percent of the long-term Federal rate . . . ."[945]

"To the extent provided in regulations, if residual interests in a REMIC do not have significant value, the excess inclusions with respect to such interests shall be the amount [of income taken into account with respect to such interests] without regard to [the daily accruals]."[946] The House Conference Committee intended "that the regulations would not apply in cases where the value of the residual interest is at least two percent of the combined value of the regular and residual interests."[947] The Committee also intended "that these regulations may apply in appropriate cases to residual interests issued before regulations are issued."[948] This 2 percent limitation may cause concern about the size of the residual interests, unless regulations lower the percentage. In addition, if residual interests do not have significant value, the "excess inclusion" rule may apply to thrifts.

A residual interest holder also must include in income any cash distributions to the extent they exceed the adjusted basis of the interest. The adjusted basis is initially the adjusted basis of the property transferred to the REMIC in consideration for the interest. The basis is increased by REMIC taxable income with respect to the interest and decreased by REMIC net loss with respect to the interest and by distributions.

The holder will recognize a capital loss if termination of the REMIC is treated as a sale or exchange of a residual interest and if the owner has an adjusted basis remaining and was holding the interest as a capital asset.

A loss from the disposition of a residual interest may be disallowed or deferred under the "wash sale" rule[949] if the holder purchases another residual interest or comparable interest in a "taxable mortgage pool"[950] within six months before or after the disposition of the residual interest "except as provided in regulations."[951]

In an "underwater REMIC," the SPV sponsor amasses a large pool of loans and then sells securities worth only a portion of the total SPV and retains the residual class.

---

[945] I.R.C. § 860E(c)(2)(A).

[946] I.R.C. § 860E(c)(1).

[947] H.R. Conf. Rep. No. 841, 99th Cong., 2d Sess. II-235 (1986), *reprinted in* 1986 U.S.C.C.A.N. 4075, 4323 (footnote omitted).

[948] H.R. Conf. Rep. No. 841, 99th Cong., 2d Sess. II-235 n.17 (1986), *reprinted in* 1986 U.S.C.C.A.N. 4075, 4323 n.17.

[949] I.R.C. § 1091.

[950] I.R.C. § 7701(i)(2) (definition of "taxable mortgage pool").

[951] I.R.C. § 860F(d).

Through this substantial residual class, the sponsor can recognize a decline in the market value of the SPV of commercial mortgages and is able to reduce its taxes. Depending on the structure, investors are protected because the residual class may act as a subordinate class that absorbs losses. Therefore, the cost of the funding for the sponsor is lower, as it provides the investors with credit enhancement.

Liquidation of REMICS. A REMIC is not taxed on a "qualified liquidation." In a "qualified liquidation," a REMIC "adopts a plan of complete liquidation, . . . sells all its assets (other than cash) within the liquidation period, and . . . all proceeds of the liquidation (plus the cash), less assets retained to meet claims, are credited or distributed to holders of regular or residual interests [during] the liquidation period."[952] The "liquidation period" begins with the adoption of the plan of liquidation and is no longer than 90 days.

Reporting Requirements. A REMIC must have the calendar year as its taxable year. It is treated as a partnership for purposes of subtitle F and therefore must file information returns. The REMIC must make its election to be treated as a REMIC on its return for its first taxable year.

At the end of each quarter, the REMIC must provide each residual interest holder with information including that holder's share of REMIC taxable income or net loss. The REMIC must also provide each regular interest holder with information including payments of interest. "Interest" includes interest actually paid, interest accrued, and original issue discount. Because a REMIC is treated as a partnership for purposes of the procedural and administrative provisions of subtitle F, the IRS may make administrative adjustments in REMIC-level administrative proceedings.

The Status of Non-REMIC SPVs. Beginning on January 1, 1992, a "taxable mortgage pool" other than a REMIC has been treated as a corporation under certain circumstances and therefore has been taxed at the entity level. This provision offers a strong incentive to elect the REMIC form for mortgage-backed securities.

A "taxable mortgage pool" is an entity other than a REMIC in which (i) "substantially all" the assets consist of debt obligations or interests in debt obligations and more than 50 percent of the obligations or interests are real estate mortgages; (ii) the entity "is the obligor under debt obligations with 2 or more maturities"; and (iii) under the terms of debt obligations on which it is the obligor, payments on these obligations bear a relationship to payments on the obligations that are its assets.[953]

---

[952] I.R.C. § 860F(a)(4)(A).

[953] I.R.C. § 7701(*i*)(2)(A).

Under this provision, a trust or partnership pay-throughs (CMO) issuer other than a REMIC will be a taxable entity. Further, a corporate pay-through (CMO) issuer will not have the privilege of making a consolidated return. A multiclass pass-throughs issuer other than a REMIC will still ordinarily be excluded from the definition of a grantor trust and taxed as a corporation.

PART III: ASSESSMENT AND FUTURE OF SECURITIZATION

Chapter 12: International/Cross-Border Securitization Issues

Since the late 1990s, foreign countries, especially Far Eastern countries such as China and Japan, have shown a strong interest in securitization. In this chapter we examine the challenges of cross-border securitization. First, the issues that surround foreign-based SPVs are considered. Next, securitization in foreign countries is profiled. The experience in China is used to detail the international application of securitization. The chapter closes with suggestions on proposed inquires for lawyers dealing with international securitizations.

This growth of international securitization may be similar to the proliferation of cell phones in countries that did not have strong and efficient telephone exchanges. The new technology has allowed them to bypass the establishment of telephone exchanges, which is costly, and supply the country with a highly efficient, less expensive and mobile communication system. Securitization has similar effects in countries with a less developed securities market and a far stronger and historically conclusive institutional intermediation, such as the People's Bank of China. This bank has spawned numerous branches that turned more or less independent with the relaxation of the political regime, and yet holds a significant amount of failed loans to State Enterprises. One way to relieve the bank and its branches of the entire loss of these "bad loans" is to securitize them, suffer a lower loss by selling the loans for less than their face value, and "clean the bank's financial statements." In Japan the interest was to some extent linked to the liberalization of the Trust Banks, when their main product, a type of bank account linked to the securities value of certain specific enterprises, had become less prevalent, if not obsolete.

Regardless of the incentives, the advantages of securitization can be attractive to some foreign countries and its use has been spreading. The American lawyer that ventures abroad does not design cross-border securitization without the active, and perhaps leading, aid of the local lawyer. On a high level, however, the issues facing such a lawyer are similar in any cross-border transaction. The following discussion is an example of the legal issues that arise when foreign law is involved.

A. Foreign Based SPVs

Securitization divides the assets and liabilities of the company by transferring the assets to a special purpose vehicle (SPV), and enabling the SPV to issue securities to raise funds in the markets. In order to access capital markets and receive better sources for finance, the SPV may be established in a foreign country and securities would be issued in capital markets of that country.

Discussion Topics

1. Halyk Savings Bank

In 2003, Halyk Savings Bank of Kazakhstan executed a $100 million securitization transaction.[954] It was the first such transaction in Kazakhstan. Halyk sold its future payment rights from the correspondent banks to an SPV based in Jersey, England. The purchase funding $100 million was underwritten by WestLB. WestLB is a universal bank based in Düsseldorf, Germany. The bank is partly owned by the German State of Nordrhein-Westfalen. WestLB is also the central institution for savings banks in Nordrhein-Westfalen. On August 30, 2002 WestLB was converted into a joint stock company (AG) and on July 19, 2005 its institutional liability and guarantor liability was abolished. This allowed WestLB to concentrate on commercial operations. During that period, England had a very large securities market, and its legal rules were quite clear, as compared to the rules of other countries.

i. Who was the servicer in this transaction?

ii. Why did the parties choose to establish an SPV in England rather than in Kazakhstan? Which law applied to the SPV? What characteristics of a law would you seek when determining the place to establish the SPV and the transaction?

iii. What law applied to the transaction? English law or Kzakstan law?

iv. What other alternative structures for the SPV did the parties have?

v. Is there any difference between a foreign and domestic SPV?

vi. What were the benefits and risks for each of the parties to the transaction?

2. AMRO Bank

In 2004, a syndicate of banks led by ABN AMRO Bank NV executed the securitization of 1.25 billion Euros in German auto loan receivables. The receivables were originated by Volkswagen Bank through a German-based securitization SPV entitled "Driver One GmbH."[955] The securities issued by

---

[954] Press Release, White & Case, White & Case Represents WestLB on Securitizations in Kazakhstan and Turkey (Oct. 15, 2003), http://www.whitecase.com/news/detail.aspx?news=549 (last visited Oct. 1, 2009).

[955] News Release, Mayer Brown, Mayer, Brown, Rowe & Maw Frankfurt Advises on First German True Sale Initiative Securitization (Dec. 9, 2004), http://www.mayerbrownrowe.com/news/article.asp?id=1922&nid=5 (last visited Oct. 1, 2009)

the SPV were rated AAA by Moody's and Fitch. This was the first German auto loan securitization of Volkswagen Bank and the first German "true sale securitization" using True Sale Initiative's securitization platform, "which was established by 13 banks and True Sale International GmbH (TSI)."

i. Why did the banks form a syndicate? Why was not one bank enough?

ii. What was the risk involved in these securitized loans, and to whom?

iii. Did each of the syndicate banks receive a portion of the securitized loans? Did each syndicate member have direct contact with the investors? Did each bank sell the securities? Or was there a lead bank that made the decisions, for example whether to waive some costs to one of the borrowers?

iv. Did the banks anticipate further such transactions?

v. Who was the servicer? Each bank or the lead bank, if any?

vi. Does "true sale" have a special meaning in this case? What law applied to the transfer of the securities to the "platform"?

3. Advanced Semiconductor

In 2005, Advanced Semiconductor Engineering Group (ASE) "complete[d] the first Taiwanese corporate cross-border trade receivables securiti[z]ation."[956] ASE was an engineering company that was paid by customers within a short term after receipt of the products. It possessed receivables from clients all over the world. The $200 million securitization of cross-border trade receivables was considered "the first cross border trade receivables securitization of obligations out of Taiwan for a Taiwanese corporate." For the Taiwanese Originator it "involve[d] the sale of trade receivables from ASE Group to an asset-backed commercial paper conduit which fund[ed] the purchase in the [U.S.] commercial paper market." What laws would Taiwan's Originator have to research?

4. Samsung

In 2001, Samsung Capital, a Korean finance company, securitized auto loan receivables supported "in an interesting transaction"[957] with credit

---

[956] ABN AMRO, Press Release, ABN AMRO Completes First Taiwanese Corporate Cross-Border Trade Receivables Securitization for Advanced Semiconductor Engineering Group (Nov. 23, 2005), http://www.corporates.abnamro.com/corporates/docs/news/23112005_cross-bordertrade.jsp (last visited Oct. 1, 2009).

[957] *Samsung Capital in First Cross-Border Performing Asset Securitization, in Ian H. Giddy, Financial Institution Risk Management: The Impact of Securitization,*

enhancement by Financial Security Assurance (FSA). This transaction "'marks the first Korean cross-border securitization of auto loans' to originate from Korea."[958] The structure of this $ 187.5 million transaction is as follows. The loans are originated by Samsung and sold to an SPV. The Korean SPV issued its note to a Cayman Islands SPV. The Cayman Islands SPV securities were guaranteed by FSA, and issued to investors. What prompted this structure?

E. Securitization in Foreign Countries[959]

Securitization in foreign countries and across country borders presents a number of different legal and business issues, in addition to the ones discussed until now. Note that the issues and citations to foreign legal rules are used only as examples, and some may be obsolete by the time this Book is published. Any securitization that involves foreign legal issues should make use of one or more local legal experts.

The following materials are intended to raise awareness and serve as guidelines; to examine issues that are unique to securitization in foreign countries, and to propose questions that a lawyer would ask the local expert. At least some of the materials touch on areas of concern on which to focus. Finally, the purpose of this section is to offer insights into possible developments of the law in this unique context. Global transactions are not new, and they have always depended on reliable intermediaries and hospitable or even interested governments. Securitization is different only in the sense that dependence on the intermediaries is relatively greater and the dependence on the governments is somewhat less. Yet, governments can render securitization too costly and therefore close the doors to it.

a. The Issues[960]

Governments may impose barriers on securitization for a number of reasons. First, the incentives of governments or the intermediaries in a country may not be as great as in other countries and may be even hostile to securitization if the country does not consider the process to be beneficial. For example, Austrian banks have less incentive to reduce their assets because they are subject to a different deposit insurance system and high level of stability in banks' reserves and in their capitalization. In addition, a universal banking system, such as the one in Austria, makes it easier for banks to raise funds in capital markets through broader range of permissible activities. The state subsidizes mortgage loans and certain business loans

---

http://pages.stern.nyu.edu/~igiddy/cases/absdealsinkorea.html (last visited Oct. 1, 2009) (seminar on Risk Management in Financial Institutions, Sogang Univ., Seoul, Oct. 2001).

958 *Id.*

959 2 TAMAR FRANKEL, SECURITIZATION § 23.1 (Ann Taylor Schwing ed., 2d ed. 2005).

960 2 TAMAR FRANKEL, SECURITIZATION § 23.2.1 (Ann Taylor Schwing ed., 2d ed. 2005).

connected to Institutions, thus diminishing the gap between demand and supply of funds, which is one of the main driving forces for securitization.

Second, a country may lack adequate Institutional systems to effectuate securitization. For example, if registration of land and mortgages is dispersed among thousands of villages and not accessible in one registration office, then securitization of mortgages is unlikely to arise. The cost of identifying the land and the mortgages would outweigh the benefits of the securitization. Similarly, if receivables and notes cannot be easily registered to publicize their transfer or the imposition of a security interest on them, then securitization of such assets is not likely for a similar reason.

Third, in some countries the legal system must be adjusted in order to accommodate the new form of transaction. The legal system may either disallow securitization or some aspect of the process or make securitization too costly. The legal system may lack rules that facilitate the securitization or are at odds with legal systems that act in global capital markets. For example, the importance of verification of relevant information cannot be exaggerated. Lack of trust increases the costs of capital and sometimes eliminates the possibility of a market altogether. One legal rule that poses special obstacles to securitizing receivables is the rule that transfers of receivables are ineffective unless the debtors are notified of, or consent to, the transfers. Similarly, if the law prohibits the establishment of a legal entity for the sole purpose of holding assets, which is the main use of an SPV, that would create a barrier to efficient securitization.

Fourth, foreign intermediaries may pose higher or different risks. Not all intermediaries are subject to strict self-regulation or government regulation. Untrustworthy intermediaries may raise the cost of securitization.

b. Bankruptcy Issues[961]

Problems arise when a cross-border securitization involves bankruptcy, such as that of the Enron Corporation. Even the identity of the home country of certain assets is hard to establish, let alone the attempt to appoint a trustee to collect all assets in all countries. A multinational corporation that faces insolvency has little protection from a particular system. Until the 2005 amendments, the federal bankruptcy courts had limited jurisdiction under former section 304 to avoid an attack on their constitutionality. Former section 304 has now been expanded significantly in scope in section 1501 et seq. "to provide effective mechanisms for dealing with cases of cross-border insolvency" in order to achieve cooperation, "greater legal certainty for trade and investment," proper administration of cross-border insolvencies to protect the creditors, debtor and other interested parties, protection and maximization of the debtor's assets, and "facilitation of the rescue of financially troubled businesses,

---

[961] 2 TAMAR FRANKEL, SECURITIZATION § 23.2.2 (Ann Taylor Schwing ed., 2d ed. 2005).

thereby protecting investment and preserving employment."[962] Section 1507 enables the court to provide assistance when consistent with the principles of comity.

The assistance is designed to reasonably assure (a) just treatment of all claimants against, or interests in, the debtor's property; (b) protecting claimants in the United States against prejudice and inconvenience in processing the claims in such foreign proceeding; (c) preventing preferential or fraudulent dispositions of property of the debtor; (d) distribut[ing] the proceeds of the debtor's property substantially in accordance with the order prescribed by this title; and, if appropriate, (e) provid[ing] an opportunity for a fresh start for the individual that such foreign proceeding concerns. In the opinion of one commentator, bankruptcy courts and judges have been able to use former section 304 to achieve legal harmony with foreign systems to a significant extent in cross-border insolvency cases. The expanded provisions in section 1501 et seq. should be allowed for even greater success.

Commentators suggest ways in which to reach conformity through principles of territorialism rather than universalism. As Chris Farley notes, each extreme has merits and demerits: "This stalemate has led to various forms of compromise including cooperative territorialism and modified universalism. Neither of these two conceptually similar ideas solves all of the problems inherent with territorialism or universalism. Specifically, under both cooperative territorialism and modified universalism, courts must consistently reach a level of unprecedented international legal cooperation. Other solutions include 'contractualism' allowing 'corporations to specify in their charter which law will apply in the event of bankruptcy,' and 'UNCITRAL, has proposed a Model Law,' but it has not been widely used."[963] He concludes that "[n]one of the proposed theories or solutions provide a sufficient resolution to the transnational bankruptcy problem; therefore, the current state of international bankruptcy law will continue indefinitely."[964]

An important lesson in the bankruptcy area may be that the need for a uniform law and uniform enforcement has been exaggerated. The difficulties of achieving such uniformity are high, and another alternative is to aim at the results themselves, regardless of how the authorities reach them. The uniformity and the consensus among the jurisdictions may be more important with respect to a few basic principles rather than the implementations of the principles. To be sure, implementation may change the result or the emphasis, but the way to reach uniformity may have to start

---

[962] 11 U.S.C. §1501(a) (2006).

[963] Samuel L. Bufford, *Global Venue Controls Are Coming: A Reply to Professor LoPucki,* 79 AM. BANKR. L.J. 105 (2005); Lynn M. LoPucki, *Universalism Unravels,* 79 AM. BANKR. L.J. 143 (2005); Alastair Smith & Andre Boraine, *Crossing Borders into South African Insolvency Law: From the Roman-Dutch Jurists to the UNCITRAL Model Law,* 10 AM. BANKR. INST. L. 135 (2002).

[964] Chris Farley, Comment, *An Overview, Survey, and Critique of Administrating Cross-Border Insolvencies,* 27 HOUS. J. INT'L L. 181, 218 (2004).

with the results, and then regress, if you will, to the way in which the results are achieved.

c. Sovereignty Issues[965]

In a cross-border securitization, as in any cross-border transaction, risks include the "sovereign" risk associated with engaging in a transaction subject to the jurisdiction of another country. Concerns with sovereign risk, whether the risk is perceived or real, present obstacles to securitization in many countries. When deciding the overall risk, investors in foreign markets, especially long-term investments, must account for the possibility of unfavorable or unpopular political changes in those countries. A sovereign state might exercise jurisdiction over an aspect of a transaction in a manner that affects legal relationships or property rights, to impact negatively the anticipated return of investors. If investors suspect that a country might nationalize assets or impose currency controls, the investors will demand a higher return as an inducement to purchase securities backed by assets located in that country or cash flows subject to that country's jurisdiction.

American and European rating agencies often impose sovereign risk "ceilings" on borrowers, preventing the debt of a borrower from receiving a rating that is higher than the rating of the borrower's home country. The rating agencies recognize that foreign currency obligations can have a higher risk element than local currency obligations. Thus, if a sovereign state receives a rating that is below investment grade (as has been the case in many Latin American countries), then the highest rating of a debt of a company within the state's borders will be that of its home state, even if the company's own rating is higher. For example, an oil company's debt securities may be rated at AAA while the debt securities of the country in which the oil and the company are located may be rated at AA. Notwithstanding the higher rating, the oil company's rating will be AA—that is, following the rating of the country.

Securitization can minimize the impact of sovereign risk in a number of ways. One way is by structuring a transaction to avoid contact with the sovereign country, thus insulating cash flows from the jurisdiction of the sovereign. For example, the parties could arrange to divert cash flows at their source to move outside the jurisdiction of the sovereign state. The parties could also agree by contract that the laws of a country other than the sovereign state would apply to any future litigation, and they could select a forum for litigation outside the home country of the debtor. Such a selection will frequently take the form of an arbitration clause, under the multinational system of arbitration treaties.

---

[965] 2 TAMAR FRANKEL, SECURITIZATION § 23.2.3 (Ann Taylor Schwing ed., 2d ed. 2005).

A second way to minimize "sovereign risk" is to structure the securitization to involve the acquisition of accounts from an entity that is important to the economy of the sovereign. For instance, when Pemex, the Mexican oil company, securitized its receivables, the rating agencies were encouraged by the fact that Pemex generated one half of Mexico's foreign currency. Because of its strong position, the dollar-denominated securities Pemex issued were rated significantly higher than Mexico's credit rating. This sort of arrangement would not account for the risk of nationalization but may reduce sovereign risk enough to gain higher rating than the sovereign country rating for a new issue representing receivables flowing into a sovereign country.

A third way in which transactions have addressed sovereign risk is through third party credit enhancement. Although private guarantees remain prohibitively expensive to include in an SPV, quasi-governmental support is an option. The International Finance Corporation ("IFC") provides some support in this area. Other possible sources of credit support are the Multilateral Investment Guarantee Agency, a member of the World Bank Group, and the Overseas Private Investment Company, a development agency of the U.S. Government, each of which provides political risk insurance.

d. Currency Issues[966]

A major risk associated with cross-border securitization involves multicurrency issues. If an issuer intends to securitize non-U.S. currency receivables denominated in a non-U.S. currency and issue U.S. dollar-denominated securities, rating agencies typically will require that a hedge be included in the structure to assure the issuer's ability to convert the payments on the receivables denominated by non-U.S. currency receivables into a sufficient amount of U.S. dollars on any day that payments are due on the securities. In cross-border securitizations involving the currencies of two or more countries, currency exchange or forward purchase agreements can often be arranged as hedges to the currency exchange risk. However, hedges with respect to many currencies and U.S. dollars are not feasible because of the effective or actual cost of such transactions. Alternatively, the exchange rate risk could be shifted to the investors. This structure has been used in some cross-border securitizations. Finally, a guarantee from a governmental or quasi-governmental agency can act as credit enhancement with respect to currency risk.

One type of international transaction involves securitization of future receivables, such as currency receivables. Securitizing "hard currency" (e.g., U.S. dollar) receivables can be useful for firms in "emerging countries." These firms generally attempt to avoid carrying currency receivables on their books and prefer to sell their receivables to obtain foreign currency in the present. Future-flows securitization

---

[966] 2 TAMAR FRANKEL, SECURITIZATION § 23.2.4 (Ann Taylor Schwing ed., 2d ed. 2005).

transactions have proven attractive to foreign investors because investors buy securities backed by receivables, and are repaid from funds that are not located in a politically risky country. Hence, where political or economic instability once rendered foreign investors reluctant to finance Latin American ventures, for example, future-flows securitization offers a risk-reducing mechanism of financing. For the buyers, such securitized assets present somewhat different "risk profiles" than do other types of securitization.

A multinational firm may wish to securitize trade receivables owned by its subsidiaries in different countries. A securitization of this type is useful to hedge the expected earnings of the subsidiaries against currency fluctuations and to provide consistency in the firm's consolidated financial statements, especially if currency exchange rates are likely to change, although, if the hedges must be "marked to market," the firm will not be able to meet the goal of consistency on its balance sheets. To hedge the future earnings of its subsidiaries, a firm will sell off receivables owned by the subsidiaries in different countries to a specially formed subsidiary. That subsidiary will, in turn, sell undivided interests in the SPV of receivables to purchasers.

e. Overcoming the Problems[967]

Notwithstanding barriers, securitization has been spreading abroad. Legal difficulties are slowly being removed as governments and regulators in Europe, Latin America, and Japan have passed laws and regulations to facilitate securitization. Securitization has made great strides in advanced industrial countries where observers note the shrinking demand for banking services.

Interest in developing a global financial business may induce the financial institutions in such countries to enter into the securitization business. France, Belgium, and Switzerland, for example, have been gearing towards a more active development of securitization, especially in order to develop international financial services businesses. In 1993, it was suggested that securitization may be particularly useful to European Institutions as the European Union's First and Second Banking Directives increase competition. In the 1990s, banks and other Institutions in Europe and the Far East began developing securitization techniques.

The ability to raise funds all over the world is attractive to companies that hold financial assets, such as receivables. The companies can persuade their governments to open the doors to securitization. Moreover, the process can help ease structural problems in the financial systems of countries. For example, it has been suggested that securitization can avert the pressure of distressed loans in banks. Securitization can also increase market discipline and induce bank prudence in granting loans. As

[967] 2 TAMAR FRANKEL, SECURITIZATION § 23.3 (Ann Taylor Schwing ed., 2d ed. 2005).

one commentator wrote: "The common thread throughout my analysis has been the importance of financially sound, reputationally strong banks in fostering capital market development by reducing information problems and conflicts of interest between debtors and bondholders, most especially in developing financial systems, such as China's, in which information structures (e.g. credit rating agencies and financial media) remain weak or non-existent."[968] Similarly, securitization can help change a traditional structure that has not fully caught up with the dynamic changes in the global financial system.

Developing countries are moving towards securitization. Argentina, Brazil, Chile and Columbia have proposed or enacted legislation or regulations to encourage securitization. For example, in 1993, the Argentine Commission Nacional de Valores (Argentine Securities and Exchange Commission) passed Resolution 237, authorizing creation of a new form of mutual fund to issue different types of securities in connection with the securitization of financial assets. In 1994, Chile enacted Law 19,301, authorizing creation of a special-purpose corporation for the exclusive purpose of acquiring residential mortgage loans and issuing securities backed by those loans. Brazil's new comprehensive legal framework was created to foster development of a real estate receivables securitization market there as traditional sources for real estate funding cannot meet demands for housing and long-term funding engendered by growth of the Brazilian economy. Brazil's Law 9,514 enables greater integration of real estate finance into capital markets and ensures a framework for securitizing real estate receivables, exempting such receivables from judicial action or foreclosure, and segregating such receivables from other actions. The law should help promote multiple business opportunities, including financing for commercial and residential developments, investment in secondary real estate receivables market, servicing and marketing of insurance products. Developing countries experienced securitization in the 1980s, when their own obligations were securitized, and that may have taught them lessons and made them effective creditors and borrowers.

Arguably, securitization of sovereign debt has created a new problem for the debtor governments and for the lenders by increasing the risk of litigation against the sovereign by individual investors. Yet apart from the market in government and government-guaranteed loans, the private sector is increasing the use of securitization to fund different projects in developing countries with the help of substantial credit enhancements.

For example, Citicorp securitized $172.1 million in securities, known as "participation certificates," backed by future credit card receivables due to Banca Serfin (a Mexican bank) from Visa International and MasterCard International. The

---

[968] Patrick J. Schena, *Banks, Distressed Loans, and the Development of Chinese Markets for Asset-Backed Securities,* 29 FLETCHER F. WORLD AFF. 35, 47 (2005).

sponsor was Serfin Trust, a New York registered trust unit of Banca Serfin, Mexico's third largest bank. The "participation certificates" offered were priced at 6.56 percent, carrying a tenor of seven years with an average life of five years. Citicorp has offered the securities in a private placement to Institutional investors in the United States. The transaction, which offered the Mexican bank financing at a lower rate than it could obtain by issuing a straight Eurobond, illustrates the movement toward increased securitization in Latin American countries. About $800 million worth of such asset-backed securities have been issued by Mexican Institutions, and more transactions are likely to develop in other Latin American countries. Latin American corporations are also engaging in securitization as a means of generating revenue to finance projects during periods of economic decline.

Two innovative financings have emerged from African countries, determined to access capital directly from the West. PTA Bank, an African government-sponsored development bank for eastern and southern Africa, securitized development bank loans (commercial paper) to exporters in the first asset-backed commercial paper program from an African issuer. Similarly, the government of the Congo securitized future royalties and taxes on oil production due from an Italian oil company. It offered secured bonds to ten banks in London active in emerging country debt markets. PTA Bank's $13 million offering has a $500 million capacity. The Investment risk involved is primarily in the political and economic instability of the high-risk emerging markets of sub-Saharan Africa. The Congo offering is not rated and is ultimately an obligation of the Congo government that is not servicing its $4.7 billion foreign debt. The deal has similar risks to investing in unstable African countries. Both deals deliberately attempt to structure their financing to reduce risks associated with investing in sub-Saharan Africa. The PTA offering provides 100 percent protection to investors through a cash collateral account maintained in the West. The Congo deal includes a "put option" that investors may exercise if one quarterly payment on bonds is missed; it also includes over-collateralization and a waiver of sovereign immunity by Congo.

f. China- A Broad Discussion

The following section summarizes an article by Chang Zhang outlining some issues concerning securitization in China. Since 1996, interest in securitization has been rising in China. The first securitization project involved securitizing fees collected on a Zhuhai Toll road. In September 1997 a second project was the securitization of future flow receivables held by the state-owned shipping company, China Ocean Shipping (Group) Co (Cosco). A third, in 1998, was a mortgage-backed securities program.[969] In 2003, China Construction Bank "[planned to issue] 5 billion yuan ($600 million) of securities backed by residential mortgage loans and China

---

[969] Nidhi Bothra, *State of Market, in Securitization Markets in China,* http://www.vinodkothari.com/secchina.htm (last visited Oct. 1, 2009).

Development Bank [planned to issue] 10 billion yuan ($1.2 million) of securities backed by infrastructure loans" under the newly administrative measures.[970] In October 2006 a utility obtained approval from China's securities regulator to securitize future cash flows. A rival utility obtained shareholder approval for a securitization transaction earlier in the year. At the same time one firm planned to sell bonds backed by commercial properties, the second such securitization in mainland China.

That year witnessed also the first commercial mortgage-backed securitization in China. It was a cross-border securitization. By a complicated ownership structure, Macquarie Wanda Real Estate Fund (MWREF), a joint venture between Macquarie and local property developer Dalian Wanda, ultimately controlled the properties. The borrower in the transaction was Dynasty Property Investment (DPIL), a Bermuda-registered special purpose company that will become 100% owned by MWREF. DPIL has 100% interests in the nine property holding companies (PHCs) that technically own the properties. The PHCs were established in Mauritius because that country's treaty with China avoided double taxation. Under the terms of the deal, the Cayman-Islands SPV (Dynasty Assets) purchased a term-loan facility extended by Citigroup and Macquarie to DPIL. The nine properties (independently valued at $475 million) were leased to 40 tenants, including internationally known names such as Wal-Mart, B&Q, KFC and Pizza Hut. The weighted average remaining lease term was 11 years, while the assets had a combined average LTV of 49.1% and debt service coverage ratio of 2.3 times. One aspect of the transaction was the high occupancy of the real estate. The average occupancy rate was 98%, and seven properties had an occupancy rate of 100%.

China's banks' strongest drive to credit securitization resembles that of the United States banks. It was the desire to reduce the large amount of non-performing loans and debt of State-owned enterprises[971] off the banks' balance sheets. Securitizations of non-performing loans took place in June 2003 and May 2004. In December 2005, there were two "pilot" issuances of asset-backed securities by banks (a mortgage-backed security and a collateralized loan obligation).

In addition to the desire to reduce non-performing loans on the banks' balance sheet, China aims at developing its bond market in order to provide corporations with financing sources in addition to bank loans.[972]

---

970 Jian Wang, *What China Can Learn from US Securitization,* INT'L FIN. L. REV., Jan. 2006, at 22, 22, *at* http://www.cadwalader.com/assets/article/010106IFLRWang.pdf (last visited Oct. 1, 2009).

971 Johnny P. Chen, Non-Performing Loan Securitization in the People's Republic of China (May 2004) (thesis), http://economics.stanford.edu/files/Theses/Theses_2004/Chen.pdf (last visited Oct. 1, 2009).

972 *See, e.g., Nation Moves to Diversify Bond Market,* CHINA.ORG.CN (Dec. 14, 2005), http://china.org.cn/english/BAT/151833.htm (last visited Oct. 12, 2009).

The Regulators. China's main regulators are the China Banking Regulatory Commission (CBRC) as well as the People's Bank of China (PBOC) and the China Securities Regulatory Commission (CSRC). CBRC and PBOC regulate bank credit asset securitization traded in the national inter-bank market, and the enterprise asset securitization traded in exchanges is under the regulation of CSRC.[973]

The Laws. The laws regulating credit asset securitization in China are the Administrative Measures on Pilot Projects of Credit Assets Securitization (APPS) jointly promulgated by PBOC and CBRC in 2005, the Trust Law of the People's Republic of China and the Administrative Measures for Supervision of Pilot Projects for Securitization of Financial Institutions' Credit Assets.[974]

The main difference between the APPS and the United States model is that the SPVs, and the transfer of assets to the SPVs are based on the trust law. SPVs are organized as trusts that issue trust certificates. These certificates may be traded only in the national inter-bank bond market.[975] For example, in the Kaiyuan case, the China Development Bank was the originator. The bank transferred assets to a trustee - Zhongcheng Trust Company, which holds large loans. The Trust Company selected a servicer and custodian to administer the assets, and issued securities to institutional investors on the National Inter-bank Bond Market.[976] This structure is similar to that in the United States.

However, under the law in China, the United States model of the SPV must be adjusted. First, the restrictions in China's Corporation Law may render the corporate form for SPVs unsuitable. China's Corporation Law seems to require that a corporation be engaged in an active business (minimum capital and reserve derived from income) while SPVs are essentially passive holders of assets. In addition, "issuing corporate bonds requires that the net assets of a limited liability company be at least 60 million yuan ($7.8 million)."[977] Further, partnership law may not be available as a form of SPV organization because China's partnership law does not recognize a limited partnership as a legal entity.

---

[973] Yang Bushing, *Legal and Regulatory Framework for China's Securitization* (Oct. 2006), e-Bulletin (Pac. Rim Advisory Council), Nov. 2006, at 20, http://www.prac.org/materials/2006_November_eBulletin.pdf (last visited Oct. 1, 2009).

[974] *Id.*

[975] *Id.*

976 *Focus: China – Securitization – July 2005*, http://www.aar.com.au/pubs/asia/focsjul05.htm (last visited Oct. 1, 2009).

[977] Jian Wang, *What China Can Learn from US Securitization*, INT'L FIN. L. REV., Jan. 2006, at 22, 22-23, *at* http://www.IFLR.com/chinasecuritization (last visited Oct. 1, 2009).

In 2001, China promulgated Trust Law, under which trust companies have managed trust property, supervised by CBRC. Under the law, trust assets are recognized as separate from the assets of the trustor, the trustee, the servicer and the holders of beneficial interests (investors). Therefore, trust assets are not exposed to the risks that the creditors of a bankrupt or liquidated originator-trustor could claim the property (unless the originator is the only beneficiary to the trust). Trust law imposes on the trustee a duty to segregate the trust property, protecting the investors and eliminating the seller's control after it transfers the property to a trust company. The assets are removed from the seller's balance sheet and the seller's creditors have no claim against the trust property. Because the trust property is insulated from the trustee's assets as well as other trust property accounts, it protects the SPV from the creditors of the trustee as well. Hence, the effect of the trust model is similar to the effect of a "true sale" under United States law.

However, China's law is ambiguous about who owns the trust property. This ambiguity creates potential risks for investors. The uncertainty about who owns the property stems from the dichotomy between the common law of trust and the civil law system.[978] The U.S. and China laws draw on different legal sources. While the United States' law is grounded in the common law, China's law is grounded in the civil law. China's securitization laws draw on both systems. China's law draws on the common law--title vests in the trustee and the beneficial interests vest in the beneficiaries, and the trustor leaves the scene. But under the civil law, property rights cannot be so divided. When the legislators in China introduced the common law of trust, they left the adjustment of the two systems open, by resorting to ambiguous words. China's trust law provides that "the settler, based on his faith in [the] trustee, entrusts his property rights to the trustee and allows the trustee to, according to the will of the settler and in the name of the trustee, administer or dispose of such property in the interest of a beneficiary or for any intended purposes."[979] It does not establish the legal status of the transfer, or state when a sale is a 'true sale.'" Under China's law it is unclear how the "seller" will be paid, especially if there is no true sale. In addition, if a trustor is also a beneficiary, the benefits the trustor receives will be subject to liquidation or bankruptcy when he becomes bankrupt.[980] This may pose risks to investors.

---

[978] *See, e.g.*, Hue (Hannah) Cao, Note, *Asset Securitization: Is It a Resolution Option for China's Non-Performing Loans?*, 28 BROOKLYN J. INT'L L., 565, 604 (2003) ("[T]he 'trust' concept is still new to China, as is to many other civil law countries. Therefore, it remains to be seen how the law will be applied and interpreted in the context of asset securitization." (footnote omitted)).

[979] *Trust Law of the People's Republic of China*, ch. I, art. 2 (Apr. 28, 2001), http://english.gov.cn/laws/2005-09/12/content_31194.htm (last visited July 15, 2009).

[980] *Id.* ch. III, art. 15.

Arguably, under China's Trust Law and the APPA, there is no sale relationship between an Originator and a trustee. On the other hand, because investors buy participations in the SPV's pool of assets, the price that investors pay for the SPV securities should become trust property rather than the property of the trustor, as is usual under trust law. It has been suggested that the Originator is entitled to be paid for the transferred assets. The Originator may be viewed as the first beneficiary, who then sells its own beneficial interests in the trust (and is therefore entitled to the compensation). However, this first step could raise problems if, for example, immediately before the transfer to investors, the Originator is bankrupt. Similar problems would arise as a result of substantive consolidation, which exposes investors to the risk of the Originator's bankruptcy.[981]

Notwithstanding the legal ambiguities, a number of highway development projects were financed through securitization, even before China enacted the Highway Law in 1996 to facilitate such transactions. Three projects securitized future revenue streams from toll charges and vehicle registration charges. The revenues from securitization were designed to finance the construction and maintenance of highways. For example, in August 1996, the Zhuhai Highway Company, acting as both originator and issuer, successfully completed a $200 million bond offering. The bond placement securitized fees derived from toll roads, bridges, and tunnels collected by the Zhuhai municipal government, annual fees for registered vehicles, and entry tolls to the city of Zhuhai.

However, a number of factors made the Zhuhai Highway securitization unusual, as compared to the run of the mill transactions. First, the City of Zhuhai completed the construction of the Zhuhai Highway before the issuance of the asset-backed receivables. Thus, the securitization merely liquefied the present value of the Zhuhai Highway's receivables for use in other Zhuhai infrastructure projects. Second, both local and national government agencies approved the transaction. Third, using the Security Law, the entire stock in the Zhuhai Highway Company was pledged to secure the Zhuhai Highway asset-backed securities interest bearing notes. Fourth, China's uncertain law did not pose a serious obstacle as long as SAFE (the State Administration of Foreign Exchange) and other regulatory authorities approved the Zhuhai Highway's private contracts stipulating investment terms, priority rights, and bankruptcy rights. At the time of the Zhuhai Highway transaction, China lacked the legal framework to create a trust. However, the parties constructed ad hoc trust accounts, approved by China Construction Bank.

But ambiguities in the law can be serious. Under China's law secured creditors have priority over the investors in the SPV with respect to the collateral security. And as

[981] Jian Wang, *What China Can Learn from US Securitization*, INT'L FIN. L. REV., Jan. 2006, at 22, 22, *at* http://www.IFLR.com/chinasecuritization (last visited Oct. 1, 2009).

stated above, there are gaps in the law governing the transfer of the assets to the SPVs, involving the form of the asset transfers, whether and how the debtors should receive the notice of the transfers, and whether the debtors should consent to the transfer. What rules apply when the sale of the assets is accompanied by the Originators' recourse and guarantees, or if the Originators have rights to any surplus collections of assets? There are various unclear registration requirements (real estate mortgages, properties originally subject to property registration, patent, trademark, and guarantees).

China has imposed limitations on foreign investments. In 1996 "the People's Bank of China promulgated the Foreign Security Procedures."[982] The law recognizes guarantees, mortgages, and leases as "foreign-related securities," limits certain kinds of assets and receivables, and provides procedures, and specifies what parties may serve as issuer. To the extent that uncertainties remain SAFE approval is the only assurance of legal compliance; and the assignments of foreign-related security rights require prior consent of the issuer and SAFE approval. The participation of foreign investors raises also the requirement of approval and regulation by more than one department, and foreign exchange controls on sending profits out of the country.

Chinese mortgage laws are not compatible with American laws. An American law mortgage involves a promissory note and a mortgage or mortgage-equivalent document. Each may be governed by different transfer forms (e.g., negotiable note or non-negotiable). Under Chinese law, there is generally only one document, and the Security Law provides that the mortgage right and the debt are inseparable.

Yet, China's registration system of mortgages transfers may require registration in many registries, for example, for land without fixtures, land with fixtures, and forest land. The registries are local and hard for investors to reach and verify ownership. Some registrars have discretion in imposing mortgage registration fees, and some have charged excessive fees. Further, it is unclear whether mortgages can be used as security for other debts, and if so, how to perfect such a pledge.

Foreclosures. Under Chinese law, if, after default, the mortgagor and mortgagee do not agree on the manner of foreclosure sale, apparently the sale must be at auction rather than negotiated sale. Because negotiated sale is more common than auction involving individual parcels and private owners, auction sales may bring inadequate prices.

Status of foreign investors. "Until recently, [China] recognized three types of holding structures. The first involves 100% ownership by an onshore entity; while the second

---

[982] Kevin T.S. Kong, Note, *Prospects for Asset Securitization Within China's Legal Framework: The Two-Tiered Model,* 32 CORNELL INT'L L. J. 237, 254 (1998) (citing Songhua Rennin Gongheguo Waihui Guanli Tiaoli [The PRC Foreign Exchange Control Regulations] (effective Apr. 1, 1996), *reprinted and translated in* CHINA L. & PRAC., Mar. 1996, at 37)),.

sees assets owned by an overseas entity with no operational presence in China. The third is a two-tier structure, where properties are owned by an onshore entity such as a Wholly-Owned Foreign Enterprise, which is 100% controlled by an offshore entity." But recently China has stated that "companies must have a Chinese presence to own property in the country."[983] _This is an impediment to cross-border securitizations.

Regulatory uncertainty. The Chinese legal system includes "legal pragmatism," which distinguishes between "paper law" (published law) and law in practice. In addition, a web of personal connections (*guanxi*) exists through and outside the legal structure. The Chinese legal system lacks transparency. "Foreigners and even Chinese citizens cannot easily access many internal regulations" as well as financial information about corporations.[984] It has been remarked that China cannot adopt "neutral rules" on securitization because the country lacks the necessary legal doctrines and rules (e.g., bankruptcy and private ownership); the judiciary still lacks experience in the area to provide guidance; and the regime is still authoritarian and may be incompatible with "neutral rules." China still lacks a general legal system such as the U.S. model of asset securitization. Rather it has a patchwork of laws concerning the organizational structure of SPVs and consequently, the nature of the transfer of the assets to the SPVs and protection of investors from the claims of the transferor's creditors.[985]

Chinese banks were burdened with non-performing loans they made in the 1990s, including loans to state enterprises. Consequently the Chinese government formed asset management companies which purchased non-performing loans from state banks, for eventual sale. The asset management companies have considered securitization as one way to dispose of the non-performing loans. However, there are limits to such securitization, including "the peculiar nature of Chinese [non-performing loans], the [immature] capital markets, and the [problem] of China's . . . legal infrastructure."[986]

While many of the non-performing loans to state enterprises cannot be securitized because the enterprises are not profitable, some types of these loans could be

---

[983] Rob Davies, *First Chinese Cross-Border CMBS Arrivess,* ASSET SECURITIZATION REP., Sept. 19, 2006, LEXIS, News Library, Arcnws File.

[984] Yuliya A. Dvorak, Comment, *Transplanting Asset Securitization: Is the Grass Green Enough on the Other Side?,* 38 HOUS. L. REV. 541, 572 (2001).

[985] Kevin T.S. Kong, Note, *Prospects for Asset Securitization Within China's Legal Framework: The Two-Tiered Model,* 32 CORNELL INT'L L. J. 237, 262-63 (1998).

[986] Hui (Hannah) Cao, Note, *Asset Securitization: Is It a Resolution Option for China's Non-Performing Loans?,* 28 BROOKLYN J. INT'L L., 565, 567-68 (2003).

securitized. Theses are: (1) non-performing commercial mortgages in the cities, which provide revenues; (2) non-performing corporate loans secured by land use rights or other real estate collateral, even though there are difficulties in enforcing the asset management companies' creditor rights and; and (3) loans to state enterprises that have a "viable business prospect."[987]

There are legal obstacles in China unique to non-performing loan securitization: First, under China's Contract Law of 1999, an assignment of assets should be approved or registered according to applicable law. Assignment of state assets may require compliance with complicated regulation and government agencies' approval. Second, a creditor petitioning for the bankruptcy of state enterprises must obtain a prior approval by other government entities, and a two-year reorganization period may be imposed in such a case. Bankruptcies of state enterprises have been rare. Third, foreign investors are subject to restrictions on the kind of SPVs that they may set up to securitize state enterprises' non-performing loans.

Recent Developments to Facilitate Securitization. The Security Law of 1995 provided uniformity in security interest law setting forth "five types of security interests" (guarantee, mortgage, pledge, lien, deposit).[988] The State Administration of Foreign Exchange (SAFE) in 1998 issued the Foreign Security Implementing Rules, clarifying the Foreign Security Procedures, which limit foreign investment.[989] China passed laws designed to facilitate financing.[990] Regulatory controls over securitization have been consolidated under one agency (SAFE).[991]

The China Banking Regulatory Commission (CBRC) allowed "pilot" securitizations of asset-backed securities[992] and the China Securities Regulatory Commission set up

---

987 Hui (Hannah) Cao, Note, *Asset Securitization: Is It a Resolution Option for China's Non-Performing Loans?,* 28 BROOKLYN J. INT'L L., 565, 567-68 (2003).

988 Kevin T.S. Kong, Note, *Prospects for Asset Securitization Within China's Legal Framework: The Two-Tiered Model,* 32 CORNELL INT'L L. J. 237, 254 (1998).

989 Kevin T.S. Kong, Note, *Prospects for Asset Securitization Within China's Legal Framework: The Two-Tiered Model,* 32 CORNELL INT'L L. J. 237, 255 (1998).

990 Highway Law, passed in 1996 "to provid[e] legal certainty" in highway financing, and Project Finance Procedures, to "provide clear guidelines regarding the approval process for 'project financing' transactions." Kevin T.S. Kong, Note, *Prospects for Asset Securitization Within China's Legal Framework: The Two-Tiered Model,* 32 CORNELL INT'L L. J. 237, 258 (1998) (Highway Law); *id.* at 260 (Project Finance Procedures).

991 Kevin T.S. Kong, Note, *Prospects for Asset Securitization Within China's Legal Framework: The Two-Tiered Model,* 32 CORNELL INT'L L. J. 237, 256-57 (1998).

992 Mimi Hu, Note, *Developing Securitization Laws in China,* 27 REV. BANKING & FIN. L.565, 587 (2008) (citing The People's Bank of China and the China Bank Regulatory Commission Announcement

a pilot program for corporate securitizations in 2005.[993] The CBRC allowed more institutional investors, (insurers, broker dealers, fund companies) to invest in securitized assets.[994] And China's tax authority clarified the tax treatment of securitizations.[995]

The State Council of the Peoples' Republic of China issued a statement in 2004 "reasserting its objective to reform and develop China's capital markets."[996]

C. Conflict of Laws and Unification (Harmonizing) of Laws[997]

Cross-border securitization involves parties or assets located in or emanating from different countries. Cutting across different jurisdictions and countries poses unique problems. Risks to parties engaging in cross-border securitization may arise from institutional and legal differences within respective sovereignties. For example, the transactions may involve countries with conflicting legal systems such as the common law and civil law systems. Litigation and enforcement may raise jurisdictional issues. Even if issues of subject matter and personal jurisdiction can be resolved, there remains the issue of choice and implementation of the law. Even when the parties designate the legal system that they select to apply to their transactions, their agreement may not always be binding or effective.

This problem is addressed in part by a movement to unify or harmonize the laws of different countries. Attempts to harmonize the laws of different countries have not been met with the governments' enthusiasm, but some steps have taken place in Europe to reach this goal. The European Union (EU) is acting to unify the laws of the members, such as the Principles of European Contract Law that set forth general rules for contract law, and these efforts are likely to enhance securitization

---

No. 7 (2005)) (promulgating rules for pilot securitization); Yuwa Wei, *Asset-Backed Securitization in China,* 6 RICH. J. GLOBAL L. & BUS. 225, 225 (2007).

[993] Jamil Anderlini, *China Gives Top Lenders Clearance to Sell Loans,* S. CHINA MORNING POST, Aug. 16, 2006, at 2, LEXIS, News Library, Arcnws File.

[994] *See China's CDO Market: Opportunities and Challenges,* Derivatives Wk., Apr. 28, 2006, LEXIS, News Library, Arcnws File (noting that CBRC was "in the process of specifying . . . whether banks, funds, brokerages, investment companies, insurance companies and branches of foreign banks are allowed to invest in [Chinese] . . . securitization products").

[995] Chris Wong, *China's First Taxation Policies on Asset-Backed Securities Released,* MONDAQ BUS. BRIEFING, Dec. 5, 2006, LEXIS, News Library, Arcnws File.

[996] Patrick J. Schena, *Banks, Distressed Loans, and the Development of Chinese Markets for Asset-Backed Securities,* 29 FLETCHER F. WORLD AFF. 35, 35 (2005).

[997] 2 TAMAR FRANKEL, SECURITIZATION § 23.4 (Ann Taylor Schwing ed., 2d ed. 2005).

in the EU. Similarly, the United Nations Commission on International Trade Law (UNCITRAL) is acting to facilitate cross-border securitization of current and future receivables.

In addition, there are interesting methods by which harmonization of rules seems to have developed. One method is by developing custom and precedent. When governments' or private organizations' proposals gain support in the courts, later courts' citations to the earlier decisions help harmonize the proposals and give them weight. This process is similar to that of the creation of a custom. This is one reason why the designers of securitized transactions have an impact on the harmonization. Their impact stems from the very nature of the process. Lawyers and other private sector organizations of persons who design the transactions contribute to creating unified structures that help cross-border securitization.

Securitization converts unique and "inflexible" assets into liquid assets, with features that are similar to those of money. Therefore, the process allows for the combination of different "inflexible" assets into one asset that can be divided into similar ones, provided there is a way to price the combined underlying assets reliably. A designer of a financial asset can combine not only different assets but also different forms and structures to fit a particular situation. Because securitized assets can be treated much like money, it is not difficult to divide securitized assets into different groups under different terms in much the same way one could divide money into different accounts or put money in the hands of others under different terms (as a gift, as a trust, as a loan, and so on). It is no longer the nature of the asset that dictates the terms of the relationship among the parties; the parties enjoy greater freedom to determine their terms, regardless of the nature of the assets. This flexibility is especially important in cross-border securitization when the same structure may not be suitable for passing through different jurisdictions. The designer can have some choice of jurisdictions to avoid or benefit from their institutions and laws. The designer's ability to create a flexible open-ended structure can help fit the structure into different jurisdictions and satisfy different parties more easily.

Discussion Topics[998]

How should a lawyer who deals in cross-border transactions approach the unique legal and accounting issues that such transactions raise? Professor Steven Schwarcz suggests an inquiry into the following issues:

a. The jurisdictions in which the financial assets originate, the SPV and the investors are located, and the regulations applicable in each of these jurisdictions,

b. The structure of the transfer of financial assets to the SPV and assurance that the transfer is a "true sale." True sale would protect the

---

[998] 2 TAMAR FRANKEL, SECURITIZATION § 23.5 (Ann Taylor Schwing ed., 2d ed. 2005).

buyers from the creditors of the transferring party and allow the transferring party to remove the financial assets from its balance sheet,

c. Issues concerning the position of the investors as against the transferor's creditors, such as perfection and priority, avoidance of fraudulent conveyance problems, consolidation and commingling problems,

d Contractual and legal restrictions,

e. Enforcement issues,

f. Currency exchange issues, and

g. Tax issues.

In their 1993 article on multi-country securitization and currency hedging, Oxenbridge and Nicolaides suggested the following inquiries:

(i) Whether collections on trade receivables are subject to withholding taxes,

(ii) Effects of securitization on capital requirements,

(iii) Maintaining deductibility of interest on the securities, and

(iv) Whether banking or other licenses are required.

D. Case Study: Facilitating Securitization in Japan

The Japan Securities Dealers Association (JSDA) announced in March 2009 that its members "shall establish procedures to properly communicate information to their customers, who are investors, regarding details and risks (including risk not reflected in the credit rating) of the underlying assets, etc. of the securitized products" they distribute (or following the distribution of said securitized products).[999] This new policy was established as a means to shore up the sagging securitization market in Japan, following the global financial crisis and strengthening investor confidence in the quality of the assets that underlie securitized products.

Securitization began to be practiced in Japan in 1990s as part of the global trend to manage credit risk and tap new sources of investment funds. Securitization growth, however, was initially stymied by the lack of a legal framework for securitization. First, perfecting the transfer of assets in Japan was costly. "Perfection of transferring loans and receivables requires notarial certification of individual loans and receivables one by one."[1000] A second cost issue was the expense of establishing an SPV. Under Japanese laws the SPV had to maintain a 10 million yen capitalization,

[999] WORKING GROUP ON DISTRIBUTION OF SECURITIZED PRODUCTS, JAPAN SEC. DEALERS ASS'N, WORKING GROUP ON DISTRIBUTIONS OF SECURITIZED PRODUCTS FINAL REPORT 3 (Mar. 17, 2009), www.jsda.or.jp/html/eigo/wg/Final_Report.pdf (last visited Oct. 2, 2009).

[1000] Hideki Kanda, *Securitization in Japan,* 8 DUKE J. COMP. & INT'L L. 359, 359 (1998).

have a minimum of three directors and retain an auditor.[1001] A third issue was the multiple regulatory bodies that controlled different aspects of the securitization transaction. Perhaps the most basic issue was the question of whether an asset-backed security was a "security" under Japanese law.

During the 1990s, a series of laws were enacted in Japan that facilitated the issuance of asset-backed securities. In 1992, the Japanese Securities and Exchange Law (SEL) was amended to allow for the Ministry of Finance to designate asset-backed securities as a security for legal purposes in Japan.[1002] By 1997, a residential mortgage trust obligation was designated as a "security" and this designation was "expanded to include a beneficial interest of a trust in which the trust property is any loan from any financial institution."[1003] Also, in 1992 the Ministry of International Trade and Industry (MITI) enacted The Law for the Regulation of Business Relating to Specified Claims (MITI Law) which allowed for the perfection of a transfer without individual notice and approval. The MITI Law thus removed a major barrier to securitizing lease receivables, auto receivables and installment credit card obligations. Analogous changes were made to Japan's Civil Code "simplifying the procedures for the perfection of transfers of debt obligations, creating new opportunities for the security[z]ation of a new range of asset classes."[1004] The high costs of creating and operating SPVs was also addressed by legislation. The SPC Law reduced the minimum capitalization and number of directors. The law also "specifically allows an SP[V] to issue ABS,"[1005] and acquire a variety of different assets, and conferred special tax advantages to the entity.

As the legal framework for securitization in Japan was clarified and strengthened, the number and value of securitization transactions increased. Securitized assets in Japan grew from 30 billion yen in 1994[1006] to approximately 11 trillion yen in 2006.[1007]

1001 *Id.* at 360.

1002 *Id.* at 369-70.

1003 *Id.* at 370.

1004 Salim Nathoo et al., *Japanese Consumer Loan Securitization: A New Asset Class,* http://www.hk-lawyer.com/1999-8/aug99-26.htm (last visited Oct. 2, 2009).

1005 Roy B. True, *New Developments in Japanese Asset Securitization: Open the Floodgates* (1998), http://www.tuj.ac.jp/newsite/main/law/lawresources/TUJonline/Corporate/assetsecwith%20glossary.html (last visited Oct. 2, 2009).

1006 YOSHITAKE HATTORI, BANK OF JAPAN, DEVELOPMENT AND CURRENT ISSUES OF JAPANESE SECURITIZATION MARKET 9 http://www.afdc.org.cn/afdc/UploadFile/200932452463657.PPT (last visited Oct. 2, 2009).

Japan dominated the Asian securitization market. (Exhibit 1) The assets that have been securitized consist of commercial and residential real estate as well as other asset-backed securities including credit card receivables and other consumer loans. In the early years of securitization in Japan, the technique was used to remove non-performing loans from large Japanese banks' balance sheets. Interest in using securitization in other areas expanded after 2000. In 2002, for example, there was an effort to securitize the revenue stream from a patent for voice synthesizing equipment, a concept encouraged by the government.[1008] From 2003 to 2007 residential mortgage-backed securities accounted for the majority of new issues. (Exhibit 2) As shown in Exhibit 3, more than 90 percent of issues have been rated A or higher. The vast majority were AAA rated. (Exhibit 3)

Securitization in Japan has grown rapidly from its inception in 1994; however, in the context of the global market for securitized assets Japan's volume was very small. (See Exhibit 4) Moreover, in Japan itself the value of securitization issues annually was less than 2 percent of bank loans outstanding.[1009] In 1998, when the legal barriers to securitization in Japan were being eliminated and the use of securitization was growing rapidly in the United States and Europe, there were expectations that Japan "[t]he world's second largest economy," should soon become the "second largest [securitization] market."[1010] The Bank of Japan reiterated the rationale for a robust securitization market in Japan in 2004 stating: "A vibrant securitization market should also encourage a better balancing of risks and returns in financial transactions including lending. This should invigorate Japanese financial institutions as new kinds of business and frontiers in financial technology begin to emerge. Furthermore, the stability of the Japanese financial system should be enhanced with

---

[1007] Author estimations from: Kousai Arimura & Yasuki Okai, *Current State of Japan's Securitization Market,* LAKYARA, Nov. 28, 2008, at 1, 3 (Exhibit 1) (Nomura Res. Inst., Ltd.), http://www.nri.co.jp/english/opinion/lakyara/2008/pdf/lkr200845.pdf (last visited Oct. 2, 2009).

[1008] *Japan Moves Towards First Patent Securitization,* MIP WK., Sept. 22, 2002, http://www.managingip.com/Article/1326865/Japan-moves-towards-first-patent-securitization.html (last visited Oct. 2, 2009)..

[1009] YOSHITAKE HATTORI, BANK OF JAPAN, DEVELOPMENT AND CURRENT ISSUES OF JAPANESE SECURITIZATION MARKET 8, http://www.afdc.org.cn/afdc/UploadFile/200932452463657.PPT (last visited Oct. 2, 2009)..

[1010] Roy B. True, *New Developments in Japanese Asset Securitization: Open the Floodgates* (1998), http://www.tuj.ac.jp/newsite/main/law/lawresources/TUJonline/Corporate/assetsecwith%20glossary.html (last visited Oct. 2, 2009).

the development of financial intermediary channels that can complement lending by financial institutions."[1011]

Despite the strong rationale for growth in the asset-backed securities market, Japan's securitization remained comparatively small. Several reasons explain this small market share. Culture plays an important role. On the consumer side, saving rates in Japan have been among this highest in the world. At the same time, Japanese consumers utilize very little credit for purchases. The combination of these factors limits the need for securitization of credit card debt or even receivables. On the originator side, banks dominate Japanese financial intermediation. Historically the banks have been very conservative, especially after the housing bubble bust in 1989 leading to non-performing loan problems. Beyond the cultural issues, legal and regulatory barriers to securitization still remain. Concerns about what constitutes a true sale, an essential ingredient for bankruptcy remoteness, remain. "The term 'true sale' has various meanings, but in a legal context in Japan, it means that even if bankruptcy proceedings . . . have commenced against the originator . . . the transfer will not be regarded by an insolvency trustee . . . as part of the originator's . . . estate subject to the proceeding."[1012] While there is no absolute test of a true sale, the following factors aid the determination: "(i) the intentions of the parties; (ii) the reasonableness of the purchase price; (iii) whether the transferor has a right to the asset transferred . . . ; (iv) whether the transferor bears the risk of the asset transferred . . . ; (v) whether or not the transferor has a right to repurchase the asset transferred . . . ; (vi) whether the transfer of assets is perfected; and (vi) whether or not the assets are offset from the transferor's account book."[1013] Another bankruptcy remoteness related issue is the risk of the servicer becoming insolvent. The SPV relies on a service provider to collect its obligations. "Under Japanese law, cash is considered to be the property of the person who possesses it. If the servicer goes bankrupt while possessing collected money, this money will be subject to the insolvency proceedings of the servicer and may be used to satisfy the obligations of the servicer."[1014] Frequent transfer of funds from the servicer to the SPV can

---

[1011] Secretariat of the Workshop on Securitization, Bank of Japan, *Report on the Workshop on Securitization (Summary),* May 21, 2004, http://www.boj.or.jp/en/type/release/zuiji/kako03/mpo0405a.htm (last visited Oct. 2, 2009).

[1012] Hajime Ueno & Takuya Shimizu, *Bankruptcy Remoteness and Securitization in Japan,* asailaw japan Rev., Jan. 2007, at 14, 14, http://www.jurists.co.jp/en/publication/tractate/docs/f_070117_hau_tks_en.pdf (last visited Oct. 2, 2009).

[1013] *Id.* at .15.

[1014] Hirokazu Ina, *in Japan, in* GLOBAL AND STRUCTURED FINANCE 2008, at 109, 112, . http://www.globalsecuritisation.com/08_GBP/GBP_GSSF08_109_116_Japan.pdf (last visited Oct. 2, 2009).

mitigate, but not eliminate, this risk. Moreover, until 2005 perfection of transfer of some assets required notification and consent of the individual obligors.

The barriers to securitization enumerated above ironically and fortunately keep the Japanese financial system from falling prey to the subprime crisis. In April 2008 after the failure of the investment bank Bear Stearns in the United States and the run on Northern Rock Bank in the United Kingdom, Nomura Research Institute reported "the subprime crisis does not appear to be having much impact on Japan's securitization market."[1015] The report noted that "spreads have widened, reflecting investor caution" and went on to suggest "[t]he market is offering advantageous opportunities for investors able to capitalize on them with sophisticated risk management."[1016] Although the volume of securitization activity in the first quarter of 2008 was 30% below a year earlier, "Japan's securitization market [was]n't as severely damaged as overseas markets, and there were no reports of mortgage loan defaults spiking, nor any deterioration in the performance of securitization transactions exposed to residential mortgage loans . . . ."[1017] By the end of 2008 it was clear that the volume of securitized transactions would fall below 2007 levels and perhaps remain at depressed levels for some time but Japan avoided the systemic failure of the financial system seen in the United States and Europe.

Japan was able to avoid the securitization crisis not only because the volume of securitized transactions was comparatively small but also because of the structure of securitization in Japan. The majority of securitization transactions in Japan were single-layer. The re-securitization of securitized products (e.g., squared and cubed collateralized debt obligations) that was prevalent in the United States and led to an understatement of risk was rare in Japan. The level of standardization of securitization in Japan also mitigated risk. Rather than rely on standards, the relationships between the parties were more based on contractual terms. On the investor side of the transaction, in Japan banks and insurers were the primary customers for the asset-backed securities. Given the conservative nature of these institutions, they were more interested in securities that offered moderate risk with moderate return "not the highly leveraged speculative products that wreaked havoc

---

[1015] Kousai Arimura, *Japanese Securitization Market Trends amid the Subprime Crisis,* LAKYARA, Apr. 10, 2008, at 2, 2, http://www.nri.co.jp/english/opinion/lakyara/2008/pdf/lkr200835.pdf (last visited Oct. 2, 2009).

[1016] *Id.*

[1017] *Japan Securitization Issuance Down 30% sSo Far in 2008*, MARKETWATCH, Apr. 18, 2008, LEXIS, News Library, Curnws File..

in the US."[1018] Consequently, subprime and securitization related losses of the big Japanese banks have been small. The attitude toward securitization remained largely positive in Japan even as the global financial crisis deepened. Exhibit 4 shows that a majority of investors had not changed their policies toward securitization products even at the end of 2008.

While the direct negative impact of the collapse of the securitization market in Japan has been small, the global financial crisis is taking a toll on the Japanese economy. Japan's GDP fell an annualized 12.7 percent in the fourth quarter of 2008, the worst decline in the country since the 1970s oil crisis as the country's exports plummeted.[1019] The IMF has forecast that Japan's economy will shrink more than 5 percent in 2009.[1020] The bank of Japan and the private sector recognize the positive role that securitization can play in supporting the Japanese economy. As the financial crisis was deepening in 2008, the Bank of Japan wrote about the importance of securitization: "Basically, these securitized products are being utilized by investors as an investment choice for effectively controlling the risk and return on an investment portfolio. They also could contribute to improving the efficiency of financial markets by providing economic entities requiring funds with a new means for fund-raising."[1021]

The Bank found that the critical requirement for a more robust securitization market was the improved ability to identify and manage risk - of the assets, structure of the product, price, marketability, etc. Managing risk in turn requires information. To this end the Bank working with the other stakeholders encouraged the formation of the Working Group on Distributions of Securitized Products. The Japan Securities Dealers Association (JSDA) as both a trade organization and self-regulatory body took a leadership role establishing rules for information disclosure. The rules cover both public offerings and private placements as well as primary and secondary

---

1018 Kousai Arimura & Yasuki Okai, *Current State of Japan's Securitization Market,* LAKYARA, Nov. 28, 2005, at 1, 6, http://www.nri.co.jp/english/opinion/lakyara/2008/pdf/lkr200845.pdf (last visited Oct. 2, 2009).

1019 Qi Wei, *News Analysis: Japan Dragged into Deeper Recession amid Global Financial Meltdown,* XINHUA GENERAL NEWS SERVICE, Feb. 16, 2009, LEXIS, News Library, Curnws File, *at* http://news.xinhuanet.com/english/2009-02/16/content_10828827.htmwww.xinhuanet.com (last visited Oct. 2, 2009).

1020 Darrel Whitten. *IMF Now Says Japan's GDP Will Fall Nearly 6% in 2009,* ISTOCKANALYST, Mar. 23, 2009, http://www.istockanalyst.com/article/viewarticle/articleid/3138120 (last visited Oct. 2, 2009).

1021 Fin. Sys. & Bank Examination Dep't, Bank of Japan, Securitized-Product Investment: Risk Management Perspectives 1 (BOJ Reports & research Papers, Paper Series of Risk Management in Financial Institutions, Mar. 2008), http://www.boj.or.jp/en/type/ronbun/ron/research07/data/ron0803a.pdf (last visited Oct. 2, 2009).

issues. The information provided is not proscribed. Rather, there is flexibility given the range of securitization structures used in Japan; although, the Standardized Reporting Information Package is a guide.

Whether the actions taken by the financial sector in Japan will bolster the securitization market is yet to be seen. But, in June 2009, a *New York Times* blogger ran a story with the headline: Securitized Debt Makes a Comeback in Japan. “Securitized debt may have been behind the mortgage crisis, but it still has it uses. Takefuji, one the largest consumer lenders in Japan, aims to raise as much as 100 billion yen, or $1 billion, by securitizing its loan book and borrowing from other institutions . . . .”[1022]

Exhibit 1
Asian Securitization Activity

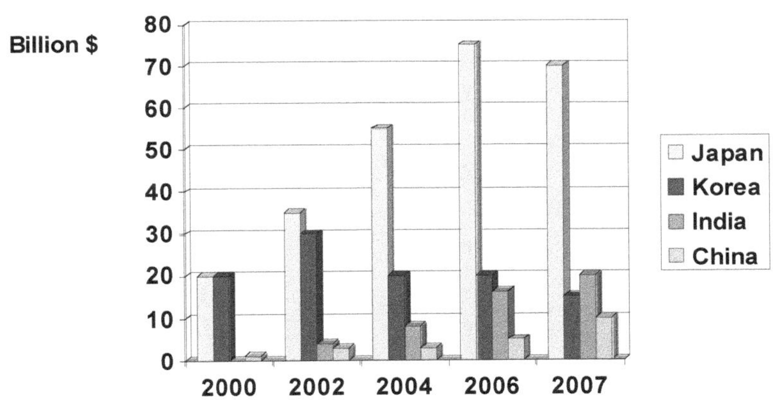

Source: Author estimation of data presented in:
Luc Can, *Asset Securitization in Asia: The Case of China and Implications for Vietnam* (2008).

[1022] *Securitized Debt Makes a Comeback in Japan,* N.Y. TIMES, June 3, 2009. http://dealbook.blogs.nytimes.com/2009/06/03/securitized-debt-makes-a-comeback-in-japan/ (last visited Oct. 2, 2009) (linking Finbarr Flynn & Takako Taniguchi, *Takefuji Aims to Raise as Much as 100 Billion Yen (Update3),* BLOOMBERG.COM, http://www.bloomberg.com/apps/news?pid=20601208&sid=a2RhUcLWmKQ8&dbk (last visited Oct. 2, 2009)).

Exhibit 2
Composition of Assets Securitized in Japan

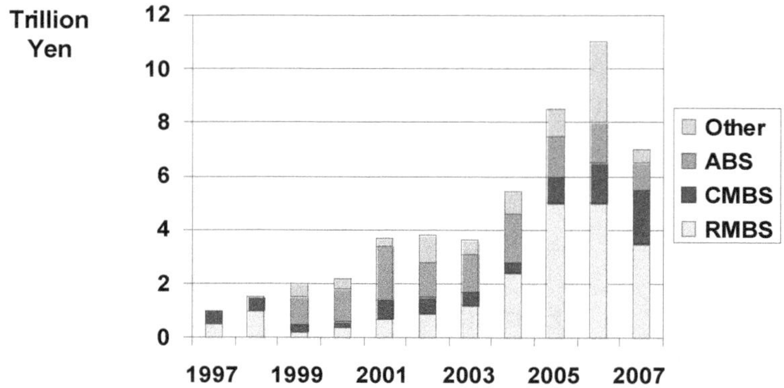

Source: Author estimations from: Kousai Arimura & Yasuki Okai, *Current State of Japan's Securitization Market*, Lakyara, Nov. 28, 2005, at 1, 3 (Exhibit 1), http://www.nri.co.jp/english/opinion/lakyara/2008/pdf/lkr200845.pdf (last visited Oct. 2, 2009).

Exhibit 3
Securitization Product Credit Ratings (as of issue date)

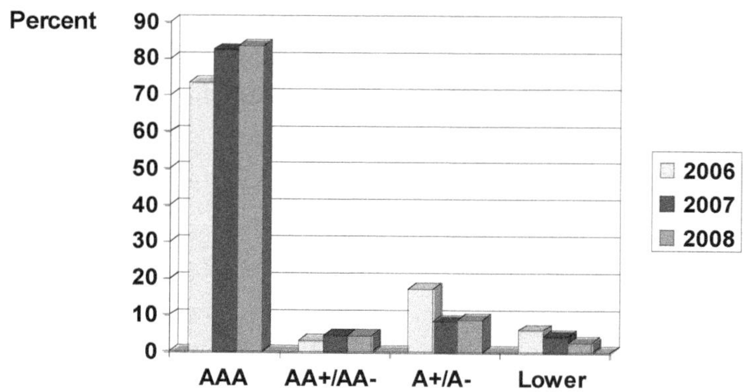

Source: Author estimation drawn from data in Luc Can, *Asset Securitization in Asia: The Case of China and Implications for Vietnam* (2008).

Exhibit 4
Impact of Subprime Problems on Japanese Securitization Activity

	Yes	No
Revised investment policies since the subprime problems?	42%	58%
What revisions were made?		
- Ceased investment in products difficult to risk -assess	75%	
- Tightened risk management	14%	
- Other	12%	

Source: Kousai Arimura & Yasuki Okai, *Securitized Product Investment and the Information Divide Among Financial Institutions*, Lakyara, Nov. 28, 2005, at 13, 13 (Exhibit 1), http://www.nri.co.jp/english/opinion/lakyara/2008/pdf/lkr200845 pdf (last visited Oct. 2, 2009).

Discussion Questions

Legal

- How do the requirements for "true sale" in Japan compare with the United States?
- How do the requirements for "perfection" in Japan compare with the United States?
- What regulatory approach could Japan use to mitigate the risk of servicers' bankruptcy?
- How does the structure and management of SPVs in Japan compare with those in the United States?

Business

- Is self-regulation by disclosure an effective tool for reducing information risk in Japan? In the United States?
- Will transparency of risk alone restore the securitization market in Japan?
- What assets are more attractive to securitize in Japan? How does the list compare with the most attractive assets in the United States?

Public Policy

- What is the role of securitization in a risk-averse financial environment?
- What is the rationale for the Bank of Japan's efforts to support the securitization market?
- How can the Japanese Securities Dealers Association balance its trade and regulatory functions?

Chapter 13: The Impact of Securitization

The purpose of this chapter is to consider the impacts of securitization on the individual participants and on the financial system as a whole. First, the impacts on borrowers such as access to credit and their relationships with lenders are explained. Next the impacts on lenders (banks) are explored including the effect of securitization on liquidity, cost of funds, risk, and competition. The impacts on non-bank intermediaries are also outlined. The final participant group examined is the investors. Here we consider the benefits, risks, and costs of securitization. The chapter concludes with a discussion of the impact of securitization on the overall financial system. A case study about the rash of mortgage foreclosures in 2007 and 2008 provides a context for weighing the totality of benefits and risk of securitization.

The financial crisis beginning in 2008 is impacting all of the securitization stakeholders. Proposals for redefining roles and regulations abound. It is too early to tell what changes will be adopted and/or mandated. Therefore the reader should understand this chapter in an historical context and be aware that new impacts of securitization are likely to emerge.

A. Impact on Borrowers [1023]

Being a limited resource, credit can be rationed. Lenders can ration credit by price, conditions, or denial. For example, banks screen out risky borrowers and deny credit to them altogether, rather than make loans on interest rates that match different risk levels. Banks also ration credit by conditions. For example, they prefer borrowers that keep "compensating balances" in their deposit accounts because these balances provide collateral, ease liquidity problems for the banks, enable an easy setoff in case of nonpayment, and may provide the banks with cheaper funds. Similarly, banks prefer long-term customers to maintain their customer base and reduce the banks' information costs. However, the environment is changing. Price is increasingly used, long-term customers have become short-term, customers manage their cash better and calculate the cost of compensating balances and banks can rely on market sources for funding.

Markets ration credit mainly by price, which signals the level of risk that a security carries. Even in the Markets, risky instruments may be rationed by means other than price, and there are borrowers that cannot sell their securities at any price. The law plays a crucial role in market rationing. Explicit disclosure may render instruments unsalable; broker-dealers are required to know their customers and avoid unsuitable

---

[1023] 1 TAMAR FRANKEL, SECURITIZATION § 5.1 (Ann Taylor Schwing ed., 2d ed. 2005).

recommendations to them, and prudence rules impose limits on the risk that regulated Institutional investors may take. As these investors transact an ever-larger portion of market trades, the overall limits on risk in the Markets increase. However, Markets offer high-risk securities to sophisticated investors and investors that could sustain losses. In the past thirty years, small investors have increasingly invested in the Markets through Institutions, such as pension funds and mutual funds. Because these Institutions are deemed sophisticated and because they can invest in high-risk securities only a small percentage of the assets they manage—although this percentage can be very high in dollar terms—may be in risky securities.

a. Access to Credit[1024]

Securitization gives incentives to create efficient credit evaluations based on statistical data. Fannie Mae has developed a list of red flag signs to help loan Originators in detecting fraudulent applicants for mortgage loans. These red flag signs include young borrowers with substantial cash (probable gift rather than earning power); high-income borrowers with relatively little cash (probable undisclosed liabilities); significant changes in deposit balances during the two months preceding the loan application; checks drawn on banks different from the checks sent with the deposit form; lines of credit that are open at the same time for no apparent reason; spouses with no credit history; even-dollar amounts of income and deductions; self-employed applicants with no estimated tax payments. FHLMC has its own extensive list of red flags, broken down into multiple categories to address the mortgage loan application, the credit report, verification of employment, paystubs, W-2 and 1099 Forms, tax returns and specific schedules, verification of deposits, bank checks, sales contract, escrow instructions, appraisal, preliminary title report or title search, HUD-1/settlement statement, and miscellaneous. Other lenders have developed their own criteria, such as the GMAC Bank Wholesale Mortgage Lending Code of Conduct and Fraud Awareness Guide. Credit reports and income tax returns are significant sources of information in addition to the appraisal, contract documents and various verifications from employers and others. Any system of guidelines for identifying potential fraud will not be completely accurate and may shift the cost to borrowers who are caught in the statistical net to show that they are able to make mortgage payments. An appropriate procedure for appeals by prospective borrowers who believe they have been unfairly denied credit should be devised, but there is no escape from imposing such a process. Although different from credit allocation, a similar process is used in IRS audits, in standardized admission tests to educational institutions seeking financial aid, and in many other situations.

[1024] 1 TAMAR FRANKEL, SECURITIZATION § 5.2 (Ann Taylor Schwing ed., 2d ed. 2005).

b. Competition Among Borrowers and Lenders[1025]

Since securitization produces savings by efficiencies, borrowers can enjoy lower cost of credit in a competitive environment because they share in the savings. In fact, the process of securitization itself increases competition in the lending Markets that are already vigorously competitive. Accordingly, borrowers benefit.

For borrowers who had a choice of raising funds in the Markets or from Institutions, securitization creates greater competition with new borrowers who can now resort to Markets. For borrowers who could obtain credit only from Institutions and those who could not obtain credit even from Institutions, securitization offers an indirect access to Markets at lower interest rates.

When lenders compete to make loans for sale, they function less as evaluators of credit and more as marketing organizations. Credit is easier to sell than other products because borrowers can be tempted to enjoy now and pay later. The problems accompanying the "hard sell" of credit have indeed appeared. They take the form of inaccurate information that persuades people to borrow even if they cannot afford it or to take risks they would not otherwise take (for example, that they will lose their homes). These problems are similar to those that appeared in the sale of mutual fund shares by installments in the 1960s and the sale of securities on margin.

There are some commentators who argue that borrowers should fend for themselves. In direct negotiations they can inquire from the lender about the terms of the loans. *Caveat emptor* should apply to them. Farmers that borrowed on the equity of their land and lost their farms as land prices tumbled should pay the price of their gullibility or greed under this analysis. Even if that approach were entirely satisfactory, however, the issue is no longer confined to particular borrowers. At least some borrowers have the opportunity to refinance, although on harsher terms, in accordance with the risk they present. If the results of gullibility and greed, or illness and other misfortunes, are mass foreclosures, unemployment, recession in regional economies, and bank failures, non-borrowers are affected as well.

One solution is to require the lenders to provide future borrowers with accurate disclosure. Indeed, many laws require disclosures, especially as to calculation of interest. Requiring more accurate information from all sellers of loans may produce an adequate screening mechanism yet maintain competition among lenders. Another solution is to tie the salespersons' rewards to the level of risk that the borrowers can take. For example, if the salesperson sells a loan, the salesperson should not receive his commission for at least 18 months, or receive only 20% of his commission upon the sale, and the rest of the commission after 18 months, if the borrower paid all his

---

[1025] 1 TAMAR FRANKEL, SECURITIZATION § 5.3 (Ann Taylor Schwing ed., 2d ed. 2005).

monthly payments. This system has been adopted in section 27 of the Investment Company Act of 1940. Banks have also adopted this approach to rein in the zeal of employees who made loans for sale. In addition, by pooling the bonuses of the loan officers, who were more conservative in their lending and the employees who made loans for sale, the loan officers had an incentive to monitor the salespersons to limit the level of risk of the loans they made.

Arguably, competition drives banks, like any other industry, to cut costs at the small customer's expense. However, competition also subjects banks to the countervailing pressure to increase quality. For example, asset management accounts in conjunction with mutual funds currently offer lines of credit, provide quality services, and show sensitivity to customers' desires. On balance, it seems that small customers are not worse off than before securitization.

c Relationships with Lenders[1026]

Large and small borrowers value long-term relationships with lenders. Implicit in these relationships is the promise of possible future credit, especially if the borrowers experience financial difficulties. Long-term relationships also reduce the information costs for lenders and provide more expedient funds for borrowers in temporary but urgent need. A bank that has made a loan for investment has a stake in the borrower's financial well-being. This aspect of the relationship is especially important for small borrowers, about whom information is not easily available (although the transactions in the deposit accounts give the bank some indication of the borrowers' situation). In addition, a bank may advise a larger customer in financial trouble on ways to restructure its loans. Such a customer values advice from a bank familiar with the customer's affairs.

Although the foregoing symbiotic relation between banks and borrowers may continue to exist in smaller communities and special circumstances, relations are increasingly impersonal. Large and small borrowers tend to shop for better rates and are less loyal to their banks; the banks return the sentiment.

As compared to banks in other countries, United States banks have not been especially active in helping customers in difficulties. A case study comparing the role of banks in solving problems of large borrowers in four countries is instructive. In Japan, a customer usually has one lead bank. While other banks participate in the customer's loans, the lead bank maintains the sole contact with the borrower and is closely associated with it. The lead bank receives current information regarding the borrower's affairs and can therefore detect trouble very early on. The case study showed that the lead bank took prompt and drastic steps upon detecting trouble. The bank's officers assumed greater influence over the customer's long-term policies and

[1026] 1 TAMAR FRANKEL, SECURITIZATION § 5.4 (Ann Taylor Schwing ed., 2d ed. 2005).

day-to-day operations. Through the bank's involvement, the probability and cost of the borrower's failure were reduced. In contrast, the particular U.S. borrower in the case study borrowed from as many as 400 banks. Its financial difficulties were discovered only when failure was imminent. The banks remained passive in the process of resolving the borrower's problems. In an exceptional case (Chrysler), the Government and Congress assumed leadership, but the usual troubled company had to find help on its own or through the bankruptcy court. While Japan and the United States represent the extremes, Germany and the United Kingdom occupy a middle ground.

United States banks more often act as creditors that seek to improve their position against other creditors regardless of the borrower's needs. Services that banks used to perform with some frequency in "workout" situations are now more often performed by the bankruptcy courts in Chapter 11 proceedings. The Markets are developing expert companies that manage corporations in trouble for rehabilitation. An example is a mutual fund manager of a fund that invests in highly leveraged companies, knowing that some of the companies were on the verge of bankruptcy. The fund invested recognizing that once the company filed for bankruptcy (or was forced into bankruptcy) the fund could take a leadership position in restructuring the company. The fund also assumed that large bank creditors would do what they had historically done and just try to mitigate losses and not try to maximize potential value.

To the extent that small borrowers benefited from a closer relationship with their banks in the past, the benefits seem to have been greatly reduced. Under a securitization regime, relationships between banks and borrowers are impersonal because the lender participates the large loan and sells small loans to an SPV. Banks can legally sell small loans without the consent of the borrowers. Large borrowers whose loans are sold by participation are sometimes notified or asked to approve, depending on the lender's policies and on how much it values its relationship with the borrowers. However, large customers rarely refuse to allow the sale of their loans, especially if they have other outstanding securities in the Markets.

Once the loan is sold, the borrower has no one to talk to, for example, if there is a need to change the loan terms. For example in the New Century bankruptcy (363(*o*)) the originator who sold the loan has neither authority nor interest in serving the borrower. The originator may continue to service the loan but has little discretion in that role. The SPV manager cannot change the terms because the SPV securities are based on the original terms of the loan. If the borrower is in financial difficulties, an impersonal foreclosure process is set in motion. The originating bank will take no part in it or will foreclose automatically; the bank has no incentive to infuse additional funds for rehabilitation. Small borrowers, especially the borrowers who bought consumer goods on installment, may be precluded by the sale of their loans to SPVs from asserting defenses against the seller of unsatisfactory products. This problem is not the result of securitization; it has been the rule in the United States for a long time, and there are statutes that address this problem. In practice, this is not what happens. Pursuant to the REMIC laws, if foreclosure is imminent, it is possible to change the terms of the loan to keep it in the securitization, including rate and term adjustments. There are triggers in the payout rules in the securitization trust that would kick in, requiring a greater portion of the cash flow to go to the more senior holders, if losses and delinquencies hit a certain percentage.

Securitization has reached the debt of borrowers in distress whose loans have been charged off by the lenders. This type of debt is sold at very deep discounts. The Originators of the SPVs are collection agencies and special departments established by lenders for collection purposes. Arguably, such Originators could be expected to tend to take all legal means to collect the debt, although some maintain that the reverse is true and that the buyers tend to help the borrowers recover, especially if the price of the loans was very low.

In addition, securitization by pooling and establishment of secondary Markets in SPV securities bring pressures for standard loan documents and underwriting. To the extent that borrowers had bargaining power under the traditional Institutional model, that power is greatly reduced when the pressure to follow standard terms effectively defeats the ability to negotiate terms more favorable to the individual borrowers' circumstances.

The development of the global capital market is a tale of two systems. While these systems should in principle reflect one another, their development has in fact diverged considerably. The international capital market has thrived and grown to unimaginable levels, however its regulation has stagnated and remains trapped in a different era. Globalization has brought with it a flourishing of the international capital market which has fundamentally changed the global economy. The magnitude and variety of international debt transactions that occur daily is truly astounding. However, the regulatory regime governing this market has lagged severely behind its economic growth, leaving both investors and the global economy vulnerable to manipulation and potential economic disaster.

B Impact on Lenders (Banks)[1027]

The problems inherent in the traditional bank structure stem mainly from the mismatch between bank assets and liabilities and lack of diversified loan portfolios. The solution this country chose many years ago was to support the fragile structure of banks by providing bank guarantees on a certain amount of deposits, granting banks a monopoly on deposits and prohibiting them from competing among themselves for deposits and to a lesser degree also for borrowers. In addition, the

[1027] 1 TAMAR FRANKEL, SECURITIZATION § 4.1 (Ann Taylor Schwing ed., 2d ed. 2005).

Government provided loans for banks with short-term liquidity problems. An attempt was made to insulate banks from market fluctuations by a fixed book value for their loans (except when the borrowers' credit deteriorated substantially) and by prohibiting banks from investing in most types of securities or engaging in investment banking.

The traditional regime could work only in stable economic conditions and only as a whole. Since the mid-1960s, economic conditions have fluctuated and bank protections have been partially dismantled by the marketplace and by Congress. Banks' deposit bases became unstable, and their losses increased as loans in their undiversified portfolios became sour. Not surprisingly, the banks' financial conditions deteriorated significantly.

a. Effect on Liquidity[1028]

Bank certificates of deposit (CDs) offer similar terms as bank deposits but are tradable. However, if they are short-term, they can pose for banks similar problems of liquidity as deposits do. That is if they are concentrated in a few hands and are not renewed. They are not likely to be renewed if the market interest rates rise above the interest rate promised under the CD. But CDs that are widely distributed do not pose less of such risk. In addition, such market substitutes for deposits can also help relieve liquidity pressures for banks, because the banks can raise funds in the markets by issuing commercial paper and CDs. Similarly, markets enable banks to raise money after they receive borrowers' commitments, rather than seek the borrowers after raising costly funds. A similar scenario appears if the banks securitize their loans. Holding securitized loans provides banks with liquidity but renders their assets more volatile to market fluctuations. The answer may be that the banks' stable deposits and assets are linked to the economy and its fluctuations, regardless of how the numbers appear in the books.

b. Effect on Cost of Funds[1029]

Securitization can provide banks with less risky and less costly funds. If the overall credit of a bank is lower than the credit of particular loans in its portfolio, the bank can raise funds less expensively by selling off these loans or using them as collateral than by issuing its own obligations. For example, if the market requires x% on the bank's CDs but only x-y% on the bank's borrowers obligations, the bank may securitize the borrowers' loans and the securities would then bear the borrowers' credit rating of x-y%. In such a securitization the bank will sell the securitized loans at a better price than the price of its own borrowing. A similar result is likely to occur if the bank raises funds and collateralized its borrowing with loans it holds, if the market demands lower interest for these loans. In addition, this process can

---

[1028] 1 TAMAR FRANKEL, SECURITIZATION § 4.2 (Ann Taylor Schwing ed., 2d ed. 2005).

[1029] 1 TAMAR FRANKEL, SECURITIZATION § 4.3 (Ann Taylor Schwing ed., 2d ed. 2005).

protect the banks from market interest risks. After all, once the bank borrows on a fixed rate and does not hold loans for sale it passes the risk of interest fluctuations to the buyers of the securitized loans.

Further, by selling loans and purchasing loan participations or loan-backed securities, banks can better diversify their loan portfolios and continue to specialize in lending to particular types of borrowers. On this count, securitization can be most advantageous for banks.

c Effect on Other Risks[1030]

Securitization by pooling allows banks and other holders of financial assets (SPVs and lead banks) to take short-term risks and shift these risks onto investors. Thus, SPVs issuing pass-throughs simply pass on whatever borrowers pay to investors. Put differently, all credit risks, prepayment risks, and market risks are transferred to the investors. Collateralized Asset Obligations allocate risks among classes of investors. The SPV issues a number of classes, called tranches. The least risky tranche receives payments from the SPV's pool first but collects lower interest. The second tranche holders receive payments second, and a higher interest rate. The third and the fourth tranches receive later payments and a higher interest rate. Timing of payment represents risk for which the later-paid tranches are compensated. In both cases, the SPVs do not bear the risks, although there is some concern that cash flow risks remain with the SPVs. That is if the SPV losses are truly substantial or there is a conflict among the tranche holders as to the amounts due to each. The assumption is that investors will diversify these risks, and that, if their portfolios are too small to do this directly, they will do so indirectly through investment companies or through other investment.

d Effect on Competition in the Banking Business[1031]

Banks have been losing lending business since nonbank intermediaries appeared about 100 years ago. This trend continued until the 1930s and then reappeared in the 1960s. One reason for the decline in banks' share of the lending market is the burden of noninterest-bearing reserves that banks must keep with the Federal Reserve Banks. Banks could choose to reduce this cost of unproductive reserves by reducing their assets and their deposits. Since reserves remained stable between the 1930s and 1960s, we can assume that banks' lending remained competitive, perhaps because they had a monopoly over a cheap source of funds (deposits). In fact, banks do not pay interest rate on their deposits, unless the deposits are very large. This strategy changed beginning in the mid-1970s when banks started to sell their assets and shrink their

---

[1030] 1 TAMAR FRANKEL, SECURITIZATION § 4.5 (Ann Taylor Schwing ed., 2d ed. 2005).

[1031] 1 TAMAR FRANKEL, SECURITIZATION § 4.6 (Ann Taylor Schwing ed., 2d ed. 2005).

deposits. It may be that the elimination of the monopoly over deposits forced the banks to take this route and securitization enabled them to do so.

Nonetheless, lending business has declined for a number of reasons. First, technology and securitization are attracting more borrowers and investors away from banks. Securitization erodes bank monopoly because it helps others to intermediate and bypass bank intermediation. Small or unseasoned companies that finance customers with good credit can use the same technique: pool their receivables and distribute shares in the SPVs, or use the receivables as collateral to obtain funds at lower interest. Second, of all the functions involved in securitization, the function of originating loans involves the highest cost and risks. Third, securitization paves the way for nonbank intermediation. It offers nonbank intermediaries a source of funds that is competitive with deposits. Nonbank lenders can effectively compete with banks; they may be more efficient and they do not bear the same costs of regulation. However, they may be subject to regulation that may be either more or less costly than bank regulation. For example, in the 2004-2007 years the regulation of mortgage bankers and hedge fund lenders was very light as compared to bank regulation.

While banks have not fared well in raising capital in the markets, their nonbank competitors have. Finance companies account for more than 50 percent of the issuers of medium-term notes, but banks account for only 17 percent of such notes, and thrifts—for only 1 percent.

More importantly, securitization has enabled *any* corporation, small or large, to become an intermediary and bypass the banks. While corporations in the past offered customers short-term credit or installment payments and discounted their customers' notes at the banks, these corporations can now sell the notes to an SPV issuing its own securities or issue commercial paper backed by these notes. Corporations have an incentive to securitize their customers' credit when the process may be less expensive than bank discounts, and if the corporations can utilize the credit of customers, higher than their own, to obtain less expensive funding. As this system develops, it will take an additional bite from the banks' borrower base, especially good credit borrowers. The cost of securitization, however, may differ from the cost of bank lending depending on the cost of establishing and maintaining the securitization system, the cost and risk of holding an inventory of the securitized loans, as compared to the cost of lending and the ongoing costs of maintaining and supervising the borrowers.

e Effect on Banks' Hegemony in Pricing Loans[1032]

The hegemony of banks as loan price setters is giving way to pricing based on loan-backed securities. As securitization of loans develops, market pricing of the securities signals the price of the loans that the banks make.

For a while, it appeared securitization was substantially reducing bank lending business. Banks took in fewer deposits, made fewer loans, and commentators predicted that the downward trend would continue. However, the market crash of October 1987 sensitized small investors to risk, and funds reverted to bank accounts, among other less risky investments. To the extent that the markets remain volatile, banks may retrieve part of their lost business as occurred after market prices declined in 1969. Bank business may even improve if investors turn their future savings toward safer investments, including bank accounts, and corporate borrowers seek bank loans at rates lower than the cost of equity. But as long as banks could not engage in both market and institutional intermediation and diversify the risks of both forms of business, bank problems were likely to persist. However, with the termination of the Glass-Steagall Act restrictions, and their ability to issue, underwrite and trade in securities, banks could engage in securitizing their loans and distributing the loan-backed securities.

The real estate market recession in the early 1990s, and the ensuing tightening of credit, led to a collapse in commercial lending by insurance companies and commercial banks. To liquidate its massive inventory of commercial mortgage loans, the RTC developed commercial real estate structured finance. After the government RTC developed the market for these securities, Wall Street investment banks filled the role of traditional lenders. Initially, firms purchased assets from RTC and pooled them to issue mortgage backed securities (MBS). After they had learned the necessary skills and the market had grown accustomed to commercial MBS (or collateral mortgage backed securities "CMBS"), investment banks now seek newly originated loans, usually ranging between $1 million and $15 million and backed by second- and third-tier properties, to securitize them. These transactions are sometimes referred to as "conduit" transactions in which investment banks purchase commercial mortgage loans from regional originators, including banks, or, increasingly, directly originate the loans to maximize their profits. After two years of conduit transactions, volume soared, accounting for nearly a quarter of total commercial MBS volume in 1995. Insurance companies and other traditional lenders that sought to regain their role as commercial lenders were forced to offer extremely favorable terms. Therefore, insurance companies, as lenders in the commercial real estate market, tend to concentrate on industrial, anchored-retail, and suburban office properties.

[1032] 1 TAMAR FRANKEL, SECURITIZATION § 4.7 (Ann Taylor Schwing ed., 2d ed. 2005).

f. Effect on Risk in the Banking Business[1033]

If the best borrowers have left banks for financing in the markets, banks must compete for borrowers who cannot resort to the markets: those about whom information is not readily available, or those engaged in complex transactions, or, worse yet, riskier borrowers that the markets have rejected. These customers involve higher information costs thus banks must learn to price correctly and this may result in the liquidation of large amounts of varied collateral, with which banks have little expertise. Therefore, today even traditional banking is new.

Securitization produces new, untested, and risky instruments. These instruments can be very volatile, reflecting fluctuations in market interest rates and even magnifying them; for example, loan-backed SPV securities that provide only for interest payments or principal payments. Further, securities based on the cash flows of SPVs, especially those that are designed and manipulated by computers, are complex and difficult to comprehend without special expertise and equipment. Thus a bank may purchase instruments that are not appropriate for it. Traditional bank analysis of credit is not helpful in evaluating a large number of guaranteed small loans of diverse borrowers held by an SPV. The kinds of risks that securitized loans pose are not the traditional risks with which banks have dealt. Asset-backed securities pose less credit risk but more market risks. However, because asset-backed securities are liquid, they may also be used by banks as a tool for managing interest rate risk. Selling loans through securitization shortens the effective maturity of the bank's loan portfolio, thus reducing interest rate risk for the seller.

In a separate effort to increase the ability of financial intermediaries to purchase MBS, and as a result of industry pressure, in 1995 the National Credit Union Administration ("NCUA") decided to relax its proposed rule limiting Corporate Credit Union ("CCU") holdings of MBS or asset-backed securities (ABS) to only approximately three percent of their assets. In addition, by classifying certain assets as securities for purposes of risk-based capital calculations, the National Association of Insurance Commissioners ("NAIC") Securities Valuation Office has made it more advantageous for life insurers to hold commercial mortgage related securities than to hold whole loans. These efforts indicate a general agreement among regulatory authorities and industry groups that holding MBS is to be encouraged, both to stimulate the availability of funds in the capital markets and to decrease the risk of Institutions holding whole loans.

[1033] 1 TAMAR FRANKEL, SECURITIZATION § 4.9 (Ann Taylor Schwing ed., 2d ed. 2005).

g. New Business for Banks[1034]

Banks may borrow and lend in the present and in the future. Securitization shifts much of the banks' traditional lending and borrowing from the present to commitments for future lending and from risk undertaking to risk bearing by guarantees. While borrowers and savers deal directly in the markets, they seek bank guarantees against the risks they take. For example, borrowers in the markets (issuers) take the risk that their securities will not be placed at the expected price or not be placed fully. The underwriters may not be willing to cover this risk. Borrowers of long-term funds may choose less expensive short-term loans, provided they secure an alternative source if the short-term loans become more expensive. To cover these risks, borrowers turn to banks for commitments to lend at the option of the borrowers. Similarly, borrowers who desire protection against volatile interest rates (as in the 1970s and 1980s) seek a bank promise to lend in the future at fixed rates.

h. Contingent Obligations[1035]

Investors in the Market are exposed to the borrowers' credit risk. Investors are also exposed to liquidity risk. For investments that are considered low risk, such as commercial paper and loan-backed securities, investors demand bank letters of credit to cover the credit and liquidity risks. Historically, letters of credit were viewed as contingent loans to bank customers. Their new use renders them a functional equivalent of guarantees or insurance commitments.

The temptation for banks to issue contingent obligations is great; these obligations offer fees today and require performance tomorrow or perhaps never, and help maintain the banks' relations with long-term customers. But these obligations expose banks to a number of risks. First, future commitments are generally harder to gauge than present ones. Second, borrowers are likely to call upon banks when money is tight, precisely when it might be as difficult for the banks to raise funds as it would be for their customers. Third, the markets may reject a particular borrower because of vague concerns about its future; the bank may share these concerns but be constrained to lend for legal or business reasons.

Whether contingent liabilities are riskier than immediate loans is an open question. Banks specialize in types of risks, pooling and diversifying them. But the method of managing current risk used by banks and regulators may be less appropriate for future (similar) contingent risk. A different technique to back contingent liabilities could follow an insurance model. The risks must be priced and funded correctly. For example, the premiums cannot be viewed as fixed fees for services.

[1034] 1 TAMAR FRANKEL, SECURITIZATION § 4.10 (Ann Taylor Schwing ed., 2d ed. 2005).

[1035] 1 TAMAR FRANKEL, SECURITIZATION § 4.1 (Ann Taylor Schwing ed., 2d ed. 2005).

Banks can also self-insure against market risks by purchasing hedging market instruments, such as options, futures, and "swaps." For example, loans at fixed rates can be offset by swapping the interest for variable rates. These instruments also enable banks to select the kind of risk they will take and fine-tune their risk management. In theory, banks can spread risks through these instruments among more parties, each able to choose the risk it is best able to bear. However, like loan-backed securities, some of these instruments are novel and involve unknown risks. In contrast to assessing credit risks, with which banks are familiar, these instruments require expertise in assessing market risks and pricing contingent liabilities with which banks are unfamiliar. Further, some hedging instruments pose new risks to banks from additional intermediaries and new or anonymous parties.

In sum, banks have been moving into a new business of underwriting contingencies, and, in the past, they took the risks during the transition and learning period. Banks have also entered into the service for fee business. This business represents lower risks and usually lower returns. However, banks have found that the business can be very lucrative, by adding offers of multiple and new services to the same customers and taking advantage of opportunities as they arise, such as providing refinancing services.

i. Servicing Loans and Market Intermediation[1036]

Traditionally, bank income was based on returns from loans and a lesser proportion from trading in Government securities and currencies, service fees, and management fees. Securitization introduces banks to new businesses. Banks that securitize their loans may retain the servicing function for these loans and provide custodial, payment agent, and trustee services to others. To the extent that the law permits, banks are expanding their services as market intermediaries. The income of the money center and regional banks reflects the entry of banks into securitization in its many-splendored variations. Money center banks, and increasingly regional banks, are deriving a greater percentage of their incomes from management fees, and there is evidence that securities transactions are becoming a major source of income for them.

As compared to investment income, fee income is safer and less volatile, but it is usually smaller than loan income and it requires service personnel and large volumes to achieve economies of scale. Furthermore, fee income is more vulnerable to competition. Credit enhancement fees compensate an Institution for taking on a considerable contingent liability. As competition continued to drive down fees, some commentators expressed concern that such low fees were inadequate to compensate banks for the level of risk assumed. Nonetheless, one 1988 survey found that a fee-based strategy was one of the most successful strategies for banks.

[1036] 1 TAMAR FRANKEL, SECURITIZATION § 4.12 (Ann Taylor Schwing ed., 2d ed. 2005).

Arguably, problems of ailing and failing banks today do not stem from new services or new products or even customer dissatisfaction but from traditional banking activity of making loans, many of which have turned sour. In addition, learning and growing pains that banks experience do not place them at a competitive disadvantage because their competitors in the markets have similar problems that seem to arise from traditional trading.

However, entry into new businesses requires restructuring. Banks have restructured at an inappropriate time, in an unstable economy. Securitization requires expertise: ability to evaluate novel instruments and act in a fast-moving environment, skills to manage large volumes of transactions, and technological capability by computers and Internet use. Many banks lack these skills and resources. Securitization may drive banks to growth, acquiring more loans for inventory (though short term) and increasing the turnover of their sales. Quick growth in lending activities can create pressure to relax lending standards and increase the risk that internal controls might fail.

In sum, securitization contributes to the banking industry's loss of traditional lending business to markets and other forms of intermediation. The law prohibits banks from engaging in many lucrative aspects of the securitization process. To compete, banks are taking on greater risks by lending to riskier borrowers or on riskier terms (e.g., long term) and are entering new businesses for which they may not be prepared. Banking has not yet been rationalized; old risks are being replaced by new risks.

j. Adjusting to the Securitization Process[1037]

A survey of the process of securitization by pooling leaves it doubtful whether banks or anyone else will undertake to perform all the functions involved in the process. Many of the functions are outside of traditional banking. The functions are regulated under different laws and require various reporting forms to different regulators and to customers; further, they often have different accounting requirements. It is difficult to integrate or even interface the necessary computer systems with those of any existing business, including the banks. Since the trend is to allow banks to perform different functions in separate legal entities, full integration may be achieved only by a bank holding company system. Entering the business of securitization requires learning. In fact, the business resembles banking only superficially. Nonetheless, money center banks have mastered the knowledge, and regional and even smaller banks are following suit.

[1037] 1 TAMAR FRANKEL, SECURITIZATION § 4.13 (Ann Taylor Schwing ed., 2d ed. 2005).

k. Legal Limitations on Bank Entry into the Securities Business[1038]

Since securitization sent banks to the capital markets, the large banks have established sales departments to distribute their own CDs and the commercial paper of their holding companies. These departments have had the capacity and a very strong incentive to continue to serve customers who have resorted to the commercial paper markets. Here banks ran into legal difficulties for many years, mainly because the former Glass-Steagall Act prohibited banks from underwriting and dealing in securities in the United States (but not abroad).

The infrastructure necessary for smooth securitization by banks was missing in many areas, perhaps even in 2007. For example, banks' assets are generally valued at the face amount of the loans they hold, and that valuation may change at discrete dates as borrowers' circumstances change. Thus, a $1000 loan is valued at $1000. If at a revision date the borrower failed to make some payments, the loan value may be reduced to $700. Securities held by banks are marked to market. As the amount of securities held by banks increases, so does variation in the value of the banks' assets. Since bank liabilities are usually fixed and do not match their assets, marking loans to market may create problems for banks. For example, the capital requirements of banks, that are the long-term obligations that they issue, such as stocks and long-term bonds, which cover short-term obligations such as the deposits, are less stable, depending on the market valuation of their assets.

l. Organizational and Cultural Changes[1039]

Securitization and competition have produced more aggressive and entrepreneurial bank managements who increasingly realize the need for risk controls, but they face a difficult task: to transform their banks into market Institutions, yet maintain for banks a more conservative culture than that of traditional securities firms. Today's world requires a large dose of both. The question is how to shift the balance to greater risk without pushing too hard, while also installing a competitive environment and transaction orientation in the organization but maintain prudence and caution. Successful leaders suggest three main keys to achieving this balance: expertise; internal risk controls, that is, taking risks knowingly, after a careful evaluation and not blindly; and preparing for the unknown, that is, being prepared for uncertainties that can neither be anticipated nor calculated.

[1038] 1 TAMAR FRANKEL, SECURITIZATION § 4.14 (Ann Taylor Schwing ed., 2d ed. 2005).

[1039] 1 TAMAR FRANKEL, SECURITIZATION § 4.15 (Ann Taylor Schwing ed., 2d ed. 2005).

The Current Process of Structural Change: In Search of a Culture.[1040] Banks reorganize in response to market demands and their own needs for protection. Money center banks are developing risk controls for their diverse, large, and fast-moving transactions, and for a business and personnel that is more transaction oriented and competitive. These controls consist of a number of components. First, global electronic information systems enable managements to ascertain the risk exposure of the entire bank at any given moment.

Second, controls involve incentive systems more suitable to the new business methods and more suitable for a new type of personnel that is more transaction oriented and competitive than in the past. These systems must instill in the workforce a "risk culture" that is strict, yet motivating. For example, to induce appropriate credit evaluation, some banks no longer give salespersons bonuses merely for producing loans. Credit decisions are not made by salespersons alone—although they may have information about the borrowers and buyers—but by two independent groups of sales and credit officers. Since loan officers are not compensated for credit evaluation, there are no incentives for them to perform the task. Therefore, bonuses to both groups depend on success in both functions, that is, on the volume of sales and appropriate risk level.

Third, banks change their internal organization to combine credit assessment and market risks in order to evaluate their exposure, control their traditional lending and funding operations, and adjust their pricing to risk. Banks can either evaluate risk first and establish their profit according to risk level or establish their profit goal and make sure that the risk is correctly priced no matter what the level of risk. In fact, banks often do both. The choice of emphasis may depend on whether risk can be correctly priced and, most important, whether part of the fees is to be allocated to loss reserves and invested as such. Since risk does not include unanticipated disasters, such as the 1973 oil crisis or the September 11 terrorist attacks, banks need additional "cushions" for these disasters. But these precautions add costs, and competition creates pressure to avoid them. It may well be that "disaster reserves" should be established by law.

All the different management systems that banks are developing aim at maximizing returns and controlling risks; all examine proposed transactions for revenue, cost of funds, control costs, and risks. The level of potential revenues determines the level of risk and control costs. Different systems may reflect the degree to which banks centralize their (global) funding and lending operations. One structure may be formal, requiring that each loan be approved by both credit and "relationship" officers, while another may give discretion to lending officers, subject to strong internal auditing.

[1040] 1 TAMAR FRANKEL, SECURITIZATION § 4.16 (Ann Taylor Schwing ed., 2d ed. 2005).

Reflecting the securitization process, banks are reorganizing by merging commercial and investment banking operations into one profit center, broadening the investment area to include interest risk management, and integrating market and credit risk management by establishing joint meetings of funding and lending management committees with interlocking membership in various degrees of formality. Bank corporate trust departments that have historically provided trustee and agency services to asset-backed securities transactions have increasingly provided additional services.

m. The Current Process of Structural Change: In Search of a Business Strategy[1041]

Securitization has changed the basic strategy of banking. Instead of lending long term for investment and borrowing short term, as they did in the past, banks are now lending long term but using the loans as inventory for trade. After loans are made, the investment group in the bank securitizes the loan and sells the securities. The strategy is to recycle assets as fast as possible, to earn fees and reduce maturity dates, and to invest any assets at variable rather than fixed rates to reduce market risks.

In a competitive environment a bank must innovate depending on its particular capabilities, the new product's risk and return, and the bank's expectations. To determine its options in the international area, a bank will evaluate the characteristics of the country involved and opportunities for domestic and cross-national arbitrage. In light of all these factors and options, the bank will set its criteria. Such a decision process has produced floating rates in an era of interest rate fluctuations; swaps to shorten the length of the maturities of loan portfolios, and futures options to lock in interest rates. Like all new and innovative techniques, use of these instruments requires expertise.

n. Will Banks Survive? The Issue of Organizational Change[1042]

There exists an extensive theoretical literature on organizational longevity and mortality that extends beyond the limits of this book. A short discussion, however, may be useful to predict the chance for survival of banks in transition. There are a number of theories on organizational survival. One theory focuses on the internal world of the organization and suggests that organizations change more slowly than the environment because of inertia; those organizations with stable performance and the ability to account rationally for their actions have a better chance for survival. The older an organization becomes, the better it can withstand internal changes. Revisions of existing interorganizational patterns endanger the existence of the organization.

[1041] 1 TAMAR FRANKEL, SECURITIZATION § 4.17 (Ann Taylor Schwing ed., 2d ed. 2005).

[1042] 1 TAMAR FRANKEL, SECURITIZATION § 4.18 (Ann Taylor Schwing ed., 2d ed. 2005).

A second theory focuses on the external environment of organizations. To survive, they must alter their structures to adjust to, and remain aligned with, outside conditions in order to match critical contingencies over time. Those organizations that develop routines for change that harmonize with environmental change will persevere. A third theory asserts that there is no relation between changes in organizations and their mortality rate. Survival is random, a matter of "luck."

These theories are complementary rather than mutually exclusive. Some organizational changes are "adaptive," while others depend on external environment and perhaps others are random. The fact that many banks have failed in their traditional businesses suggests that organizational changes to align with the new environment are crucial if banks are to survive. Changes in strategies, such as rapid growth without adjusting controls and other internal structures, may be fatal. Yet, the theory that old organizations that undergo structural changes become "new" and therefore more vulnerable is probably correct as well. Thus, change is crucial to the survival of banks but it makes them weaker.

Reorientation in the banking system is most dangerous because after half a century of strict regulation banks have lapsed into a deep inertia. While reorientation is less risky to an organization when change is implemented quickly (reducing disruption and uncertainty) "frame-breaking" involves internal and external opposition because of personnel anxiety and commitment to the status quo, political coalitions, the difficulty of maintaining control during the transition period, and pressures by outside constituencies (customers, suppliers, regulatory agencies, and local communities). Therefore, such changes require a strong leadership.

The recipe for successful leadership in transforming an institution is shrouded in mystery. Clearly, it requires a unique talent. A leader must define the new mission, select and acquire the appropriate technology, revise policies, change values and organizational structure, reassure the personnel, and provide inspiration and a new network of information.

Small and large banks are weaker today. While small banks are less adversely affected by securitization, they also lack the resources to reorganize properly. Large banks are more adversely affected by securitization but have more resources for drastic restructuring and can bring in new teams of managers to replace traditional ways of thinking and a commitment to the old ways. The quality of bank managements in recent years has indeed improved. They are ready to take more risks and are more sensitive to market signals. Yet, the metamorphosis of banks is extremely difficult. Banking business is very complex, especially if it combines wholesale and retail commercial banking, securitization activities, and other permissible market activities. The survivors will be those who find their niche, acquire expertise, and establish a culture of flexibility—the ability to change in response to the environment. One can only speculate as to what these banks of the future will look like.

C. Effect of Securitization on Nonbank Intermediaries[1043]

Securitization has facilitated expansion of traditional nonbank intermediaries and entry of new ones. Among the old ones are the auto companies' finance subsidiaries that have provided loans to purchasers of cars. Among the new ones are SPVs that serve as Institutions. For example, an Institution, financed by Institutional investors, "recycles" bank loans to the banks in the form of securities. The banks sell their loan portfolios to the SPV and receive from the SPV securities, for which a secondary market will be developed. Such a transaction has provided enough legal issues to occupy lawyers and regulators for quite a while.

Securitization by substitution has taught borrowers and savers to shop for alternatives all over the globe, to "manage cash" and to take into consideration the value of float (short-term money in transit). These developments propelled the use of market intermediaries at the expense of Institutions. Market intermediaries have increasingly provided Institutional-like intermediation, for example, by making "bridge loans" to issuers. Both market intermediaries and Institutions have diversified their business abroad and both provide various forms of intermediation in which they cooperate and compete. While banks underwrite and distribute securities, market intermediaries lend (or obligate to lend) like banks. In a large issuance of securities, the two may act together in both capacities.

a. Effect of Securitization as a New Business and Added Regulation[1044]

New businesses expose nonbank intermediaries to risks stemming from the new businesses and the risks of learning new businesses. These intermediaries are therefore learning and restructuring either before or after experiencing losses. The culture of market intermediaries is beginning to resemble that of Institutions, just as Institutional culture is beginning to resemble that of market intermediaries. As Institutions become more competitive and aggressive, market intermediaries are becoming more cautious and conservative.

The first nonbank Institutional intermediaries to enter new business were life insurance companies. Since these companies offered safe and low returns on savings, they saw their market share shrink from the effects of rising inflation and stock market prices during the late 1950s and 1960s. Therefore, life insurance companies developed annuities and life insurance tied to the performance of equity securities. This new business required that the companies comply with a different regulatory

---

[1043] 1 TAMAR FRANKEL, SECURITIZATION § 4.20 (Ann Taylor Schwing ed., 2d ed. 2005).

[1044] 1 TAMAR FRANKEL, SECURITIZATION § 4.20 (Ann Taylor Schwing ed., 2d ed. 2005).

regime, that is, the securities acts, including the Investment Company Act of 1940. The transition was not without cost. However, life insurance companies carry an amazingly diversified business of financial intermediation, which includes instruments similar to bank certificates of deposits, private placement of securities, mergers and acquisitions advisory and financing business, management of investment companies and distribution of investment company shares, property and casualty insurance, insurance of SPVs or loan-based securities, and other innovative instruments that combine insurance and securities components.

Insurance companies have learned to live with a multitude of state regulators, the SEC, and the Labor Department (which regulates pension fund managers). If a study were done of the evolution of the insurance business, the results might help other intermediaries that are now undergoing the process.

b. The Net Capital Rule

Like most other intermediaries that deal with other people's money in the financial Markets, broker-dealers must maintain a minimal amount of capital under the SEC's "net capital Rule." The Rule "is intended to ensure that broker-dealers have sufficient liquid capital to protect the assets of customers and to meet their obligations and responsibilities to other broker-dealers."[1045] In calculating the value of their assets for purposes of determining their required net capital, the market value of their securities is reduced by certain percentages ("haircuts"). These haircuts "provide[] a capital cushion against adverse market movements and other risks faced by the firms including, liquidity and operational risks."[1046]

Mortgage-backed securities "issued or guaranteed as to principal or interest by the United States or any agency thereof" are assigned haircuts based on the length of time to maturity.[1047] The longer the maturity, the higher the "haircut" would be.

Mortgage-backed securities present problems under the Rule because partial principal payments are often made earlier than the maturity date, thus shortening the effective maturity. In December 1997, the SEC proposed an amendment to the Rule, which would determine the haircut of a "Pass-Through Mortgage-Backed Security" in accordance with its market value relative to its par value. The Rule would therefore take into consideration the shortened maturity of the instruments resulting from partial earlier payments.

[1045] 62 Fed. Reg. 67,996 (Dec. 30, 1997); see 34-39455 (Dec. 17, 1997).

[1046] 62 Fed. Reg. 67,996 at 67,996 (Dec. 30, 1997).

[1047] 17 C.F.R. § 240.15c3-1(c)(2)(vi)(A)(1) (2009).

D. Impact on Investors

a. Effect of Securitization on Investors[1048]

Markets offer investors a rich variety of securities. Very few instruments are barred by law from the Markets. By and large, borrowers are free to offer investors securities on any terms and in any amount. In competitive Markets, investors benefit from the efforts of issuers to differentiate their securities from those of others. In contrast, banks, insurance companies, and other Institutions have been traditionally constrained by law to offer a relatively small variety of instruments on terms that were partially designed and limited by law. The amounts of Institutional offerings have also been limited by legal requirements of capital and reserves. Institutional issuers have had less incentive to innovate since they were legally protected, in various degrees, from competition within and from outside their industries.

b. Benefits: Choices and Diversification[1049]

Securitization expanded the variety of market offerings for investors. Through the process, investors gain access to loans that they could not have acquired before or could have acquired only at great cost. Securitization offers investors a choice of such loans in a liquid form, to sell, trade, or hold long term. Variety may be confusing and increase information costs, but sophisticated investors soon find out which new instruments offer a meaningful difference and which are merely "gimmicks."

Discussion Topics

1. Were the sub-prime loans gimmicks?
2. Were investors tricked into buying these securities?

Securitization is limited only by the extent of the legal constraints on the originating Institutions. SPVs that issue asset-backed securities are free, like other issuers, to design the terms and determine the amounts of the securitized loans they issue. By separating the holding of loans from their origination, securitization releases issuers from the legal limitations on the terms of the securities they offer and allows them to focus more on the investors' needs.

Securitization offers investors greater flexibility in designing and diversifying their portfolios. SPVs reduce risks for investors by partial diversification; the SPVs hold loans of the same kind but diversify in terms of borrower location, collateral, or various other factors. Securities issued by SPVs involve different risk levels, thus allowing investors to diversify their own portfolios as they choose. In addition,

---

[1048] 1 TAMAR FRANKEL, SECURITIZATION § 5.6 (Ann Taylor Schwing ed., 2d ed. 2005).

[1049] 1 TAMAR FRANKEL, SECURITIZATION § 5.7 (Ann Taylor Schwing ed., 2d ed. 2005).

investors can diversify their own portfolios by issuers, investing in part in securities of enterprises and part in securities of Institutions (the SPVs). Investors that desire particular types of loans can buy shares in SPVs that hold such loans and at the same time diversify the risk from failure of any particular SPV by holding the securities of different SPVs. In some cases investors may benefit from the special expertise of SPV Originators (e.g., the expertise of collection agencies).

Bank Regulators are Concerned that Banks May Lower Their Credit Standards in Making Loans Intended for Sale. This concern for bank investors (and indirectly for other investors) can be addressed through the banks' internal organization by requiring that the decision to approve the loan be made independently from the decision to securitize the loan.

The credit risk to investors varies with the borrower and the collateral, guarantees, and credit support, if any. Therefore, the credit risk posed by SPV securities depends on the creditworthiness of the borrowers, that is, the type of assets that the SPV holds, and on the collateral and on any additional third-party guarantees (credit enhancement) backing the securities.

Risk increases with unstable economic conditions that may affect the value of the collateral and the creditworthiness of the borrowers. For example, if the starting interest rate for mortgages increases but the rate of real estate appreciation (equity growth of the collateral) falls, the interest increase may not be matched with future cash flow from the borrowers. Although banks have a long-term interest in maintaining their lending standards, the need to raise short-term income can create an incentive to lower lending standards, resulting in losses to investors.

Loans made for sale are tailored to the buyers' requirements and sold before or immediately after they are made. The terms of these loans as to risk and interest may not be as advantageous to the investors as the loans made by the initial lender for investment. Lenders that make loans specifically intended for sale may tend to generate loans with higher credit risk than lenders who make loans to hold in their own investment portfolios.

c. Information Costs[1050]

Securitization by pooling imposes high information costs on investors because SPVs hold many illiquid loans of different borrowers. Historical default experiences of similar SPVs are not useful because even SPVs of similar assets may have been structured differently from the current SPVs and because unstable economic conditions make predictions based on past experience less reliable. Documentation for some types of loans (mortgages) is cumbersome and, for others (credit card

[1050] 1 TAMAR FRANKEL, SECURITIZATION § 5.8.2 (Ann Taylor Schwing ed., 2d ed. 2005).

receivables), is unreliable, since borrowers do not sign all the documents. Third, bankruptcy laws and the laws governing the foreclosure of the collateral, especially mortgages, are diverse and uncertain. In addition, securitized loans can be very complex and require expertise that some investors do not possess. Therefore, investors must rely on other sources to evaluate the SPVs' assets, such as loan originators, insurance companies, SPV trustees, appraisers, and rating agencies. To the extent that investors' reliance on these others to evaluate loans in the SPV or the SPV's securities is misplaced, investors may suffer losses. For example, the appraisers in the recent sub-prime debacle had incentives to overestimate the value of real property (a lot of drive-by appraisals) and the unregulated rating agencies were seen as being unreliable.

Asset-backed securities pose for investors a somewhat unique type of risk because the securities represent portions of a cash flow from a pool of loans rather than specific amounts. For example, securities that promise all the interest payments from an SPV composed of loans pose not only the credit risk that borrowers will fail to pay but also the risk that borrowers will prepay the loans. The latter risk depends mainly on market interest rates: if rates fall, prepayments will increase, and, if rates rise, prepayments will decrease, contrary to the lenders' interests. In addition, prepayment of "interest only" securities may eliminate the securities' source of payment altogether and result in horrendous losses. Asset-backed securities can be complex. They may require full information on what the SPVs contain, high level expertise, and the right software to determine and verify both the underlying assumptions on which the securities are based and their price.

Securitization has been used by investment bankers to repackage for sale securities that could not be sold directly, called "kitchen sink" bonds, also known as "by-product bonds." Arguably, these bonds do not resemble the securities that the Market rejected, because the bonds are pooled with other securities and senior classes of the new SPV enjoy credit enhancement. Nonetheless, there is concern that these securities pose substantial risks and that the securities will be sold to unsophisticated investors without adequate disclosure.

For all investors, asset-backed securities pose serious risks of valuation. Asset-backed securities valuation can be problematic if the securities are custom-made, designed in particular terms for the particular fund. In such a case, the securities do not have a Market and their valuation depends on the judgment of the fund's board of directors; that valuation might not be as accurate as the market valuation. In addition, many asset-backed securities are sold to sophisticated investors in "private placements" and by definition do not have liquid Markets. Yet another issue arises because "valuation of asset-backed securities often has a behavioral dimension not present with core derivatives and structured notes."[1051] Mortgages may be paid off if the property underlying the security is sold or the borrower refinances; partial prepayments occur whenever the borrower elects to pay more than the specified monthly payment. Significant variation between actual prepayment behavior and the anticipated prepayment behavior can materially affect the value of mortgage derivatives. Valuation is therefore especially important for such securities.

Some mortgage loans' values were based not only the ability of the borrowers to pay back the loans but on the value of the real estate collateral.[1052] Lenders justified their pricing of the sub-prime equity loan, the location of the property or the race or sex of the borrower appears to continue to be indications of a borrower's creditworthiness. That, however, is not convincing when the borrowers bought homes in locations which did not reflect the borrower's standard of living.

Both the Markets and legislation have addressed some of these drawbacks. The Markets usually require appraisals and ratings for asset-backed securities. Institutional lenders, appraisers, and, to a lesser extent, rating agencies, are regulated with respect to lending and other activities involved in the securitization process. As investment banks increased their originating activities in the 1990s, great advances have been made to standardize the terms of loans and the resulting mortgage-backed securities, particularly in the area of commercial loans. To bring further standardization (particularly for originators not working in conduit programs), Capital Consortium, a group of representatives from the Mortgage Bankers Association of America, the National Association of Realtors and the National Realty Committee, issued a set of guidelines. The guidelines consist of a standardized capital markets mortgage template, a due diligence checklist, data element guides and a list of suggested legislative and regulatory reforms. In addition, the laws and the regulators impose disclosure requirements on the creation and distribution of asset-backed securities.

d Liquidity Risk[1053]

Asset-backed securities have different degrees of liquidity, depending on the depth of the secondary Markets in which they are traded. For example, since the Market in mortgage-backed securities is much larger than the Market in other asset-backed securities, mortgage-backed securities are more liquid. Securities that are issued in a

---

[1051] Henry T.C. Hu, *Hedging Expectations: "Derivative Reality" and the Law and Finance of the Corporate Objective,* 73 TEX. L. REV. 985, 999-1000 (1995), *reprinted in* 21 IOWA J. CORP. L. 3, 16 (1995).

[1052] Cassandra Jones Havard , *Invisible Markets Netting Visible Results: When Sub-Prime Lending Becomes Predatory,* 26 OKLA. CITY U.L. REV. 1057 (2001).

[1053] 1 TAMAR FRANKEL, SECURITIZATION § 5.8.4 (Ann Taylor Schwing ed., 2d ed. 2005).

private placement have a more limited liquidity. If the SPV issues bonds, it offers investors liquidity if the bonds are short term.

e. Market Risk: Prepayment[1054]

Investors in SPVs that hold consumer debt are exposed to the risk that the borrowers will prepay their loans, if the borrowers are legally entitled to prepay their loans at any time, without penalty. When interest rates fall, these loans will be prepaid to be refinanced at a lower rate. But this is precisely the time when investors prefer obligations of a higher interest rate to cash which can be loaned at lower interest. Because prepayments are unpredictable except in their rough relation to the rise and fall of interest rates, they make it difficult for investors to plan their investments. To reduce this risk, issuers have prepared prepayment models based on various assumptions. In addition, many SPV securities may be divided into classes that shift the prepayment risk from one class of securities to another.

In addition to credit and market risks, SPV assets and investments in SPV obligations involve the risk that the borrowers might prepay the loans, if they have the legal right to do so. Since prepayments are unpredictable, they make it harder for investors to plan long-term.[1055] Prepayments expose investors to higher risk of interest rate fluctuations. The lenders get the short end of the stick both ways. They are locked into interest rates even if the rates rise, and are left with cash when the interest rates fall. Publicly held bonds usually grant the issuer a right to "call" a limited percentage of the outstanding bonds (and refinance at a lower rate). The choice of the particular prepaid bonds is usually made by lottery, to avoid suspicion of favoritism.

There are laws that entitle mortgagors and certain other consumers to prepay their loans at any time without penalty. Therefore, mortgage-backed securities could have shorter and less predictable maturities than bonds, and investment in mortgages could be more vulnerable to interest rate fluctuations than investment in bonds. It turns out, however, that there are many states which do not offer such protection to the mortgagors, and when the interest rates under the mortgage documents rise sharply, and to more than the market rates, borrowers who wish to pre-pay their loans and refinance them found that they had to pay very steep penalties which in fact prevent them from refinancing. As we shall see, the design of SPV securities reflects an attempt to reduce the investors' risk when the state laws allow mortgagors to pre-pay their loans without penalty. This risk cannot, however, be entirely eliminated. The risk makes it hard to determine the rate of return on the loans, and therefore the price of the SPV securities funded by these loans.

[1054] 1 TAMAR FRANKEL, SECURITIZATION § 5.8.5 (Ann Taylor Schwing ed., 2d ed. 2005).

[1055] 1 TAMAR FRANKEL, SECURITIZATION § 2.5.5 (Ann Taylor Schwing ed., 2d ed. 2005).

Cash flows for each class can be determined only by assuming a prepayment rate, and a variety of prepayment benchmarks and assumptions are available. The realized rate of return depends on the actual prepayment rate as compared with the assumed rate. The price of a high return pass-through security selling at a premium may fall if the realized prepayment is higher than the assumed prepayment and the cash flow has to be reinvested in lower yield investments. If the yield on the securities is current, the value of the securities will not change (the prepaid cash can be invested at the same yield). No fixed conservative assumption about prepayments is possible because of the asymmetric response to fast and slow prepayments of mortgages.

Other market risks may arise. For example, the value of collateralized mortgage obligations backed by a foreign government can deteriorate as a result of changes in the currency exchange rates.

f. Legal Risks[1056]

As the materials in this Book show, asset-backed securities pose risks for investors that stem in part from uncertain legal rules. Law has lagged behind the market developments. The rights of the securities holders and the SPVs are unclear when the borrowers or SPV Originators fail or when conflicts arise among the parties.

As securitization spread, so did fraudulent practices that caused enormous losses to investors. A notable example is the Enron Corporation whose managers used this form to transfer Enron's assets to SPVs that were managed by Enron's managers. The SPVs sold participations in the SPVs backed by Enron's stock. Enron's liabilities and debts could be hidden through the creation of SPVs. Securitization is complex and can be used to disguise the nature of the transactions, as the Enron Corporation did. Because securitization of assets can be continuous, as more assets are acquired and securitized, one SPV can hide the shortfall of another by buying from the other its securities at an inflated price. The managers of such SPVs are in fact operating a Ponzi scheme. The scheme is destined to failure and discovery but not until the losses to investors increase. Both complexity and the participation of many actors in this transaction can give rise to fraud at one or more of the junctures of the transaction. The recent cases have shown that the gatekeepers such as the investment bankers, the accountants and the lawyers do not always provide protection to investors.

[1056] 1 TAMAR FRANKEL, SECURITIZATION § 5.8.6 (Ann Taylor Schwing ed., 2d ed. 2005).

g. Investors' Risk: Lack of Prudence[1057]

SPVs pose for investors the kinds of danger posed by other Institutions with long-term obligations. These Institutions can follow a speculative, extravagant, or irrational business plan, and even become insolvent, yet continue to exist for a long period without detection, because they can raise new funds from investors to cover the shortfall. Such Institutions may pay a higher return to investors than the rate they earn from borrowers, spend excessively for overhead and management compensation, or rely on speculative future events that may not materialize. Unless Institutions fund their long-term liabilities conservatively, those who hold the Institutional obligations when the Institutions finally fail will suffer substantial losses. SPVs that issue equity and hold long-term debt pose similar dangers for investors (unless their portfolios are fixed).

E. Risk to the Overall Financial System

a. Does Securitization Make Sense?[1058]

Although Markets develop only under certain conditions, if Markets exist, they are a less expensive form of intermediation than Institutions. We noted that Markets develop only when certain cost-saving devices are available. To repeat, securities must be standardized, and the amounts must not be too large. If savers desire nonstandard instruments, or if borrowers will not or cannot produce standard documents in sufficient amounts, or if the preferences of investors and borrowers do not match, the parties must resort to Institutions that borrow from one party and lend to the other, each on its own terms. For these parties, Institutions are less costly than Markets. Nonetheless, as a system of intermediation, Institutions may be more costly for a number of reasons.

First, Institutions provide custom-made treatment and traditionally maintain larger physical facilities and a higher ratio of permanent personnel than market intermediaries. Second, the greater the disparity between the terms of the loans from Institutions to borrowers and the loans to Institutions from savers, the more precarious the financial structure of Institutions will be. Institutions must keep "cushions" (capital and reserves) to cover the mismatch between their assets and liabilities. And these cushions increase with the mismatch. The costs of these cushions are absorbed by the borrowers and investors. For example, assume that a bank owes depositors $100 million, and lends to borrowers $100 million. The borrowers' risks are high, and the loans are valued at $90 million. The bank must keep a reserve to cover any shortfall. If the value of the loans declines further to $80 million, the bank must increase the loan loss reserve. In that case the bank cannot

[1057] 1 TAMAR FRANKEL, SECURITIZATION § 2.5.4 (Ann Taylor Schwing ed., 2d ed. 2005).

[1058] 1 TAMAR FRANKEL, SECURITIZATION § 1.4 (Ann Taylor Schwing ed., 2d ed. 2005).

show a profit and cannot pay a dividend to its shareholders-investors. In addition, the bank might have to raise the interest rate that it charges borrowers, provided it can do so in light of its competitors.

Third, the intrusion into Institutions' operation by government regulation is greater, and presumably more costly, than the intrusion into the Markets. While Markets are regulated mostly by disclosure requirements, Institutions are regulated by substantive rules affecting their managements' decisions and financial structure.[1059]

Fourth, it can be argued that, as compared to Markets, information costs (about borrowers) can be relatively higher for Institutions. On the one hand, information embodied in price is less costly especially if the information is complex and detailed. After all, market prices present the aggregate information of many traders. Therefore, to the extent that market prices for Institutions' loans are not available, information costs for Institutions are relatively higher. In addition, because the relationships between the borrower and the banks are unique, the higher number of customers increases the costs to the banks more than the cost to Markets.

On the other hand, banks gain information from the demand accounts that the borrowers have with the banks and the contacts with the borrowers. Therefore, the quality of Institutional information may be higher than market price information. But this advantage is being eroded as the dependence of borrowers on Institutions has weakened, and available technology allows Markets to transfer and retrieve large amounts of credit information. Arguably, this technology has tilted the scales to benefit Markets since it allows for quick transfer of information, and the sooner information can reach decision makers, the sooner price disparities stemming from ignorance will equalize.

Moreover, the larger the number of information-collectors, the cheaper the information is. As compared to Markets, Institutional lending involves a smaller number of information collectors (loan officers, their supervisors, and government examiners) and the cost to each collector, and especially to the Government, is higher.

Traditionally, however, Institutions have had a greater incentive to gather accurate information about borrowers because Institutions expect income from the loans and bear the borrowers' credit risk, while market intermediaries seek fees from trading and rarely bear long-term credit risk. Securitization has eroded the higher quality of

---

[1059] Conservative measures to keep Institutions financially sound may conflict with short-term goals of their managements and shareholders. Moreover, market discipline through public information conflicts with the benefits of privacy for borrowers and can expose Institutions to the risk of runs and failures. Thus, whether wholesale or retail, if Markets can be formed, the costs to savers, borrowers, and regulators will usually be lower.

Institutional information as Institutions convert from long-term investors in loans into sellers of, or short-term investors in, loan-based securities, and their loan officers to sales personnel.

The Government's information costs in valuing bank assets are higher than these costs in market regulation because small depositors do not gather this information and are not effective monitors of banks. In fact, timely information to depositors can cause "runs" on banks. Since depositors are traditionally risk-averse, they might withdraw their funds on the slightest rumor. Few believe that the securities Markets are perfectly efficient. But many agree that market information and its timely disclosure are more quickly reflected in market prices, although the benefit of this efficiency may be debated.

b. The Efficiency Argument

Because securitization utilizes market intermediation at some junctures of the process, it captures the advantages that Markets have, as compared to Institutions. Calculating the benefits and costs of securitization by SPVs is complex. Initial lending is performed in the traditional way. However, the existence of secondary Markets in loan-backed securities gives loan originators incentives to adopt better prepared, more standard documents and procedures, even for loans that ultimately may not be sold. In addition, it is less costly to evaluate investments in SPVs than to evaluate investments in traditional Institutions because SPVs hold similar loans (e.g., mortgages) while Institutions often do not. Moreover, the benefits from market price of loan-backed securities spill over to reduce information costs for lenders that deal with the same or similar borrowers. The regulators of Institutions that hold loan-backed securities and the investors in these Institutions can use the market price of these securities to value the Institutions' assets.

This transformation is not without its problems since the whole regulatory system is based on the face value of loans, which is fixed. At a certain level of deterioration, the law requires the bank to increase its loan loss reserve, and, at the lowest point, the loan reserve covers the face value of the loan. If bank loans fluctuated with market prices, the regulatory system would have to be changed. The transition period poses difficult questions. In addition, it is not clear that market prices are the most accurate for valuing credit risk. If the bank has insider information about the borrower that leads the bank to different valuation of the loan, should market prices prevail? If not, would the bank's valuation "lead" the Market without disclosure?

Even though securitization pooling reduces the incentives of initial lenders to collect and evaluate information about the borrowers, because those who make loans for sale rather than investment bear less credit risk, the Markets have created a number of counterincentives. For example, loan origination fees are calculated as a percentage of interest payments for the duration of the loan, thus tying the originator's fees to the creditworthiness of the borrowers. Other parties are added to the evaluation process: those who pool the loans, the trustees managing the SPVs that hold the loans, the underwriters of the SPVs' securities, guarantors, rating agencies, and appraisers of the collateral for the loans. These measures are not necessarily sufficient, as will be discussed later.

c The Other Side of the Argument

Not everyone agrees that securitization is more efficient than traditional financing. The disagreement is especially strong when securitization takes the form of structured financing. In such a case, a corporation can reduce financial assets by selling them to an independent SPV to pay its secured debtors. The unsecured debtors may be left with fewer assets to satisfy their claims against the corporation. Whether this scenario is always correct is subject to much debate. However, structured financing by a corporation can lead to robbing the investors, as the Enron Corporation's story has demonstrated.

In that case the losses of Enron Corporation were hidden by creating SPVs, transferring losing assets to the SPVs and guaranteeing the value of the assets by pledging the shares of Enron Corporation. The investors in the SPVs did not rely on the assets in these SPVs but on Enron's shares. In fact, the SPV allowed Enron to cycle losing assets through a subsidiary and receive payment by pledging its shares.

d Enforcing the Parties' Contracts

In the secondary Markets, investors are exposed to the risk that their trading partners will renege on their obligations. In a volatile market a buyer might be tempted to renege on the trade if the market price falls, and the seller might renege on the trade if the market price rises. This risk of reneging, however, has been eliminated to a great extent, if brokers are involved. Custom and law have shifted the enforcement costs from the contract parties to the brokers. Because brokers have the incentive to execute transactions and earn their commissions, they were given powers and imposed with the duties to ensure enforcement. A broker may not execute a sale unless the broker has the sold securities in his possession, or a purchase unless the broker has in his possession the cash to pay for the securities. If he does not, then he is responsible for the trade. In practice, few Market transactions through brokers are breached by "trading partners." This enforcement, however, does not reach to the lenders or the borrowers of the loans that back the securities. Brokers' enforcement is not complicated. Broker-dealers may not buy or sell securities without possessing the securities to be sold or the money to buy the securities. Thus, the traders in securities are assured of their bargain, but the lenders are not.

Neither the lenders nor the borrowers have a say regarding the sale of the obligations. Borrowers have no control over the buyers of their obligations, or whether the buyers are reasonable or predatory creditors. The borrowers know only the servicers to whom they must send their mortgage payments.

e. Disciplining the Borrowers

Both Markets and Institutions discipline borrowers. Markets "grade" large borrowers' performance by ratings and public information and punish them by price. Small borrowers are evaluated by the lenders and, if they do not pay their debt, are punished by higher interest rate and low availability of loans. Borrowers' performance affects the decisions of lenders and investors, and through them, the behavior of borrowers.

Borrowers' managements heed the Markets for several reasons: to reduce the cost of funds for their corporations; to increase the price of their own stock holdings; or to obtain the satisfaction of heading a successful enterprise. While Markets discipline borrowers by pricing the securities, Institutions such as banks can discipline borrowers by withholding funds and cashing the collateral. In addition, Markets and Institutions can exercise their powers under trust indentures or loan agreements to enforce the collection of loans upon the occurrence of certain events.

Securitization by pooling into SPVs and distributing SPV securities increases market supervision of borrowers, as the Markets take over at the outset when securities are formed. Institutions make loans for sale and lose the contact with the borrowers and their ability to influence the borrowers who do not pay. The servicing agents have some monitoring power over the borrowers but no ability to act on their information. Unless they are required to take back defaulted loans, servicing agents have little incentive to enforce loans, since this costly process is not usually well compensated. Thus, market discipline of borrowers is predominant. This idea applies also outside the United States. For example, Patrick J. Schena suggested that China has been avoiding the disruptions that visited other countries in Southeast Asia during the 1990s.[1060]

f. Disciplining the Intermediaries

Both market intermediaries and Institutions are regulated, but Institutions are also regulated as to the type of their liabilities (obligations to savers) and assets (obligations they receive from borrowers). As competition and pressures to innovate have produced a variety of Institutional obligations, the cost of regulating Institutions has risen. Consequently, regulators are attempting to shift at least part of their monitoring and disciplining functions to the Markets. Since Institutions have become

---

[1060] Patrick J.. Schena, *Banks, Distressed Loans, and the Development of Chinese Markets for Asset-Backed Securities,* 29 FLETCHER F. WORLD AFF. 35 (2005).

more dependent on Markets for funds, Markets can discipline Institutions better than in the past. Investors' perceptions determine banks' cost of equity capital and have even made banks vulnerable to takeovers. Public information about Institutions and their assets and operations is increasing as the FDIC may require disclosure of its sanctions against banks. Although it is unclear to what extent these exposures are effective, compared to the negligible discipline imposed by small insured depositors, these new market pressures seem more effective. And since securitization also makes price information about bank assets public, the process should have a cost-saving effect in disciplining banks and perhaps other Institutions.

g. The Danger of Fraud in Securitization[1061]

The events of the 1990s, including the Enron Corporation debacle, suggest that securitization may raise serious risks for investors when the process is used by unregulated entities and helped by gatekeepers who have ceased to watch the gates or obey the law. When issuers and market makers remain unregulated, important (incriminating) information is buried in mounds of documents, and conflicts of interest are permitted, then securitization becomes a great tool for misappropriating other people's money.

One factor that could contribute to the investors' risk is the complexity that securitization can present. Another factor is the need of this process for multiple actors, each of whom can defraud investors. The third factor is that the Markets are not necessarily the best and especially not the quickest detectors of hidden fraud. Therefore, the failure of the private sector gatekeepers such as the lawyers, accountants, investment bankers and underwriters to keep the gate closed can be catastrophic. The fact that fraud by securitization, especially if it takes the form of a Ponzi scheme, can be hidden for some time creates a serious threat of a "market run" when investors are inclined to sell their shares even at a loss to escape larger losses. Such a run can depress securities prices below their economic value. The reaction to the dangers posed by securitization, however, was not focused on the process as much as it was focused on the actors. The law on the books, though enough to prosecute for fraud, was expanded to impose strict and sometimes costly preventive measures. These measures applied to corporate governance and gatekeepers. Securitization as a process was left untouched. As Professor Steven Schwarcz recognized, there are important differences between what happened at Enron Corporation and securitization proper. Unlike the Enron-SPV transactions, securitization proper "transfers risk from the originator to the SPV and its investors; and transfer of risk is, and should be, central to the accounting determination of non-consolidation," making all parties better off, and no other parties worse off. Generally, the debt has a lower interest-rate cost than the originator's corporate debt, and makes liquidity "available to companies unable to borrow, keeping them out of

---

1061 1 TAMAR FRANKEL, SECURITIZATION § 3.4.4 (Ann Taylor Schwing ed., 2d ed. 2005).

bankruptcy (and thus enhancing creditor recovery)." "In comparison, secured debt, unlike securitization, has a more ambiguous impact on the expected value of unsecured creditor claims."[1062]

F. Case Study: A Million Home Foreclosures – How Could It Happen?

Ask people to define the American Dream and you will hear phases such as "freedom, equal rights and equal opportunity," "a better life for my children," and "economic prosperity." When asked for an example of the dream, home ownership is often cited. The Federal National Mortgage Corporation, Fannie Mae, the largest source of mortgage financing in the U.S., once stated in its annual report: "At Fannie Mae, we are in the American Dream business. Our Mission is to tear down barriers, lower costs, and increase the opportunities for homeownership and affordable rental housing for all Americans."[1063]

Why is homeownership so important? Historically, home ownership was tied to the right to vote. More recently, owning your home provides a broad array of financial and social benefits. The financial benefits are based on government policies that encourage homeownership. Property taxes and mortgage interest payments are deductable from personal income taxes providing a very tangible incentive to own a home rather than rent one. A substantial, yet hidden, tax opportunity cost is that home owners do not pay taxes on the implicit rent they pay themselves. If the house were owned by a third party, the landlord would pay income tax on the rent. A second financial benefit to home ownership has been the steady appreciation of real estate; you could "make money" while you slept. Your home is a source of collateral for borrowing. The equity that was built up in the value of a home could be tapped for cash to meet extraordinary expenses or temporary loss of income. Finally, the home is the retirement savings account for many Americans. When people retire, their house is sold, they receive another very generous tax avoidance, and they live off the cash generated from the sale of the house.

Beyond these financial incentives, home owners also gain social benefits. Because your home is often one of your largest investments, there is a strong incentive to take responsibility for not only your own house but also for your neighborhood since locale is a primary determinant of housing value. The resulting "involvement" behavior yields a range of positive social outcomes including impacts on children, health, and crime. With respect to children: "Research in this area has found large

---

[1062] Steven L. Schwarcz, *Asset Securitization and Secured Lending: Securitization Post-Enron,* 25 CARDOZO L. REV. 1539, 1551, 1559, 1562 (2004).

[1063] FANNIE MAE, 2001 ANNUAL REPORT inside front cover, http://www.fanniemae.com/global/pdf/ir/annualreport/2001/fullreport.pdf;jsessionid=BWP01XOHKVOK1J2FQSISFGQ (last visited Oct. 8, 2009).

positive impacts of homeownership on educational outcomes, such as test scores and graduation rates, and social outcomes, such as teenage pregnancy."[1064] Improved health outcomes are also correlated with homeownership. For example, home owners are more likely to remediate lead paint in the home than are renters. Even political participation is linked to home ownership. Substantially more homeowners vote than do renters. One study found that homeowners were 16% more likely to vote in local elections than renters.[1065] Another reported that the homeowners voting rate was 69% compared to 44% for renters.[1066]

The dream of homeownership became a reality for a growing portion of Americans over the past half century. From the turn of the century through the 1940s, approximately 45% of U.S. households were homeowners. The baby boom and post-war programs that increased credit availability helped boost homeownership to 63% by 1965. The ownership percentage remained in the 60-65% range for the next three decades. The ten year period from 1995 to 2005 saw another spurt in homeownership. By 2005, 69% of U.S. households owned their own homes.[1067] (Exhibit 1) Minority homeownership rates accounted for a significant portion of the growth. For example, Hispanic ownership rates increased from 41% in 1994 to almost 50% in 2005.[1068] Several factors explain the recent rise in home ownership. First, home prices homes were rising rapidly. Median home prices of new homes sold in the United States increased from $163,500 in January 2000 to $254,400 in January 2007.[1069] (Exhibit 2) The price increases put pressure on new home buyers to "act now or be priced out of the market later." Second, interest rates for mortgages to finance the purchase of a home were at comparatively low levels. Mortgage interest rates were in the 5.5% to 6.5% range between 2003 and 2007 compared to 7% to 8.5% in the 1990s. This era of less expensive money and rising home prices encouraged new home buyers into the market and encouraged existing owners to upgrade to more expensive homes. A third explanation was the extension of

---

1064 ROBERT D. DIETZ, THE SOCIAL CONSEQUENCE OF HOMEOWNERSHIP 4 (2003), http://www.newtowncdc.org/PDF/social_consequences_study.pdf (last visited Oct. 8, 2009).

1065 William M. Rohe et al., *The Social Benefits and Costs of Homeownership: A Critical Assessment of the Research* 18 (Joint Center for Hous. Stud. of Harvard Univ., Oct. 2001). http://www.jchs.harvard.edu/publications/homeownership/liho01-12.pdf (last visited Oct. 8, 2009).

1066 ROBERT D. DIETZ, THE SOCIAL CONSEQUENCE OF HOMEOWNERSHIP 5-6 (2003), http://www.newtowncdc.org/PDF/social_consequences_study.pdf (last visited Oct. 8, 2009).

1067 EDWARD M. GRAMLICH, SUBPRIME MORTGAGES 2 (2007).

1068 John C. Weicher, *Homeownership: Patterns, Trends and Policies* 5 (Hudson Inst., May 18, 2006), . http://www.hudson.org/files/publications/2006_bsc_weicher.pdf (last visited Oct. 8, 2009).

1069 U.S. CENSUS BUREAU, MEDIAN AND AVERAGE SALES PRICES OF NEW HOMES SOLD IN THE UNITED STATES, http://www.census.gov/const/uspricemon.pdf (last visited Oct. 8, 2009).

mortgage credit to subprime borrowers, those individuals who do not have the income or assets to qualify for conventional mortgages.

Throughout the 20th Century a vast majority of Americans financed their dream of home ownership with a loan collateralized by a mortgage on the home, known as a conventional mortgage. The standard mortgage during the second half of the 20th century was a 30 year fixed interest loan, averaging 6 percent for most of the period.[1070] The amount of the mortgage was in the range of 80-90 percent of the value of the home. The mortgage process was essentially local: the home buyer went to a local bank for the loan; the bank used a local appraiser to verify the value of the home; the bank evaluated the repayment risk of the borrower and issued or rejected the application. Often the bank held the mortgage during its life. If a repayment problem arose, the borrower and bank could jointly work to resolve the issue. In order to increase the amount of funds available for mortgage loans, the Federal National Mortgage Association (Fannie Mae) and the Federal Home Loan Mortgage Corporation (Freddie Mac), government sponsored agencies, purchased some of the loans from local banks. Taking these loans off the banks' books enabled the lending institutions to offer more mortgages. In turn, Fannie Mae packaged the mortgages into securities and sold them to third party investors.

At the dawn of the millennium, a new loan product was introduced for borrowers whose credit position would not qualify them for a conventional mortgage. These "less than prime" borrowers (or commonly referred to as subprime borrowers) were offered loans even thought they had poor past credit, minimal income and limited assets. The rationale for the lender was that if the borrower defaulted the appreciation in home value would cover the costs of foreclosure on the property and that it could be readily sold to another buyer. The subprime mortgages were primarily offered by mortgage bankers rather than traditional banks, whose prudential regulations limited offering such loans.[1071] With mortgage bankers and construction firms that sought buyers, there arose an army of mortgage brokers, who contacted potential buyers and offered loans to finance purchase of homes. An additional mortgage bankers' enticement was "teaser" rate loans which offered very low interest payments and/or interest-only repayment for a period of time. Of course, the rates and payments ballooned after a few years. For example, many adjustable rate mortgages offered fixed and low interest rates for the first two years of the loan replaced by higher and adjustable rates for the remaining loan period. Borrowers took the bait; subprime loans soared to more than $600 billion in 2005.[1072] (Exhibit 3) The rapid growth of mortgage loans including to subprime borrowers was enabled

---

[1070] EDWARD M. GRAMLICH, SUBPRIME MORTGAGES 2 (2007).

[1071] *Id.* at 7.

[1072] *Id.* at 6.

by declining denial rates. (Exhibit 4) The potential for profits in this new model could be presumed from the growth in the number of independent mortgage brokers. That number grew from 7000 in 1987 to 53,000 in 2004.[1073]

The assumption of ever-increasing home prices, which supported the subprime loans, was erroneous. The escalation in home prices was a bubble; and like all bubbles it burst. Over-building and speculation peaked and were replaced by slowing home sales and declining prices. In 2004 and 2005, the building of 1.6 and 1.7 million new privately owned housing units was started. In 2007 the number fell to just over 1 million.[1074] Existing home sales also slowed. Exhibit 5 shows that the inventory of existing homes increased steadily from 2005 to 2007. New home inventory also were at high levels. Weak demand rapidly translated into falling home prices. Median existing home prices in many cities across the U.S. fell more than 5-10% between 2006 and the end of 2007. In some locations the drop was even more precipitous. In Riverside, California, for example, prices in 2008 were 25% lower than a year earlier.[1075] The bottom line to the housing statistics was that once prices started to drop, a vicious cycle began: falling home prices, defaults, falling home prices, defaults.

The macroeconomic impacts of the housing crash were quick to take hold. Overall economic growth as measured by GDP slowed from 2.8% - 3.6% in the period leading up to the bubble bursting in 2006 to an annualized 0.9% in the first quarter of 2008. The residential investment component for GDP declined more than 15% in 2007 alone. (Exhibit 6) Unemployment grew from 4.6% in January 2007 to 5.7% in July 2008.[1076] In the construction industry unemployment exceeded 11% in April 2008.[1077] More than half a million construction jobs were lost since the building

---

1073 *Id.* at 19.

1074 U.S. CENSUS BUREAU, NEW PRIVATELY OWNED HOUSING UNITS STARTED IN THE UNITED STATES, BY INTENT AND DESIGN (Table Q-1), http://www.census.gov/const/startsusintentq.pdf (last visited Oct. 9, 2009).

1075 LAWRENCE YUN, AFTER THE CLEAN UP 30 (May 29, 2008), 30, http://media.miamiherald.com/smedia/2008/06/12/17/NAR_Chief_Economist_Dr_Yun_RAMB_Miami_Congress__June_2008_.source.prod_affiliate.56.pdf (last visited Oct. 9, 2009).

1076 U.S. Dept. of Labor Statistics, *Unemployment Rates by Demographics, January 2007* (Feb. 6, 2007), http://www.bls.gov/opub/ted/2007/feb/wk1/art02.htm (last visited Oct. 9, 2009);News, Dept. of Dabor Statistics, U.S. Dep't of Labor, The Employment Situation: July 2008, http://www.bls.gov/news.release/archives/empsit_08012008.pdf (last visited Oct. 9, 2008).

1077 *Industry Employment Hits 11%,* ENR.COM (May 28, 2008), http://enr.ecnext.com/coms2/article_necoar080528b (last visited Oct. 9, 2009).

industry peak in September 2006.[1078] Talk of recession increased with headlines such as "Credit Woes Hinting at Consumer Recession."[1079] Fears of banks' failure triggered by exposure to bad loans caused the first runs of banks in more than a decade. In February 2008, Federal Reserve Bank Chairman Ben Bernanke stated that "[t]here probably will be some bank failures."[1080] Four months later his prediction proved all too accurate. IndyMac Bank which had $32 billion in assets became the second largest bank failure in the history of the country. The bailout of the bank's depositors by the Federal Deposit Insurance Corporation (FDIC) is expected to cost $4 to $8 billion.[1081] The psychological impact of the failure was captured in the words of one depositor who "leaned on the locked doors, pleading with an employee inside: 'Please, please, I want to take out a portion.' All she could do was read a two-page notice taped to the door."[1082] The overall impact of the housing crisis (and soaring oil prices) led to the lowest level of consumer confidence in years. (Exhibit 7)

A "perfect storm" brewed in the subprime market. The loans which looked secure when housing prices were rising became problematic. A slowing economy meant that many mortgage holders, especially those who lost their jobs, found it harder to make their monthly payments. At the same time, the teaser rates, which enticed many to take loans they really could not afford beyond the low introductory rate period, were converting to the higher rates. The option of selling the home to pay off the loan was unrealistic in face of a slow real estate market with falling prices. Many subprime borrowers were not required to make a down payment on the home. Consequently in the first few years of homeownership they had not built any equity in their home. Others who had equity often took a second mortgage on the home to tap the cash value that had accrued. Borrowers increasingly found it less expensive to simply turn over the keys to the loan holder and walk away from the house rather than try to meet the monthly mortgage payments.

[1078] Economic News Release, Bureau of Labor Statistics, The Employment Situation: July 2008,(Aug. 1, 2008), http://www.bls.gov/news.release/archives/empsit_08012008.htm (last visited Oct. 9, 2009).

[1079] Luke Mullins, *Credit Woes Hinting at Consumer Recession,* U.S. NEWS & WORLD REP., Nov. 10, 2007, at 38, LEXIS, News Library, Curnws File..

[1080] Patrice Hill, *Bernanke Expects Bank Failures,* WASH. TIMES, Feb. 29, 2008., at A01, LEXIS, News Library, Curnws File.

[1081] Kathy M. Kristof & Andrea Chang, *Federal Regulators Seize Crippled IndyMac Bank,* L.A. TIMES, July 12, 2008, at A1, LEXIS, News Library, Curnws File, *at* Kathy M. Kristof & Andrea Chang, *IndyMac Bank Seized by Federal Regulators,* L.A. TIMES, July 12, 2008, http://articles.latimes.com/2008/jul/12/business/fi-indymac12 (last visited Oct. 6, 2009).

[1082] *Id.*

For those who provided the loans, the "insurance" of foreclosing and selling the house to a new buyer became infeasible as prices fell, financing became tight and new, credit-worthy buyers were hard to find. Nevertheless, the number of foreclosed homes grew. Exhibit 8 shows that the foreclosure rate rose since 2005. The 2008 level was roughly two times the historical level.[1083] The number of foreclosures in the remainder of 2008 and 2009 is expected to remain at unprecedented levels.

The impact of foreclosures of homes that served as collateral for subprime mortgages was felt in urban and rural communities. In the Crown Heights and Bedford-Stuyvesant neighborhoods of Brooklyn, New York, 25% of homes with subprime loans were in the foreclosure process in October 2007.[1084] The subprime crisis hit the farm belt as well. The delinquency rate on subprime loans in Iowa was more than 14% with more than 5% in foreclosure.[1085] Foreclosure rates were almost double that rate for the subset of subprime loans that were adjustable rate mortgages.

The economic drain by foreclosures was significant for borrowers, lenders, neighborhoods, and municipalities. Estimates of the total costs per foreclosure were in the $80,000 range.[1086] Borrowers lose any equity that they accumulated at foreclosure. Moreover they bear the costs of moving and finding new accommodations. Beyond the financial losses, the emotional costs can be large especially for families whose children must be uprooted. Put in human terms: "One child in every classroom in America is at risk of losing his/her home because their parents are unable to pay their mortgage."[1087] The lenders face the direct cash costs of completing the foreclosure process and the loss in market value of the home at the time of resale. Given the weak housing market and the glut of homes for sale,

---

1083 LAWRENCE YUN, AFTER THE CLEAN UP 6 (May 29, 2008), http://media.miamiherald.com/smedia/2008/06/12/17/NAR_Chief_Economist_Dr_Yun_RAMB_Miami_Congress__June_2008_.source.prod_affiliate.56.pdf (last visited Oct. 9, 2009).

1084 *Report: Subprime Foreclosures Rampant in Brooklyn,* BROWNSTONER, Jan. 28, 2008, http://www.brownstoner.com/brownstoner/archives/2008/01/report_subprime.php (last visited Oct. 9, 2009).

1085 Patrick Madigan, Assistant Attorney General, Iowa, *Subprime Foreclosures,* 2 (2007 HousingIowa Conference, Oct. 23, 2007), http://www.iowafinanceauthority.gov/documents/filelibrary/2007_housingiowaconference/october_23/subprime_lending_part_ii_where_do_we_go_from_here/Patrick_Madigan.pdf (last visited Oct. 9, 2009) (noting also that delinquency rate on subprime ARMs was 16.95%, the "highest level on record," and that over 8% of subprime ARMs were in foreclosure).

1086 *Id.* at 7.

1087 NEIGHBORWORKS AMERICA FORECLOSURE STATISTICS,, http://www.docstoc.com/docs/3732648/housing-market-statistics (last visited Oct. 8, 2009).

foreclosures are bringing in only 50 cents on the dollar.[1088] The lender's loss is even greater if an inflated appraisal of the house was used to justify the initial mortgage.

Beyond the direct participants in the subprime drama, "40.6 million neighboring homes will experience devaluation because of subprime foreclosures that take place nearby."[1089] The Center for Responsible Lending estimated that each single family home foreclosed in a neighborhood reduced the value of the surrounding homes by 0.9% or on average $5,000. The loss is estimated to be 1.4% in lower-income areas.[1090] Thus the total property value loss for the country totals $223 billion. The states with the largest devaluations are California ($61 billion), New York ($37 billion), Florida ($20 billion) and Illinois ($15 billion).[1091] While almost all areas have been affected by the subprime problem there are some counties where the impact has been huge. The losses of housing value in Los Angeles CA, Cook IL, Kings NY and Miami-Dade FL counties are estimated to be $27, $13, $12, and $10 billion respectively.[1092]

The lower property value had a cascading effect on municipalities whose budgets were funded through local property taxes which were reduced as home values dropped. At a time when local needs especially for housing assistance are growing cities and towns have less funds available for support. The local governments are also facing direct cash outlays associated with foreclosures. "[T]he foreclosure of a single-family house, especially one that leaves the home vacant and unsecured, may, in some cases, cost cash-strapped municipal governments in excess of $30,000 per property. Typical costs include loss of tax revenue, increasing policing, building inspections, legal expense, administrative costs to manage the foreclosure policy and more."[1093]

[1088] John C. Dugan, Comptroller of the Currency, Remarks Before the Nat'l Foundation for Credit Counseling Spring Meeting 4 (Apr. 24, 2007), http://www.occ.gov/ftp/release/2007-44a.pdf (last visited Oct. 8, 2009).

[1089] Center for Responsible Lending, *Subprime Spillover* 1 (CRL Issue Paper, Jan. 18, 2008), http://www.responsiblelending.org/mortgage-lending/research-analysis/subprime-spillover.pdf (last visited Oct. 8, 2009).

[1090] *Id.*

[1091] *Id.* at 2.

[1092] *Id.* at 3.

[1093] Nat'l Multi Hous. Council, *Collateral Damage: The Municipal Impact of Today's Mortgage Foreclosure Boom*, http://www.nmhc.org/Content/ServeContent.cfm?IssueID=722&ContentItemID=3489&siteArea=Resources (last visited Oct. 6, 2009).

1,000,000 foreclosures is so large a number it is hard to grasp its importance; yet, each 1 of the million has its own human story. A single mother of three lived in her South Chicago home. Health problems forced the mother onto long term disability. The insurance payments in conjunction with funds provided by her working children enabled the family to make ends meet. When the daughter lost her job, the family could not continue to meet their mortgage payments. A subprime lender offered to refinance her home with a fixed-rate mortgage. At the closing, however, the terms were not what she had been told: “They lied to me . . . . [I]t’s going to be fixed rate for one year and then adjustable every six months.”[1094] She reluctantly signed. “You’re at the closing, and you don’t want to lose your home, and you don’t have other options open . . . .”[1095] Her hopes that it would all turn out alright did not materialize. The need to replace her furnace, some pipes, and her washing machine put her finances into the red. Her failure to meet mortgage payments led the lender to begin actions to take her house. Her story actually has a happy ending. A community-based non-profit organization helped her find a mortgage loan that she could afford, and she was able to remain in her home. A million other homeowners might not have been so lucky. Research on the “tipping point” that results in homeowners defaulting shows that 32% experience a job loss and 25% have a health crisis.[1096] The desperation associated with the possible loss of one’s home is illustrated in a January 2008 story carried by CNNMoney. An Indiana homeowner “offered to pay a neighbor $5,000 to help her burn down her house and make it look like a botched rape attempt - all in order to claim $80,000 in insurance money”[1097] to solve her financial problems.

The subprime crisis continued to intensify during 2008. Senator Charles Schumer, the chair of the Joint Economic Committee, published a timeline of the subprime crisis in July 2008. The following entries[1098] demonstrate the breath and depth of the crisis:

[1094] Dona DeZube, *The Tragedy of Foreclosure,* BRIGHT IDEAS (NeighborWorks Am., Washington, DC), Summer 2006, 6, 12, http://www.nw.org/network/pubs/brightIdeas/documents/brightIdeas_Summer2006complete_000.pdf (last visited Oct. 6, 2009)..

[1095] *Id.*

[1096] NEIGHBORWORKS AMERICA, FORECLOSURE STATISTICS, http://www.docstoc.com/docs/3732648/housing-market-statistics (last visited Oct. 8, 2009).

[1097] Jon Birger, *Will Foreclosures Spark an Arson Boom?,* CNNMONEY, Jan. 10, 2008, http://money.cnn.com/2008/01/09/news/economy/birger_arson.fortune/index.htm (last visited Oct. 6, 2009).

[1098] SEN. CHARLES E. SCHUMER, CHAIRMAN, JOINT ECONOMIC COMM., SUBPRIME MORTGAGE MARKET CRISIS TIMELINE (July 2008), ,

- January 15: Citigroup the largest bank in the U.S. announced that its mortgage portfolio dropped in value by $18.1 Billion. . . .
- January 30: Standard and Poor's announced it would be cutting the credit ratings of $534 billion in subprime mortgage backed securities.2 . . .
- February 29: A report from market analysts at UBS shows that losses within the financial sector from subprime mortgage back (sic)securities could reach $600 billion. . . .
- March 16: Investment bank Bear Stearns announced that it will sell itself to JPMorgan Chase for $2 a share – a 93% discount on the current stock price. . . .
- April 29: First quarter data . . . revealed a 112% jump in foreclosure filings compared with the same period last year. . . .
- May 21: [E]xactly five years after the peak in the housing boom, mortgage applications now stand at one-third of the volume at the high point in May 2003.
- June 5: For the first time in history, more than one million homes are now in foreclosure.

Whenever a bubble busts and many people are hurt, politicians, the media and everyday citizens ask the questions: How did this happen? Who is responsible? How should the problem be rectified? How should it be prevented in the future?

The "how" and "who" are clear with 20-20 hindsight. First, risky loans were not only offered but encouraged. Low introductory rate loans, known as "exploding ARMs" (adjustable rate mortgages), enticed borrowers into loans that could not be repaid in the long run. Second, there was weak underwriting. Those offering loans were at best lax, and in some cases fraudulent, in offering loans to borrowers who were highly unlikely to have sufficient funds to keep mortgage payments current. Some of these loans were linked to costly fees if timely payments were not made. The fees were designed to strip the homeowners' equity first, and then lead to foreclosure without the opportunity for refinancing. Third, the loan originators lacked accountability for the loans' risks. The vast majority of subprime loans were packaged and sold to investors in the secondary market. The originators held no residual responsibly for the repayment of the loans. Their incentive was to close loans and sell them as quickly as possible. Finally, there was minimal oversight over the process. The mortgage brokers who originated the loans were largely unregulated; they did not carry the prudential obligations of traditional banks. The backstop protectors,

---

http://jec.senate.gov/index.cfm?FuseAction=Reports.Reports&ContentRecord_id=0d3fa2c7-acc9-3b31-a3e6-a00e1c2d8378&Region_id=&Issue_id= (last visited Oct. 6, 2009).

appraiser of the property, and agencies that rated for investors the securities backed by the packages of mortgages, failed to provide realistic guidance.[1099]

One frustrating element of the current crisis is that the news about the problems associated with subprime lending was not new. Although the number of subprime loans was lower in the 1990s, there was ample evidence showing the problems with this form of lending. Between 1995 and 1999 the number of subprime foreclosures in Boston nearly tripled, while foreclosures of conventionally financed homes were cut in half.[1100] Mortgage delinquencies increased by almost 50% between 2000 and 2003.[1101] (Exhibit 9) Nevertheless, lenders continued to offer subprime loans at an increasing rate. Why did lenders continue to make loans that they knew were problematic? According to an economist at the Mortgage Brokers Association: "Because investors continued to buy the loans."[1102]

In the multi-billion dollar subprime debacle there is blame for all parties. Borrowers entered into loans that they should have realized were unsustainable. Lenders aggressively marketed such loans in many cases knowing that the likelihood of repayment problems was high. They consummated the loans; however, because they assumed that rising housing prices would "make them whole" and in any case they would not be held to account for the bad loans. According to Federal Reserve Board Chairman Ben Bernanke many loans were "inappropriate for or misled the borrower."[1103]

1099 ELLEN SCHLOEMER ET AL., LOSING GROUND: FORECLOSURES IN THE SUBPRIME MARKET AND THEIR COSTS TO HOMEOWNERS 5 (2006), http://www.responsiblelending.org/mortgage-lending/research-analysis/foreclosure-paper-report-2-17.pdf (last visited Oct. 9, 2009).

1100 Harold L. Bunce et al., *Subprime Foreclosures: The Smoking Gun of Predatory Lending?, in* HOUSING POLICY IN THE NEW MILLENNIUM CONFERENCE PROCEEDINGS 257, 265 (Susan M. Wachter & R. Leo Penne eds.,2001), http://www.huduser.org/publications/pdf/brd/12Bunce.pdf (last visited Oct. 9, 2009).

1101 Tim Dunne & Brent Meyer, *Subprime Statistics,* FED. RESERVE BANK OF CLEVELAND (Apr. 5, 2007), http://www.clevelandfed.org/research/trends/2007/0407/07ecoact.cfm (last visited Oct. 9, 2009).

1102 *Mortgage Servicing Practice: Hearing on H.R. 3221 Before the H. Comm. on Financial Services,* 110th Cong. (2008), LEXIS, News Library, Curnws File (statement of Julia Gordon, Policy Counsel, Center for Responsible Lending).

1103 Press Release, Statement of Chairman Ben S. Bernanke, Federal Reserve Board, July 14, 2008, http://www.federalreserve.gov/newsevents/press/bcreg/bernankeregz20080714.htm (last visited Oct. 9, 2009); *Mortgage Servicing Practice: Hearing on H.R. 3221 Before the H. Comm. on Financial Services* 110th Cong. (2008), LEXIS, News Library, Curnws File (statement of Julia Gordon, Policy Counsel, Center for Responsible Lending) (quoting press release)..

The appraisers were to provide critical insight into the value of homes to support mortgage loans. Accurate valuations are required to reduce the risks to those who hold the loans, or the loan backed securities. After all, it is the value of property that provides the collateral for the loan holder in the case of default. While appraisers "must perform assignments with impartiality, objectivity, and independence, and without accommodation of personal interest,"[1104] there is ample evidence that they routinely provided valuations that were greater than the true value to the property in order to close loans. For example, New York Attorney General Andrew Cuomo filed suit on behalf of the people of New York against First American Corporation (and its eAppraiseIT unit) alleging that they "have abdicated their role in providing 'third-party, unbiased valuations'" by allowing eAppraiseIT's customer's "loan production staff to hand-pick appraisers who bring in appraisal values high enough to permit [customer] loans to close . . . . This wrongful conduct constitutes a deceptive, fraudulent, and illegal business practice. It violates New York law as well as federal law and regulations."[1105]

Some of the blame also falls on the investors. The subprime mortgages were sold to very sophisticated investors, including banks such as Citibank and Bank of America. Some of the largest investment banking firms, such as UBS and Merrill Lynch, were also investors in subprime mortgages. One can only presume these companies either failed to conduct appropriate due diligence or were convinced that the rising housing market and growing economy would secure their loans. In either case their subprime investments have led to multi-billion losses. In the case of Bear Stearns, over the second weekend in March 2008 a deal was made for JPMorgan Chase to buy the venerable investment firm for a mere $2 per share. The Federal government provided $30 billion in guarantees to assure that the transactions would close.[1106] Only a week earlier Bear Stearns stock traded at $50![1107] In 2007, the company's stock stood at

---

1104 USPAP, *Ethics Rule*, http://commerce.appraisalfoundation.org/html/2006%20USPAP/ETHICS_RULE.htm (last visited May 21, 2008).

1105 People v. First Am. Corp. 3 [Supreme Ct.],*Id.* at 3. http://www.oag.state.ny.us/media_center/2007/nov/EA%20Complaint.pdf (last visited Oct. 9, 2009)

1106 *With the Collapse of Bear Stearns and the Federal Reserve Heavily Involved in the Banking Business, the Question Many Traders Are Likely to Ask Is, 'Who's Next?,'* PR NEWSWIRE, Mar. 18, 2008, LEXIS, News Library, Curnws File.

1107 David Roeder, *Did Rumors Help Sink Bear Stearns?; Company, SEC Checking It Out; Some Big-Time Investors Got Caught Outside the Loop,* CHI. SUN-TIMES, Mar. 23, 2008, at 23, LEXIS, News Library, Curnws File.

$170.[1108] The collapse had a direct cause – excessive exposure to mortgage-backed securities associated with subprime loans.

The investors have explained their lack of homework by their reliance on credit rating agencies (CRAs). The CRAs evaluate the quality of debt and structured finance offerings for investors. Moody's Corporation, the first credit rating agency in the world, began rating bonds in the U.S. in 1909. Since that time Moody's and other CRAs have provided ratings on most government and private debt offerings and more recently on structured finance opportunities. The ratings are intended to provide potential investors with "forward-looking opinions that speak to the relative probability that principal and interest will be repaid in a timely manner."[1109] Concerns about the reliability of ratings surfaced in the 1980s when the Washington Public Power Supply System could not repay more than $2 billion in debts. Those obligations were rated highly by the CRAs.[1110] The questions intensified at the outset of the 21st century especially with the failure of Enron. The reliability and objectivity of CRAs ratings are once again being questioned in conjunction with the subprime. Chair of the Senate Committee on Banking, Senator Dodd, opened a September 2007 hearing on the role of the credit agencies in the subprime market stating: "Families all across this nation continue to struggle to hold on to their homes . . . because of abusive and predatory subprime lending. These loans were facilitated by Wall Street with the support of credit rating agencies."[1111] A particular concern has been raised about the potential conflict of interest between the rating agencies and those "customers" who seek to sell the investments that the CRAs rate. While the industry has strenuously defended its ratings and protections against conflicts, an

---

1108 *With the Collapse of Bear Stearns and the Federal Reserve Heavily Involved in the Banking Business, the Question Many Traders Are Likely to Ask Is, 'Who's Next?,'* PR NEWSWIRE, Mar. 18, 2008, LEXIS, News Library, Curnws File.

1109 MOODY'S INVESTORS SERVICE, CODE OF PROFESSIONAL CONDUCT 3 (2007), http://www.moodys.com/cust/content/Content.ashx?source=StaticContent/Free+Pages/Regulatory+Affairs_Documents/professional_conduct.pdf (last visited Oct. 9, 2009)..

1110 *See* U.S. SEC. & EXCH. COMM'N, SEC REPORT ON THE ROLE AND FUNCTION OF CREDIT RATING AGENCIES IN THE OPERATION OF THE SECURITIES MARKETS 10 (2003), http://www.sec.gov/news/studies/credratingreport0103.pdf (last visited Oct. 9, 2009) (noting that SEC and Congress "reviewed the regulatory treatment of credit rating agencies" at the time of the Washington Public Power Supply System's "large scale credit default").

1111 *Impact of Credit-Rating Agencies: Hearing Before the Sen. Comm. on Banking, Housing, and Urban Affairs,* 110th Cong., LEXIS, News Library, Curnws File (statement of Chairman Christopher J. Dodd); Press Release, Sen. Chris Dodd, Statement of Senator Dodd, Chairman of the Senate Committee on Banking, Housing and Urban Affairs, on Hearing Entitled "The Role and Impact of Credit Rating Agencies on the Subprime Credit Markets." (Sept. 26, 2007), http://banking.senate.gov/public/_files/dodd.pdf (last visited Oct. 9, 2009)..

S&P's representative acknowledged that "we have learned hard lessons from the recent difficulties in the subprime mortgage area."[1112]

One more actor in the subprime saga has the burden of accountability for the continuing crisis – the mortgage servicers. These companies provide the administrative services that link the borrower to the investor; they collect payments from the borrower and pay them to the investor. The servicer works for the investor. The agreement between these parties typically dictates how modifications to the loans can be structured. The terms often limited the opportunity to help find a solution for borrowers who were delinquent or in default. Even if a servicer wanted to renegotiate the terms of a loan, tax issues often limited flexibility. Finally, the financial incentives for servicers favor highly automated processes not individual time consuming renegotiations.

The outlook for solving the subprime problem in the near future is bleak. The testimony of the Center for Responsible Lending's Julia Gordon before the U.S. House of Representatives Committee on Financial Services in July 2008 provides a compelling case for concern: "Just one year ago, some in the mortgage industry claimed that the number of coming foreclosures would be too small to [be significant]. No one makes that claim today. . . . Projections by Fitch Ratings indicate that 43% of recent subprime loans will be lost to foreclosure, and at least two million American families are expected to lose their homes to foreclosures over the next two years."[1113] A study of the survival function of home mortgages in Cleveland illustrates the continuing vulnerability of subprime loans. As shown in Exhibit 10 only 60% of subprime mortgages to white homeowners are still current with no foreclosure actions taken after 36 months. The number falls to 40% for black subprime mortgage holders.[1114] "What's more, industry projections forecast that by

---

[1112] *Impact of Credit-Rating Agencies: Hearing Before the Sen. Comm. on Banking, Housing, and Urban Affairs,* 110th Cong., LEXIS, News Library, Curnws File (testimony of Vickie A. Tillman, Executive Vice President, Standard & Poor's Credit Market Services).

[1113] *Mortgage Servicing Practice: Hearing on H.R. 3221 Before the H. Comm. on Financial Services,* 110th Cong. (2008), LEXIS, News Library, Curnws File (statement of Julia Gordon, Policy Counsel. Center for Responsible Lending).

[1114] Claudia Coulton et al., *Pathways To Foreclosure: A Longitudinal Study of Mortgage Loans, Cleveland and Cuyahoga County, 2005-2008,* at 10 (Center on Urban Poverty and Community Development, Case Western Reserve Univ.,June 2008), http://blog.case.edu/msass/2008/06/23/Pathways_to_foreclosure_6_23.pdf (last visited Oct. 9, 2009).

2012, 1 in 8 mortgages – that's all mortgages, not just subprime mortgages – will fail."[1115]

The primary response of Congress, regulators and politicians to the crisis in the first half of 2008 was to encourage the servicers to reduce the number of foreclosures because the servicers were the only link between the borrowers and investors. As detailed above, this approach was hindered by legal and business issues that make changing the terms of loans problematic. The rapid escalation in foreclosures was strong evidence that the voluntary program was not sufficient to solve the problem. As the second half of 2008 began there were calls for more legislative and regulatory actions. A UBS analyst captured the rationale for intervention: "[W]hen markets fail, lenders and borrowers need some sort of regulatory and legislative framework within which to manage problems, rather than be forced to act in the chaos of the moment."[1116]

Legislative proposals to resolve the current crisis and avoid another in the future would require loan servicers to "engage in loss mitigation prior to foreclosure"[1117] and to assure that the homeowner could afford the new terms. Another proposal would require the servicers of ARM mortgages to notify borrowers of rate increases prior to the change. A House bill would delay foreclosures for up to nine months if the borrower continued to pay the minimum monthly obligation of the loan's teaser rate. There have even been calls to extend the power of bankruptcy courts to modify loans to include those of primary residences.

The discussions around remedying the subprime crisis have also called into question the financial/legal arrangement that allowed the packaging and reselling of mortgages to third party investors and separated borrowers from lenders, that is – securitization.

[1115] *Mortgage Servicing Practice: Hearing on H.R. 3221 Before the H. Comm. on Financial Services* 110th Cong. (2008), LEXIS, News Library, Curnws File (statement of Julia Gordon, Policy Counsel, Center for Responsible Lending).

[1116] *Id.*

[1117] *Id.*

Exhibit 1
Homeownership of U.S. Households

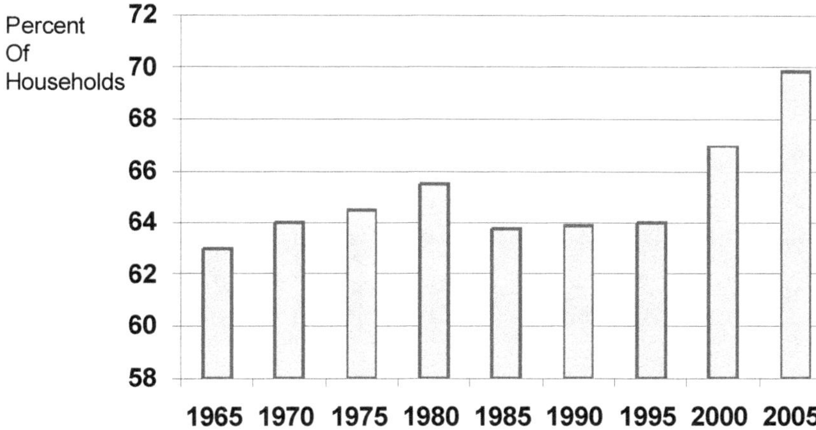

Source: U.S. Census Bureau, Historical Census Of Housing Graphs: Homeownership, http://www.census.gov/hhes/www/housing/census/historic/hograph.html (last visited Oct. 8, 2009).

Exhibit 2
Median Housing Prices

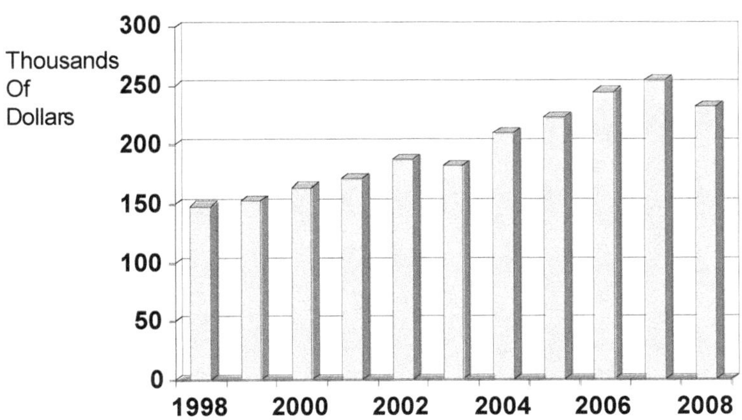

Source: U.S. Census Bureau, Median and Average Sales Prices of New Homes Sold in the United States, http://www.census.gov/const/uspricemon.pdf (last visited Oct. 8, 2009).

Exhibit 3
Value of Subprime Mortgage Originations

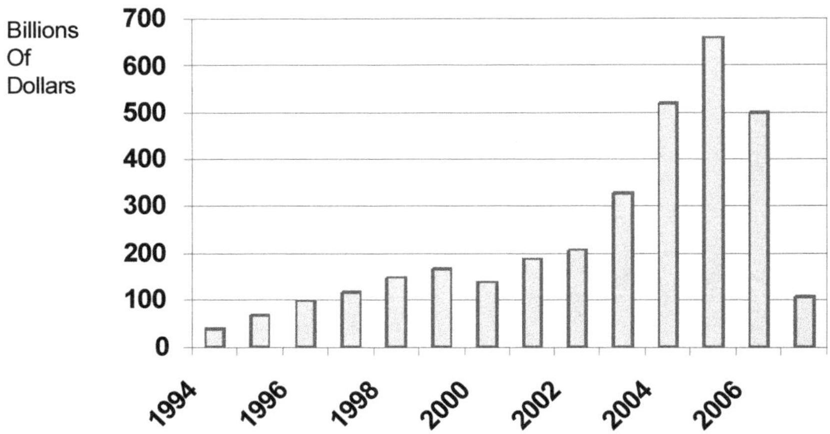

Source: Lawrence Yun, After the Clean Up 2 (May 29, 2008), http://media.miamiherald.com/smedia/2008/06/12/17/NAR_Chief_Economist_Dr_Yun_RAMB_Miami_Congress__June_2008_source.pr od_affiliate.56.pdf (last visited Oct. 9, 2009).

Exhibit 4
Conventional Mortgage Denial Rates

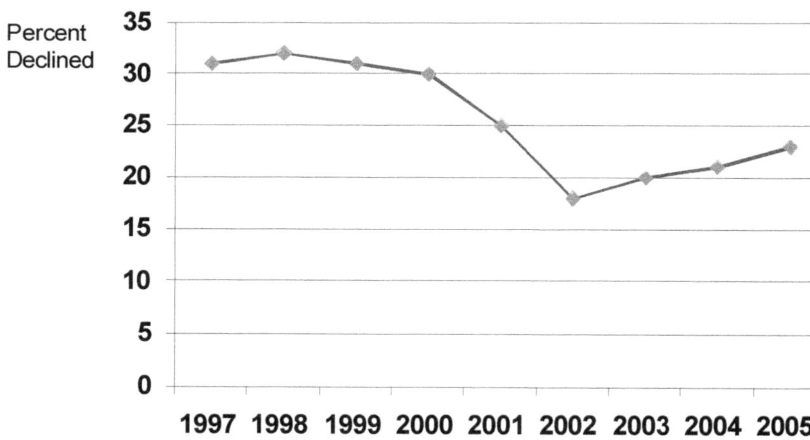

Source: Edward M. Gramlich, Subprime Mortgages 6 (2007) (author interpretation of data).

Exhibit 5
Inventory of Existing and New Homes
Thousands of Homes

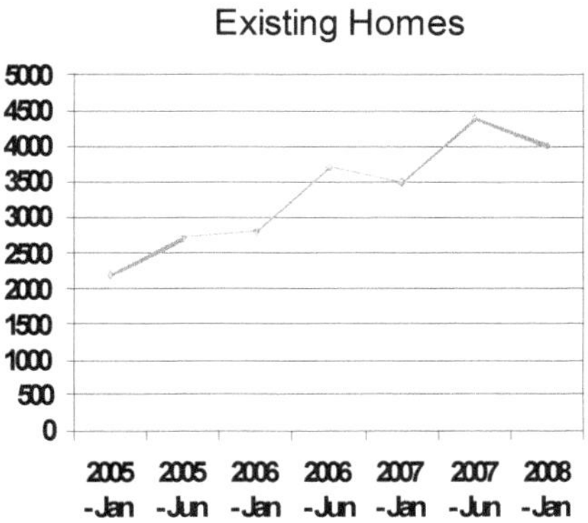

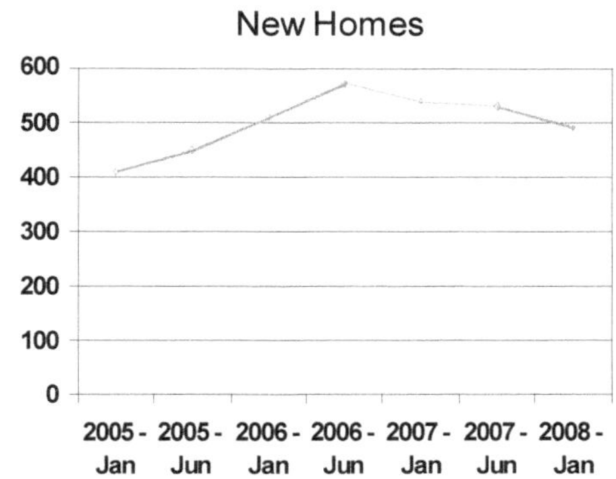

Source: Lawrence Yun, After the Clean Up 24-25 (May 29, 2008), http://media.miamiherald.com/smedia/2008/06/12/17/NAR_Chief_Economist_Dr_Yun_RAMB_Miami_Congress__June_2008_source.pr od_affiliate.56.pdf (last visited Oct. 9, 2009).

Exhibit 6
Real Gross Domestic Product

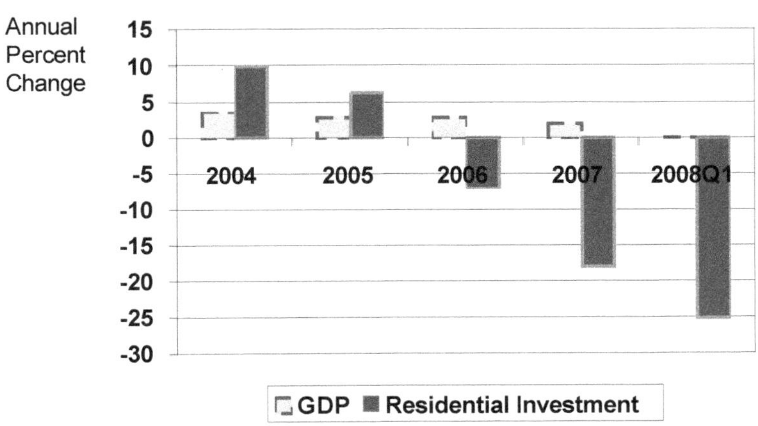

Source: News Release, Bureau of Econ. Analysis, U.S. Dep't of Commerce, Gross Domestic Product: First Quarter 2009 (Advance) Table 1 (BEA 09-17, Apr. 29, 2009), http://www.bea.gov/newsreleases/national/gdp/2009/pdf/gdp109a.pdf (last visited Oct. 8, 2009).

Exhibit 7
Consumer Confidence
(2007-2008)

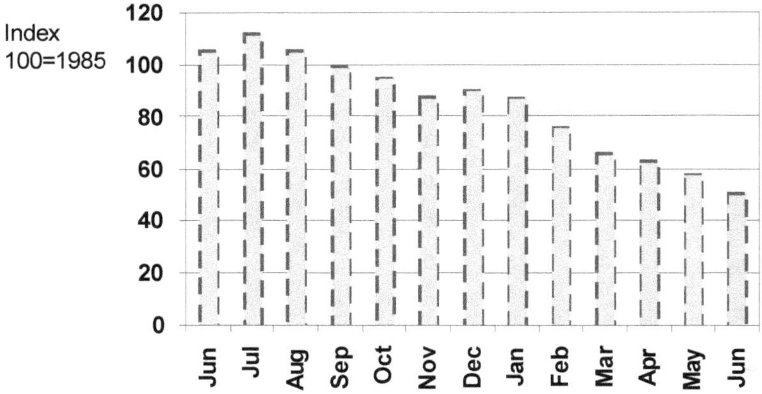

Source: Conference Board, Consumer Confidence Index

Exhibit 8
Foreclosure Rates

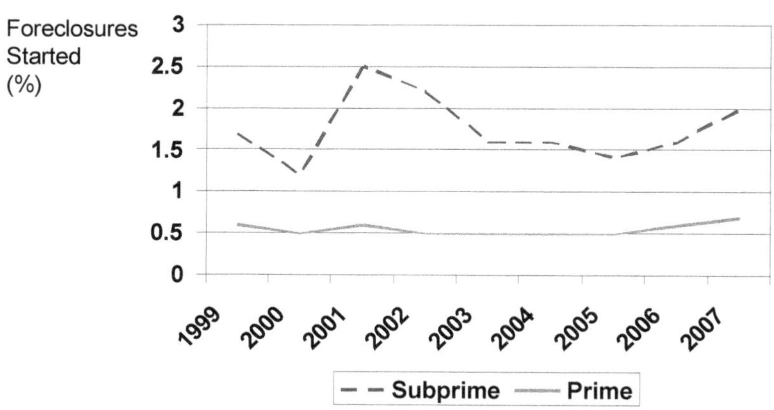

Source: Tim Dunne & Brent Meyer, *Subprime Statistics*, Fed. Reserve Bank of Cleveland (Apr. 5, 2007), http://www.clevelandfed.org/research/trends/2007/0407/07ecoact.cfm (last visited Oct. 9, 2009).

Exhibit 9
Mortgage Delinquency Rates

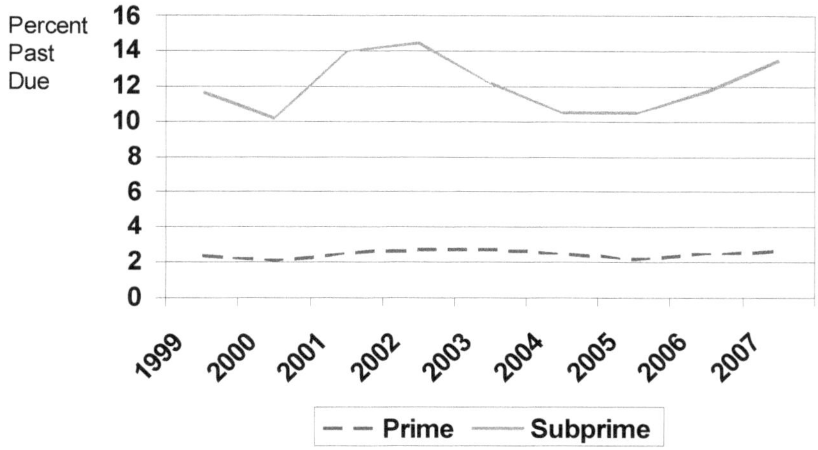

Source: Tim Dunne & Brent Meyer, *Subprime Statistics,* Fed. Reserve Bank of Cleveland (Apr. 5, 2007), http://www.clevelandfed.org/research/trends/2007/0407/07ecoact.cfm (last visited Oct. 9, 2009).Chapter 13 (subprime)

Exhibit 10
Mortgage Survival Rates

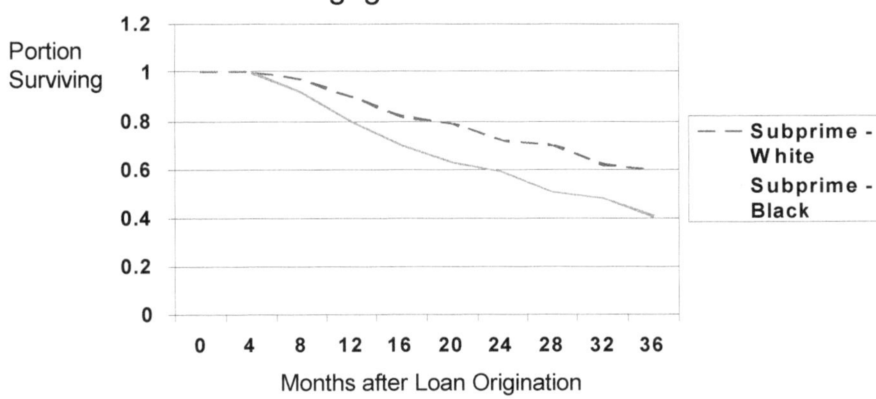

Source: Claudia Coulton et al., *Pathways To Foreclosure: A Longitudinal Study of Mortgage Loans, Cleveland and Cuyahoga County, 2005-2008,* at 10 (Center on Urban Poverty and Community Development, Case Western Reserve Univ., June 2008), http://blog.case.edu/msass/2008/06/23/Pathways_to_foreclosure_6_23.pdf (last visited Oct. 9, 2009).

Discussion Questions

Legal

- What are the legal restrictions on re-negotiating loans?
- To whom does the servicer own an obligation to?
- Can the federal government require servicers to postpone foreclosures if the borrower remits minimal payments?

Business

- What are the incentives of the loan originators, the servicers, and the investors?
- Why did sophisticated investors get caught with non-performing subprime loans?
- Is the subprime an example of market failure?
- How much reliance should an investor place on appraisals and ratings?
- Why did the subprime have such a large impact on the overall economy?
- Who is hurt by a liquidity crunch?

Public Policy

- Should subprime loans be banned?
- Should restrictions be placed on the use of "teaser" rate loans?
- What is the rationale for the federal government guaranteeing the sale of Bear Stearns?
- What are the social costs of the subprime crisis?
- What is the role of regulation in preventing another subprime disaster?

Chapter 14: The Future of Securitization

This final chapter provides an analysis of securitization and offers a case study about covered bonds, a variant of securitization that could be either a complement or competitor to securitization. The chapter ends with predications about the future of securitization.

A. Analysis [1118]

What brought about securitization? Why did it not come before? And is it here to stay? A number of circumstances contributed to the emergence of securitization.

First, banks were losing ground in relationship to the Markets. New technology for information retrieval and recording facilitated domestic and international securities trading. This technology drastically reduced the costs of securities trading and made information available almost instantaneously all over the globe. As a result, banks were losing their historical competitive advantage over market intermediaries in acquiring information about customer-borrowers, and Markets were gaining a larger share of the intermediation business.

Second, regulators pressed the banks to increase their equity and long-term debt capital. In the bear market of the 1970s, this capital was very expensive. Therefore, banks took an alternative route, increasing their capital by reducing their assets (and short-term liabilities). To reduce assets, banks had to sell loans, and to sell loans efficiently they needed to securitize them.

Third, investors favored securitization and Markets. Many investors preferred to invest part of their portfolios in the Markets and part in Institutions. Securitization allowed investors to invest in SPVs (Institutions) while also gaining market efficiencies. Further, investors favored the Markets because the investors' risk-tolerance for market volatility has increased as memories of the Great Depression dimmed, and investors' concern with inflation made Markets more attractive as a hedge.

While these advantages tilted the scales toward market intermediation, an unstable economic environment brought to the fore the weaknesses inherent in banks' financial structure. Inflation in the 1970s, followed by stagnation and the "credit crunch" in the 1980s, threatened the banks' financial situations. One of the weaknesses of banks is rooted in their main function: their usefulness as intermediaries. The banks intermediate between savers and borrowers whose

[1118] 1 TAMAR FRANKEL, SECURITIZATION §§ 1.6, 2.11 (Ann Taylor Schwing ed., 2d ed. 2005).

preferences are incompatible. Depositors desire the most liquid and safest place to keep a portion of their transaction money, while borrowers offer far riskier and long-term obligations. The banks' beneficial service for the parties and the economy makes banks' structures risky because their liabilities and assets are mismatched. Paradoxically, this mismatch provides the banks with a "spread." They can charge borrowers more than they pay for the depositors' money. However, because this mismatch requires the banks to keep substantial "cushions" to support their risky structure, it also reduces the banks' profitability.

Yet, if banks are so frail, how did they remain stable and healthy for so many years? The answer can be found in the legal system of monopolies for banks, in government support for banks, in depositors' patterns of behavior, in bank practices, and in the long relative stability of interest rates in the United States. Banks were granted a legal monopoly on deposits. The law prohibited competition over deposits between banks and others. In addition, the law precluded competition for deposits among banks by fixing the interest rate that all banks were allowed to pay for deposits. Further, small deposits were insured by the Government, adding value to no-interest or low-interest bank deposits and assuring the stability of the deposit base.

The pattern of the depositors' behavior also helped bank stability because depositors behaved in a fairly predictable manner. The amounts of deposits that were withdrawn nearly matched the amounts deposited. For temporary liquidity problems, banks could borrow from the Federal Reserve System's "discount window." Thus, banks were assured of inexpensive and stable funding.

The banks' monopoly over borrowing was also tight. Few borrowers could raise funds abroad. Competition among banks for borrowers was limited to geographical areas, at least until the 1960s. No one else could profitably enter the lending business. Consumer banks, mortgage companies, and factoring companies remained small because the cost of their funds was higher than the cost of deposits for banks. Since these lenders had to charge borrowers more, they offered little competition to banks.

Banks' practices helped reduce the gap between the risk levels of their liabilities and assets. Rather than make long-term loans to risky enterprises, banks made mostly short-term loans for working capital to seasoned enterprises. These prudent lending policies reduced the banks' liquidity and credit risks. The privilege and duty of long-term funding for housing was bestowed on savings and loan associations; this activity rendered their capital structure even less rational than that of banks. Risk capital came mainly from venture capital companies. Small consumer banks, mortgage companies, and factoring companies catered to those who did not have the necessary credit rating for, or contacts in, the banks.

Paradoxically, the stability of banks was also enhanced by the fact that their loans were illiquid. Until default, loans were carried on the books at face value, regardless of small fluctuations in the risk level of the borrowers or larger fluctuations of market interest rates. This legal regime made the banks stable and profitable—at a price. That price became too high when the environment in which banks operated changed. Economic pressures made bank monopolies highly unfair to all depositors. Government exemption for large depositors made these monopolies most unfair to the small depositors. As savers withdrew their money from deposits and savings accounts, they dried up bank deposit funding and thrifts' capital for housing.

In addition to unstable economic conditions, a fundamental change has occurred in the philosophy underlying government regulation of banking. Social and political attitude militated against bank monopoly. The Government chose securitization as the solution to intermediation problems with which banks could not cope. This solution initiated the dismantling of the traditional bank monopoly.

The Government played a crucial role in eliminating bank monopolies and paving the way to securitizing debt. The Government actively initiated and developed the process of securitization by pooling, creating and financing agencies to securitize mortgage loans as a solution to the tight credit in the housing capital Market. This analysis may explain why securitization did not appear before the 1970s. It was triggered by economic conditions, a new technology, and a different government policy, all of which emerged in the 1970s.

B. Case Study: Covered Bonds – Complement or Competition

In Mid-2008 Secretary of the Treasury Henry Paulson spoke at a press conference on the financial crisis about the need to increase credit availability in the housing market. He noted Fannie Mae and Freddie Mac were continuing to fund 70 percent of residential mortgages. However, private label securitization of mortgages had significantly diminished. He expressed confidence that the private label market would recover but he went on to say: "We also believe it is useful to explore additional mortgage financing options to complement more traditional funding models."[1119] His suggestion: covered bonds, a $3 trillion source of mortgage funds in Europe.

Covered bonds are secured debt instruments issued by banks which are collateralized by a dedicated pool of mortgages. The mortgages remain on the balance sheet of the bank and the bank holds capital reserves to cover potential losses on the underlying mortgages. The interest and principal repayment of the bonds are a secured bank

---

[1119] Secretary Henry M. Paulson, Jr.
Statement on Covered Bond Best Practices (July 28, 2008), http://www.treas.gov/press/releases/hp1101.htm (last visited Oct, 12, 2008), .

obligation and are not linked directly to the cash flow from the mortgage pool. In the event of a prepayment or default of mortgages in the pool, the bank adds new mortgages into the pool so that the net value of the collateral and cash flow stream remain unchanged. Thus, the investor does not face exposure to the mortgage market, rather the exposure is to the financial health of the bank offering the bonds. But even in the worst case of a bank failure, the investor could take possession of the underlying assets. A Morgan Stanley managing director summarized the risk profile of covered bonds as follows: "This is basically an interest-rate product. They are triple-A rated and secured. They have the backing of double-A and single-A banks. There is not a lot of credit risk to these deals."[1120]

Covered bonds date back to the 18th century when aristocratic landowners under the egis of Frederick the Great sold "Pfandbriefe" or bonds secured by real estate. Two hundred years later, Pfandbriefe are widely used to increase the liquidity in the mortgage market throughout Europe. The covered bond market in Europe has grown dramatically since 2000 (38 percent between 2003 and 2007 alone) and "has developed into the most important privately issued bond segment in Europe's capital markets"[1121] Of new covered bond issues in 2007, two thirds were secured by mortgages with the remainder primarily backed by public sector loans. (See Exhibit 1) Institutions in Denmark and Germany have been the primary issuers of covered bonds accounting for more than half of covered bond activity in Europe. Spain, France and the United Kingdom account for the most of the remainder of European covered bond issues. (See Exhibit 2)

The European Central Bank attributes the growth in covered bonds to the low risk nature of investment as most bonds are AAA rated.[1122] Exhibit 3 shows that 100 percent of covered bonds were rated AAA in France and Ireland. In Germany 96 percent of bonds carried that rating. The Central Bank's assessment has been borne out by the resilience of covered bond values even in the case of a significant downgrade in the rating of the issuing institution. Allgemeine Hypothekenbank Rheinboden AG (AHBR) was one of Germany's largest mortgage banks and had more than $55 billion in covered bonds outstanding in 2005. In that year, the bank's rating was significantly downgraded. Its financial strength rating was dropped to a level suggesting that the bank might need to be rescued. Nevertheless, the yields on

---

[1120] Donna Mitchell, *U.S. Covered Bond Market Takes Flight,* ASSET SECURITIZATION REP. June 18, 2007, LEXIS, News Library, Arcnws File, *at* http://www.securitization.net/knowledge/article.asp?id=141&aid=7414 (last visited Oct. 12, 2009).

[1121] EUROPEAN CENTRAL BANK, COVERED BONDS IN THE EU FINANCIAL SYSTEM § 3, at 8 (Dec. 2008), http://www.ecb.int/pub/pdf/other/coverbondsintheeufinancialsystem200812en_en.pdf (last visited Oct. 12, 2009).

[1122] *Id.* § 3.2, at 10.

its covered bonds hardly changed indicating that investors were confident the future interest and principal payments on AHBR's covered bonds would be made.[1123]

A special law-based framework supports the covered bond market in 26 European countries. The bonds issued under this framework provide "preferential risk weightings in the hands of certain regulated investors."[1124] The European Covered Bond Council identifies four essential features of covered bonds. First, "[t]he bond is issued by – or bondholders otherwise have full recourse to - [credit institutions] subject to public supervision or regulation."[1125] The right is unrestricted and unconditional. Second, the "[b]ondholders have a claim against a cover pool of financial assets in priority to the unsecured creditors of the credit institution."[1126] The covered assets are primarily real estate mortgages -- specifically excluding equities, commodities and other intangible property. A set of minimum standards apply to the quality of the assets in the pool. For example, most countries set a maximum loan-to-value ratio of 60-80 percent.[1127] The cover pool is typically "ring-fenced" to separate the assets from the general obligations of the issuing institution. This provides bondholders priority if the institution becomes insolvent. Third, "[t]he credit institution has the ongoing obligation to maintain sufficient assets in the cover pool to satisfy the claims of covered bondholders at all times."[1128] Not only does the value of the pool value have to exceed the value of the issued bonds (i.e. overcollateralization) but also the pool value must be maintained on an ongoing basis. Thus, new assets must be added to the pool if some pool assets mature or default. Fourth, the covered bond obligations are subject to special supervisions (typically in the form of a monitor and periodic audits) focused on the stability of the asset pool rather than the overall safety and soundness of the institution itself.

The investors of covered bonds include banks, structured investment vehicles and insurance/pension funds. Banks accounted for 45 percent of purchases in the primary market. Covered bonds are particularly attractive assets for banks because they "have a 10% risk weight in most countries, compared to 50% for residential MBS tranches

---

[1123] Frank Packer et al., *The Covered Bond Market,* BIS Q. REV., Sept. 2007, at 43, 53, http://www.bis.org/publ/qtrpdf/r_qt0709f.pdf (last visited Oct. 12, 2009).

[1124] European Covered Bond Council, *ECBC Essential Features of Covered Bonds,* http://ecbc.hypo.org/Content/Default.asp?PageID=367 (last visited Oct. 12, 2009).

[1125] *Id.*

[1126] *Id.*

[1127] Frank Packer et al., *The Covered Bond Market,* BIS Q. REV., Sept. 2007, at 43, 48, http://www.bis.org/publ/qtrpdf/r_qt0709f.pdf (last visited Oct. 12, 2009).

[1128] European Covered Bond Council, *ECBC Essential Features of Covered Bonds,* http://ecbc.hypo.org/Content/Default.asp?PageID=367 (last visited Oct. 12, 2009).

with the same rating."[1129] Structured investment vehicles and insurance/pension funds accounted for 37 percent and 18 percent of primary market purchases respectfully. This distribution of investors stands in contrast to purchases of asset-backed securities where structured investment vehicles are more prominent. (See Exhibit 3)

European covered bonds have fared comparatively well during the 2007-2008 financial crisis. During 2007, as credit tightened, the swap-spreads on covered bonds in the secondary market did widen. However, the magnitude of the spread was far less than that for senior financial debt. (See Exhibit 4) In the primary market the financial turmoil was initially advantageous as banks sought to acquire covered bonds as safe assets. As the financial crisis intensified at the end of 2008 and governments began guaranteeing bank debt, the demand for covered bonds weakened and few new issues were offered.

Looking to the future of the covered bond market in Europe, the European Central Bank expects "in the near term, risk averse investors may find government guaranteed bank debt relatively attractive to those covered bonds which do not benefit from an explicit government guarantee. However, covered bonds are likely to be issued again once general investor confidence returns and dislocations in funding markets ease substantially."[1130] The Central Bank is also considering proposals to shift the trading in the secondary market from an over-the-counter model to a more efficient and transparent marketplace via established electronic trading platforms.

In the United States the covered bond market was slow to develop for several reasons. First, the mortgage-backed securities (MBS) market flourished throughout the 1990s and until 2007. The comparatively higher returns on MBS and the perceived low risk of these investments kept covered bonds out of the market. A second concern "was the regulatory uncertainty surrounding the enforceability of the senior claim of the covered bondholders on the cover pool."[1131] Since bank depositors are generally considered the most senior claimants, would the pool of mortgages collateralizing the covered bonds be used to pay off depositor claims before the covered bond holders? This regulatory risk increased in 2007 when bank laws were amended "to include an automatic stay, for as long as 90 days, of any

---

1129 Frank Packer et al., *The Covered Bond Market,* BIS Q. REV., Sept. 2007, at 43, 46 n.2, http://www.bis.org/publ/qtrpdf/r_qt0709f.pdf (last visited Oct. 12, 2009).

1130 EUROPEAN CENTRAL BANK, COVERED BONDS IN THE EU FINANCIAL SYSTEM § 5.1, at 25 (Dec. 2008), http://www.ecb.int/pub/pdf/other/coverbondsintheeufinancialsystem200812en_en.pdf (last visited Oct. 12, 2009).

1131 O. Emre Ergungor, *Covered Bonds: A New Way to Fund Residential Mortgages,* FED. RESERVE BANK OF CLEVELAND, July 15, 2008, http://www.clevelandfed.org/research/commentary/2008/0708.cfm (last visited Oct. 12, 2009).

attempt to foreclose on a failed bank's property or to affect its rights under a contract."[1132]

Despite the uncertainty about the superiority of the covered bondholders' claims, Washington Mutual successfully completed a $26 billion covered bond offering in the fall of 2006.[1133] Interestingly, the offering was denominated in Euros indicating that the target investors for these securities were Europeans not Americans. The first dollar priced covered bond offering was made by Bank of America in 2007. The Federal Deposit Insurance Corporation (FDIC) described these transactions as follows: "an IDI [insured depository institution] sells mortgage bonds, secured by mortgages, to a trust or similar entity ('special purpose vehicle' or 'SPV'). The pledged mortgages remain on the IDI's balance sheet, securing the IDI's obligation to make payments on the debt, and the SPV sells covered bonds, secured by the mortgage bonds, to investors. In the event of a default by the IDI, the mortgage bond trustee takes possession of the pledged mortgages and continues to make payments to the SPV to service the covered bonds."[1134]

The potential for expansion of the covered bond market in the United States increased greatly with the July 2008 FDIC policy statement on covered bonds. "The Policy Statement provides that the consent of the FDIC, as conservator or receiver, is provided to covered bond obligees to exercise their contractual rights over collateral for covered bond transactions conforming to the Interim Policy Statement no sooner than ten (10) business days after a monetary default on an IDI's obligation to the covered bond obligee . . . ."[1135] The Statement defines a covered bond "as a non-deposit, recourse debt obligation of an IDI with a term greater than one year and no more than thirty years, that is secured directly or indirectly by a pool of eligible mortgages or, not exceeding ten percent of the collateral, by AAA-rated mortgage bonds."[1136]

Qualifying bonds must meet a set of standards. First, the bonds must be issued "with the consent of the IDI's primary federal regulator in which the IDI's total covered

---

[1132] Donna Mitchell, *U.S. Covered Bond Market Takes Flight,* ASSET SECURITIZATION REP. June 18, 2007, LEXIS, News Library, Arcnws File, *at* http://www.securitization.net/knowledge/article.asp?id=141&aid=7414 (last visited Oct. 12, 2009).

[1133] *Id.*

[1134] Fed. Deposit Ins. Corp., Covered Bond Policy Statement, 73 Fed. Reg. 43,754, 43,754 (July 28, 2008) (footnote omitted), *at* Press Release, Fed. Deposit Ins. Corp., Covered Bond Policy Statement (July 15, 2008), http://www.fdic.gov/news/news/press/2008/pr08060a.html (last visited Oct. 7, 2009).

[1135] *Id.* at 43,757.

[1136] *Id.* at 43,758.

bond obligations at such issuance comprise no more than 4 percent of an IDI's total liabilities."[1137] A second requirement is that the bonds be secured by "perfected security interests under applicable state and federal law on performing eligible mortgages on one-to-four family residential properties, underwritten at the fully indexed rate, relying on documented income, a limited volume of AAA-rated mortgage securities, and certain substitution collateral."[1138] The policy explicitly excludes "[s]ecurities backed by tranches in other securities or assets (such as Collateralized Debt Obligations)" as acceptable collateral.[1139]

Shortly after the FDIC policy statement was released the U.S. Treasury Department issued a set of best practices for residential covered bonds. The practices specify that the issuer can be a bankruptcy-remote SPV or a depository institution. Illustrative structures for both direct and SPV issued bonds are provided. (See Exhibits 5 and 6) "[T]he cover pool must be owned by the depository institution. Issuers must provide first priority claim on the assets to bond holders and the assets in the cover pool must not be burdened by other liens. The cover pool's assets and liabilities must be clearly identified on its books and records."[1140] The practices reiterate the requirements for collateral in the cover pool specified by the FDIC noted above and add that loan-to-value ratio be less than 80 percent and that negative amortization loans are excluded from the cover pool. The best practices specify that the issuers continuously overcollateralize the pool by at least 5 percent. The Treasury practices also limit the amount of covered bonds issued by an institution to 4 percent of its liabilities.[1141] Under the best practices guidelines, the "[c]overed bonds may be issued as registered securities or may be exempt from registration under securities laws"[1142]. However, "[i]ssuers must receive consent to issue Covered Bonds from their primary federal regulator. . . . Only well-capitalized institutions should issue Covered Bonds."[1143]

The best practices also detail that in the event of insufficient asset coverage the issuer has one month to correct the deficiency or the Trustee may terminate the program. If a federally insured issuer failed, the FDIC can "1) continue to perform

---

[1137] *Id.* at 43,757.

[1138] *Id.*

[1139] *Id.*

[1140] Ofc. of Public Affairs, U.S. Treasury Dep't, Fact Sheet: Treasury Releases Best Practices for Residential Covered Bonds (July 28, 2008), . http://www.treas.gov/press/releases/reports/factsheet.pdf (last visited Oct. 7, 2009).

[1141] *Id.*

[1142] DEP'T OF THE TREASURY, BEST PRACTICES FOR RESIDENTIAL COVERED BONDS 15 (2008), http://www.treas.gov/press/releases/reports/USCoveredBondBestPractices.pdf (last visited Oct. 7, 2009).

[1143] *Id.*

on the Covered Bond transaction under its terms; 2) pay-off the Covered Bonds in cash up to the value of the pledged collateral; or 3) allow liquidation of the pledged collateral to pay-off the Covered Bonds."[1144]

As the financial crisis deepened at the end of 2008, Secretary Paulson's call for the development of a covered bond market had yet to materialize. However, the FDIC policy and Treasury's best practices provide a framework for creating such a market in the future.

Exhibit 1:
Collateral for European Covered Bond Issues in 2007

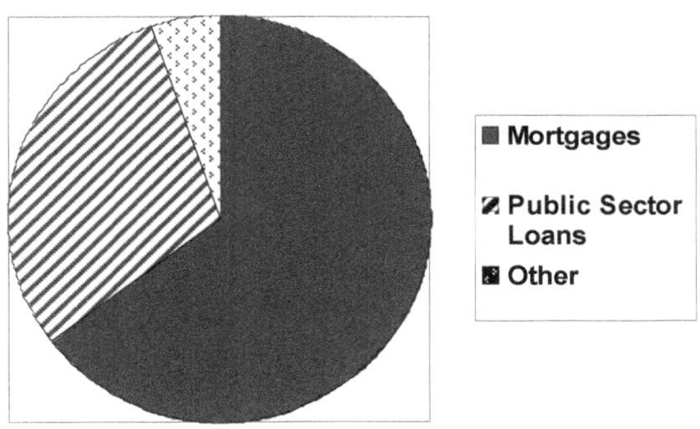

Source: European Central Bank, Covered Bonds in the EU Financial System Statistical Annex at 31 (Dec. 2008), http://www.ecb.int/pub/pdf/other/coverbondsintheeufinancialsystem200812en_en.pdf (last visited Oct. 12, 2009).

[1144] *Id.* at 16.

Exhibit 2:
Total Covered Bonds Outstanding in the EU
by Residence of the Borrower in 2007

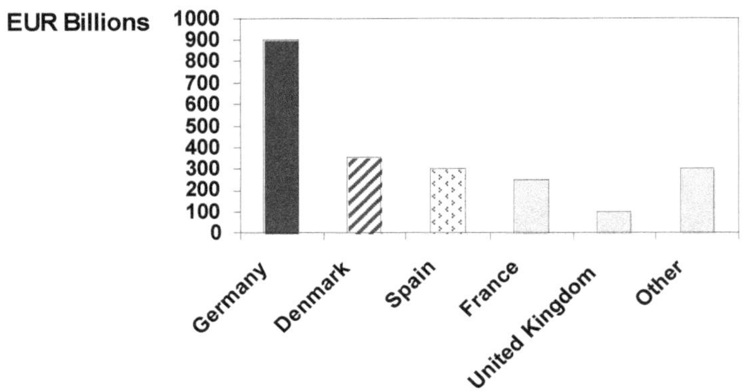

Source: European Central Bank, Covered Bonds in the EU Financial System § 3. at 9 Chart 2 (Dec. 2008), http://www.ecb.int/pub/pdf/other/coverbondsintheeufinancialsystem200812en_en.pdf (last visited Oct. 12, 2009).

Exhibit 3:
Investors in Covered Bonds and Asset -Backed Securities

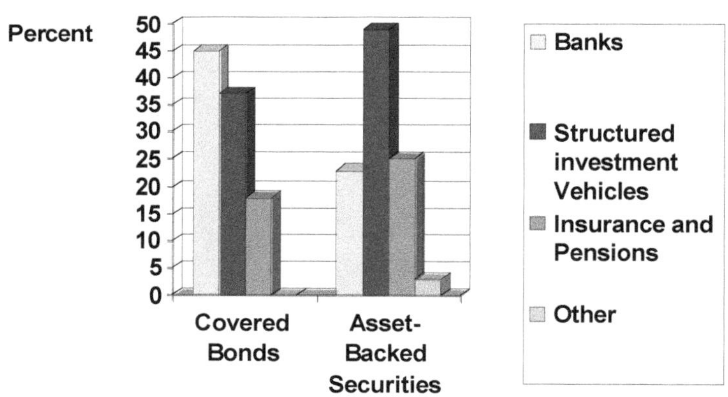

Source: Author estimates drawn from data in Frank Packer et al., *The Covered Bond Market,* BIS Q. Rev., Sept. 2007, at 43, 47, http://www.bis.org/publ/qtrpdf/r_qt0709f.pdf (last visited Oct. 12, 2009).

Exhibit 4:
Swap Spreads of Covered Bonds and Senior Financial Debt

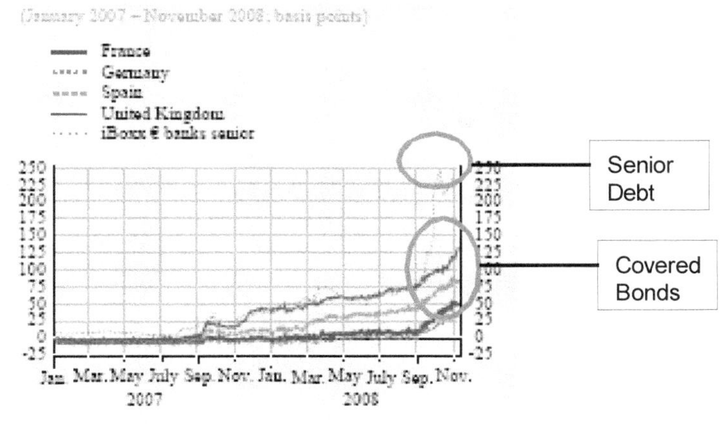

Source: European Central Bank, Covered Bonds in the EU Financial System § 5.1, at 23 Chart 6 (Dec. 2008), http://www.ecb.int/pub/pdf/other/coverbondsintheeufinancialsystem200812en_en.pdf (last visited Oct. 12, 2009).

Exhibit 5:
Illustrative Structure for Direct Issuance of Covered Bonds

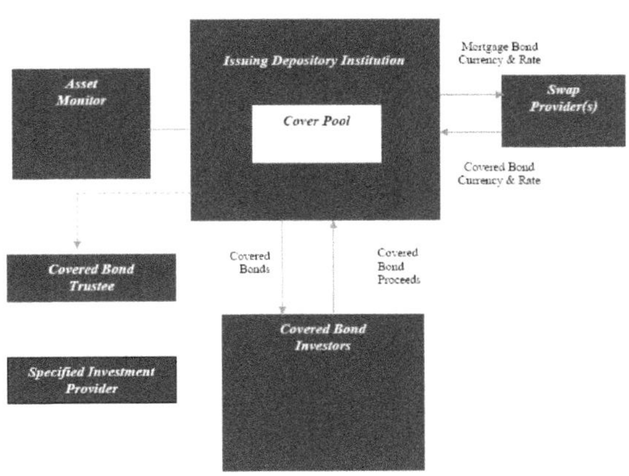

Source: Dep't of the Treasury, Best Practices for Residential Covered Bonds 17 (2008), http://www.treas.gov/press/releases/reports/USCoveredBondBestPractices.pdf (last visited Oct. 7, 2009).

Exhibit 6:
Illustrative Structure for SPV Issuance of Covered Bonds

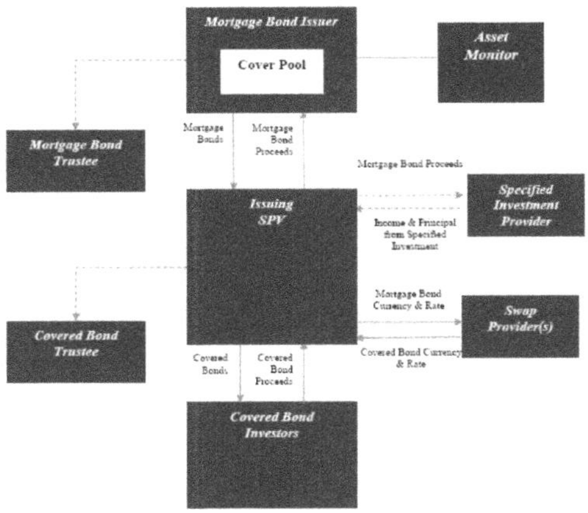

Source: Dep 't of the Treasury, Best Practices for Residential Covered Bonds 18 (2008), http://www.treas.gov/press/releases/reports/USCoveredBondBestPractices.pdf (last visited Oct. 7, 2009).

Assignment:

1. What are the similarities and differences between covered bonds and mortgage-backed securities?
2. What are the advantages and disadvantages of covered bonds?
3. Why has the European Market in covered bonds expanded rapidly, while it has yet to gain a toehold in the United States?
4. Under what circumstances would covered bonds be most attractive in the United States?
5. Are there legal/regulatory barriers to the successful development of the covered bond market in the United States?
6. Do you consider the development of a covered bond market in the United States a threat to the mortgage-backed securities market?
7. What is the outlook for the covered bond market in the United States in 2009 and beyond?

C. Case Study: Securitization as Part of the Solution to the Financial Crisis - Term Asset-Backed Loan Facility

Automobile sales plunged in 2008 as the financial industry's problems became an economic crisis. New vehicle sales dropped from 16.1 million in 2007 to only 13.2 million in 2008.[1145] The drop in sales equaled approximately $80 billion of sales loss to the economy. The falling sales led to a $30.9 billion loss in 2008 at General Motors (GM) alone.[1146] The US Big Three automakers combined lost more than $46 billion in that year. The US manufacturers were not alone in reporting red ink. For the first time since World War II, Toyota projected a 350 billion yen net income loss for fiscal year 2009 (ending March 31, 2009).[1147] Fears of a massive economic dislocation from the failure of US auto manufacturers led the government to provide $13 billion of loans to GM and Chrysler to keep the companies afloat and an assurance of more funding upon presentation of approved restructuring plans. While a portion of the vehicle sales decline was attributed to consumers tightening their belts during uncertain times and the general recession, policy makers believed that a lack of credit also limited purchases.

The purchase of a new vehicle represents one of the largest expenditures that most Americans make. With the average price for a new car in 2008 at $28,000, it is easy to understand why the vast majority of cars are purchased on credit. The manufacturers have understood for decades that they need to provide consumers both quality cars and attractive financing. The major manufacturers established financing arms to facilitate the loan origination process. For example, General Motors Acceptance Corporation (GMAC) was created in 1919. Its mission was to help dealers and consumers finance auto purchases. To increase car sales, financing representatives are located at the dealerships so that once a customer decides to make the purchase, the loan can be arranged and the deal sealed within minutes. By the beginning of the 21st century, GMAC had financed $1 trillion dollars of auto and truck purchases around the globe.[1148]

[1145] Michelle Krebs & Bill Visnic, *2008 U.S. Auto Sales Are Worst Since 1992,* AUTO OBS., Jan. 05, 2009, http://www.autoobserver.com/2009/01/2008-us-auto-sales-are-worst-since-1992.html (last visited Oct. 12, 2009).

[1146] *Automotive Industry Crisis, Times Topics,* N.Y. TIMES, http://topics.nytimes.com/top/reference/timestopics/subjects/c/credit_crisis/auto_industry/index.html?scp=1-spot&sq=auto%20bailout&st=cse#articles (last updated Apr. 27, 2009) (last visited Oct. 12, 2009).

[1147] TOYOTA MOTOR CORP., FINANCIAL SUMMARY, FY2009 THIRD QUARTER 1, http://www.toyota.co.jp/en/ir/financial_results/2009/q3/summary.pdf (last visited Oct. 12, 2009).

[1148] GMAC Fin. Servs., *History,* http://www.gmacfs.com/us/en/about/who/who_history.html (last visited Oct. 12, 2009).

The auto financing companies provided loans to "prime" borrowers who had strong credit histories, assets, and cash flows to support the repayment of the loans. The desire to boost sales and the availability of low cost capital as well as the opportunity to securitize and sell the obligations post-2000 resulted in offers of loans to less creditworthy borrowers. By 2006, more than one fourth of the auto asset-backed securities were based on nonprime borrowers or subprime loans.[1149] The capital to provide the loans came from internally generated profits, debt financing, or the investors in these loan backed securities. Securitization of auto loans dates back to the 1980s, and has grown to a multi-billon source of funds. The role of securitization typically increases with profit pressures such as the pressures during a recession. The role of securitization declines during periods of economic prosperity when the car manufacturers are flush with cash. Exhibit 1 shows that securitization of auto loans grew from less than $20 billion in 1994 to more than $110 billion in 2006. As the financial crisis deepened and credit dried up in 2008, securitization of auto loans declined to $40 billion. Securitization has shrunk in other areas which had been active in prior years, including securitization of credit card receivables, student loans and small business loans.

In late 2008, as the economic crisis lengthened, policy makers continued to search for ways to revive the financial system. The freeze in the credit markets, which began in 2007, intensified in 2008 as shown by the London Interbank Offered Rate (LIBOR) spread. The initial focus of the government's economy recovery program was to "unfreeze" the credit markets. Despite the infusion of hundreds of billions of dollars of capital into the banking system, these institutions seemed unwilling to make loans for fear that consumers would not be able to repay them. Thus, policy makers faced a "Catch-22." The economy could not recover because the banks would not lend, and the banks would not lend until the economy recovered. Consequently, the availability of consumer and small business credit was very limited. According to the Federal Reserve: "The ABS markets historically have funded a substantial share of consumer credit and SBA-guaranteed small business loans. Continued disruption of these markets could significantly limit the availability of credit to households and small businesses and thereby contribute to further weakening of U.S. economic activity."[1150]

The Federal Reserve decided that jump-starting securitization was necessary to improve capital availability and in turn stimulate the economy. On November 25, 2008, the Federal Reserve announced the establishment of the Term Asset-Backed Securities Loan Facility (TALF), "a facility that will help market participants meet the credit needs of households and small businesses by supporting the issuance of

---

[1149] Fitch Ratings, *In the Auto ABS Driver's Seat,* Nov. 2006, at 5.

[1150] Press Release, Bd.d of Governors of the Fed.l Res. Sys. (Nov. 25, 2008), http://www.federalreserve.gov/newsevents/press/monetary/20081125a.htm (last visited Oct. 7. 2009).

asset-backed securities (ABS) collateralized by student loans, auto loans, credit card loans, and loans guaranteed by the Small Business Administration (SBA)." "Under the TALF, the Federal Reserve Bank of New York (FRBNY) will lend up to $200 billion on a non-recourse basis to holders of certain AAA-rated ABS backed by newly and recently originated consumer and small business loans. The FRBNY will lend an amount equal to the market value of the ABS less a haircut and will be secured at all times by the ABS. The U.S. Treasury Department--under the Troubled Assets Relief Program (TARP) of the Emergency Economic Stabilization Act of 2008--will provide $20 billion of credit protection to the FRBNY in connection with the TALF."[1151]

Under this program the Federal Reserve Bank of New York will offer non-recourse loans to investment funds organized and managed by an investment manager based in the United States. In addition, the funds must have an account relationship with a US primary dealer. The offer was designed to provide funding by facilitating loan securitization rather than by directly providing funding to consumers or businesses. Consequently, the minimum loan size to borrowers must be $10 million. Moreover, the Federal Reserve has restricted the eligible collateral to those asset-backed securities that have received the highest rating from two or more nationally recognized rating agencies. The assets that are qualified to participate in the program are "auto loans, student loans, credit card loans, equipment loans, floorplan loans, small business loans fully guaranteed . . . by the U.S. Small Business [Administration], or receivables related to residential mortgage servicing advances."[1152] These loans must be new or recently issued.

The TALF loans are offered monthly with a planned end date of December 2009. The loans are for three years with interest payments due monthly and full principal due at the end of the three year term. "TALF loans will not be subject to mark-to-market or re-margining requirements."[1153] While there is a $10 million minimum for a loan there is no upper limit. "The interest rate on TALF loans secured by ABS backed by federally guaranteed student loans will be 50 basis points over 1-month Libor. The interest rate on TALF loans secured by SBA Pool Certificates will be the federal funds target rate plus 75 basis points. The interest rate on TALF loans secured by SBA Development Company Participation Certificates will be 50 basis points over the 3-

---

[1151] *Id.*

[1152] Federal Reserve Bank of New York, *Term Asset-Backed Securities Loan Facility: Frequently Asked Questions,* Apr. 21, 2009, at 4, http://www.newyorkfed.org/markets/FAQ_Blackline_042109.pdf (last visited Oct. 7, 2009).

[1153] Federal Reserve Bank of New York, *Term Asset-Backed Securities Loan Facility: Terms and Conditions,* http://www.federalreserve.gov/newsevents/monetary20081125a1.pdf (last visited Oct. 7, 2009).

year Libor swap rate. For TALF loans secured by other eligible fixed-rate ABS, the interest rate will be 100 basis points over the 1-year Libor swap rate for securities with a weighted average life less than one year, 100 basis points over the 2-year Libor swap rate for securities with a weighted average life greater than or equal to one year and less than two years, or 100 basis points over the 3-year Libor swap rate for securities with a weighted average life of two years or greater. For TALF loans secured by other eligible floating-rate ABS, the interest rate will be 100 basis points over 1-month Libor."[1154]

The Federal Reserve will protect itself against the loss of value of the collateral assets in the program by requiring borrowers to take a "haircut" or to obtain a loan for less than the value of the collateral that supports the loan. The amount of the "haircut" varies, based on the type of asset and the average life of the asset-backed security. For example, auto loans to prime borrowers with an average life of less than one year require a 6% haircut as compared to a 12% haircut for a similar loan to a low credit borrower with an average life of 3-4 years. The "haircut" required for student loans with an average life of less than 1 year is 5% for government guaranteed loans and 8% for privately issued loans.[1155] Borrowers also pay an administrative fee to the Federal Reserve of 5 basis points of the loan amount.[1156]

The reaction to the TALF program in the investment community has been cautious optimism. Commentators agree that the objectives of the program are appropriate – thaw credit markets and increase the consumers' ability to reenter the market for autos, and provide small businesses with access to capital, and students with loans to engage in higher education. The chairman of the private equity company Blackstone "said he expects the plan to be successful at bringing investors back into these markets."[1157] The co-chief investment officer at Pacific Investment Management Co. was less optimistic: "It may be the same problem we have with banks. . . . You can bring the horse to water, but they (sic) may not drink."[1158] As of this writing it was

---

[1154] Federal Reserve Bank of New York, *Term Asset-Backed Loan Facility: Terms and Conditions* (Apr. 21, 2009), http://www.newyorkfed.org/markets/talf_Terms_090421.html (last visited Oct. 7, 2009).

[1155] Federal Reserve Bank of New York, *Term Asset-Backed Securities Loan Facility: Frequently Asked Questions,* Apr. 21, 2009, at 14-15, http://www.newyorkfed.org/markets/FAQ_Blackline_042109.pdf (last visited Oct. 7, 2009)..

[1156] *Id.* at 14.

[1157] Liz Rappaport & Jon Hilsenrath, *Fed Moves to Free Up Credit for Consumers,* WALL ST. J., Mar. 4, 2009, at A1, LEXIS, Busfin Library, Wsj File, *available at* http://online.wsj.com/article/SB123609012856118765.html (last visited Oct. 7, 2009).

[1158] *Id.*

too early to tell the impact of the TALF program. However, the importance of securitization in general, and the potential of the TALF program in particular, was captured in a book entitled *Animal Spirits* by Nobel Laureate George Akerlof and Yale professor Robert Shiller: "TALF shows us that there are two sides to creative finance: It may have gotten us into this crisis. But its genius may also get us out of it."[1159]

Exhibit 1
Auto ABS Issuance by Dollar Volume

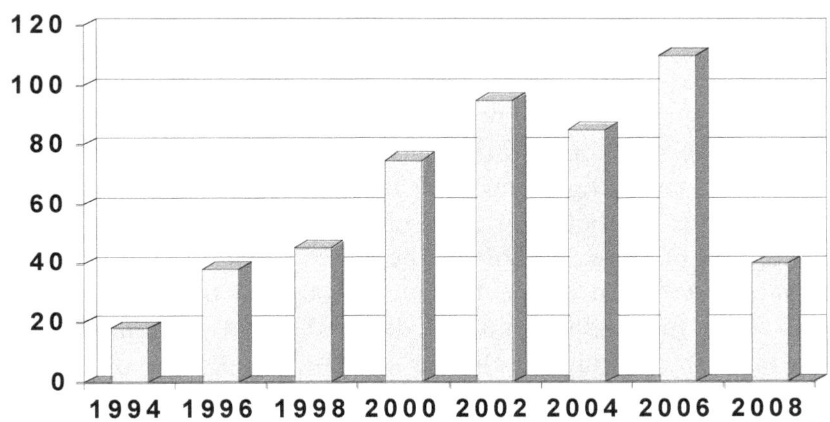

Source: Author estimate drawn from data in Fitch Ratings, *In the Auto ABS Driver's Seat*, Nov. 2006; Fitch Ratings, *In the Auto ABS Driver's Seat*, Feb. 2009.

Discussion Topics

Law

- Does the Federal Reserve have the authority to establish the TALF program? Does it have to seek Congressional approval?
- Who should be authorized to establish and manage the TALF?
- Does the fact that under the TALF loans are collateralized by the government involve legal issues? What information would you like to have in order to evaluate the price of the loans?

Business

- Does government backing, essentially public subsidies, distort private sector investment?
- Is the TALF program attractive to investors?

[1159] GEORGE A. AKERLOF & ROBERT J. SHILLER, ANIMAL SPIRITS 92 (2009).

Public Policy

- Should the federal government be in the business of facilitating securitization?
- Do non-recourse loans create a moral hazard?
- Does the amount of the "haircut" sufficiently protect the American taxpayer?

D. Predictions and Conclusions

Authorities can be cited to current and past situations, and even they are open to debate and uncertainty. Authorities for prediction are harder to prove. Therefore, the suggestions in this concluding section are based on no authorities but for the authors' overview of the subject and sense of possibilities. In the mid-1980s, securitization was but a twinkle in a few people's eyes. It evolved into a movement that is spreading all over the globe. Looking back at the changing environment, one can better understand why. Among the reasons for the spread of securitization is the rise of market power, the creation of information systems that transcend physical and political boundaries, emerging technology that allowed risk shifting forms, and the surfacing of numerous symbols that represent physical assets. Most important is the acceptance and trust in these symbols as the stores of value, the recognition of their importance and the creation of mechanisms to support their acceptance and trust. Securitization has a far reaching impact. In a way that is similar to the Internet, securitization must, by definition, change a balance and view of power. It creates money and allows for power transfer; it empowers numerous intermediaries and requires their cooperation. It creates incentives for cooperation among international and political governments, as well as among private sector actors. It requires trust and its supportive mechanisms.

Securitization also opens the door to new types of fraud and abuse of trust. It calls for self-protection, market protection, and multi-government regulation. When one mechanism is strong, the other can weaken, but they must work in tandem to produce this complex financial and social process. The industrial era is called a revolution because it allowed for mass production of raw materials. Financial systems opened the door to mass production of financial assets. Securitization opens the door to the conversion of "raw materials" in the form of financial assets into mass produced financial assets. In fact, it represents the final step in an industrial age of financial assets. Like the industrial age, securitization facilitates different social structures, laws, and cooperative efforts. The prediction is that if it is allowed to continue, and if its abuse is controlled and regulated, securitization can have an enriching financial, social, political and international impact on individuals and nations everywhere.

This section was written in 2006, before the crash of 2008. Nonetheless, we do not withdraw it. The issue is how to maintain the good in securitization while preventing and controlling the bad.

Predictions are dangerous. No one's crystal ball is clear, even in highly predictable cases, such as if the sun will rise tomorrow morning. Nonetheless, we all try to predict the future, even of complex things such as the fate of securitization as part of the financial system. In 1991, when the first edition of Frankel's treatise was published, she dared to ask whether securitization is here to stay, and suggested that it is. The horrendously bad experience of securitization starting in year 2007 does not suggest, however, that securitization will disappear. But if we do not learn from this experience then maybe we do not deserve this unique and beneficial financial tool. Throughout this course we may have received quite a bit of information of what went wrong and why securitization of mortgage loans failed. We dwelt on the subprime loans, and the creation of a bubble both in the securities markets and in the real estate market. We know that large institutions that are too large to fail ought not to gamble and risk the entire system and economy. The main questions are: How to keep securitization and benefit from it without allowing its destruction on the one hand, and without a heavy handed treatment that will squeeze the benefits of securitization to reduce its rich offerings, on the other hand. How can we allow beneficial innovations while preventing destructive innovations? How can the market become well-informed about the value and risk of asset-backed securities and avoid gambling? If we can perceive the ways in which this goal can be achieved, we might dare predict that securitization will remain a useful financial tool. If, however, there is no way to prevent the recurrence of the events that have brought us the crisis of 2008 then perhaps securitization might not remain a tool in the future and will shrivel and die.

List of Cases

U

W

Z

Index

A

B

C

H

I

L

M

N

O

P

R

S

www.ingramcontent.com/pod-product-compliance
Lightning Source LLC
LaVergne TN
LVHW062244200926
348484LV00006B/1609
9781600420955